COMPENDIUM
of the
MIRACULOUS

DEACON ALBERT E. GRAHAM

TAN Books
Charlotte, North Carolina

All interior images are under public domain in the United States of America via Wikimedia Commons unless otherwise mentioned.

Cover design by Caroline Green

Cover image: Virgin with Child appearing to St. Francis de Sales, 1691, by Carlo Maratta (1625-1713), oil on canvas, 335x205 cm / G. Dagli Orti / De Agostini Picture Library / Bridgeman Images

ISBN: 978-1-5051-1136-1

Published in the United States by

TAN Books

PO Box 410487

Charlotte, NC 28241

www.TANBooks.com

Printed in the United States of America

Contents

Foreword

Michael O'Neill, *the Miracle Hunter*

Miracles happen every day. Even in our modern world—even in the United States—claims of the supernatural abound. A recent study showed that 61 percent of Americans believe that they have witnessed something that could be considered miraculous. Everyone has something to say about miracles. For believers, they stand as proof positive that God is a loving Father actively interacting with His creation. For skeptics and atheists, miracles—while particularly distasteful—need to be countered with some explanation. After all, if miracles do imply some sort of divine intervention, then that is a problem for those that do not believe in God. Both sides are well beyond the point of being able to accept British philosopher David Hume's famous but circular out-of-hand dismissal: Miracles are impossible because miracles can't happen.

That which the average person today considers miraculous most likely will not be the fodder for a serious Vatican-level investigation. A miracle (from Latin *mirari,* "to wonder") is something that is rare, without natural explanation, and is worked for the good, implying divine intervention. (Things that are simply unknown or inexplicable are considered mysteries or marvels.) People find inspiration in their favorite sports team making a great comeback, finding their lost cell phone, or uncharacteristically light traffic on a day when they are already running late. Even those cases of a person's hardened heart being opened to faith, the healing of family wounds, or landing a job in desperate times, while seemingly clearly showing the hand of God, will never get classified as a true miracle by Church authorities.

The cases that people from all faiths seem to get excited about are those healing miracles in which a dire medical condition has been unexpectedly reversed. It is a common misconception that the leaders of the Catholic Church are very eager to learn of new medical miracle stories so that they might quickly rubber stamp an approval and publicize them to get new members into the pews on Sunday. But it turns out that the Church, while celebrating some very famous examples of the miraculous with specific feast days in the General Roman Calendar—I am thinking here particularly of the miracles associated with Fatima, Lourdes, Guadalupe, Mt. Carmel, and Divine Mercy—is not all that eager to hear of new miracle claims and probably is more likely to wish these distractions would go away and that the faithful might return to a normal practice of the faith.

In fact, other than when attention must be paid to the crowds that begin to form around a very public event, the Catholic Church only investigates medical miracles in the case of those related to Our Lady of Lourdes and those that arise when the Consulta Romana at the Vatican is investigating the potential medical miracles considered as proofs of intercession in sainthood causes.

And, too, the criteria that the Church uses is almost impossibly strict, relying on the very old Lambertini criteria, so named for an Italian cardinal Prospero Lambertini (later Pope Benedict XIV) born in the

1600s. For a cure to be considered truly miraculous, it must be a healing of a severe medical condition not liable to go away on its own, instantaneous, complete, and lasting. And perhaps most difficult of all in our modern era when most everyone sees their doctor is that there can be no medical treatment that relates to the cure. The cases considered are those that occur before a treatment or surgery has begun or afterwards when the medical professionals have recognized that their treatment was ineffective.

Other types of investigated phenomena—strange to the outside world, but beautiful to the Catholic—are incorruptible bodies of some saints, weeping statues and icons, the stigmata (bearing the wounds of Christ), Eucharistic miracles, and Marian apparitions. Each case involves a unique process of investigation and validation and may result in some official declaration either way. When it comes to private revelation where divine messages are allegedly transmitted through a seer, the Church will render three possible judgments: *non constat de supernaturalitate* (maybe), *constat de supernaturalitate* (positive), or *constat de non supernaturalite* (negative). All three give a comment on the supernatural character of the event. Even in those very famous examples of Church-approved apparitions with messages for the world like Lourdes, Fatima, and Guadalupe, there is no requirement for the faithful to believe in them or incorporate the devotions into their lives of faith. Unlike the miracles of Christ in the Gospels, the faithful can safely ignore them if they find them distracting, not credible, or not meaningful.

For all the healthy skepticism and proper grounding that is advisable when approaching claims of the miraculous, one cannot but marvel at the variety and preponderance of such phenomena. Even if only the tiniest fraction of these reports

can be taken seriously, there still exists a very large number of cases that cannot be easily ignored. The Church has, albeit rarely, declared events to be "worthy of belief" through official statements and encouragement of devotions stemming from the occurrences in question. Even more rarely, the Vatican, without need to publicly validate the findings of a local bishop, will give signs of recognition such as the visit of a pope or papal legate with a golden rose, the composing of an official prayer, the building of a basilica, the establishment of a feast day, or the canonization of an associated saint.

The impact of miracles on the Church is noteworthy. The two major bookend miracles of Christ's life—the Incarnation and the Resurrection—are the very reasons for the existence of Christianity in the first place and, as such, are embraced universally by the faithful. One need only remember that Catholics embrace Christ's great miracle of the Eucharist in churches around the world at every hour of every day when they receive the body, blood, soul, and divinity of Jesus Christ under the auspices of bread and wine. The stories of saints—especially according to pious tradition and early hagiographies—abound with accounts of amazing healing powers and other miraculous phenomena in both incredible variety and persistent repetition.

Some of the most famous Catholic sacramentals—the rosary, the scapular (in various colors) and the Miraculous Medal—all have resulted from a miracle. Five of the largest twelve churches by square footage in Christendom likewise have a supernatural backstory. Some of the largest faith movements and religious orders, including the Franciscans, Servites, and Mercedarians amongst others, trace their origins to a miracle experienced by their founders. Millions upon millions of faithful travel to the famed sites of miracles every year, with some reports indicating Lourdes receiving four million, Fatima five million, and Guadalupe nine million visitors annually. The alleged apparition site of Medjugorje has received between thirty and forty million pilgrims since the apparition claims began in 1981. Similarly, millions of Filipinos gather each year in a procession celebrating the purportedly miraculous image of Christ, the Black Nazarene. It is clear to see that miracles continue to impact the faithful even today and are indicative of a great longing for the supernatural among all peoples.

With the many famous cases of miracles and the strong interest of the faithful, one might wonder if the Vatican maintained a website cataloguing them or had a publicly accessible library collection of the books and manuscripts reporting on such phenomena. The Secret Vatican Archives, inaccessible to most, contain such information, but not for the average Catholic who wants to bolster his or her faith with the great accounts of divine intervention in our world. And this is where a comprehensive, encyclopedic book is needed and, thus happily, the *Compendium of the Miraculous* comes forth to fill that void.

Deacon Albert E. Graham, in this well-researched and meticulously sourced volume, presents the incredible variety of supernatural phenomena that the Catholic Church has witnessed, investigated, validated, and celebrated over the centuries. (And even this tome is not exhaustive.) His unique and thorough approach and the magnificent artistic treatment that TAN Books has given it make this book an invaluable asset and a treasure to anyone interested in the breadth and the depth of supernatural experience to which the Catholic Church has borne witness in the two millennia since Christ. It will remain a centerpiece in my library, and I hope in yours as well.

ACKNOWLEDGMENTS

I owe a debt of gratitude to the following people who directly or indirectly helped me bring this labor of love to fruition. To Fernande, my loving wife, who put up with my time away from the family and spent many hours proofreading the manuscript. To Drs. Angelo and Jane Collura who initially looked over the work and suggested textual and stylistic changes. To Patricia Lynn Morrison, editorial director at ICS Publications, who pointed out some factual errors and problematic areas in which changes needed to be made. To my sons Michael and Stephen and daughters Monique, Elisabeth and Kristina who encouraged me and bailed me out of innumerable computer glitches while I was putting this work together. To faithful parishioners Eugene and Christine Ambrogio, Matthew and Phyllis Laidley for reading and critiquing the entire book and recommending changes. To Deacon Anthony Barrasso and Fr. John Reutermann who helped clarify some doctrinal issues. Most especially to Fr. Samuel Plummer, a former employee of TAN Books before his ordination to the priesthood, who actually brought the first draft of this work to the attention of the editors of TAN Books.

Introduction

Can You Hear Me Now?

Whoever believes in God also admits that God can communicate with the beings He created. Since the beginning of time, God, in fact, has been speaking to our minds and hearts. He walked and talked with our first parents. Throughout the history of salvation, He has spoken to His saints and prophets by way of visions, apparitions, dreams (see Nm 12:6), and inner voices. The Old Testament specifically mentions some of His cameo appearances to men, such as when He led the Israelites in the wilderness by a pillar of cloud by day and a pillar of fire by night as well as when He descended in a cloud to talk to Moses. Of course, His greatest gift to mankind was when "for us men and our salvation, He sent His Son down from heaven by the power of the Holy Spirit to become incarnate of the Virgin Mary and be made man." While among us, the Son, the second person of the Blessed trinity, was in constant communication with the Father in prayer. And, on two occasions, the Father appeared in a cloud and spoke to humankind identifying Jesus as His beloved Son. These events took place at Jesus's baptism in the Jordan and His transfiguration on a high mountain.

Moreover, before the Fall of mankind, our first parents lived in a state of personal intimacy with God. This was revealed to us in Genesis where it was said that God walked and talked with Adam and Eve in the Garden "in the cool of the day" (Gn 3:8). Man's first experience with a supernatural voice thus comes at the very beginning of his creation. Whereas man heard the first supernatural voice from God Himself, it was Eve who heard the first voice from the preternatural: that of Satan disguised as a snake or a serpent (see Gn 3:1, 4–5). It is also interesting to note that God spoke out directly to Adam after he had sinned and asked, "Where are you?" (Gn 3:9). The conversation between God and our first parents takes up the next nine of the twenty-four total passages in chapter 3 of Genesis.

After the first man and woman sinned, there was a radical disruption of their harmonic relationship with the Creator. They immediately lost the grace of original holiness. Their expulsion from the Garden symbolizes the separation between God and the human race. Man's sin had placed a veil between God and mankind. However, God never stopped seeking us. He continued to pursue us and reveal Himself to us. He communicated to us gradually, in stages, through words and deeds.

Throughout the Old Testament, God, in various ways and according to His sovereign will, reveals Himself, His truth, and His program to His people. He made these things known sometimes through a prophet, sometimes through events, and sometimes through great wonders.

In the period before Abraham, revelation was frequently given to individuals. God speaks at various times to Adam and Eve, to

Cain (see Gn 4:6), Hagar, Job, Joshua, and probably many others of whom there is no written record. The primary idea is that of direct (private) revelation rather than the impartation of a message to be delivered subsequently to others. The knowledge of Job and his companions about God and His ways is proof that prior to written Scripture God had revealed Himself. While the written Word had its primary purpose in preserving Revelation in infallible accuracy for future generations, direct (private) revelation had to do largely with contemporary problems and need for truth and guidance which would later be afforded by the complete written Word.

God Spoke Through the Prophets

A prophet may be defined as one who with inward eyes open to the eternal realities "sees the vision of the Almighty" (Nm 24:4) and, inspired by this vision, speaks in burning words of that which was seen. To adapt Emerson's phrase, he is a seer who becomes a sayer. God communicates to the prophets by word or by visions. The Lord puts His words into the mouths of these individuals (see 1 Kgs 22:14; Jer 1:9; 15:19b; Ez 2:7; 3:1; 3:10). In most cases, God gave direct revelation to those who were publicly known as prophets. However, He did not exclusively limit revelation to them. To receive a revelation or a vision does not make one a prophet unless it is accompanied by the command to proclaim the Word of God.

There was a succession of true prophets called by God to make known His will to successive generations. As the spokesmen and messengers for the Deity, the prophets were commissioned by Him to speak in His name. They conveyed His words to His people at a given moment in time, regardless of whether or not the people wished to hear them (see Ez 3:11; Jer 2 ff). The message of the prophets primarily dealt with the past, reminding the people of God's dealing with them. Their message was frequently that of specific guidance in the midst of a crisis. Many times their message was one of warning of judgment to come for sin. They spoke of future events. They did not specify when the events would occur. These events could even change or be modified depending on the repentance of the audience (see Is 38:1–2; Jer 1:1; 3:1–10). Exhortation was given to worship God and obey Him. They conveyed God's message to the audience by words, miracles, signs, and in non-verbal ways.

The Old Testament begins with the development of the interaction between God and humanity; then, the interaction between God and Israel, his holy, chosen people (see Ex 19:3–6; 1 Pt 2:9–10). The interaction occurs first within the context of the covenants between God and Noah (see Gn 9:8–17). Before Abraham there were a few individuals who had the distinctive character of prophets. As already noted, revelation during this period was more frequently given to those who had no part in the prophetic office. The prophetic ministry of Noah is then noteworthy in this regard. God speaks to this righteous man about the wickedness of humanity. Most of Genesis 6 and 7 concerns God's conversation with Noah. His prophetic ministry was probably far richer than that which appears on the pages of Genesis.

The earliest religious leaders of Israel, such as Abraham (see Gn 20:7) and Moses (see Dt 34:10), were sometimes called prophets. God called Abraham (see Gn 17:1–22) to be the ancestor of the faithful, and, from that covenant, this interaction moves forward to the covenant between God and Israel through Moses at Sinai (see Ex 19ff). Abraham's life affords an advance in the history of prophecy. He is distinctly known as a prophet to whom God speaks and who is blessed by God. To him is given abundant revelation of his peculiar place in history and of God's great purpose to be realized through him. Notably absent, however, is the command to deliver a message. He received a revelation but had no message to be communicated to others except in so far as it is recorded in the Scriptures. Following Abraham, and in the same period, God spoke to Isaac and Jacob confirming the revelation given to Abraham and adding to it.

Moses was considered the greatest of the Old Testament prophets. He was the first prophet through whom the new faith was mediated. He had a large prophetic ministry as well as a more extended revelation. Moses enjoyed the distinctive call of a prophet when God appeared to him in the burning bush. To him God spoke, not in vague visions, but face to face (see Nm 12:7–8). The Creator communicated to him His plan for His chosen people. The Lord commanded Moses to tell the Israelites, "If you will obey my voice and keep my covenant, you shall be my own possession among all peoples; for all the earth is mine" (Ex 19:5). Moses' office was recognized by all the people. The prophets that followed continued to reveal God's unfolding plan for His people. In this sense, God's revelation was public; that is, it was meant for a whole people, not for individuals. The prophets of the Old Testament generally exercised a public function and a permanent ministry as God's spokesmen for the public revelation.

During the period of the early kings, beginning with Samuel and ending with the so-called writing prophets, a definite advance is made in prophetic history. The prophet comes into his own. He is regarded not only as a seer, one to whom visions and revelations are given, but also as a divinely chosen representative of God set apart, in many cases, to an entire lifetime of prophetic ministry. Prophets such as Samuel, Nathan, Elijah, and Elisha were prominent in this period. Their prophetic utterances, however, dealt largely with contemporary problems.

The prophetic warnings of the coming exile with the accompanying revelation of the glory of the future kingdom are exemplified in the great prophets of this era, namely Isaiah, Jeremiah, Ezekiel, and Daniel. It is interesting to note that the primary source for the title "Son of Man" originates with the Old Testament prophet Daniel, who describes this mysterious figure in his night visions (see Dn 7:13). Revelation after the exile is found in the likes of Ezra, Nehemiah, Haggai, Zechariah, and Malachi.

All the covenants of the Old Testament ended in Jesus Christ. His purpose was to complete what the covenants set out to do: to restore sinful humanity to the fullness of its proper relationship with God in creative love.

Methods God Used to Convey His Messages

At least four methods of special revelation were used by God in making known His mind to His prophets. The character of the revelation is supernatural in nature and consists primarily of:

The spoken word (locutions): historical appearances of God in created symbols are witnessed by the Scriptures. As the epistle to the Hebrews says, "In many and various ways God spoke of old to our fathers by the prophets; but in these last days he has spoken to us by a Son" (1:1–2). This speaking, then, of the personal transcendent God took place according to Scripture in the most diverse manners. The prophet who is to become the mouthpiece of God for man hears a voice (see Ez 1:28). It is evident from such New Testament instances such as the baptism of Christ in the Jordan (see Mt 3:17), the transfiguration on Mt. Tabor (see Mk 9:7), and the appearance of Christ to St. Paul that God sometimes speaks vocally in the presence of others and did so on several occasions. In the Old Testament, God spoke in a similar way. At Mount Sinai, for instance, God spoke in such a way to Moses that the people could also hear with the express purpose of validating Moses as a prophet of God (see Ex 19:9). In the case of the call of Samuel (see 1 Sm 3:1–14), the voice of the Lord was so real, so similar to a human voice, that it was mistaken for that of Eli's in the first three instances. In some instances, God used a communication similar to a human voice, and in other instances, He may have spoken directly to the heart of man with such reality that the effect is produced without the use of actual words.

A secondary means of revelation is that of dreams. Divine messages in dreams appear throughout the Bible, sometimes standing as the center of the story (see Mt 1:20; 2:19).[1] In biblical times, prophets and apocalyptic visionaries were moved by the Holy Spirit to dream dreams and see visions disclosing possibilities that would otherwise have been hidden from human eyes. This method of revelation was commonly accepted as a normal way for God to speak. Scripture is replete with such examples. In most instances, the one to whom God speaks is not a prophet, as illustrated in the case of Abimelech (see Gn 20:3, 6), Laban (see Gn 31:24), the butler and baker of Pharaoh, and in the dream of Pharaoh himself. In the rebuke delivered to Miriam

and Aaron for murmuring against Moses, God said, "If there is a prophet among you, I the Lord make myself known to him in a vision, I speak with him in a dream" (Nm 12:6). In some cases, the revelation was given during a sleep supernaturally imposed, as in the case of Abraham (see Gn 15:12) and Daniel (see Dn 10:9). It is prophesized in Joel 3:1 that the future period would involve many instances of this kind of revelation. God uses dreams in Scripture to warn of coming events or judgments (Pharaoh or Nebuchandazzer) or to give specific guidance or direction. St. Joseph is warned in a dream to flee to Egypt (see Mt 2:13) and to return from Egypt (see Mt 2:19–20). The Magi are warned in a dream to avoid Herod after they visit the child Jesus (see Mt 2:12). Pilate's wife is warned in a dream to abandon the case against Jesus (see Mt 27:19).

Thirdly and closely associated with dreams as a means of revelation were visions and apparitions. The very term seer as applied to prophets had reference to seeing visions. Visions and apparitions related in the Sacred Scriptures are numerous both in the Old and New Testaments. Hence they are confirmed in their supernatural authenticity by divine inspiration and by the Magisterium of the Church. From the Church's patristic origins to our days there have been numerous visions and apparitions which have turned the history of the Church. The person involved was fully conscious at the time. This probably was the case of Isaiah in the two incidents noted (Is 1:1; 6:1). Ezekiel had a similar experience (see Ez 1:1). Micaiah's vision of heaven belongs in the same category (see 1 Kgs 22:19).

That God may enter into communication with man through visions and dreams is asserted in Numbers 12:6 and still more explicitly in Job 33:14–16: "For God speaks in one way. . . . In a dream, in a vision of the night, / when deep sleep falls upon

---

[1] New Catholic Encyclopedia (NCE). prepared by the editorial staff of Catholic University of America. 1st ed. 18 v., NY, McGraw Hill Book Company, (1967) v.4, pp.1056–1057.

Moses and the Burning Bush, Domenichino (1581–1641)

men, / while they slumber on their beds, / then he opens the ears of men." Dreams and visions are always mentioned as two distinct phenomena in the Bible. Job complained of being frightened of dreams and terrified by visions (see Jb 33:15–16;7:14), and Daniel, like some other prophets, was described as having understanding of both dreams and visions (see Dn 1:17). The saints of the Old Testament, like Jacob and many of the prophets, were in communication with God and His messengers in their dreams.

The prophet has a vision (see Is 2:1). He sees God's revelation in pictures and in symbols (see Jer 1:13; 24:1); angels appear delivering a heavenly message (see Lk 1:11, 26 ff.). One comes across no fewer than a dozen incidents in the lives of Abraham, Isaac, Jacob, and Moses, the first patriarchs of Judaism, in which God was allegedly encountered in a dream, a vision, or in something even more concrete. Most of Genesis and the first half of Exodus are accounts of these encounters. Five separate encounters are attributed to Abraham, including one in which the Lord "appeared," accompanied by two other beings (see Gn 18). One also encounters the apparition of God in His appearance to Moses in the Burning Bush.

In the case of the earlier prophets, the visions came spontaneously and were comparatively simple in form and contents (cf. Am 7–9; Is 6). Amos saw coming disasters for Israel in a vision (see Am 7:1). He is called the prophet of justice because of his visions of impending justice. The more sensitive Hosea felt the touch of God's love in the tragedy of his home and became the prophet of love. But, with the later prophets, the visions became more and more elaborate. The kingly Isaiah saw the Holy One on His throne high and lifted up, and became the prophet of holiness. Ezekiel saw the vision of the glory of Lord God and became the prophet of regeneration. The seers, of whom Samuel is the most important example, received revelations from God (see 1 Sm 9:15) in visions and dreams (see Nm 24: 3; 1 Sm 3:10–14).

A fourth element, often present in supernatural revelation, was that of trances or ecstasies. Ecstasies are regarded in Sacred Scripture as such means of divine communication (see Acts 10:10; 11:5; 22:17;[2] Cor 12:2–5; Rv 4:2).[2] They are incidental to the impartation of the message of God and often accompanied visions, as in the case of Ezekiel (see Ez 8:3). It is difficult to distinguish ecstasies and dreams in some cases since the supernaturally imposed sleep is similar to a trance (see Gn 15:12; Dn 10:9). It is clear that ecstasies in themselves are not very important in the transmission of revelation.

Throughout the Old Testament, we see a personal God who deliberately makes Himself known and heard to various people over the course of human history.[3] God communicated His revelations to them not only by word (locutions) but by dreams, visions, and ecstasies. The prophets were interpreters of the mind and purpose of God, in the fullest sense of the term. They had seen the vision of the Almighty, and their purpose was to make the vision real to their followers.

The tendency of these multifarious sorts of divine communications varies widely according to the phase of the history of salvation in which the visionary lives and which he is intended to influence.

---

[2] Ibid., p. 1056.
[3] Michael Freze. S.F.O. *Voices, visions and apparitions* (VVA). Huntington, Ind., Our Sunday Visitor, 1993, p.108.

New Testament Revelation: God Speaks to Us Through His Son

Revelation in the New Testament is basically the same as in the Old. After God had spoken many times and in various ways through the prophets, He spoke to us through His Son, the incarnate Word of God (see Heb 1:1–2). The incarnation of Jesus Christ in human history was a specific revelation of God which exceeded anything which the Old Testament prophets could offer. Jesus, the Eternal Word, was sent to dwell among men and make known to them the innermost things of God. He was sent as a man to men to speak the words of God, and He brings to perfection the saving works that the Father gave Him to do. By His whole presence and self-revelation, by words and actions, by signs and miracles, especially by His death and glorious resurrection from the dead, and finally by sending the Spirit of truth, He completes Revelation and brings it to perfection, sealing by divine testimony its message that God is with us to free us from the darkness of sin and death and to raise us up to eternal life. Jesus and His Church were seen as the fulfillment of the salvific plan of God of which the prophets spoke. The Father's self-communication, made through the Word in the Holy Spirit, remains present and active in the Church today and for all time to come.

The New Testament includes numerous accounts of post-Resurrection appearances and visions of Jesus. He appeared to Mary Magdalene, to the disciples without St. Thomas, to the disciples including St. Thomas, to the two disciples at Emmaus, to seven fishermen on the shore, to St. James, St. Paul, and to more than five hundred brethren at once.

In the New Testament, the first heavenly

apparitions and messages came from God's mighty angels. In Matthew's Gospel, one finds the first supernatural sign through the voice and appearance of the heavenly archangel Gabriel to St. Joseph. In this discourse, Gabriel encourages Joseph to marry Mary explaining that her pregnancy was of a miraculous nature (see Mt 1:18–23). An angel, probably Gabriel, warned Joseph in a dream to flee to Egypt and announced when it was safe to return (see Mt 2:13). The angelic apparitions came first in Luke's Gospel as well when Gabriel appeared to the priest Zechariah and informed him that his elderly wife would bear a child (see Lk 1:11). Angels instructed Deacon Philip to go to Gaza to meet the eunuch (Acts 8:26–40) and told the centurion Cornelius to invite St. Peter to his home (see Acts 10:1–4, 30). St. Paul had a vision of his guardian angel that appeared and prophesized that the ship on which he was sailing as a prisoner would be wrecked in a terrible storm but all passengers on board would be saved (see Acts 27:22–24). When the Sadducees arrested and imprisoned the twelve apostles (see Acts 5:17–21) an angel appeared to them and opened the prison doors. Later on, during St. Peter's imprisonment at the hands of King Herod (see Acts 12:6–11), an angel appeared and freed him from his chains. The whole book of Revelation was given to John as a supernatural revelation when he was "in the Spirit." It is a revelation from the Lord who spoke to him in "a loud voice like a trumpet" (Rv 1:9–11) as well as a record of visions of heaven and paradise given in the Spirit and through the ministry of angels from whom things were made known to him.

Throughout the New Testament, a normal channel of supernatural communication is through the voice of an angel of God. As mentioned above, the book of Revelation, for example, records many instances of angelic appearances and voices. The Almighty uses these creatures to deliver supernatural messages, to warn people of danger, or to help those in trouble. God's voice is thus often expressed through the voice of the angels who assist Him in His plan for salvation.

God Continues to Make Himself Known Through His Creatures

Since the death of the last apostle and the public revelation of His Son, the communication of God with man has not ceased. The lack of any divine communication would contradict the history of the Church as well as God's Word in Scripture.

We know from Scripture that visible signs and wonders will accompany the followers of Jesus generation after generation: "And these signs will accompany those who believe" (Mk 16:17). Moreover, God continues to be close to His people. Jesus assured us of this when He said: "I am with you always, to the close of the age" (Mt 28:20). Scripture makes it clear that the faithful have and will experience supernatural wonders. It proclaims that dreams, visions, and apparitions will occur throughout the history of the Church: "And in the last days it shall be, God declares, / that I will pour out my Spirit upon all flesh, / and your sons and your daughters shall prophesy, / and your young men shall see visions, / and your old men shall dream dreams; . . . And I will show wonders in the heaven above / and signs on the earth beneath" (Acts 2:17, 19; see also Jl 3:1).

Whatever God has communicated to these privileged souls can add nothing to the deposit of Christian faith. Private revelations of this nature may be granted for the personal good of individuals and also to stir up among Christians a more faithful

Shrine of Our Lady of Banneux. Photo by Anuja Mary Tilj / Shutterstock

adherence to the gospel. Though they are not meant to present new doctrines, private revelations do play a positive role in the life of the Church. They draw attention to what in the faith is likely to meet the particular needs of the times.

Private revelation can never end as long as God continues to deal personally with man and be present in human history. God still intervenes directly in human affairs through voices, visions, apparitions, locutions, miracles, signs, and wonders. He uses others as catalysts for these signs to come about: the Blessed Virgin Mary, angels, saints, beati, venerables, et al. Authentic messages from the Lord have been passed on from these dead holy ones to the living recipient (visionary) who might be fully awake and going about normal activity, or else be in various states of altered consciousness, from those semiconscious states which immediately precede and follow sleep to the deep relaxation

of profound prayer and on into ecstasy and rapture as well as to those who are fully asleep.[4]

In the twentieth and twenty-first centuries alone, more Marian apparitions and messages for the world have occurred than at any other time in Church history. In fact, it is claimed that some 378 reports of Marian apparitions in thirty-two countries have come forth in the few years between 1923 and 1975. Out of all these claims, at least 95 percent of them involve Marian messages for the seers, their parish, the Church, and the world. Since 1973, the supernatural messages in particular have become even more common—perhaps double the total number recorded in the previous fifty years.[5]

Twenty-two Marian Apparitions were seriously studied between 1931 and 1950, and only two were approved (Beauraing and Banneux in Belgium). Six remained undecided in 1952, and the remaining fourteen were rejected.[6] Since then, the Akita Marian phenomena experienced by Sister Agnes Katsuko Sasagawa were approved as genuinely supernatural in origin by Bishop John Ito on April 22, 1984, after consulting with the Holy See. The Marian apparitions which took place in Le Laus, France, in 1664 to the visionary Benoite Rencurel were approved in 2008. In 2010, the apparitions of Our Lady to Adele Joseph Brise in Champion, Wisconsin, in 1859 became the first Marian apparition approved by the Catholic Church in the United States. Over the last several decades, apparitions of Mary have proliferated throughout the United States and the world. Her apparitions, visions, and locutions have produced a networked spiritual family that emerges like precious

[4] Patricia Treece. *Apparitions of Modern Saints. Appearances of Therese of Lisieux, Padre Pio, Don Bosco, and Others, Messages From God to His People on Earth*. Ann Arbor, Mich.: Charis, 2001, p. 33.

[5] Freze, VVA, op cit., 103.

[6] NCE, 1967, op. cit., v.12, p.446.

flowers in the early dawn of springtime.[7]

As we will see in this study, many of the saints, blesseds, venerables, and other holy people mentioned herein, during and since apostolic times, have claimed to have seen the Lord and talked with Him just as we talk to one another. Many of them have experienced extraordinary mystical phenomena. These include such supernatural phenomena as hearing heavenly voices, dreaming otherworldly dreams, seeing supernatural visions and apparitions of Mary, angels, saints, patriarchs, prophets, demons, and the suffering souls in purgatory, experiencing ecstasies, and receiving private revelations.[8]

Such phenomena continue to be experienced by people living today among laity and clergy, Catholics and Protestants, devout and casual believers alike. A poll taken in 1995 found that about 40 percent of the population say God speaks to them personally.[9] If you take a poll in a typical Christian congregation, you will probably discover that a cross-section of parishioners has had very deep supernatural encounters with God. Most have had at least a few occasions of dramatic answer to prayer, some have seen physical healings of various kinds, still others have heard the voice of God speaking to them or may have had a vision or apparition of Jesus, Mary, a saint, or an angel. Speaking more generally, one would be safe to say that millions of God's people have had some sort of religious experience at one time or another. There is compelling evidence that we are serving a living Savior: a God who still directly intervenes in human affairs through voices, visions, apparitions, locutions, miracles, signs, and wonders—a

God who promised to remain close to His people because of His overflowing generosity and love for them. Again, Jesus assured us of this when He said, "I am with you always, to the close of the age" (Mt 28:20). God's voice is something one has to listen for—"the still, small voice" that spoke to the prophet Elijah.

It is the purpose of this work to relate any private revelation that may have been revealed to some of God's people and to try and assess its credibility and authenticity. Another intention of the author is to explore a vast array of supernatural and concomitant phenomena experienced by saints, blesseds, and other of the faithful. In the process, mystical phenomena such as apparitions, visions, dreams, and locutions that have been approved by the Church will be examined. Another section of this work will examine those special favors and promises made by Jesus and Mary to various saints. Lastly, short biographies of specific saints, blesseds, venerables, and other holy people who have experienced a private revelation or some type of concomitant mystical phenomena such as levitation, bilocation, discernment of spirits, the stigmata, etcetera will be explored. It is through mystical experiences such as visions, powerful dreams, and locutions that God touches our lives. He is a God of love, and love longs to communicate. If you are like most people, you need a word of encouragement from the Lord. Say, with Samuel, "Speak, for your servant hears" (1 Sm 3:10).

"Today when you hear his voice, / do not harden your hearts" (Heb 4:7; see also Ps 95:7–8).

---

[7] Connell, T. *Meeting with Mary; Visions of the Blessed Mother*. N.Y. Ballantine Books, 1995, p.347; see also *Washington Post*, Oct. 14, 1994, p.A1.
[8] Ibid., p.5.
[9] *Washington Times*, Dec. 5, 1995, p.A15.

Saint John the Evangelist on Patmos by Hieronymus Bosch

Divine Revelation

Divine Revelation is the self-manifestation of God. It is the Creator's self-disclosure or communication of hidden truths that are not normally accessible to man. Through Divine Revelation, God chooses to communicate the eternal decisions of His will regarding the salvation of men. Out of love for mankind, He discloses the mystery of His own Trinitarian life and invites us all to share ultimately in this inner life.

God has revealed Himself historically to man by gradually communicating His own mystery in great deeds and in words. Divine Revelation is thus a complex reality consisting of the inspired Word as the formal element and of the historical event as the material element.[10] This Revelation was not broken off by our first parents' sins. After the Fall, God buoyed mankind up with the hope of salvation by promising redemption. If one grants that God has created man for a supernatural destiny, one must admit that He has revealed that destiny to us together with the means of attaining it. The divine economy is the fulfillment of God's plan of salvation, fully developed in His mind from eternity and fully revealed in Jesus Christ. Before the Incarnation, God's plan was known only obscurely. After the ascension of Christ and the coming of the Holy Spirit at Pentecost, God's plan of loving goodness, formed from all eternity in Christ for the benefit of all men, was fully revealed. It is the substance of that apostolic preaching which is preserved in its integrity for each generation.[11]

Through Abraham, Noah, Moses, and the prophets, God prepared His people, through His covenants with them, to accept the salvation destined for all humanity. God then revealed Himself fully by sending His own Son in whom He has established His covenant forever. As the self-manifestation of the Father, Jesus perfected Revelation by fulfilling it through His words and deeds.

As the Dogmatic Constitution on Divine Revelation of the Second Vatican Council (no. 4) specifically states: "After God had spoken many times and in various ways through the prophets in these last days, He has spoken to us by a Son (Heb. 1:1–2). The revealer-son is described as bearing the very stamp of God's nature (Heb. 1:3), as being the 'image of the invisible God' (Col. 1:15). He sent His Son, the eternal Word who enlightens all humankind, to live among them and to tell them about the inner life of God. Hence Jesus Christ sent as 'a man among men and women,' speaks 'the words of God' (Jn. 3:34), and accomplishes the saving work which the Father gave Him to do (see Jn. 5:36;17:4).

---

[10] Avery Dulles, S.J. *Models of Revelation*. Garden City, NY, Doubleday Books, 1983, p. 66.

[11] Catechism of the Catholic Church (CCC). Liguori, MO., Libreria Editrice Vaticana, 1994, nos. 50, 66, 122, 260.

As a result, He Himself—to see who is to see the Father (see Jn. 14:9)—completed and perfected revelation and confirmed it with divine guarantees. He did this by the total fact of His presence and self-manifestation—by words and works, signs and miracles, but, above all by His death and glorious resurrection from the dead, and finally by the sending of the Spirit of truth.[12] The revealer-Son disclosed that God the Father was with us, to deliver us up from the darkness of sin and death, and to raise us up to eternal life. Jesus Christ is thus the Mediator and at the same time the fullness of all revelation.[13] Since the Son is the Father's definite Word, there will be no public Divine Revelation after Him.

Jesus Christ in whom the entire Revelation of the most high God is summed up, then commanded the apostles to preach the Gospel, which had been promised beforehand by the prophets, and which He fulfilled in His own person and promulgated with His own lips.

In the Gospel or Sacred Scripture, God is explained beyond our ability to know Him. It is His word in as much as it is consigned to writing under the inspiration of the Holy Spirit. Thus, the Father's self-communication made through the Word in the Holy Spirit remains present and active in the Church today and for all time to come.[14]

Primarily then, Revelation is the act of God, seen in the progressive unfolding of His eternal plan of salvation in Christ, by which He manifests and communicates Himself to men, calls the Church into being, and demands the loving respect of assent and obedience. Secondarily, it is the body of truth that is made known through God's unfolding plan. The nature of Revelation can be seen both in the Old Testament (OT) and the New Testament (NT), which together make up the complete deposit of Sacred Scripture.[15] Sacred Scripture is thus considered by most Christians to contain the whole of Revelation and is itself the final revelation of God.[16]

There are two types of Divine Revelation: public or universal revelation which is contained in the Sacred Scripture and in the Deposit of the apostolic Tradition and is transmitted by the Magisterium (teaching authority) of the Church. Public revelation ended with the preaching of the apostles and is a matter of faith and belief for everyone. The other is called private or special revelation. With regards to this type of revelation, belief in it is not required by the Church, even when found credible and she approves it. By this approbation, the Church only intends to declare that nothing is to be found in it that is contrary to faith or morals and that it can be accepted without danger and even with advantage.[17]

---

[12] Vatican Council II, 2nd (1962–1965): Constitutions, Decrees, Declarations The Basic Sixteen Documents. general editor Austin Flannery, Northport, N.Y., Costello Publishing Co. 1975; *Dogmatic Constitution on Divine Revelation of the Vatican Council II, Dei Verbum*, (no.4), pp. 98–99.

[13] Dulles, op.cit., p. 155.

[14] Vatican Council II, op.cit. pp. 97–106.

[15] New Catholic Encyclopedia. Catholic University of America, 2nd ed. 15 v. Detroit, Mich., Thomson-Gale 2003, v.12, p. 187.

[16] Dulles, op.cit., p. 38.

[17] Augustin Poulain, S.J. *Revelations and visions: discerning the true and the certain from the false or the doubtful*; translated by Leonora L. Yorke Smith; edited and with an introduction by Frank Sadowski. NY, Alba House, 1998. p. 29.

Public Revelation

For Catholics, a distinction is thus made between public and private revelation. Public revelation is, as presented above, God's choice to reveal Himself through His Son. It is called public revelation because Christ said that it was to be given to all nations (see Mt 24:14; 28:19; Mk 13:10; Lk 24:47). It will never pass away, and no new public revelation is to be expected before the glorious manifestation of our Lord, Jesus Christ.[18] This revelation, which God has given to all people for all ages, is preserved in twin sources of revelation: Sacred Scripture and Sacred Tradition. These make up the heritage of faith, which is most often referred to as the Deposit of Faith. This body of teachings came from Christ directly or through the prophets before Him and apostles after Him. This Deposit has never changed. It is the substance of the Faith. All who accept Christ in faith must accept all the truths handed down in these two sources of revelation. To them is added a third component: the Magisterium, or teaching authority of the Church. Sacred Tradition, Sacred Scripture, and the Magisterium, in accord with God's most wise design, are so linked and joined together that one cannot stand without the others. All three together and each in its own way, under the action of the one Holy Spirit, contribute effectively to the salvation of souls. Thus everything essential to the Faith has been already revealed through the Scriptures and interpreted through the wisdom of the Magisterium, which is guided by the inspiration of the Holy Spirit.[19]

Sacred Scripture, or the Bible, is God's word recorded in writing by human authors inspired by the Holy Spirit. No book will ever be added to or deleted from Sacred Scripture (see Rv 22:18–19). Sacred Tradition is the transmission of the Deposit of Faith from one generation to another under the magisterial guidance of the Church, which proclaims, explains, and applies the revealed truths throughout the centuries. Sacred Tradition is thus the passing on of the Word of God which Jesus entrusted to the apostles. The apostles and their successors, the Fathers of the Church, guided and enlightened by the Holy Spirit, whom our Lord identified as the Spirit of Truth, have preserved, expounded, and preached these revealed truths. The Church maintains Sacred Tradition: Christ's teachings that have never been written down and which supplement and clarify the truths contained in Sacred Scripture. Sacred Tradition is thus "the collection of revealed truths which the Church has received through the apostles in addition to inspired Sacred Scripture which it preserves by the uninterrupted continuity of the apostolic teaching office (Magisterium)."[20] Pedagogically, Sacred

---

[18] Vatican Council II: op. cit., p. 99.

[19] Ibid., pp. 103–104.

[20] G. van Noort. *Dogmatic Theology*, v.3, *The Sources*

Tradition can be more helpful than Sacred Scripture when it comes to understanding certain revealed truths such as the Incarnation and the Trinity. Other examples of Sacred Tradition include the Nicene and Apostle's Creeds.[21] Sacred Tradition is thus also important as an interpretive medium. It is a "living thing." It is dynamic and alive. It is one primary way the Lord is with us, even to the end of the age.[22]

The New Testament consists of information that exists in Sacred Tradition and was written down by the Church under the inspiration of the Holy Spirit, so the Church is the only organization from which one can get the New Testament intact.[23] Together Sacred Scripture and Sacred Tradition form one Deposit of Revelation, "for both of them, flowing out from the same divine well-spring, come together in some fashion to form one thing and move towards the same goal."[24]

In these definitions, an important point is emphasized: while public revelation is complete, "it has not been made completely explicit; it remains for the faithful to gradually grasp the full significance of public revelation contained in the Scriptures and tradition of the Church."[25] Herein lies the role of the Magisterium or the Church's teaching authority, instituted by Christ and guided by the Holy Spirit, which seeks to safeguard and explain the truths of the Faith. The job of interpreting accurately the Word of God, oral or written, has

been given only to the Magisterium of the Church, which exercises it in the name of Jesus Christ.[26] This means that the task of interpretation has been entrusted to the bishops in communion with the successor of Peter, the bishop of Rome.[27] The Magisterium is thus exercised in two ways: extraordinarily, when the pope and ecumenical councils infallibly define a truth of faith or morals that are necessary for one's salvation and that has been constantly taught and held by the Church, and ordinarily, when the Church infallibly defines a truth of the Faith that (1) is taught universally and without dissent, (2) must be taught or the Magisterium would be failing in its duty, (3) is connected with a grave matter of faith or morals, or (4) is taught authoritatively.[28] All faithful Catholics are bound to accept these revealed truths with a divine faith. To deny these revealed truths would be considered heresy akin to denying the mystery of the incarnation of our Lord, the Real Presence of our Lord in the Holy Eucharist, or the existence of hell.[29]

---

of Revelation. Westminster: Newman, 1961, 1963, no. 138, p. 139.

[21] Francis Xavier Schouppe. *Hell and How to Avoid Hell.* Rockford, Illinois, TAN Books and Publishers, Inc. 1989, p. 142.

[22] Devin Rose. *If Protestantism is True.* Lexington, Ky.,Unitatis, 2011, pp. 135–36.

[23] Kevin Orlin Johnson, PhD. *Apparitions: mystic phenomena and what they mean.* Dallas, Texas, Pangaeus Press, 1995. p. 284.

[24] Vatican Council II, op.cit., no. 9, p. 102.

[25] CCC, op.cit., nos. 66–67.

[26] Vatican Council II, op.cit., no. 10, p. 103.

[27] CCC, op.cit., no. 85.

[28] Peter Stavinskas, Rev., ed. *Catholic Dictionary.* Huntington, Indiana, Our Sunday Visitor Publishing Division, 2002. pp. 484–85; see also see CCC, nos. 77, 85–88, 95, 888–92, 2032–36.

[29] William P. Saunders. *Straight Answers II; answers to 100 more questions about the Catholic faith.* Baltimore, Md., Cathedral Foundation Press, 2003, p. 15.

Private Revelation

The previous explanation does not imply that since the death of the last apostle, the communication of God with man ceased, or that after Jesus Christ all revelations are impossible. The lack of divine communication would contradict the history of the Church as well as God's Word in Scripture. Although there are many cases of pseudo-visionaries and false revelations, there are numerous visionaries, apparitions, locutions, and revelations that fulfill the conditions that the theological critique requires as signs of authenticity.

Creditable private revelation consists of all non-contradictory communications from God approved by the Church that have occurred since the deposit of public revelation was closed at the death of St. John the Apostle (c. 6–104). Since that time, there can be no public revelation, although private revelation to certain individuals for the direction of their lives is not excluded.[30] Private revelation may be a simple and fairly routine matter like the answer to a simple prayer, or it may be by way of an extraordinary event like an apparition or a locution, a miraculous healing, or some other recognized mystic phenomenon. It may be a sort of reminder of something to an individual person by God, delivered sometimes by way of an angel or saint. Revelation can never end as long as God continues to deal personally with man and be present in human history.[31] God still directly intervenes in human affairs through voices, visions, apparitions, locutions, miracles, signs, and wonders. He uses others as catalysts for these signs to come about: the angels, the saints, the Blessed Virgin Mary, etc. In modern times, revelation can also be authenticated through miracles and fulfilled prophecies.[32]

Again it must be stated that no creditable private revelation, however, can contradict or override public revelation.[33] When the Church intervenes in private revelations, it does so in order to determine its compatibility with public revelations. As a consequence, if it finds that the private revelation contradicts the public revelation, it declares it false, as God cannot contradict Himself. If it finds agreement in both, it allows the private revelation to be admitted. Generally the Church does not go further than this. Still, though less frequently, on finding sufficient reasons that give credit to the supernatural character of a private revelation, the Church can declare it as such. By doing so, it does not oblige the faithful to admit this declaration as of "catholic or ecclesiastical faith" but guides them prudently so that they can admit it by human faith, with the warrant of a serious investigation and the testimony of an ecclesiastical authority which

---

[30] Johnson, op cit., p. 364; Dulles, op.cit., p. 229.

[31] Dulles, op.cit., p. 105.
[32] Ibid., p. 22.
[33] Johnson, op.cit., p. 364.

The Conversion of Saint Augustine (1430–1435), Fra Angelico (1395–1455).

emits the declaration.[34] So, in essence, acceptance of even those private revelations declared creditable is not required of Christians, only permitted. Private revelations thus never receive any assent from the Church. Even the Church's official approval just says that these extraordinary events contain nothing contrary to the Faith, that they are probable, not that they are undoubted, that they are "worthy of belief," not that they must be believed.[35] The important thing to remember about a private revelation or any other extraordinary personal phenomenon is that, as far as the Church is concerned, it is not essential to the Faith, even if approved by the Church.[36]

A private revelation, as such, can be differentiated from a religious experience. A religious experience means any subjective state suggesting to the individual the presence or action of the divine or transcendent reality.[37] A private revelation, on the other hand, gives the impression of being beyond the control of the individual. In Book VIII, 7 of his *Confessions*, St. Augustine describes his conversion after reading Romans 13:13 as a personal internal response to grace. He had no vision or locution or direct response to grace.[38] However, throughout the ages, individuals have experienced a private or particular revelation from God; that is, a message given them in a vision, apparition, dream, locution or in a state of rapture, or ecstasy and the like for the greater service of the Church. They are historical facts based upon human testimony.

As alluded to above, some of these so-called "private revelations" have been recognized

[34] Jordan Aumann, O.P. *Spiritual Theology.* London, England, Contiuum, 1980 [reprinted 2006], p. 429.

[35] Johnson, op.cit., p. 288; Stavinskas, op.cit., p. 614.

[36] Johnson, op.cit., p. 285.

[37] Benedict J. Groeschel. *A still, small voice; a practical guide on reported revelations.* San Francisco, Ignatius Press, 1993, p. 151.

[38] Ibid., p. 137.

by the authority of the Church. Although genuine private revelations do not add anything new to the primary or essential truths of our faith—that is, truths already contained in the Deposit of Faith—they, nonetheless, highlight and accentuate certain truths of the Deposit that may be eclipsed or ignored at a particular moment of history, thereby causing harm to the spiritual life of the People of God. Consequently, it might be legitimately suggested that each authentic instance of private revelation contains a dogmatic truth or truths specifically needed at a particular moment in the life of the Church. Private revelations may recommend a particular devotion, exhort to penance, give certain instructions, warn against certain doctrines, recommend a spiritual doctrine or manner of life, and so forth.[39] So private revelation's role is not to improve or complete Christ's definite revelation but to help the faithful live more fully by it in a certain period of history. As evidenced by Fatima, Lourdes, Knock, Guadalupe, and many other approved private revelations, the Lord gives them to mankind as a means of encouragement. Guided by the Magisterium of the Church, the *sensus fidelium* (mind of the faithful) knows how to discern and welcome in these revelations as whatever constitutes an authentic call of Christ or His saints to the Church.[40] So to re-emphasize, the only thing that a private revelation can do, at best, is just nudge one back to the truth of public revelation or of some fact of it, drawing one's attention to some essential point of that doctrine and the way in which to apply it in one's life.[41]

Although the Church wisely claims that divine truth is revealed through the sacred deposits of Scripture and the teaching body of the Church, some are, nevertheless, called individually to respond to God's intervention in their lives. To neglect this duty would be as much of a serious sin as to discredit a truth revealed for the universal Church through divine faith.

Types of Private Revelation

Private revelations are communications made to individuals by God Himself (usually through Jesus Christ) or through the Blessed Virgin Mary, the angels, or the saints. Experts in the field usually classify these communications or messages into three types: absolute or a simple statement of a truth or mystery, as when St. Bernadette Soubirous (1844–1879) heard the words, "I am the Immaculate Conception," conditioned, which is usually a threat or promise based on some conditions, such as the promises made to St. Margaret Mary Alacoque (1647–1690), or denunciatory, which is usually a condemnation or threat of future punishment,[42] as when St. Dominic (1170–1221) had a vision of an angry Christ in 1217 whereby He threatened to chastise Rome for its transgressions. The denunciatory revelation may also be conditioned, as was in the case of Rome with Mary's intercession to save Rome and the prophecy of Jonah concerning the destruction of Nineveh. If a revelation refers to the future, it is ordinarily called a prophecy, although prophecy as such abstracts from time and place.[43] Private revelations may proceed from a natural, a diabolical, or a supernatural source, and even if the revelation is supernatural in origin, the seer may unwittingly distort its meaning.[44]

To reiterate, the first thing that must be

---

[39] Karl Rahner. *Visions and Prophecies.* [VAP], Translated by Charles Henkeyand Richard Strachan. Freiburg, Herder, 1963. p. 18.
[40] CCC, op.cit., no. 67.
[41] Johnson, op.cit., p. 286.

[42] NCE, 1st ed. op.cit., v. 10, p. 173.
[43] Aumann, op.cit., p. 429.
[44] NCE, 2nd ed, op.cit., v. 10, p. 108.

said again about private revelations is that they must not clash with public revelation and that the only persons obliged to believe them are the ones who are convinced that they are supernatural in origin. Thus the faithful may reject all private revelations if they choose not to believe in them after conscientious reflection.

Prospero Labertini, an Italian cardinal who later became Pope Benedict XIV (1740–1758), wrote four hundred pages of instructions on how to properly investigate cases involving mystical phenomena, miracles, and sanctity. In his work *On the Beatification and Canonization of the servants of God*, the pope stated that one can give private revelations only prudent acceptance as probable. "Prudence," he said, "dictates that before giving assent to any private revelation, one should exert every effort to discern whether or not it is worthy of credence."

As regards the faithful, the general principle is that one is free to inquire and to prayerfully discern which private revelations are true and which are false. Pope Benedict XIV, writing about the partially approved revelations of St. Hildegard of Bingen by Pope Eugene III (1145–1153), St. Bridget of Sweden by Pope Boniface IX (1389–1404), and of St. Catherine of Siena by Pope Gregory XI (1370–1378), taught authoritatively that "persons other than the recipient who accept a private revelation will do so simply on human faith, after making a prudent decision according to which the aforesaid revelations are probable, and piously to be believed."[45]

Cardinal Jean-Baptiste-Francoise Pitra (1812–1889), an outstanding Benedictine scholar who edited the writings of St. Hildegard of Bingen, says basically the same: "Everyone knows that we are fully at liberty to believe or not to believe in private revelations, even those most worthy of credence. Even when the Church approves them, they are merely received as probable and not as indubitable. They are not to be used in deciding questions of history, natural philosophy, philosophy, or theology which are matters of controversy between the Doctors [of the Church]. It is quite permissible to differ from these revelations even when approved, if we are relying on solid reasons, and especially if the contrary doctrine is proved by unimpeachable documents and definite experience."[46]

Granted that the Church assumes no further responsibility, a question then arises: "What is the last word regarding the actual authority of private revelations? They have the value of the testimony of the person who witnesses to having received them, nothing more or less. Now this person is never infallible. It is evident, then, that the points vouched for are never absolutely certain—except in the sole case where a miracle is worked directly in favor of the attestation. In a word, private revelations have only a pure human or probable authority."[47]

The closest that the Church usually comes to endorsing private revelations is to say that she finds some of them credible and worthy of belief, whereby one may believe with moral certitude that what is taught or encouraged in these messages will bring one closer to God, to the imitation of the ways of Christ, and help people live more integrated, Gospel-centered lives.[48]

---

[45] De Canon., Book III, ch. Liii, no. 15; Book II, ch. xxxii, no. 11. Eng. Trans. *Benedict XIV on Heroic Virtue*, vol. III, ch. xiv cited byAugustin Poulain in *The Graces of Interior Prayer*, Translated by Leonora L. Yorke Smith. St. Louis, Mo., B.Herder Book Co., 1950. p. 320; see also Augustin Poulain S.J.. *Revelations and visions*, op.cit., pp. 29–30.

[46] Poulain, *Revelations*, op.cit., p. 30 cites Cardinal Pitra's Book on St. Hildegard, p. xvi.

[47] Ibid., p. 30, cites Fr. Toulemont on Private revelations in Review, Les Etudes, 1866, p. 61.

[48] Freze, VVA, op.cit., p. 128.

However, as regards belief in private revelations, it is said that Pope Urban VIII (1623–1644) once declared: "In cases which concern private revelations, it is better to believe than not to believe, for, if you believe, and it is proven true, you will receive all the benefits of grace for believing. If you believe, and it should be proven false, you will receive some benefits of grace anyway because you believed it to be true." Thus, one's clear conscience and moral certitude are taken into account by God, who judges each person by his or her sincere heart.[49]

Authentic (Credible) Revelations

The closing of public revelation does not mean that God has withdrawn into eternal silence. On the contrary, the history of the Church is replete with examples of private revelation given to individuals to be shared and to have wide circulation. If the investigations and the judgment of the Church declare that a particular vision and private revelation may be believed with human faith, this ecclesiastical approbation in itself is not necessarily infallible. The approbation implies that such a revelation can show good grounds for human credibility and does not contradict the Deposit of Faith. Like all important acts of the Church's pastoral authority, it deserves to be respectfully obeyed by the faithful.[50]

The Church has never been long without saints or holy persons who received from God authentic private revelations. Early on there were the desert fathers such as St. Anthony of Egypt (251–356). In medieval times there were great mystics like St. Hildegard of Bingen, St. Gertrude the Great, and St. Bridget of Sweden who wrote books containing revelations they received. More spectacular, in a way, were those persons called by God in private revelation to a mission in the Church, such as St. Catherine of Siena who brought about the return of Pope Gregory XI from Avignon to Rome. Other saints who were commissioned by God in private revelation to work for the creation of a liturgical feast such as Blessed Juliana of Cornilion (1192–1258) for the feast of Corpus Christi and St. Margaret Mary Alacoque for the feast of the Sacred Heart. In another class of private revelations, also generally involving a mission, are the modern Marian apparitions, among which Lourdes and Fatima are best known. There are also the "revelations" of the mystics and saints, often unconnected with any visible mission but providing spiritual guidance for the Church, such as the two Carmelite mystics St. Teresa of Avila and St. John of the Cross.[51]

Can one ever be morally certain that a private revelation is purely divine? Yes, one can, for when God wills it, He can give complete certainty while the revelation lasts, at any rate, to the person receiving it. The light and the evidence are of such strength that any kind of doubt is impossible. One can also be certain that a private revelation made to another person is purely divine. The Old Testament prophets furnished indubitable signs of their mission.[52] A visionary or seer who perceives a private revelation does so in one of two ways. If it is a so-called "express revelation," the recipient knows with absolute certainty that the revelation is of divine origin. This certainty is experienced through an inner conviction of the heart as well and is based upon a clear conscientious reflection. With an express revelation, God illumines the soul by inspirations or motives that were not originally sought out through preconceived desires rooted in vanity, curiosity, or attachments to extraordinary things.

---

49 Ibid., p. 122.
50 Rahner, op.cit., 83.

51 NCE 2nd ed., op.cit., v. 12, 201.
52 Poulain, *Revelations*, op.cit., rav, 65.

Rather this revelation (vision or locution) is initiated solely by God, who makes His presence known with absolute certainty to the recipient involved. Express revelations, visions, or locutions should never be desired or sought lest the evil spirit use such desires to deceive the one who seeks such things. Authentic supernatural experiences are always unexpected and unpredictable. God gives them to whomever He wills whenever He wills. Acceptance of these facts helps to promote humility, sincerity, and a clear conviction of conscience. The other type of revelation is that which is perceived by instinct. In this case, the recipient may be unable to distinguish whether these revelations are conceived of divine instinct or through one's own spirit. Because of such uncertainty, the visionary risks being victim of his or her own imagination, suggestive powers, or deceptions and illusions brought about by the powers of darkness. Because it is often difficult to distinguish the express revelation from that which is believed to be true through an instinct or "inner hunch," consultations with a wise and learned director is a necessary step toward advancement in the spiritual life.[53]

When a miracle is performed and it is stated that it is worked with this intention, or when circumstances show this to be the case, it is undeniable proof of the divine nature of the revelation.[54]

Anyone declared a saint, blessed, or venerable by the Church, as well as any pope, should be believed when they claim to have received some type of private revelation from heaven. There are a number of private revelations that have been accepted by the mind of the faithful and approved by the temporal authority of the Church.

The following Catholic saints, for instance, have received authentic messages from the Lord or His mother and have had them sanctioned by the Church: St. Hildegard of Bingen, Blessed Juliana of Cornillon, St. Gertrude the Great, St. Bridget of Sweden, St. Catherine of Siena, St. Vincent Ferrer, St. Teresa of Avila, St. John of the Cross, St. Margaret Mary Alacoque, St. Bernadette Soubirous at Lourdes, and St. Catherine Laboure. The various apparitions of our Blessed Mother also are private revelations whereby she has spoken on behalf of her Son. Some of the most famous are the apparitions of Guadalupe in Mexico (1531); Paris, France (1830); La Salette, France (1846); Lourdes, France (1858); Pontmain, France (1871), Knock, Ireland (1879); and the children at Fatima in Portugal (1917).[55] Sometimes a private revelation may alter major events, as did the call of St. Joan of Arc (1412–1431), who in a single year changed the course of European history. And as already mentioned, Saint Catherine of Siena, following personal inspirations she received, was successful in calling Pope Gregory XI back from Avignon thus preserving the sovereignty of the papacy from royal domination.[56]

It also sometimes happens that a private revelation leads to the execution of some bold enterprise like the establishment of a new devotion; for instance, the foundation of a religious congregation or pious association or the remodeling of the constitution of another. Such a revelation may also relate to the correction of the relaxed state of a certain group of persons, the building of a church, the inauguration of some work for which the available resources are insufficient, the preaching of a more refined spirituality which God is supposed to have reserved for our time, etc.[57]

As regards a private revelation given to institute a new devotion, one only has to look at the scapular of Mount Carmel,

[53] Freze, op.cit., pp. 304–5.
[54] Poulain, *revelations*, op.cit, p. 66.

[55] Saunders, op. cit., p. 15.
[56] Groeschel, op.cit., p. 26.
[57] Poulain, *revelations*, op.cit, p. 91.

Joan of Arc Receiving a Vision from the Archangel Michael (1876),
Eugène Romain Thirion (1839–1910).

the devotion to the Sacred Heart, and the Miraculous Medal to see that God favored these works in a special manner. These revelations have withstood the test of time and scrutiny and have produced great fruits of grace on all sides.[58]

On the other hand, caution must be exercised by the Church in validating a private revelation that suggests starting a new devotion. An extreme example of this is the case of Blessed Juliana of Cornillon mentioned above. She had a revelation instructing her to work for the establishment of a feast in honor of the Blessed Sacrament; however, she did not present this instruction to theologians for almost twenty years. Juliana encountered only opposition and persecution with her attempts to reform the convent where she served as superior. Eventually she had to leave and wandered around for twenty years until her death. Only long after her death did her revelations get any real hearing because a priest whom she knew in Liege, Belgium, became Pope Urban IV (1261–1264). The result was that the feast of Corpus Christi was finally celebrated in the universal Church over one hundred years after Blessed Juliana had her revelation.[59]

Questionable Revelations

Questionable revelations are far more numerous than approved ones. Father P. Deletter, SJ, a theologian who writes extensively on this subject, states that twenty-two Marian apparitions were seriously studied between the years 1931 and 1950, and only two were approved (Beauraing and Banneux in Belgium). Six remained undecided in 1952, and the remaining fourteen were rejected.[60] No fewer than two hundred apparitions were reported in the vicinity of Lourdes after the experience of St. Bernadette Soubirous. None of these were ever taken seriously. The case of St. Joan of Arc shows that sometimes decisions made on revelations can be reversed. Joan died condemned as a witch by the Church court in a decision approved by the University of Paris and was exonerated twenty-five years later and eventually canonized. Although the process of canonization does not consider the question of the authenticity of visions and revelations, Joan's acceptance as a saint certainly dismisses the charge that her visions were satanic and evil. One gets some real credibility from canonization although, as we will see, a saint may be wrong about a vision.[61]

[58] Ibid., pp. 92–93.

[59] Groeschel, op. cit., pp.112–13.
[60] NCE, 1st ed. op.cit., v. 12, p. 446.
[61] Groeschel, op.cit., p. 41.

Erroneous Revelations

A person who is the recipient of an authentic revelation, even a canonized saint, may indeed make theological errors in understanding that revelation or in reporting experiences that are not authentic revelations.[62] Piety, humility, and personal honesty are absolute prerequisites before a vision can possibly be considered genuine, but they are no proof of its authenticity because these qualities are no protection against error.[63] Private revelations come through the prism of the recipient's personality and experience. No matter how objective their origin in the mercy of divine grace, no matter how unexpected and unsolicited, revelations are all more or less defined within the subjectivity of the individual.[64]

There are many examples of these "erroneous revelations" in the lives of the saints. St. Peter, for instance, at the Transfiguration, became completely overwhelmed by the objective experience. His subjectivity then took over and he suggested building booths, as the Jewish people do at Sukkoth, for Christ and the apparition of the two prophets (see Mt 17:1–8). It is this subjective element that opens the door to misunderstanding and even error. Canonization of a saint does not at all guarantee the truth of an alleged private revelation. For example, St. Norbert of Xanten (c. 1080–1134) was absolutely certain that the anti-Christ would appear in his lifetime. St. Catherine of Siena and St. Veronica of Binasco believed Our Lady told them in a vision that she was not conceived immaculate. Apparitions of Christ delivered impossible etymologies to St. Mechtild of Hackenborn and St. Gertrude the Great. St. Hildegard of Bingen attributed her knowledge, which was no means always correct, to immediate divine illuminations and dictation. St. Vincent Ferrer declared on the authority of his visions that the end of the world was imminent. It was later declared that this was a conditional prophecy and that God postponed the destruction of the world because of the works of the saint.[65] St. Ignatius of Loyola determined through discernment that one series of mystical visions he experienced was generated from the "evil spirit," even though at the time they seemed to be from the Holy Spirit.[66] The historical contradictions between the various saints and venerables such as Sts. Bridget of Sweden, Elizabeth of Schonau, Maria Maddalena de' Pazzi, Blessed Anne Catherine Emmerich, and Venerable Mary of Agreda in regard to the different dates of the death of the Blessed Mother are well known.[67]

Father Augustin Poulain, SJ (1836–1919), the author of *The Graces of the Interior Life* which was first published in 1901 in France under the title of *Des Graces D'Oraison*, reports on these historical contradictions. For instance, he states that these visionaries all had different death dates for the Blessed Virgin Mary. St. Bridget reported that Our Lady died fifteen years after the death of Christ (Book vii, ch.xxvi); Blessed Anna Catherine Emmerich said it was thirteen years (Life of the Blessed Virgin, pt. II, ch. xii); Venerable Maria of Agreda reckoned twenty-one years, four months, and nineteen days (Cite mystique, Part III, Book VIII, ch. xix); and St. Elizabeth of Schoenau reported a year and a half (Bolland, June 18, No. 110). They cannot all be right. The pious believer should be aware that a visionary may have taken the vision

---

[62] Ibid., p. 49.
[63] Rahner, op.cit., p. 76.
[64] Groeschel, op.cit., pp. 49–50.

[65] Rahner, VAP, op.cit., p. 66.
[66] http://www.catholicculture.org/docs/doc_view.cfm?recnum=515.
[67] Rahner, op.cit., p. 67.

too literally and should have understood them allegorically and spiritually.[68]

Some saints, in their visions of Jesus on the cross at Calvary, perceived that there were three nails only; others saw four. Those who saw three nails include St. Maria Maddalena de' Pazzi and Blessed Anne Catherine Emmerich. St. Clare of Montefalco and St. Veronica Giuliani had the three nails imprinted on their hearts. St. Bridget of Sweden, on the other hand, saw four nails. Consequently, it is clear that God did not choose to settle this controversial question by revelation.[69] Now, if these saintly women knew error, we must not be surprised to find self-deceptions occurring in the case of other visionaries whose sanctity is by no means established. Father Poulain cites five general reasons why authentic revelations may contain errors.

First, a divine revelation may at times be interpreted wrongly by the person who receives it. This may be due primarily to the obscurity of the revelation. God, at times, gives only a partial comprehension of its import. His communication has a deep meaning that is not understood; it is taken in the everyday sense. A sad example of this was in the misunderstanding of St. Joan of Arc. She had an interior locution concerning her death, but misinterpreted both the date and the manner. She says in her words: "I inquired of my voices whether I should be burned; and they answered me that I should trust in the Lord and that *He would aid me.* . . . St Catherine told me that I would *receive succor.*" St. Joan states that she interpreted this utterance as indicating her deliverance. She adds: "As a rule, the voices tell me that I shall be *delivered by a great victory.* And afterwards, they say, '*Fear not because of your martyrdom. It will bring you at last to Paradise.*'" These predictions were quite accurate. But St. Joan did not see their real significance. She thought, as she herself explains, that the word *martyrdom* meant "the great pains and adversity that she suffered in prison" and "the deliverance by a great victory" caused her to think of something quite different than her death.[70]

Second, a tendency to use a revelation to write history rather than to use it symbolically. It is imprudent to seek to remake history by the help of the saints' revelation. Many of the revelations of persons whose sanctity and doctrine have been approved by the heads of the Church contradict each other.[71]

Third, the tendency of the visionary to mix subjective expectations and preconceived ideas with the action of divine grace.[72] Ideas that appeal to our own desires and preconceived ideas in matters of doctrine or history and also the recollection of anything that has struck us vividly in reading or conversation may be wrongly attributed to divine influence either during an ecstasy or in close union with God.[73] Perhaps the most celebrated revelation of this type is that of St. Catherine of Siena's 1377 ecstasy in which Our Lady told her that she was not immaculately conceived.[74] This is most likely a classic example of where a saint deceived herself as a result of preconceived ideas. St. Colette, the founder of a reform of the Poor Clares, brought preconceived ideas into her visions. In accordance with the belief of her directors, she began by holding that St. Anne, the grandmother of Jesus, had been married three times and had had several daughters. She believed that she saw St. Anne appear to her with all her supposed family.[75] St. Catherine dei Ricci was perhaps also influenced by preconceived ideas. St. Catherine

---

[68] Poulain, op.cit., p. 62.
[69] Poulain, Ibid., pp. 38, 62.
[70] Poulain, ibid., pp. 33–34 cites *La Vraie Jeanne d'Arc* by P. Ayrolles, vol II, ch. v, no. 4, p. 161.
[71] Poulain, Ibid., p. 39.
[72] Groeschel, op.cit., p. 59.
[73] Poulain, op.cit., pp. 40–41.
[74] Groeschel, op.cit., p. 59.
[75] Poulain, op.cit., pp. 41–42.

was devoted to the Italian religious Dominican reformer Girolamo Savonarola (1452–1498). She strove to make him an object of public veneration as a prophet and martyr. Savonarola often appeared to her surrounded by glory and twice cured her suddenly of a serious illness. These appearances seemed an obstacle at first to Catherine's beatification because Pope Alexander VI (1492–1503) had excommunicated Savonarola and declared him a heretic. He was burned at the stake. Pope Benedict XIII (1724–1730) resolved the issue by separating the saint's virtues from her visions. This led to the principle that when a servant of God is canonized, it is his or her virtue that is canonized and not his or her visions.[76]

Fourth, a subsequent altering or amplification of the testimony after the revelation. This has led to visionaries revealing details decades later which were never mentioned in their original testimony. Perhaps it is an error in memory that is the source of reports that the Blessed Virgin instructed the children of Fatima to pray for the souls in hell. This would be a theological impossibility.[77] There is also a great danger when the written revelation is very long and yet has been received almost instantaneously. St. Bridget of Sweden recognizes that this is sometimes so in her own case. It is not rash to believe that not all the words used were supplied by the revelation and that the thoughts were not given in detail. They were developed later by the person who received them.[78]

Lastly, errors made in good faith by those who record the testimony. Secretaries, for instance, may easily alter the text without any wrong intention, for their own personality intervenes in the choice of expressions. They sometimes, with a certain amount of good faith, think they can add whole

sentences under the pretext of making the thought clearer. Examples of where the accuracy of the text is disputed are those of Venerable Mary of Agreda, Blessed Catherine Anne Emmerich, and Marie Lataste. Compilers likewise sometimes modify revelations. For example, in the first German edition of Catherine Emmerich's works, it was said that St. James the Greater (d. 42) was present at the Blessed Virgin's death. It was later seen that this statement was incompatible with the chronology of events in the Acts of the Apostles, and this erroneous phrase was removed in the Ratisbon edition of her work.[79]

False Revelations

Father Benedict Groeschel, a Capuchin Franciscan friar, was a psychologist, spiritual writer, pastoral counselor, and director of spiritual development for the New York Archdiocese. He employed the term "false revelation" in cases where the recipient and supporters are mistaken, but they are all in good faith. Here, a sincere person honestly believes the revelations came from God and reflect the special operation of divine grace. Saint Elizabeth of Schonau and her bizarre elaboration of the already fantastic Saint Ursula (4th c.) legends which were clearly false revelations may be an example of this. The conclusion in her case is that even a heroically virtuous person may respond to grace in a way that is strongly affected by subjective expectations and needs.[80]

Father Groeschel says there are many possible causes of false revelation. He cites severe mental illness, especially a certain kind of paranoid schizophrenia, and hallucinatory experiences of a pseudo-mystical type as examples. The internationally known lecturer and retreat master

---

76 Ibid., pp. 45–46.
77 Groeschel, op.cit., p. 66.
78 Poulain, op.cit., p. 49.

79 Ibid., p. 50.
80 Groeschel, op.cit., p. 71; NCE, 1st ed. op.cit., v.5, 283.

relates that once convinced of their divine call, these unbalanced persons may feel justified in fabricating evidence and imagining extraordinary spiritual experiences. This self-importance may even make them feel justified in misleading others. Because of their subjective sincerity, they tend to be very convincing. Subjectively, they are not lying, so they don't experience guilt. Though deluded, they are certainly not frauds. Father Groeschel further states that false revelation may occur in fairly well-balanced persons who encounter some of the more untypical functions of the human mind. He also mentions the case of open falsification done for pious motives. The editors of the works of St. Catherine of Siena, for instance, have been accused of changing her testimony on the denial of the Immaculate Conception.[81]

Both Groeschel and Poulain maintain that editing went on in the writings of Venerable Maria of Agreda whereby objectionable parts were deleted and suppressed.[82] Even if one of the revelations is false, it does not follow that it should be the same with the saint's ecstasy, for ecstasy is much less subject to illusion.[83]

The desire for revelations also exposes the soul to deception. St. Augustine relates that his mother, Saint Monica (c. 331–387), only just barely escaped falling into illusion by this means. As she was striving to convert him, she wished to know by revelation the outcome of her endeavors. False visions were the results.[84]

Desiring to punish a presumptuous feeling in St. Catherine of Bologna at the outset of her religious life, God permitted that she should not detect the diabolic action in her for some length of time in spite of the disquiet that accompanied it. Feeling herself favored with great graces, she had said audaciously to the devil: "Know that you could send me no temptation without my perceiving it?" After this imprudent challenge, she had false apparitions of Our Lord and the Blessed Virgin for five years. Catherine then fell into a dreadful spiritual aridity until God finally enlightened her completely with regard to this temptation.[85]

Fraudulent Revelations

False mystic events, whether produced by fraud or by delusion, claim to clarify the Faith in incorrect or improper ways, and, without exception, they try to add to Christ's teachings or preach exemptions from them, or they purport to correct something that Christ said.[86]

According to Poulain, there are five causes of absolutely fraudulent revelations. The first is from persons who are untruthful and, in bad faith, claim to have received these revelations.[87]

Frauds have a long history in Christianity beginning with Simon Magus in the Acts of the Apostles (8:9). These people knowingly fabricate revelations and exploit paranormal phenomena. They can be individuals of extreme piety such as the Franciscan nun Magdalena of the Cross who was thrice abbess of her monastery at the beginning of the sixteenth century. Complete with a self-inflicted stigmata and the ability to levitate above the earth, with ecstasies and a gift of prophecy, she even convinced others that she lived without food (inedia). She enjoyed a reputation for extreme holiness for several decades. Bishops, clergy, great nobles, and

---

[81] Groeschel, op.cit., pp. 43–44, 67.

[82] Poulain, op.cit. p.50; Groeschel, op.cit., p. 68.

[83] Poulain, op.cit., p. 31.

[84] Ibid., p. 78; see also St. Augustine, *Confessions*, Bk. VI, ch. xiii.

[85] Ibid., p. 91, citing from Bolland, March 9, Second Life, No. 10 and following.

[86] Johnson, op.cit., p. 305.

[87] Poulain, op.cit., p. 51.

even inquisitors flocked to her. For thirty years, she succeeded in deceiving thousands, including a large number of Spanish theologians who prided themselves in not being easily taken in.[88] Some of her predictions were questionable and some were just wrong, but just enough of them came true to keep people guessing.[89] However, in danger of death, she confessed that the whole thing was a fabrication and that, in fact, she inflicted the stigmata on herself. By her own admission she said that she had sold her soul to Satan in return for all these deceptive gifts, and she actually had to be eventually subjected to exorcism to remove the devil's control over her will.[90]

The Poem of the Man-God by the mystic Maria Valtorta has created a great deal of popular interest in recent years. It has created a false impression that it has papal approval when, in fact, it has not. In actuality, this work was placed on the *Index of Forbidden Books* by Pope John XXIII (1958–1963) on January 5, 1960. It has been evaluated as a heap of pseudo-religiosity and placed in a well-known category of mental sickness. Its author has been described in the preface of this publication as having spent the last decade of her life in a state similar to catatonic schizophrenia.[91] It should be pointed out, however, that the Index was abolished in 1965. Maria's work still has its detractors and supporters even to this day. Since 1993, the Catholic Church has remained silent on its position with respect to *The Poem of the Man-God.*

The second cause of fraudulent revelations, according to Poulain, are those which are received by a person who is in good faith but who may have been deceived by his or her overactive imagination or mind.[92]

The third cause of fraudulent revelations stem from an illusion or special disease of the memory, which consists in thinking that certain facts are remembered, although they never existed. Certain minds invent stories and sincerely persuade themselves that the incidents occurred. They are inventors in good faith. They are earnest people who believe what they say, and this from the very moment of saying it.[93]

The fourth cause of fraudulent revelations are a result of the devil giving false revelations or visions. He is able to appear as an "angel of light"—even as Christ and the Blessed Virgin, as witnessed in the lives of many saints.[94] Satan's action may sometimes be recognized by the circumstances of the vision. He can also produce alienation of the sensible faculties, trying to counterfeit the divine ecstasy. An example of this was the action of the devil in the seventeenth century upon Nicole Tavernier (Nicole of Reims), a young woman who had many visions of Jesus and appeared to possess the most extraordinary graces. She was approved and consulted by a number of pious persons and even seemed to labor for the conversion of souls.[95] It was only as Nicole became more and more self-enamored that Blessed Marie of the Incarnation (Barbe Acarie) and St. Francis de Sales saw that while her visions and other gifts were real, they were not from God. "Jesus" was a dark spirit playing on Nicole's egocentricity to incite her to the pride that turns one away from God in self-absorption.[96]

The fifth cause of fraudulent revelations are the inventions of falsifiers. Political

---

[88] Groeschel, op.cit., pp. 45–46.

[89] Johnson, op.cit., pp. 305–6.

[90] Groeschel, op.cit., p. 46; Poulain, op.cit., p. 51.

[91] Groeschel, op.cit., pp. 58–59.

[92] Poulain, op.cit., p. 52.

[93] Ibid., pp. 53–54.

[94] Gerard J.M. van Den Aardweg. *Hungry souls; supernatural visits, messages, and warnings from purgatory.* Rockford, Ill., TAN Books and Publishers, 2009, p. 20.

[95] Poulain, op.cit., p. 55.

[96] Treece, op.cit., p. 28; see also *Barbe Acarie, wife and mystic. A biography* by Lambert C. Sheppard, NY, David McKay Co. Inc. 1953, pp. 36, 60–62.

prophecies have often been their hand-iwork. They were inspired by motives of political or pecuniary interest. These abound particularly at times of great polit-ical or religious upheaval.[97]

Rules for Discernment

It must be again stressed that since public revelation was brought to its completion in Jesus Christ, no new public revelation can be expected until the Second Coming of Christ. The only complete direct revela-tion of God came through the Divine Per-son of Our Lord Jesus Christ. He alone has known the Father as He is (see Jn 14:8–11). Beyond this, faith tells us that the entire public revelation is kept free from substan-tive distortion by the power of the Holy Spirit.[98]

Private revelations, on the other hand, are extraordinary phenomena given for the good of the individual or for others in the Church. As such, they are not a proof of the holiness of the individual who receives them. As previously mentioned, Pope Ben-edict XIV set forth a fundamental principle in this regard. He noted that "heroic virtue must be established before mystical phe-nomena and miracles may be presumed to be of divine origin. And, in fact, even when mystical phenomena are judged authentic, they have no influence on the candidate's sanctity."[99] In every case, private revela-tion must be understood and interpreted in light of the revelation made by Christ and proclaimed by His Church.

The rules for discerning private revela-tions can be summarized as follows:(1) Any revelation that is contrary to the public teaching on faith or morals must be rejected. God does not contradict Himself. (2) Any teaching contrary to the common teaching of theologians or that claims to settle an argument among schools of the-ology is gravely suspect. (3) If some part or detail of a private revelation turns out to be false or erroneous, it is not necessary to reject the entire revelation; the remainder may be authentic. (4) The fact that a proph-ecy comes true is not a proof that the rev-elation was from God; it could have been the mere unfolding of natural causes or the result of a superior natural knowledge on the part of the seer. (5) Private revelations that are very detailed or deal with useless matter or mere curiosity should be rejected as not divine. The same is to be said of those that are detailed, lengthy, and filled with a superfluity of proofs and reasons. Divine revelations are generally brief, clear, and precise. (6) The person who receives the revelation should be carefully examined as regards physical and mental health, moral character, and his or her virtues, such as obedience and humility. Serious doubt arises if the individual displays excessive mortifications, suffers nervous affliction, is subject to periods of great exhaustion or great depressions, or is eager to divulge the revelation or exult him or herself.[100] (7) The immediate fruits that are produced in the soul by the revelation should be care-fully examined.[101]

Revelations that are due to Satan always end in a strong inclination to evil or the hindrance of good.[102] Evil tendencies com-ing from the devil may not show them-selves at the onset. What the devil cannot

---

[97] Poulain, op.cit., pp. 56–57.

[98] Groeschel, op.cit, pp. 27, 29.

[99] Joan Carroll Cruz. *Mysteries, Marvels, Miracles in the Lives of the Saints*. Rockford, Illinois, TAN Books and Publishers, Inc. 1997, p. xv.

[100] Aumann, op.cit., p. 430.

[101] Adolphe Tanquery, *The spiritual life; a treatise on ascetical and mystical theology*. Tournai, (Belgium), Desclee & Co.,1932. Translated by the reverend Herman Branderis. Rockford, Illinois, photo reproduction by TAN Books and Publishers, Inc. 2000. p. 706.

[102] Poulain, op.cit., p. 32.

do is to incline the soul toward solid virtues in a real and durable manner.[103] Eusebius Amort (1692–1775), a German Jesuit theologian, deduced some 125 rules for the discernment of spirits that were largely directed against Venerable Mary of Agreda's *Mystical City of God*.[104]

Moreover, St. John advises us in Scripture: "Do not believe every spirit, but test the spirits to see whether they are of God" (1 Jn 4:1). St. John further explains that the Holy Spirit will not fail to guide us when human reason may err: "When the Spirit of truth comes, he will guide you into all the truth" (Jn 16:13).

So keep in mind that private revelations may proceed from a natural, a diabolical, or a supernatural force, and even if the revelation is supernatural in origin, the seer may unwittingly distort its meaning.[105]

The virtue of obedience indicates authenticity in mystical phenomena because it springs from the virtue of humility. Humility can only come from God, just as pride comes only from the devil, and humility is generally considered the first and principal sign by which the value of purported mystic phenomenon is judged.[106] Humility is the virtue most opposed to our nature and the one virtue of which Satan has the greatest horror.[107]

The devil himself is obliged to obey the Church that speaks for Christ (see Mk 3:15; Phil 2:10). So the mystic's absolute obedience to the Church is a necessary safeguard against the devil's wiles and snares. That is why obedience is really the central test of the validity of any purported mystic activity, and only a priest, a person consecrated to God's service through the sacrament of Holy Orders administered by a bishop who stands himself in unbroken apostolic succession, can exercise the authority that mystics and demons alike are compelled to obey.[108]

For one thing, a confessor or any priest can order a person in an ecstatic state out of an ecstasy or call the levitator down. This is referred to as the recall, but when you think about it, it is God who obeys. God is the cause of the phenomenon. In these cases, the mystic who is caught up in an ecstasy cannot hear anything with their bodily ears except for the commands of the priest. Whether by willful fraud or pathological delusion, the counterfeit, false mystic won't obey these commands.[109]

Revelations Made by Christ and the Saints About . . .

Heaven

In my father's house are many rooms; if it were not so, would I have told you that I go to prepare a place for you? (Jn 14:2)

Blessed are the pure in heart, for they shall see God. (Mt 5:8)

But nothing unclean will enter [heaven]. (Rv 21:27)

What no eye has seen, nor ear heard, / nor the heart of man conceived, / what god has prepared for those who love him. (1 Cor 2:9)

For the gate is narrow and the way is hard, that leads to life, and those who find it are few. (Mt 7:14)

You, therefore, must be perfect, as your heavenly Father is perfect. (Mt 5:48)

No one is good enough to get to heaven.

---

[103] Ibid., p. 71.
[104] Ibid., p. 131.
[105] NCE, 1st ed. op.cit.,v.10, 173.
[106] Johnson, op.cit., pp. 313–14.
[107] Poulain, op.cit., p. 72.

[108] Johnson, op.cit., pp. 57–58.
[109] Ibid., p. 311.

Assumption of the Virgin, Francesco Botticini (1446–1498)

Heaven is the pure abode of God. Anyone who gets there must be pure like God. Holiness is an essential attribute of every inhabitant of heaven. They are all pure of heart, for no one else can see God.[110] We are all sinners unworthy to enter heaven. Christ had to pay a penalty for our sins by His sacrifice on the cross. He thus cleared the way for the rest of us to enjoy eternal happiness. Our job is to acknowledge that we are sinners, repent of our misdeeds and accept Christ's sacrifice for our sins. Finally, we must then strive to become morally innocent like little children and emulate Christ by seeking purity of heart.

There have been any number of real experiences of apostles, canonized saints, beati, venerables, and genuine mystics, however, who were absolutely convinced of having had real visits to (and not just mere visions of) heaven (although not enjoying the actual beatific vision), hell, and purgatory. In some cases, the soul seems to have gone out of the body, leaving it, whether or not in an ecstatic state—seemingly dead.[111] St. Peter had such an experience of ecstasy on Mount Tabor when, along with Sts. James and John, he was given a wonderful vision of Christ's glory, a foreshadowing of the kingdom of heaven. In ecstasy, St. Peter exclaimed, "Lord, it is well that we are here" (Mt 17:4). St. Paul could not nail down the exact nature of his real experience when he said he "was caught up to the third heaven"(2 Cor 12:2).

Those whose souls have been allowed to visit heaven often describe it in terms of figures and scenes familiar to earthly sense faculties. The privileged persons see paradise gardens, hear glorious choirs of saints and angels singing ineffable songs, and smell celestial fragrances. They especially see Jesus (in His humanity) and the Blessed

---

[110] F. J., Boudreau, S. J. *The happiness of heaven: The joys and rewards of eternal glory.* Baltimore, John Murphy & Co., 1872, Rockford: TAN Books, 1984. pp. 141; see also Rv 21:27.

[111] Albert J. Hebert, Fr. S.M. *Saints Who raised the dead; true stories of 400 resurrection miracles.* Rockford, Illinois, TAN Books, 1986. p. 95.

Virgin Mary in great beauty and splendor. They experience great joy and happiness and hate to "return" to earth again.[112]

Heaven is indeed a state of happiness for those who have died in Christ. It brings full lasting satisfaction to the whole of our being through our union with the Holy Trinity in Christ together with all the members of the mystical body.[113] Our happiness will come, first and foremost, from our complete union with God, our spirit overflowing with His love, at last beholding Him as He is, the beatific vision.[114] The beatific vision is thus the essential happiness in heaven. It consists of three acts: the first being the sight or vision of God. This means that the intellect, which is the noblest faculty of the soul, is suddenly elevated by the light of glory and enabled to see God as He is by a clear and unclouded perception of His divine essence. The vision of the divine essence is the root or source of the beatific vision.[115] The second element of the beatific vision is an act of perfect and inexpressible love. The blessed see God as He is, and, therefore, they love Him spontaneously, intensely, and supremely. The third element of the beatific vision is an act of exceeding joy, which proceeds spontaneously from both the vision and the love of God. It is an act by which the soul rejoices in the possession of God, for without it, this last act could have no existence and the happiness of the blessed would not be complete.[116] The beatific vision means that God unites the soul to Himself, and the soul, without losing its created nature or personal identity, is transformed into the likeness of God. It comes to share "in the divine nature" (2 Pt 1:4).

In the beatific vision, "we shall be like him, for we shall see him as he is" (1 Jn 3:2). Some extraordinary souls have achieved what appears to be a near-complete or partially complete vision of God during their earthly lives. Yet even they fall short of seeing the full glory and purity of God on earth. Since St. Paul stated that "what no eye has seen, nor ear heard, / nor the heart of man conceived, / what God has prepared for those who love him" (1 Cor 2:9), we must believe that the beatific vision is a reality that occurs in the life to come.

St. Faustina Kowalska

St. Faustina Kowalska speaks of such happiness in the vision of heaven she had on November 27, 1936:

> Today I was in heaven in spirit, and I saw its inconceivable beauties and the happiness that awaits us after death. I saw how all creatures give ceaseless praise and glory to God. I saw how great is this happiness in God, which spreads to all creatures, making them happy; and then all the glory and praise which springs from this happiness returns to its source; and they enter into the depths of God, contemplating the inner life of God, the Father, the Son, and the Holy Spirit, whom they will never comprehend nor fathom. The sight of this great majesty of God, which I came to understand more profoundly and which is worshiped by the heavenly spirits according to their degree of grace and the hierarchies into which they are divided, did not cause my soul to be stricken with terror or fear; no, not at all! My soul was filled with peace and love; and the more I came to know the greatness of God, the more joyful I become that He is as He is. And I rejoice immensely in His greatness and am delighted that I am so little because, since I am little, He carries me in His arms and holds me close to His heart.[117]

---

[112] Ibid., p. 237.

[113] Lord, Bob and Penny. *Visions of heaven, hell and purgatory* (VHHP). np. 1996. p. 28

[114] CCC, op.cit., no. 163.

[115] Boudreau, op.cit. pp. 8–9.

[116] Ibid., pp. 10–12.

[117] Sophia Michalenko, Sister, *The life of Faustina Kowalska; the authorized biography*. Ann Arbor,

St. Christina the Astonishing

St. Christina the Astonishing, during an ecstatic rapture, described her vision of heaven as a beautiful place, full of love and the peace of God. She was said to have been present before the eternal throne of God. There, in the heavenly kingdom, God's presence was constantly felt and everyone experienced great joy.[118]

St. Lydwina of Schiedam

St. Lydwina of Schiedam, during an ecstasy in which she was admitted to heaven, saw its beauty and those of its inhabitants as well as heard heavenly music and the voices of angels. She reported heaven to be a great festal hall in a palace, with crystal and gold goblets and with Jesus and Mary presiding over a love feast with the elect at the tables. More often, Lydwina ran with her guardian angel in a beautiful garden of Eden with marvelous trees and flowers.[119]

St. Bernardine of Siena

St. Bernardine of Siena, who raised four people from the dead to include Blasio Massei, an eleven-year-old boy from Cascia, near Naples, relates that after having come back from death, Blasio, in speaking of heaven, told, in particular, of the great multitude of angels around the throne of God and of the Blessed Virgin Mary's great beauty and glory.[120]

St. Clare of Montefalco

St. Clare of Montefalco was given gifts of heavenly visions often during the time of Christmas. During one of her ecstasies, she saw the heavenly court of saints inviting her into heaven. She related that her bridal party, the saints and the angels, were awaiting her, her Bridegroom was standing at the High Altar, and God the Father was presiding. On another occasion, on the feast of the Epiphany, she felt herself being drawn up again into the celestial surroundings. She went into such an ecstasy that she was lost to the entire world for thirty days. During this time, she witnessed God's judgment of the souls. But it was like nothing she had ever heard or seen. There was no anger, no guilt, no trial. Actually, God did not judge anyone; they judged themselves. She could see them convicting themselves of all they had done in their lives, and condemning themselves because of their sins, and exacting for themselves their own punishments, their own condemnation.[121] God also graced his holy servant with a vision of the Blessed Trinity. The "little nun" beheld her triune God in three distinct Persons, yet in one Substance, equal. St. Clare wrote that even should God come to her and ask what gift He could give her, there would be nothing she could desire that would equal this vision of her Lord in His glorious Trinity.[122]

St. Hyacinth

The day before St. Hyacinth died, he saw a brilliant light come down from heaven. On the light's great beam there descended a long procession of bright angels who escorted Our Lady as their queen. Our Lady motioned to Hyacinth and said, "Behold," and at that instance the heavens opened. Hyacinth saw Mary advance in majesty to the throne of the Most High. There was a great silence while the Eternal Father placed upon her head a crown of flowers and stars. Mary then turned to St. Hyacinth and said "Behold, Hyacinth! This crown is for you." Then the vision ended.[123]

Mich., Charis Books, 1999. p. 141.
[118] Freeze, VVA, p. 222.
[119] Hebert, op.cit., p. 239
[120] Hebert, op.cit., pp. 112–13, 238.

---

[121] Lord, VHHP, op.cit., pp.107–9.
[122] Ibid., pp. 108–9.
[123] Hebert, op.cit., pp. 237–38.

St. Alphonsus Rodriguez

St. Alphonsus Rodriguez relates that, being transported to heaven in an ecstasy, he saw and knew all the blessed together, and each one of them separately, as if he had passed his whole life with them.[124]

St. Gertrude the Great

St. Gertrude the Great had visions of liturgies celebrated in heaven on major feast days, such as Christmas and the Exaltation of the Holy Cross, as well as on major saints' feast days, such as that of St. Augustine. On Gaudete Sunday, the third Sunday of Advent, for example, Gertrude was not feeling well and complained to Jesus that she could not hear Mass. So Jesus offered to celebrate Mass for her, bringing her into the celestial court.

After describing the scenes in heaven as Jesus intoned the *Kyrie eleison* and *Christe eleison*, the Son of God then rose from His royal throne and, turning to God the Father, intoned the *Gloria in Excelsis* in a clear and sonorous voice. At the word *Gloria*, He extolled the immense and incomprehensible omnipotence of God the Father; at the words *in excelsis*, He praised His profound wisdom; at Deo, He honored the inestimable and indescribable sweetness of the Holy Spirit. The whole celestial court then continued in a most harmonious voice. *Et in terra pax bonae voluntatis.*

"Our Lord being again seated on His throne, St. Gertrude sat at His feet, meditating on her own abjection, when He inclined toward her lovingly."

Following the *Gloria*, Jesus read the Collect, and "St. John, the Evangelist then rose, and stood before God and her soul. He was adorned with a yellow garment, which was covered with golden eagles. He commenced the epistle."

Gertrude the Great, 1763, Miguel Cabrera (1695–1768)

Another evangelist chanted the Gospel, and Gertrude was invited to chant the Credo and the Mass proceeded.

At the time of the *Sanctus*, "the Virgin Mary, the effulgent Rose of Heaven, who is blessed above all creatures, chanted the *Sanctus, Sanctus, Sanctus*, extolling with the highest gratitude by these three words the incomprehensible omnipotence, the inscrutable wisdom and the ineffable goodness, of the Ever-Blessed Trinity, inciting all the celestial choirs to praise God for having made her most powerful after the Father, most wise after the Son, and most benign after the Holy Spirit."

The saints then continued the *Domine Deus Sabaoth*. When this was ended, Gertrude saw Our Lord rise from His royal throne and present His blessed Heart to His Father, elevating it with His own hands and immolating it in an ineffable manner for the whole Church.

"At the moment the bell rang for the elevation of the Host in the Church, it appeared as if Our Lord did in Heaven what the priest

---

[124] Vie from his Memoirs, Appendix No. 275 cited in Poulain, R*evelations*, op.cit., p. 17.

did on earth. The saint was entirely ignorant of what was going on in the church or what the time was. As she continued to be amazed by so many marvels, Our Lord told her to recite the *Pater Noster.*"[125]

St. Teresa of Avila

During an ecstasy, St. Teresa of Avila saw a priest she knew being transported upward by a "Heavenly Army of Angels." In another vision of heaven, St. Teresa saw a religious surrounded by angels standing very close to God. On many occasions, in her visions, she saw all the Jesuits, Franciscans, Carmelites, Dominicans, and Augustinians "together in heaven with white banners in their hands."[126]

St. Maria Magdalena de' Pazzi

St. Maria Magdalena de' Pazzi was also allowed by God to see the soul of her mother as well as several of her fellow sisters in the glory of heaven. In one of her ecstasies, she witnessed one of her deceased sisters who had suffered greatly toward the end of her life ascending into heaven. When she was having this vision of the sister, Our Lord told the Carmelite that the soul of the sister had only spent fifteen hours in purgatory. He said this was because she had atoned for her transgressions during her life with her suffering on earth and because of the plenary indulgences she had received.[127]

In St. Maria Magdalena de' Pazzi's convent was another very pious, obedient, and humble sister named Sister Benedicta. She had a very short illness before the Lord called her home. At the morning Mass following her death, St. Maria Magdalena lapsed into ecstasy. While the good sisters were singing the *Sanctus*, God gave St. Maria Magdalena the gift of seeing the good and holy sister's glorified body as it will be after the Last Judgment. She was clothed in glory with a star as a reward for her kindness and generosity in dealing with all situations. She had rings of precious stones on all her fingers. The Lord told St. Maria Magdalena these rings were for her faithfulness to her vocation and for her uncompromising obedience to the Rule. Then, for her love of Jesus crucified, He placed a golden crown on her head.[128]

St. John (Don) Bosco

St. John (Don) Bosco's vision of heaven took place in 1861 over a period of three nights. Each night it continued where it had left off the night before.[129] It consisted of a large group of his young people and himself trying to climb an enormous mountain at the top of which was a fire they could make out as God. All along the mountain people were climbing trying to reach the top. Don Bosco's group had to go down into a great valley and cross a lake to be able to begin their ascent up the mountain. The lake separating them from the mountain was filled with blood and dead bodies with arms and legs broken strewn over the lake. A sign at the lake read "Through blood," which he was told meant the blood of the martyrs who had already reached the top of the mountain. The blood of the Lamb also flowed in this lake. The dead bodies symbolized those who tried to destroy the Church. Their bones were scattered over the shores of the lake. Another sign read "Through water." Don Bosco was told this was the water which flowed from the side of Christ and through which all men must be baptized before they can enter into the kingdom. They continued along the path and came to another lake and another sign which

---

[125] Paul Likoudis, "German Mystic; A Guide to a Eucharistic Jesus," *The Wanderer*, (Nov. 17, 2005), p. 9, see also *Revelations of St. Gertrude.*

[126] Lord, VHHP,.op.cit., p. 160.

[127] Ibid., p. 210.

[128] Ibid., p. 211.

[129] Ibid., p. 244.

read "Through fire." This was explained to be the fire of the charity of God and His saints. These are the flames of love and desire through which all must pass who have not gone through the blood or water. They continued to search for a path up the mountain. They saw a large plaza and other valleys beyond it. These valleys turned out to be distractions from going to heaven, such things as laziness, stubbornness, concupiscence, gluttony, and things of man's lower nature. After taking a road that was leading them downward toward hell, they finally found the right road, went through the boulders, and came to a dangerous bridge which would bring them to the foot of the mountain. They then began their ascent up the mountain, encountering many obstacles. As Don Bosco got closer to the summit, he looked down to see the young people in his group down below him doing silly things like resting and chasing butterflies. He went down and gathered each member of his group like sheep and told them to continue up the mountain. As he began his ascent back up the mountain, he tripped over a stone and woke up. That was the end of the dream. The dream was very symbolic; for instance, the three great lakes are the Church; the mountain is the Oratory; the ongoing struggle to bring all his young men up the mountain to heaven. The people in pain along the way are those in purgatory. The boys lollygagging on the side of the mountain are those who allow unimportant things to take up their time, when they should be concentrating on reaching the Kingdom.[130]

---

[130] Ibid., pp. 245–49; suggest reading *Don Bosco's Memoirs of the Oratory* and *Dreams, Visions and Prophecies of Don Bosco*.

Near Death Experiences

Contemporary accounts of returns from the other world in near death experiences (NDEs) seem to intimate that heaven is open to almost everyone with little attention being paid to one's service to God— or negligence towards Him—on earth. Most have had a very comforting and fairly pleasant view of death. The temporarily departed usually experience another dimension of being, a feeling of warmth and peace, go through a dark tunnel, are met by welcoming relatives and friends, and experience a "being of light" who is warm, personal, comforting, and reassuring. Some of them resist returning. Others reluctantly return out of a sense of obligations to loved ones. Some change their lives. Most do not fear death any longer. Obviously these modern "returnees" did not meet their judge for a final sentence of reward or punishment.[131]

Raymond Moody's book entitled *Life after Life* and successor books on the subject of near death experience have evoked loud reaction from conservative Christians who see these books as a satanic trick designed to lull us into a false sense of security about the future life, to lure us into occult practices such as astral projection, to beguile us into accepting the advances of demons disguised as departed spirits and to sell us a secular (but fundamentally diabolic) bill of goods about salvation without Christ.[132]

Dr. Maurice Rowlings, author of *Beyond Death's Door*, also points out that there may be a possibility of deceit here from the false "angel of light." Satan could deceive a person into believing he is experiencing clinical death when he has not actually died at all.[133] The purpose of this is to make

---

[131] Hebert, op.cit., pp. 256–57.
[132] Carol Zaleski. *Otherworld Journeys; accounts of near death experience in medieval and modern times.* NY, Oxford University Press, 1987, p. 185.
[133] Hebert, op.cit., p. 258.

us complacent about our salvation, promoting presumption of God's mercy and thus laxity to draw more souls into hell. It seems strange that "souls"—even those of Christians—coming back from clinical death experiences seem to learn nothing of purgatory or hell, experiencing only a state vaguely resembling heaven.[134] Moreover, the so-called "being of light" that most "returnees" encountered issues no warning to the "dead" person to examine his soul to see if he is in the grace of God. The state of sanctifying grace, as we know from divine revelation, is the absolutely necessary "ticket to heaven."[135]

Hell

The teaching of the Catholic Church affirms the existence of hell and its eternity.[136]

The state of definite self-exclusion from communion with God and the blessed is called hell.[137]

"And I tell you, you are Peter, and on this rock I will build my church, and the powers of death shall not prevail against it" (Mt 16:18).

The punishment for original sin is the loss of the beatific vision, but the punishment of actual sin is the torture of eternal hell.[138]

"Enter by the narrow gate; for the gate is wide and the way is easy, that leads to destruction, and those who enter through it are many" (Mt 7:13).

"More souls go to hell because of sins of impurity than for any other reason."[139]

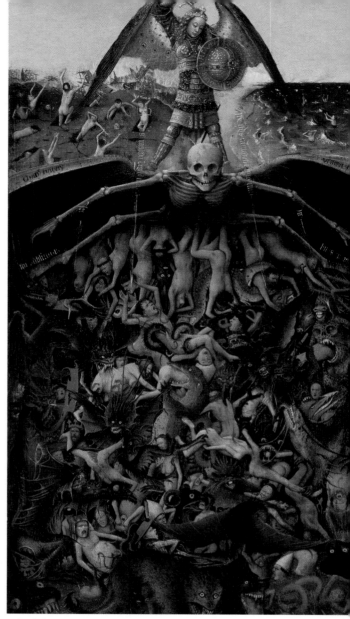

Last Judgment, 1440–4, (detail) Jan van Eyck. Everett - Art / Shutterstock

Is there a hell? The concept of hell is mentioned 146 times in the Bible. If we add gehenna to this figure, it is another 12 times.[140] It is referred to as the nether world in the Old Testament 69 times.

If we say there is no hell, we make Jesus a liar. In the New Testament, seven times hell is referred to as the nether world and twelve times as Gehenna (see Mt 5:22, 29,

---

[134] Ibid., p. 259.

[135] Ibid., pp. 260–61.

[136] CCC, op.cit., no. 1035.

[137] Ibid., no. 1033.

[138] Pope Innocent III (1198–1216), Letter to Humbert, Archbishop of Arles, 1201.

[139] Our Lady of Fatima in an apparition on May 13, 1917 to Jacinta Marto.

[140] Lord, VHHP, op.cit., p. 33.

30; 10:28; 18:9; 23:15, 33; Mk 9:43, 45, 47; Lk 12:5; Jas 3:6). In Revelation, we see hell referred to as Hades three times (Rv 6:8; 20:13, 14).

Though He was love incarnate, Jesus gave extremely severe warnings about hell. For example, when he said in Mark 9:43–48: "And if your hand causes you to sin, cut it off; it is better for you to enter life maimed than with two hands to go to hell, to the unquenchable fire. And if your foot causes you to sin, cut it off; it is better for you to enter life lame than with two feet to be thrown into hell. And if your eye causes you to sin, pluck it out; it is better for you to enter the kingdom of God with one eye than with two eyes to be thrown into hell, where their worm does not die, and the fire is not quenched."

God predestines no one to go to hell; for this, a willful turning away from God (a mortal sin) is necessary, and persistence in it until the end.[141] To die in mortal sin without repenting and accepting God's merciful love means remaining separated from Him forever by our own free choice.[142]

"The teaching of the Church affirms the existence of hell and its eternity. Immediately after death the souls of those who die in a state of mortal sin descend into hell, where they suffer the punishments of hell, 'eternal fire.' The chief punishment of hell is eternal separation from God, in Whom alone man can possess the life and happiness for which he was created and for which he longs."[143]

We became heirs to hell, which had not been planned for us, because of the sins of our first parents, Adam and Eve. Since the day when, in the terrestrial paradise, the enemy of the human race took the form of a serpent in order to tempt our first parents, the devil has shown himself to men in a sensible form. The struggles of St. Anthony in the desert against the visible attacks of the enemy are well known as also in more recent times are the devil's visible attacks on Sts. Martin de Porres, Ignatius of Loyola, John Vianney, Pio of Pietrelcina (Padre Pio), and others. As St. Paul says in 2 Corinthians 11:14, Satan often transforms himself into an "angel of light" in order to seduce souls.

St. John Damascene

St. John Damascene (675–749) of Damascus, Syria, declared Doctor of the Church by Pope Leo XIII (1878–1903) in 1890, once told of a story about a St. Josaphat (c. 1580–1623) who received a vision of hell. During a state of ecstasy, Josaphat was taken to a dark place full of horror, confusion, and frightening specters. There, in hell, was a pool of sulfur and fire in which the damned souls were immersed. Devouring flames issued forth from this pool with howls and screams of agony piercing the air. A supernatural voice from heaven confirmed the fact to Josaphat that this was the reality of hell where all damned souls are sent for their eternal suffering.

St. Clare of Montefalco

St. Clare of Montefalco describes a vision in which she could see her own sins; defects which she would have never seen as wrong before all of a sudden took on grave significance, calling for severe consequences. She saw thousands and thousands of demons in front of her. They shrieked at her: "You must come down here! We're waiting for you!" A condemned soul rushed past her being pulled by demons with rakes and hooks; they were hurled into the darkness right in the line of a huge demon who smashed the soul with a huge iron. St. Clare goes on to say that the fury of the shrieking and the pitch of the

---

[141] CCC, op.cit., no. 1037.
[142] Ibid., no. 1033.
[143] Ibid., no. 1035.

outcries were impossible to describe they were so horrible. The frightening thing for St. Clare was she was not sure if these souls were going down into hell or purgatory.[144]

St. Lydwina of Schiedam

St. Lydwina of Schiedam once had a vision of hell during an ecstasy. Hell appeared to her like a great dark abyss, frightening to the sight and filling one with horror. Heartrending screams and curses issued forth from this abyss, the sounds of the suffering souls who were damned. Confused with this vision at first, Lydwina's guardian angel appeared to her and revealed that it indeed was a true vision of hell.[145]

St. Frances of Rome

St. Frances of Rome, foundress of the Oblates, once saw a vision of hell. It was so horrendous she could not speak of it without sobbing uncontrollably. The vision of hell and its horror, the excruciating agony of its tenants, tormented her more than any sufferings she had endured on earth.[146]

St. Faustina Kowalska

On October 20, 1936, St. Faustina Kowalska went on an eight-day retreat. During that time, she was shown the abysses of hell with its various torments. St. Faustina swears that by the order of God, it was granted to her to have visited the abysses of hell so that she might tell souls about it and testify to its existence. She describes it thusly:

> Today, I was led by an angel into the chasms of hell. She described it as awesomely large and extensive and a place of great torture. The kinds of torture I saw: the first torture that constitutes hell is the loss of God; the second is perpetual remorse of conscience; the third is that one's condition will never change; the fourth is the fire that will penetrate the soul without destroying it—a terrible suffering, as it is a purely spiritual fire, lit by God's anger; the fifth is continual darkness and a terrible suffocating smell. And despite the darkness, the devils and the souls of the damned see each other and all the evil, both of others and their own; the sixth is the constant company of Satan; the seventh is horrible despair, hatred of God, vile words, curses and blasphemies. These are the tortures suffered by all the damned together, but that is not the end of the sufferings. There are special tortures destined for particular souls. These are the torments of the senses. Each soul undergoes terrible and indescribable sufferings, related to the manner in which it has sinned. There are caverns and pits of torture, she relates, where one form of agony differs from another. I would have died at the very sight of these tortures if the omnipotence of God had not supported me. Let the sinner know that he will be tortured throughout all eternity, in those senses which he made use of to sin. I am writing this at the command of God, so that no soul may find an excuse by saying there is no hell, or that nobody has ever been there, and so no one can say what it is like. The devils were full of hatred for me, but they had to obey me at the command of God. What I have written is but a pale shadow of the things I saw. But I noticed one thing: that most of the souls there are those who disbelieved that there is a hell. When I came to, I could hardly recover from the fright. How terribly souls suffer there![147]

---

[144] Freze, op.cit., p. 223.
[145] Lord, VHHP, op.cit., p. 131.
[146] Michalenko, op.cit., pp. 136–37.

---

[147] Michalenko, op.cit., pp. 136–37.

Children of Fatima

On July 13, 1917, Our Lady showed the Children of Fatima (ten-year-old Lucia Dos Santos and her cousins Jacinta Marto, aged seven, and Francisco Marto, aged eight) a vision of hell and told them what the vision meant. In her fourth memoir, written at the request of her bishop, Sister Lucy (1907–2005), one of the seers, describes the vision of hell that Our Lady showed them as follows:

> She opened Her hands and rays [of light] appeared to penetrate the earth, and we saw, as it were, a vast sea of fire. Plunged in this fire, we saw the demons and the souls [of the damned]. The latter were like transparent burning embers, all blackened or burnished bronze, having human form. They were floating around in that conflagration, now raised into the air by the flames which issued from within themselves, together with great clouds of smoke. Now they fell back on every side like sparks in huge fires, without weight or equilibrium, amid shrieks and groans of pain and despair, which horrified us and made us tremble with fright. (It must have been this sight which caused me to cry out, as people say they heard me.) The demons were distinguished [from the souls of the damned] by their terrifying and repellent likeness to frightful and unknown animals, black and transparent like burning coals. That vision only lasted for a moment, thanks to our good Heavenly Mother, Who at the first apparition [May 13, 1917] had promised to take us to Heaven. Without that, I think that we would have died of terror and fear.[148]

Jacinta Marto (left, seated) and Lúcia Santos, 1917

The children of Fatima spoke about a sea of fire, filled with devils and the souls of people, black or bronzed, burning fiercely, ghastly screams of indescribable pain coming out of them, being sucked into a river of fire, like molten lava, embers of burnt skin flying off their charred bodies. The demons could be distinguished from the people in that they looked like ghoulish, deformed animals.[149]

The youngsters were quite disturbed by the vision of hell. The Blessed Virgin told them that "Many souls go to hell because there is no one to pray and make sacrifices for them."[150] Our Lady was trying to desperately warn us, through these children, of the horrors that await those who break relationship with Jesus.[151]

[148] "Sister Lucy of Fatima describes the vision of hell," The Fatima Network, http://www.fatima.org/essentials/facts/hell.asp; see also "Fatima in Lucia's own words, Third and Fourth memoir, the vision of hell," http://www.concernedcatholics.org/printable/pr-hell.htm; http://www.bibleprobe.com/fatimvisionofhell.htm.

[149] Lord, VHHP, op.cit., p. 271.
[150] Hebert, op.cit., pp. 265–66.
[151] Lord, VHHP, op.cit., p. 275.

Their vision was as real as if the children were right there with the damned souls tossing about. It was an experience that utterly changed many lives, including their own. After this vision, the children performed great acts of penance and self-denial seldom heard of in little children.[152]

St. Teresa of Avila

St. Teresa of Avila, one of the great mystic saints, was shown a vision of hell.[153] She states that while praying one day, she found herself in the middle of hell. The saint wrote that the entrance resembled a very long straight alley, like a very low oven, dark and narrow. The ground, she said, was covered by what looked like very filthy, muddy water. A nauseatingly foul stench attacked her senses from the water that was stirred up by the many vile reptiles slithering through it. As her eyes adjusted to the darkness, she spotted on one side of the pathway, a cavity in the wall. The horrible, frightening sight before her was as nothing compared to what she felt there. She writes that she felt a fire in her soul and the most unbearable bodily pains she had ever known—including the excruciating spasms resulting from the shrinking of her limbs, the physical and spiritual torment caused by the devil—could not compare with the agony she experienced in her soul, "a sense of being constrained, a stifling, an anguish so keen, a sorrow so abandoned and afflicted" she could not describe it adequately. She said that it seemed as if "her soul was cutting itself to pieces." She felt herself crumbling into pieces, being in a place so evil and she so helpless to escape, with no hope or any

consolation, no place to sit or to lie down, no room at all. The walls, where they had placed her, tightened around her, closing in on her, suffocating her. Although she was enveloped in utter darkness, she could see everything that was horrible to behold in this deep black hole.[154]

St. Veronica Giuliani

St. Veronica Giuliani was shown and felt the pains of both hell and purgatory. She wrote: "At that moment I was once again shown hell opened, and it seems that many souls descended there, and they were so ugly and black that they struck terror in me. They all dropped down in a rush, one after the other, and once they entered these chasms, there was nothing to be seen but fire and flames."

St. Veronica devoted her life to keeping souls from ending up there by offering herself as a victim soul to hold back the hand of the God of Justice.[155]

St. John Bosco

On April 19, 1868, St. John Bosco began a series of dreams in which he was led by a heavenly guide (possibly his guardian angel) on a journey to hell. He states that they descended along a road which became very steep. Then, at the bottom of the precipice, at the entrance of a dark valley, an enormous building loomed into sight, its towering portal tightly locked, facing our road. He says he became smothered by a suffocating heat, while a greasy, green-tinted smoke lit by flashes of scarlet flames rose from behind those enormous walls which loomed higher than mountains.

There was an inscription on the portal which bore the words "The place of no reprieve." Don Bosco realized that he was

---

[152] Hebert, op.cit., p. 240.

[153] See Teresa of Avila, Book of Her Life 32, 1–5; also Teresa of Avila, Saint. *The Complete Works of St. Teresa of Jesus*, 3 vols. translated and edited by E. Allison Peers from the critical edition of P.S. Vero de Santa Teresa, London, Sheed and Ward, 1946. Johnson, op.cit., p. 250.

[154] Lord, VHHP, op.cit., pp. 153–54.

[155] Bob and Penny Lord. *Visionaries, Mystics and Stigmatics Down Through the Ages* (VMS). Westlake Village, CA, Journeys of Faith, c. 1995, p. 267.

at the gates of hell. The aide led him all around this horrible place. At regular distances, bronze portals like the first overlooked precipitous descents; on each was an inscription, such as "Depart from me, you cursed, into the fire prepared for the devil and his angels" (Mt 25:41) or "Every tree that does not bear good fruit is cut down and thrown into the fire" (Mt 7:19). They trudged along to the edge of a precipice facing the first opening to hell.

These were huge bronze doors. The guide continued to bring him deeper into the bowels of hell. They passed prophetic inscriptions on the walls and then came to a courtyard. The guide said to him, "From here on, no one may have a helpful companion, a comforting friend, a loving heart, a compassionate glance, or a benevolent word. All this is gone forever."

The two then entered into a large cave. They stood on a platform, sort of an observation deck. For as far as Don Bosco could see there were mountains and abysses of white-hot flames. He said if it had been possible to measure the temperature, it would have been thousands of degrees. He could not begin to describe the horror before him. He could see boys plummeting down into the center of the white-hot cave crying out ghastly, shrill, ear-piercing screams as they fell to the bottom. Some of these boys began clawing the skin off their own bodies. Others were covered with worms and vermin which were biting at their vital parts, their hearts, eyes, hands, legs, every part of their bodies. At given points, the ceiling of hell would open up and show these boys their companions who had saved themselves and were sitting in heaven in the bosom of the Lord. This made the boys in hell even angrier, causing them more pain.

After walking Don Bosco through all the corners of hell, and his guide showing him which sins merited each type of eternal punishment, Don Bosco asked him what he could do to ensure that his boys never end up in hell. The guide told him, "Keep telling them that by obeying God, the Church, their parents, and their superiors, even in little things, they will be saved." Don Bosco asked, "Anything else?" "Warn them against idleness. Because of idleness, David fell into sin. Tell them to keep busy at all times, because the devil will not have a chance to tempt them."

Then the guide began to lead him out of hell. As they passed the last gateway, he told Don Bosco he would have to touch the wall to experience a little of what eternal suffering felt like. "Only one touch, so that you may say you have both seen and touched the walls of eternal suffering and that you may understand what the last wall must be like if the first is so unendurable." The guide showed him an extremely thick wall. He said, "There are a thousand walls between this and the real fire of hell. A thousand walls encompass it, each a thousand meters thick and equally distant from the next one. Each measure is a thousand miles. This wall therefore is millions and millions of miles from hell's real fire. It is just a remote rim of hell itself."

At that, the guide presses Don Bosco's hand against the wall. The pain was so excruciating that it awakened him. His hand was burning. Even the next day, as he was telling the boys of his dream, his hand was still red and swollen and blistered. And that was from touching the outer wall, millions of miles from the fire of hell.

It was as if the Lord had wanted Don Bosco to pass through this to impress upon everyone the seriousness of sin and the righteous punishment of hell.[156]

---

[156] Lord, VHHP, op.cit., pp. 241–44.

St. Bernadette

St. Bernadette never actually had a vision of hell as much as she experienced the sounds of hell during one of the times Our Lady appeared to her. This occurred during the fourth apparition, which took place on Friday, February 19, 1858. Our Lady had no sooner appeared to Bernadette when the child heard the most horrible roaring sounds, much like screaming and raving, very low and guttural at first, very angry. These sounds started off with a low rumble and then graduated to loud yells. In his book on St. Bernadette, Abbe Francois Trochu describes her experience as follows: "At a certain time, the apparitions seemed different from before. Suddenly loud yells belched from the Gave [River]. They challenged, crossed, collided with one another, like the clamor of a brawling crowd. One voice more furious than the rest, dominated them all and roared out: 'Get out of here! . . . Get out of here!' Bernadette guessed rightly that the threatening curse was by no means addressed merely to her humble self, but was an attack directed beyond her to the Vision of Light standing above the child."

"The Vision merely glanced in the direction of the rushing stream. This single look, one of sovereign authority, reduced the invisible mob to silence: the enemy of all good would not drive her from the grotto where she gave her audiences."[157]

It appeared that all the powers of hell were roaring, using the Gave River as their vehicle, to disrupt and even stop the apparitions.[158]

Sister Josefa Menendez

Sister Josefa Menendez

Sister Josefa Menendez, a privileged mystic who bore the stigmata and whose life was filled with ecstasies, raptures, visions, apparitions, and whose soul was mystically transported to hell, describes the horrible realities of hell in her spiritual autobiography called *The Way of Divine Love*. "Many curse their tongues, their eyes, whatever was the occasion of their sin. . . . The majority accuse themselves of sins of impurity, of stealing, of unjust trading, and that most of the damned are in hell for these sins." In her journal entry dated March 22, 1923, she states that among the many souls falling into hell was a child of fifteen who cursed her parents for not having taught her to fear God nor that there was a hell. In her entry for September 28, 1922, she states that "on one occasion when I was in hell, I saw a great many priests, religious and nuns, cursing their vows, their orders, their Superiors, and everything that could have given them the light and the grace they had lost."[159]

[157] Francis Trochu. *Saint Bernadette Soubirous 1844–1879* English [from an old catalog] NY, Pantheon Books, Inc., [1958; c1957]. See also., Francis Trochu. *Saint Bernadette Soubirous*. Rockford, Ill.: TAN Books and Publishers, 1993. p. 64.

[158] Lord, VHHP ,op cit., p. 253.

[159] Freze, VVA, op.cit. pp. 224–25; Josefa.

Saint Teresa of Ávila Interceding for Souls in Purgatory, Peter Paul Rubens (1577–1640)

Purgatory

The Catholic Church gives the name purgatory to the final purification of the elect, which is entirely different from the punishment of the damned.[160]

He made atonement for the dead, that they might be delivered from their sin. (2 Mc 12:45)

But nothing unclean shall enter [heaven]. (Rv 21:27)

Purgatory is a place of real and terrible suffering, where even saintly souls must expiate their sins and faults. As Our Lord said, "Truly, I say to you, you will never get out till you have paid the last penny" (Mt 5:26).

Purgatory exists because God is both just and merciful. Purgatory is like a "refiner's fire" (Mal 3:2). It refines and purifies those who, at the moment of death, are not good enough for an immediate heaven or bad enough for hell. In purgatory, all remaining love of self is transformed into love of God. Thus, "all who die in God's grace and friendship, but still imperfectly purified, are indeed assured of their eternal salvation; but after death they undergo purification, so as to achieve the holiness necessary to enter the joy of heaven."[161] The Church gives the name purgatory to this final punishment of the elect, which is entirely different from the punishment of the damned.[162] It is sometimes referred to as an "agony of love." St. Catherine of Genoa says that although purgatory is incomparably painful because we see all the horror of our own sins, it is incomparably joyful because God is with us there and we are learning to endure His truth and His light. It is also joyful because all those in purgatory have already passed the Particular Judgment and are assured of their eventual entrance into heaven.[163]

The existence of purgatory logically follows from two facts: our imperfection on earth and our perfection in heaven. At the moment of death, most of us are not completely "sanctified," even though we are "justified" or saved by having been baptized into Christ's body and thereby having received God's supernatural life into our souls, having accepted Him by faith and not having rejected Him by unrepented mortal sin. But in heaven, we will be perfectly sanctified, with no lingering bad habits or imperfections in our souls. Therefore, for most of us, there must be some additional change, some purification, between death and heaven. This is purgatory.

Unlike heaven and hell, purgatory is only temporary. Purgatory takes away the temporal punishment still due to our sins after baptism. Faith and repentance have already saved us from the eternal punishments due to our sins; that is, hell. There are only two eternal destinies, not three: heaven or hell, being with God or without Him. The Church commends prayers, almsgiving, indulgences, and works of penance undertaken on behalf of the dead to bring them into heaven.[164] Private revelations reveal that the suffering of the souls in purgatory can be relieved by these actions.

Some of the means the living can undertake to avoid purgatory are imploring God to grant you His grace and a holy, happy death and no purgatory, obeying God's will in all things, doing penance and accepting

---

Menendez, *The Way of Divine Love; The Meaning of the Sacred Heart to the World and a Short Biography of His Messenger Sister Josefa Menendez, Coadjutrix Sister of the Society of the Sacred Heart of Jesus.* Rockford, Ill., TAN Books, 1973, pp. 501–3.

[160] CCC, op cit. no. 1031.

[161] Ibid., no. 1030.

[162] Ibid., no. 1031.

---

[163] Catherine of Genoa, St. *Purgation and Purgatory, The Spiritual Dialogue,* translated and notes by Serge Hughes; introduction by Benedict Groeschel. NY, Paulist Press, 1979 (Western Spirituality Series) pp. 71 ff.

[164] CCC, op.cit., no. 1032.

all suffering, forgiving all injuries and offenses, avoiding all mortal sins and deliberate venial sins, breaking off all bad habits, performing random acts of kindness and charity, praying often for the souls in purgatory, confessing weekly, receiving Holy Communion daily, and visiting the Blessed Sacrament as often as possible.[165]

Protestants in Purgatory

Protestants who save their souls but do not merit heaven directly will find themselves in purgatory like everyone else. The fact that they do not believe in purgatory will not relieve them at all of the necessity of going there. God's truth is still the truth, no matter what we as individuals might believe about it.

Blessed Anne Catherine Emmerich revealed that the souls of Protestants languish the longest and suffer the worst in purgatory because they generally have so few friends and relatives to pray for them.[166]

The main reason for Protestant opposition to purgatory is that it cannot co-exist with fundamentalism's notion of salvation. The Catholic doctrine of purgatory thus collides with the Protestant doctrine of *sola fide*, whereby we are saved by faith alone. For Fundamentalists, salvation comes by "accepting Christ as one's personal Savior." Aside from that one act of acceptance, no acts—meaning no good deeds and no sins—make any difference with respect to one's salvation. If one is *"born again"* in Fundamentalism's sense, salvation has already occurred, and nothing can keep one from heaven. If not *"born again,"* one is damned. In Fundamentalism's scheme of things, purgatory would be superfluous since cleansing before entering heaven would be unnecessary, and God ignores the un-cleanliness of every soul by "covering" the soul's sinfulness.[167]

Protestants also argue against purgatory on the basis of their principle of *sola scriptura* ("the Bible alone"). After all, they argue, where in the Bible do we find purgatory? However, the reality of purgatory is found in Scripture, though not the word—just like the Trinity or Incarnation are not in Scripture either, yet those doctrines are taught in it. For instance, Scripture speaks of a cleansing spiritual fire (see 1 Cor 3:15; 1 Pt 1:7). The two facts mentioned in the last paragraph are found in Scripture: that at death many of us are still imperfect (see 1 Jn 1:8) and that in heaven we will be perfect (see Mt 5:48; Rv 21:27). Put these two facts together and purgatory necessarily follows. Scripture also teaches us to pray for the dead: "that they might be delivered from their sin" (2 Mc 12:46)—which is impossible for those in hell and already finished for those in heaven. Scripture also distinguishes sins that cannot be forgiven either before or after death from sins which can be forgiven after death (see Mt 12:31). Finally, the Church, which Scripture calls "the pillar and bulwark of the truth" (1 Tm 3:15), has always taught and has solemnly and officially defined purgatory as a divinely revealed dogma (Councils of Florence in the fifteenth century and Trent in the sixteenth century).[168] Catholics hold that Christ empowered the Church to give infallible interpretation of the Bible and did not leave it to be self-interpreted.

---

[165] Francis Xavier Schouppe. *Purgatory: Explained by the Lives and Legends of the Saints Translated from the French.* Rockford, Illinois, TAN Books, 1986. pp. 368 ff.

[166] Ibid., *Purgatory*, op.cit., p. xxv.

[167] Karl Keating. *Catholicism and Fundamentalism: The Attack on "Romanism" by "Bible Christians,"* San Francisco, Ignatius Press, c 1988. p. 195.

[168] CCC, op.cit. no. 1031.

Some Saints, Blesseds, and Venerables Who Have Seen Purgatory

A strong theological tradition recognizes that deceased human souls can and do visit the living after death for various reasons and in various modes.[169] It is clear that this is only done "according to the disposition of Divine providence" and not as a common occurrence. St. Thomas Aquinas says that "separated souls sometimes come forth from their abode and appear to men," and this can be for "intimidation" (i.e., damned souls) or for "instruction" (i.e., redeemed souls). He also claims that souls may appear to others "in order to seek our suffrages" (i.e., souls in purgatory).[170] Such apparitions can also be due to a special intervention into the human sphere by a demon creating a deception or an angel appearing in human form to communicate a message.[171]

Very many canonized saints, blesseds, venerables, and holy and faithful souls in Catholic history have had frequent contacts with souls from purgatory while they were alive. They provided great help to them through their prayers and sacrifices. God permits suffering souls to appear before the living for their relief and in order to excite our compassion and make us conscious of how terrible are the rigors of His Justice against those faults which we consider trivial.[172]

The vision of purgatory has been granted to many holy souls. St. Catherine de' Ricci descended in spirit into purgatory every Sunday night. St. Lydwina de Schiedam, while in ecstasy, penetrated into this place of expiation and was led by her guardian angel into the subterranean dungeons, where she saw with extreme compassion the torments of the poor souls plunged in flames. In like manner, an angel led Blessed Osanna of Mantua through this dismal abyss. St. Veronica of Binasco, St. Frances of Rome, and many others had visions exactly similar, with impressions of terror.[173]

During one of their ecstasies, both St. Bridget of Sweden and Venerable Maria Villani (1584–1670) were transported in spirit, at different times, to purgatory. The latter experienced the pain of purgatory's fire touching her forehead. The pain was so acute as to cause her ecstasy to cease.[174] Venerable Sister Paula of St. Theresa (1603–1657) had an extraordinary devotion to the souls in purgatory. She was rewarded with miraculous visions and frequently transported in spirit to this place of suffering.[175] Venerable Mother Agnes de Langeac (1602–1634), a Dominican religious, while in ecstasy, was also taken in spirit to a place of expiation where she saw many souls in the midst of flames.[176] Venerable Archangela Panigarola (d. 1525), a Dominican religious and prioress of a monastery, was conducted by an angel in spirit into purgatory where she saw the soul of her father plunged in an icy pond for his tepidity in the service of God and his indifference with regard to the salvation of souls.[177]

St. Nicolas of Tolentino was likewise transported to purgatory where he saw a vast multitude of souls of all ages and

---

[169] Herbert Thurston, Fr. SJ. *Ghosts and Poltergeists* (GAP). Chicago, Henry Regnery Co., 1954 Thurston, Ghosts and Poltergeists, p. 205.

[170] Paul Joseph Glenn, *A Tour of the Summa*. Rockford. Ill., TAN Books and Publishers, 1978, p. 435; see also Thomas Aquinas, Saint. *Summa Theologiae / St. Thomas Aquinas*; translated by fathers of the English Dominican Province. complete English edition in five volumes. Westminster, Md., Christian Classics, 1981, c 1948. Suppl. 69.2–3.

[171] Hospers, John, "Is the Notion of Disembodied Existence Intelligible?" In *Immortality*. Paul Edwards (ed.) New York, Macmillan, 1992. pp. 279–82; Aquinas,op.cit., 69.3.ad 6.

[172] Schouppe, *Purgatory*, op.cit., pp. xxxvi–xxxvii.

[173] Ibid., pp. xxxviii, 80.

[174] Ibid., pp. 117, 289.

[175] Ibid., p. 183.

[176] Ibid., p. 229.

[177] Ibid., p. 342.

conditions prey to diverse tortures too horrible to behold.[178]

After his canonization, St. Bernardine of Siena is said to have led an eleven-year-old named Blasio Massei into the regions of hell, purgatory, and heaven.[179]

The twelfth-century Belgian St. Christina the Astonishing, who experienced death at the age of thirty-two and then came back to life before burial, reported that "her soul had been conducted by angels to a very gloomy place called purgatory where she said, "souls were subjected to excessive torments."[180] St. Gertrude the Great (c. 1256–1302) also descended with Jesus into the depths of purgatory and was devastated by what she saw.[181]

One day, while praying in the garden of the Convent with the other religious, St. Maria Maddalena de' Pazzi became enraptured in ecstasy and saw before her the pits of purgatory opening. She later shared that she heard a voice beckoning her to follow and witness the pain the Poor Souls in purgatory had to endure. The other sisters heard her say, "Yes, I will go." She began to pace in circles, round and round the spacious gardens, for two hours, hesitating at times, as if in great pain. She later confided that these were times when she contemplated the suffering of the Poor Souls before her in purgatory. Her back bent, as if carrying the sorrow of the world, her tiredness increased and her strength seemed to be ebbing away. As she saw the intense agony of the Poor Souls, the blood drained from her face; she wrung her hands helplessly, tears streaming from her eyes.[182]

Part of the mission of Sister Josefa Menendez, a victim soul whose cause for beatification is now being promoted, was that of expiation and reparation for the sinners of the world as well as the poor souls in purgatory. Josefa was one of those privileged few who was mystically taken down to purgatory to see the suffering souls. Pitying their state, she constantly implored the Lord to release them through her expiatory sufferings. Jesus granted her request, for she was made to know that because of her heroic sacrifices and prayers, many souls were released into their heavenly home.[183]

Blessed Anne Catherine Emmerich would often communicate with the poor souls in purgatory via her angel, who led her safely through this place of purification in order that she might visit those who implored her aid. In turn, this victim soul would pray and suffer in order to help free them from their pain and to help gain their entrance into their heavenly kingdom.[184]

Satisfied Debts and Duration of Purgatory

Sister Lucia, the eldest seer at Fatima, surmises that the intensity of the love of God with which the soul crosses the threshold into eternity—along with the weight of sins not atoned for—determines the duration of the process of purification. Therefore, the fire of purgatory is individual, person-bound, and does not equally affect all souls.[185]

However, the Lord, through the mystics, tells us that it is better to suffer a thousand days on earth (in reparation for our sins) than one hour in purgatory. St. Thomas Aquinas maintains that the least pain of purgatory surpasses all the sufferings of this life, whatsoever they may be.[186] Thomas a

---

178 Ibid., p. 208.
179 Ibid., pp. 84–86.
180 Ibid., pp. 45–46.
181 Lord, VHHP, op.cit., p. 97.
182 Ibid., p. 197.
183 Michael Freze, S.F.O. *They Bore the Wounds of Christ: The Mystery of the Sacred Stigmata* (TBWC), Huntington, Ind., Our Sunday Visitor, 1989, p. 274.
184 Ibid., p. 166.
185 Van Den Aardweg, op.cit., p. 14.
186 Schouppe, *Purgatory*, op.cit., p. 34.

Kempis (c. 1379–1471) states in the *Imitation of Christ* that "one hour of Punishment [in purgatory] will be more bitter than a century of penance on earth."[187]

St. Catherine of Genoa's *Treatise on Purgatory* is one of the finest revelations we have on the subject. Our Lord gave Catherine deep knowledge of purgatory. In it she states that "He who purifies himself of his faults in this present life satisfies with a penny a debt of a thousand ducats ($300,000); and he who waits until the other life to discharge his debts, consents to pay a thousand ducats for that which he might before have paid with a penny." The Lord, through other mystics, tells us that it is better to suffer a thousand days on earth (in reparation for our sins) than an hour in purgatory.[188]

In a vision, St. Frances of Rome was told that for each mortal sin committed and forgiven, a payment of seven years of reparation in purgatory was necessary to erase it from the soul. Since the damage by each mortal sin affects the world differently, some more deadly and lasting, the length of time and punishment differs. The type of pain and suffering measured out to each of these souls was in proportion to the type of sin, the damage done by the sins, and the number of wounds inflicted on the Lord's Sacred Heart by these sins.[189] This seven-year term should be taken as an average penalty since mortal sins differ in enormity.[190]

It says in Scripture that the just man falls seven times (a day) (see Prv 24:16). If we suppose that even the best of us commits ten faults (venial sins) a day, then in a year's time we have 3,650 faults. If we round that off to 3,000 per year, then at the end of ten years, we have 30,000 faults. If we live to be seventy, we have 210,000 sins to atone for. Even if we expiate half of these by penance and good works, we have 105,000 faults to atone for. Suppose on the average, each fault requires one hour of expiation in purgatory, this means approximately twelve and a half years in purgatory. Thus, a good Christian who watches over himself, who applies himself to penance and good works, finds himself liable for about twelve and a half years in purgatory. This calculation is lenient, allowing only one hour to expiate a venial sin. If expiating a venial sin in purgatory requires a full day there, we are looking at something like three hundred years. If you have debts resulting from remission of a mortal sin, then, as St. Frances of Rome says, one needs seven years for the expiation of just one mortal sin. We can see here that even the best of us can find ourselves in purgatory for many years and even for centuries.[191] For those of us who have not paid our debt on earth, we have to clear the invoice due the Lord in purgatory.

In Catherine of Genoa's (1447–1510) *Treatise on Purgatory*, she writes: "Either in this life or in the life to come, the soul that seeks union with God must be purged by 'The Fiery Love of God.' The holy souls are purged of all the rust and stains of sin which they have not rid themselves of in this life. The fire of purgatory is first of all The Fiery Love of God."

God told her that the soul is like gold; once all the impurities are burned away, no matter how great the fire is, it can do no harm to the soul. He keeps the soul in the flames of His Divine Love until every stain of sin is burned away and the soul reaches the highest perfection it is capable of (each according to its own vocation and

---

[187] *Imitation of Christ*/Thomas a Kempis. Translated and with an introduction by Leo Sherley–Price. Baltimore, Md., Penguin Books, 1956, Book 1, chap., 24, p. 60.
[188] Schouppe, Purgatory,op.cit., pp. 367–68.
[189] Lord, VHHP, op. cit. pp. 131–32.
[190] Schouppe, *Purgatory*, op.cit. p. 16.

[191] Ibid., pp. 91–92.

capacity), and once this is accomplished, the soul rests completely in Him.[192]

Our souls are meant to be like a room flooded with sunlight, only the light is the light of the Son, not the sun; the Creator, not the creation. The Lord told St. Catherine that the sun cannot penetrate a covered surface (like a dark shade which will not allow light to flow into a room), not through any defect in the sun but simply from the blockage of the covering; so it is with the rust of sin which darkens the soul; it blocks the Son's love from coming through.[193]

She writes:

> The source of all suffering is either original or actual sin. God created the soul pure, simple, free from every stain, and with a certain beatific aspect toward Himself. It [the soul] is drawn away from Him by Original Sin, and when Actual Sin is added afterwards, this draws the soul still further away from God; and as the soul removes itself more and more from Him, its sinfulness increases and its communication with God decreases, till there is less and less of Him and more and more of the dark shade of sin blocking the soul from Him.[194]

> The Poor Souls in purgatory are in a state of the greatest joy. In fact, no happiness can be found worthy to be compared with that of a soul in purgatory except that of the saints in Paradise; and day by day this happiness grows as God flows into these souls, more and more as the hindrance to His entrance is consumed. [The stain of sin] is the hindrance and the fire burns away [the stain of sin] so that more and more the soul opens itself to the Divine inflowing. At the same time, the souls endure a pain so extreme that no tongue can be found to tell it, nor could the mind understand its least pang if God by special Grace did not show (reveal) so much. All guilt has been removed from their souls. Only [the stain of sin] remains.

> As the purified spirit finds no repose but in God for whom it was created, so the soul in sin can rest nowhere but in hell, which by reason of its sin has become its end. The same thing is true of purgatory: the soul leaving the body, and not finding in itself that purity in which it is created, and seeing also the hindrances which prevent its union with God, conscious also that only purgatory can remove them, casts itself quickly and willingly therein. And if it did not find the means ordained for its purification, it would instantly create for itself a hell worse than purgatory, seeing by reason of this impediment it is hindered from approaching its end, which is God; and this is so great an ill that in comparison with it the soul esteems purgatory as nothing. True, it is like hell; and yet in comparison with the loss of God it is as nothing.[195]

St. Catherine relates that the Divine Essence is so pure—purer than the imagination can conceive—that the soul, finding in itself the slightest imperfection, would rather cast itself into hell than appear so stained in the presence of the Divine Majesty. Knowing then that purgatory was intended for its cleansing, it throws itself therein and finds there that great mercy, the removal of her stains.[196]

---

[192] Lord, VHHP, op.cit., p. 141; Catherine of Genoa, *Purgation and Purgatory*, op.cit., p. 79; J. Sadlier, *Purgatory: Doctrinal, Historical and Poetical.* NY, D & J Sadlier & Co., (1886), pp. 23–24.

[193] Lord, VHHP, op.cit., p. 142.

[194] Ibid., pp. 142–43.

[195] Ibid., p. 144.

[196] Schouppe, *Purgatory*, op.cit., p. 72; Reginald Garrigou-Lagrange, O.P. *Life Everlasting and the Immensity of the Soul; A Theological Treatise on the Four Last Things: Death, Judgment, Heaven and Hell.* trans. By Rev. Patrick Cummins, O.S.B. Rockford, Ill., TAN Books and Publishers, Inc. 1991, p. 192.

Souls Being Purified in Purgatory, relief, photo by Zvonimir Atletic / Shutterstock

Location of Purgatory

St. Thomas Aquinas tells us that no one can say with certitude where purgatory is located. The most common opinion among theologians is that it is in the bowels of the earth, not far from the hell of the reprobates. St. Robert Bellarmine (1542–1641), one of the two Jesuit Doctors of the Church, states that theologians are almost unanimous in teaching that purgatory, at least the ordinary place of expiation, is situated in the interior of the earth.[197]

God frequently showed St. Teresa of Avila the souls she had released from their suffering and their entrance into heaven. They generally came forth from the bosom of the earth.[198] St. Maria Maddalena de' Pazzi (1566–1607) likewise witnessed the soul of one of her deceased sisters issue from the earth on the way to heaven.[199]

Description of Purgatory

St. Frances of Rome, foundress of the Oblates, made her visions known at the request of her spiritual adviser, Venerable Canon Matteotti. She wrote that having passed through the unbearable inferno of hell, she was carried into purgatory by her celestial angel. There, she saw neither the utter hopelessness nor the endless pitch-black gloom she had seen in hell. Instead, it seemed as if they were in a fog where the bright hope of life eternal with Jesus was trying to cut through. Here, in this level of purgatory, the pain of the poor souls was seeing that glimmer of divine hope and yet not being able to see God in His beatific vision. Although these souls suffered intensely, their pain was lessened by the presence of angels who came to visit and help them in their suffering.

St. Frances said that purgatory is composed of three distinctly different levels, each one worse than the other. They were said to be situated one beneath the other and occupied by souls consigned based on the seriousness of the offense and the debt owed. The deeper they are interred, the longer the time before their delivery.

---

[197] Schouppe, *Purgatory*, op.cit., p. 8; see also Bellarmine *Catechism Rom*, Chap. 6, para. 1.
[198] Schouppe, *Purgatory*, op.cit., pp. 11–12.
[199] Ibid., p. 14.

The angel brought St. Frances to the lowest level of purgatory, to a cavern filled with roaring fire, its red-hot flames cutting through the black smoke that darkened the cave. But as horrible as it was, St. Frances said it was not as hot as in hell. As her eyes adjusted to the darkness, she could see bodies being plunged into what appeared to be a cauldron of raging fire, its flames enveloping them, pulling them down. She was told that these souls had committed mortal sins, had confessed, and were absolved by a priest but had not sufficiently expiated during life the wrong done by their act against God.[200]

Although the souls here are enveloped in the same flames, their sufferings are not the same; they differ according to the number and nature of their former sins. In this lowest level of purgatory, the saint beheld laics and persons consecrated to God. The laics were those who, after a life of sin, had had the happiness of being sincerely converted; the persons consecrated to God were those who had not lived according to the sanctity of their state.[201]

The angel then led St. Frances into the intermediate purgatory. This region was destined for souls who had not sinned as seriously as those of the lowest dungeon, nor caused irreparable damage by their transgressions. As their souls were not free from the ugly blemishes that are a result of sin, they were required to spend time in purgatory; but because of God's justice, they did not need to spend time suffering the intense punishment of souls in the dungeons below. This dungeon had three distinct compartments.

The first was an immense cavern of ice, sharp icicles threatening the souls below. The cold in there was indescribably intense. She could see the poor souls trying to warm themselves to no avail, as ice seemed to be hemming them in, closing in on them, surrounding them; the walls, the floor, the ceiling, nowhere to get away from the endless freezing cold.

Next, there was an underground prison of boiling oil and pitch. The sickening odor of burning flesh filled the area. She could see the poor souls covered with black pitch writhing in pain. No matter what they did, they could not escape the boiling petroleum nor the sticky hot, black mess which clung to them.

In the third and last level, she saw souls struggling not to drown in what appeared to be a pond filled with liquefied metal resembling molten gold or silver. Had these souls attached too much importance to the rewards of the world, counting the graces from the Lord as nothing in comparison?

St. Frances then visited the upper dungeon. She does not go into detail on this level of atonement, only that this is the place where the poor souls condemned themselves upon seeing that one time before the Lord how they had transgressed against Him. The souls in this dungeon have the anguish which the poor souls in purgatory say is the most painful, the absence of the beatific vision.[202]

St. Lydwina de Schiedam also was led by her guardian angel into the mysterious regions of purgatory where she saw dwellings, prisons, divers dungeons, one more dismal than the other.[203] She saw suffering souls trapped in various pits or wells. Some souls appeared as though on fire and even took on the characteristic of molten metal, so much were they being purged for their transgressions. St. Lydwina also saw the guardian angels of these victims, who faithfully stayed with them in their darkened wells. She was repeatedly asked to pray and

---

[200] Lord, VHHP, op.cit., p. 132.
[201] Schouppe, *Purgatory*, op.cit., p. 16.

[202] Lord, VHHP, op.cit., pp. 133–34.
[203] Schouppe, *Purgatory*, op.cit., p. 22.

suffer for them, and she did so heroically throughout the remainder of her life.[204]

St. Maria Magddalena de' Pazzi, a Florentine Carmelite, received a vision of purgatory just shortly before her death. During a state of ecstasy in the convent garden, Maria Magddalena was led in a mystical transport to the very depths of purgatory. There, she saw everyone from religious to simple souls imprisoned in different levels of dark dungeons. They were screaming in pain, tormented constantly by demons and the burning flames of purifying fire. In one part, the children who died without repenting of their venial sins were kept. Their sufferings were slight and did not last very long.[205]

She saw their guardian angels beside them strengthening and sustaining them with their presence.[206] In another area reserved for greater sins, souls would cry out in anguish for the agony of their pain. Many of these souls had lived a life of hypocrisy. Further down were those guilty of impatience and disobedience.[207] The impatient as well as the disobedient and uncharitable souls looked as if they had been pinned under a huge cement pillar. There were also those souls who pretended to be and do good, who gained the confidence of innocent lambs only to lead them astray and oftentimes into hell.[208] As St. Maria Magddalena descended deeper into the pits of purgatory and looked at the suffering of the poor souls, she was filled with pity and dismay for these souls who had lost all their earthly smugness and self-assuredness. They looked as helpless as the rich man who asked for a drop of water from Lazarus (see Lk 16:19–31).[209]

St. Maria Magddalena next entered a part of purgatory much like hell (possibly the bottom pit of purgatory). This was one of the deepest levels of purgatory, most resembling the region of hell. As she approached what appeared to be a bottomless pit, she saw souls writhing in pain, their suffering beyond description. She had entered the level of purgatory reserved for compulsive liars. The punishment in purgatory (for these souls) is severe because although these sins have been confessed and absolution has been granted, the damage they did was so far-reaching, oftentimes affecting whole families, churches, communities, countries, the world. For a lie is like a pebble thrown into a body of water: the small ripple spreads and spreads covering the entire area, affecting the river which spills into the ocean, covering the universe.[210] These lying souls are said to be confined in a place in the vicinity of hell and have had molten lead poured into their mouths.[211]

When St. Maria Magddalena approached the next dungeon, she was told these were souls who sinned through weakness. She was surprised to see them in a separate dungeon from those who were paying for their damage done by sinning through ignorance. All about her, she saw frantic flames licking at the already scorched souls. The fire was more furious than had been in the dungeon of ignorance. The difference between the two types of sins seemed to be that those who sinned out of ignorance had to pay a debt for the harm done, but their sin was done unwittingly. They knew no better, while the souls in this dungeon knew full well the seriousness of the sin and its repercussions but chose to do it nonetheless. They paid not only for the damage done to their own souls but for the harm done to other souls.[212]

---

[204] Freze, TBWC, op.cit., pp. 161–62.
[205] Freze, VVA, op.cit., p. 230.
[206] Lord, VHHP, op.cit., p. 198.
[207] Freze, VVA, op.cit., p. 230.
[208] Lord, VHHP, op.cit., p. 198.
[209] Ibid., p. 199.

[210] Ibid., p. 200.
[211] Schouppe, *Purgatory*, op.cit., p. 20.
[212] Lord, VHHP, op.cit., p. 201.

Christ's Descent into Limbo, 1470–75, Andrea Mantegna (1431–1506)

The saint next saw the souls who had chosen the false gods of materialism for whom no amount of money and possessions was enough. They lived each day to protect what they had and to get more and more of that which they did not need but instead desired. Their possessions became the keepers and they the slaves. She saw all the blindness of avarice (the overindulgent love of temporal or earthly things, especially riches). She saw all these souls being thrown into the fire, like raw crude metal which needs to have all earthly impurities burned away so that only precious gold remains.[213]

St. Maria Magddalena saw souls who had been soiled by impure thoughts and actions. Impure and unholy thoughts begin in the mind and then travel to other members of the body. Her next stop was a dungeon that was filled with an unbearable stench, infested by filth and mire, diseased souls bearing the marks of such highly fatal, infectious, and contagious diseases, such as the bubonic plague (the social ills of our time: syphilis, AIDS, etc.). She was almost overcome by waves of nausea, the sight and smell was so offensive. She was told that this was the place for those whose souls had been tainted by impure actions. The pestilence and decay here choked and smothered her so she could barely breathe. She had to flee to the next place.[214]

The next area of purgatory she visited was dedicated to those souls whose focus in life

---

[213] Ibid., p. 202.

[214] Ibid., pp. 203–4.

was to be popular, to be admired, to be looked up to. Their aims were ambitious, to the exclusion of any and all human feelings for others; their philosophy being the ends justify the means, to do whatever it takes to succeed. Such souls were seen as being now held in a dungeon of obscurity, with no one to console them. They chose the respect of men over the divine respect of God. The respect of humans died with them, and now much of their suffering like the others in purgatory was the longing to behold the divine image of that God to Whom they gave second place on earth.[215]

Coming almost to the end of her journey, the saint saw the souls of those who prayed when they needed help from the Lord but, like the nine lepers, never thanked Him. When their petitions were granted, they soon forgot it was the work of the Lord and began to believe Satan's lie that it was their own doing and not the Lord's, or that it was due to circumstances not miracles that the course of their lives had changed for the better. These souls were immersed in a pool of boiling, bubbling, molten lead, many of them barely able to stay afloat.

The saint's last stop was a place of the least pain and suffering. It was filled with those souls who had not committed any grave wrongdoing but out of lack of prudence had been guilty of lesser faults, venial sins. The problem with these sins is that they could have led to more serious mortal sins. They chose not to listen to the warning of their guardian angel when they were doing something that could lead them astray and they, through pride or lack of wisdom, or just plain desire, chose to ignore the messenger of God and commit these minor infractions; then it is God's justice that they be cleansed of these imperfections by sharing to a lesser degree the suffering of the other Poor Souls in purgatory.[216]

Saints' Encounters With Simple Souls and Relatives in Purgatory

Souls in purgatory have been allowed by God to return to earth as apparitions to reveal His justice as well as His mercy in dealing with immortal souls. The story about Saul and the Witch of Endor (see 1 Sm 28:7–20) shows that God can permit a departed soul to appear to a living person to disclose things unknown to them, to ask for help or for prayers.[217]

Stories of purgatorial visitations, appearances, and revelations may also be found from the lives of: Sts. Thomas Aquinas, Margaret of Cortona, Gertrude the Great, Bridget of Sweden, Catherine of Genoa, Teresa of Avila, Francis de Sales, Margaret Mary Alacoque, John Vianney, Blessed Catherine of Racconigi,[218] Ambrose, Bonnaventure, Dominic, Efraim, Augustine, Francis of Assisi, Francis Xavier, Pio of Pietrelcina, Nicolas of Tolentino, Peter Damian, Victor, Faustina Kowlaska, Bernard of Clairvaux, Gregory the Great,[219] Philip Neri, Clare of Montefalco, John Bosco,[220] Malachy, Lutgardis, Elizabeth of Portugal, Vincent Ferrer, Louis Bertrand, Peter Claver, Paul of the Cross, Blessed Christina of Stommeln, Blessed Elizabeth von Reute, Blessed Maria of the Passion of Our Lord Jesus Christ, Blessed Henry Suso, and Denis the Carthusian.[221]

In some mysterious way, the deceased is present, there and then, in the place and in the moment he appears. At the onset of an apparition, the seers and bystanders often observe physical phenomena such as atmospheric changes, a gust of cold wind,

---

[215] Ibid., pp. 204–5.
[216] Ibid., pp. 205–6.

[217] Johnson, APP, 117; see *The New American Bible*. South Bend, Indiana, Greenlawn Press 1987, p. 269, note 28:12; Hebert, op.cit. p. 262.
[218] Hebert, op.cit., p. 240.
[219] van den Aardweg, op.cit., pp. 80–81.
[220] Lord, VHHP, op.cit., p. iii.
[221] Schouppe, *Purgatory*, op.cit., pp. 18, 92, 206, 264, 285, 356.

crackling sounds, a strange and sudden silence. The spirit develops its figure and form out of a hazy cloud or mist, or starts as a passing shadow. It is not unusual for animals to perceive something physical. These souls appear in variant forms or figures. They either come in the figure of the person they were in life with their typical clothes, enveloped in flames, or again as deformed humans with remarkable symbolic features that represent their sins and/or punishments—sometimes even as humanized animals or animalized humans. These suffering souls from purgatory are as a rule recognizable by their eyes and mouth.[222] At times, a familiar priest, religious, relative, friend, or neighbor appears to beseech sacrifice and intercession from the living saint or holy person on their behalf. Kings, soldiers, and even a pope have begged for intercessions.[223]

Saint Maria Magddalena de' Pazzi saw her brother in one of purgatory's dungeons. He had led a truly Christian life. He had received the many graces which enabled him to do so. His responsibilities were great, but he failed to fulfill them as he should. There were faults he had not atoned for while still alive. He pleaded with his saintly sister to receive 107 Holy Communions to help him make restitution for the times he had not put the Lord first in his life. She did as he requested, all the while pleading with the Lord on his behalf.[224]

St. Elizabeth of Portugal's daughter, Queen Constance, made known to her mother after her sudden death that she was condemned to languish in the depths of purgatory for a long time. Constance said she would be delivered only if the Holy Sacrifice of the Mass was celebrated for her every day for the space of a year. At the end of a year, Constance appeared to her mother clad in a brilliant white robe as she was about to enter heaven.[225]

The sister of St. Vincent Ferrer, the celebrated wonder worker of the order of St. Dominic, appeared to him some days after her death in the midst of flames. She said she was condemned to undergo intolerable torments until the day of the Last Judgment. She requested her brother celebrate thirty Masses for her. Upon the fulfillment of this request, his sister again appeared to him surrounded by angels and soaring to Heaven. Thanks to the virtue of the Divine Sacrifice, a long term expiation was reduced to thirty days. This shows us the powerful effect of the Mass when God is pleased to apply it to a soul.[226]

St. Catherine of Siena had God agree to exempt her father's soul from expiation in purgatory in return for her to suffer in her lifetime the pain meant for him. When her father's soul separated from his body, Catherine was seized with the most violent pains. These remained with her until her death.[227]

The Angelic Doctor, St. Thomas Aquinas, had his deceased sister who had been the abbess of St. Mary's Convent in Capua appear to him asking for his suffrages. He was able to obtain her deliverance. She told him that their brother Arnold was in heaven but their brother Landolph was still in purgatory and needed assistance.[228]

As already mentioned above, Venerable Archangela Panigarola (16 c.), a Dominican religious and prioress of a monastery, was conducted by an angel in spirit into purgatory where she saw the soul of her father plunged in an icy pond for his tepidity in the service of God and his

[222] van den Aardweg, op.cit., p. 78.
[223] Freze, TBWC, op.cit., p. 161.
[224] Lord, VHHP, op.cit., p. 206; Schouppe, *Purgatory*, op.cit., pp. 59, 244.
[225] Schouppe, *Purgatory*, op.cit., p. 206.
[226] Schouppe, *Purgatory*, op.cit., pp. 96–97; Freze, VVA, op.cit., p. 229.
[227] Schouppe, *Purgatory*, op.cit., p. 312.
[228] Ibid., p. 348.

indifference with regard to the salvation of souls.[229]

The souls in purgatory would appear to St. Margaret of Cortona and beg her to offer all her suffering to diminish their pain and anguish. Two merchants who were slain suddenly who only had time to say an act of contrition before death (which incidentally spared them from eternal damnation) pleaded with her to help them. They were suffering excruciating pain to pay for the wrongs they had committed against people who had trusted them. They told Margaret they would have no relief until these debts were paid on earth. They asked her to go to the families and make amends to those whom they had cheated. Margaret fulfilled their wishes and the souls never appeared again. Margaret offered all her mortifications and sufferings for the release of poor souls in purgatory. When she was dying, she saw an army of souls that had been delivered from purgatory forming an honor guard to escort her to heaven.[230]

Venerable Frances of Pampeluna (Mother Frances of the Blessed Sacrament), who was favored with several visions of purgatory, reports about a tolerably good Christian who passed fifty-nine years in purgatory on account of seeking his ease and comfort and another with a strong passion for gambling being retained there for sixty-four years. Still another soul was said to have been condemned to a long stretch in purgatory for not having truly submitted to the Divine will upon her deathbed.[231]

Stigmatic Blessed Anne Catherine Emmerich described the corporeal visions of souls in purgatory who appeared to her. She described them as being buried in darkness, tortured with thirst, heat, and sometimes extreme cold; other times these images appeared the color of grey. These

darkened features are thought to reflect the state of their impure soul in purgatory, burning from the flames of purification. All of these souls were continually tormented by evil spirits according to where they happened to be in purgatory. Those who had sinned the most frequently or seriously were placed in the lower depths of purgatory, which is very close to the borders of hell. Here, the flames of purgation burn far more violently and the poor souls suffer more intensely and for longer periods of time since they have more to atone for before they are released into heaven. In these lower levels, the evil spirits are able to attack their victims more directly and with greater force. Yet a poor soul is often able to appear to some on earth seeking prayers and sacrificial offerings, for God has allowed those here on earth to make atonements as satisfaction for their sin. They cannot help themselves, for the time of merited grace is during our earthly lives, not later.[232]

Saints' Encounters With Religious in Purgatory

Divine Justice is relatively severe toward souls called to perfection who have received much grace. As Christ tells us in Scripture: much will be required of the person entrusted with much, and still more will be demanded of the person entrusted with more (see Lk 12:48).

There are incidents whereby even the holiest of souls have to undergo expiation in purgatory. St. Margaret Mary Alacoque speaks of her Jesuit confessor Saint Claude de la Colombiere (1641–1682), who died in the odor of sanctity at Paray-le-Monial, France on February 15, 1682. Because of some negligence in the practice of divine love his soul was deprived of the vision of

---

[229] Ibid., p. 341.

[230] Lord, VHHP,.op.cit., pp. 83, 85.

[231] Schouppe, *Purgatory*, op.cit., pp. 128, 395.

[232] Freze TBWC, op.cit., p. 161; see also Karl, Erhard Schmoger, *Life of Anne Catherine Emmerich*, 2 v., NY, F. Pustet & Co., 1885.

God from the time it left his body until the moment when his remains were consigned to the tomb. There is also the example of a truly holy person, Father Louis Corbinelli, SJ, who also died in the odor of sanctity in Rome in 1591, had to pass through the flames of purgatory before being admitted into the presence of God.[233]

Then there is the celebrated apparition of Pope Innocent III (1198–1216). The Holy Father presided at the Council of Lateran in 1215 and was one of the greatest pontiffs who ever filled the chair of St. Peter. On July 16, 1216, the same day he died, Pope Innocent III appeared to St. Lutgardis from the depths of purgatory enveloped in flames. This vision occurred in her monastery at Aywieres in Brabant. Startled that the Holy Father could end up in such a place, Lutgardis questioned him about his status. He explained that he needed to expiate three faults committed while still on earth which might have caused his eternal perdition. He related that he had obtained pardon for them through the intercession of the Blessed Virgin Mary but still needed to make atonement for these faults. The pope revealed that his suffering would last for centuries but he was allowed by Mary to appeal to St. Lutgardis for her help.[234]

Venerable Frances of Pampeluna reports seeing priests and bishops in purgatory. One day she said she saw a poor priest in purgatory whose fingers were eaten away by frightful ulcers. He was being punished for having at the altar made the sign of the cross with too much levity and without the necessary gravity. She reports that, as a rule, priests remain in purgatory longer than laymen. And that the intensity of their torments is in proportion to their dignity. One priest had to spend forty years in purgatory for his neglect in allowing a person to die without the sacraments and another forty-five years for performing the sublime functions of his ministry with a certain levity. She then mentions two bishops detained there for five and forty-five years respectively for seeking special privileges.[235]

Blessed Anna Marie Taigi reports seeing a priest who had been held in great esteem while on earth for his preaching and charismatic gifts suffering brutal, torturous agony in purgatory because instead of giving glory to God, he centered on himself, drawing the faithful to himself and not the Savior.[236]

St. Severin (d. 403), archbishop of Cologne and a truly virtuous man, is said to have spent six months in purgatory because of the haste with which he recited the Holy Office and that he sometimes said it at an hour not appointed by the Church.[237]

The souls of the religious were those who had not kept the vows they had professed. St. Frances of Rome recognized the soul of a priest (in purgatory) who was very well known. The priest had led a truly priestly life, faithfully administering the sacraments and pasturing his flock. His only sin had been an intemperate need to gorge himself at meal time, seeking the reward from God's creation rather than from God alone.[238]

St. Bernard of Clairvaux (1090–1153) tells of a priest who was in purgatory to expiate the sin of tepidity in his religious life. Other religious souls suffer there for negligence in their service to God. Still others tell of their laxity in preparing for Holy Communion.[239]

One night while at prayer, a recently

---

[233] Schouppe, *Purgatory*, op.cit., pp. 362–65.
[234] Schouppe, *Purgatory*, op.cit., p. 95; Freze, VVA, op. cit., p. 228.
[235] Schouppe, *Purgatory*, op.cit., p. 139.
[236] Lord, VMS, op.cit., p. 312.
[237] Schouppe, *Purgatory*, pp. 138–39.
[238] Lord, VHHP, op.cit., p. 133.
[239] Schouppe, *Purgatory*, p. 131–35.

deceased friar named Pellegrino of Osimo appeared to St. Nicholas of Tolentino. He told Nicholas he was in the pits of purgatory suffering the most excruciating pain. He pleaded with his old friend to have Mass said for him and other souls who had implored his aid. Pellegrino brought Nicholas into the pits of purgatory so he could see firsthand the suffering of those asking for his intercession. Before him were a multitude of souls of all ages and conditions experiencing terrible torment. Nicholas broke out in tears and asked his superior for permission to dedicate his Masses as well as all his prayers toward the deliverance of poor souls from purgatory. By the end of the week, Pelegrino again appeared to Nicholas. This time he was on his way to heaven. The other souls were in the same way, clad in white garments and enveloped with a bright heavenly light.[240] St. Nicholas is the champion of the souls in purgatory.

Saint Margaret Mary Alacoque also reports seeing a vision of one of her deceased convent sisters in purgatory. The bed where she lay was covered with sharp spikes that tore into her flesh. The sister revealed that her punishment was due to her sin of sloth and negligence while observing her religious rule on earth. This same soul also claimed to be tortured in her heart on account of certain wicked sentiments and in her tongue as a punishment for her uncharitable words.[241]

One day while praying before the Blessed Sacrament, St. Maria Magddalena de' Pazzi saw the tortured soul of one of her sister religious who had passed on recently. She saw her rising painfully from the earth encircled by leaping flames wrapping themselves around her body. The only thing that kept them from scorching the sister's body was a sparkling white robe covering her, shielding her from the blazing fire. This nun had been faithful to the Rule. She had led a pious life. Saint Maria Magddalena was puzzled and curious as to why this religious was appearing to her in such a state. The sister explained that she had grudgingly spent time before the Blessed Sacrament while she was alive. And now she was being denied her Spouse's beatific vision.[242]

Once again, St. Maria Magddalena saw in purgatory another one of her religious sisters who had recently died. This nun was known for her piety, but she was found guilty of not having appreciated God's grace on three different occasions.[243] Religious are granted special graces to practice their vocations faithfully and fully. With religious, these gifts are imparted by the Perfect Spouse Who provides them with all His heart. Jesus's heart is wounded when His religious, His brides, refuse His gifts. Such is what happened to this sister in purgatory. She rejected an infusion of grace she received on one of the Church's feast days. Although she was supposed to dedicate this day to the Lord, this sister chose to do some embroidery instead. She heard that inner voice to observe this solemn feast in prayer and meditation, but she chose to disobey and follow the dictates of the world.[244] On another occasion, knowing there was a problem in the community and that she should tell her superior, the nun chose to remain silent. Her third fault was her inordinate attachment to loved ones on earth. She found herself becoming more and more involved with the concerns and ongoing demands of her family.[245] St. Maria Magddalena began to pray for her soul, and sixteen days after her death, the sister appeared to her and announced her deliverance from purgatory. She told the

---

[240] Lord, VHHP, op.cit., pp. 67–68.
[241] Freze, VVA, op.cit., p. 231.
[242] Lord, VHHP, op.cit., p. 195.
[243] Schouppe, *Purgatory*, op.cit., p. 157.
[244] Lord, VHHP, op.cit., p. 207.
[245] Ibid., p. 208.

saint that she had to make atonement for the times she ignored God's grace and put the world before Him.[246]

Venerable Catherine Paluzzi relates that a holy religious who died in her arms was not admitted to eternal beatitude until she had passed an entire year in purgatory.[247]

The holy stigmatic St. Gertrude the Great mentions in her *Revelations* that she was once visited during an ecstasy by a former religious from her own convent. This pious soul had been remarkable for her tender devotion to the Blessed Sacrament. She was thought by her community to be in heaven, but this nun from purgatory explained how even the slightest stain of sin must be purged before one can enter heaven.[248]

The deceased sister was shown to Gertrude standing before the throne of God surrounded by a brilliant halo and in rich garments. However, she appeared to be troubled and her eyes were cast down as though she were ashamed to appear before the face of God. She told Gertrude that she was entirely unworthy to appear before the Immaculate Lamb because she still had some stains on her soul which she contracted on earth. She asserted that to approach the Son of Justice, one must be as pure as a ray of light. She had not yet acquired the degree of purity the Lord requires of His saints. Only the border of her garment shone with light and glory. She related that to wear the celestial robe not even a shadow of sin should be retained.[249]

The Pains of Purgatory

According to the saints, there is great diversity in the corporal pains of purgatory.

Although fire is the principal instrument of torture, there is also the torment of cold, the torture of the members, and the torture applied to the different senses of the human body. The diversity of suffering seems to correspond to the nature of the sins, each of which demands its own punishment.[250] For Scripture tells us, "One is punished by the very things by which he sins" (Ws 11:16).

The soul has to be pure, without blemish, to enter paradise. Stains on the soul have to be removed by the purifying flames of purgatory.[251] Sin produces a double effect on the soul which we call the debt of guilt and the debt of pain (remains of sin); it renders the soul not only guilty but deserving of pain or chastisement. Now, after the guilt is pardoned, it generally happens that the pain remains to be undergone, either entirely or in part, and this must be endured either in the present life or in the life to come.[252] Souls in purgatory cannot obtain the least relief for themselves because their time of merit has passed; they can no longer merit, they can but suffer, and in that way pay to the terrible justice of God all that they owe, even to the last penny (see Mt 5:26).

In purgatory, as in hell, there is the double pain: the pain of loss and the pain of sense. The pain of loss consists of being deprived for a time of the sight of God, who is the Supreme Good, the beatific end for which our souls are made. It is a moral thirst which torments the soul.[253] Speaking of the pain of loss, St. Teresa of Avila, in the *Castles of the Soul* (Part 6, ch. 11), expresses it thusly: "The pain of loss or the privation of the sight of God exceeds all the most excruciating sufferings we can imagine, because the souls urged on towards God as to the

---

[246] Ibid., p. 209.
[247] Schouppe, *Purgatory*, op.cit., p. 107.
[248] Freze, TBWC, op.cit., p. 162.
[249] Schouppe, *Purgatory*, op.cit., pp. 71–72; Freze, TBWC, op.cit., p. 162.

[250] Schouppe, *Purgatory*, op.cit., p. 78.
[251] Lord, VHHP, op.cit., p. 116.
[252] Schouppe, *Purgatory*, op.cit., pp. 111–12.
[253] Ibid., p. 32.

St Catherine of Genoa's passage from Purgatory, by Carlo Giuseppe Ratti (1737-1795). St Catherine's Church, Genoa, Italy, 18th century. / G. Dagli Orti /De Agostini Picture Library / Bridgeman Images.

center of their aspirations, are continually repulsed by His Justice." According to all the saints and the Doctors of the Church, the pain of loss is much more acute than the pain of sense.[254]

The pain of sense, or sensible suffering, is the same as that which we experience in our flesh. Its nature is not defined by faith, but it is the common opinion of most Doctors of the Church that it consists of fire and other species of suffering.[255] The pain of sense has different degrees of intensity. It is less terrible for those souls that have no grave sins to atone for or who, having completed the most rigorous part of their expiation, approach the moment of their deliverance.[256]

As regards the severity of these pains, St. Catherine of Genoa, in her treatise on purgatory (ch. 2, 8), says, "The souls endure a torment so extreme that no tongue can describe it, nor could the understanding conceive the least notion of it, if God did not make it known by a particular grace.[257] However, since these pains are inflicted by Infinite Justice, they are proportioned to the nature, gravity, and number of sins committed. Each one receives according to his works, each one must acquit himself of the debts with which he sees himself charged before God. It follows that souls undergo various kinds of sufferings in purgatory with different degrees of expiation for sin. Some of these sufferings are incomparably more severe than others. The same fire torments the damned and purifies the elect.[258]

St. Francis de Sales, on the other hand, says that while it is true that the sufferings of the holy souls in purgatory are great, there is an inner satisfaction which is there enjoyed so that no prosperity nor contentment on earth can equal it. The souls are in continual union with God. They are perfectly resigned to His will. They purify themselves willingly and lovingly so as to not appear before God with the stains with which they see themselves disfigured. They are consoled by angels, especially their guardian angel. They are assured of their eternal salvation and filled with a hope that can never be disappointed in its expectations.[259]

St. Catherine of Genoa, in her *Treatise on Purgatory*, states that "the Divine Essence is of such purity that the soul, unless she be absolutely immaculate, cannot bear the sight. If she finds in herself the least atom of imperfection, rather than dwell with an imperfection in the sight of the Divine Majesty, she would plunge herself into the depths of hell. Finding in purgatory a means to blot out her stains, she casts herself into it."[260] The soul wishes to be there in the state wherein God pleases, and as long as it shall please Him. The soul cannot sin, nor can it experience the least movement of impatience, nor commit the slightest imperfection. The souls love God more than they love themselves, and more than they love anything else. They love Him with a perfect, pure, and disinterested love. They are consoled by angels. They are assured of their eternal salvation and filled with a hope that can never be disappointed in its expectations. Their bitter anguish is soothed by a certain profound peace.[261]

Saint Teresa of Avila said that she thinks

---

[254] Ibid., pp. 37, 40.

[255] Ibid., p. 32.

[256] Ibid., p. 69.

[257] Ibid., p. 37.

[258] Ibid., pp. 32–33.

[259] Schouppe, *Purgatory*, op.cit., pp. 35–36, see also *Esprit de St. Francoise de Sales*, ch. 9, 16.

[260] Schouppe, *Purgatory*, op.cit., p. 72; Sadlier, op.cit., p. 26; Catherine of Genoa. St. *A Treatise on Purgatory*. Translated by Charlotte Balfour & Helen Douglas Irvine. London, Sheed &Ward, 1946, p. 78.

[261] Schouppe, *Purgatory*, op.cit., p. 36 from *Esprit de St. Francis de Sales*, ch. 9, p. 16.

the greatest pain in purgatory has to be the knowledge that Jesus is just beyond and you cannot be with Him. It has to be similar to when a beloved has been left behind by the other spouse. You know he or she is alive but not with you to love or be loved by. The only relief is we are promised that in the case of purgatory, through the prayers of those on earth, there will someday be that union with Jesus that we long for as He welcomes us Home.[262]

On a visit of Blessed Catherine of Racconigi to purgatory, she is also said to have brought back an agonizing wound from a mere spark that had fallen on her cheek. The suffering caused by that simple spark surpassed all the painful maladies she had endured.[263] Venerable Maria Villani, a Dominican religious, begged a soul in purgatory to allow her to feel something of what she suffered, and immediately it appeared as though a finger of fire touched her forehead. The pain which she experienced instantly caused her ecstasy to cease. The mark remained, and so deep and painful was it that two months afterward it was still to be seen and caused the nun most terrible suffering.[264]

St. Stanislaus Kostka, a Dominican from Poland, was in the middle of saying the Rosary when a poor soul from purgatory appeared to him in a vision. This female told Stanislaus that the sufferings on earth are nothing compared to those in purgatory. To prove her point, she asked Stanislaus to put out his hand. Suddenly a drop of sweat from the visitor fell upon his skin. Stanislaus screamed with agony as the liquid burned a hole in his hand. The departed soul claimed this was only a portion of the pain she continuously felt in the depths of purgatory. Moved with compassion, Stanislaus continued to offer his prayers and penances for the poor souls in their state of purification.[265]

St. Catherine of Ricci had so great a devotion to the souls in purgatory that she suffered in their place on earth that which they had to endure in the other world.[266]

The mercy of God is exercised with regard to purgatory in a threefold manner: 1) in consoling the souls; 2) in mitigating their sufferings; 3) in giving to ourselves a thousand means of avoiding these penal fires. In the first place, God consoles the souls in purgatory through the Blessed Virgin and through the holy angels. He consoles the souls by inspiring them with a high degree of faith, hope, and Divine love—virtues which produce in them conformity to the Divine Will, resignation, and the most perfect patience. "God," says St. Catherine of Genoa, "inspires the soul in purgatory with so ardent a movement of divine love, that it would be sufficient to annihilate her were she not immortal. Illumined and enflamed by that pure charity, the more she loves God, the more she detests the least stain that displeases Him, the least hindrance that prevents her union with Him.[267]

Venerable Sister Paula of St. Theresa (1603–1657), a Dominican religious, being rapt in ecstasy one Saturday and transported in spirit to purgatory, witnessed the Queen of Heaven surrounded by a multitude of angels to whom she gave orders to liberate those souls who had honored her in a special manner and conduct them to heaven.

St. Peter Damian tells us that on the feast of the Assumption, the Blessed Virgin each year delivers thousands of souls from purgatory. The faithful believe Our Lady delivers those souls who, having worn the holy

---

[262] Lord, VHHP, op.cit., p. 152.
[263] Schouppe, *Purgatory*, op.cit., pp. 61–62.
[264] Ibid., pp. 120–21, 289.

[265] Freze, VVA, op.cit., p. 230.
[266] Ibid.; Schouppe, *Purgatory*, op.cit., pp. 175, 287.
[267] Ibid., pp. 169–70.

scapular, enjoy the Sabbatine privilege and afterward gives relief and consolation to other souls who have been particularly devoted to her.[268]

According to Venerable Sister Paula of St. Theresa, she witnessed a great number of souls plunged into flames in purgatory. Close to them, she saw Our Savior attended by His angels who pointed out, one after the other, several souls whom He wished to take into heaven. Those were souls, according to Christ, who had performed great acts of charity and mercy during their lifetime.[269]

The Doctors of the Church teach that the tutelary mission of the guardian angels terminates only on the entrance of their clients into paradise. If, at the moment of death, a soul in the state of grace is not yet worthy to see the face of the Most High, the guardian angel leads it to the place of expiation and remains there with the soul to procure for that soul all the assistance and consolations in his power.[270]

How to Help the Poor Souls in Purgatory

St. Francis de Sales, a Doctor of the Church, opines that "we do not sufficiently remember our dear departed; their memory seems to perish with the sound of the funeral bells."[271]

St. Bridget of Sweden was given knowledge of the souls of the dead. She knew whether or not they were in purgatory, what the nature of their punishment was, and in what way prayers and alms on earth could free them from their sufferings.[272]

The souls in purgatory can be delivered

An Angel Frees the Souls of Purgatory, 1610, Ludovico Carracci (1555–1619)

from their suffering before the great day of judgment by the merits of our prayers, alms, fasts, penances of any kind, stations of the cross, indulgences, and above all the Holy Sacrifice of the Mass offered up for them. The Holy Mass is the most powerful means of assisting the souls in purgatory. Jesus also allows us to offer all the works we perform in the state of grace to Him for the relief of our brethren in purgatory. God then applies these works to those souls according to His Justice and Mercy.[273]

Saint Juan Masias purportedly liberated over a million souls from purgatory by his many daily Rosaries and visits to the Blessed Sacrament. Many of these souls came back to him when he was at prayer to thank him for his help.[274] The poor souls

---

[268] Ibid., p. 180.

[269] Ibid., pp. 183–84.

[270] Ibid., pp. 182–83.

[271] Ibid., p. xxxiii.

[272] Stephen Fanning, *Mystics of the Christian Tradition*. London, NY, Routledge, 2001, p. 133.

[273] Schouppe, *Purgatory*, op.cit., pp. 44, 192.

[274] See Juan Masias in *Dominican Saints* online http://

are grateful and are able to effectively pray for their benefactors while in purgatory or after their entry into heaven.[275]

As noted earlier, St. Elizabeth of Portugal's daughter Constance made known to her mother that she could be delivered from purgatory only if the Holy Sacrifice of the Mass was celebrated for her every day for the space of a year.[276] The sister of St. Vincent Ferrer requested her brother celebrate thirty Masses for her. Upon the fulfillment of this request, his sister again appeared to him surrounded by angels and soaring to heaven. Thanks to the virtue of the Divine Sacrifice, a long-term expiation was reduced to thirty days. This shows us the powerful effect of the Holy Sacrifice of the Mass when God is pleased to apply it to a soul.[277]

Saint Clare of Montefalco had a vision of a woman suffering excruciating pain in purgatory. She asked the Lord for permission to partake in the poor soul's agony and He agreed. Clare shared the stripes meant for the woman, paying in part for the sins of the poor soul as Our Savior, before her, had accepted the flagellation due us for our sins. After enduring unfathomable suffering, it was revealed that the soul could be helped by her husband giving alms to those whom she had named.[278]

Another effective way to assist the poor souls in purgatory is the so-called Heroic Act of Charity toward the souls in purgatory which was approved by the sovereign pontiffs Benedict XIII (1724–1730), Pius VI (1775–1799), and Pius IX (1846–1878). This act of charity consists in ceding to the souls in purgatory all our works of satisfaction. That is all the works of our life and all the suffrages which shall be given to us after our death, without reserving anything to expiate our own sins. We deposit them all into the hands of the Blessed Virgin so that she may distribute them according to her good pleasure to those souls which she desires to deliver from purgatory. The formula of the Heroic Act is as follows: "O Holy and Adorable Trinity, desiring to co-operate in the deliverance of the souls in purgatory, and to testify my devotion to the Blessed Virgin, I cede and renounce in behalf of those holy souls all the satisfactory part of my works, and all the suffrages which may be given to me after my death, consigning them entirely into the hands of the most Blessed Virgin, that she may apply them according to her good pleasure to those souls of the faithful departed whom she desires to deliver from their sufferings. Deign, Oh my God, to accept and bless this offering which I make to Thee at this moment. Amen."[279]

St. Thomas Aquinas says in his *Summa* that "suffrages for the dead are more agreeable to God than suffrages for the living; because the former stand in more urgent need thereof, not being able to assist themselves, as are the living."[280] It was revealed to St. Bridget of Sweden that he who delivers a soul from purgatory has the same merit as if he delivered Jesus Christ Himself from captivity.[281] She also declares in her revelations that she heard the voice of an angel blessing those on earth for their prayers and good works for the suffering souls in purgatory.[282]

St. Philip Neri who had a tender devotion to the souls in purgatory confided that many of these souls appeared to him after their death to ask his prayers or to thank him for what he had already done for them.[283]

---

willingshepherds.net/lives.
[275] van den Aardweg, op.cit. p. 125.
[276] Schouppe, *Purgatory*, op.cit., p. 206.
[277] Ibid., p. 97.
[278] Lord, VHHP, op.cit., p. 106.

[279] Schouppe, *Purgatory*, op.cit., pp. 265–66.
[280] Glenn, op. cit., p. 436, Supplem. Q. 71, art. 2.
[281] Schouppe, *Purgatory*, op.cit., p. 280.
[282] Ibid., p. 316.
[283] Ibid., p. 319.

A holy person in the city of Castello who was rapt in ecstasy at the moment when St. Margaret of Cortona died related that she saw a multitude of souls that the saint had delivered from purgatory form a procession to escort her to paradise.[284]

Eminent Jesuit theologians such as St. Robert Bellarmine and Francisco Suarez (1548–1617) attest that even though souls in purgatory cannot pray for themselves, they can obtain great graces for us. To this extent, St. Catherine of Bologna who had a special devotion to the holy souls in purgatory stated that "when I wished to obtain any favor from our Father in heaven, I have recourse to the souls that are detained in purgatory. I entreat them to present my request to the Divine Majesty in their own name, and I feel that I am heard through their intercession.[285]

St. Gertrude the Great is especially invoked for living sinners and souls in purgatory. In a vision, Jesus had told her that a certain prayer would release one thousand souls from purgatory each time it is said. The prayer was extended to include living sinners as well: "Eternal Father, I offer Thee the Most Precious Blood of Thy Divine Son, Jesus, in union with the Masses said throughout the world today, for all the Holy Souls in Purgatory, for sinners everywhere, for sinners in the universal church, those in my own home and within my family. Amen."[286]

How to Avoid the Pains of Purgatory

1. Daily prayer

2. Frequent confession

3. Frequent Mass and Holy Communion

4. Regular penance

5. Daily Rosary

6. Offering up your death and all its circumstances entirely to God

7. Offering up your daily crosses, burdens, and duties completely to God

8. The sacrament of anointing (plus Holy Viaticum), which purifies the soul from the temporal punishment of sin and spares it from the pains of the other life. To produce their effects, a soul must receive it with the requisite dispositions. If one is in the state of grace, he or she need not go to confession before receiving anointing. But confessing before anointing will maximize the removal of punishment due for sin and heighten the other spiritual and physical benefits of the sacrament.

9. Have confidence in God's mercy

10. Have a true submission to God's will on your deathbed[287]

---

[284] Ibid., p. 318.

[285] Ibid., pp. 337–39.

[286] Rosemary Guiley. *The Encyclopedia of Saints*. NY, Facts on File, c 2001. pp. 133–34.

[287] Schouppe, *Purgatory*, op.cit., pp. 390, 395; see also Plenary and Partial Indulgences. Learn about indulgences and how to get them. In the work entitled: *Manual of Indulgences, Norms and Grants*. Apostolic Penitentiary. Washington, D.C., USCCB, 2006.

Madonna and Child with Souls in Purgatory, Luca Giodarno (1634–1705)

Extraordinary Mystical Phenomena

The classic Christian writers say that all our knowledge of God comes to us from three sources. First, He is manifested in the natural world and its creatures, and realization of this is "natural theology." Next, He has declared Himself to us in history in many varying degrees, but supremely in and through the Christian revelation. This aspect of truth is expressed in "dogmatic theology." Last, He is found through the soul's secret and direct experience, and that is called "mystical theology."[288]

Parisian and former Princeton philosopher Jacques Maritain argued that there are several valid ways of knowing, including the empirical, the metaphysical, and the mystical.[289] Extraordinary mystical phenomena refers to those extraordinary psychosomatic manifestations that sometimes occur in authentic mystics but do not fall within the normal manifestations of the mystical state. They could be given for the good of others or they could be interpreted as a witness to the sanctity of the individual for the edification of the Church.[290]

Extraordinary mystical phenomena do not occur in the normal development of the spiritual life but proceed from a supernatural cause distinct from sanctifying grace, the virtues, and the gifts of the Holy Spirit. Therefore, they are classified as charisms (free gifts) and since charisms neither presuppose grace in the soul of the individual nor flow from sanctifying grace, they are no proof of the sanctity of the individual. Some charisms are true miracles; others are supernatural in cause but do not necessarily surpass the powers of created nature and thus are called "epiphenomena" of the mystical life and are "paranormal" in relation to mystical activity.[291]

Mystical theology is the science which deals with supernatural phenomena. It signifies a particular, hallowed, and sacredly hidden knowledge of God and the things of God.[292] The knowledge of God that one receives in the mystical state is experiential. No one knows God like those souls who have experienced Him intimately and directly, especially within the union of love.[293] Evelyn Underhill, in her work entitled *Mystics of the Church,* defines mysticism as " the direct intuition or experience of God."[294]

Since the mystical state is essentially

---

[288] Evelyn Underhill. *The Mystics of the Church.* New York, Schocken Books, [1964]. pp. 14–15.

[289] Dean L. Overman, *A case for the existence of God*; forward by Robert Kalita; afterword by Armand Nicholi. Lanham, Md., Rowman & Littlefield, c 2009, p. 21.

[290] Aumann, op.cit., pp. 424–25.

[291] NCE 2nd ed., op.cit., v. 10, 106.

[292] Montague Summers, *The physical phenomena of mysticism, with especial reference to the stigmata, divine and diabolical.* London, NY, Rider and Co., 1950. Reprinted by Kessinger Publishing, pp. 52–53.

[293] Freze, TBWC, op.cit., p. 93.

[294] Underhill, op.cit., p. 9.

constituted by the operation of the gifts of the Holy Spirit and since God is the primary mover in the operation of the gifts, it follows that all truly extraordinary mystical phenomena must be attributed to God. But the identification of such extraordinary mystical phenomena becomes exceedingly difficult when we consider that the human organism may present identically the same external manifestations as a result of natural or diabolical causes.[295]

Considered exclusively as paranormal, extraordinary mystical phenomena could be attributed to one of three possible causes: God, occult natural powers, or diabolical influence. As long ago as 1783, the Promoter of the Faith, the future Pope Benedict XIV, laid it down in *De Beatificatione et Canonizatione Servorum Dei* that no supernatural phenomenon was to be attributed to the power of the Holy Spirit unless all possible natural or diabolical explanation has been investigated and excluded. As such, the following rules of discernment concerning paranormal phenomena were established:

1. No extraordinary phenomenon may be attributed to a supernatural—i.e., divine—cause as long as a natural or diabolical explanation is possible;

2. The extraordinary phenomenon is not of itself an indication of the sanctity of an individual, for God could grant charisms to a person in mortal sin and even work miracles through such persons;

3. Normally it would be rash to petition God for charisms or miracles since none of these phenomena flow from sanctifying grace, the virtues, and the gifts of the Holy Spirit; and

privileges of this kind could in fact be damaging to the spiritual life of an individual;

4. No extraordinary phenomenon is necessary for the attainment of sanctity;

5. The extraordinary phenomena, when they come from God, are generally classified as charisms and are primarily for the good of the faithful and not the one who receives them, although accidentally the individual may benefit from them;

6. Because of the impossibility of identifying the cause of some of the extraordinary phenomena, the investigator should consider primarily the effects of the phenomena on the life of the individual who has experienced them.[296]

St. Bonaventure of Bagnorea, the Seraphic Doctor, said there are two ways to truth: the simply rational, which proceeds by way of abstraction from sense experience, and the mystical, which proceeds by way of intuition or inner apprehension. The first is the natural way, the second the supernatural.[297] He says that mysticism is "an act of the intelligence, which, set free from all that can let or hinder, and purified by the grace of God, concentrates its gaze upon the supernatural vision of things eternal, and having seen intellectually, and seeing, known and being certain, remains rapt in blissful admiration."[298]

---

[295] Aumann, op.cit., p. 421.

[296] Benedict XVI, Pope. *On the beatification and Cononization of the Servants of God*. De Canon., Book III, ch. Liii, no. 15; Book II, ch. xxxii, no. 11. Eng. Trans. Benedict XVI on Heroic Virtue, vol. III, ch. Xiv, NY:Edward Dunigan and Brother, 1850.

[297] Jose De Vinck, *The Works of Bonaventure*; cardinal, seraphic doctor and saint Paterson, NJ, St. Anthony Guild, Press, 1960-1970, v. 2, t. 1.

[298] Summers, op.cit., p. 52.

The "mystic way" entails three stages of purgation, illumination, and union. By "purgation" is usually meant the purification of character and detachment from earthly interests. The term "purgative way" is sometimes applied, for instance, by St. John of the Cross to the gradual spiritualization of the mystic's prayer, especially the painful struggles and obscurities which accompany the transition from the stage of meditation on religious themes and figures to the beginnings of real contemplation. By "illumination" is meant that peaceful certitude of God and perception of the true values of existence in His light, which is the reward of a surrendered will. Finally, by "union" is meant that perfect and self-forgetting harmony of the regenerate will with God which makes the full-grown mystic capable of "being to the Eternal Goodness what his own hand is to man." This is the true "spiritual marriage" of the soul: a union with God so completely established that it persists unbroken among the distractions of the world. It leads to total self-abandonment.[299]

St. Teresa of Avila once described the "experience" of mystical theology as "a feeling of the presence of God that comes upon me unexpectedly so that I could in no way doubt He was within me or I totally immersed in Him. The soul is suspended in such a way that it seems to be completely outside itself. The will loves, but the memory, it seems to me, is almost lost."[300] When the soul is suspended and enraptured in this state, the intellect ceases to work. In this state, God bypasses the intellect and senses and goes directly to the heart and soul, where He has promised to make His dwelling place for those in the state of sanctifying grace.[301]

Credible mystic phenomenon are free acts of God, not anything that the mystic himself does. You cannot set a person up as an example because of something that somebody else did to him, and usually against his will.[302]

The genuine activity of a mystic is, by definition, a pull by God away from this world. Spiritual gifts are not given for the recipient's benefit but for the benefit of others, and they always bring with them the severe worldly trials of being a channel for the extraordinary activity of God.[303]

Mystical phenomenon can happen to correct our course.[304] Since the Apostles, there have been thousands of canonized saints who have had credible mystical experiences. These experiences do not necessarily give them a short route to sainthood. They are subject to the same intense scrutiny that any other candidate would get.[305]

A mystic may be defined then as a person who lives a contemplative life and attains, or who believes in the possibility of attaining, insight into mysteries transcending ordinary human knowledge as by immediate intuition in a state of spiritual ecstasy. Mystical knowledge has the same object as the knowledge of faith and theology, but its method is more intuitive and direct than discursive and scientific. Christian mysticism is distinctive in the prominence it gives to the notion of union (with God) over that of absorption. The mystic retains his or her personal identity in the relationship of mystical knowledge and love. The mystical relationship is thus a truly personal relationship between a created person and the triune personal Creator.[306]

---

[299] Underhill, *Mystics*, op.cit., pp. 26-28.
[300] Book of Her Life, Autobiography, Chapter 10, 74; *Teresa of Avila* by Peers, v. 1, no. 10, 58.
[301] Freze, TBWC, op.cit., p. 91.

[302] Johnson, op.cit., p. 301.
[303] Ibid., p. 332.
[304] Ibid., p. 352.
[305] Ibid., pp. 301–2.
[306] *The Random House College Dictionary*, Laurence Urdang, editor in chief. NY, Random House, 1973, p. 882.

God must invite these souls and gift them with the necessary grace to live a life of spiritual union with Him.[307]

Specific Charismatic Phenomena

Charismatic phenomenon can be defined as something extraordinary, out of the course of nature, a marvel, a wonder, or even as something abnormal.[308] We know from Scripture that visible signs and wonders will accompany the followers of Jesus generation after generation: "And these signs will accompany those who believe" (Mk 16:17). Moreover, God continues to be close to His people. Jesus assured us of this when He said "I am with you always, to the close of the age" (Mt 28:20). Scripture makes it clear that the faithful will experience supernatural wonders. It proclaims that voices, visions, and apparitions will occur throughout the history of the Church: "And in the last days it shall be, God declares, / that I will pour out my Spirit upon all flesh, / and your sons and your daughters shall prophesy, / and your young men shall see visions, / and your old men shall dream dreams; . . . And I will show wonders in the heaven above / and signs on the earth beneath" (Acts 2:17, 19).

Visions and apparitions form part of the charismatic dimension of the Church which is conjugated with its ministerial dimension, though it should be mentioned that the ministerial dimension is a charism in itself. As cited in *Lumen Gentium* no. 12: "It is not only through the sacraments and ministries that the Holy Spirit makes the people holy, leads them and enriches them with His virtues. [He] allots His gifts 'to each person as He wishes' (1 Cor.12:11). He also distributes special graces among the faithful of every rank. By these gifts, He makes them fit and ready to undertake various tasks and offices for the renewal and building up of the Church."[309]

It observes that extraordinary gifts "are not to be rashly desired, nor from them are the fruits of apostolic labors to be presumptuously expected. Those who have charge over the Church should judge the genuineness and orderly use of these gifts, and it is especially their office not to quench the Spirit but to test everything (and) retain what is good."[310]

The above text gives us an insight to understand the meaning that visions, apparitions, and private revelations have in the life of the Church. They belong to its charismatic dimension and constitute a demonstration that Christ is present among us until the end of the age (see Mt 28:20) and that the Holy Spirit, the soul of the Church, acts on it and gives it life. Divine favors or mystical gifts are given by the Holy Spirit for various reasons: in some cases to enlighten and to guide a specific person or to bring him or her to divine union with God; in others to promote a certain style of spirituality, inspiration, edification, or illumination of the faithful; for conversion or a certain form of pastoral action, etc. Although divine favors may be considered to be any ordinary gifts that the Holy Spirit gives to the faithful, nevertheless this term is usually reserved for special graces or charisms of those intimately connected with the ways of the interior life.[311]

Mystical gifts shone brightly in the early centuries of Christianity which followed the apostolic age, especially among the martyrs and the anchorites of the desert. We need only look at St. Stephen, the deacon and first martyr. In the midst of his

---

[307] Stavinskas, op.cit., pp. 529–30.
[308] Freze, TBWC, op.cit., p. 91.
[309] Cruz, MMM, op.cit. p. xi.
[310] Vatican Council II, *Lumen Gentium*, op.cit. no. 12, p. 17.
[311] Ibid., 17; 1 Th 5:, 19–21.

Martyrdom of St. Stephen, oil on canvas (ca. 1645), Bernardo Cavallino (1616-1656), Museo del Prado, Madrid, Spain.

torture of stoning, the heavens opened and Jesus enthroned in glory came to console and fortify him in a sublime vision. After his example, many of the Christians on their way to martyrdom were lifted to the highest degrees of the mystical life. Their visions and ecstasies were frequent.[312]

Mystics then are a highly privileged group of individuals who serve as the means of communication between God and mankind.[313] They may manifest charismatic or mystical phenomena which are spiritual events that characterize an extraordinary outreach by God to an individual soul. These phenomena are apostolic in nature. Such phenomena do not occur in the normal development of the spiritual life. They are also referred to as charisms.

These supernatural gifts are not given by God to the mystic for their benefit but, if genuine, for the benefit of others.[314] True mystics are always obedient to the Church's authority. Mystical favors are bestowed on both men and women—and many of the greatest mystics are women.[315]

Such concomitant mystical phenomena or charisms may include agility, apparitions, aureoles, ardors (flames) of love, bilocation, blood prodigies, bodily incorruptibility, cardiac phenomena, cardiognosis, compenetration of bodies, discernment of spirits, dreams, ecstasies, exchange of hearts, gift of tears, gift of tongues, hematidrosis, hierognosis, inedia, insomnia, levitation, locutions, mystical transport,

[312] Freze, VVA, op.cit., p. 302.

[313] Albert Fargas. *Mystical Phenomena Compared with Their Human and Diabolical Counterparts; A Treatise on Mystical Theology in Agreement with the Principles of St. Teresa Set Forth by the Carmelite Conference of 1923 at Madrid by Msgr. Albert Farges*, translated from the French by S.P. Jacques. London: Burns, Oates & Washbourne, Ltd. 1926, pp. 21–22.

[314] Jose De Vinck, *Revelations of Woman Mystics; From the Middle Ages to Modern Times*, NY, Alba House, 1985, p. viii.

[315] Ibid.

mystical marriage, miraculous cures of their diseases, odor of sanctity, odor of sin, prophecy, rapture, sensitivity, stigmatization, supernatural empery over nature, telekinesis, vision through opaque bodies, heart wounds, and visions. They may occur in any intensity or combination, in addition to bearing the marks of the Passion (stigmata).[316]

Below is a list of some of the supernatural wonders, divine gifts, or mystical phenomena experienced by those designated by the Church: saints, blesseds, venerables, and other holy souls.

Visions

A vision or apparition is the supernatural perception of an object naturally invisible to man. We say "supernatural" to distinguish true visions and apparitions from the illusions or hallucinations that proceed from natural causes or the fraudulent visions and apparitions produced by diabolical power. The object of a supernatural vision or apparition may be anything at all that exists: God, Christ, Mary, the blessed angels (see St. Bruno above), devils, the souls in purgatory—any living being or even an inanimate object.[317]

These supernatural events are constants in the history of salvation. The Bible speaks so often about them, relating God's revelation to people with these manifestations, that we can consider them to be one of its central themes.

Visions and apparitions usually include some kind of message or teaching, generally oral. This is what is ordinarily called "private" revelation. It is also possible for this kind of revelation to take place without a vision or an apparition (a locution for example). Although, of course, an authentic revelation, though without a message, is a revelation itself, while proving the existence of the supernatural by making visible invisible realities. To admit or not to admit the possibility of visions and apparitions depends on one's position concerning the possibility that realities which are beyond the material field of positive methods of investigation could exist and be perceived.

Who believes in God also admits that God can communicate with the beings He created. This possibility, of course, does not guarantee that a concrete phenomenon is a communication with God. It is necessary to critically analyze each phenomenon in order to guarantee it as a supernatural occurrence. The existing difficulties to reach this analysis is not cause to say they are not valid, thus rejecting their authenticity "a priori," or to adopt a systematically negative or skeptical attitude.

Particular or private revelations are of two kinds: the one consists of visions, the other of apparitions. Some moral theologians make a distinction between visions and apparitions and some mystics use the two terms interchangeably.[318] An apparition that includes more than one figure, or that recreates an historical or future event, symbolically or realistically (as in the book of Revelation), is sometimes called a vision.[319] A vision might be defined as seeing a scene or participating mystically in some episode of Christ's life or Mary's, while the appearance of a single figure, Mary or an angel for instance, might be called an apparition. Many seem to use the words interchangeably. One just needs to find each writer's definition of them.[320] More specifically, by visions is meant the perception of an object that is naturally invisible to man. They are subjective lights infused by God into the understanding of His creatures in order to discover in them

---

[316] Johnson, op.cit., p. 162.
[317] Aumann, op.cit., pp. 425, 426.

[318] Johnson, op.cit., p. 16.
[319] Ibid., p. 356.
[320] Ibid., pp. 16–17.

Vision of St. Bernard with Sts. Benedict and John the Evangelist, ca. 1504, Fra Bartolomeo

His mysteries. (A mystery is one of the teachings of the Church that can only be known by revelation, not by reason.) Such are the visions of the prophets, St. Paul (c. 1–5–67), or St. Bridget of Sweden and many other saints. These visions usually take place when the subject is in a state of ecstasy. They consist in certain mysterious representations, which appear to the eyes of the soul and which must not always be taken literally. Frequently they are figures, symbolic images which represent in a manner proportionate to the capacity of our understanding, things purely spiritual, of which ordinary language is incapable of conveying an idea.[321]

Visions and apparitions are confirmed in their supernatural authenticity by divine inspiration and by the Magisterium of the Church. From the Church's patristic origins to our days there have been numerous visions and apparitions which have turned the history of the Church. The first apparitions were to Adam and Eve. The Old Testament is replete with angelic appearances to Abraham, Jacob, Elias, Daniel, Agar, Judith, Tobias, etc. Even God Himself appeared to Moses. This carries through in the New Testament with angelic appearances to Peter, Paul, and Joseph and Mary in the Annunciation. Heavenly beings appear during the nativity of Christ, His transfiguration and resurrection, as well as in the Apocalypse in which John describes his vision of the whole heavenly Jerusalem. The whole Bible is the transcript of one apparition after another.

Historical apparitions of God in created symbols is witnessed by the Scriptures. God who spoke, as the epistle to the Hebrews says (1:1 ff.), in partial and various ways to our ancestors through the prophets, in these days He spoke to us through a Son. This speaking, then, of the personal transcendent God took place according to Scripture in the most diverse manners. The prophet who is to become the mouthpiece of God for men hears a voice (Ez 2:1 ff.); he has a vision (Is 2:1 ff.; Nm 12:6); he sees God's revelation in pictures and in symbols (Jer 1:13; 24:1 ff.); angels appear delivering a heavenly message (Lk 1:11; 1:26 ff.); the divine communication can happen in a dream (Mt 1:20; 2:19); it may occur while the seer is in ecstasy (Acts 10:10; 11:5; 22:17; 2 Cor 12:2–5; Rv 4:2). The tendency of these multifarious sorts of divine communications varies widely according to the phase of the history of salvation in which the visionary lives and which he is intended to influence.[322]

As stated above, a supernatural vision is a charism through which an individual perceives some object that is naturally invisible to man. They are primarily for the good of others.[323] In *The Literal Meaning Of Genesis* (Ch. 14, 185–98), St. Augustine distinguishes three kinds of visions: corporeal,

---

[321] Schouppe, *Purgatory*, op.cit., p. xxxv.

[322] Rahner, op.cit., pp. 14, 15.
[323] NCE, 2nd ed, op.cit., v. 14, 562.

Liberation of Saint Peter, Follower of Hendrick ter Brugghen (1588–1629)

imaginative, and intellectual. A corporeal (sensible) or bodily vision uses the usual powers of sight; the other two kinds of vision do not. An imaginative (imaginary or spiritual) vision is where the experience takes place as a result of the activity of the human imagination, apart from the usual organs of sense. St. Augustine refers to it as thinking of our neighbor when that person is absent. An intellectual vision is an experience by means of which we receive understanding "through an intuition of the mind."[324]

In a corporeal (sensible) vision, the eyes perceive an object that is normally invisible to the sense of sight caused by God through an angelic power, the devil, or by a purely natural phenomena (optical illusion). A material being is formed, or seems to be formed, outside of us, and we perceive it like anything else that is around us.[325] They are like three dimensional bodily images of Jesus, Mary, angels, or saints.[326] We read of such a vision in chapter 21 of Revelation where St. John relates the description and excellence of the heavenly Jerusalem which he beheld as it descended from heaven. If the same corporal vision is experienced by many people, the vision may be said to be exterior.[327] St. Anthony of Padua covered the Infant Jesus with his kisses. This indeed was a corporal vision which was witnessed by the owner of the house where

[324] Phillip H. Wiebe, *Visions of Jesus; Direct Encounters from the New Testament Today.* NY, Oxford University Press, 1997, p. 21.

[325] Poulain, op.cit., p. 3.
[326] Freze, VVA, op.cit., p. 78.
[327] Freze, VVA, op.cit., p. 211.

the saint lodged.[328] Another example of such a vision was St. Peter at the gate of Rome where he threw himself at the feet of the vision saying the well-known words "Quo vadis, Domine," ("Lord, where are you going?") whereupon the Lord replied "I am going to Rome to be crucified."[329] The image is very real to the visionary, who often claims to hear a voice and at times is even able to be physically touched. Such was the case again with St. Peter after King Herod arrested him and threw him in prison. It was an angel who appeared to him in a vision, tapped him on the side, awakened him, freed him from his double chains, and led him out to safety (Acts 12:1–11).

Visions may be produced in four ways. The first manner is objective. The body is really that of a person appearing. It is its substance that acts upon our eyes. The nature of exterior or corporal visions is possible for seeing Our Lord or the Blessed Virgin whose bodies and souls are in heaven but cannot occur with angels and disembodied spirits. It was thus that Our Lord showed Himself to St. Mary Magdalen after His resurrection in the likeness of a gardener, and to the disciples at Emmaus as a traveler. The second manner is also objective. A body that exists materially, but as a borrowed body which is then admittedly formed by the ministry of angels. God thus makes use of secondary causes for works which angels are capable of executing. The third manner may be called semi-objective. There is no longer any true body, but there is still something material outside the person who sees it; namely, luminous rays similar to those that a body would have been capable of emitting.[330] The fourth manner is purely subjective. The angels imprint the image of the object directly upon the retina. When the seer of the vision is the only one to perceive it, St. Thomas Aquinas is inclined to think that the vision is purely subjective. At Lourdes, for instance, St. Bernadette Soubirous was the only one to see and hear the Blessed Virgin.[331]

An imaginative vision is one in which God imprints certain images into our mind that are either preexistent or new. These visions often occur in a state of sleep or moment of contemplation; otherwise they occur in the state of ecstasy. Imaginative visions are by far the most numerous in the lives of the saints.[332] These images are supernaturally placed in the imagination of the recipient in order to impart a divine truth, to warn, or to inspire.[333] For instance, the scenes in the Apocalypse and described by St. John, the seer of Patmos, or as with St. Joseph in Matthew 2:13–15, a dreamlike vision may occur in order to warn one of impending danger. The vision also may be symbolic (the ladder in Jacob's dream), personal (the vision of the Sacred Heart to St. Margaret Mary), or dramatic (the vision during the mystical espousal of St. Catherine of Siena).[334] They can serve to excite or inspire one's faith or action, give a sense of profound peace in the soul, and produce desires to excel in the virtues or in the practice of perseverance in faith.[335] Corporeal and imaginative visions occur in the imaging faculty of the mind. They must be distinguished from visionary hallucinations by reason of their origin which is not from pathology.[336] Imaginative visions come suddenly and last a short time. They cannot be controlled or predicted. They are particularly subject to the influence of the evil spirit, who often works on the

---

[328] Poulain, op.cit., p. 22.
[329] Stravinskas, op.cit., p. 633.
[330] Poulain, op.cit., p. 19.

[331] Poulain, op.cit., p. 20; St. Thomas, Summa III, q 76, art 8, c (see Glenn, op.cit., p. 382).
[332] Farges, op.cit., p. 332.
[333] Freze, VVA, op.cit., p. 78.
[334] NCE, 2nd ed.,op.cit.,v. 14, p. 562.
[335] Freze, VVA, op.cit., p. 307.
[336] Groeschel, ASSV, op.cit., p. 157.

imagination and senses in order to deceive the faithful while appearing "as an angel of light" (2 Cor 11:14). Since they are subject to diabolical illusion or excesses of the imagination, one ought never to seek out extraordinary visions. If they do occur vividly and with great impression, the privileged soul is urged to seek spiritual direction for guidance and discernment.[337]

St. John of the Cross took a dim view of corporeal and imaginative visions, and of revelations that involve bodily sensations and feelings. His view expressed in *Ascent of Mt. Carmel* is that "between spiritual things and all those bodily things exists no sort of proportion whatever. And thus it may always be supposed that such things as these are more likely to be of the devil than of God; for the devil has more influence in that which is exterior and corporeal, and can deceive a soul more easily thereby than by that which is more interior and spiritual." But he conceded that God uses visions on occasion, for God prepares people in stages to receive the revelations that come through faith alone. His advice was that those who experience such things should not rely on them or accept them, but "always fly away from them, without trying to ascertain whether they are good or evil; for the more completely exterior and corporeal they are, the less certainly are they of God."[338]

An intellectual vision is a supernatural vision in which God imprints upon the intellect thoughts or ideas of a truth or mystery of the Faith. These are perceived by the mind alone and do not rely upon the bodily senses for its vision. For this type of vision is one by which a supernatural

revelation is instantaneously infused upon the mind, whereby one understands the meaning of a divine truth instantly without the aid of human effort or reason.[339] The image is infused by God directly into the intellect of the privileged soul.[340] Such was the case with St. Teresa and several mystical saints, when the mind was supernaturally enlightened without sensible images as to some fact naturally invisible such as the presence of God, of which the soul is clearly conscious, or again of the Holy Trinity, of whom these saints believed that they had a more or less clear vision; when the mind is enlightened by truths naturally inaccessible, such as the explanation of mysteries, the foresight of events to come, including contingent future things, then the vision is said to be purely intellectual.[341]

St. Augustine considers intellectual visions superior to the other two kinds of visions, for they are not susceptible to deception while the other two are. Intellectual visions—when infused into the mind—are free from diabolical influence because the devil cannot penetrate, influence, or capture the pure will of man; this is reserved to God and God alone. Hence the will of man is joined with the infused vision from God that unites one to a supernatural and heavenly state. The intellectual vision is perhaps the closest image a soul can receive to the beatific vision we are all promised one day in heaven.[342]

Intellectual visions are of the supernatural order when the object known exceeds the natural range of the understanding (e.g., the essence of the soul), certain existence of the state of grace in the subject of another, and the intimate nature of God and the Trinity when it is prolonged for

---

337 Freze, VVA, op.cit., pp. 212, 307.
338 Wiebe, op.cit., p. 29; see also John of the Cross, Saint. *The Collected Works of St. John of the Cross.* Ascent of Mt. Carmel, translated by Kieran Kavanaugh and Otilio Rodriguez. Washington, D.C., ICS Publications, c 1991, ch. 11, para 3, 7; ch. 17, 4, p. 132.

339 Freze, VVA, op.cit., pp. 78, 309.
340 Ibid., p. 212.
341 Farges, op.cit., p. 325.
342 Freze, VVA, op.cit., p. 213, NCE, 1st ed., op.cit., v. 10, 173.

a considerable time. St. Teresa of Avila says that such a vision may last for more than a year. The intervention of God will be recognized especially by its effects, persistent light, Divine love, peace of soul, inclination towards the things of God, the constant fruits of sanctity. The intellectual vision takes place in the pure understanding and not in the reasoning faculty. If the object perceived lies within the sphere of reason, intellectual vision of the supernatural order takes place, according to the Scholastics, by means of species acquired by the intellect but applied to God Himself or illuminated especially by God. If it is not within the range of reason, it takes place by the miraculous infusion into the mind of a new species. Intellectual visions of the supernatural order, such as the mystery of the Trinity, point indisputably to a very high degree of mystical union.[343]

St. Hildegard of Bingen's visions were cerebral, unaccompanied by emotions except those of weariness and infirmity; but she visualized the whole theology of creation and redemption and then reported her apocalyptic vision. Like St. John the Evangelist, she says, "And I heard a voice from heaven saying . . ." and insists repeatedly, "These things are true."[344]

Like St. Augustine before him, St. Thomas Aquinas, who experienced interior visions himself, was inclined to consider the supernatural truth seen in intellectual visions superior to that found in other kinds of visionary experience. However, reflecting on the annunciation of the Blessed Virgin Mary, in which the Angel Gabriel visibly appeared, St. Thomas concludes that a combination of corporeal and intellectual vision is more excellent than the intellectual vision alone. When an angel causing a

The Star of Bethlehem, Frederic Leighton (1830–1896)

corporeal vision enlightens the intellect at the same time, the percipient is prevented from being deceived.[345]

The three kinds of visions, far from being mutually exclusive, may occasionally be reunited in one single complex vision characterized and described by its dominant feature. The vision of the star by the Magi was both external and intellectual. External, for they followed its progress, disappearance, and reappearance; intellectual, for they understood its hidden meaning.[346]

---

[343] "Intellectual Visions," http://www.new advent.org/cathen.

[344] Kathleen Jones, *Women Saints: Lives of Faith and Courage.* Maryknoll, NY, Orbis Books, 1999, p. 8.

[345] Wiebe, op.cit., p.25; Summa, 1, 111, 3; 2, 174.2.

[346] Farges, op.cit., p. 325.

Some visions are, at once, corporeal, imaginative, and intellectual. Examples of the three kinds of vision united together seems more rare, however. There is one suggested by St. Augustine in the biblical vision of Balthazar, when he saw the mysterious hand writing on the wall: Mane, Thecel, Phares (Dn 5:25). At the sight of this, the king fixed the image of it in his mind and later understood its fatal meaning. In the New Testament, St. Paul's vision on the road to Damascus may be considered a triple vision: corporal or outward when he saw the heavenly light which blinded him, or contemplated in spirit Our Lord appearing and speaking to him; imaginative, when he saw the features of Ananias, whom the Lord sent to lay hands on him; finally intellectual, for he understood the will of God in his regard, which was revelation to his intelligence.[347] In the New Testament there is also the Annunciation and St. John's vision of the whole heavenly Jerusalem, and the visions of St. Stephen which fit this category.

Blessed Julian of Norwich's visions took three forms: "Corporal," which probably meant perceived with the physical senses; "Corporal and yet more spiritual" (imaginative), which probably meant a combination of sensory and inner perception; and "spiritual" (intellectual), which probably referred to an inner visioning seen with the spiritual eye only.[348]

All genuine visions and apparitions must be understood in line with a divine message or lesson that the image is sent to impart. In other words, these heavenly signs do not occur merely for emotional or sensation comfort; rather, a divine message or illumination of some aspect of the Faith must accompany such experiences or the visions and/or apparitions may be

considered a personal or diabolical illusion.[349] As early as the fourth century, Christian leaders offered advice to visionaries to assist them in determining whether their experiences were divine or diabolical. Scripture itself speaks of an evil spirit that might come "as an angel of light" (2 Cor 11–14), giving expression to the belief in deceptive powers of diabolical forces to produce an inaccurate physical likeness of Jesus in a percipient. This vision is said to be deemed objective but not genuine.[350] St. Athanasius, bishop of Alexandria, suggested that an apparition should be asked who it is and where it came from, adding: "And if it should be a vision of holy ones they will assure you, and change your fear into joy. But if the vision should be from the devil, immediately it becomes feeble." He noted that demons greatly feared the sign of the cross and were given to making worldly displays, threatening death, and "capering and changing their forms of appearance."[351] St. Martin of Tours experienced an allegedly deceptive appearance of Christ. Martin said to the visitor who appeared to him in royal garment and crown that he would not acknowledge him unless he appeared with stigmata and the cross, whereupon the vision vanished.[352] More contemporary, the devil is also said to have used diabolical tricks to deceive St. Padre Pio. These were said to include appearances as an "angel of light" and the alteration and destruction of letters to and from his spiritual directors. The Capuchin was said to have been able to distinguish between real appearances of Jesus, Mary, and the saints and the illusions created by the devil by carefully analyzing the state of his mind and the feelings produced in him during these appearances.[353]

---

[347] Acts 9:12; Farges, op.cit., pp. 325–26; Tanquery, *The Spiritual Life*, op.cit., p. 702.
[348] Guiley, op.cit., p. 198.

[349] Freze, VVA, op.cit., p. 79.
[350] Wiebe, op.cit., p. 36.
[351] Ibid., p. 29.
[352] Ibid., p. 28.
[353] St. Pio of Pietrelcina, Wikipedia, note 11.

As already stated, most authentic visions will be imaginative ones.[354] These are visions of material objects, seen without the assistance of the eyes. They are perceived by the imaginative sense. Genuine Christian mysticism is highly suspicious of alleged imaginative visions if they occur outside the context of proper mystical graces. Both St. John of the Cross and St. Theresa of Avila express the opinion that true visions and revelations are not granted to a soul until it has reached the stage of mystical betrothal.[355] Intellectual visions are visions perceived by the mind alone without any interior image, like St. Teresa of Avila's vision of the Holy Trinity. Visions that occur in an ecstasy or in a dream belong to one of the last two categories, for, normally, the action of the eyes is suspended during the ecstasy.[356] At times, an imaginative vision can occur during an ecstasy or even produce it.[357] St. Teresa never had corporal (bodily) visions but only imaginative ones. By this she meant that she never saw the object of her visions with her physical eyes but with the "eyes of her soul."[358] Commenting on the object of intellectual visions of Christ, she says, "Without a word, inward or outward, the soul clearly perceives who it is, where He is and occasionally what He means. Why or how she perceives it, she knows not, but so it is."[359]

No visions are essential to sanctity. It is possible to become a saint without them. It should be noted that God has also granted visions to sinners whom He wished either to convert or to punish: such as the visions of Balthazar, Heliodorus, Balaam, and Saul (St. Paul) before his conversion. Among sinners, however, visions are very rare, and therefore must always seem suspect and attributable to illusion or to the devil until there is proof to the contrary. And even among the saints themselves, they should never be accepted without serious examination.[360]

Normally, however, God chooses holy, pious, pure, and humble servants to be His instruments of prophetic and visionary signs. Moreover, the seer must be totally resigned to the will of God and obedient to His impulses of grace.[361] Some of the most well-known and authenticated visions have also occurred to simple people, usually children, who are not looking for anything like this at all—for instance the children of La Salette and Fatima, or Saint Bernadette. Others simply were folks who were praying, like Saint Margaret Mary Alacoque or Saint Catherine Laboure or the peasant people of Knock in Ireland. They had no thought of ecstasy.[362] However, most of the seers have been far advanced in the spiritual life living a life of total prayer and sacrifice and a deep love for God.[363] Of the thousands of beati and canonized saints throughout history, at least 80 percent have been priests, brothers, or nuns; the others have typically lived solitary single lives in the lay state, or they were widowed before receiving the gift of voices, visions, and apparitions. Again, it must be acknowledged that there have been some exceptions to this rule, such as St. Catherine of Genoa, St. Helena (250–330, St. Nicholas of Flue (1417–1487), Blessed Anna Maria Taigi, and others.[364]

Divine visions never produce scandal, disorder, or trouble in the Church, while diabolical visions inevitably engender evils.[365]

[354] Rahner, op.cit., p. 41.

[355] Ibid., pp. 58–59.

[356] Poulain, op.cit., p. 3.

[357] Ibid., p. 10.

[358] St. Teresa, *Life* 28, op.cit., v. 1, p. 179; Rahner, op.cit., p. 33.

[359] Poulain, op.cit., p. 23.

[360] Farges, op.cit., pp. 326–27.

[361] Freze, VVA, op.cit., p. 82.

[362] Groeschel, ASSV, op.cit., pp. 137–38.

[363] Freze, VVA, op.cit., p. 82.

[364] Ibid., p. 90.

[365] Farges, op.cit., p. 337.

Characteristics of a genuine vision, as attested by those who have experienced them in the past, are the following:

- A real vision arrives suddenly and unexpectedly by the Holy Spirit.

- At first it stirs and agitates the soul, but immediately afterwards floods the visionary's soul with a sense of peace and great joy.

- It does not last long.

- It leaves a strong desire for perfection and abundant gifts with which to practice the Christian virtues, especially profound humility and modesty of conduct.

- It remains impressed for a long time on the mind of the recipient.

- The true vision cannot be provoked, sought, or dismissed at will.[366]

The so-called "fruits of an authentic vision or apparition" may include:

- physical healing from serious, even terminal illness,

- emotional healing, often with visible, radical personality improvement, particularly in behavior toward others,

- spiritual growth from egotism into greater other-centeredness,

- rescue in a life-threatening situation, either from natural peril such as fire or flood, man-made peril such as enemy troops, or self-destruction,

- a new direction in life, particularly regarding vocation,

- a new acceptance—even joy—in carrying some burden (including illness or facing one's own or others' deaths),

- and resolution of spiritual questions or difficulties.[367]

Again, it behooves us to mention that the visionary is responsible if a vision and its transcendent cause is misinterpreted. God does not deceive man, but man deceives himself.[368]

Apparitions in General

An apparition is a type or category of a vision. It is a visible, physical, three-dimensional appearance of a supernatural (heavenly) or preternatural (diabolical) source.[369] It may be defined as the appearance of a being that is not normally visible to human sight.[370] If vision is a genus, apparition is a species which tells us much more than a simple vision. The appearances of Our Lord to His apostles after His resurrection, or to St. Paul after His ascension, or again that of the Immaculate Virgin at Lourdes, were outward or corporal visions to which the word "apparition" may more fittingly be applied, for it expresses an outward reality, visible or tangible, which is perceived by our senses and not merely an image or idea in the mind.[371]

When one speaks of heavenly "apparitions" concerning the experience of authentic visionaries, we limit the understanding of apparitions to people or spirits—Jesus, the Blessed Virgin Mary, archangels, guardian angels, the saints, a soul in purgatory, or a diabolical spirit. If the images extend to a nonhuman or spiritual dimension, then we are dealing in the realm of visions. Visions that are not apparitions occur in many

---

[366] Zsolt Aradi, *The Book of Miracles*. Farrar, Straus and Cudahy Co. NY, 1956. p. 27; Freze, VVA, op.cit., p. 212.

[367] Treece, *Apparitions*, op.cit., p. 29.
[368] Rahner, op.cit., p. 36.
[369] Freze, VVA, op.cit., p. 211.
[370] Johnson, op.cit., p. 356.
[371] Farges, op.cit., p. 324.

Apparition of Saint Michael at the Castle of Sant'Angelo, Jaume Huguet (1412–1492)

ways: images of heaven, hell, and purgatory; celestial visions; visions from the early Church; visions depicting specific experiences in the lives of the saints, etc. One should keep in mind that a vision per se is not an apparition, although the two are usually found together. For example, whenever Jesus appears to a visionary, it is usually in the context of another vision or experience: He may appear surrounded by the vision of a cross, the Eucharist, or He may appear riding the white horse of the apocalypse. Michael Freze, the author of *Voices, Visions and Apparitions*, states, "In these cases, it is very important that one interpret the experience in its full context, including both the apparition and the associated vision in the process. Without this overall context, a wrong or faulty interpretation may occur and lead the faithful astray."[372]

One must also distinguish between apparitions and appearances. Jesus appeared to St. Mary Magdalen, St. Peter, Cleopas, and an unidentified man on the road to Emmaus; His twelve disciples; more than five hundred brethren at once; St. James; seven of the apostles again; and St. Paul himself after His resurrection. He told His apostles to touch and feel His hands and side to see that He was not a ghost (or apparition) but real and to give Him something to eat. Normally what we call "apparitions" do not eat and drink.[373] The visiting parties are usually Our Lord, the Blessed Virgin, the angels, and the saints—very holy people; but sometimes they are "ordinary" people such as souls from purgatory.[374]

Apparitions are objective phenomena which have a real exterior object. They simply mean an occasion when a presumably sane and sincere person reports "seeing" and "hearing" a heavenly visitor, usually the Blessed Virgin Mary. It should be noted that in the specific Marian apparitions mentioned below, ordinarily, only the alleged visionaries were able to see the apparition.[375] However, Our Lady has also appeared to numerous individual saints, beati, and venerables. For example, while kneeling before the altar of Our Lady, the Mother of God appeared to St. Alphonsus Mary Liguori and requested he become a priest.[376] The Virgin Mary appeared to Saint Mariam Baouardy (Mary of Jesus Crucified) to address her wound after a Moslem attacker had slit her throat and left her for dead.[377] Venerable Maria of Jesus had conversations with Mary during the times Mary appeared to her.[378] Moreover, there are multiple appearances of the Mother of God with her Son where the Blessed Virgin witnessed mystical marriage and espousal ceremonies between Jesus and a specific saint.

An apparition may also be defined as the phenomenon of a heavenly being touching the senses, communicating directly with the intellect and the consciousness. They are remarkable occurrences that seem to defy the laws of our natural world and point to the existence of a world beyond.[379] Many of the miracles associated with apparitions take place in close conjunction with the Eucharist.[380]

In an apparition, such a person's presence or communication is made obvious together with his body as it was made known on earth. It is a manifestation of a "person" who is temporarily bodiless, living as a disembodied soul in expectation of the resurrection at the end of the world.

---

[372] Freze, VVA, op.cit., p. 79.
[373] Hebert, op.cit., p. 26.
[374] Ibid., p. 234.

[375] Groeschel, ASSV, op.cit., p. 160.
[376] Fargas, op.cit., p. 31.
[377] Sarah Gallick. *The Big Book of Women Saints.* San Francisco, Harper, c 2007, p. 251.
[378] See Santos y beatos Latino–Americano on the internet.
[379] Johnson, op.cit., pp. 16–17.
[380] Ibid., p. 99.

Whatever the methods or means by which God allows saints or others to appear in apparitions, the recipients of such "visions" experience and refer to them just as if the person appearing were actually there in his or her body. The apparitions are usually radiant and accompanied by a strong but soft and beautiful light unknown to earthly experience. There seems to be something unforgettable about genuine apparitions as the visionaries can recall them in remarkable detail. Good spiritual directors should be able to differentiate the real thing from illusions and hallucinations.[381]

The Church has always understood that there is a definite distinction between creditable apparitions and psychological phenomena like illusions, hallucinations, or dreams. Psychological events come from inside the person himself, but the evidence implies that apparitions have an objective and independent reality of their own. An illusion is seeing something real but not as it really is. They are different by nature from apparitions, which have no material substance and are not usually seen by all the people present. An hallucination is the appearance of something that does not exist, and it usually happens through the action of some psychoactive substance or extreme emotional stress. Apparitions are very distinct from hallucinations. Apparitions can happen without emotional stress, certainly without drugs or other factors that alter one's consciousness. Apparitions persist. Hallucinations fade. Apparitions cannot be induced. One cannot make God do something like that. Apparitions often convey information that the seer did not have before and could not have had by natural means, which no hallucination can do.[382] Moreover this information may constitute a message of some importance for the whole world. Apparitions are not dreams either. Dreams happen when people are asleep but apparitions happen to people who are wide awake and, often, who are not thinking about anything supernatural at the time.

It is not necessary to actually have functional bodily eyes to see an apparition. Blessed Sibyllina Biscossi for instance was blind from the age of twelve, and Venerable John of Saint-Samson (1571–1636) was blind since he was three, but they both saw visions and apparitions anyway, as did St. Lutgardis, who was blind during the last eleven years of her life.[383]

St. Thomas Aquinas says the soul has its own five senses and mystics and visionaries are given the extraordinary grace of being in touch with these senses, which most of us are not. Through the soul's eyes, the mystic sees apparitions. Through the soul's hearing, they sense heavenly voices or music. Their spiritual smell is opened to the celestial fragrances so often experienced around apparitions.[384]

The visions and apparitions related in the Sacred Scriptures are numerous both in the Old and New Testaments. In the Old Testament, one comes across no fewer than a dozen incidents in the lives of Abraham, Isaac, Jacob, and Moses, the first patriarchs of Judaism, in which God was encountered in a vision or in something even more concrete.[385] Most of Genesis and the first half of Exodus are accounts of these encounters. Five separate encounters are attributed to Abraham, including one in which the Lord "appeared," accompanied by two other beings.[386] One also encounters the apparition of God in His appearance to Moses in the Burning Bush.

---

[381] Hebert, op.cit., p. 235.
[382] Johnson, op.cit., pp. 110–12.
[383] Ibid., pp. 114–15.
[384] Ibid., p. 115; see also *Summa* 1, 75–79, q 51, article 2.
[385] Wiebe, op.cit., p. 212.
[386] Ibid., p. 249, see note 1; Genesis 18:1–2.

In the New Testament, the first heavenly apparitions and messages came from God's mighty angels. In Matthew's Gospel, one finds the first supernatural sign through the voice and appearance of the heavenly Archangel Gabriel to St. Joseph. In this discourse, Gabriel encourages Joseph to marry Mary, explaining that her pregnancy was of a miraculous nature (Mt 1:18–23). An angel, probably Gabriel, warned Joseph in a dream to flee to Egypt and announced when it was safe to return (Mt 2:13). The angelic apparitions came first in Luke's Gospel as well when Gabriel appeared to the priest Zechariah and informed him that his elderly wife would bear a son (Lk 1:13). Angels instructed Deacon Philip to go to Gaza to meet the eunuch (Acts 8:26–40) and told the gentile Cornelius to invite St. Peter to his home (Acts 10:1–4, 30). St. Paul had a vision of his guardian angel who appeared and prophesized that the ship on which he was sailing as a prisoner would be wrecked in a terrible storm but all passengers on board would be saved (Acts 27:22–24). When the Sadducees arrested and imprisoned the Twelve Apostles (Acts 5:17–21), an angel appeared to them and opened the prison doors. Later on, during St. Peter's imprisonment at the hands of King Herod (Acts 12:6–11), an angel appeared and freed him from his chains. In the book of Revelation, St. John claims that Christ Himself sent an angel to him to make things known. Many other angelic voices are heard throughout the book of Revelation (Rv 1:1; 5:2; 9:1; 9:14–17ff).

The Church exercises great care in investigating reports of apparitions and most are not found authentic. However, if an apparition is deemed authentic, it does not mean that Catholics have to believe in the appearance. It simply means that those who do believe will not be harmed by believing. The most that any post-biblical apparition gets is that there is nothing in the report or in its implication that is contrary to the Faith and that it is "worthy of belief"[387] in the supernatural character of the event. (Merely finding it not contrary to church teaching puts it in the "non constat" category, but moral certainty of a miracle elevates it to the "constat de supernaturalitate" category.)

Well–substantiated apparitions are worthy of belief and devotion, particularly such great appearances as those of Our Lord to St. Margaret Mary Alacoque, a nun of the Visitation Order in France, concerning devotion to His Sacred Heart. St. Margaret Mary was praying before the Blessed Sacrament and the Risen Christ appeared before her and showed her His Sacred Heart. Christ regularly appeared to her on the first Friday of every month and requested that a special feast day be celebrated in the Universal Church to honor His Sacred Heart. It was to be observed every year on the first Friday after the Feast of Corpus Christi, the feast honoring the Body of Christ in the Eucharist.[388]

One would especially think that the apparition of Our Lady to Saint Bernadette Soubirous at Lourdes represents the highest form of supernatural experience. However, according to such writers as Saint Teresa of Avila and Saint John of the Cross (both Doctors of the Church), this kind of extraordinary apparition accompanied by an exterior locution represents the lowest form of divine communication. In fact, such an apparition can be given by divine providence to a random group of very ordinary souls as happened in Knock, Ireland in 1879.[389]

Most saints are canonized without ever seeing an apparition, and a person can see an apparition, even a credible one, without

---

[387] Ibid., p. 14, see also Tanquery, op.cit., p. 701.
[388] Ibid., pp. 4–6.
[389] Groeschel, ASSV, op.cit., pp. 149–50.

ever coming close to canonization; e.g., the cases of the visionaries Mariette Beco (b. 1921), Albert and Fernande Voison, Melanie Mathieu (1831–1904) (Sr. Mary of the Cross), Estelle Faguette, and Maximin Giraud.[390]

Saints like St. Teresa of Avila fought her apparitions and locutions for two solid years, begging God with all her might to take them away, whether they were from the devil or from Him, but to no avail. At one point Christ tried to reassure her, "I treat only my friends this way." She answered, "No wonder you have so few." Many other visionaries like St. Catherine of Ricci and St. Margaret Mary Alacoque begged God to leave them alone, sometimes in those very words: "Leave me alone, Lord." Blessed Anna Maria Taigi (1769–1837) would even add, "[because] I have [house] work to do."[391]

Having looked at hundreds of apparitions over the centuries, moral theologians have distinguished three different categories of these events: corporeal, imaginative, and intellectual.

Like visions, most common kinds of apparitions are called corporeal (exterior or ocular) because they show an apparent bodily solidarity and are perceived by the eyes of the body. Apparitions of incorporeal substances (angels and departed souls) cannot be seen in this earthly life because they are of the spiritual order. Yet, on rare occasions, God sometimes allows these saintly souls to see heavenly or spiritual beings when He sends them as messengers, protectors, or to plead for the prayers and sacrifices of the chosen soul. When this happens, the spiritual beings temporarily take on a material body in order for one to recognize and converse with them. Such is the case with guardian angels, poor souls in purgatory, the saints, Jesus, and the Blessed Virgin Mary.[392] The Angel of Peace who appeared in the clouds of Fatima in the spring of 1916 was probably this kind of apparition because all of the children saw him in that form.[393]

Another kind of apparition is called imaginative. This type of apparition is perceived by the eyes of the soul, without the aid of bodily sight, while the mystic is asleep or awake. It cannot be dismissed at will.[394] An imaginative vision is that sense inside one that can receive and comprehend direct communications from some supernatural agency to your soul. So when one of these occurs, a person gets a clear image of the external entity—God, an angel, a saint, or a devil—in what one might call "one's mind's eye."[395] Imaginative apparitions fall into three subclasses: they may be symbolic (Jacob's ladder, Gn 28:10–22), personal (St. Margaret Mary's experience of the Sacred Heart), or dramatic (Mystic Marriage of St. Catherine of Sienna).

Apparitions can also be intellectual; these, as St. John of the Cross explained, are so–called because "all that is intelligible to the intellect, the spiritual eye of the soul, causes spiritual vision, just as all that is physically visible to the material eye causes bodily vision." The intellectual apparition is a simple intuitive knowledge acquired without any natural means like study and with no help from the bodily senses. St. Teresa of Avila described it as being as if the food were already placed in the stomach without eating it or knowing how it got there.[396] While praying on St. Peter's Day one year, St. Teresa of Avila had her first intellectual apparition. She saw nothing with her bodily eyes or with her soul.

---

[390] Johnson, op,cit., p. 13.
[391] Ibid., pp. 80–81.

[392] Freze, TBWC, op.cit., p. 160.
[393] Johnson, op.cit., p. 116.
[394] Ibid., p. 356.
[395] Ibid., p. 117.
[396] Ibid., p. 356.

She just felt Christ beside her. This kind of apparition is a simple intuitive knowledge that you just know without the aid of your bodily senses.[397]

As with an imaginative vision, the mystic can be asleep or awake, but an intellectual apparition can last hours or days. Only God can produce an intellectual apparition because only God has access to the human intellect. But an overactive imagination or the devil can cause events that seem to the recipient to be a real apparition of any of these kinds.[398] The interesting thing is that mystics can usually tell the difference among the kinds of apparitions. Blessed Julian of Norwich knew that her apparition of the scourging was imaginative, not corporal, because as the torrent of hot blood ran to where it should have fallen, it disappeared.[399]

All apparitions are specific in the sense that only those intended to experience them can do so. Because all genuine apparitions are outreaches by God, none can be induced or summoned at the will of the recipient, and very few can be predicted.[400]

Marian Apparitions

Apparitions of the Blessed Virgin Mary are sometimes accompanied by a host of glorious phenomena, such as visions of angels, heavenly music and singing, miraculous healing, luminosities, ecstatic states, extrasensory perception, and prophesying. The apparitions may be apocalyptic in nature, with Mary exhorting people to prayer and righteous living, and to build churches or shrines in her honor. She also warns of dire consequences if people continue their sinful ways, such as the end of the world. She bestows secret prophecies on a select few who perceive her. In this respect, Mary has taken over the primary functions of the prophets of old, who were transported to heaven to receive the same admonitions and prophecies from God. But Mary, out of her love for humanity and her loyalty to those devoted to her, is able to intercede with an angry God on humanity's behalf.[401]

The Congregation for the Doctrine of Faith has established in the 1978 Document "Norms of the Congregation Regarding the Manner of Proceeding in the Discernment of Presumed Apparitions or Revelations" that to proceed with verifying a proposed Marian apparition, a report must be compiled. Among other things, the report should include information on the observed facts of the case. An examination of the messages should then be made. The content cannot contradict the Christian faith. A medical-psychological examination of the visionary should be undertaken to guarantee his or her health and normalcy and to eliminate the possibility of hallucinations. The spiritual fruits of the message should also be evaluated. These fruits might include such things as a conversions, a return to the Faith of those who have left, vocations, the morality and ecclesiastical nature of the message and its cooperation in the evangelization of the world, and possible miraculous cures. Once verified and authenticated by ecclesiastical authority, these extraordinary manifestations are considered worthy of belief, but the faithful are free to choose if they adhere to them or not.

It should be duly noted that, to date, the Medjugorje apparitions claimed by 6 children in Bosnia-Hercegovnia starting in 1981 have not been officially approved by the Church although as of 2018 were under Vatican investigation.

---

[397] Ibid., pp. 117–18.
[398] Ibid., p. 356.
[399] Ibid., p. 117.
[400] Ibid., p. 356.

[401] Guiley, op.cit., p. 387.

In the twentieth and early twenty-first centuries alone, more Marian apparitions and messages for the world have occurred than at any other time in Church history. In fact, it is claimed that over 250 reports of Marian apparitions in thirty-two countries have come forth in the few years between 1923 and 1975. Out of all these claims, at least the vast majority of them involve Marian messages for the seers, their parish, the Church, and the world. Since 1973, the supernatural messages in particular have become even more common—perhaps double the total number recorded in the previous fifty years.[402]

Twenty-two Marian Apparitions were seriously studied between 1931 and 1950 and only two were approved (Beauraing and Banneux in Belgium). Six remained undecided in 1952 and the remaining fourteen were rejected.[403] Since then, the Akita Marian phenomena experienced by Sister Agnes Katsuko Sasagawa starting in 1973 were approved as genuinely supernatural in origin by Bishop John Ito on April 22, 1984, after consulting with the Holy See. The Marian apparitions which took place in Le Laus, France, in 1664 to the seer Benoite Rencurel were recently officially approved in Laus. In 2010, the apparition of Our Lady to Adele Joseph Brise which took place in Robinsonville (now Champion)Wisconsin in 1859 became the first Marian apparition approved by the Catholic Church in the United States.

Guadalupe, Mexico 1531
Our Lady of Guadalupe

One of the first of the Marian-age apparitions occurred to a Mexican Indian peasant named Juan Diego in 1531. He was a member of Mexico's Chichimeca tribe who had converted to Christianity.[404] One day while on his way to Mass on the feast of

The Virgin of Guadalupe

the Immaculate Conception in 1531, Juan passed the hill of Tepeyac when he heard music and saw a glowing cloud over the summit of the hill illuminated by a sort of a rainbow. He then heard a voice calling his name. He climbed the hill and saw the figure of a young marvelously beautiful mestiza girl who appeared to be about fourteen years old.

The girl spoke to him in Nahuatl, his native language, identifying herself as the Ever Virgin Mary, Mother of the True God. She requested that a temple be built upon this site "to make my Son manifest" and asked Juan to relay her intentions to the bishop-elect of Mexico City. This simple man failed to convince the bishop the first time and reported this to Our Lady. She requested he try again. The next time, the bishop asked for some proof, a confirming

---

[402] Freze, VVA, op.cit., p. 103.
[403] NCE, 1967, op.cit., v. 12, p. 446.
[404] Gallick, op.cit., p. 372.

sign from heaven. Our Lady directed him to the barren hilltop of Tepeyac to gather Castilian roses which were in bloom during the middle of winter. Mary then rearranged the roses in his Tilma, a poncho-like garment woven of maguey fiber.

Appearing before the bishop, he opened his tilma and let the fresh Castilian roses spill out. When the bishop looked up at Juan Diego, he saw a miraculously imprinted image of the Mother of God on the tilma. Our Lady told Juan she wanted her image to be known as the Ever Virgin, Holy Mary of Guadalupe. A third confirming sign was the cure of Juan Bernardino, Juan Diego's uncle, who had been gravely ill. Following the apparition, some nine million Mexicans were baptized.

Like the Shroud of Turin, another image "not made by human hands" (*acheiropoieta* in Greek), the image of Guadalupe has been studied and analyzed by scientists and art historians for more than a century. To date, no natural explanation for the image has ever been found.[405] According to the laws of nature, the unique image of the Virgin on coarse cactus cloth should have disintegrated in around 30 years, especially since it had been exposed to the open air for so long. Another marvel is that it has been scientifically demonstrated that in an ophthamalgic effect the eyes of the image of Our Lady contained the reflected image of Juan Diego, as would be the case with a photograph, but not with a painting.[406] Juan Diego (c. 1474–1548) was beatified on May 6, 1990 at the Basilica of Our lady of Guadalupe by Pope John Paul II.[407]

Laus, France 1664
Our Lady of Laus

Benoite Rencurel (1647–1718) (Benedicta Rencurel) was born in Saint-Etienne d'Avancon (Laus) in the Southern French Alps. In May of 1664, the Blessed Virgin started appearing to her every day for four months thereafter. The Lady told Benedicta that her name was Mary and told her to "pray continuously for sinners." Benedicta told the woman who owned the flocks she attended about the apparitions, but the woman did not believe her. The owner then secretly followed the little shepherdess one day, and although she did not see the apparition, she did, however, hear Mary's voice tell Benedicta that her own soul was in danger. The woman was so deeply moved by the message that she turned her life around. This shepherdess of Laus had numerous apparitions of Mary throughout the rest of her life, for more than fifty years. Her apparitions were the longest single series of apparitions in history recognized by the Church. She also saw the Child Jesus as well as Jesus as an adult.[408] In all, Benedicta received five visions of Jesus, who showed her His suffering so that she could participate in His passion. Our Lady requested that a house be built in Laus for priests, with the intention of drawing people to greater conversion. The holy site now draws 120,000 pilgrims annually. Numerous physical healings have also been associated with the site, especially when oil from the sanctuary lamp is applied according to the directives which the Virgin Mary gave to Benedicta. During a Mass celebrated in the Basilica of Notre Dame in Laus, France, on May 4, 2008, Bishop Jean-Michel de Falco of Gap officially approved these apparitions. As previously noted, these were the first Marian apparitions to be approved in the twenty-first century by the Vatican and the Church in France.[409]

[405] Johnson, op.cit., p. 202–12; Guiley, op.cit., p. 387.

[406] Hebert, op.cit., p. 217.

[407] *New Catholic Encyclopedia. jubilee volume. The Wojtyla years.* Detroit, MI: Gale Group in association with the Catholic University of America, c 2001, p. 516; Connell, op.cit., pp. 51ff.

[408] Wiebe, op.cit., p. 20.

[409] Sister Mary Jean Dorcy, O.P. *Saint Dominic's*

Apparition of the Virgin to St. Catherine Laboure, Le Cerf, (fl.1835) / Private Collection / Archives Charmet / Bridgeman Images

Paris, France 1830
Our Lady of the Miraculous Medal

On July 18, 1830, Catherine Laboure, a nun with the Sisters of Charity in the motherhouse of the Daughters of Charity in Paris, France, was awakened at 11:30 p.m. by the sound of her name being called. She saw a child of about four or five years old with golden hair, whom she took to be her guardian angel. The angel told her to go to the convent chapel. Upon

Family: The Lives of Over 300 Famous Dominicans. Rockford, Il., TAN Books, 1983, pp. 476–78.

arrival there, she found it brilliantly lit. The Blessed Virgin appeared at midnight and delivered her customary messages of exhortation to prayer. She asked Catherine to undertake a mission that would require her suffering and also gave her prophecies. Mary appeared to Catherine again on July 19 and on November 27. At these times, she appeared hovering over a globe of the world, with arms extended and rays of light radiating from her hands. Catherine saw a message in the apparition that read, "Mary conceived without sin, pray for us who have recourse to you." This concept of Mary as conceived without sin influenced the Church's dogma of the Immaculate Conception, which was pronounced by Pope Pius IX in the year 1854. Another image represented the letter "M" on top of a cross that was placed over the hearts of Jesus and Mary. Our Lady then told Catherine, "Have a medal struck on this model." As many as a billion medals have since been made, bringing countless blessings and graces to the faithful. The sign of the Miraculous Medal is one that reveals a trust in the providence and protection under the mantle of Mary and her Son, Jesus Christ.[410]

La Salette, France 1846
Our Lady of La Salette

On September 19, 1846, eleven-year-old Maximin Giraud and fourteen-year-old Melanie Mathieu were attending their individual herds of cows in the little village of LaSalette in the French Alps when they encountered the Blessed Virgin, who spoke to them in French and the local patois. Mary wore a headdress capped by a crown ringed with roses. Her long white dress and slippers were decorated with pearls, and her slippers also had gold buckles and roses.[411] Our Lady told the children that because of lack of faith in the area, the region was suffering economic disaster, and she urged the people to come back to God. The messages of our Lady concerned trust in Jesus, the necessity of daily prayer, participation in the Eucharist, and the need for conversion and reconciliation with God. Mary said that the two sins most distressing to her were neglect of the Sunday Mass obligation and misuse of her Son's name.[412] The great miracle of La Salette was the general conversion that spread across

Statue depicting Our Lady of La Salette, photo by DyziO/Shutterstock

the region.[413] This was the first Marian apparition in which prophetic "secrets" allegedly were given to the visionaries.[414] Our Lady spoke to each of the visionaries alone and entrusted each with a secret. In 1850, the secrets were revealed only to Pope Pius IX.[415] There is controversy surrounding the secrets, which supposedly dealt with the wickedness of some priests, blinding of people to faith, materialism, spiritualism, and vice of all kind as well as persecution of the Church and suffering of the Holy Father. She gave encouragement for the faithful to remain watchful, to pray, and to be obedient to the will of God. A spring of water was discovered in the place where the Blessed Mother appeared to the children, and miracles of physical healing began to be associated with the water. A

[410] Freze, VVA, op.cit., p. 275; Guiley, op.cit., p. 388.

[411] Guiley, op.cit., p. 388.

[412] *The Wanderer*, Feb.3, 2005, p. 2.

[413] Johnson, op.cit., p. 227

[414] Randall Sullivan, *The miracle detector: an investigation of holy visions.* NY: Atlantic Monthly Press, c 2004, p. 167.

[415] Aradi, op.cit., p. 223.

beautiful basilica now welcomes pilgrims to this site.[416]

Lourdes, France 1858
Our Lady of Lourdes

On February 11, 1858, the Blessed Virgin appeared to fourteen-year-old Bernadette Soubirous (1844–1879) near the river Pau in the French Pyrenees. Our Lady appeared in the Grotto of Massabielle. Bernadette described her as "a lady in white" who smiled at her and prayed the Rosary. There were a total of eighteen apparitions in all beginning on February 11 and ending on July 16, 1858. As a result of the apparitions, Bernadette reportedly experienced ecstasies, some lasting an hour. Through this humble peasant girl, Mary called for heartfelt prayer, especially meditations of the Rosary, which illuminate the life of Christ, penance, the conversion of sinners, attendance at Mass, and especially service to the sick and the poor. Three secrets were also alleged to have been imparted to Bernadette. Finally, Mary told Bernadette that she had come from heaven and was the Immaculate Conception (March 25), a significant title, and in 1954, Pope Pius XII (1939–1958) defined the Immaculate Conception of Mary in dogmatic form. At Mary's request, a chapel was built in 1871 upon the site of her appearance. It has grown to become one of the great churches of southern France. A miraculous spring has gushed forth from this site, and thousands of healings have been reported ever since with 70 (as of 2019) having been declared medically inexplicable by the International Lourdes Medical Commission (CMIL). Up to six million pilgrims visit Lourdes each year.[417]

Dalat cathedral. Stained glass window. Our Lady of Lourdes: An image depicting Mary appearing on the grotto, in front of Bernadette Soubirous. Dalat. Vietnam / Godong / Bridgeman Images

Champion, Wisconsin 1859
Our Lady of Good Help

Adele Joseph Brise was born in Dion-le-val in the Belgian province of Brabant on January 30, 1831. As a child, she suffered an accident with lye that resulted in the loss of an eye. In the mid-1850s, her family immigrated to America and settled in Robinsonville (Champion) near Green Bay, Wisconsin. In early October 1859, she reported seeing an apparition of a woman dressed in dazzling white and a starry crown which seemed to float above the fields. The following Sunday, October 9, 1859, on her way to Mass, she saw the vision a second time. After Mass, on her way home, the lady appeared a third time. Adele asked her who she was and what she wanted of her. The woman identified herself as: "the Queen of Heaven who prays for the conversion of sinners and I wish you to do the same." Adele was then given

---

[416] Connell, op.cit., pp. 73–77.
[417] Guiley, op.cit., p. 388; Connell, op.cit., p. 79.

a mission to gather the children in this wild country and teach them what they should know about salvation. She went on to dedicate her life to prayer, especially for the conversion of sinners and to the catechesis of children. After this command, Adele helped to build a chapel along with a school. The chapel, now the National Shrine of Our Lady of Good Help, is located in the community of Champion, Wisconsin, about sixteen miles northeast of Green Bay. This apparition was formally approved on December 8, 2010, by the bishop of Green Bay, David L. Ricken, thus becoming the first Marian apparition approved by the Catholic Church in the United States. Adele Brise died on July 5, 1896, and was buried near the chapel.[418]

Pontmain, France 1871
Our Lady of Hope

On January 17, 1871, at Pontmain in the Brittany section of France, twelve-year-old Eugene Barbadette witnessed a smiling Lady of great beauty in the winter sky above and between two stone chimneys of a neighbor's house. His ten-year-old brother, Joseph, also saw the figure as did some of the other children of Pontmain. The lady appeared in a dark-blue robe and was encircled with stars. It was seen also by little neighbor girls, nine-year-old Jeanne-Marie Lebosse and her eleven-year-old sister, Francoise. Both saw the beautiful Lady and described her as the boys had done. Four children together with twenty-five-month-old Augustine Boitin saw a large red crucifix, bearing the figure of Jesus Christ near the Blessed Virgin. Baby Augustine reached out toward the apparition and cried out "Jesus." In all, including Eugene Friteau, six children saw the apparition. Mr. and Mrs. Barbadette saw nothing upon visiting the site and accused their children of lying or dreaming. Later on, the boys saw Mary again, but

Stained Glass Depicting Our Lady of Hope

nobody else did. The nuns at their school came to investigate the site, but nothing was seen. These apparitions and messages lasted that night for about two hours. Mary's message to the four children centered on the need for more prayer and trust in God. The Virgin, once smiling, appeared sad at the state of the world. At this time, the Franco-Prussian War, which had started in 1870, was bringing sorrow and death upon thousands of French citizens. This apparition coincided with the German Army's imminent advance on the town of Pontmain, when it received orders to turn around. Our Lady of Hope is a treasure of the French

---

418 LA Times, December 15, 2010; see also Wikipedia.

people, for ten days after her apparition in Pontmain, a full armistice was signed, ending the Franco-Prussian war. This is the great miracle of Pontmain.[419]

Pellevoisin, France 1876
Our Lady of Pellevoisin

The apparition of Pellevoisin was accorded to Estelle Faguette (1843–1929), an incurably sick woman, in February, 1876. During the night of February 14, Estelle was on the verge of death because of acute peritonitis, pulmonary tuberculosis, and an abdominal tumor. She was given only a few hours to live. Estelle claimed the Blessed Virgin approached her and told her to have no fear. She then promised Estelle five more days of suffering in honor of the wounds of Jesus and appeared to her each of those nights with words of wisdom, rebuke, and comfort. Estelle was miraculously healed following the fifth day and was honored with ten more visits from Mary during the following months. On the seventh visit on July 2, 1876, Mary entrusted Estelle with a secret. The Blessed Mother was described as completely surrounded in light and dressed in white. She would often appear with arms outstretched. Mary emphasized that she wanted to convert sinners and revealed that devotion to the Sacred Heart of Jesus was an especially dear and effective means to obtain grace. She related that Estelle was chosen to proclaim and spread devotion to a scapular of the Sacred Heart and instructed her to go to the prelate to promote the design and usage of this scapular. On the feast of the Immaculate Conception, December 8, Mary also released "raindrops" filled with the graces she could bestow from "His Heart" such as piety, salvation, and health. Although never declaring the apparitions as "worthy of belief" in the supernatural character of the events, the bishop and Pope Leo XIII heeded the Virgin's message through Estelle, and a Confraternity of Our Mother All Merciful was established in Pellevoisin in 1894 to promote devotion to the Sacred Heart scapular.[420]

Knock, Ireland 1879
Our Lady of Knock, Queen of the Angels, Apparition of Our Lady of Knock

On a rainy night of August 21, 1879, Our Lady appeared outside St. John the Baptist Church, County Mayo, Ireland, to fifteen persons. The apparition was first seen by a woman who had gone to lock up the church and who ran into a friend. They saw what they thought at first were statues, but curious about them, they moved closer. They saw they were alive and were very much amazed. Our Lady, with St. Joseph at her right hand and St. John the Evangelist on her left. They appeared motionless in a blaze of light and all dressed in white. Mary also wore a golden crown with a golden rose at her brow. And St. John wore a mitre as a bishop would. Mary stood praying with her eyes and hands raised toward heaven. Behind them all was an altar with a large cross. At the foot of the cross was a Lamb. There were angels surrounding the cross in adoration.

Others came, and altogether the apparition was ultimately witnessed by fifteen people of various ages and both sexes. The apparition lasted two hours, from 7:30 p.m. to 9:30 p.m. on August 21. It was followed by miraculous healings. This was one of the few Marian apparitions where no words were spoken or messages given.[421]

Once approved by the Commission of Inquiry, Knock became one of the great Marian shrines and has been the scene

---

[419] Johnson, op.cit., pp. 239–44; Freze, VVA, op.cit., pp. 276; Connell, op.cit., pp. 81–83.

[420] http://www.miraclehunter.com/marian_apparitions/approved_apparitions/pellevoisin; Aradi, op.cit, p. 242; Freze, VVA, op.cit., p. 275.

[421] Freze, VVA, op.cit., pp. 268–69.

Statue of Our Lady of Knock, Knock Shrine, photo by Michael McLaughlin

of hundreds of cures. People have subsequently referred to Our Lady of Knock under her ancient title Queen of the Angels.[422]

Fatima, Portugal 1915–1917
Our Lady of Fatima

The Marian apparitions at Fatima started with an angel, silent and distant in the clouds. In 1915, eight-year-old Lucia dos Santos was tending sheep on Mount Cabeco and was eating lunch with her companions Maria Justino, Maria Rosa Matias, and Teresa Matias when they saw a figure in the sky in the form of a large angel. It appeared twice more later that year. In 1916, Lucia was tending sheep again with her cousins Jacinta Marto, aged six, and Francisco Marto, aged eight. This time a beautiful young man, whiter than snow, about fourteen or fifteen years old

[422] Connell, op. cit., pp. 84–85; Aradi, op.cit., p. 243.

appeared to them. He told them, "Do not be afraid. I am the Angel of Peace. Pray with me." Kneeling on the ground, he bowed down until his forehead touched the ground and told the children to repeat these words three times:

"My God, I believe, I adore, I trust, and Love you! I ask pardon of you for those who do not believe, do not adore, do not trust, and do not love you."

Then rising, he said:

"Pray thus. The hearts of Jesus and Mary are attentive to the words of your prayers."

A few months later, the angel appeared to them again and demanded, "Pray, Pray very much! The most holy hearts of Jesus and Mary have designs of mercy on you. Offer prayers and sacrifices constantly to the Most High."

He identified himself as the Guardian Angel of Portugal and went on to say, "Make every possible sacrifice. Offer it to God as an act of reparation for the sins by which He is offended, and in supplication for the conversion of sinners. Above all, accept and bear with submission all the suffering which the Lord allows in your lives. In this way you will draw down peace upon your country. I am the Guardian Angel of Portugal."

When this angel next appeared in the fall of 1916, he was holding a chalice in his left hand with the host suspended above it, from which drops of blood fell into the chalice. Leaving the chalice suspended in the air, the Angel knelt down beside the chalice and repeated three times: "Most Holy Trinity, Father, Son and Holy Spirit, I offer you the Most Precious Body, Blood, Soul and Divinity of Jesus Christ, present in all the tabernacles of the world, in reparation for the outrages, sacrileges, and indifference by which Himself is offended. And through the infinite merits of His most Sacred Heart, and the Immaculate

Lúcia Santos, Jacinta and Francisco Marto, 1917,
photo attributed to Joshua Benoliel

Heart of Mary, I beg of you the conversion of poor sinners."

Then, rising, he took the Host and chalice again. He placed the Host on Lucia's tongue and shared the Blood from the chalice between Jacinta and Francisco, saying as he did so: "Take and drink the Body and Blood of Jesus Christ, horribly outraged by ungrateful men. Make reparation for their crimes, and console your God."

It took some time for the children to come out of this ecstasy.[423] Then, about noon on May 13, 1917, while tending their sheep, the Blessed Virgin Mary appeared before them and in Portuguese told them that she was from heaven and asked them to accept whatever sufferings God would send them. She said, "I ask you to come here for six consecutive months, on the thirteenth day, at this same hour. I will tell you later who I am and why I have come to you. I shall return here again a seventh time."

Again the beautiful Lady from heaven spoke saying, "Do you want to offer yourselves to

God, to endure all the sufferings He may allow, as an act of reparation for the sins by which He is offended and as a supplication for the conversion of sinners?"

When the children responded, "We will do as you ask," the beautiful Lady opened her hands and great streams of light radiated upon the children and they were allowed to see themselves in God. In parting, the Lady revealed herself as "Our Lady of the Rosary" and told them to "say the Rosary every day to earn peace for the world and the end of war."

The Lady promised to appear to the children again. The second apparition of Fatima occurred on June 13, 1917. No more than fifty people were present. This time the beautiful Lady from heaven asked the children to add the following prayer of reparation after each decade of the Rosary: "O my Jesus, forgive us our sins, save us from the fires of hell, lead all souls to heaven, especially those in most need of your mercy."

Then the beautiful Lady now identified as the Mother of God made a promise to the world in the name of her Divine Son. This promise to the three visionaries came to be known as the first secret of Fatima. She said, "I promise salvation to those who embrace devotion to my Immaculate Heart. Their souls will be loved by God as flowers placed by me to adorn His throne. These souls will suffer a great deal, but I will never leave them. My Immaculate Heart will be their refuge, the way that will lead them to God."

The third apparition took place on July 13, 1917. On that day, thousands gathered. The children fell into ecstasy. During this apparition, the Blessed Lady promised to perform a cosmic miracle on October 13, 1917. As recounted by Sister Lucy of Fatima in her memoirs:

> She opened Her hands once more, as she had done the two previous months

[423] Johnson, op.cit., pp. 246–48.

Our Lady of Fatima, Charles Bosseron Chambers, Restored Traditions

[May 13, June 13, 1917]. The rays [of light] appeared to penetrate the earth, and we saw, as it were, a vast sea of fire. Plunged in this fire, we saw the demons and the souls [of the damned]. The latter were like transparent burning embers, all blackened or burnished bronze, having human form. They were floating around in that conflagration, now raised into the air by the flames which issued from within themselves, together with great clouds of smoke. Now they fell back on every side like sparks in huge fires, without weight or equilibrium, amid shrieks and groans of pain and despair, which horrified us and made us tremble with fright. (It must have been this sight which caused me to cry out, as people say they heard me). The demons were distinguished [from the souls of the damned] by their terrifying and repellent likeness to frightful and unknown animals, black and transparent like burning coals. That vision only lasted for a moment, thanks to our good Heavenly Mother, Who at the first apparition [May 13, 1917] had promised to take us to Heaven. Without that, I think that we would have died of terror and fear.[424]

Lucia recounts that the Blessed Mother then imparted to the three what has been referred to as the second secret of Fatima.

You have seen hell where the souls of poor sinners go. To save them, God wishes to establish in the world devotion to my Immaculate Heart. If what I say to you is done, many souls will be saved, and there will be peace in the world. The war will end [WWI], but unless people cease to offend God, another, even worse will break out during the pontificate of Pope Pius XII [1939–1958].When you see a night illumined by an unknown light, then know that this is the great signal that God gives you that He is about to punish the world for its crimes, by means of war, famine, and persecutions of the Church and of the Holy Father. To prevent this, I shall ask for the consecration of Russia to my Immaculate Heart and a Communion of Reparation on the first Saturdays of each month. If my requests are heeded, Russia will be converted, and there will be peace. If not, she will spread her errors throughout the world, causing wars and persecutions of the Church. The good will be martyred; the Holy Father will suffer grievously. Several nations will be annihilated. Finally, my Immaculate Heart will triumph. The Holy Father will consecrate Russia to me, and she will be converted, and a period of peace will be granted to the world.[425]

A third secret was entrusted to the three visionaries on this date.[426]

The fourth apparition took place on August 13. There was a crowd of about fifteen thousand. This time there were no visionaries as the authorities had them put in jail.

On August 15, the visionaries were freed and returned to their village. The Blessed Mother urged them to pray the Rosary every day and again told them that she would perform a miracle in the last month's apparition.

By the time of the sixth apparition on September 13, 1917, the crowd had swelled to thirty thousand. In response to what the beautiful Lady wanted of the visionaries, she replied:

Let the people continue to say the Rosary every day to obtain the end of war. In the last month, in October, I

---

[424] "Sister Lucy of Fatima describes the vision of hell," The Fatima Network, http://www.fatima.org/essentials/facts/hell.asp; Fatima in Lucia's own words," Third and Fourth memoir, the vision of hell; http://www.concernedcatholics.org/printable/pr–hell.htm.

[425] Lucia of Fatima, *Fatima in Lucia's Own Words*. Edited by L. Kondor (Fatima, Portugal: Postulation Centre, 1976), pp. 60–63, 104, 107; Johnson, op.cit., pp. 250–51.

[426] Connell, op.cit., p. 102.

shall perform a miracle so that all may believe in my apparitions. If they had not taken you to the town to prison the miracle would have been greater. St. Joseph will come with the Baby Jesus to give peace to the world. Our Lord will also come to bless the people. Besides, Our Lady of the Rosary and Our Lady of Sorrows will come.

The famous "cosmic miracle," or "miracle of the sun," took place on October 13, 1917 just as the three Portuguese peasant children had predicted several months in advance. On this date, a huge crowd of upwards of seventy thousand people made up of all ages and conditions, comprising believers and non-believers, gathered at the Cova da Iria where the children said the miracle would take place. These people stood in the pouring rain for several hours on that day. Shortly after midday, the clouds parted and the people saw the sun turn different colors while apparently spinning on its axis. This lasted about ten minutes. Immediately after that, the entire crowd saw the sun plunge toward the earth. They were terrified for it seemed like the end of the world. When they looked again the sun was in its accustomed place. Our Lady had predicted this sign as early as the first apparition (May 13). Moreover, although this mass of people had been standing in pouring rain for a long time, each member of the crowd discovered he or she was completely dry. These unprecedented, inexplicable, and terrifying solar events were witnessed by tens of thousands of people to include many others who were within a radius of thirty miles. Hundreds, including anti-Catholics, testified to this supernatural event without a single dissenting voice.[427]

In her memoirs, written at the request of her bishop, Lucia related that next to the

A photostatic copy of a page from Ilustração Portuguesa, October 29, 1917, showing the crowd looking at the "miracle of the sun"

sun she saw Saint Joseph holding the Child Jesus, and Our Lady, resembling Our Lady of Mount Carmel, was in white with a blue mantle. Our Lord, she says, along with Saint Joseph, was blessing the world.[428]

Among the messages imparted to the children from the Virgin Mary were the three secrets of Fatima. Lucia was instructed to reveal these secrets and did so in her 1930s memoirs, after the other seers had died. Francisco died on April 4, 1919 and Jacinta on February 20, 1920. (Both were beatified

---

[427] Thomas Crean, O.P. *God is no delusion: A refutation of Richard Dawkins.* San Francisco, Ignatius Press, c 2007, pp. 56–57; Freze, VVA, op.cit., p. 265; Sullivan, op.cit., p. 424.

---

[428] Christopher Rengers, O.F.M.Cap., *The Youngest Prophet.* NY, Alba House, 1986. pp. 58–59; see also Lucia of Fatima, *Her own words to the nuclear age: The memoirs of Sr. Lucia By John Haffert.* Asbury Park, N.J.:101 Foundation, 1993.

by Pope John Paul II on May 13, 2000 and canonized by Pope Francis on May 13, 2017.) As the only surviving visionary at Fatima, Lucia joined the Order of Carmel of St. Theresa at Coimbra in Portugal. She was known there as Sister Mary of the Immaculate Heart (1907–2005).[429]

The so-called secrets are usually divided into three parts. The first secret was a terrifying vision of Hell. The second secret appeared to predict the end of WWI, the Bolshevik revolution and its effects on the Christian faith, and the start of WWII. The third prophecy had the Virgin Mary speaking of a "bishop dressed in white," who would "fall to the ground as though dead under gunfire." This apparently referred to the assassination attempt on Pope John Paul II (1978–2005) by Mehmet Ali Agca in St. Peter's Square on May 13, 1981. This took place on the same day and at the same hour that Our Lady first appeared at Fatima. The pope credited his miraculous recovery to the intercession of Our Lady of Fatima, who is celebrated on May 13. After the pope recovered from this attempt on his life, he visited Fatima to give thanks to Mary for his survival. He placed one of the gunman's 9mm bullets in the crown of the Virgin's statue. He also re-consecrated the world to Mary's Immaculate Heart.[430]

The revelation of the three children of Fatima was meant to have a far-reaching effect. These children had no knowledge of history or geography. They reported the Virgin Mary's request that the Rosary be widely recited throughout the world so that many people would be led to penance and prayer for world peace, especially for the conversion of Russia.[431]

[429] Connell, op.cit., p. 116.
[430] Johnson, op.cit., pp. 252ff; Gallick, op.cit., p. 51; Freeze, VVA, op.cit., p. 265; Guiley, op.cit., pp. 161–62; http://www.guardian.co.uk/obituaries/story; Sister Lucia dos Santos /obituaries / Guardian unlimited; Sullivan, op.cit., p. 396.
[431] Groeschel, op.cit., p. 34.

Beauraing, Belgium, 1932–1933
Our Lady of Beauraing

On November 29, 1932 at 6:30 p.m. in Beauraing, a little town near Namur in French-speaking Belgium, Albert Voison, age eleven, and his sister Fernande, age fifteen, went to school to pick up their sister Gilberte, age thirteen. They were with two others: Andree Degeimbre, age fifteen, and his sister also named Gilberte, age thirteen. After picking up Gilberte Voison, all the children initially saw the Virgin walking in the air above a grotto that had been constructed to represent Lourdes at a convent school they attended. Mary was dressed in white with her feet obscured in a cloud.

The children returned each night, although the apparitions did not always occur. They would stand on the street just outside the convent walls, and slowly a crowd would gather to watch them. The visionaries would say the Rosary and, when the Lady appeared, fall to their knees. Their faces "became beautiful" and they kept repeating their prayers in unison for as long as the ecstasy lasted. In this state of ecstasy, the children were the only ones who saw the Virgin. Their ecstatic state was often tested by observers who stuck pins into them and flashed lights in their eyes.

In all, the visionaries received a total of thirty-three supernatural apparitions of the Blessed Virgin between November 29, 1932 and January 3, 1933. Our Lady conveyed specific secrets to each of the children. Her messages concerned prayer, the faith life, the importance of the family, and living according to the Gospel. She also told the children that she wanted them to always be "really good," to sacrifice themselves, and to love Christ and their neighbor.

More specifically, the Virgin appeared to Fernande on December 29 with a heart of gold surrounded by rays. The next day, two more of the children saw the same heart. The following day, the others also saw the heart. The message accompanying the heart vision was: "Pray always."

Mary announced January 3, 1933 as the day of her last appearance. Some thirty thousand people gathered for the event, at which time she said she would speak to each of the children individually. When she initially appeared on January 3, only four of the children saw her. Speaking to the four individually, she identified herself as the Immaculate Virgin and the Mother of God, Queen of Heaven, and said her task was the conversion of sinners.

Fernande, the oldest of the children, seemingly left out of the last apparition, remained at the site after the other four departed. Then she and some of the gathered crowd heard a loud noise and saw a ball of fire on the hawthorn tree. The Lady reappeared and asked if Fernande loved her and her son. Given an affirmative reply, she said, "Then say the Rosary and practice self-denial." She then disappeared for the last time.

As with Banneux, mentioned below, Our Lady had asked for a chapel to be built on the site of the apparitions (December 17, 1932). Over two hundred thousand pilgrims visit the shrine every year.[432]

The local bishop waited two years to appoint the standard commission to investigate the apparitions. It did not report for some time, and only in 1943 were public devotions authorized.[433]

Banneux, Belgium, 1933
Our Lady of Banneux

Two weeks after the apparitions at Beauraing had ceased, on the night of January 15, 1933, an eleven-year-old girl named Mariette Beco in Banneux, Belgium, while looking out a window for her brother, saw a radiant young lady in the yard. The Lady was wearing a white gown with a blue belt. An oval light surrounded her body. She had a rosary in her right hand, which was joined to the left in an attitude of prayer. A golden rose was on her right foot.[434]

Mariette was the least likely of any visionary. She was described by her bishop as being farthest away from God of any child in the village.[435] However, two days after seeing the vision, for the first time in several months, Mariette attended Mass. She told the priest what had happened. The priest suggested that she had merely seen a statue of the Virgin at Lourdes. Mariette refuted this by noting that the Lady she had seen was more beautiful. On several occasions as she followed the Lady, Mariette fell abruptly to the ground. On the third occasion, she knelt near a ditch and was told that the water had been reserved for the Virgin. On the following evening, Mary identified herself as "the Virgin of the Poor." She emphasized that she had come to relieve suffering and to comfort the sick and the poor and reiterated her designation of the water at the ditch: "This spring is reserved for all the nations—to relieve the sick."[436]

"The Virgin of the Poor" appeared to Mariette eight times during that winter at usually around seven o'clock in the evening. During the March 2 apparition Mary called herself the "Mother of the Savior, the Mother of God." Our Lady took leave of

[432] Aradi, op.cit., p. 252; Johnson, op.cit., pp. 257–58; Freze, VVA, op.cit., p. 262.

[433] J. Gordon Melton, *The encyclopedia of religious phenomena.* Detroit, MI: Visible Ink Press, 2008. pp. 27–28; see also article by Donal Anthony Foley in *The Wanderer*, Jan. 10, 2013, p. 7B.

[434] Melton, op.cit., p. 28; see also Donal Anthony Foley article in *The Wanderer*, Jan. 17, 2013, p. 4B.

[435] Johnson, op.cit., p. 258.

[436] Melton, op.cit., p. 28.

Our Lady of Grace, Charles Bosseron Chambers, Restored Traditions

Mariette on March 2nd and, most unusual for a Marian apparition, placed her hands on her head and gave her a secret which she was not to reveal. The girl collapsed and then wept uncontrollably for hours afterwards and told everyone that the Lady would not return.

During the apparitions, a miraculous spring came out of the ground in Banneux. Shrines have been built in both Banneux and Beauraing. There have been said to be thousands of reported cures, physical as well as spiritual, recorded at each site. Two at Beauraing have been declared miraculous. After the apparitions, Mariette Beco married and led a quiet family life.[437]

Akita, Japan, June 12, 1973
Our Lady of Akita

In 1973, Our Lady gave Sister Agnes Katsuko Sasagawa, a member of the Servants of the Eucharist in a convent at Yuzawadai on the outskirts of Akita, Japan, three messages through a statue of Mary. Bathed in a brilliant light, the statue became alive and spoke with a voice of indescribable beauty. The nun's guardian angel also appeared and taught her how to pray. The wooden statue from which the voice came wept 101 times from January 4, 1975 until September 15, 1981. It also perspired abundantly and the perspiration sent out a sweet perfume. Its right palm bled from a wound having the form of a cross. Hundreds of people witnessed these events over a hundred times. Scientific analysis of the blood and tears from the statue provided by Professor Sagisaka of the Faculty of Legal Medicine of the University of Akita confirmed that the blood, tears, and perspiration were of human origin.

After eight years of investigating the Akita apparitions and after consulting with the

Carved wooden statue of Our Lady of Akita, Japan

Holy See, Bishop John Ito on April 22, 1984 approved the apparitions as genuinely supernatural in origin. He also authorized throughout the entire diocese the veneration of the Holy Mother of Akita, saying: "The message of Akita is the message of Fatima." The main message is a coming chastisement for an unrepenting world. A terrible punishment from a fire that will fall from the sky and annihilate large numbers of people.[438] Another part of the Akita message reads: "The work of the devil will infiltrate even in the Church in such a way that one will see cardinals opposing cardinals, bishops against bishops."[439]

[437] Johnson, op.cit., pp. 258–59; Freze, VVA, op.cit., p. 261.

[438] Freze, VVA, op.cit., p. 261.
[439] http://www.tldm.org/News10/Akita.htm; Connell, op.cit., pp. 129–46.

Medjugorje, Yugoslavia, 1981– Our Lady of Medjugorje

Beginning on June 24, 1981, six Croatian youths from the village of Bijakovici in the parish of St. James in Medjugorje, a mountain town in the region of Herzegovina in Western Central Yugoslavia, reported receiving almost daily apparitions of the Blessed Virgin Mary, at first on Mount Podbrdo ("Hill of Apparitions"). The six visionaries—Vicka Ivankovic (b. July 3, 1964), Mirjana Dragicevic (b. March 18, 1965), Marija Pavlovic (b. April 1, 1965), Ivan Dragicevic (b. May 25, 1965), Ivanka Ivankovic (b. April 21, 1966), and Jakov Colo (b. June 3, 1971)—reported to have seen the "Gospa" (Croatian for Madonna) in the form of a three-dimensional, external apparition, during which time the visionaries collectively entered an ecstatic state that medical and scientific researchers from Milan and the French University of Montpellier have described as "removed from the spatio-temporal order."

Bishop Pavao Zanic in May 1986 ruled negatively about the experiences at Medjugorje. In October 1986, a bishop's commission of twelve members was formed, presided over by Cardinal Franjo Kuharic, Archbishop of Zagreb. They overruled Bishop Zanic. It was felt the latter made up his mind prematurely and did not follow the criteria set down in the 1978 Vatican document. It was given the judgment of "not established as supernatural", neither confirming or denying the reality of the apparitions and leaving it open for further study.

The messages received from the Madonna who comes as the "Queen of Peace" are presented both as an authentic embodiment of Catholic doctrine and as a post-conciliar formulation of the Marian messages transmitted at Lourdes and Fatima. The messages are heavily colored with apocalyptic overtones and words about the reality of heaven, hell, purgatory, and the devil.

The essence of the messages received for more than nine years in more than three thousand apparitions[440] can be summarized into six foundational themes. The Medjugorje message calls for a more resolute faith in the one God and in Jesus Christ as the one mediator to the Father, combined with faith in the apparitions themselves as a means of special graces and conversion. The call to prayer requests a greater generosity of Christian prayer that accentuates the daily recitation of the fifteen decade Rosary, an invitation to daily Mass, the praying of Sacred Scripture, and a consecration of each person and family to the Sacred Heart of Jesus and the Immaculate Heart of Mary as a means of total abandonment to God.

It was reported that the Madonna requested a strict fast (bread and water) initially every Friday, and later on Wednesdays as well, in reparation for sin and for the conversion of sinners. The call to penance comprises a general call to Christian self-denial offered for sinners. The message also asks for an interior change of heart to God made possible through greater faith, prayer, fasting, and penance. A monthly sacramental Confession is specified as a principal constituent of authentic conversion. In essence then, the preeminent Medjugorje theme was the call to peace. It requests an interior peace of Christ in the heart of every person, obtained by consistent faith, prayer, fasting, penance, and conversion. Significant world chastisements because of humanity's failure to convert, to take place within the lifetime of the visionaries, are also part of the Medjugorje message, but the acceptance of divine peace, in spite of upcoming internal events, remains the heart of the reported Marian message.[441]

---

[440] Sullivan, op.cit., p. 229.

[441] NCE, 2nd ed , op.cit., v. 9. pp. 466–67; Freze, VVA op.cit., pp. 271–72; Sullivan, op.cit.;

The Blessed Mother is said to have disclosed ten secrets about the future of the world during daily apparitions to Mirjana in 1981 and 1982. These secrets have been written on a parchment that only Mirjana can read. They were reportedly given to the other visionaries at an appointed time through the permission of the Virgin. The apparitions and daily messages end when a visionary receives all ten secrets from the Gospa. As of this writing, it is believed that all the visionaries have received the ten secrets. Mirjana explained that the first secret will break the power of Satan. The third secret has been described by all six visionaries as a permanent, indestructible, and beautiful sign on Apparition Hill (Mount Podbrdo), the site of the first apparition of the Blessed Mother, for all the world to see. The last three secret messages are reportedly very grave for the world.

Visionaries Vicka and Jacov claimed to have visited heaven, hell, and purgatory with the Blessed Mother. Many extraordinary phenomena have accompanied these alleged apparitions: physical healings, miracles of the sun (spinning, pulsating, changing colors, etc.), mass conversions, nocturnal luminous signs, crosses that glow, and so on. Although widely accepted by many faithful, the Vatican has, to date, made no official judgment regarding the Medjugorje apparitions. Millions of pilgrims have visited Medjugorje since 1981.

Dreams (Supernatural)

Divine messages in dreams appear throughout the Bible, sometimes standing as the center of the story. In biblical times, prophets and apocalyptic visionaries were moved by the Holy Spirit to dream dreams and see visions disclosing possibilities that would otherwise have been hidden from human eyes.[442] That God may enter into communication with man through visions and dreams is asserted in Numbers 12:6 and still more explicitly in Job 33:14–16: "God does speak . . . in a dream in a vision of the night, when deep sleep falls upon men as they slumber in their beds: it is then He opens the ears of men." Dreams and visions are always mentioned as two distinct phenomena in the Bible. Job complained of being frightened of dreams and terrified by visions (Job 33:15–16; 7:14) and Daniel, like some other prophets, was described as having understanding of both dreams and visions (Dn 1:17).

Two kinds of dreams can be distinguished: those which require no interpretation from a second person and those whose meaning is hidden from the dreamer. The former include Solomon's dream at Gibeon; Jacob's understanding the implication of angels ascending and descending a stairway between heaven and earth with the Lord standing beside him saying: "I, the Lord, am the God of your forefathers Abraham and the God of Isaac" (Gn 28:12–13; see picture above); and in the New Testament, Pilate's wife grasping the import of her dream about Jesus (Mt 27:19). Other dreams need interpretation such as the dreams of Pharaoh (Gn 41:1–36) and Nebuchadnezzar (Dn 2:1–45; 4:1–27). Joseph and Daniel respectively were the gifted interpreters of their dreams.

Sometimes the whole course of divine revelation pivots on a dream, as when St. Joseph's dream prompted him to take the Child Jesus to Egypt and keep Him safe during Herod's persecutions. (Mt 2:13). The dream thus may be a legitimate vehicle of divine revelation, in which case God Himself provides for proofs attesting to the divine origin of dreams. He also takes care of dream interpretation, for he

---

Connell, op.cit., pp. 202–33.

[442] Dulles, op.cit., pp. 159–60.

Jacob's Dream, 1715, by Joseph Goupy

Dream of Solomon, 1694–1695, by Luca Giordano

is the ultimate source of the dreamer's knowledge.[443]

Supernatural manifestation and revelation of God to man may be produced as a kind of mystic experience in the imagination during sleep, as in a dream, or when awake, in ecstasy. Dreams and ecstasy are regarded in Sacred Scripture as such means of divine communication.[444] Poulain believes that some of the states Holy Scripture calls prophetic sleep may perhaps in reality have been ecstasies.[445] God uses dreams in Scripture to warn of coming events or judgments (Pharaoh or Nebuchadnezzar) or to give specific guidance or direction. St. Joseph is warned in a dream to flee to Egypt (Mt 2:13) and to return from Egypt (Mt 2:19–20). The Magi are warned in a dream to avoid Herod after they visit the child Jesus. They depart for their country by another way (Mt 2:12). Pilate's wife is warned in a dream to abandon the case against Jesus (Mt 27:19).

The signs by which the supernatural origin of a dream may be recognized are: 1. a dream divinely sent is always extremely reasonable and directive, without any diversion of romantic imaginings; 2. the dream affords intelligible and wise guidance, or may foretell, in plain fashion, some future event; 3. a divine dream leaves a complete and ineffable impression, and is remembered in detail and in its entirety, whereas natural dreams are often complicated and confused in detail and not easy to recall; 4. a divine dream is often sent to two or more persons simultaneously without any previous discussion or mutual conversation concerning the subject of the dream. Such a dream was when Our Lady appeared in their sleep to St. Peter Nolasco (c. 1182–c. 1256), St. Raymond of Penafort (1175–1275), and King James of Aragon

[443] NCE, 1st ed, op.cit., v. 4, p. 1055.
[444] Ibid, p. 1056.
[445] Poulain, RAV, op.cit., p. 3

(121–1276), directing that the Mercedarian Order be founded in her honor.[446]

St. Thomas Aquinas acknowledged that, because of biblical tradition, some dreams come from God. For the most part, he said, dreams come from demons, false opinions, and natural causes such as conditions of the body. It was not unlawful to divine from dreams as long as one was certain that the dreams were from a divine source and not from demons.[447]

Divine revelation through dreams occurred frequently in the Old and New Testaments. In most of the cases recorded, the dream is expressly said to have come from God. Some specific examples of dreams in Scripture are the following:

- Abimelech, king of Gerar: of God, "Return Sarah to Abraham." Genesis 20:3–7
- Jacob (at Bethel): of God, a stairway and a promise to Abraham of His intentions and His help. Genesis 28:10–17
- Jacob: of God "Go back to Canaan." Genesis 31:10–16
- Laban the Aramean: God appeared to him in a dream and warned him not to harm Jacob. (31:24)
- Joseph: of sheaves bowing down. Genesis 37:5–8
- Joseph; of the sun, moon, and eleven stars. Genesis 37:9–11
- Pharaoh's cupbearer and baker: interpreted by Joseph. Genesis 40:9–23
- Pharaoh: of seven fat cows and seven skinny cows. Genesis 41
- Gideon: of a loaf of barley bread, a tent, and a victory. Judges 7:13–14

- Solomon: of God, and a request for wisdom. 1 Kings 3:5–14
- Nebuchadnezzar; of gold, silver, bronze, iron, and clay statue, told and interpreted by Daniel. Daniel 2:1–45
- Nebuchadnezzar: of a tree, interpreted by Daniel. Daniel 4:2–27
- Daniel: of four beasts, and more. Daniel 7
- Joseph: of an angel, "Marry Mary." Matthew 1:20–21
- Magi: of a message, "Do not return to Herod." Matthew 2:12
- Joseph: of an angel "Flee to Egypt." Matthew 2:13
- Joseph (in Egypt): of an angel, "Return to Israel." Matthew 2:19
- Pilate's wife; of Jesus, "Have nothing to do with Him." Matthew 27:19[448]

As we have seen from the above, the saints of the Old Testament, like Jacob and many of the prophets, were in communication with God in their dreams. So was St. Joseph, who in a dream was advised what to do with Jesus and Mary. It seems that in the first centuries of Christianity God often communicated with His elect in this way. St. Polycarp (c. 49–155), St. Cyprian (c. 200–258), and St. Perpetua (c. 181–203) experienced such messages in dreams and visions.[449] God spoke to Saint John Bosco (1815–1888) in dreams and John himself would visit people in their dreams. After a dream of Our Lord and Our Lady at age nine, this future saint was determined to become a priest. It was in that dream that the Blessed Virgin told him to "care for her

---

446 Summers, op.cit., p. 64.
447 Guiley, op.cit., pp. 327–28.

448 Peter Klein, Rev. *The Catholic Source Book.* Edited by Peter Klein. 3rd ed. Dubuque: Brown–Roa, c. 2000, p. 130.
449 Aradi, op.cit., p. 159.

flock of sheep." From this moment on God spoke to John Bosco in dreams. He often-times had an angel or saint as a dream interpreter. In his dreams, the founder of the Salesian Order also foresaw the exact revelation of events (including deaths) that were to occur.[450] In fact, John Bosco sometimes saw in his prophetic dreams the state of the souls of his boys in the Oratory. For sixty years he experienced remarkable vision-like dreams, which were so lively and vivid that he would often awaken exhausted the next morning. Some of his dreams and prophecies are said to fit into the realm of the psychic or the para-psychological.[451]

There is an historical dispute as to the sort of sign the pagan Emperor Constantine (c. 280–337) received. Eusebius of Caesarea (c. 260–329), the bishop of Caesarea in Palestine and one of the earliest Church historians, says that Constantine saw a waking vision of a cross surrounded by a brilliant, fiery light in the sky of the IHS Christogram, a Greek symbol for Christ. Lactantius later claimed that the Emperor saw Christ in a dream. Both agreed however that the omen informed Constantine that he would conquer his rival Maxentius under the sign of Christ.[452] Deeply impressed with this experience, the Emperor had the standards of his soldiers altered to bear not only the cross, but also the holy monogram X and P, which represent the first two letters of Christ's name in the Greek alphabet.[453]

Locutions

"Oh that today you would hear his voice: Harden not your hearts." (Psalms 95:7–8; Heb 4:7)

Apparitions that are heard rather than seen are called locutions (or auditions) whether they are heard physically through the ears or spiritually through the heart. Locutions may be defined then as supernatural words or statements received internally in a clear, distinctive manner. Although locutions are not subject to external stimulus or the use of the physical senses, nevertheless, the words they convey are very real and convincing to the recipient of such divine favors.[454] Locutions (auditions) can occur in dreams, as part of visions, or alone during waking consciousness.[455]

Man's first experience with a supernatural voice comes at the very beginning of his creation! Was this voice a literal sound heard by the human ear? We cannot know according to the evidence presented in Genesis. Perhaps it was a locution that Adam experienced: an internal voice heard and clearly perceived without the aid of the external auricular sense.

A similar experience of an inner locution occurred to Adam's mate, Eve, but this voice is quite different. Whereas man heard the first supernatural voice from God Himself, it was Eve who heard the first voice from the preternatural—that of Satan, disguised as a snake or a serpent. The voice from the serpent questions Eve about obeying God the first time he speaks (Gn 3:1, 4–5).

It is also interesting to note that God spoke out directly to Adam after he had sinned and asked "Where are you?" (Gn 3:9). This conversation between God and our first parents takes up the next nine passages out of twenty-four total in chapter three of Genesis.

[450] *Forty Dreams of St. John Bosco*, op.cit., xi, pp. 3ff; Cruz, MMM, op.cit., p. 200.

[451] Groeschel, op.cit., p. 153; Bert Ghezzi, *Mystics and miracles: true stories of lives touched by God.* Chicago, Loyola Press, c 2002, p. xii.

[452] NC, 1st ed. v. 4, op.cit., p. 227.

[453] Cruz, MMM, op.cit., p. 527; Guiley, op.cit., pp. 82–83.

[454] Freze, VVA, op.cit., p. 310.

[455] Guiley, op.cit., p. 383.

The Creation of Adam, 1511, Michelangelo Buonarroti

In a later story about Cain's murder of Abel, God has a supernatural conversation with Cain that takes up nine verses of chapter four. When we get to the story of Noah, God speaks to him about the wickedness of humanity. The greater part of Genesis 6 and 7 concerns God's talk with Noah.

Throughout the Old Testament, we see a personal God who deliberately makes Himself known and heard to various people over the course of human history. Throughout the New Testament, a normal channel of supernatural communication is through the voice of an angel of God. The Book of Revelation, for example, records many instances of angelic appearances and voices. The Almighty uses these creatures to deliver supernatural messages, to warn people of danger, or to help those in trouble. God's voice is thus often expressed through the voice of the angels who assist Him in His plan of salvation.

The significance of this discourse on Adam and Eve is that we can come to realize that God Himself can and does speak to people from time to time in the course of human history. Likewise, we learn that as is the case with many saints throughout history who claimed to experience heavenly voices, the clash between a heavenly communicator with the diabolical is readily apparent. Satan will also appear to humans through physical manifestations and/or voices. This is an important mystery to understand—this mystery of iniquity—for the saints and mystics throughout the ages have repeatedly experienced this manifestation of good and evil during their contacts with the supernatural. Satan is all too quick to counter with his own preternatural intervention.[456]

Although it frequently happens that an apparition or vision is accompanied by a locution, it is possible for either to occur without the other. A locution is an affirmation or statement supernaturally effected. Like visions and apparitions, locutions can be divided into auricular (exterior), imaginative, and intellectual.[457]

Auricular (exterior) locutions are words perceived by the human ear. Sounds are received, but they are produced supernaturally. Sometimes they are called auricular supernatural words, but usually just locutions. They are the most frequently reported mystic phenomena. Imaginative locutions are also composed of words

456 Freze, VVA, op.cit., pp.106–7.
457 Aumann, Spiritual theology, op.cit., p. 427.

The Infant Samuel Hearing the Voice of God, 1776, by Joshua Reynolds

but they are received directly without the assistance of the ear. They are perceived in the imagination. Intellectual locutions are simple communication of thought without words, and consequently without the use of any definite language. They are concepts perceived immediately by the intellect. They reportedly parallel the ways in which spiritual beings communicate with each other.[458]

The locutions of St. Michael and St. Catherine of Alexandria (d.c. 310) to St. Joan of Arc or of the crucifix of San Damiano to St. Francis of Assisi were one or the other of these kinds of locution because they consisted of words understood. Those saints gave direct quotations of what they heard.[459]

One can tell imaginative locutions from the auricular kind because they are directed specifically to a person. Nobody else around can hear them. Blessed Agnes of Jesus at age seven heard a voice telling her that if she wished to be delivered from the great spiritual anguish she was suffering and protected against all her enemies, she should make herself a slave of Jesus and Mary. Likewise, Blessed Clare of Rimini one day at Mass heard a voice that bade her to pray with more fervor and attention. She became a Franciscan tertiary and resolved to expiate her former sinful life by living a life of penance. St. Jane Frances de Chantal was informed by an interior voice of the death of her friend St. Francis de Sales. The German stigmatic Theresa Neumann heard an inner voice which appeared to be that of St. Therese of the Little Flower who told her that "more souls have been saved through suffering than by the finest sermons."[460] Saint Teresa of Calcutta's (1910–1997) private letters reveal that she began her charitable ministry in Calcutta after receiving an interior locution from Jesus in 1947.[461]

Unlike prophecy, locutions are generally for the consolation or enlightenment of the one who receives them and thus differ from *gratiae gratis datae* (grace that sanctifies others) in the strict definition. Auricular or imaginative locutions could proceed from any one of three causes: natural, diabolical, or supernatural. Intellectual locutions could proceed from natural or supernatural causes. It is beyond the power of the devil to produce a truly intellectual locution.[462]

St. John of the Cross had a somewhat different view regarding intellectual locutions. He divided intellectual locutions into successive, formal, and substantial. He gives the name of successive intellectual locutions to a kind of dialogue or

---

[458] Ibid.; see also Poulain, rav, op.cit., pp. 1–2.

[459] Johnson, op.cit., pp. 118–19.

[460] Sullivan, op.cit., p. 395.

[461] Sidney Callahan, *Women who hear voices; the challenges of religious experience*, NY/Mahwah NJ, Paulist Press, 2003, p. 97.

[462] NCE, 1st ed. op.cit.,v. 10, p. 173; NCE, 2nd ed., op.cit., v. 8, p. 953; NCE, 2nd ed., op.cit., v. 10, p. 108.

conversation between the Holy Spirit and the soul. He says it is discursive reasoning rather than an instantaneous intuition, and although it is under the direction of the Holy Spirit, the human intellect plays its part. Therefore the actual functioning of the human intellect in this type of locution, he opines, requires the operation of the imagination, with the result that error can proceed from the human side of the dialogue. The devil, St. John claims, can indirectly affect successive locutions by influencing the imagination. Similar locutions occur in the natural phenomenon of the dual personality, although the effects are noticeably different from the effects of truly supernatural successive locutions.

Formal intellectual locutions, the Carmelite mystic maintains, are those words or statements which come to the mind from without and do not involve the activity of the intellect itself, except to receive them. Unlike the successive locutions, they may be infused into the mind when it is thinking of something entirely different. When they are truly supernatural, they produce virtuous effects in the soul and impart great illumination and certitude. Although the devil cannot directly influence the intellect, St. John asserts that an individual may be deceived by the devil so that the phenomenon itself cannot easily be distinguished by its effect. The saint advises that souls should never act according to their own opinions or accept the locutions without much reflection and the counsel of others.

Substantial intellectual locutions, St. John contends, are basically the same as formal locutions, but with this difference: what is stated is effected immediately. They are similar to the creative word of God. According to St. John of the Cross, there is no possibility of deception or the influence of the devil in substantial locutions.[463]

As already mentioned above, locutions as extraordinary phenomena could be caused by God or the devil or proceed from natural causes. Imaginative locutions are words perceived in the imagination during sleep or in waking hours. St. Teresa says they occur outside ecstasy. She says they come frequently unexpected when the mind is occupied by other things.[464] Since they, too, could be supernatural, diabolical, or natural in origin, the rule for discernment is to study the effects produced in the individual. Locutions of supernatural origin cannot be produced at will; they are distinct, causing fervor, peace, humility, and obedience. When St. Bernadette Soubirous was in a trancelike state at Lourdes, she simply reported instructions as if she had heard them "from the Lady" with her own ears. She "heard" the words, but the witnesses did not hear them.[465]

Intellectual locutions are words or statements perceived immediately by the intellect without the aid of the external senses or imagination. These words are heard whether or not they are thought about before or during the time they occur, or even if one is thinking about something totally different at the time they are heard. For this reason, they are very precise and the recipient has no doubt of their supernatural origin.[466] Sometimes they are directly infused; at other times, they are a supernatural coordination of naturally acquired ideas. It is beyond the power of the devil to produce truly intellectual locutions.

---

463 NCE, 1st ed., v. 8, op.cit., p. 953; NCE, 2nd ed., v. 8, op.cit., p. 747; Aumann, op.cit., pp. 427–28.
464 Poulain, RAV, op.cit., p. 6; see also Teresa of Avila, *Life*, op.cit., xxv, p. 6.
465 Groeschel, op.cit., p. 155.
466 Freze, VVA, op.cit., p. 305.

Intellectual interior locutions are thus those that are communicated without words. St. Teresa of Avila says this is a foretaste of the way communication occurs in heaven, the blessed understanding each other without speaking.[467]

Since locutions are often closely associated with visions (and apparitions), the same rules and distinctions concerning visions (and apparitions) may likewise be applied to locutions. Locutions are unmerited and freely given graces in the sense that they do not proceed from the normal development of the spiritual life. They differ somewhat from the usual charismatic gifts given for the benefit of others in the sense that they can bring much consolation and many blessings to the soul that receives them. They should not be desired, except for the substantial locutions, of which St. John of the Cross says: "Blessed is the soul to whom the Lord speaks the substantial locution."[468]

Saint Anthony of Padua Exonerates his Father Accused of Murder, by Willem van Herp

Agility

Agility is the phenomenon of apparently instantaneous transfer or movement of a material body without seeming to pass the intervening space.[469] It implies the power of instantaneously transporting oneself from place to place with the rapidity of thought to the most distant parts of God's universe. Likewise, in this world one can be able, in the twinkling of an eye, to send one's thoughts on the wings of electricity across a whole continent, or the vast expanse of the ocean. This phenomenon would be something of an anticipated agility of the glorified body. After the resurrection, we shall all possess that power in our very bodies because they shall rise as spiritual bodies, entirely under the control of the soul.[470] The ability to traverse space and time instantaneously, or the ability to traverse space with supernatural force or alacrity, is recorded in the lives of many of the saints. Some of the saints instantaneously were said to move over long distances or were transported from one place to another without passing through the

---

[467] Johnson, op.cit., p. 119.
[468] NCE, 1st ed., v. 8, op.cit., p. 953.

[469] Aumann, op.cit., p. 435.
[470] Boudreau, op.cit., pp. 83,110; Aumann, op.cit., p. 436.

intervening space and then returned in the same manner.[471]

St. Anthony of Padua is but one example of this mystic ability to transcend time and space. One of the best documented cases of this phenomenon was when the saint once took a trip from Padua, Italy to his home town of Lisbon in Portugal within a day's timeframe. His father, it seems, had been arrested and accused of murdering a young nobleman in Lisbon, Portugal. When the matter was made supernaturally known to St. Anthony, he asked his superior's permission to leave the monastery in Padua where he lived to travel on foot to Lisbon. While in route, he found himself miraculously transported to Lisbon in time to speak in defense of his father. He convinced the authorities to travel to the victim's grave and commanded the corpse, in the name of God, to speak out. According to the story, the corpse sat up and declared his father guiltless. When Anthony reappeared in Padua, he had been absent two nights and a single day.[472]

Likewise, Venerable Anthony Margil, a Franciscan missionary often called the "Flying Father," possessed the gift of agility because he could cover so many miles barefoot in such a short period of time. It was nothing short of a miracle for him to traverse forty or fifty miles a day over rough terrain. Testimonies from his brother and soldier companions attest to the fact that he literally walked on water as he crossed swollen streams and rivers on his apostolic journey to convert hundreds of thousands of Indians in Spanish America.[473]

Saint Margaret Mary Alacoque Contemplating the Sacred Heart of Jesus, 1765, by Corrado Giaquinto

Ardors (Flames of Love) (Incendium Amoris)

Ardors refer to the mystic phenomenon of bodily heat that far exceeds the norm. These are burning sensations in the body without apparent cause. They are also called "flames of love" and are regarded as a manifestation of the mystic's intense love of God. These ardors take the form of simple but preternaturally high body temperatures. They range from simple interior heat, an extraordinary heat perceived in the area of the heart and sometimes spreading throughout the entire body, to intense ardors where the heat becomes unbearable and cold applications must be used to assuage the burning sensation, and finally to material burning where the heat reaches such a point of intensity that the mystic's clothing is scorched or his or her skin is blistered, especially around the heart.[474]

---

[471] NCE, 1st ed, op.cit., v. 10, p. 173; v. 2, p. 559.

[472] Cruz, MMM, op.cit., p. 90; Johnson, op.cit., pp. 130–31; Hebert, op.cit., p. 244.

[473] Miriam Horvat, Venerable Antonio Margil of Jesus, Apostle of New Spain. http://www.traditioninaction.org/Margil.

[474] NCE, 2nd ed., v. 10, op.cit., p. 108; NCE 1st ed., op.cit., v. 10, p. 173; Aumann, op.cit., p. 431.

Although these flames of love are confined to a particular part of the body such as the chest or the face, they are sometimes accompanied by other mystic phenomenon like the aureole or by natural symptoms like a nearly unquenchable thirst. They do not injure the body. Ardors are not said to rank very high in the catalogue of mystic gifts.[475] This fire and heat originates from the heart of Jesus as "the living source of these flames."

St. Margaret Mary Alacoque in her *Autobiography* tells of a vision in which "the Divine Heart of Our Lord being opened, there issued from it a flame so ardent that," she said, "I thought I should be consumed, for I was totally penetrated by it."[476] Another time, Margaret Mary writes that "Our Lord showed her His heart as a burning furnace."[477] The burning love that God bears for human kind suggests a comparison with the flames of charity.

One time, St. Catherine of Siena reported to her confessor that when she received Communion, "I wondered how I would go on living in such an excess of ardor and love."[478] St. Gerard Majella who also experienced this mystical phenomenon, tells us that "God is a consuming fire. When He enters a soul, He inflames it, and its affections become sometimes so intense that they appear even on the body."[479] St. Philip Neri seemed to glow visibly with the flames of love. He kept his windows open and never wore a coat, even in the winter, because the heat of his ardors were so intense.[480] A more current example of this "fire and heat of love" is demonstrated in

the life of St. Padre Pio. His ardors were so intense that when he became ill in 1917 and his temperature taken, it reached at times 120–125 degrees Fahrenheit, resulting in several broken thermometers. His extraordinarily high fevers broke all natural and scientific rules. Padre Pio confirmed himself that the fevers were those of the fire and heat of love. He said he was "consumed by love for God and neighbor."[481]

Venerable Serafina di Dio was a visionary, ecstatic, and stigmatic Carmelite nun of the Capri convent. Serafina received the stigmata on her hands and feet which were clearly seen by many. Her heart was allegedly pierced through by a golden dart received during a vision of the Divine Child. When she was rapt in prayer after Holy Communion, her sister nuns claimed to see Serafina with her face glowing like a red flame and her eyes sparkling fire. "It burned them if they but touched her." Her sister religious repeatedly had heard her say that she was consumed with a living fire and that her blood was boiling as if there was molten lead in her veins.[482]

Venerable Maria Villani, a stigmatic Dominican nun of Naples, was said to be wounded in the heart and side by a fiery spear of love. This wound was attested to by three of her confessors. Maria drank an excessive amount of water each day to counterbalance the heat produced by the fire of love sparked by the flaming arrow. She was a furnace of love, consumed by an almost insupportable flame of love which dominated all her thoughts. A surgeon who made an incision in her heart during an autopsy was, along with other witnesses, amazed to see "smoke and heat exhaled from her heart, a veritable furnace

---

[475] Johnson, op.cit. pp. 356–57.

[476] St. Margaret Mary Alacoque, *The Autobiography of St. Margaret Mary Alacoque*, Rockford, Ill.: TAN Books and Publishers, 1995. pp. 69–70.

[477] Cruz, MMM, op.cit., pp. 173–74; St. Margaret Mary Alacoque, op.cit., p. 95.

[478] Cruz, MMM, op.cit., p. 175.

[479] Ibid., p. 173.

[480] Johnson, op.cit., p. 319.

[481] Cruz MMM, op.cit., p. 183; Hebert, op.cit., p. 241.

[482] Summers, op.cit., pp. 71, 195–96; Herbert Thurston, Fr., S.J., *The Physical Phenomena of Mysticism* edited by J. H. Crehan. Chicago, Henry Regnery Co., 1952. p. 218; Cruz, MMM, op.cit., p. 181.

St. Philip Neri at Mass by Giandomenico Tiepolo

of divine love." The heat was so intense that the surgeon had to wait for the body to cool down before extracting the heart, but even then the heart was hot enough to burn his hands.[483]

St. Maria Maddalena de' Pazzi was transformed by a sudden burst of overwhelming love. Father Fabbrini, her biographer and confessor, states that the heat she attributed to the celestial flame which consumed her burned so fiercely in her that she could not bear wearing woolen garments in the midst of winter. She also drank large quantities of cold water to assuage the flames. St. Peter of Alcantara was obliged to unfasten his habit to go out into the chilly winter air so torrid were the feelings of fire that burned and broiled in his breast.

It is recorded that St. Philip Neri, overcome by divine love, sometimes swooned as he said Mass. On one occasion, it was said that an illness for several days was because the flame of interior supernatural love so scorched and blistered his throat.

Blessed Anna Maria Taigi would often fall as if struck by lightning after receiving Communion and remain on the ground a long time burned in the sweet flames of divine love. Some others who exhibited this phenomenon include St. Catherine of Genoa, St. Stanislaus Kostka and the Venerable Ursula Benincasa.[484]

It should be noted that this phenomenon could also be caused by the devil or some pathological condition and, therefore, is not necessarily to be attributed to a supernatural cause.[485]

Aureoles and Luminous Radiance (Lights and Rays of Love)

This phenomenon consists in the resplendent light or luminous irradiance that emanates at times from the bodies or stigmatic wounds of mystics, especially during contemplation or ecstasy. There are countless cases recorded. It is sometimes called "luminous effluvia" and is considered an anticipation of the radiant splendor of a glorified body.[486] There have been many instances of saints and other holy persons, particularly contemplative ecstatics, who have been seen with light, halos, and aureoles around them. Sometimes the light has flooded the room of the person in ecstasy, calling attention to the graces he or she would have preferred to keep hidden. At other times, witnesses have seen a light falling in a shaft upon them or radiating from their figures.

The earliest Western example of bodily luminosity comes from Judaism. When Moses came down from Mount Sinai after a face-to-face conversation with the Divine Majesty, his face shone so radiantly that the Israelites were afraid to come near him

---

[483] Thurston, op.cit., pp. 219–20.

[484] Summers, op.cit., pp. 71, 72.

[485] NCE, 1st ed., v. 10, op.cit., p. 173.

[486] NCE, 1st ed., v. 10, op.cit., p. 174; Johnson, op.cit., p. 357; Cruz, MMM, op.cit., p. 159.

Transfiguration fresco, 1441, by Fra Angelico

until he covered it with a veil (Ex 34:29–35). For Christians, the best known example of luminosity is the incident in Jesus's life called the Transfiguration (Mt 17:1–2; Mk 9:2). Here we learn of light surrounding Our Lord when He was on a high mountain with Saints Peter, James, and John. Scripture tells us: "He was transfigured before their eyes. His face shone like the sun, His clothes became as white as light." Jesus showed them a wonderful vision of His glory, a foreshadowing of the kingdom of heaven. Again, we hear of the first Christian martyr, St. Stephen, whose face shone like that of an angel while being stoned to death (Acts 6:15).

St. Stephen mentioned above is only one of many saints who died while illuminated in ecstasy. During the first three hundred years of Christianity, many Christians were tortured and killed and went to their deaths in ecstasy. From the radiant martyrs and transfigured saints could possibly have come the "halo" in Western art.[487]

Other specific saints who have been reported to appear gloriously radiant include St. Catherine of Ricci and St. Bernadette, the latter when she saw Our Lady

---

[487] Patricia Treece. *The mystical body; an investigation of supernatural phenomena*, [mb], NY, Crossroad Pub. Co. c. 2005, p. 32.

in the grotto of Massabielle at Lourdes. St. Phillip Neri and Venerable Anthony Margil were said to be often raised in ecstasy and rapture surrounded by light. At times their faces were said to glow with celestial radiance. St. Gaspar del Bufalo was witnessed to have a luminous cross upon his head when in ecstasy. In some of his rapturous states, he was said to be "all afire in the face."[488] While in the palace of King Ferdinand I of Naples, the King witnessed St. Francis of Paola floating in mid-air while in ecstasy praying fervently, his whole body glowing in light. Blessed Henry Suso was reportedly seen while in ecstasy with a light streaming from his heart.[489] During her luminous ecstasies, the face of St. Maria Maddalena de' Pazzi became inflamed and her eyes shone as a seraph.[490]

St. Bernardino Realino while alive was seen by witnesses with an extraordinary radiance coming from his countenance which they said dazzled them on numerous occasions. Likewise, Sts. Paul of the Cross and Juan Masias were reportedly seen with rays of light streaming from their face and head at times.[491]

Other saints such as Sts. Ignatius of Loyola, Francis de Sales, Charles Borromeo, Anthony Mary Claret and Joseph of Anchieta were said to be surrounded by a brilliant heavenly light when preaching or when offering the holy sacrifice of the Mass.[492] The cell of St. Philip Neri was often radiant with light thought to be emanating from his body. St. Jean Baptiste Marie Vianney, the Curé of Ars, often spent sixteen to eighteen hours a day in the cramped, stifling confessional. While in this dark setting, several penitents claimed to witness a transparent and unearthly radiance emanating from their confessor's face. One witness saw two fiery rays projecting from the priest's face, his features being completely hidden by the brightness of their light.[493] A priest who visited Ars testified under oath that he saw the cure's forehead "encircled by an aureole" and "his countenance transfigured."[494]

While celebrating Mass, there was reported to be a radiant globe, a supernatural light of the aureole, often appearing over the head of St. Martin of Tours. Others who had been claimed to exhibit this phenomenon while celebrating Mass, included St. Francis of Posada. Observers thought they had seen a brilliant light emanate from his body which illuminated the whole altar. The same was said of St. Peter Julian Eymard (1811–1868) and St. John of the Cross, the latter of whom was seen to sometimes have a halo, a celestial brightness radiating from his head.[495] St. Maximilian Kolbe (1897–1941) a Polish Franciscan who died heroically at Auschwitz, also appeared to be illuminated by an unearthly radiance when he said Mass.[496]

St. Julie Billiart (1751–1816) was reportedly often seen with a halo of light around her head whenever she went into an ecstatic state. Some even stated that Julie's face would frequently take on a Christ-like appearance.[497] St. Clare of Assisi also was said to experience illumination. The sisters of her community commented that at times "she came from prayers with her face so shining that it dazzled the eyes of those who beheld her.[498] St. Frances de Sales' face was also claimed by many to glow with an unearthly light.[499] Several nuns reported

[488] Ibid., p. 45.
[489] Cruz, MMM, op.cit., pp.163–64.
[490] Ibid., p. 175.
[491] Dorcy, op.cit., p. 407; Cruz, MMM, op.cit., p. 169.
[492] Thurston, op.cit., p. 164.
[493] Cruz, MMM, op,cit., p. 171.
[494] Treece, MB, op.cit., p. 56.
[495] Johnson, op.cit., pp. 133–34; Freze, VVA, op.cit., p. 44.
[496] Treece, MB, op.cit., p. 51.
[497] Freze, VVA, op.cit., p. 44.
[498] Cruz, MMM, op.cit., p. 162.
[499] Summers, op.cit., p. 62.

The Death of Saint Dominic (1221) - Fra Angelico or il Beato (1400-1455), v. 1432 / Bridgeman Images

seeing the face of St. Teresa of Avila as "shining resplendently" on several occasions.[500] St. John Bosco was yet another saint believed to have a halo glowing around his head and his body illuminated during times of deep prayer and during the elevation of the host.[501] It was said that Blessed Ambrose Sansedoni (1220–1286) sometimes was seen surrounded by a "circle of glory": a mystical light filled with birds of brilliant plumage.[502]

Many saints who were granted visions of Our Lord or the Blessed Virgin Mary claimed that the light surrounding the heavenly visitor was more brilliant than that of the sun. The witnesses were saved from blindness by a special softness of that celestial light. Sometimes the face of a saint or a holy person is transfigured, like that of St. Benedict Joseph Labre, to appear similar to that of Christ.[503] The illustrious St. Vincent Ferrer reported that he saw his friend St. Collette more than once with her face streaming with light during ecstasies. Nuns and friars of her order reported that after receiving Holy Communion, "she was all enraptured and transfigured, and remained in this state as if in a trance. And when she returned to herself, sometimes her face was thought to be like an angel's, so beautiful and bright."[504] St. Catherine of Siena was likewise said to be transfigured at times.

Some saints were perceived to be radiant and beautiful as they lay dying, seeming sometimes to be in the flower of youth despite their aging, emaciated, or tortured bodies. St. Francis of Assisi, St. Dominic, St. Anthony of Padua, St. Teresa of Avila, and St. Rose of Lima are but a few of those so glorified. St. Francis of Xavier

[500] Cruz, MMM, op.cit., p. 165.
[501] Freze, VVA, op.cit., p. 45; Treece, MB, op.cit., p. 57.
[502] Guiley, op.cit., p. 17.

[503] Hebert, op.cit., p. 251.
[504] Cruz, MMM, op.cit., p. 164.

(1505–1552), the exhausted missionary, had a beautiful appearance in death. St. Catherine of Ricci's face glowed. Her body was radiant and gave off a perfume. Likewise, St. Stanislaus Kostka's face is said to have shone with a most serene light at his death. At his death, witnesses said a triple crown seemed to encircle the head of St. John of the Cross and his face shone with a brilliant pallor. Upon the demise of St. Rita of Cascia, an astounding light reportedly emanated from the stigmatic wound on her forehead. It shone and glistened like a jewel and the little worms in the stigmata wound were transformed into sparks of light. At the death of Blessed Henry Suso, sparks of fire were reported coming from all over his body. St. Louis Bertrand's entire body was thought to shine at death like pure crystal and, like that of many other saints, remained incorrupt.[505]

Bilocation

Bilocation is one of the most stupendous of all extraordinary mystical phenomena and one of the most difficult to explain. This is a fairly common occurrence in the lives of the saints and mystics. It consists of the supernatural gift whereby the same physical person appears in two different places simultaneously. If the apparent bilocation is caused supernaturally, the body is physically present in one place and represented in the other place in the form of an apparition. One of the two appearances of the mystic is probably a corporal apparition. One who sees the bilocation actually experiences a real bodily apparition of the person, though sometimes a feeling of that person's presence is all that is experienced. Some souls who have claimed to bilocate actually feel themselves leave their present surroundings and instantly appear in a new location, while realizing that they are still where they were before.

St. Padre Pio explained the phenomenon to someone by saying he was sometimes in two places at the same time by "a prolongation of personality." Bilocation is called by others "visionary participation," which indicates their view that the bilocator sees rather than goes. That makes bilocation a synonym for clairvoyance, the ability to see actions or objects which are physically far removed in space and time. Taking an opposite view, some authorities say bilocation is the ability to induce a vision in a targeted recipient. Blessed Anne Catherine Emmerich, who allegedly bilocated frequently, said, "the (guardian) angel calls me and I follow him."[506]

The soul which bilocates generally does so because another person is in need of his or her assistance or intercession, usually where there is a serious illness, an extreme danger from a diabolical attack, or with the approach of death.[507] It should be understood that this mystical gift is not given for the convenience of the recipient, but to aid him in helping his fellow man or in performing a function some distance away that had been forgotten. Often the recipient of this gift employs it to attend the dying, to comfort, to edify and instruct others, and for many other reasons.[508] It is similar to the agility enjoyed by spiritual beings who exist outside the bounds of time and space.[509] The most noteworthy cases among saints, beati, and venerables with the gift of bilocation include St. Nicholas of Myra (d. c. 352), St. Clement, St. Francis of Assisi, St. Anthony of Padua, St. Colette, St. Francis of Paola, St. Francis Xavier, St. Philip Neri, St. Catherine of Ricci, St. Drogo (1102–1186), St. Joseph Cupertino, St. Martin de Porres, St. Paul of the Cross, St. Alphonsus Liguori, St.

---

[505] Hebert, op.cit., pp. 251–52.

[506] Treece, MB, op.cit., p. 19.
[507] Freze, TBWC, op.cit., p. 304.
[508] Cruz, MMM, op.cit., p. 1.
[509] NCE, 2nd ed., v. 2, op.cit., p. 396–97; v. 10, p. 108.

Gerard Majella, St. Benedict Joseph Labre, St. John Bosco, St. Padre Pio, St. Angelo of Acri, Bl. Mary of Jesus Crucified, Bl. Maria of the Passion of Our Lord Jesus Christ, Venerables Maria of Jesus, Mary of Agreda, Anthony Margil, Teresa Helena Higginson, and, in today's world, allegedly Fra Elia, who was born in 1960.

Credible witnesses have, on a number of occasions, claimed to see St. Alphonsus Liguori preaching while at the same time being in the confessional. On September 21, 1774, while in a prolonged ecstasy at his church in Naples, this saint was seen attending to a dying Pope Clement XIV (1769–1774) in Rome. St. Joseph of Cupertino also was reported to have bilocated to come to the assistance of dying souls on their deathbed.

Although St. Martin de Porres spent all of his religious life at the Monastery of the Holy Rosary in Lima, Peru, he was seen, according to reliable witnesses, at different times in Mexico, China, Japan, Africa, the Philippine Islands, and perhaps even in France.[510]

Venerable Mary of Agreda, a Spanish nun, also had the gift of bilocation, and in some of her ecstasies, she said she was teaching Christianity to people in foreign lands. She is said to have bilocated to America more than five hundred times between 1620 and 1631. Our Lord had commanded her to go there to teach the natives. A vision of her, known as the "Lady in Blue," was simultaneously reported teaching the native Tiguas and Caddoes Indians in the areas of what are now New Mexico and Texas.[511]

Although he never left his friary in San Giovanni Rotundo after 1918, St. Pio of Pietrelcina (Padre Pio) apparently paid visits to some of his friends through bilocation. He would come to the aid of those

Mary Agreda Evangelizing in the Americas. Image from mariadeagreda.org

who were seriously ill or close to death. Witnesses from all over Italy and as far as Hawaii and even Uruguay reported that the friar appeared to them for several minutes, solid and alive, comforted them, and then disappeared.[512]

St. Mary de Cervello (c. 1230–1290), who was referred to by seamen in danger as Sor Maria del Socors, was frequently claimed to have been seen walking on water or hovering over stricken ships, while all the time she was in deep ecstasy in her convent.[513]

St. Catherine of Ricci also had the gift of bilocation and reportedly had frequent conversations and mystical visits with St. Philip Neri (1515–1595) and St. Maria Maddalena Pazzi (1566–1607), neither of whom she had ever met, while they were

---

[510] Cruz, MMM, op.cit., pp. 1–4.
[511] Ibid., pp. 6–8, 17.

[512] Johnson, op.cit., p. 132.
[513] NCE, 1st ed., v. 9, op.cit., p. 387.

in other locations and she was in her convent at Prato.[514]

Adrienne von Speyr claimed to bilocate to Nazi concentration camps during World War II in order to comfort the suffering there. Guided by her guardian angel, she was also said to have been transported to seminaries, abandoned churches, and various convents throughout the world.[515]

Blood Prodigies

Blood prodigies include phenomena such as prematurely hot blood (a form of ardors), copious bleeding during mystic states or the stigmata, blood issuing as sweat (hematidrosis), bleeding Hosts, blood flowing from images, liquefaction of ancient but incorrupt blood, anomalies in the physical weight of such blood, and transformation of wine during transubstantiation, etc.[516]

Tears of Blood and bloody sweat consist of an effusion of blood from the pores of the skin, especially on the face and forehead, or a bloody effusion from the eyes similar to the manner of tears. There are cases in medical history of the bloody sweat, called in medicine hematidrosis.[517] This is a pathological condition brought on by severe stress which causes tiny blood vessels to rupture in the sweat glands. The night before His execution, His disciples reported seeing Jesus in agony on the Mount of Olives in the Garden of Gethsemane. He was in such agony and He prayed so fervently that His sweat became like drops of blood falling on the ground (Lk 22:44).

Certain stigmatics—for example, St. Lutgardis, a Cistercian nun, St. Veronica Giuliani, a Capuchin Poor Clare Abbess, St. Gemma Galgani, an Italian mystic, and

Blessed Catherine of Racconigi, a Dominican tertiary—all reportedly suffered the sweat of blood.

One of the most unusual mystical phenomena is that of liquefaction whereby a preserved deceased person's blood loses its hard crumb-like characteristics and miraculously changes back into liquid as fresh as it was when that person was alive. One of the first examples of this type of phenomenon was that of St. Nazarius of Rome (d.c. 68) who was beheaded in Milan for preaching the Faith during the persecutions of Emperor Nero. Witnesses attest that his blood was still liquid with a fresh, red color several hundred years after his death.[518]

One of the better known cases of liquefaction of blood is that of St. Januarius (d.c. 305), the bishop of Benevento, Italy, near Naples. After his decapitation, his followers removed the remains and collected two vials of blood, as was the custom regarding martyrs. The miracle of liquefaction first took place in 1389 while a priest was holding a flask of his blood during a procession. The coagulated blood began to liquefy and bubble, an occurrence that took place afterward eighteen times a year. In more recent years, the liquefactions have taken place three times a year; on September 19, the feast day of the Saint; on December

Drawing of the reliquary containing the two ampoules holding St. Januarius' blood, from *Die Gartenlaube*.

514 Cruz, MMM, op.cit., p. 6.
515 Freze, VVA, op.cit., p. 35.
516 Johnson. op.cit., pp. 357–58.
517 Aumann, ST, op.cit., p. 434.

518 Freze, VVA, op.cit., p. 32.

16, which is the anniversary of the eruption of Mt. Vesuvius in 1631; and on the first Sunday in May, which commemorates the relocation of the relics to Naples. The color of the blood changes from dark red to almost black to a bright vermillion. The viscosity changes as well, with the blood being sometimes gummy, at other times very fluid. Everything about this blood is phenomenal, especially the times when the blood liquefies and forms tiny bubbles that rise up to the surface and collect into a foam. The liquefaction has occurred for over six hundred years.[519] No satisfactory scientific explanation has been adduced to this phenomenon and devout Neapolitans accept it as a miracle.[520]

The blood of St. Andrew Avellino (1521–1608) also reportedly bubbled in a vial. On the anniversary of his death, the hardened blood was said to liquefy and bubble (similar to the blood of St. Januarius) when brought out for veneration. The blood is said to bubble every year on the anniversary of his death.[521]

The blood collected from St. Clare of Montefalco and placed in a beaker has been known to liquefy at times and even to boil up and bubble.[522] Blood from the severed incorrupt right arm of St. Nicolas of Tolentino has, on occasion, gushed with fresh blood, a portent which is taken to foreshow some impending calamity. More than twenty-five effusions of liquid blood are recorded from his arm, and some of these are recent in date.[523] Likewise, blood collected in phials from Venerable Passitea Crogi (1564–1615), a stigmatic Capuchian nun of Siena, has been known to liquefy

on occasion.[524] Her blood, in fact, has been known to change into a rosy-hued fluid that increases in size until it almost fills the entire phial.[525] Other saints whose blood exhibits liquefaction include: St. Stephen (d.c. 35), the first Christian martyr; St. Pantaleon (d.c. 305); St. Patricia (d.c. 665); and St. Bernardino Realino.

Another condition which defies explanation is the flow of fresh blood that proceeded from a number of the saints' bodies many years after their death. This spectacle was observed eighty years after the death of St. Hugh of Lincoln (1140–1200) when the head separated from the neck.[526] The mortal wound on the forehead of St. Josaphat (c. 1580–1623) bled twenty-seven years following his death. Forty-three years after the death of St. Germaine de Pibrac, fresh blood was found to have miraculously flowed from her nose. Thirty-six years after his death, the body of St. Peter Regaldo (c. 1390–1456), a Spanish Franciscan, was exhumed and several fingers removed at the request of Queen Isabella who wanted them as relics. The amputation of the fingers elicited a flow of fresh red blood. A similar phenomenon occurred eighteen months after the death of St. John of the Cross; a decision was made to amputate the three fingers of his right hand which had held the pen used by the saint in his writings. As soon as these were detached, the hand filled with blood, which continued flowing freely, "as from a living person." As already mentioned above, forty years after the death of St. Nicholas of Tolentino, a copious flow of blood issued from his severed arms. This phenomenon was to occur several times over the next four hundred years. Upon the exhumation of the body of St. Catherine of Bologna, a piece of skin was pulled off one of her feet and fresh

---

[519] Cruz, MMM, op.cit., pp. 324–26.
[520] John J. Delaney, *Pocket dictionary of saints.* Abridged ed. Golden City, NY, Image Books, 1983, p. 266.
[521] Guiley, op.cit., p. 19.
[522] Summers, op.cit., p. 135.
[523] Ibid., p. 137.

[524] Ibid., p. 139.
[525] Cruz, MMM, op.cit., p. 337.
[526] Ibid., p. 366.

red blood instantly flowed from it. Three months after her death, she twice bled from the nose so copiously as to fill a cup with the blood.[527] Likewise, the incorrupt heart of St. Francis de Sales was imbued with his blood almost three hundred years after his death.[528]

Bodily Elongation and Shrinkage

This phenomenon has been witnessed not only in the lives of a few saints but also in certain spiritualists, although in the latter case one might suspect trickery or diabolical intervention. If it occurs in the life of a mystic, there is always a question as to its purpose. The fact remains that in these cases the body or limb of the individual has visibly elongated to proportions far beyond the normal.[529] It is claimed, for instance, that certain stigmatics had the power to extend or shrink their bodies. The arm of the Italian sixteenth-century stigmatic Blessed Stephanie Quinzani purportedly grew longer while she was reliving the moment of Jesus being nailed to the cross.[530]

Much the same was noted of St. Catherine of Genoa. Her arm was said to have become elongated during agonies preceding her death. "The arm [reportedly] grew more than a half of a palm longer than it was by nature." In the nineteenth century, the French stigmatic Marie-Julie Jahenny, having predicted what would happen, produced a whole series of contractions and enlargements in the course of one performance. This occurred on

Friday, October 1, 1880 in the presence of five witnesses along with Dr. Imbert-Goubeye. At that time, her head seemed to shrink into her body to just about the level of her shoulders, her whole frame shriveled into a sort of a ball, each of her shoulders seemed to protrude at right angles to her collarbone, the right side of her body enlarged while the left shrank to virtually nothing, and her tongue swelled to enormous proportions.[531]

The seventeenth-century nun and ecstatica Veronica Laparelli was observed to stretch out until the length of her throat seemed to be out of all proportions in such a way that she was altogether much taller (at least by ten inches) than usual. Similar elongation phenomena are cited in the life of Mother Constante Maria Castreca and Venerable Domenica of Paradiso.[532]

Cardiac Phenomena

Cardiac phenomena include those mystical events associated with the physical heart of a mystic, symbolically referring to charity, God's overwhelming love of humankind. They include heartbeats audible to crowds or distant bystanders, immense enlargement of the heart, cardiac ardors, images and imprints of religious symbols, or flesh formations of the Instruments of the Passion actually revealed in a heart during autopsies, etc.[533]

For instance, the heart of St. Clare of Montefalco, an Italian mystic of the Augustinian Order, was graced with an apparition of Our Lord during which He said to her: "I have sought a place in the world where I might plant my Cross and have found no better site than your heart." After her death, her larger than average heart was extracted and examined. It was reported

---

527 Ibid., pp. 330–37.
528 Ibid., p. 79.
529 Aumann, op.cit., p. 439.
530 Thurston, op.cit., pp. 201–2; Ian Wilson, *Stigmata: An investigation into the mysterious appearance of Christ's wounds in hundreds of people from medieval Italy to modern America*, San Francisco: Harper and Row, c. 1989, p. 134.

531 Wilson, op.cit., p. 111.
532 Thurston, op.cit., pp. 198, 200.
533 Johnson, op.cit., p. 357.

Christ Appearing to St. Clare of Montefalco

to bear tiny but distinct symbols of Our Lord's Passion, all composed of cardiac tissue. These figures included the crucifix, which was about the size of one's thumb, the column and cord of the flagellation, the Crown of Thorns, the lance, the sponge and the three nails.[534]

In 1700, St. Veronica Giuliani, a Capuchin nun, drew a picture of the instruments of the Passion indicating their location in her heart. She said they were imprinted on her heart during a vision of Christ. This sketch was confirmed at her autopsy thirty hours after she died. A post-mortem examination performed in the presence of a bishop and many witnesses showed her heart bore a number of the figures corresponding to those she had drawn. In fact, the marks on her heart were almost the same as those of St. Clare of Montefalco mentioned above.[535]

Blessed Margaret of Castello who was often heard to exclaim, "Oh, if you only knew what I have in my heart!" was reportedly

marked similarly. Upon death, her heart was examined and in it were discovered three pellets or pearls on which were carved religious symbols which some recognized as being the images of Our Lord, the Blessed Mother, and St. Joseph.[536]

On his deathbed, the "flying friar" St. Joseph of Cupertino asked the Lord to take his heart and burn and tear it. When his heart was examined after death, it was found that the tissue around the heart was shriveled, the ventricles were without blood, and the heart itself withered and dry. It would seem that his deathbed request that his heart be taken and burned had actually been realized long ago and that one might say that the condition of the heart was the effect of the burning love of God.

During the Easter season of 1544, while praying in the catacomb of Saint Sebastian, St. Philip Neri felt in an extraordinary way "filled with God." At that time, he received a vision of a globe of fire that entered his mouth and fell into his heart. During this ecstasy, Philip felt something as large as his fist in his chest. At once he began to experience loud palpitations of the heart. After his death, an autopsy revealed that the swelling that had existed from that experience was caused by two broken ribs which were raised to form an arch over his enlarged heart. The pulmonary artery was very large but the other organs appeared normal. The doctors attested that the cause was supernatural and could not explain how Philip had lived without experiencing extreme pain.[537]

A ferita, heart wound, or transverberation was discovered later after the death of Blessed Mary of Jesus Crucified (1846–1878). The surgeon who removed her heart at death perceived a deep wound, triangular in shape, which appeared as though it had

---

[534] Cruz, MMM, op.cit., p. 72.
[535] Ibid., p. 73; see also Aradi, op.cit., p. 164.
[536] Ibid., pp. 76–77.
[537] Ibid., pp. 177–78; see also Johnson, op.cit., p. 149.

been inflicted by a broad sword.[538]

During St. Francis de Sales' autopsy, his heart was removed and placed in a silver coffer in the Church of the Visitation in Lyons. A clear oil has exuded from the relic at intervals throughout the years. His incorrupt heart was seen to be imbued with his blood almost three hundred years after his death. Like St. Francis, the heart of St. Jane Frances de Chantal was extracted at her death. It is also said to swell at times like a heart under the pressure of sorrow.[539]

Some saints, such as St. Catherine of Sienna, the Venerable Ursula Benincasa, and St. Catherine of Ricci, have received a grace that is called "change of heart". We do not know its nature, only that something takes place in the material heart. Other saints have spoken of having entered into the heart of Jesus.[540]

Cardiognosis (Reading of Hearts)

The ability to know the secret thoughts of others and to see the state of their souls is known as cardiognosis or the "reading of hearts". It entails the ability to see into the minds and hearts of others, to know their thoughts, desires, and sins. In the language of parapsychology, the ability to know the thoughts and desires of others would be called clairvoyance.[541]

This gift enables one to discern the condition of another's soul; for example, whether they are living in God's grace or in the state of mortal sin. The certain knowledge of the secret thoughts of others is completely supernatural. The devil has no access to the spiritual faculties of men; namely, their intellect and will. No human being can know the mind of another unless

Therese Neumann, 1926, photo by Ferdinand Neumann, German Federal Archives

it is in some way supernaturally communicated by God.[542] Numerous saints possessed the knowledge of the secrets of hearts.

Some of these gifted people have been able to see the intimate details of one's past, present, or future. By such means, they help in the reformation of souls. It is an extraordinary gift given to some of God's favored ones for the sanctification of those whom he puts in their care.[543] Sts. Joseph of Cupertino, Catherine of Siena, and Maria Maddalena de' Pazzi enjoyed this favor so habitually that persons were often unwilling to encounter them without first having cleansed their consciences.[544]

Therese Neumann displayed this remarkable ability to read hearts. She was aware of a person's thoughts and intentions before they were spoken or not actually spoken at all. She also had a privileged knowledge of

---

[538] Summers, op.cit., p. 238.
[539] Cruz, MMM, op.cit., pp. 79–80.
[540] Poulin, RAV, op.cit., p. 23.
[541] Guiley, op.cit., pp. 384–85.

[542] NCE, 2nd ed., v. 10, op.cit., p. 108; Aumann, op.cit., p. 430.
[543] Freze, TBWC, op.cit., pp. 175, 178.
[544] Poulain, RAV, op.cit., p. 80.

the individual's former life.[545] Therese used this ability to help uncover those impediments which hindered the spiritual progress of the soul; furthermore, she helped to expose the types and degrees of personal sin in people with the intention of leading them closer to God.[546]

St. Catherine of Siena, whose works explore the highest and untrodden realms of the spirit and soar profoundly to the very throne of God,[547] had the ability to read souls. St. Catherine and St. Lydwina of Schiedam, who also could read souls, were able to disclose to transgressors sins only known to them and God.[548]

St. Philip Neri's gift of reading hearts was exercised frequently in the many hours he spent in the confessional when a sin had been forgotten or a penitent had withheld telling of a grievous sin out of shame. St. John Vianney often spent from sixteen to eighteen hours in the confessional each day. He had insight into men's minds and souls and could read the minds and hearts of his penitents. The Curé of Ars, as he was known, assisted many of these penitents in the revelation of their sins which he was aware of through divine inspiration. Due to the long lines, some penitents waited for days to confess. The saint often invited certain persons to confess before others because of an interior insight telling him that these individuals should speak to him without further delay.[549]

It has been said that St. John Bosco had the ability to know "the mystery of hearts, the secrets of conscience, men's innermost thoughts as well as the future and end of anyone's life." He saw consciences in the confessional as if they were open books. He also had the ability to discover hidden sins and to relate all the sins of his penitents so that it was practically impossible to leave his confessional with any grave sin on one's conscience.[550] Blessed Mary of Oignes often knew by vision and revelation the temptations and secrets of the hearts of the persons who consulted her.[551]

St. Gerard Majella read souls, hearts, and thoughts so frequently that he sent many sinners back to the confessional to confess sins that they had deliberately withheld. St. Paul of the Cross not only knew the condition of souls and their forgotten and unconfessed sins but also correctly advised many on the correct course they should take in spiritual and temporal matters.[552] St. Padre Pio also was very much aware of those who came before him to confession who were secretly living in a state of sin. Oftentimes, he could be extremely harsh with these people, even refusing them absolution or spiritual direction until they mended their ways.[553] St. John of Sahagun was gifted with special powers to penetrate the secrets of conscience so that it was not easy to deceive him, and sinners were almost forced to make good confessions.[554]

Likewise, St. John Joseph of the Cross was said to be able to read the thoughts of those who came to consult him as clearly as though they had been written words. St. Joseph of Cupertino knew the consciences and sins of those with whom he came into contact. He would often approach people to remind them to confess hidden sins. When they replied that they were not conscious of any hidden sins, the saint would reveal the time, place, and circumstances

[545] Johannes Steiner, *Therese Neumann: A portrait, based on authentic accounts, journals and documents*, Staten Island, NY, Alba House, 1967, pp. 58–59.

[546] Freze, TBWC, op.cit., p. 17.

[547] Summers, op.cit., p. 67.

[548] Cruz, MMM, op.cit., p. 260.

[549] Ibid., pp. 263, 272.

[550] Ibid., pp. 258, 273–74.

[551] http://my.tbaytel.net/nitesky/christian/miracles.htm. *Miracles Will Follow the True Church.* [Miracles], p. 5.

[552] Cruz, MMM, op.cit., pp. 268–69.

[553] Freze, TBWC, op.cit., p. 176.

[554] Miracles, op.cit., p. 5.

of the offenses against God.

Blessed Anna Maria Taigi could discern the secret thoughts of persons who were present as well as far off.[555]

Some other saints and beati with insight into men's hearts, souls, and minds include: Sts. Anthony of Padua, Francis of Paola, Peter Claver, Ignatius of Loyola, Alphonsus Liguori, Maria Maddalena de Pazzi, Faustina Kowalska, Pacifico of San Severino,[556] Marianna de Jesus Paredes y Flores, Gaspar del Bufalo, Francis of Posada, Blessed John of Alvernia, Blessed Villana de Botti, Blessed Elizabeth von Reute, Blessed Stephanie de Quinzanis, Saint Marie of the Incarnation, Blessed Mary of Jesus Crucified, and Theresa Neumann.

Compenetration of Bodies (Subtility)

This phenomenon occurs when one material body appears to pass through another material body. It is generally held to be philosophically impossible, although much remains to be learned concerning the quantity, weight, and distribution of parts in a body. In the apparent compenetration of bodies, one of the bodies could be an immaterial representation of a body; or it is possible that a body might enjoy the anticipated quality of subtility that is characteristic of a glorified body.[557] Subtility means that our risen bodies will be endowed with the power of penetrating all things, even the hardest substances, as easily as the sun's rays penetrate a clear crystal. This is the power which Our Blessed Lord possessed and exercised when He arose from the dead and emerged from the sealed tomb without removing the stone that covered the mouth of the sepulcher.

He simply passed through it with His glorified body. Again, after eight days, when the apostles were gathered together, "Jesus came, although the doors were locked, and stood in their midst, and said 'peace be with you'" (Jn 20:19). This is an anticipated supernatural gift with which we shall be clothed, because we must rise similar to the glorious body of Jesus Christ.[558]

Penetrating locked doors or other material substances has also been done by the saints. St. Rita of Cascia, for instance, was a widow who tried a number of times to enter a convent as a religious but was refused because of her age. Finally a few of her patron saints—St. Augustine, St. John the Baptist, and St. Nicolas of Tolentino—took her in the middle of the night and placed her right within the convent, all the doors of which remained locked. The sisters then saw the hand of God and accepted Rita into their convent.[559] This miracle was reminiscent of the Lord miraculously appearing in the midst of the Apostles on Easter Sunday when the doors were locked, or when He emerged from His sealed tomb. St. Patrick (389–461);[560] St. Raymond of Pennafort (1175–1275), a famous Dominican preacher;[561] St. Martin de Porres,[562] a Peruvian Dominican; and Venerable Anthony Margil, a Franciscan missionary, are all said to have possessed the gift of subtility which enabled them to enter dwellings through closed doors.[563]

---

[555] Ibid., p. 540.
[556] Miracles, op.cit., p. 5.
[557] NCE, 1st ed., v. 10, op.cit., p. 174.

[558] Boudreau, op.cit., p. 84.
[559] Hebert, SWRD, op.cit., p. 245.
[560] Ghezzi, MM, op.cit., p. 158.
[561] Cruz, MMM, op.cit., p. 100.
[562] Ibid., p. 94, see also Guiley, op.cit., p. 227.
[563] See Miriam Horvat, *Venerable Antonio Margil of Jesus, Apostle of New Spain.* http://www.traditioninaction.org/Margil.

The Miracles of St. Francis Xavier by Peter Paul Rubens

Cures and Miraculous Healings

A miracle may be defined as a phenomenon in nature which transcends the capacity of natural causes to such a degree that it must be attributed to the direct intervention of God.[564] Miraculous healings might include a reversal of the symptoms of a disease, the regeneration of healthy flesh where none was before, or the restoration of function to a damaged organ, with or without physical restoration of the organ's structure. However, spontaneous or unusually rapid remission of disease, no matter how well timed, is not generally investigated as miraculous unless it is accompanied by unquestionably supernatural phenomena.[565] Miracles are performed for the glory of God and the good of men.

It should also be noted that many miraculous healings have occurred and are still occurring today at the Marian apparition sites such as at approved apparition sites like Fatima, Lourdes, Laus, Knock, Banneux, and Beauraing, and alleged apparition sites like Medjugorje.

Blessed Anna Maria Taigi worked many miracles of healing. She is said to have cured hundreds and even thousands of afflictions, like a neighbor child's diphtheria and her own daughter's torn eyeball, just by touching.[566] St. Padre Pio has a long history of miraculous cures. A few worthy of mention include the son of Count Marzotta, whom he cured of blindness, Gemma Di Giorgi, who was born with no pupils but was able to see after his intercession, and the Countess Baiocchi of Gavinana, whom he healed of an incurable disease. He cured others of such things as extreme pneumonia, tongue diseases, kidney failure, heart and thyroid disease, etc.

A modern day Padre Pio is claimed to be Fra Elia, an Italian stigmatic, who is said to have miracle-working capabilities.

Some other saints and beati with the gift of miraculous healing while alive include St. Francis of Assisi, who cured many people of various illnesses, diseases, and deformities. One time Francis healed a man of his leprosy after washing him and rubbing sweet herbs on him with his holy hands.[567] St. Louis Marie Grignion de Montfort cured the sick and made the blind see. Numerous miraculous cures were attributed to Sts. Clare of Montefalco, Catherine of Siena, Frances of Rome, Camillus de Lellis, Joseph of Cupertino, and Gaspar del Bufalo.

Restoring hearing to the deaf were cures performed by Sts. Patrick, Vincent Ferrer, Francis of Paola, Francis Xavier, and Paul of the Cross. The aforementioned saints along with Sts. Bernard of Clairvaux, Malachy O'Morgair, Hyacinth, Philip Benizi, Rose of Lima, blessed Margaret of Castello, and Blessed Peter de Geremia (1381–1452) were said to have restored mobility to the lame. Some saints and beati who restored sight to the blind include Sts. Ambrose, Remy of Rheims (437–530), Martin de Porres de Porres, Andrew Bobola (1592–1657), and Blessed Jane of Signa.[568] As already mentioned, St. Pio of Pietrelcina (Padre Pio) cured the son of the count Marzotta of blindness and Gemma Di Giorgi, who was born with no pupils, was able to see after his intercession.[569] Some saints who restored speech to the mute include Sts. Martin of Tours, Patrick, Bernard of Clairvaux, Vincent Ferrer, Francis Xavier, and Jean Marie Vianney.

Many saints performed supernatural healing of the sick. St. Martin of Tours once kissed a leper at Lerroux and another time

---

[564] Aradi, op.cit., p. 16.
[565] Johnson, op.cit., p. 359.
[566] Ibid., p. 41.

[567] Freze, TBWC, op.cit., p. 182.
[568] Miracles, op.cit., pp. 15–16.
[569] Freeze, TBWC, op.cit., p.182.

embraced a leper in Paris. On both occasions the disease disappeared instantly. St. Clare of Assisi and St. Felix of Cantalice (1515–1587) healed many people who came to them in need just by making the sign of the cross.[570]

One of the more incredible gifts of healing which defies all known laws of nature is that of raising people from the dead. As unbelievable as this may seem, many such cases are on record. Even before the coming of Christ, God had blessed some of His servants with the power to raise the dead, as in the case of both Elijah (1 Kgs 17:17–24) and Elisha who raised young boys back to life (2 Kgs 4:17–37). We also know from Scripture of three instances of Christ Himself restoring life to other persons: the son of the widow of Nain (Lk 7:11–17), the daughter of Jairus (Mt 9:18–26; Mk 5:22–43; Lk 8:41–56), and of course the famous case of Lazarus who had been entombed for four days and had begun to decompose (Jn 11:11–44). There is also the case of the disciple Tabitha (Dorcas) from Joppa in the Acts of the Apostles, who fell sick and died and was brought back to life by St. Peter (Acts 9:36–42), and the young man Eutychus, who was brought back to life by St. Paul (Acts 20:12). Jesus says in Matthew 10:8, "Cure the sick, raise the dead, cleanse lepers, drive out demons." One of the main reasons God gives some of His chosen souls the ability to raise the dead is to remind people of Christ's glorious resurrection.

St. Martin of Tours performed many miracles in his lifetime including raising three people from the dead. He is also credited with many posthumous miracles. St. Ambrose (340–397) raised from the dead a boy named Pansopius. St. Patrick of Ireland (389–461) is reported to have raised at least thirty-nine people from the dead, some of whom who had been buried a long

St. Anthony Raises a Dead Man by Jacob van Oost

time. St. Francis Xavier raised a man who had been dead who after death had even begun to smell. He is recorded to have raised many people from the dead with a sprinkle of Holy Water and the Sign of the Cross. St. Benedict of Nursia (480–547) raised a child from the dead and a monk who had been crushed in a construction collapse.[571] St. Anthony of Padua known as the "wonder worker of Padua," healed the sick and is credited with raising a dozen people from the dead. St. Dominic brought several back to life to include a Cardinal's nephew who had been thrown from a horse. St. Elizabeth of Hungary (1207–1231) likewise raised a number of people from the dead to include three children,

---

[570] Miracles, op.cit., pp. 17–18.

[571] Ibid., pp. 13–15.

St Hyacinth Raising a Drowned Child by Francesco Vanni

an adolescent, and a stillborn infant.[572] St. Hyacinth is credited with restoring scores of people back to life and bringing dying people back to full health. St. Margaret of Cortona had miraculous healing powers in her lifetime which continued after her death. She is credited with raising a dead boy back to life.

St. Nicholas of Tolentino is reported to have resurrected over a hundred dead children, including several who had been under water for days.[573] St. Agnes of Montepulciano performed many miracles including the raising of a drowned child from the dead. St. Hyacinth brought back to life a drowned boy whose body was recovered the day after he died. Likewise, St. Gerard Majella raised a baby who had

drowned and was dead for over an hour. In the same vein, St. Sharbel Makhluf raised a two-year-old infant who had drowned and had turned purple.[574]

St. Catherine of Siena raised her dead mother Lapa Benincasa from the dead through her prayers and pious tears. Lapa lived to the ripe old age of eighty-nine. St. Vincent Ferrer was a celebrated miracle worker. In 1412, while preaching before a crowd of thirty thousand in Salamanca, he brought to life, for some fifteen minutes, a dead woman being carried to the cemetery. He is credited with performing some forty thousand dazzling miracles as well as raising a total of twenty-eight persons from the dead.[575] St. Francis of Paola was credited with many miracles to include raising his dead nephew and at least five other people to life. One man he brought back to life had allegedly been hanging from the gallows for three days.[576] St. Bridget of Sweden and her daughter, St. Catherine of Sweden, are credited with raising several persons back to life who had been pronounced dead.[577]

St. Colette is said to have raised many dead people to life again to include a young nun who was already in her coffin and a child who had been buried. She is also credited with giving life to many stillborn infants.[578] St. Ignatius Loyola performed some hundred or so miracles to include bringing back to life a man named Lassani who had hanged himself.[579] St. Teresa of Avila reportedly raised her six-year-old nephew Gonzalo from his premature death.[580] St.

---

[572] Freze, VVA, op.cit., pp. 69–70.

[573] Miracles, op.cit., p. 13; Hebert, op.cit., pp. 158, 162; see also Lucy Gorden, "He Raised 100 Children from the Dead," in *Inside the Vatican*, July 2005, pp. 42–43.

[574] Miracles, op.cit., pp. 13–15.

[575] Hebert, op.cit., pp. 106, 166–67.

[576] Ibid., p. 114; see also Miracles, op.cit., p. 14.

[577] Ibid., p. 86; see also Freze, VVA, op.cit., p. 71.

[578] Freze, VVA, op.cit., p. 71; Rene Biot, *The enigma of the stigmata*, translated from the French by P. J. Hepburne–Scott. New York, Hawthorne Books, [1962], p. 79.

[579] Miracles, op.cit., p. 14.

[580] Freeze, TWBC, op.cit., p. 181.

Philip Neri, who was said to have the ability of curing people just with the touch of his hand, is also credited with raising the dead in his lifetime and through his intercession after his death.[581] Remarkable miracles followed the preaching of St. Louis Bertrand to include bringing two people back to life and another thirteen were raised through his intercession after his death.[582] St. Martin de Porres was said to perform many miraculous cures including raising a fellow monk from the dead. St. Gerard Majella was called a wonder-worker for his many miracles, including restoring two dead infants back to life.[583] Bl. Columba of Rieti, a Dominican tertiary, raised several people back to life. Bl. Augustine of Biella (1430–1493) once brought back to life a deformed un-baptized infant long enough to baptize him.[584]

Many cures and healings are attributed to the intercession of saints and beati after their death. Some 136 miracles attributed to St. Benedict Joseph Labre occurred in fewer than two months following his death.[585] Many persons who were incurably ill were healed at the gravesite of St. Catherine of Bologna. St. Peregrine Laziosi known throughout the world as "the Cancer Saint," is known to have cured many afflicted with various diseases during his lifetime. It is said that during the thirty-two years prior to his canonization in 1726 there were over 300 miracles attributed to him and authenticated by Church officials. Likewise, over 200 miracles have been attributed to the intercession of Blessed Margaret of Castello after she expired.[586] Through the intercession

of St. Rose of Lima, upon her demise, two people were raised to life and many sick people to include lepers were cured.[587]

After their deaths, cures also began to be reported through the intercession of many saints, including Sts. Francis of Assisi, Hyacinth, Nicholas of Tolentino, Catherine of Genoa, Paschal Babylon, Marianna de Jesus Paredes y Flores, and Sharbel Makhluf.

Another area of miraculous healing that is often overlooked concerns the conditions of spiritual bondage and diabolical oppression or possession, which are, in effect, the gift of deliverance or exorcism. Jesus was the first exorcist. He regularly performed exorcisms during His earthly ministry as known through the many scriptural examples of people being cured who were possessed by demons. The four Gospels contain numerous examples of our Lord driving out and commanding such foul spirits. He commands the unclean spirits and they obey Him (Mk 1:32–34). He even liberated a victim having a demon via long distance as noted in Matthew 15:21–28 and Mark 7:24–30 when he healed the Canaanite woman's daughter. Christ differentiated illness from possession in many passages. In Matthew's Gospel, it says, "He cast out the spirits with a word, and healed all who were sick," (Mt 8:16) and, "[they] brought Him the sick . . . [and the] demoniacs . . . and He healed them" (Mt 4:24). He also healed those afflicted with complete diabolic possession as noted in the case of the Gerasene demoniac (Mt 8:28–32; Mk 5:1–20) who demonstrated great rage and who had superhuman strength allowing him to break chains and shackles. Another case of serious possession from childhood was the boy who had a demon which nine apostles could not cast

[581] Hebert, SWRD, op.cit., p. 123.

[582] Freze, VVA, op.cit., p. 72.

[583] Hebert, SWRD, op.cit., pp. 142, 153–54.

[584] Ibid., p. 136, see also Miracles, op.cit., p. 14.

[585] NCE, 2nd ed, v. 8, op.cit, pp. 267–68.

[586] Joan Carroll Cruz, *The incorruptibles; A study of the incorruption of the bodies of various Catholic saints and beati.* Rockford, Illinois, TAN Books and

Publishers, Inc. 1977, pp. 111,116 [in future, Cruz, Inc.]

[587] Hebert, op.cit., p. 141; Miracle, op.cit., p. 14.

Saint Martin Healing the Possessed Man, 1630, by Jacob Jordaens

The Possessed Boy at the Foot of Mount Tabor by James Tissot

out (Mk 9:14–29; Lk 9:38–43). The victim is said to have become mute, thrown himself down on the ground, and had seizures. The demon is said to have wanted his death. Mark 9:21 states that the victim had this affliction from childhood. It revealed that the victim was guiltless. Christ commented that "this kind [of possession] cannot be driven out by anything but prayer and through fasting" (Mk 9:29). This also tells us that the success of exorcisms is not automatic but often requires much time, in addition to faith and prayer (and sacrifice on the part of the exorcist).

Jesus repeatedly stressed the ability to expel demons among the specific powers that He wanted to pass on to His apostles and their successors (Mk 3:5). As such, He explicitly commissioned His followers to take up His ministry of demon expulsion and spiritual warfare. He handed the power to drive out demons to the twelve apostles first, then to the seventy-two disciples, and finally to all those who believe in Him (Mk 3:14–15; Mt 10:1:7–8; Jn 14:11–12). Luke 9:1–2 specifically says that the first power Jesus conferred on the apostles was that of casting out evil spirits. He gave them the power as well as the authority over all demons and to cure diseases. Jesus says, "In my name they will cast out demons" (Mk 6:7;16:17). Upon their return, the seventy-two disciples said, "Lord, even the demons are subject to us in your name" (Lk 10:17). The strength of the exorcism lies solely in the name of Jesus. We can only presume that Judas also performed miracles and expelled demons even though Satan later entered him.

At the dawn of the Church, disciples could expel demons on the strength of Christ's mandate (Mk 16:17). After the apostolic age, the primitive Christians continued to exorcise demons. St. Justin Martyr (c. 100–165) speaks of numberless demoniacs throughout the whole world who were exorcised by Christian men in the name of Jesus Christ. Origen (c. 185–254) remarks that the name of Jesus expelled myriad evil spirits from the souls and bodies of men. St. Cyril of Jerusalem (c.315–386) notes that the invocation of the name of God scorches and drives out evil spirits like a fierce flame. These remarks are typical of the attitude of the early Church, for which an exorcism was an invocation of God against the harassment of devils. In the early Church, exorcisms were performed by lay persons as well as by clerics. Gradually, in the West, the Church began to limit the authority to exorcise. Today, the use of the power of exorcism is restricted by ecclesiastical law. Ecclesiastic appointments of exorcists has become the norm. The rite of solemn exorcism requires special permission from the ordinary and is given only to priests of piety and prudence.

Some of the other saints renowned for casting out demons include Sts. Benedict

(480–547), who was one of the first to exorcise demons in a particular location, at Monte Cassino, Italy where there was formerly a temple of Apollo that offered pagan sacrifices to the gods;[588] Ambrose (340–397),[589] Cosmos and Damian (4 c.),[590] and Cuthbert, the latter of whom put demons to flight both from his own person and others who were possessed; Sts. Guthlac, Malachy, Anthony of Padua, Agnes of Montepulciano,[591] Frances of Rome, Francis of Paola, Ignatius Loyola, Philip Neri,[592] Joseph of Cupertino, Vincent Pallotti (1795–1850);[593] Pio of Pietrelcina,[594] Bl. Augustine of Biella, Bl. John of Salerno (13c),[595] and St. Margaret Fontana, the latter of which would fend off all their encounters with demons with holy water, the Sign of the Cross, or the name of Jesus. Sts. Martin de Porres, Rita of Cascia,[596] Jean Marie Baptiste Vianney, Alphonsus Liguori, and Bl. Mary Fortunata Viti (1827–1922) all dismissed demons with the Sign of the Cross.[597] St. Paul of the Cross once freed a soldier from the torments of the devil by placing the holy rosary around his neck. Sr. Josefa Menendez dismissed a demon by holding up her rosary before him. Relics such as the cincture of St. Lydwina of Schiedam and a silver reliquary carried by St. Jean-Marie-Baptiste Vianney in his pocket were used to perform

exorcisms.[598] It is said that St. Catherine of Siena in the fourteenth century was so holy that priest exorcists who could not expel demons usually brought the afflicted persons to her to be immediately freed of their demons.[599]

St. Francis de Sales was also renowned as a healer, being especially effective in cases of possession. He was said to have cured over four hundred people with this affliction.[600] St. Vincent Ferrer's hagiographers claim that he delivered seventy people from diabolical possession. This Spanish Dominican is said to have had such power over demons that it was often simply enough for him to just touch a possessed person for him to be freed.[601] At times, people suffering diabolical obsession or possession were brought to St. Francis of Assisi for deliverance. Although he did not always see a physical manifestation of the devil, Francis often spoke to the evil spirits and they at times spoke back.[602] On the day of his ordination, St. Peter of Atroa (773–837) is said to have exorcised a possessed man at the door of the Church.[603]

Dark Night of the Soul

In speaking about this spiritual cleansing, the Catholic Dictionary describes the "dark night of the soul" as the purification by which God draws one to Himself and to a deeper sanctity. This period is marked by purging of self-love and a feeling of abandonment by God. One cannot "see" Him as before. The "dark night" is a transitory prelude to "mystical marriage" and occurs only for those who have attained contemplation. [Rev. Peter M.J. Stavinskas,

[588] Joan Carroll Cruz, *Angels & Devils*. Rockford, Illinois, TAN Books and Publishers, Inc, 1999. pp. 251–52 (in future, Cruz, A&D).
[589] Freze, VVA, op.cit., p. 69.
[590] Tomas Dale Cowan, *The way of the saints: prayers, practices and meditations.* NY, NY: Putnam, c1998, p. 126.
[591] See Bolland, March 9; *First Life*, Book III, 33, 37.
[592] Johnson, op.cit., pp. 325–26.
[593] David Hugh Farmer. *The Oxford Dictionary of Saints.* Oxford, NY, NY: Oxford University Press, 2004, p. 409.
[594] Freze, VVA, op.cit., p. 253.
[595] Dorcy, op.cit., pp. 28–29.
[596] Cruz, A&D, op.cit., p. 223.
[597] Ibid., p. 233; see also Freze, VVA, op.cit., p. 288.

[598] Ibid., pp. 234–36.
[599] Gabriele Amorth, Fr. *An Exorcist: More Stories.* Ignatius Press: San Francisco, 2002. pp. 92–93.
[600] Fanning, op.cit., p. 162.
[601] Hebert, op.cit., p. 166.
[602] Freze, VVA, op.cit., p. 289.
[603] Miracles, op.cit., p. 4.

Catholic Dictionary Revised, Huntington, Indiana, Our Sunday Visitor, 2002, p.240]

The phrase "dark night of the soul" comes from a poem by St. John of the Cross (1542-1591), a Spanish Carmelite monk and mystic, whose "Noche oscura del alma" is translated "The Dark Night of the Soul." This eight stanza poem outlines the soul's journey from the distractions and entanglements of the world to the perfect peace and harmony and union with God. According to the poet, the "dark night of the soul" is synonymous with traveling the "narrow way" that Jesus spoke of in Matthew 7:13-14.

The monk taught that one seeking God will cast off all attachments to this world and live a life of austerity. Before attaining union with God, however, the soul must pass through a personal experience of Christ's passion. The time of testing and agony is accomplished by confusion, fear, and uncertainty—including doubts of God—but on the other side are Christ's glory, serenity and a mystical union with God.

The dark night is not pleasant, but to the end that it allows one to approach nearer to God and His love, the poet calls it a "happy night" and a "night more lovely than the dawn." At the end of one's journey, he concludes, God takes away all feeling, leaving the traveler senseless except the presence of God Himself.

From a theological standpoint, the concept of a "dark night of the soul" fits with Catholic teaching of purgatory and of earning God's favor through penance and other works. However, the idea of a step-by-step process of self-denial and affliction culminating in glory is not taught in Scripture. Jesus predicted that His followers would face persecution (John 16:20), but he also gives His peace to those same followers (John 14:27). A believer has God's peace

Detail of St. John of the Cross from The Virgin of the Carmen with Saint Teresa and Saint John of the Cross by Juan Rodríguez Juárez

now, he doesn't have to experience a "dark night" first (Romans 5:1). The child of God is already seated "in the heavenly realms in Christ Jesus." (Ephesians 2:6). Neither Jesus nor the apostles ever taught a "dark night of the soul."

The ideas contained in the "Dark Night of the Soul" have been applied in the contexts outside of Catholicism. Protestants have been known to use the phrase to describe a period of questioning one's salvation. And the phrase is sometimes used generically to describe any type of mental, emotional, or spiritual anguish.

The Dark night of the soul may also be referred to as a period of spiritual aridity or desolation. Some of our most beloved saints have experienced this mystical phenomenon. The list includes St. Teresa of Avila, St. Teresa of Calcutta, St. Therese of Lisieux, St. Gemma Galgani, St. Maria Maddalenna de'Pazzi, St. Alphonsus Liguori, St. John of the Cross, and St. Ignatius of Loyola. It is said that St. Ignatius experienced the loss of faith, hope and love and offered insights on how to deal with this spiritual darkness.

It should be noted that each of us is influenced by spiritual inspirations throughout our lives. We are always in a state of either consolation or desolation. We may be oblivious to these spiritual states unless we enter a "school of discernment" and learn how to become aware of their influence.

Why would God allow this? St. Ignatius offers three reasons. The first reason deals with following the false logic of counter inspirations. When we make wrong decisions in our thoughts, words and deeds, God allows us to experience the darkness of our sins as a holy warning. This experience of desolation is meant to stir our consciences and return us to authenticity.

The second reason is that God wants to awaken our whole being—spirit, mind and body—to become aware of our hidden wounds. Desolation reveals the ways in which sin has taken root in our spirits, minds and bodies. Spiritual progress is possible only when we "wake up" and confront these damaging patterns. We might feel discouraged by the darkness at such times. In this moment, however, we must reaffirm our hope in the Lord, who is gradually uprooting the source of darkness in our being, with our cooperation.

St. Ignatius reminds us that when we feel lost, God is closer to us than ever.

The third reason deals with desolation that appears during times of spiritual advancement. One example might be a period of peace in divine inspiration after a period of purification marked by struggle. At such times, we may be tempted to believe that we have "arrived" and have reached the end of our spiritual journey. This is an illusion. When we find ourselves in these moments of pride and self-satisfaction, the counter-inspiration of desolation returns. God allows desolation at these times as a warning, to remind us that although we have grown in authenticity and holiness, we are still susceptible to the narcissism and destructive pride that will halt our progress.

St. Ignatius developed guidelines for how we should act when we feel the discouragement, hopelessness, and frustration that accompany spiritual desolation.

First, he taught that we should never change course when in desolation. He warned that it is a clear sign of counter-inspirations at work when we feel compelled by an "anxious urgency" to reach a decision or engage in action.

Second, he said that during times of desolation, we need to redouble our efforts to open and orient our hearts to God, even if it feels useless. Prayer, examination of conscience, and simple penance or fasting is helpful as we seek God's grace [cf. Mark 9:29]

The third guideline is to remember that God will give us the grace we need, building on our natural abilities. When we feel overwhelmed by temptations, or the darkness of spirit associated with disordered attractions and compulsive behaviors, there is always sufficient grace for salvation, even if the counter inspirations indicate otherwise.

Finally, we must be intentional in our efforts to cultivate patience and perseverance in the religious practices of our faith when influenced by the counter inspirations of desolation.

As St. Paul said: "For I am convinced that neither death, nor life, nor angels, nor principalities, nor present things, nor future things, nor powers, nor height, nor depth, nor any other creature will be able to separate us from the love of God in Christ Jesus, Our Lord." [Romans 8:38-39]

It is important to remember that God holds you fast during the divine inspirations of consolation, and holds you even closer during the cleansing times of desolation.

Affirm your faith in God, hold fast to your spiritual disciplines and the practices of your faith, and seek stability and fidelity both in times of peace and calm and in times of turbulence and struggle. Then God will fill you with peace. [The Wanderer, Catholic Replies, March 15, 2018, p.5B]

St. Alphonsus Liguori [1696-1787] was the founder of the Order of the Congregation of the Most Holy Redeemer (Redemptorists). For the last few years of his life, he experienced deep spiritual depression and he went through a "dark night of the soul." But this period was replaced by a time of peace and light when he experienced visions, ecstasies, made prophecies that were later fulfilled, and reportedly performed miracles. He was declared a Doctor of the church in 1871 by Pope Pius IX. [Cruz, Eucharistic Miracles, 249; Delaney, 360-361]

St. Camilla Battista Varano [1458-1524] suffered through a period of spiritual aridity to become a great mystic and an advocate of devotion to the Sacred Heart of Jesus. [Magnificat, May 2013, 410]

St. Elizabeth Ann Seton [1774-1821] along with Sts. John Vianney and Augustine suffered from depression. In a 2003 address,

St. John Paul II emphasized the role of prayer in the lives of depressed persons. He recommended the praying of the psalms and the rosary as ways to experience the tenderness of Christ's gaze and the love of His mother. [M, Jan. 2014, 394]

St. Jane Frances de Chantal [1572-1641] experienced periods of Spiritual aridity and more than once suffered the torments of the dark night of the soul. [Delaney, 144]

St. Gemma Galgani [1878-1903] experienced spiritual aridity and abandonment by God in the last year of her life. In Feb. 1901 the Lord told her "Your suffering shall greatly increase and a new life shall begin for you." Her ecstasies came to a complete cessation during the last 8 or 10 months of her life, and she looked as if she was abandoned by the Lord. An observer claimed she was participating in all the trials of Our Crucified Lord, especially the abandonment. She was enveloped in the same darkness the crucified savior had experienced on the cross. During the fall of 1902, the dark night of the soul became for her darker and more frightening. During her prayers and ecstasies, Gemma often pleaded with Jesus to make her die with Him. [Padre Enrico Zoffoli C.P. La Povera Gemma, 1959, pp.972-979]

St. Margaret of Cortona [1247-1297] was a native of Laviano, Tuscany, Italy. At the age of 17, she moved in with a rich nobleman and bore him a son. Nine years later her lover was murdered and she resolved to change her lifestyle. She made a public confession. She was filled with self-loathing and remorse and went through three years of spiritual despair and aridity. After her purification came to an end she became a Franciscan tertiary. From this time, Jesus began to speak to Margaret in prayer, calling her "my child." [M, Sept. 2016, 106, Delaney, 381]

Vision of St Maria Magdalena di Pazzi by Pedro de Moya

St. Maria Maddalena de' Pazzi (aka Mary Magdalen de' Pazzi) [1566-1607] was born in Florence, Italy and baptized Catherine. She joined the Carmelites in 1582 taking the name of Mary Magdalen when professed the following year. At the time of her profession Maria experienced a plethora of mystical graces—all well-documented. Christ drew her into a "mystical marriage" and she bore the stigmata and an invisible crown of thorns. Soon thereafter, she was called to live without God's graces and became seriously ill, during which she experienced an abandoned state which she called "the lion's den" [dark night of the soul]. She practiced great mortifications and spent five years in the depths of spiritual depressions and aridity. She suffered urges to rail against God, including blasphemy and profound doubt, as well as temptations to harm herself through gluttony, impurity and suicide. This last dark trial was conquered with the help of Mary, at whose altar Maria Maddalena left the knife she had planned to use to end her life. She did not emerge from this state until around 1590. This Carmelite mystic had the gifts of prophecy and the ability to read people's minds and to perform miracles of healing. She is also said to have received Holy Communion from the hands of the Savior Himself. Her utterances while in ecstasy and descriptions of her revelations were copied down by some of the sisters in the convent and were later published. [Delaney, 453-454; Cruz, Eucharistic Miracles, 262; M, Feb. 2018, 209]

St. Teresa of Calcutta [1910-1997] was born as Agnes Gonxha Bojaxhiu in Skopje, modern Macedonia. She suffered the spiritual trial of interior desolation known as "the dark night of the soul." After her death in 1997, the publication of Teresa's private letters showed that she had suffered from an almost continuous darkness lasting over 40 years, the feeling of being rejected and unwanted from the moment her work had begun. In time, the "tunnel" was revealed to her as a share in the spiritual abandonment suffered by the very poor she served, a communion with the darkness Christ had experienced on the cross. Her extraordinarily fruitful vocation continues to be manifest in the work of her order [Missionaries of Charity], carried on by priests, brothers, lay volunteers, and over 4,500 sisters in 133 countries. [M, Sept. 2004, 66; M, Jan. 2017, 294; M, Feb. 2018, 324, 325]

St. Therese of Lisieux [1873-1897] was born in Alencon, Normandy, France to (Saints) Louis and Zelie Martin. By the time she lay dying, ravaged by tuberculosis, she had lived through a final dark night in which she tasted the atheist's unbelief. [M, Feb. 2017, 147]

Bl. Elizabeth the Good [1386-1420] (aka Elizabeth Achler) was born in Waldsee, Germany. She became a Franciscan tertiary in Reute at age fourteen. Shortly after this, she was afflicted with the interior trials of spiritual aridity and desolation. Moreover, she was subjected to diabolical visions. She enjoyed ecstasies, visions of heaven and purgatory, went for months without food and at times displayed the stigmata, which bled on Fridays and during Lent. [M, Nov. 2003, 343; Delaney, 23]

Bl. John of Penna [c.1193-1271] was born at Penna, Ancona, Italy. He joined the Franciscans and founded several Franciscan homes in France. He experienced visions and had the gift of prophecy, but was also afflicted with several periods of spiritual aridity. [Delaney 325, Habig, Franciscan Book of Saints; Wikipedia]

Bl. Mary of Turin (aka Mary Fontanella) [1661-1717] was born at Baldinero, near Turin, Italy. She entered the Carmelite convent of Santa Cristina in Turin taking the religious name of Mary of the Angels. For three years she suffered the painful purgative mystical experience known as the "dark night of the soul," and was subjected to diabolical attacks. At the conclusion of this great spiritual aridity, she attained a high state of prayer and began to experience numerous mystical experiences. [M, Dec. 2003, 216; Delaney, 231]

Bl. Pina Suriano [1915-1950] experienced a dark night of the soul because her parents were opposed to her becoming a nun. [M, May 2005, 303]

Diabolical Apparitions and Molestation

A diabolical apparition is a preternatural (not supernatural) appearance of a bodily form whose origins are demonic in nature. During many false voices, visions, or apparitions, the devil himself may appear in disguise as "an angel of light "(2 Cor 11–14), or one of his cohorts may appear on his behalf. The diabolical apparition may also be purposely frightening in nature, designed to scare, confuse, or intimidate the visionary or to make him or her lose faith. Diabolical apparitions are extremely dangerous and are not to be taken lightly because physical harm from diabolical attacks, sometimes to the point of death, may occur if the demonic spirit is provoked or challenged in any way. Visionaries who experience voices, visions, or apparitions must be extremely careful that they are not being deceived by a diabolical spirit. In normal cases, the type of spirit will reveal itself in time through a series of clues: the apparition may be missing something or appear odd and out of character (such as a human with one eye or no mouth); an eerie or uncomfortable feeling exists in the presence of the apparition (fear, extreme cold, nausea, etc.); a teaching or message that will contradict a truth of Scripture or the Church; or the apparition will react violently against the sight of religious objects or at the words of Our Lord, the Blessed Virgin Mary, St. Michael the Archangel, various saints, or other supernatural beings.[604]

God in His Providence sometimes allows a person in a state of grace to be afflicted, obsessed, and even possessed by a demon. Sts. John Bosco, Gemma Galgani, and Giovanni Calabria (1873–1954) were said to be possessed by the devil for their own

---

[604] Freze, VVA, op.cit. ,pp. 301–2.

Temptation of St. Anthony by Matthias Grünewald

sanctification. Thus God can use the devil to accomplish His purposes.[605]

Since the day when, in the terrestrial paradise, the enemy of the human race took the form of a serpent in order to tempt our first parents, the devil has shown himself to men in a sensible form. Violent diabolical attacks are often the case with God's chosen victim souls. The struggles of St. Anthony in the desert against the visible attacks of the enemy are well known[606] as also in more recent times are the devil's visible attacks on St. John Vianney and others. As St. Paul says in 2 Corinthians 11:14, Satan often transforms himself into an angel of light in order to seduce souls.

The King of Mystics, Our Lord Himself, was tempted by the devil. Mystics who try

---

[605] Thomas J. Euteneuer, Rev. *Exorcism and the Church Militant.* Front Royal, VA: Human Life International, 2010, pp. 37, 215.

[606] St. Athanasius, *St. Antony of the Desert (251–356).* Rockford, Illinois: TAN Books and Publishers, Inc. 1995. pp. 29–34.

to attain spiritual heights are special objects of Satan's enmity. St. Paul was one of the earliest reported saints to be assaulted and beaten by a demon. He wrote, "That I might not become too elated, a thorn in the flesh was given to me, an angel of Satan, to beat me, to keep me from being too elated" (2 Cor 12:7). He is saying that the Lord kept him humble by giving him this thorn in the flesh, this messenger of Satan to torment him. We know also of the satanical persecutions of St. Anthony of Egypt who, during his long life, saw Satan in many forms and had such terrifying visions of him that he prayed on his knees to dispel them.[607] While living in solitude for some twelve to fifteen years, St. Anthony engaged in struggles with and was beaten by the devil and had torments and temptations that are legendary. When this holy man later moved to the desert, he was known to have had power over demons. He is said to just rebuke them by remarking that they must be very weak to come in such numbers against one little old man.[608]

Demons attempt to produce aggravations to the five senses. They have assaulted the sense of sight by appearing in frightening forms, such as armed men, repulsive animals as well as lions, dragons, bulls, large black dogs, cats, wolves, wild boars, toads, spiders, snakes, etc. All of which threaten to attack the saints. They have attacked the sense of hearing by uttering cries, blasphemies, obscene words, moanings, shrieks, and noises of all kinds, such as those that afflicted the Curé of Ars and so many other saints. They have assaulted the sense of taste by, for example, defiling in a terrible way everything that was to be eaten by Sister Veronica, a Capuchin nun. They have afflicted the sense of smell with strong and unpleasant odors that were noticed

Guillaume de Toulouse Tormented by Demons, by Ambroise Fredeau

not only by the saint involved but by many others that were near the saint. Such an instance took place when St. Frances of Rome once thought a corpse in a state of full decomposition had been brought near and its matter applied to her face. Her garments retained the odor even after several washings. Assaulting the sense of touch is a very frequent tool of the devil, when he afflicts the body with beatings, scratchings, biting, and kickings, sometimes causing serious injuries. We are told that Blessed Agnes of Jesus was beaten twice a week for four years before her profession. Padre Pio suffered miserably at the hands of demons, as did many other saints.[609]

St. Christina of Stommeln was constantly harassed, beaten, battered, and bruised by fiends. Her many assaults by demons almost drove her to commit suicide. St. Juan Masias had demons tempt and reproach him on the night of his profession. He was attacked bodily by them at

---

[607] Ibid., pp. 29–38; see also Aradi, op.cit., p. 44.
[608] Johnson, op.cit., p. 325.

[609] Cruz, A&D, op.cit., p. 185.

this time and over the next twelve years of his life. Sts. Nicholas of Tolentino, Louis Marie Grignion de Montfort, and Theodore of Alexandria (5 c.) were said to have been beaten frequently by demons during their lifetime.[610] St. Gemma Galgani was so hateful to Satan that he waged a continual war against her and tortured her by bruises and blows, attempting the most abominable deceits to entrap her. She wrote that the devil smeared the pages she was writing on with black hoof-prints and carbon from the fires of hell. These marks can still be seen on the pages of her writings.[611]

St. Colette saw the devil during her adolescent years. He later tormented her appearing in various animal forms such as a roaring black lion and a huge dragon. He also appeared to her in "loathsome human form." She would often dismiss these demons with her crucifix and holy water. However, once she was so roughly treated by these creatures that she laid half-dead on the floor of her cell.[612]

The Curé of Ars, St. John Vianney, once said that the evil one only tempts those souls that wish to abandon sin and those that are in the state of grace. The others belong to him: he has no need to tempt them. The Curé of Ars added that "the greatest of all evils is not to be tempted because there are then grounds for believing that the devil looks upon that soul as his property."[613]

St. John Vianney himself was sensibly persecuted by devils. After 1824, his few hours of nocturnal sleep were said to be interrupted and disturbed by diabolical attacks such as strange phenomena, deafening nocturnal noises, insulting conversation, cruel beatings, and, once, a fire in his bed. At night the infernal enemy would rouse him from his few hours' sleep by thundering blows upon the doors and walls of the presbytery.[614] On December 4, 1826, this simple priest claimed that the devil took form in his room and vomited in front of him. Another time, this saintly soul witnessed the devil in the form of a serpent at a sick parishioner's home. On still another occasion the Curé of Ars described seeing Satan in the form of a black dog at three a.m. in the morning.[615] These diabolical onslaughts continued to torment the saint for the remainder of his life and were attested to by dozens of impeccable witnesses.[616] Toward the end of his life, St. Godric (c. 1069–1170) experienced preternatural phenomena believed to be of diabolic origin. These were remarkably similar to those recorded of St. John Vianney mentioned above.[617]

Both Blessed Anna Maria Taigi and stigmatic Sister Josefa Menendez (1890–1923) were also said to have been assaulted by demons in ways reminiscent of St. John Vianney. Satan was given great power over both of them. Blessed Anna Maria Taigi had demons appear to her in horrible forms. They frequently disturbed her prayers by suggesting unclean imaginings and doubts against the faith.[618] Sister Josefa experienced great temptations by Satan against her vocation. He would hound her soul throughout most of her remaining life. It was said that she had been showered with blows that fell from invisible fists day and night, during the times she was impatient and especially when she was praying. Like St. John Vianney, she was buffeted, bruised, and thrown to the ground, and

---

[610] Johnson, op.cit., p. 325.
[611] Lord, VMS, op.cit., p. 341.
[612] Cruz, A&D, op.cit., pp. 172, 199.
[613] Freze, TBWC, op.cit., p. 133.

[614] Bert Ghezzi, *Voices of the saints: A 365–Day Journey with our Spiritual Companions*. Chicago: Loyola Press, 2000, pp. 634–35; [referred to as Ghezzi, VOS in future]; Summers, op.cit., p. 70.
[615] Freze, VVA, op.cit., p. 289.
[616] Summers, op.cit., p. 70.
[617] Farmer, op.cit., p. 227.
[618] Ibid., p. 52.

her clothing burned on her very body. Josefa survived but was severely burned in this attack. There are few who have experienced as many diabolical attacks as this humble victim soul of God.[619] Blessed Helen dei Cavalcanti (1396–1458) suffered demonic temptations to commit suicide. She was often bruised and twice had her leg broken by the evil one.[620]

Blessed Catherine of Racconigi is also said to have been persecuted by devils disguised as men, beasts, birds, and corpses, but she was defended by saints and angels who took her to heaven, hell, and purgatory.[621] St. Gerard Majella was also reportedly assaulted by demons who annoyed him on many occasions. After their physical attacks when he was bruised all over with blows, Gerard used a few drops of holy water to instantly heal his wounds.[622] St. Padre Pio was likewise plagued by encounters with demons, being attacked by them both spiritually and physically. In fact he was reportedly beaten by them frequently and even seriously injured. His blood-stained pillow can still be seen in his cell at Our Lady of Grace Friary in San Giovanni Rotunda.[623]

St. Teresa of Avila claims to have rarely seen Satan in a bodily form, although she knew of his presence through a vision. The saintly nun reported experiences in which diabolic agents sought her undoing but said she would use holy water to put them to flight.[624] One time, however, when she was sixty-two years old, she is said to have broken her arm when she was thrown down the stairs by demonic means.[625]

There is also the strange saga of St. Catherine of Bologna. Desiring to punish a presumptuous feeling in her at the outset of her religious life, God permitted that she should not detect a diabolic action in herself for some length of time, in spite of the disquiet that accompanied it. Feeling herself favored with great graces, Catherine had said audaciously to the devil: "Know that you could send me no temptation without my perceiving it?" After this imprudent challenge, she had false apparitions of Our Lord and the Blessed Virgin for five years. Catherine then fell into dreadful spiritual aridity until God finally enlightened her completely with regard to this temptation.[626] Blessed Mary of Jesus Crucified (Miriam Baouardy) was said to have fought off demonic possession for a period of forty days.[627]

St. Margaret of Cortona also had confrontations with demons. Once when an evil spirit appeared seeking to terrify her, her guardian angel also appeared to comfort her. The angel told her that he is the guardian of her soul which is an exalted abode of God.[628] Blessed Veronica of Binasco's guardian angel was likewise always with her to help her when she experienced mistreatment by demons.

The devil tried to seduce St. Flora of Beaulieu (1300–1347), and when flattery failed, he used satanic logic: if she did not "agree to delight in the flesh and lose her chastity," he said he would make her life so miserable that she would give up all hope of salvation. Despair was the greatest sin,

[619] DeVinck, *Revelations*, op.cit., p. 82–83.

[620] Joan Carroll Cruz, *Secular saints, 250 canonized and beatified lay men, women and children*. Rockford, Illinois: TAN Books and Publishers, 1989. p. 299 [referred to as Cruz, SS in future].

[621] Gallick, op.cit., p. 274.

[622] Cruz, MMM, op.cit. ,p. 515.

[623] Freze, TBWC, op.cit., p. 284; Johnson, op.cit., p. 325.

[624] Poulain, RAV, op.cit., p. 24 citing *Life*, ch. xxxi, 10; Cruz, MMM, op.cit., p. 515, Wiebe, op.cit., p. 17.

[625] Johnson, op.cit., p. 325.

[626] Poulain, RAV, op.cit., p. 91 citing Bolland, March 9, *Second Life*, no.10ff.

[627] Gallick, op.cit., p. 251.

[628] A.M. Hiral, *The Revelation of Margaret of Cortona*, tr. R. Brown. St. Bonaventura, NY, 1952.

and since there was no forgiveness for it in this world or the next, the devil reasoned, it would be far better for Flora to get the carnal sin over with, then confess and do penance. Of course, Flora rejected this argument, and the more the devil taunted her, the more she prayed. An angel is said to have given Flora a symbolic sword to drive the devil away from her heart. She also fought off the evil one by telling him, "God, without whom you can do nothing, orders you to stop testing me."

Like many other mystics, Blessed Benevenuta Bojani (1255–1292) struggled with the devil. He appeared to her under the most horrifying forms. However, once he appeared as a handsome young man who taunted her and urged her to explore the pleasures of the world with him. When Benevenuta refused, he lifted her into the air and threw her on the floor. Benevenuta called upon Our Lady and fought back. Once she even knocked the devil to the floor and put her foot on his neck while she gave him a piece of her mind. The devil is said to have appeared to Blessed Mary of the Angels (1661–1717) often in the form of a cat. He tempted her to destroy herself. She finally emerged from this temptation with great mystical gifts.[629] The devil who feared Blessed Catherine of Racconigi's influence over souls persecuted and tortured her. He appeared to her in many forms. Her weapon against him was the aspiration "Jesus, my hope!"[630]

St. Lydwina of Schiedam was also the object of violent diabolical attacks throughout her saintly life, as is so often the case with God's chosen victim souls. Frequently harassed and beaten by the evil spirits, she courageously looked to the cross for her liberation.[631] St. Joseph of Cupertino underwent relentless attacks by the devil.

Detail of Demons from Descent of Christ to Limbo, by Andrea di Bonaiuto

The "evil one" tried to drown him, kill him by running him through with a sword, and destroy him by gossip.

St. Veronica Giuliani suffered from misunderstandings caused by some of her close relatives, and her soul was plunged into darkness. Satan was not long in seizing the chance to drive her to despair, and he attacked her spirit relentlessly, suggesting to her that her devotions were wrong and bringing to mind her past sins. In the first year of her religious life, she suffered the slings and arrows of the devil through her sister novices. The "evil one" took on the identity of some of her fellow sisters accusing her of vile misconduct. When that was not enough to destroy her, Satan abused her physically, inflicting wounds, bruising her body mercilessly. The Lord gave her the strength not only to withstand these assaults, but to infuriate the devil as she laughed at his stupid antics.[632]

[629] Gallick, op.cit., pp. 297, 329, 379.
[630] Dorcy, op.cit., p. 272.
[631] Freze, TBWC, op.cit., p. 260.
[632] Lord, VMS ,op.cit., pp. 138, 151, 265.

There is also the well-known case of Magdalena of the Cross. The devil stood before her and said, in essence, if you want, I will see that you get a reputation for sanctity that will last at least thirty years; that way, you will get all of the attention and worldly glory that you could possibly desire. Magdalena agreed to this and Satan kept coming back telling her what to do and how to do it. She instantly regretted her agreement because his appearance was so unspeakably hideous that she could hardly stand it. Magdalena was a great success in her career, serving three times as Abbess of her convent. Satan gave her all kinds of physical phenomena mimicking genuine mystical events. In the end Magdalena confessed to everything and had to be exorcised.[633]

Blessed Alexandrina Maria da Costa was also diabolically assaulted and tormented with horrendous temptations against the faith and with injuries inflicted on her body. Her body was allegedly covered with purplish bruises from the blows received by the evil one. This went on for some ten years until she finally broke loose from his chains.[634]

Venerable Teresa Helena Higginson was continually tormented by the devil who tried to get her to doubt the truth of her revelation regarding the devotion to the Sacred Head of Jesus. She reported to her confessor that the devil beat, dragged, and choked her, roused her when asleep, and threw her out of bed.[635] Venerable Dominica of Paradiso also suffered from diabolical attacks, with blows and burns, one of which brought on blindness in her right eye.[636]

Blessed Anne Catherine Emmerich once received blows to the face from the devil that appeared to her in the form of a great, black dog. Another time, the evil one tried to hurl her down a ladder. She even experienced icy-cold hands grabbing her at her feet, with the intention of throwing her to the ground.

The devil was quick to prey on Marthe Robin who was taking sinners away from him through her sacrificial sufferings. One night, Satan had struck her in the face, breaking two of her teeth. After she entered the Third Order of St. Francis in November of 1928, he continued to manifest himself, threatening to destroy her if she continued to serve God. But Marthe was a strong-willed soul with a divinely-guided mission. In the end, the devil would lose out to this faithful young woman.[637]

St. Catherine of Siena was said to be tormented by diabolic visions as much as ecstasy ravished her. Once, while traveling on a donkey, the devil caused her to be thrown off and she fell headlong into a deep ravine.[638] St. Rose of Lima's bouts with the devil are well known. The evil one frequently threatened and assaulted this child-like saint of God.[639] Her contemporary St. Martin de Porres was visited three times by the devil who tried to deflect him from the path of his faith, but each time he managed to defeat him. The first time the devil took the form of a man who accosted him at the bottom of a flight of stairs. The second time Satan and other demons appeared in his cell one night, hit and shook him, and set his cell on fire. The third time was shortly before Martin's death. This time the devil's tactic was to tell him how saintly he was, trying to make Martin suffer by tempting him to feel vain and superior. This time the Virgin Mary,

[633] Johnson, op.cit., pp. 323–24; Summers, op.cit., pp. 216–18.

[634] Freze, TBWC, op.cit., p. 279.

[635] Paul Hafner, Fr. "Teresa Helena Higginson" in *Inside the Vatican*, March 2005, pp. 60–61; see English translation of Cecil Kerr's *Teresa Helena Higginson, Servant of God* on freespace.virgin.net/ crc.english/thh/.

[636] Biot, op.cit., p. 31.

[637] Freze, TBWC, op.cit., pp. 139, 285–86.

[638] Cruz, A&D, op.cit., p. 198.

[639] Freze, TBWC, op.cit., p. 266.

Temptation of Saint Hilarion by Octave Tassaert

Sts. Dominic, and Vincent Ferrer joined him, and together they pushed the devil away again.[640]

Sts. Hilarion (c. 291–371), Pachomius (c. 292–348), and other holy anchorites also were persecuted by demons. Diabolical trials and molestations might also be cited in the lives of Saint Margaret Fontana (d. 1513), Saint Angela of Foligno, Sts. Frances de Sales, Paul of the Cross, and John Bosco. Some other saints and beati who had encounters with or fierce temptation by demons include Sts. Cuthbert, Guthlac, Elizabeth of Schonau, Peter Celestine, Ignatius Loyola, Catherine Thomas, Bernadette Soubirous, Faustina Kowalska, John of St. Samson (d. 1636), Blessed Villana da Botti, Blessed Elizabeth von Reute, Blessed Mary of the Angels (1661–1717), and Blessed Maria of the Passion of Our Lord Jesus Christ.

Discernment of Spirits

Infused discernment of spirits is a charismatic gift which is granted by God to certain individuals. It is extremely rare, even among the saints, but when it occurs, it is infallible because it is the result of an interior movement of inspiration received from the Holy Spirit, who cannot err.[641] This charism entails the infused gift to see or sense spirits and to determine their nature by their effects. It is a supernatural intuition.[642] Discernment of spirits means that the person can recognize the nature of the spirits involved in supposed mystic phenomena, distinguishing devils from angels, saints, or God Himself (1 Cor 12:10).[643] Sts. Anthony of Egypt, John of Sahagun, Veronica of Binasco, Ignatius of Loyola, Gerard Majella, Vincent de Paul, and Padre Pio, to name a few, all had supernatural visitations and possessed the gift of discerning good and evil spirits.

It is said that six demons presented themselves to St. Frances of Rome one day in the form of six beautiful doves. The saint saw this deception and they then changed into crows and tried to injure her. On another occasion, seven demons appeared to her in the form of seven lambs declaring that they symbolized the seven gifts of the Holy Spirit. She again recognized them and they changed into wolves and tried to attack her. Frances fended off all her encounters with demons with holy water, the Sign of the Cross, or the name of Jesus.[644]

The devil is also said to have used diabolical tricks to increase Padre Pio's torment. He would also appear to him in the form of various friends, colleagues, his confessor and superiors, even in the form of the reigning pontiff and of Jesus, Mary, St. Francis,

---

640 Guiley, op,cit., p. 228.

641 Aumann, op.cit., p. 399.
642 Poulain, RAV, op.cit., p. 97.
643 Johnson, op.cit., p. 45.
644 Ibid., p. 325; see also Bolland, March 9; *First Life*, Book III, no. 37; Poulain, RAV, op.cit., p. 87.

and his guardian angel. These were also said to include apparitions as an "angel of light." This holy Capuchin was able to distinguish between the real apparitions and the illusions created by the devil by carefully analyzing his state of mind and the feelings produced in him during the apparitions. He recognized the diabolical ruse by a certain feeling of apprehension and disgust, and to prove the true identity of the apparitions, he insisted that the demon utter words of praise to Jesus Christ, an order the entity always refused. Whereas diabolical visions gave Padre Pio an uneasy and unholy feeling, actual visions of holy persons gave him a feeling of love, exhilaration, and contentment.[645]

Satan once appeared to St. Martin of Tours as an "angel of light" saying he was Christ. He was clad in a royal garment with his head encircled with a diadem. Martin said that he would not recognize him as the Savior unless he saw him with the stigmata and the Cross, whereupon the diabolical phantom vanished, leaving behind an intolerable odor.[646] Demons showed themselves to St. Maria Magdalena de' Piazzi in the form of the Eternal Father, Our Lord, and, at other times, as the Holy Spirit or one of Maria's own angelic protectors. She was able to see through all these disguises as the devil eventually betrayed himself.

Demons have been known to appear in more pleasing and celestial forms, such as in the form of the Blessed Virgin Mary. Once, St. Peter Martyr had such a vision of Mary. He held high a pyx with a consecrated host and addressed the false vision with the words "If you are the Mother of God, adore your son." The devil left in dismay.[647]

Ecstasy

It is within the realm of the mystical experience that the state of ecstasy is found. Genuine mystical ecstasy is an outreach by God. It is the spiritual state of being pulled by God out of one's normal state of existence into intimate union with Him. It is a mystical enrapture of the body and soul. It is a state of heightened consciousness in which one is infused with joy, awe, wonder, rapture, and love. During genuine ecstasy, the bodily senses cease to function and the soul very nearly leaves the body as in death.[648] True ecstasy is supernatural, sacred, and worthy of respect from us.[649]

Following the affective state of prayer, ecstasy is the first true stage of the divine union that involves the transmission of divine mysteries and impulses directly to the soul, as well as the infusion of divine love into the depths of one's very being. It is in the so-called ecstatic state that a visionary might receive divine messages and/or experience visions and apparitions of Christ, His Mother Mary, the angels, and the saints. It is in this state that the wounds of love, including the Sacred Stigmata, impress themselves upon the body of the chosen one. Ecstatics often receive prophecies and revelations during this initiation into the divine union, both for private use and for public exhortation or instruction. And here the chosen soul begins to experience a host of supernatural phenomena, be they extraordinary charisms for the benefit of the faithful, or inspirations and delights that invite the soul to a more intimate relationship with God.[650]

Supernatural ecstasy may be defined as a state which, while it lasts, includes two elements: the one, interior and invisible, when the mind rivets its attention on a

---

645 Cruz, A&D, op,cit., p. 182.
646 Ibid., p. 170.
647 Ibid., pp. 177–78.

648 Johnson, op.cit., p. 359; NCE, 2nd ed., op.cit., v. 5, p. 60.
649 Farges, op.cit., p. 444.
650 Freze, TBWC, op.cit., p. 145.

Saint Francis of Assisi in Ecstasy by Anthony van Dyck

Saint Teresa of Avila in Ecstasy, 1652, by Bernini

religious subject; the other, corporeal and visible, when the activity of the senses is suspended so that not only are external sensations incapable of influencing the soul but considerable difficulty is experienced in awakening such sensations, and this difficulty is experienced whether the ecstatic himself desires to do so or others attempt to quicken the organs into action.

While in this state, the visionary does not react to external stimuli in a normal way. He or she can be poked, burned, or tickled, for example, without showing any signs of reaction. The eyes do not blink when touched or when the individual is startled, nor do they dilate when a bright light is placed directly upon them. Even one's blood pressure and nerve reactions do not alter when there are repeated attempts to do so. Many tests with sophisticated machines have confirmed these facts concerning authentic ecstatic experience.[651] Reportedly, the visionaries from Medjugorje collectively entered into such an ecstatic state that medical and scientific researchers from Milan and the French University of Montpellier described them as "removed from the spatio-temporal order." St. Theresa of Avila first experienced ecstasy at age forty-three, but Venerable Mary of Agreda was given that gift at age eighteen. St. Peter of Alcantara experienced his first ecstasy at age six, and Sts. Hildegard of Bingen and Catherine of Siena and many others experienced it at the age of four.[652]

In Christian mysticism, ecstasy is a temporary state that accompanies contemplative prayer; it is an intense, though passing,

[651] Freze, VVA, op.cit., p. 303.
[652] Johnson, op.cit., p. 33.

awareness of the soul's union with God which may be either pleasant (as when sensory awareness is gently suspended) or painful (as when the soul is suddenly "seized away" from its senses). A person in ecstasy is usually radiant in the face and unaware of anything around him (including things touching him). Ecstasy is the by-product of prayer, whose object is not to produce an experience but to progress in the love of God.[653] Because the soul is not purified enough to stand in His constant presence while in this earthly life, ecstatic moments are generally short. Nevertheless, they affect the soul permanently with an infusion of the divine love that a lifetime of normal effort could not achieve.

Some of the most profound ecstatic experiences that every stigmatic has known are those called the Passion ecstasies. In this state, the victim relives the Passion scenes of Gethsemane, the Way of the Cross, and even Calvary itself, where the "mystical death" occurs. Here the stigmatic participates in every suffering that Christ endured during those last moments of His life. St. Francis of Assisi, the first officially recognized stigmatic in history, was granted the favor of suffering the Passion. He received the Five Sacred Wounds during an ecstatic state while on Mt. Alverna, Italy two years prior to his death.[654] One of the greatest examples of the Passion ecstasies can be found in Theresa Neumann, who experienced more than seven hundred separate visions of the sufferings of Christ from 1926 up to her death in 1962. It is said that these ecstasies were each divided into roughly thirty-five to fifty individual visions, lasting every week for half the year from Thursday evening through late Friday or early Saturday. Blessed Alexandrina da Costa suffered some 180 Passion ecstasies in her lifetime, which included the agony,

the scourging, the crowning of thorns, and the vision of Mother Mary at the foot of the Cross.[655]

In Sacred Scripture, ecstasy accompanies the communication of God's word to the prophets. Ecstasy in the Old Testament is sometimes indicated when it is said that the Spirit of the Lord came upon someone (Nm 11:25; 24:2; 1 Sm 10:6, 10; 19:20; 2 Kgs 3:15; Ex 3:14; 11:24) and, in some cases, when an individual is said to "behave like a Prophet" (Nm 11:25; 1 Sm 10, 5–6, 10, 13; 19:20). In the New Testament, Jesus is depicted as experiencing a kind of ecstasy at key moments such as His baptism (Mk 1:9–11); and His Transfiguration (Mk 9:2–8). St. Peter also had such an experience of ecstasy on Mount Tabor when, along with Sts. James and John, he was given a wonderful vision of Christ's glory and a foreshadowing of the kingdom of heaven. In ecstasy, St. Peter cried out, "Lord, it is good for us to be here." Ecstatic visions befell Zechariah (Lk 1:67–69), Sts. Stephen (Acts 7:55), Peter (Acts 10:10, 11:5), and John (Rv 1:10). At Pentecost, the gathered disciples are dramatically possessed by the Holy Spirit (Acts 2:2–4). The most important New Testament ecstatic figure, however, is St. Paul. In the New Testament, both Sts. Peter and Paul are said to have gone into ecstasy while praying (Acts 10:10; 22:17). Luke clearly presents St. Paul's conversion and other key events in his life as ecstatic (Acts 9:3–19; 16:9–10; 18:9–10; 22:17–21; 26:12–19). Most importantly, St. Paul describes himself in 2 Corinthians 12:1–4 as a man "caught up in the third heaven" who was put in mysterious communication with the divinity and "heard things that cannot be told."[656] St. Bonaventure relates in his Life of St. Francis that Francis learned things in his ecstasies that he (also) would never

---

[653] Stavinskas, op.cit., p. 285.
[654] Freze, TBWC, op.cit., pp. 147–48.
[655] Ibid. pp. 150–52.
[656] NCE, 2nd ed, op.cit., v. 5, pp. 60–61.

disclose to any man as long as he lived.

Some of the early anchorites experienced ecstatic rapture. St. Macarius of Egypt (c. 300–390) was nearly always in ecstasy and communed thus with God almost the whole day. St. Arsenius (c. 355–450) remained so during whole nights. Ecstasy among the anchorites was often accompanied by visions.[657]

A large number of other saints have been granted ecstasies from the spirit of God. Normally the ecstatic sees and hears nothing around him or her and cannot speak. Many mystics like St. Frances of Rome and Theresa Neumann could hear only their confessors but no one else.[658] A state of ecstasy isn't just slipping off into some kind of a daydream, but a genuine mystic phenomenon: being drawn, gently or powerfully, by God into a sort of spiritual embrace. It's being pulled by an external agency—God—out of one's normal state of existence.[659]

An ecstasy may be accompanied by concomitant physical phenomena such as bilocation, levitation, inedia, radiating light, supernatural odors, and, in some cases, the impression of the stigmata.[660] As said previously, genuine mystical ecstasy is a partial separation of the soul from the body. But because the soul does not separate entirely from the body, the body sometimes moves upward with the soul. This is levitation, an ecstatic state in which the mystic simply rises from the ground and stays there usually for a fairly short period of time, caught up in the contemplation of the Divine,[661] although there are instances whereby the ecstatica remain in ecstasy for longer periods of time or experience an uninterrupted series of ecstasies. St. Ignatius was

in ecstasy a week; St. Collette a fortnight, and St. Mary Maddalena de' Pazzi, as long as forty days. Venerable Passitea Crogi experienced a four-day ecstasy. Blessed Osanna d'Andreasi and Saint Angela of Foligno both had ecstasies of three days duration while Blessed Archangela Girlani and Venerable Beatrice Mary of Jesus had ecstatic experiences lasting twenty-four hours. St. Thomas of Villanova remained for twelve hours in ecstasy and suspended in the air, rigid as a marble statue.[662]

St. Catherine dei Ricci, Bl. Elisabetta Canori-Mora, and Venerable Ursula Benincasa are examples of those whose ecstasies were so frequent as to be almost uninterrupted. Then there is the case of Sts. John of the Cross and Teresa of Avila who both allegedly went into ecstasy and levitated while once walking together and speaking about Jesus.[663] Blessed Maria Mancini of Pisa (1355–1431) likewise would go into ecstasy while walking along the street[664] as did Bl. Anna Maria Taigi. The latter reportedly used to slip into an ecstasy in the middle of the street, tying up traffic, if she happened to see a cross or an image of Jesus or Mary.[665] St. Catherine of Siena went limp into ecstasy at will.[666] Marie Julie Jahenny was completely insensitive to pain or intense light during her ecstasies.[667]

Thus, ecstatic states involve the exaltation and the inexpressible joy of unencumbered communication with God. St. Maria Maddalena de' Pazzi, the so-called "Ecstatic Saint," was favored with multiple and intense ecstasies. Her ecstasies were rich experiences of union with God and marvelous insights into divine truths.

---

[657] Farges, op.cit., p. 24.
[658] Johnson, op.cit., p. 125.
[659] Ibid., p. 46.
[660] Summers, op.cit, p. 96; Farges, op.cit., p. 453.
[661] Johnson, op.cit., pp. 126–27.

[662] Farges, op.cit., pp. 171, 452.
[663] Johnson, op.cit., p. 76.
[664] See http://irondequoitcatholic.org/php/Bl/ MaryofPisa.
[665] See http://michaeljournal.org/taiga.
[666] Ghezzi, MM, op.cit., p. xii.
[667] Miracles, op.cit., p. 6.

Ecstasy of St Margaret of Cortona, 1622, by Giovanni Lanfranco

During one of her ecstatic states, St. Clare of Montefalco is said to have seen the heavenly court of saints inviting her into heaven. She related that her bridal party, the saints and the angels, were awaiting her, and Jesus, her bridegroom, was standing at the high altar and God the Father was presiding. While rapt in ecstasy, St. Gertrude the Great saw her guardian angel bearing her prayers to the throne of the Divine Majesty presenting them to the three Divine Persons and imploring them to hear her petitions. St. Miguel de los Santos, like several other saints, reportedly received the mystical exchange of his heart with the Sacred Heart of Jesus while in ecstasy.

St. Frances Borgia's contemplation of the Eucharist, while in ecstasy, was so profound that his Masses, like those of St. Padre Pio, took too long to be offered in public. St. Sharbel Makhluf once went so far into a suspended state of ecstasy as to ignore the lightning that singed his vestments when it struck the altar on which he was celebrating Mass.[668]

It should be noted that if a person has reached the stage of ecstasy, there is a probability in favor of having a private revelation, but nothing more, since the ecstatic saints have sometimes suffered from illusions, and their imagination came into action either during or after the divine visitation.[669] In order to judge whether ecstasies are divine, one needs to apply the same principles regarding the person's character as in the case of revelations.[670] Another key element for the discernment of credible ecstasies is whether or not they function to create holiness, good order, and loving community in the relations of the peoples of God among themselves and with their neighbors.[671]

There are numerous servants of God mentioned throughout this work who reportedly experienced ecstasies. Here are a few that are not mentioned: Sts. Monica (331–387), Bonaventure (1225–1274), Zdislava Berka (1210–1252), Aloysius Gonzaga, and Blessed Marcolino Amanni (1317–1397).[672]

Exchange of Hearts

Since the heart is regarded as the seat of affections and emotions, it seems appropriate that the heart would figure in the mystical life of saints. And that the Lord would want to reside there.[673] The exchange of hearts is a mystical phenomenon which consists in the extraction of the heart of the mystic and the substitution of another, presumably the heart of Christ. After the phenomenon occurs, the mystic often bears a

---

668 Johnson. op.cit., pp. 46–47.
669 Poulain, RAV, op.cit., p. 73.
670 Ibid., p. 96.
671 NCE, 2nd ed., v. 5, op.cit., p. 61.
672 Miracles, op.cit., p. 6.
673 Cruz, MMM, op.cit., p. 66.

wound and then a scar over the place in which the substitution of hearts was made. How can this phenomenon be explained? It can hardly be doubted to have occurred, granted the testimony that is given in the lives of so many of the saints. The only plausible explanation is that it is strictly miraculous. The difficulty revolves around the apparent substitution of the heart of Christ for the heart of a human being. Pope Benedict XIV gave the most plausible theological explanation when he stated in his eulogy of St. Michael de los Santos that the exchange of hearts was a mystical and spiritual exchange.[674] In her apparitions, Christ represented himself to St. Lutgardis as showing her His Heart. She was perhaps the first saint in whom the mystical exchange of hearts was effected.

St. Catherine of Siena experienced an exchange of hearts with the Lord. While in ecstasy, Jesus opened the left side of her chest and placed His Heart within it saying, "As I took your heart away, now, you see, I am giving you Mine, so that you can go on living with it forever." He closed the opening He had made but as a sign of the miracle, a scar remained. In a vision, the Lord extracted the heart of Venerable Dominica of Paradiso, a Florentine member of the Dominican Order, from her chest and submitted one of burning fire. She had been ill before this vision but after it regained her health. St. Margaret Mary Alacoque had many apparitions of Our Lord in which He gave instructions for the implementation of the devotion of the Sacred Heart. In her autobiography, she writes that Our Lord "asked me for my heart, which I begged Him to take. He did so and placed it in His own adorable Heart, where He showed it to her as a little atom which was being consumed in this great furnace, and withdrawing it hence as a

Saint Catherine of Siena Exchanging Her Heart with Christ
by Giovanni di Paolo

burning flame in the form of a heart.[675] St. Maria Maddalena de' Pazzi, the so-called "Ecstatic Saint," experienced the most supreme mystery of exchange of Hearts. Our Lord took His Sacred Heart from His breast and placed it within the bosom of the Carmelite, exchanging His Heart for her own.[676] St. Michael of the Saints who, it is said, lived in a constant state of rapture and seemed more an angel than a man, received, on a day he was in ecstasy, the mystical exchange of his heart with the Sacred Heart of the Lord.[677]

Some others who received the grace of the exchange of hearts include St. Catherine dei Ricci, Blessed Maria of the Passion of Our Lord Jesus Christ, and Saint Mariam Thresia Chiramel Mankidyan (1876–1926).[678]

---

674 Aumann, ST, op.cit., p. 434.

675 Cruz, MMM, op.cit., pp. 73, 75, 558.
676 Summers, op.cit., p. 194.
677 Cruz, MMM, op.cit., pp. 75–76.
678 See http://mariamthresia.org/?p+206.

Flevit super illam (Latin); He wept over it, 1892, by Enrique Simonet

Gift of Tears
(Gift of Compunction)

This charism is the spiritual and emotional reaction to the pervading sorrows for sin that accompanies spiritual awareness and knowledge, often won by heroic ascetic practices. The tears may be spiritual or bodily, or both, but the gift differs from purely psychological fits of depression in that it usually brings with it consolation. It is often the first discernable mystic gift, differing in substance and quality from the tears of penitence that characterize advancement in ascetic practice.[679] Symeon, the new theologian (949–1022), calls the Gift of Tears the "Baptism of the Holy Spirit." Eastern writers say that while Baptism cleanses us from past sins, the Gift of Tears reflects God's washing us of our present sins. They call it the "Second Baptism."

Jesus, the ultimate victim soul, wept for the people of Jerusalem (Lk 19:41). How often St. Peter and St. Mary Magdalen must have thought about their sins and expressed their grief to the Lord. Mary, especially, after seven demons were cast out of her (Lk 8:2) and Peter after realizing he had denied knowing Christ and going out to weep bitterly (Mt 26:75).

St. John of God was hit so hard by tears during his conversion that his behavior became erratic and he was locked up as a lunatic for a period of time.[680] Even St. Francis of Assisi, the most cheerful saint imaginable, wept so much in private that he contracted a serious eye disorder from it. He went entirely blind during the last years of his life.[681] Many of the associates of St. Dominic recall the tears he shed while praying, being unable to "stop himself from bursting out loudly, so that even at a distance people could hear him roaring and crying." St. Lutgardis wept tears in such abundance that her biographer commented that he once saw such floods of tears that he could scarcely bear it without weeping himself.[682] St. Maria Maddalena de' Pazzi beheld in a supernatural

[679] Johnson. op.cit, pp. 365–66.

[680] Guiley, op.cit., p. 186.
[681] Johnson. op.cit., p. 36.
[682] Fanning, op.cit., pp. 93, 97.

way all the sins of the world and the malice of them. She became drowned in tears and could not stop crying until Sts. Augustine and Catherine of Siena appeared to her and turned her sorrow into joy.[683] St. Louis Marie Grignion de Montfort had the gift to trigger the gift of tears in those who came to jeer at him or stone him.[684] St. Ignatius of Loyola recorded daily visitations of tears. He sometimes spent the whole night weeping aloud for his sins.[685] A vision of the Trinity affected him so much that he could not keep from weeping and sobbing.[686] The Russian bishop St. Tikhon of Zadonsk was especially favored with the gift of tears. At times while celebrating Mass he would weep and sob audibly even though many were in attendance. The same could be said about St. Padre Pio who cried almost continually while saying Mass. Blessed Mary of Oiginies was given to abundant tears that flowed down in streams. Her weeping became so loud that a priest had to ask her to control herself. St. Catherine of Siena also disrupted church services by her loud weeping (218). Nilus of Sora (c. 1433–1508), St. Gregory the Great (540–604), and Francisco de Osuna (1492–1540) affirmed tears as one of the essential gifts of the Holy Spirit.[687]

Blessed John Liccio (1400–1511), a Dominican priest for ninety-six years, was frequently in ecstasy and was what might be called an "easy weeper," any strong emotion caused him to dissolve in a flood of tears. Mary Razzi (1552–1600) also possessed the "gift of tears." Most of her tears were shed for man's ingratitude to God.[688] Some others who experienced the gift of tears phenomenon include: Bl. Augustine of Biella, Sts. Paul, Patrick, Gemma Galgani, John Climacus (579–649), Gertrude the Great, Francis de Sales, John of the Cross, Margaret Mary Alacoque, Teresa of Avila, and Margaret of Ypres (1216–1237).[689]

Gift of Tongues

This mystical phenomenon does not deal with tongues as they pertain to the charismatic movement. Instead, the gift of tongues treated here involves saints speaking in their own language, but being understood by many others who speak a different language. This preternatural gift also known as glossalalia is described by St. Luke as what happened at Pentecost. Scripture says: "These signs will accompany those who believe. . . . They will speak new languages" (Mk 16:17). Many saints were given this ability, including St. Anthony of Padua. Brother Ugolino describes an incident in his book entitled *The Little Flowers of St. Francis* when St. Anthony was preaching before the Pope and Cardinals from different countries. Inspired by the Holy Spirit, he explained the Word of God so effectively that all present heard and understood every one of his words as if he had spoken in each of their languages.[690] It is also said that while preaching in Italy he spoke in perfect Italian and while in France he preached in French although he had never studied these languages. St. Vincent Ferrer, the celebrated Dominican, delivered his sermons in Latin or Limousin, the language of his native Valencia, but reliable writers attest that all his hearers, French, Greeks, Germans, Sardinians, Hungarians, and Italians, understood every word he spoke.[691] He made himself

---

683 Summers, op.cit., p. 194.

684 Johnson. op.cit., p. 94.

685 Ibid., p. 55; see also Fanning, op.cit., pp. 154, 218.

686 Raphael Brown, *Saints Who Saw Mary.* Rockford, Illinois, TAN Books and Publishers, 1994, p. 113.

687 Fanning, op.cit., pp. 51, 95, 218.

688 Dorcy, op.cit., pp. 240, 345.

689 Fanning, op.cit., p. 99.

690 Raphael Brown, *The little flower of St. Francis.* Garden City, NY: Image Books, 1958, p. 130.

691 Cruz, MMM, op.cit., pp. 240–41, 529.

The Pentecost by Antonio Palomino

understood through the gift of tongues.[692] This so-called "Angel of Judgment" enjoyed tremendous success making converts by the tens of thousands, especially in Spain where he converted thousands of Jews and Moors.[693] St. Francis Solano (1549–1610), known as the "Wonder Worker of the New World," was sent to convert the Indians in Argentina, Brazil, Paraguay, and Peru. He learned the difficult Indian languages in a very short time and he, likewise, was understood wherever he went.[694] St. Louis Bertrand, a Dominican missionary, was sent to preach to the Indians of Panama. He was also favored with the gift of tongues and often spoke in languages with which he was naturally unfamiliar.[695] St. Dominic de Guzman, on one occasion, enabled himself and some of his fellow monks to converse with German monks in their own language. A language which was unknown to them.[696] Other saints said to have been favored with this ability include: Sts. Philip Benizi (1233–1285), Bernadine of Siena, Ignatius Loyola, Francis Xavier, Martin de Porres, Jean-Marie Baptiste Vianney, and Padre Pio.[697]

Hierognosis

This phenomenon relates to a mystic ability to recognize immediately any person, place, or thing that is holy, blessed, or consecrated and to distinguish it from those things that are not.[698] St. John the Baptist recognized Christ when they both were in utero (Lk 1:44). Those with this gift, for instance, can also determine if a Host has been consecrated or not; if an object has or has not been blessed; the presence of a good or evil spirit (see discernment of spirits); as well as the ability to find lost or hidden objects and holy relics. Many with this gift have been able to discern various relics that have been venerated by the faithful: authentic pieces of the True Cross;other cherished relics of the Passion; bones and articles of clothing from various saints; relics of the Apostles; relics of the Blessed Virgin Mary, etc.[699]

Hierognosis transcends the power of nature and cannot be explained naturally or pre-ternaturally. There is no way in which one could distinguish a blessed or consecrated article from those that are not holy objects. But it should be noted that, whereas many mystics have manifested an almost magnetic attraction for holy objects, the devil or those under his power have manifested the greatest revulsion or horror when any blessed article is brought near them.[700]

Blessed Anne Catherine Emmerich, Sts. Catherine of Siena, Frances of Rome, and Catherine of Genoa had the ability to recognize holiness or evil in any person, place, or thing. There have also been specific mystics who could distinguish, by a kind of spiritual perception, the sacramental presence, recognizing an unconsecrated Host from one that was consecrated. Blessed Sibyllina Biscossi had a lively sense of the Real Presence. One day a priest was going past her window with Viaticum for the sick. She knew that the Host was not consecrated, and told him so. He investigated and it turned out she was right.[701] Theresa Neumann[702] along with Marie-Julie Jahenny, the so-called "Breton Stigmatic," for instance, also possessed this marvelous gift of virtually detecting the Real Presence in the Blessed Sacrament. Both Louise Lateau, a Franciscan tertiary, and Ms. Jahenny could also distinguish blessed

---

[692] Guiley, op.cit., p. 343.
[693] Delaney, op.cit., p. 499.
[694] Cruz, MMM, op.cit., pp. 243–44.
[695] Dorcy, op.cit., p. 317.
[696] Guiley, op.cit., p. 93.
[697] Miracles, op.cit., p. 20.
[698] Aumann, ST, op.cit., p. 431.
[699] Freze, TBWC, op.cit., pp. 178, 180.
[700] Aumann, ST, op.cit., p. 431.
[701] Dorcy, op.cit., p. 174.
[702] Summers, op.cit., p. 60.

objects from those that were not blessed. Ms. Lateau could only retain a Host that had been validly consecrated. She was once given an unconsecrated wafer and suffered intolerable pains.[703]

There have also been saints and holy persons who could feel the presence of the Savior in the Blessed Sacrament. Such was the case of St. Rose of Lima and Venerable Mary of Agreda.[704] Theresa Neumann is said to have felt the sacramental presence of the Savior in the divine Host. She is said to not only have felt the Lord's presence but perceived His presence in others who had just received Communion. She also felt Him in Viaticum and when passing by a Church. Theresa also had the faculty of receiving the sacred Host in a state of "exalted repose." When the Host was placed on her tongue, it disappeared spontaneously so that no movement of deglutition could be perceived. Theresa felt that the sacred species remained in her almost up to the moment of her next Communion.[705]

Some others such as the Franciscan Saint Angela of Foligno and Bl. Ida of Louvain could reportedly taste the presence of the Lord. Still others like the Premonstratensian Sts. Herman Joseph, Catherine of Siena, and Philip Neri could smell a heavenly fragrance in the Host. Sts. Paschal Babylon, Joseph of Cupertino, and Bl. Henry Suso claimed to hear the Lord in the Host. Very many holy persons to include Sts. Catherine of Siena, Joseph of Cupertino, Veronica of Binasco, Bl. Mary of Oignes, Venerable Dominica of Paradiso, and Venerable Teresa Helena Higginson were said to be able to miraculously see Christ in the Host.[706]

Incorruptibility (Supernatural)

Incorruptibility is the complete absence after many years (it may be centuries) from normal cadaver putrefaction. This phenomenon can be caused by any number of unusual but purely natural factors, and it does not, in itself, carry any particular importance in mystic theology.[707] Many of the saints' bodies often remained fragrant, supple, and un-decayed against all the normal laws of death. This is another reminder that God will raise the body on Judgment Day. Two of the most remarkable cases of this phenomenon are those of St. Bernadette Soubirous, who died in 1879, and St. Catherine Laboure, who died in 1876. St. Bernadette's body rests in a glass case in her convent in Nevers, France, where it is visited by thousands of pilgrims each year. St. Catherine Laboure's body rests in a glass case in the chapel of the motherhouse of the Sisters of Charity at 140 Rue du Bac, in Paris. The book by Joan Carroll Cruz entitled *The Incorruptibles* cites 102 cases of incorruption of canonized saints, beati, and venerables.

Saints' bodies like that of St. Louis Bertrand have remained incorrupt for 350 years; eleventh-century miracle workers St. Cuthbert and St. Romuald (951–1027) for over 400 years, and Blessed Margaret of Savoy for over 500 years.[708] Never embalmed bodies such as that of St. Agnes of Montepulciano and Blessed Mattia Nazzarei of Matelica (1252–1319) have remained whole and incorrupt for hundreds of years.[709]

Parts of bodies like the tongues of the great preachers Sts. Anthony of Padua[710] and John Nepomucine (c.1340–1393) and

---

[703] Biot, op.cit., p. 61.
[704] Summers, op.cit., p. 60.
[705] Biot, op.cit., pp. 68–70.
[706] Summers, op.cit., p. 60.

[707] Johnson. op.cit., p. 361.
[708] Cruz, Inc, op.cit., pp. 53, 146, 185.
[709] Ibid., pp.107–8; see also Cruz, MMM, p. 369.
[710] Guiley, op.cit., p. 31.

Reliquary containing the incorrupt body of Saint Bernadette, photo by Jabonsbachek

Blessed Battista Varani (1458–1524);[711] the right foot of St. Camillus de Lellis; the finger of St. Catherine of Siena,[712] the right hand of St. Stephen, King of Hungary (975–1038),[713] both hands of St. Catherine Laboure; the arms of St. Nicholas of Tolentino;[714] the skull of St. Agatha (d. 251);[715] the hearts of Sts. Clare of Montefalco, Teresa of Avila, Camillus de Lellis, Francis de Sales, Jane Frances de Chantal, Vincent de Paul (1580–1660), Veronica Giuliani, Catherine Laboure, and Jean Baptiste Marie Vianney were all found to be incorrupt after their deaths.[716]

Several saints' bodies, such as those of Sts. Catherine of Bologna, Sharbel Makhluf, and Pacifico of San Severino, which were consigned to the grave without a coffin for a period of time before being reburied, remain unsullied. The bodies of other saints left exposed for weeks before burial such as those of Sts. Angela Merici, Bernardine of Siena, and Theresa Margaret of the Sacred Heart remained without decay.[717]

The bodies of the following saints were consigned to the grave without a coffin or whose coffin was packed with lime for a period of time before being reburied remain incorrupt:

St. Josaphat, the archbishop of Polotsk, Poland, was hacked and beaten to death and his remains thrown into the Dvina River at Vitebsk, Russia. His mutilated body remained in the water for five days before it was retrieved and interred at Biala in Podlesie. Five years after his death, his remains were found perfectly incorrupt and pliable. When the body was reexamined twenty-seven years later, the mortal wound on the forehead of the saint opened and discharged fresh red blood.[718]

---

[711] Johnson. op.cit., p. 155.

[712] Cruz, Inc, op.cit., p. 222.

[713] Cruz, SS, op.cit., p. 684.

[714] Cruz, Inc, op.cit., p. 97.

[715] Freze, VVA, op.cit., p. 42.

[716] Cruz, Inc, op.cit., pp. 104, 190, 230, 240, 249, 253, 273, 285.

[717] Ibid., pp. 34–35, 295.

[718] Ibid., pp. 36, 232–33; see also Cruz, MMM, op.cit., p. 373; Delaney, op.cit., p. 286.

St. Francis Xavier was buried on the island of Shngchuan, within sight of Canton, China. His wooden coffin was packed with lime. Ten weeks later, his casket was raised and the body found to be perfectly preserved under the layer of lime. One hundred forty-two years after his death, his body was reexamined and had the appearance of that of a living man. The body of the saint is enshrined in the Basilica of Bom Jesus in Goa, India.[719]

The body of St. John of the Cross also had a layer of lime placed over it to hasten its reduction. Nine months later, it was found to be perfectly preserved. His incorrupt body can be found today enshrined in a reliquary in Segovia, Spain.[720]

The body of St. Paschal Baylon was likewise covered with quicklime at death so that the flesh would be quickly consumed. However, the saint's body was found to be incorrupt nine months later when exhumed. It even exuded a marvelous fragrance and there was perspiration on his brow and his limbs remained supple.[721]

Perhaps one of the most remarkable cases of a beautiful appearance in death was that of St. Lydwina of Schiedam. In life, she had been wasted by plague and had suffered so many ailments that her body seemed to be held together only by her clothing. This Dutch mystic and victim soul had also been disfigured by a cleft in her forehead. Her ulcers and wounds along with the cleft disappeared completely at her death, giving way to a serene and beautiful appearance. She became as fresh and fair as if she were a young girl of seventeen smiling in her sleep.[722]

At the time of his death, St. Anthony of Padua was described as also being worn thin. His face was haggard by continuous fasting and unceasing labors and he was "enfeebled to the verge of decrepitude." However, after death, his body assumed the incomparable beauty of youth.[723] A similar wonder was the body of St. Therese of the Little Flower. The nuns who prepared her body for burial stated that she seemed no older than twelve or thirteen years old, although she died at age twenty-four after terrible spiritual and physical sufferings.[724] The same could be said of St. Catherine of Bologna whose face became so fresh and beautiful after her death that she looked like a girl of fifteen who had just fallen asleep.[725]

Blessed Alexandrina Maria da Costa had predicted that her body would not remain incorruptible but would turn to ashes without any signs of decomposition. This happened exactly as she said it would and her ashes have been known to emit a heavenly perfume.[726]

Inedia (Mystical Fasts or Supernatural Abstinence)

One gift that has mystified the best minds from the world of science and medicine is that which is known as inedia. This is an absolute and total abstinence from all nourishment beyond the limits of nature.[727] Such an ability to live without material food, other than the bread of the Blessed Sacrament, usually lasts for extended periods of time.[728] Included in this phenomenon is the absence of the elimination of any bodily waste. Many inediacs are also frequent ecstatic visionaries and some are stigmatics.[729]

---

[719] Ibid. pp. 172–73; Cruz, MMM, op.cit., p. 291.

[720] Cruz, MMM, op,cit., pp. 292–93.

[721] Thurston, PPM, op.cit., p. 248; Cruz, MMM, op.cit., pp. 293–94.

[722] Cruz, MMM, op.cit., p. 301; Cruz, SS, op.cit., p. 435.

[723] Cruz, MMM, op.cit., pp. 299–300.

[724] Hebert, SWRD, op.cit., p. 252.

[725] Cruz, MMM, op.cit., p. 303.

[726] Freze, TBWC, op,cit., p. 280.

[727] NCE, I, op.cit., v. 10, p. 174.

[728] Johnson. op.cit., p. 361.

[729] Treece, MB, op.cit., p. 116.

Christ in the Wilderness, 1872, by Ivan Kramskoi

Before the time of Our Lord, who, by His example, consecrated the complete fast of forty days, we have seen Moses, on Mount Sinai, abstaining from all food for the same length of time, before receiving from God the Tables of the Law. So also Elias, after having eaten of the mysterious bread given him by the angel, walked for forty days and nights to Horeb without having need to eat.[730]

Many saints or holy persons have been known to survive for years or decades without food or drink, except for the Holy Eucharist, the Bread of Life.[731] The first mystic whose inedia was examined,

documented, and recorded was Bl. Alpais (d. 1211).[732] If ever it can be sufficiently verified that this inedia is of supernatural origin, it must be considered a suspension of the natural law and a presage, as it were, of the glorified body.

Saint Angela of Foligno was the first person known in history to have lived with total abstinence. She survived this miraculous condition for twelve years without taking any nourishment. Angela is said to have lived solely on Communion brought to her by angels from heaven.[733]

Probably the greatest case of inedia on record and one that has been the most

---

[730] Farges, op.cit., p. 559.
[731] Hebert, SWRD, op.cit., p. 314.

[732] Johnson, op.cit., p. 147.
[733] Biot, op.cit., p. 59; Freze, TBWC, op.cit., p. 185.

thoroughly investigated and best documented is that of the lay stigmatic Theresa Neumann who lived without food from 1922 to 1962. It began in 1922 with a throat infection which made it impossible for her to swallow food or even a drop of water and lasted to her death forty years later. After this, she lost all desire for food. She took only a small particle of the consecrated Host, with a sip of water, but after September 1927, she did not even take the water. From 1930 on, she did not have any bodily discharges and no urine, no feces, no menses. Aside from this, she enjoyed robust health and even steadily gained weight despite her proven abstinence. This was remarkable because she bled so profusely on those Fridays when she relived blow-by-blow the Passion of Christ that her clothing, bed linen, and mattress were completely soaked in blood.[734]

At the age of twenty, St. Catherine of Siena, had a vision of the Sacred Heart whereby she promised the Lord to fast for the salvation of souls. She then declined all food, even bread and water. Whenever she was forced to eat anything, she became sick with violent retching pains. Her inedia lasted about eight years.[735]

St. Catherine of Genoa's life was marked by frequent ecstatic absorptions and by long, mysterious fasts (inedia) during which she was unable to take food. It is claimed that for twenty-three Lents and as many Advents, the saint took no solid food at all but occasionally drank a glassful of a beverage made up of water, vinegar, and pounded salt.[736]

It is also alleged that St. Lydwina of Schiedam, the Dutch mystic and victim soul,

subsisted virtually on nothing except a small communion wafer once a week for twenty-eight years; as did the Venerable Dominica of Paradiso for twenty years; Blessed Nicholas Von Flue for nineteen years; Blessed Elisabeth von Reute for fifteen years;[737] Blessed Anne Catherine Emmerich for the last twelve years of her life[738] and Blessed Catherine of Racconigi for ten years. Following visions of Jesus and the Blessed Virgin Mary, St. Lutgard began the first of her three-year fasts for the reparation of sinners during which she lived on nothing but bread and weak beer.[739]

In modern times, Louise Lateau, the Belgian stigmatic took no food except weekly communion after March 30, 1871 until she died in 1883.[740] Throughout this time, according to Dr. Imbert-Goubeyre, she produced nothing from her bowels, and her urine output was no more than two spoonful a week, though her monthly periods were normal.[741] Any solid food caused her acute suffering. She is also among the inediacs who did not drink. Even working on the farm in the heat of summer, she did not need even a spoonful of water. Somehow spared dehydration and nourished by no more than the Eucharistic wafer, Louise continued with farm labors for five years until the age of twenty-six. In May 1876, she became bedridden. She died seven years later at thirty-three, having sworn to the end that she had neither eaten nor drunk anything for a dozen years.[742] Theresa Neumann ate very little from 1926 until her death in 1962.[743]

---

[734] Johnson, op.cit., pp. 148–49; Freze, TBWC, op.cit., pp. 186–87.
[735] Cruz, MMM, op. cit., pp. 249–50; Freze, TBWC, op.cit., p. 174; Biot, op.cit., p. 59.
[736] Thurston, op.cit., p. 213; see also Cruz, MMM, op.cit., p. 253.

[737] Ibid., p. 341.
[738] Johnson, op.cit., p. 261.
[739] Cruz, MMM, op.cit., pp. 248, 255.
[740] Summers, op.cit., p. 166.
[741] Wilson, op.cit., p. 113.
[742] Treece, MB, op.cit., p. 119.
[743] Freeze, TBWC, op.cit., p. 281.

After eighteen years of invalidism, on Good Friday 1942, the now thirty-eight year old ecstatic visionary Blessed Alexandrina Maria da Costa believed Christ said to her: "You will not take food again on earth. Your food will be my flesh; your blood will be my divine blood, your life will be my life. You receive it from me when I unite my heart to your heart." So for the last thirteen years of her life, she was imbued with the mystical phenomenon of being nourished solely by the Eucharist.

By 1932, Marthe Robin had given up eating altogether except for the Holy Eucharist (inedia). For forty-nine years, from 1932 to her death in 1981, she neither drank nor ate anything. The only thing that entered her body was the tiny Eucharistic wafer.[744]

Marie-Julie Jahenny showed a marked disinclination to eat from the onset of her stigmata. Her inedia lasted over five years. Throughout this period there was no excretion, either liquid or solid.[745] A twelve-year abstinence from food (always, of course, excepting the consecrated Host received in Holy Communion) was observed in the case for Maria-Dominica Lazzari,[746] and St. Gemma Galgani went without food except the Blessed Sacrament from Pentecost in June 1902 until her death on April 11, 1903.

Some other saints and beati who ate hardly anything except the Eucharistic bread include: Sts. Walburga, Rita of Cascia, Maria Maddalena de Pazzi, Rose of Lima, Mariana de Jesus Paredes y Flores, Blessed Mary of Oignies, Blessed Columba of Rieti,[747] and Blessed Maria of the Passion of Our Lord Jesus Christ, the latter of whom is said to have subsisted during the last years of her life only on the Eucharist.[748]

Saint Andre of Montreal kept a hectic schedule, but throughout most of his life, he ate nothing but a wheat flour softened in hot water and seasoned with salt.[749]

Infused (Mystical) Knowledge

This is a supernatural act whereby God places in the soul the gift of divine knowledge.[750] This knowledge is beyond one's intellectual skills. It has been miraculously bestowed upon saints, mystics and others of all ages so that they may be able to better understand and explain the most difficult and intricate problems of psychology and theology.[751] Genuine infused knowledge never contains anything contrary to the Deposit of Faith nor anything in addition to it.[752]

The first instance of infused knowledge is that of Adam and Eve, who came from the hands of the Creator with every aptitude and all knowledge necessary or useful for existence. In the words of Sirach (17:5–8,) God gave them counsel, and a tongue, and eyes, and ears, and a heart to devise, and He filled them with the knowledge of understanding. He created in them the science of the spirit. He filled their heart with wisdom and showed them both good and evil. The first trial which Adam made of this innate knowledge on all the beings of creation was to confer a suitable name on each of the animals which God brought before him.

In the Old Testament, we see figures such as King Solomon who was one of the most brilliant examples of infused knowledge and wisdom. He was able to discourse on all things. In the New Testament, Jesus appeared to the disciples in Jerusalem and opened their minds to understand the scriptures (Lk 24:45).

---

[744] Treece, MB, op.cit., pp. 131, 135.

[745] Wilson, op.cit., p. 113.

[746] Thurston, op.cit., p. 341.

[747] Cruz, MMM, op.cit., pp. 247–55.

[748] Freze, TBWC, op.cit., p. 187.

[749] Cruz, MMM, op.cit., p. 256.

[750] Freeze, TBWC, op.cit., p. 312.

[751] Summers, op.cit., p. 66.

[752] Johnson, op.cit., p. 36.

Illumination from the Liber Scivias showing Hildegard receiving a vision and dictating to her scribe and secretary

Several poor nuns, unable to read or write, like Sts. Catherine of Siena, Rose of Lima, and Blessed Osanna of Mantua, who on account of this ignorance were not able to recite the divine office in choir, or correspond by letter with eminent directors or holy persons, learned, in a supernatural manner, to read and write. Others such as St. Catherine de'Ricci, learned to say the rosary or to recite the canonical office by the same means. St. Catherine of Alexandria, patroness of philosophers, was undoubtedly assisted by supernatural lights in the victorious controversy she sustained against the fifty sophists who were enlisted against her by the Emperor Maximin. Men who hardly knew how to read, like St. Joseph of Cupertino, or simple women, like Sts. Hildegard or Colette, were consulted by scholars and masters in theology, who wondered at the extent of their wisdom. St. Hildegard was even consulted as to certain difficulties drawn from the books of the Old and New Testaments, and although unable to read the text, she understood the sense of it marvelously and learnedly explained it.

The immense knowledge that has immortalized the name of St. Albert the Great (1200–1280) was to a great extent a free gift of God, who, in order to convince him of this, withdrew it from him during the last three years of his life. His disciple St. Thomas often declared that God alone was his teacher in the acquisition of natural and divine knowledge, which he possessed in so marvelous a degree.[753] Perhaps the most remarkable example of infused knowledge is that of St. Catherine of Siena mentioned above whose works explore the highest and un-trodden realms of the spirit and soar profoundly to the very throne of God.[754]

St. Francis of Assisi had things revealed to him which he said he would never disclose to anyone as long as he lived.[755] St. Guthlac claimed an angel revealed many mysteries to him which it would not be lawful to discuss.[756] When St. Antony wished to know something of which he was ignorant, he had but to pray to God, who, by symbolic and often prophetic visions, immediately gave him knowledge—whence the gifts of prophecy, long-distance vision, and discernment of spirits of which we read so often in the life of this saint.[757]

Some saints and beati were given insights into the most abstruse mysteries of the Faith. Saint Angela of Foligno received revelations on the inner life of the Trinity, on the extension of the Incarnation in the Eucharist, and on the greatness and power of God. The flood of intellectual illumination she received so quickly was followed

---

[753] Farges, op.cit., pp. 440–41.
[754] Summers, op.cit., p. 67.
[755] Johnson, op.cit., p. 250.
[756] Cruz, Inc, op.cit., p. 59.
[757] Farges, op.cit., p. 24.

by eight days of ecstasy, during which time she lay motionless and was unable to speak. In 1309, while dying, Jesus is said to have shown her the royal robe of light with which a soul is clothed at death.[758] St. Augustine and his mother, St. Monica, shared a great vision of the Trinity and the Godhead in Ostia, the port city of Rome.[759] St. Clare of Montefalco also displayed signs of infused knowledge. God graced her also with a vision of the Blessed Trinity where she beheld her Triune God in three distinct Persons, yet in one substance, equal.[760] St. Paschal Baylon was likewise granted marvelous insights into the mysteries of religion and his counsel was sought by learned and saintly persons.[761]

Sts. Martin de Porres and Gerard Majella[762] as well as Blesseds John of Alvernia (1259–1322) and Stephanie Quinzani along with Venerable Dominica of Paradiso[763] received infused theological knowledge which enlightened their minds. To this list we might also add Sts. Bonaventure, Bridget, Lydwina, Alphonsus Rodriguez, Thomas Aquinas, Teresa of Avila, and John of the Cross whose mystical insights could not spring from a human brain or be devised by man. It could only spring from the heart of God and from the splendors of His revelation.[764]

Other holy but uneducated persons received special instruction from Mary or Jesus. St. Joseph of Cupertino, for instance, received no formal education, and yet he was easily able to resolve the most complex problems in mystical theology, which professors of the science were at a loss to interpret and understand.[765] Our Lady appeared to Blessed Emily Bicchier several times to teach her how to pray.[766] Previously mentioned Blessed Osanna of Mantua, a Dominican nun, was also miraculously instructed by Our Lady in an instant on how to read and write so that the humble nun became a great model of the spiritual life. We possess forty-two letters replete with the highest mysticism, which she addressed to priests and religious.[767] Marie Lataste said Christ explained to her all the truths of the Faith in terms she could understand, verbal statements, visions, or parables.[768] Although ignorant about music, St. Godric composed hymns which he said were taught him during visions of the Blessed Virgin Mary.[769]

To other saints, like the brothers Cosmas and Damian, is attributed the infused knowledge of medicine.[770] St. Padre Pio had knowledge of souls in the other world. He once told a mother whose son was missing in action that her son must be alive because he could not find him in the other world.[771]

Insomnia (Supernatural Lack of Sleep)

It is recorded of some saints that they had the mystical ability to live on scarcely any sleep at all or to forego sleep for long periods of time without any adverse effects on their general health. This supernatural lack of sleep is called insomnia. St. John of the Cross, for instance, could forego sleep for long periods of time.[772] St. Catherine of Siena hardly slept except for thirty minutes

---

[758] Wiebe, op.cit., p. 19.

[759] Johnson, op.cit., p. 170.

[760] Lord, VHHP, op.cit., p. 108.

[761] NCE,1st. ed., op.cit., v. 10, p. 1049.

[762] Cruz, MMM, op.cit., pp. 257, 264.

[763] Dorcy, op.cit., pp. 252, 285–86.

[764] Farges, op.cit., p. 441, Poulain, RAV, op.cit., p. 17.

[765] Summers, op.cit., p. 67.

[766] Dorcy, op.cit., p. 126.

[767] O. P. Procter, Rev. STL. *Short Life of the Dominican Saints.* London, Kegan, Paul, Trench, Trubner & Co. ltd., 1901, pp. 175–76.

[768] Johnson, op.cit., p. 312.

[769] Cruz, MMM, op.cit., p. 480.

[770] Farges, op.cit., p. 440.

[771] Cruz, MMM, op.cit., p. 277.

[772] Johnson, op.cit., pp. 147, 361.

every two days,[773] and St. Catherine de' Ricci is known to have slept but one hour a week.

Sts. John Joseph of the Cross, Marianna Paredes y Flores, and Padre Pio slept but a few hours per night.[774] The Franciscan St. Colette is said to have spent a whole year without sleeping while Agatha of the Cross (1547–1621), a stigmatic Spanish Dominican nun from Toledo, reportedly did not sleep at all during the last eight years of her life.[775] St. Lydwina de Schiedam, a victim soul, slept very little, if at all, during the last seven years of her life.[776]

Sts. Peter of Alcantara, Christina the Astonishing,[777] Blessed Anna Maria Taigi, and Therese Neumann also required very little sleep.[778] The Belgian peasant girl Louise Lateau reportedly never slept. She allegedly passed her nights in contemplation and prayer, kneeling at the foot of her bed.[779] Marthe Robin stated that from 1932 to her death in 1981, she had been unable to sleep.[780]

These holy insomniacs are said to have remained energetic and to have experienced no adverse effects on their health nor to have suffered from exhaustion.[781]

Invisibility

One of the most mysterious and astounding wonders exercised by the power of God was that of saints and others who became invisible before the eyes of witnesses. Some saints have been reported as being mystically hidden.[782] This is reminiscent of the events in Christ's life when He walked unseen through the crowds as he was about to be hurled off a cliff (Lk 4:29–30), slipped away in a crowd (Jn 5:13), and hid Himself when He was about to be stoned (Jn 8:59), arrested (Jn 12:37), and heralded as a king (Jn 6:15). He also vanished from the sight of the disciples while at the table with the disciples from Emmaus (Lk 24:30–31).

One of the saints who possessed this extraordinary ability was St. Francis of Paola who was known during his lifetime as "The Miracle Worker." While visiting the city of Bormes, he was reportedly surrounded by enthusiastic fans that were tearing away at his clothing. Finding it impossible to make his way through the crowd and embarrassed by their adulation, the saint reportedly suddenly disappeared before the people's eyes, much to their confusion. His companions would later find him waiting for them outside the city walls. He offered no explanation for his disappearance but as his biographer noted: "Evidently he had willed to become invisible to human eyes during his period of deep prayer, as he had done on occasions before."[783] On another occasion, because of his opposition to the King, Francis was ordered arrested. Although the king's soldiers searched the church and many times passed by him, Francis remained invisible to them.[784] It was also said that he could make himself invisible whenever he wished to travel undetected, or to have quiet moments for prayer and meditation.[785]

St. Gerard Majella, a holy lay-brother, also was said to possess the gift of becoming invisible. Once while making a day-long

---

[773] Hebert, op.cit., p. 243.
[774] Freze, TBWC, op.cit., p. 188; Freze, VVA, op.cit., p. 220; Farges, op.cit., p. 566.
[775] Summers, op.cit., p. 63.
[776] Johnson. op.cit., p. 147.
[777] Hebert, op.cit., p. 243.
[778] Johnson. op.cit., p. 147.
[779] Thurston, op.cit., p. 351.
[780] Treece, MB, op.cit., p. 136.
[781] Summers, op.cit., p. 63.
[782] Johnson, op.cit., p. 208.
[783] Cruz, MMM, op.cit., pp. 206–7.
[784] Ghezzi, MM, op.cit., p. 136.
[785] Guiley, op.cit., p. 117.

retreat of prayer and recollection in his room in the Caposele monastery, he was summoned to the Father Rector. The saint could not be found although everyone in the house searched for him. His room, which measured ten feet square, was examined several times. On being asked where he had been later when he appeared for Holy Communion, the saint replied that he had been in his room. He explained that "fearing to be distracted in my retreat, I asked Jesus for the grace to become invisible."[786]

St. Clement Mary Hofbauer (1751–1820), the patron Saint of Vienna, while praying before the altar of St. Joseph in a Warsaw church, was reportedly seen by hundreds of people in the church to completely disappear in a cloud which slowly enveloped him. In his place, the congregation saw a celestial vision. A woman of great beauty appeared in his place and smiled at the worshippers.[787]

St. Peter of Atroa (773–837) found himself to be a wanted man due to his support of the use of icons. He is said to have escaped the imperial troops seeking him by miraculously becoming invisible.[788] Legend has it that a powerful king was about to ambush and assassinate St. Patrick (389–461) and his associates, but miraculously they all became invisible. The only thing that the king observed was some deer passing by and voices chanting "Christ be in me . . ."[789] Likewise, it was reported that a man pursued by enemies took refuge in St. Lydwina of Schiedam's room. When the man's enemies followed him into the room, they could not see him standing there.[790]

St. Martin de Porres and Fr. Paul of Moll (d.1896), a Flemish Benedictine known as "Wonder-Worker of the Nineteenth Century," are also said to have experienced this phenomenon of invisibility.[791] Once when enemies arrived in St. Martin's room to harm him, he turned invisible. He also helped others by cloaking them with invisibility. On another occasion, two escaped prisoners took refuge in his monastery cell. He had them kneel and pray. When authorities came to search the monastery, including Martin's cell, the criminals could not be found. Martin later advised them to mend their ways.[792]

Mary Razzi (1552–1600), a Dominican tertiary, is also said to have been favored with the gift of making herself invisible. If she wanted to hear a sermon without having the preacher know she was there, she merely made herself invisible. It was also said that sometimes, when in line for confession, and not ready to go in, she became invisible, letting everyone else go ahead of her.[793]

Levitation

Levitation is the elevation of the ecstatic above the ground without visible cause and its suspension in the air without natural support. If the elevation is slight, it is called ascensional ecstasy.[794] Numerous saints reportedly have levitated while in ecstasy or prayer, sometimes for extended periods and sometimes in a kneeling position. Levitation comes on spontaneously, an up-rushing force that lifts and sustains the saint.[795] This phenomenon may also appear in the form of ecstatic flight where the body rises to great heights or an ecstatic walk or ecstatic march where the body seems to glide rapidly over the ground.[796]

---

[786] Cruz, MMM, op.cit., p. 208.
[787] Aradi, op.cit., p. 180.
[788] See St. Peter of Atrroa in the patron saints index.
[789] Ghezzi, VOS, op.cit., p. 191; Ghezzi, MM, op.cit., p. 158.
[790] Johnson, op.cit., p. 208.

[791] Cruz, MMM, op.cit., pp. 208–9.
[792] Guiley, op.cit., p. 228.
[793] Dorcy, op.cit., p. 345.
[794] Farges, op.cit., p. 536.
[795] Guiley, op.cit., p. 384.
[796] Tanquery, op.cit., p. 711; Aumann, ST, op.cit., p. 437.

Sometimes the saint, blessed, or venerable who possesses this ability will soar high into the air. St. Francis of Assisi was seen raised above the ground on many occasions. He once reportedly levitated so high that he quite literally disappeared from sight, according to his close companions; at other times, one simply floats or glides above the ground. A true well-authenticated levitation cannot as yet be naturally explained.[797] All levitations are not signs from God however. They must all be investigated.

In the case of Venerable Mary of Agreda, her body was said to lose all weight during levitation, so that if one breathed on it, it moved like a feather in the breeze.[798] The sisters of her convent would often open the shutters of the choir so that Mary, also known as the "Lady in Blue," could be seen levitating for two or three hours after communion.[799]

St. Joseph of Cupertino, an Italian Franciscan friar, is by far the most astounding case of levitation on record. His elevations and aerial flight had been observed on more than one hundred occasions. He would fly over the heads of others and remain suspended in the air for long periods of time. He flew to holy statues and to altars both indoors and outdoors. His levitations and aerial flights were attested to by numerous reputable eyewitnesses.[800] In fact, Joseph levitated at will so frequently and so forcefully that he often took with him the brothers that he grabbed to steady himself.[801] It is said that he would actually be suspended in air eighteen to thirty-five feet and remain suspended in this ecstatic manner from fifteen minutes to as long as six hours at a time. While in Rome to visit the Holy Father, Joseph went into ecstasy

St. Joseph of Cupertino in ecstasy by Felice Boscaratti

at the sight of Pope Urban VIII and rose from the ground until the head of his order called him to his senses. The pope marveled at this phenomenon and told the Father General that he himself would bear witness to the occurrence should the saint die during his pontificate.[802] On another occasion, Joseph flew about seventy yards from the door of the friary to a very heavy thirty-six-foot cross which ten men could not lift. He lifted it up like a straw and placed it in a hole prepared for it.[803] His ecstatic flights earned him the title the "flying friar." He

[797] NCE, 2nd ed., v. 10, op.cit., p. 108.
[798] Aumann, ST, op.cit., p. 437.
[799] Johnson, op.cit., p. 128.
[800] Guiley, op.cit., pp. 192–93.
[801] Johnsonm, op.cit., p. 128.

[802] Cruz, MMM, op.cit., p. 32.
[803] Thurston, op.cit., p. 15; Lord, VMS, op.cit., p. 140.

Saint Dominic Levitating While Resurrecting a Boy, by Pedro Berruguete

"flew" in the air so often, in fact, that he is now the patron saint of air travelers and pilots.[804]

St. Christina the Astonishing was thought to have died at age twenty-one from a severe seizure that made her cataleptic. During her funeral Mass, she suddenly recovered and was reportedly seen by the entire congregation levitating to the roof of the church. Ordered down by the priest, she did so at once under holy obedience, landed on the altar, and related that she had been to heaven, hell, and purgatory, and that she had been returned to earth with a ministry to pray for the souls in purgatory.[805] Christina could also not stand the odor of other people because she could smell the sin in them, and would climb trees or buildings, hide in ovens or cupboards, or simply levitate to avoid contact with them.[806]

St. Teresa of Avila used to try to resist the raptures and ecstasies that would bring on levitation and would beg her fellow nuns to hold her down so she would not be embarrassed before the others. St. John of the Cross was reportedly witnessed levitating by many while in ecstatic prayer. Once when walking and talking about Jesus with St. Teresa of Avila, both allegedly went into ecstasy and levitated.[807] Another time, St. John was said to be seen levitating in the chapel with his head touching the ceiling, having been lifted up during prayer.[808] On one occasion, a story recounts that St. Gerard Majella started to levitate while speaking to a prioress through the iron grill of the convent parlor, and he likewise took hold of the grill and it bent like wax as he rose into the air.

Innumerable saints have been reported to levitate to great heights, thus, defying the law of gravity. As with St. Margaret Mary Alacoque and innumerable other saints, this ecstatic state happens mostly during Mass, at the moment of receiving the Eucharist, or while in adoration before the Blessed Sacrament.[809] It is reported that during such an ecstasy and levitation that St. Catherine of Siena received the Holy Stigmata.[810] She was said to have levitated many times throughout her life for as long as it would take to say the Miserere but only high enough so that people could pass their hands under her. St. Philip Neri occasionally hurried through Mass because he wanted to avoid levitating. He often had to lean against the altar to keep from collapsing in rapture at the consecration.[811] Sts. Dominic[812] and John Bosco[813] were also allegedly seen by witnesses to levitate while in ecstasy during Mass. St. Francis of Posadas was said to experience many levitations which he tried to resist, but without success. On one occasion, supposedly his body remained suspended in the air during the consecration. On numerous other occasions, while celebrating Mass, observers claimed to see a brilliant light emanate from his body which illuminated the whole altar.[814] Blessed Ambrose Sansedoni of Siena (1220–1287) levitated during preaching. Stories say that St. Thomas of Villanova, while preaching one day in his cathedral, suddenly went into ecstasy and remained suspended in the air for twelve hours. Blessed Giles of Santarem (c.1185–1265) of the order of St. Dominic reportedly remained suspended in the air in ecstasy for whole nights without it being possible to bring him back down to earth.[815]

---

[804] Hebert, SWRD, op.cit., p. 244.
[805] Freze, VVA, op.cit., p. 34.
[806] Delaney, op.cit., p. 117.
[807] Johnson, op.cit., pp. 76, 128.
[808] Guiley, op.cit., p. 183.

[809] Johnson, op.cit., pp. 47, 128.
[810] Cruz, MMM, op.cit., p. 39.
[811] Johnson, op.cit., pp. 47, 128.
[812] Thurston, op.cit., p. 7.
[813] Guiley, op.cit., p. 178.
[814] Cruz, MMM, op.cit., pp. 30, 169.
[815] Farges, op.cit., p. 537.

Several times the sisters of the Convent del Sacco said they saw St. Agnes of Montepulciano levitating five or more feet from the ground.[816] On one occasion, she reportedly was seen rising in the air to venerate a crucifix on a high wall.[817] St. Peter de Alcantara (1499–1562) was said to sometimes be seen raised fifteen feet or more off the floor until his head touched the roof. On other occasions, stories say he soared like a bird to the top of trees or again flew up with arms outstretched to embrace a crucifix that was up high. St. Bernardino Realino was seen rapt in ecstasy levitating about 2 ½ feet off the ground.[818] Blessed Anna Maria Taigi experienced ecstasies while engaged in household chores and was reported to have occasionally levitated.[819]

Around Christmas time of 1745, it was related that while St. Alphonsus Liguori was preaching about Mary at a church in Foggia, a picture there of the Blessed Mother became animated. Accounts say that as she moved within the frame of her portrait, the faithful in the pews gazed in wonder and were startled when a ray of heavenly light left the Virgin's face and rested on that of the saintly preacher, giving it a marvelous glow. At the words, "My Lady, is it your pleasure to play with me?" the saint fell into an ecstasy and was said to be raised bodily in the air several inches from the floor.[820]

Maria de Moerl, a stigmatic, was confined to her bed due to illness. On the Feast of Corpus Christi in 1834, while in ecstasy, she was said to have levitated from her bed and was transfigured with an angelic beauty, arms extended, and her stigmata shining with a clear crystal light. Friends and neighbors were said to have witnessed this phenomenon.[821]

Ecstasy of Peter of Alcántara by Francesco Fontebasso

The reported instances of St. Martin de Porres being raised from the ground while rapt in a profound ecstasy before a crucifix were numerous. Several priests who had witnessed these levitations gave depositions to this effect for the process of his beatification. Once, while St. Paul of the Cross was giving a mission on the island of Elba and during the most fervent part of his sermon, he reportedly walked off the platform, through the air, and over the heads of the people and then returned as if nothing had happened. Another time, during a rapture, he supposedly rose in a chair to a height of five or six feet. The Syrian Carmelite nun Blessed Mary of Jesus Crucified is said to have soared in the air to the top of a lime tree until she was commanded by her superior to come down. In her haste to obey, she left one of her sandals in the top branches where it was discovered the next day.[822]

St. Francis of Paola was said to be seen by the King of Naples in 1483 floating in mid-air, his whole body glowing with light, his

[816] Cruz, MMM, op.cit., p. 30.
[817] Hebert, SWRD, op.cit., p. 133.
[818] Thurston, op.cit., pp. 18, 22.
[819] Cruz, SS, op.cit., p. 52.
[820] Cruz, MMM, op.cit., p. 24.
[821] Summers, op.cit., p. 167.
[822] Cruz, MMM, op.cit., pp. 26–29.

hands clasped while in profound ecstasy.[823] One day at Mass, kneeling before the Blessed Sacrament, St. Thomas Aquinas had an apparition of Our Lord who said to him, "You have written well of the sacrament of My Body." Struck with ecstasy, St. Thomas reportedly levitated and remained suspended off the floor long enough for the phenomenon to be witnessed by everyone present."[824] Even a dead body has been seen to levitate. The corpse of St. Rita of Cascia had been seen to rise to the top of her reliquary on several occasions.[825] Sister Maria della Passione (d.1912), who had been very sick on a certain day, was supposedly seen being carried up the stairs to her cell by an invisible force, without her feet even once touching the floor.[826]

Other saints, blesseds, and venerables seen levitating include: Sts. Milburga (d.c.722),[827] Stephen of Hungary (975–1038), Francis Xavier (1505–1551),[828] Rose of Viterbo, Ignatius of Loyola, Rita of Cascia,[829] Thomas of Cori (1655–1729), John Vianney, Maria Maddalena de' Pazzi,[830] Michael de Sanctis, Peter Claver, Alphonsus Rodriguez, Pacifico of San Severino,[831] Juan Masias,[832] Benedict Joseph Labre,[833] Vincent de Paul (c. 1580–1660), Andre Hubert Fouret (1752–1834), Gaspar del Bufalo, Maddalena di Canossa (1774–1835), Joseph Benedict Cottolengo (1786–1842), Gemma Galgani, John of Sahagun, Malachy O'Morgair,[834] Blessed Jutta of

Prussia (1200–1260),[835] Blessed Jane of Orvieto,[836] Blessed Margaret of Castello, Blessed Flora of Beaulieu,[837] Blessed James of Bitetto,[838] Blessed Lodovica Albertoni (1473–1533),[839] Venerable Antonio Margil, Venerable Passitea Crogi,[840] Venerable Beatrice Mary of Jesus (1632–1702),[841] Venerable Maria Villani,[842] as well as a whole host of others.[843]

In modern times, holy persons such as Sts. Sharbel Makhluf, Gemma Galgani, Padre Pio, Andre Bessette, Venerable Teresa Helena Higginson, and Theresa Neumann have been reported to levitate.[844]

It should be noted in this section that, in contrast to ecstatic lightness, saints have exhibited the inverse phenomenon of superhuman heaviness. St. Joseph of Cupertino, whose ecstatic flights are matter of legend, occasionally remained stretched on the ground, adhering so intensely thereto that none of his brethren were able to move him. Analogous accounts are to be found in the lives of Sts. Lucy of Syracuse (d.304), Agnes, sister of St. Clare, Blessed Mary of Oignies, Blessed Agnes of Jesus, and many other ecstatics.[845]

Miraculous Transport

Miraculous transport deals with those saints and holy persons who, at one time or another, moved about in unusual ways to transcend space. Sometimes they moved with unusual speed, or by using an unlikely vehicle for traveling. They may have arrived

[823] Farges, op.cit., p. 27; Cruz, MMM, op.cit., p. 30.
[824] Johnson, op.cit., p. 107.
[825] Cruz, MMM, op.cit., p. 41.
[826] Aradi, op.cit., p. 89.
[827] Freze, VVA, op.cit., p. 34.
[828] Farges, op.cit., p. 537.
[829] Cruz, MMM, op.cit., pp. 39–40.
[830] Johnson, op.cit., pp. 127–29.
[831] Thurston, op.cit., p. 31.
[832] Johnson, op.cit., p. 128.
[833] Freeze, VVA, op.cit., p. 34.
[834] Miracles, op.cit., p. 8; Aradi, op.cit., p. 89; Treece, MB, op.cit., pp. 175–77, 186.
[835] Gallick, op.cit., p. 137.
[836] Dorcy, op.cit., p. 136.
[837] Cruz, MMM, op.cit., p. 33, 36.
[838] Ibid., p. 423.
[839] Freeze, VVA, op.cit., p. 34.
[840] Thurston, op.cit., pp. 19, 29.
[841] Ibid., p. 118.
[842] Cruz, MMM, op.cit., p. 21.
[843] See *Proceedings of the Society for Psychical Research*, Part 90, May 1924.
[844] Treece, MB, op.cit., p. 185.
[845] Farges, op.cit., p. 539.

at their destination suddenly without being aware of having traveled or of what took place while they were between one destination and the other.[846] An old term used in psychical research to describe this phenomenon is teleportation.[847]

On one occasion, St. Hyacinth, "the so-called Polish St. Dominic," rushed into a burning convent chapel set afire by invading Tartars. His purpose was only to remove the Blessed Sacrament and hide it as a protection from desecration. Our Lady told him to take her statue out of the chapel also. Her statue was large and heavy but Mary perhaps miraculously lightened it so he could carry both items. St. Hyacinth then crossed the Vistula River on his cloak carrying the Blessed Sacrament and the statue of Our Lady and saved them both from desecration at the hands of the invading Tartars. He reportedly often used his cloak to sail great distances over water. In the saint's Bull of canonization, it was noted that over four hundred people witnessed his walking on the waters of the Vistula River near Visgrad in Moravia.[848]

A relative of St. Hyacinth, namely St. Ceslaus (1184–1242), is also said to have crossed a raging river on his cloak, staying dry in the process. St. Bernardine of Siena crossed a river on a cloak that was thrown down on top of the water.[849] Other saints who used a mantle or cloak to traverse great distances over water include Sts. Gerard Majella, Francis of Paola, and Raymond of Penafort (1175–1275), the latter of whom is said to have traveled from the island of Majorca to the harbor of Barcelona by means of his cloak. Blessed Jane of Signa (1244–1307) crossed the Arno River kneeling on her cloak more than once. The Franciscan friar, St. Francis Solano

(1549–1610) was also said to use his mantle to cross rushing streams.[850]

As related earlier, St. Anthony of Padua's father was arrested and accused of murdering a young nobleman in Lisbon, Portugal. When the matter was made supernaturally known to St. Anthony, he asked his superior's permission to leave the monastery in Padua, Italy where he lived to travel on foot to Lisbon. While in route, he found himself miraculously transported to Lisbon in time to speak in defense of his father. He convinced the authorities to travel to the victim's grave and commanded the corpse, in the name of God, to speak out. According to the story, the corpse sat up and declared his father guiltless. When Anthony reappeared in Padua, he had been absent two nights and a single day.

St. Martin de Porres also possessed the gift of mystical transport. On two occasions, witnesses attested that while darkness was falling and his being at a considerable distance from the monastery, the saint prayed and both he and his companions were suddenly transported to the doors of the monastery in the brief space of a moment.[851]

St. Anthony Mary Claret, founder of the Claretians, also had this gift. While a seminarian, he lived at Vich in the rectory of Don Fortunato Bres, his friend and advisor. Many years later, Bres, on his way to Mass one winter day, slipped on ice and broke his leg. He asked for Anthony, who was many miles away, to be notified. Ten minutes later, Anthony arrived. The route was snow-covered, and it was snowing at the time, but Anthony was not wet. He said that "an irresistible impulse" had caused him to come to Don Fortunato.[852]

Venerable Anthony Margil, a Franciscan missionary, converted hundreds of

846 Cruz, MMM, op.cit., p. 87.
847 Guiley, op.cit., p. 384.
848 Cruz, MMM, op.cit., p. 89.
849 Miracles, op.cit., p. 22.

850 Cruz, MMM, op.cit., pp. 97–100.
851 Ibid., pp. 90, 94–95.
852 Guiley, op.cit., p. 28.

St. Rita of Cascia miraculously transported to the Augustinian convent of Cascia near Spoleto, by Nicolas Poussin

thousands of indians, an estimated eighty thousand in Guatemala alone. Anthony was also called the "Flying Father" because he could cover so many miles in such a short period of time. It was nothing short of a miracle for him to cover forty or fifty miles a day over rough terrain. Stories from his brother and soldier companions attest to the fact that he literally walked on water as he crossed swollen streams and rivers on his apostolic journey. This capacity to pass from place to place with great speed is also known as the gift of agility.[853]

Venerable Teresa Helena Higginson professed on one occasion to have been transported to a country she supposed to be in Africa, finding herself among a primitive people whose habits and customs she described in great detail.[854]

Blessed Anne Catherine Emmerich claimed that her guardian angel led her on mystical journeys to places in the Holy Land during the life and times of Jesus and the apostles.[855]

Others who have exhibited this type of supernatural phenomenon include the Franciscan mystic St. Peter of Alcantara, St. Peter Regalado (d. 1456), Blessed Catherine of Racconigi,[856] and Therese Neumann.[857]

Multiplication

Multiplication is the miraculous increase of any substance. Many saints were said to increase food and money in accordance with the needs of others. Jesus multiplied fishes and loaves to feed the multitudes (Mt 14:15–21; 15:32–38; Mk 6:36–44; 8:2–9; Lk 9:12–17; Jn 6:5–13). Jesus says in John 14:11, 12 "Believe that I am in the Father and the Father is in me or else believe because of the works themselves. Amen, amen, I say to you, whoever believes in me will do the works that I do, and will do greater ones than these."

In the Old Testament (1 Kgs 17:10–14) there is the story of Elijah and the widow which took place during a severe drought. The widow served Elijah the last of the flour and oil she had. Elijah told her not to fear starvation because the Lord said, "The jar of flour shall not go empty, or the jug of oil run dry, until the day when the Lord sends rain upon the earth." This all came to pass and the widow and her son were able to eat for a year.

Many saints performed this type of miracle. St. Peregrine Laziosi, known as the "Cancer Saint," was said to have frequently multiplied wheat and wine during a famine.[858] Blessed Stephanie de Quinzanis used to multiply wine, flour, and even money for the poor.[859] It is said that St. Joseph of Cupertino would pray, place his hands upon what little there was to eat, and what came about was the multiplication of honey, bread, wine, and whatever food there was before him. At other times, he simply called upon Our Lady to intercede, and behold, food miraculously increased.[860] St. Benedict the Moor (1526–1589) multiplied food in his sixteenth-century kitchen. It is reported that angels helped

---

[853] See Miriam Horvat, http://www.tradition inaction.org/Margil.
[854] Wilson, op.cit., p. 119.
[855] Freze, VVA, op.cit., p. 35.
[856] Cruz, MMM, op.cit., p. 97.
[857] Wilson, op.cit., p. 119.

[858] Cruz, Inc., op.cit., p. 115.
[859] Proctor, op.cit., p. 4.
[860] Lord, VMS, op.cit., p. 151.

Miracle of the Loaves and Fishes, 1750, by Juan de Espinal

him prepare meals and run the kitchen.[861] At the prayers of St. Peter Gonzalez (1190–1246), bottles were refilled with wine and bread was found in the wilderness.[862] St. Benedict (c.480–547) reportedly had two hundred sacks of flour miraculously appear outside his gate to supply not only for the needs of his famished monks but for the many poor who daily knocked at the door of the monastery.[863]

St. Ivo Helory of Kermartin (1253–1303) reportedly fed hundreds of people from a single loaf of bread.[864] Some of the other saints and beati who possessed this gift of multiplication include: Sts. John Gualbert (999–1073), Thomas of Villanova (1488–1555), Martin de Porres, Paul of the Cross, Jean–Baptiste Marie Vianney,[865] Cuthbert,[866] Isadore the Farmer (1070–1130), Dominic, Francis of Assisi, Elizabeth of

---

[861] Cowan, op.cit., pp. 6, 68.

[862] Miracles, op.cit., p. 10.

[863] Cruz, MMM, op.cit., p. 117.

[864] See http://www.Catholicwonderworkers.

[865] Miracles, op.cit., p. 10.

[866] Cruz, MMM, op.cit., p. 437.

Hungary (1207–1231), Zita (1218–1278), Philip Benizi (1233–1285), Catherine of Siena, Frances of Rome, Collette, Francis of Paola, Teresa of Avila, Maria Maddalena de' Pazzi, Rose of Lima, Francis Regis (1597–1640), Gerard Majella (124–125), Andrew Hubert Fournet (1752–1834), John Bosco, Joseph Benedict Cottolengo (1786–1842), Philip Benizi (1233–1285), Blessed Gerard of Monza (d.1207), Blessed Alvarez of Cordova (d.1420), Blessed John Liccio (d.1511), Blessed Peter of Tiferno (d.1445), Blessed Anna Maria Taigi, as well as many others.[867]

Mystical Marriage

Mystical marriage is the highest mystical state that can be attained this side of heaven. It runs the gamut from the "spiritual betrothal" to the "spiritual marriage" to the "full mystical union."[868] The mystical union with the divine is a reenactment of the Blessed Virgin Mary's fiat to the Lord, of whom she gave herself freely, totally, and unconditionally. Our Mother Mary is the prototype of all heavenly spouses who are joined to the love that is God, since she was so intimately absorbed in divine love. Many holy souls have been invited to share in the Virgin's divine espousal, thus becoming a part of the heavenly family of God.

Besides being called mystic marriage, mystic union, or the transforming union, this intimate union of the mystic soul with God is also referred to by some as the "exchange of hearts" (see entry for exchange of hearts). In any event, this state is where the soul receives the blessings of the spiritual marriage with the heavenly spouse as a sign of her total union with God.[869] It is termed "marriage" only symbolically and can occur between God and any human

Mystical Marriage of Saint Catherine of Sienna by Ceraiolo

soul regardless of bodily gender.[870] The essentials of the mystical marriage are an intellectual vision of the Holy Trinity and especially of Jesus Christ together with some intellectual locution in which mutual consent is given and vows of fidelity exchanged. The presence of Our Lady is necessary to the fulfillment of the mystical marriage since Her Son will not give Himself in wedlock without the consent and approval of His Mother.[871] Departed saints may also participate in the ceremony. Records exist of nearly one hundred saints experiencing mystical marriage, with fifty-five of them receiving a mystical ring.[872]

According to Saint Angela of Foligno, the divine transformation can occur in three different ways: The first unites the soul to the will of God (the conforming union); the second unites the soul with God Himself (the mystical union and espousal); the

---

867 Ibid., pp. 116–38.
868 Rahner, op.cit., p. 57.
869 Freze, TBWC, op.cit., pp. 202, 204.

870 Johnson, op.cit., p. 362.
871 Summers, op.cit., p. 72.
872 Guiley, op.cit., p. 385.

third unites the soul in God and God in the soul (the spiritual marriage).[873]

Before participating in mystical marriage, there is a time of spiritual betrothal (espousal) which is comparable in a small way to an earthly courtship, but the soul must have reached a high degree of sanctity. St. John of the Cross in *The Living Flame of Love* says that in the betrothal (espousal) there is only a mutual agreement and willingness between the two and the bridegroom (Christ) graciously gives jewels and ornaments to his espoused. Spiritual or mystical marriage, on the other hand, is a total transformation in the beloved. Each partner surrenders the entire possession of self to the other. When spiritual or mystical marriage between God and the soul is consummated, there are two natures in one spirit and love. Since mystical marriage is a spiritual union, it should not be surprising, then, that not only female saints have been so privileged but a number of male saints have been graced as well with this exalted state.[874]

Pope Benedict XIV states that mystical marriage is a phenomenon which makes the recipient more pleasing and closer to God.[875] It denotes the state of a human soul living intimately united to God through grace and love. In a more restrictive sense, mystical marriage refers to what is recognized in mystical theology as a "transforming" union between a soul and God, requiring extraordinary graces, and to which God calls only a few particularly privileged persons. Both St. Teresa of Avila and St John of the Cross in their works[876]

recognize the "transforming" (permanent) union as distinct from and higher than mere spiritual betrothal (temporary). Mystical marriage constitutes a consummate union of love; a total possession; a fusion of "lives,"—the soul is made one with God without losing its identity. It is a total union involving the transformation of the substance of the soul by sanctifying grace and the transformation of the faculties by divine light and love.[877] The initiative in this matter and the choice of souls to whom this union is granted belongs to Christ.[878] On November 18, 1572, at the age of fifty-seven, while receiving communion from the hands of St. John of the Cross, St. Teresa of Avila reportedly received the favor of the spiritual marriage or mystical union.[879]

The substitution of the heart of the mystic for the symbolic heart of Christ (see exchange of hearts), or the bestowing of a ring to designate the mystical espousal or mystical marriage, could also be effected in an imaginative vision.[880] This most perfect degree of mystical union with God is the mystic's goal. It rises through and above ecstasy and is a sure foretaste of heavenly bliss.[881] It is the most sublime experience of the saints.

When a stigmatic has been favored with the mystical marriage, the Lord has often appeared with the Blessed Virgin Mary in a heavenly celebration that witnesses the divine espousal between Christ the Groom and His beloved, spotless bride. Many heavenly saints were present during such

---

[873] Freze, TBWC, op.cit., p. 206.

[874] Cruz, MMM, op.cit., pp. 141–43; see also Kavanaugh, *The Collected Works of St. John, The Living Flame of Love*, stanza 3, ch. 24, 619.

[875] Cruz, MMM, op.cit., p. x.

[876] Teresa of Avila, Saint, *Interior castle*, translated and edited by E. Allison Peers from the critical edition of P. Silverio de Santa Teresa Garden City, NY: Doubleday, 1961,7, ch.2; John of the

Cross, St. *Spiritual canticle*. translated by E. Allison Peers; 3rd rev. ed., Garden City, NY: Image Books, [1961], stanzas 12–27.

[877] See *Ascent of Mount Carmel* 2, 5, 6 in John of the Cross, Saint. *The Collected Works*.

[878] NCE, 1st ed., op.cit., v. 10, pp. 170–71.

[879] Poulain, RAV, op.cit., pp. 5–6; Teresa of Avila, *Life*, op.cit., pp. xxxiii, 2.

[880] NCE, 2nd ed., op.cit., v. 10, p. 108.

[881] Summers, op.cit., p. 72.

visions at the time of the spiritual marriage. St. Catherine of Ricci once saw the presence of St. Thomas of Aquinas and St. Mary Magdalen; St. Catherine of Siena had Sts. John, Paul, and Dominic in her midst; St. Mary Maddalena de' Pazzi described the appearances of St. Augustine and St. Catherine of Siena. Venerable Marina de Escobar enjoyed the company of St. Joseph on her heavenly day of union.[882]

Mary favored some with mystical espousal to her. She called St. Joseph Herman her chaplain and her spouse being betrothed to him in mystical marriage. She also confirmed his surname "Joseph" given him by his brothers in religion.[883]

Other saints, beati, and venerables who experienced mystical marriage to Our Lord have been: Sts. Gertrude the Great, Colette, Veronica Giuliani, Jean-Baptiste Marie Vianney,[884] Faustina Kowalska, Kateri Tekakwitha (1656–1680),[885] Rose of Lima, Catherine of Bologna, Saint Angela of Foligno,[886] Blessed Catherine of Racconigi, Blessed Stephanie de Quinzani,[887] Blessed Elisabetta Canori-Mora,[888] Blessed Clara Isabella Fornari,[889] Venerable Teresa Helena Higginson,[890] Venerable Joan Mary della Croce (1603–1673), Marie-Julie Jahenny,[891] Venerable Giovanna Maria della Croce, Venerable Marina de Escobar, and, more recently, Celestine Fenouil.[892] and Mariam Thresia Chiramel Mankidyan (1876–1926).[893] Blessed Christina of

Stommeln, who had visions of the Christ child since she was five years old, was mystically married to Jesus at the age of ten.[894]

Mystical Ring

A ring of precious metals or jewels may be given in mystical marriage or in ecstasy.[895] Just as in earthly marriages, a ring is given as a visible sign, so the good Lord often gives a heavenly ring to those who are privileged to participate in this mystical union. The marriage and the ring-giving sometimes takes place in a ceremony in which the Blessed Virgin or one or more of the saints take part.[896] Records show that about fifty-five of nearly one hundred of those who experienced mystical marriage received a mystical ring.[897] In addition, Dr. Imbert-Gourbeyre compiled a list of close to a hundred persons who were admitted to the mystical nuptials, some of whom had experienced the heavenly espousal and some the heavenly marriage itself. In his study, he found that forty-three of the fifty-five examples of those who have received the mystical ring also have been stigmatics.

How does the mystical ring appear to those who bear them and others? Sometimes the ring is not visible to others, although the recipient can always see it. At other times the ring is visible to others, or it might appear as a mark, indentation, or reddening of the skin as it encircles the finger. With some, such as St. Catherine of Siena and Blessed Osanna d'Andreasi, it was only visible to them alone. For others such as St. Catherine of Ricci, it was often visible to others. Let us look at a few of these examples more closely.[898]

The mystical marriage of the Seraphic mother, St. Catherine of Siena in the year

882 Freze, TBWC, op.cit., p. 205.

883 Summers, op.cit., p. 158; NCE, lst ed., op.cit., v. 6, p. 1072.

884 Cruz, MMM, op.cit., pp. 148–51.

885 Lord, VMS, op.cit., pp. 186, 425.

886 Farges, op.cit., p. 179.

887 Cruz, MMM, op.cit., pp. 147–48.

888 Summers, op.cit., p. 106.

889 www.saints.sqpn.com–blessed–clara–Isabella–Fonari.

890 Thurston, op.cit., p. 132.

891 Johnson, op.cit., p. 69.

892 Thurston, op.cit., pp. 132, 139–40.

893 http://mariamthresia.org/?p+206.

894 http://www.newadvent.org/cathen/03724a.htm.

895 Guiley, op.cit., p. 384.

896 Cruz, MMM, op.cit., p. 143.

897 Guiley, op.cit., p. 385.

898 Freze, TBWC, op.cit., p. 205.

The Mystic Marriage of St. Catherine of Ricci

1367, was accompanied by celestial phenomena of the most extraordinary and exalted kind. Our Lady and Our Lord appeared to her, accompanied by a vision of saints, Sts. John the Evangelist, Paul, Dominic, her spiritual father, and King David, who played sweetly on a harp of gold. Our Lady presented the humble virgin to Christ. Whereupon Our Lord, taking her hand in His, placed upon her finger the wedding ring of four Orient pearls and a diamond which shone like the sun. "Thou art my spiritual Spouse in faith, and one day thou shalt be wedded to me forever in Paradise," came the Divine words and slowly the heavenly vision faded from the sight of the enraptured saint.[899] Hers is the best known example of an invisible espousal ring.[900]

The most interesting of all cases of mystic espousal accompanied by physical and external phenomena is that of St. Catherine de Ricci.[901] On Easter Sunday of 1542, Our Lord appeared to her in a vision, clothed in glory, carrying a resplendent cross on His shoulder, and wearing a magnificent crown on His head, accompanied by the glorious Virgin Mary, Sts. Mary Magdalen and Thomas of Aquinas, and another blessed one of her order. Mary begged her divine son to take Catherine for His bride. Jesus consented and took a shining gold ring[902] adorned with a magnificent diamond and enameled in red, from the index finger of His left hand, and while the Blessed Virgin held Catherine's hand, Jesus placed this beautiful ring on the forefinger of Catherine's left hand in commemoration of their mystical espousal. After the ecstasy, some nuns described the ring as being of gold and set

[899] Summers, op.cit., p. 74.
[900] Thurston, op.cit., p. 130.

[901] Ibid., p. 135.
[902] Farges, op.cit., p. 178.

with a large, brilliant diamond in it,[903] but others saw it only as a swelling and reddening of the flesh which various experiments could neither duplicate nor erase.[904] Catherine reportedly bore one of the best-documented mystic rings.[905]

St. Gertrude the Great had her first mystical experience with Christ on January 27, 1281 when a bond of love was revealed between Our Lord and her.[906] He revealed His Heart to her and placed seven golden circlets in the form of rings on her hand, one on each finger and three on the signet finger.[907]

St. Veronica Giuliani bore a ring of mystical espousal said to have taken place on April 11, 1694.[908] She called it her ring of love or her ring of the Cross. It seemed to be made somehow from her living flesh with a white or yellow stone as big as a bean which warned her of approaching sufferings. It also consisted of a raised stone as large as a pea and red in color. It was periodically seen by witnesses.[909] Likewise Blessed Stephanie de Quinzanis was given a beautiful ring during a vision of the Lord as a token of her espousal to Him.[910] This ring was said to have been seen by many people. Some others who have received espousal rings from Our Lord include St. Clare of Montefalco, Blessed Osanna of Mantua,[911] Blessed Giovanna Maria Bonomo,[912] and Marie-Julie Jahenny.[913]

Venerable Marina de Escobar (1554–1633) is said to have celebrated the mystical marriage twice, once at the age of forty-eight and again at the age of fifty-seven.[914] She received an espousal ring by Our Lord, and St. Joseph was said to have assisted at one of these ceremonies.[915] In 1644, an espousal ring with five diamonds was given to Venerable Giovanna Maria of the Cross.

St. Colette had an espousal ring presented to her and placed on her finger by St. John the Evangelist on behalf of Our Lord as a token of espousal.[916] St. Jean-Baptiste Marie Vianney, also known as the Curé of Ars, was one of the few men said to experience mystical espousal to the Lord. He reportedly wore a golden ring of extraordinary brilliance.

We are told that the Blessed Virgin appeared to Blessed Catherine of Racconigi one time while she was praying and told her that the Child Jesus wanted to take her as His Spouse. Her first betrothal took place in the presence of angels and saints to include Sts. Catherine of Siena and Peter Martyr (c. 1205–1252). Jesus appeared as a child of Catherine's own age. It was Our Lady herself who placed the ring of espousal on Catherine's finger. A second mystical espousal took place when Catherine took her vow of virginity. At that time a mark of a ring is said to have appeared upon her finger.[917]

---

903 Thurston, op.cit., p. 137.
904 Guiley, op.cit., p. 63.
905 Johnson, op.cit., p. 69.
906 Guiley, op.cit., p. 13.
907 Cruz, MMM, op,cit., p. 148; see also Gertrude the Great. *The life and revelations of St. Gertrude the Great*, Christian Classics. Inc. Westminster, Md. 1983, p. 115.
908 Cruz, MMM, op,cit., p. 150.
909 Johnson, op.cit., p. 6.
910 Cruz, MMM, op,cit., p. 148.
911 Freze, TBWC, op.cit., p. 205.
912 http://nouvl.evangelization.free.fr.giovanna.
913 Johnson, op.cit., p. 69.

914 Biot, op.cit., p. 72.
915 NCE, v. 5, op.cit., p. 538; Thurston, op.cit., p. 140.
916 Thurston, op.cit., p. 139.
917 Cruz, MMM, op,cit., pp. 147, 151.

Anne Catherine Emmerich, 1885, by Gabriel von Max

Mystical Sensitivity

Mystical sensitivity is the experience of bodily reactions to a vision. For instance, it occurs when a mystic who witnesses an event in the life of Christ feels the heat, cold, pain, etc. that would be experienced by a person physically present at the event.[918] Blessed Anne Catherine Emmerich's visions of Christ's Passion present such a case. During these visions she reportedly said she felt physically whatever the saints, or Christ felt to include the heat, the cold, the distress, everything.[919]

Odor of Sanctity (Sweet Odors)

The odor of sanctity is a phenomenon associated with supernaturally sweet fragrances emitted by saints during their lifetime or at death. These odors often resembled those of violets, lilies, scented roses, orange blossom, cinnamon, or other spices, like musk,

Benjamin, etc.[920] These scents can be given off from a live, visible, sanctified body; the stigmata wound or blood of a saint; apparent communication from a live saint who is not present (invisible bilocation); an object or place strongly associated with a living saint who is not present; the death of some saints; the corpses of some saints; an object or place strongly associated with a dead saint, including the grave; apparent communication by a dead saint or in regard to a dead saint without any link to any material object or visible body; and visible after-death appearances by saints.[921]

Such sweet and persistent odors are classified as miraculous by Pope Benedict XIV, although the phenomenon could be caused by the devil or by autosuggestion. However, if it is a true mystical phenomenon, it is interpreted as a sign of the sweet odor of glory and a testimony to the holiness of an individual.[922] The odor of sanctity might be detected during prayer or ecstasies; some saints reportedly smelled sweet all the time.[923] Certain saints' earthly visits, such as Sts. Therese of Lisieux and Padre Pio, have often been associated with numinous odors.[924]

At the very beginning of the Christian era, perfumes were introduced as elements proper to the worship of God. Myrrh, an aromatic gum resin, and frankincense were offered to the Christ child by the three Magi. We read in John 12:3 where St. Mary Magdalen, in the house of Simon, took a liter of costly perfumed oil made from genuine aromatic nard and anointed the feet of Jesus. She then dried His feet with her hair and the entire house was filled with the fragrance of the oil. It is not surprising that the sweet aroma of

---

[918] Johnson, op.cit., p. 365.
[919] Ibid., p. 261.

[920] Poulain, RAV, op.cit., p. 103; Johnson, op.cit., p. 362.
[921] Treece, MB, op.cit., p. 141.
[922] NCE, I, v. 10, op.cit., p. 174.
[923] Guiley, op.cit., p. 385.
[924] Treece, MB, op.cit., p. 36.

perfumes should be associated with virtues, goodness, and holiness of God's saints. Agreeable fragrant odors called the gift of perfume or the odor of sanctity have been noted as emanating from the living or dead body of many saints during their lifetime or at their death either directly from their body or from the site of their grave. These fragrances or perfumes also lingered around the articles these people used when alive.[925]

While alive, the stigmatic wounds of Venerable Francesca dal Serrone gushed blood that was fragrant with the odor of sweet violets every Friday.[926] A flowery perfume emanated from the wounds of St. Gemma Galgani, day and night, winter and summer, although her wounds continued to putrefy and resist any kind of medication.[927] The Dominican nun Blessed Agnes of Jesus was said to diffuse a "celestial perfume,"[928] as did the body of St. Helen of Hungary.[929] St. Veronica Giuliani was known to have emitted a sweet fragrance from her wounds that penetrated the entire confines of her convent.[930] It is also said that Marie Rose Ferron, the American stigmatic known as "Little Rose," gave off a sweet aroma from her wounds. The scent was noticed by hundreds of her admirers.[931]

St. Lydwina of Schiedam, the victim soul and stigmatic whose body was ravaged by numerous afflictions had sweet delicate aromatic fragrances, like ginger and cinnamon, emanate from her wounds.[932] Later on, after receiving the stigmata, these scents were replaced by those of fresh roses, violets, or lilies, symbols of humility and chastity.[933] A hundred years after her death, the linen with which her stigmata was enveloped was still filled with perfume.[934] Padre Pio's wounds gave forth a perfume between rose and violet flowers which does not resemble any artificial perfume.[935]

Some other saints who were known for the sweet-scented wounds which they possessed include: Blessed Humliana (1219–1246), Blessed Ida of Louvain, Blessed Lucy of Narni, Venerable Dominica of Paradiso, and Blessed Jeanne Marie de la Croix (1666–1736).[936] St. Gerard Majella was often permeated with a heavenly odor. When he was dying, even his vomit smelled sweet.[937]

In modern times, we have the case of St. Padre Pio whose stigmatic wounds emitted a heavenly perfume unlike any artificial perfume. It reportedly had a scent likened to roses, violets, and carnations. This aroma was noticed by many and defied "all scientific explanation."[938] A small cloth stained with the saint's old blood kept in a cabinet of his doctor's office for a long time emitted a perfumed smell in the office. Blessed Mary of Jesus Crucified (Miriam Baouardy) also emitted a sweet odor from her open stigmata wounds.[939] The saints and beati mentioned above are just a few of those who emitted the odor of sanctity during their lifetime.

These scents are reaffirmations that the wounds are of a supernatural nature, for normal wounds tend to fester and leave foul odors. Moreover, the smell of old blood can be downright putrid.

---

[925] Cruz, MMM, op.cit., p. 49.
[926] Summers, op.cit., p. 169.
[927] Johnson, op.cit., p. 136.
[928] Thurston, op.cit., p. 231.
[929] Farges, op.cit., p. 556.
[930] Cruz, MMM, op.cit., p. 57.
[931] Freze, VVA, op.cit., p. 53.
[932] Cruz, MMM, op.cit., p. 52.
[933] Johnson, op.cit., p. 90.
[934] Farges, op.cit., p. 556.
[935] Frank M. Rega, *Padre Pio and America.* Rockford, Ill.: TAN Books and Publishers, 2005, p. 176.
[936] Freze, TBWC, op.cit., p. 188.
[937] Guiley, op.cit., p. 131.
[938] Cruz, MMM, op.cit., pp. 60–61.
[939] Treece, MB, op.cit., pp. 147–48.

Many other saintly persons have been known for their sweet bodily aroma while alive. Among the many such privileged souls are Sts. Hermann (d. 1230),[940] Aldegundis (c. 630–690), Dominic, Catherine of Bologna, Joseph of Cupertino, Thomas of Villanova, Raymond of Penafort, Willibrord (c. 658–739), Agnes of Montepulciano, Maria Maddalena de' Pazzi, Rose of Lima, Louis Bertrand, Blessed Clare of Rimini, Blessed Catherine of Racconigi,[941] Raymond Nonnatus (1204–1240), Margaret of Cortona, Frances of Rome, Francis Xavier, Elizabeth of Portugal (c. 1270–1336), Bernardino Realino, Paul of the Cross, Maria Soledad (1826–1886), Blessed Mary of Oignies,[942] Blessed Agnes of Jesus, and Blessed Mary of the Angels.[943] It is said that a radiant light surrounded St. Catherine of Ricci when she fell into ecstasy and, at the same time, a sweet smelling flowery fragrance filled the room. More than twenty nuns attested to the celestial fragrance that clung to her and lingered in the room where she died. Some compared this "odor of sanctity" to violets, but most could not liken it to anything on earth.[944] The same was said about the celestial fragrance that surrounded Blessed Ida of Louvain.[945]

Other holy individuals emitted powerful but pleasant odors after death. St. Teresa of Avila carried a sweet fragrance throughout her life and even after her death. Teresa's cell room was saturated with this heavenly aroma, and reports of her grave giving off the same scent are well known. Her incorrupt body was said to exude a powerful scent of supernatural roses.[946] St. Flora of Beaulieu (1300–1347) died in the odor of sanctity, surrounded by the fragrance of roses and lilies.[947]

The odor of sanctity was so strong about the body of St. Benedict that it even penetrated and was perceived around his clothing. St. Mary Francis of the Five Wounds (see Gallo, Maria) (1715–1791), a Franciscan nun and stigmatic, died in the odor of sanctity. We are told that a delicious mysterious fragrance clung not only to her habit but to everything she had touched during her lifetime.[948]

During the nine days before his burial, a heavenly fragrance pervaded the sickroom of St. John of God and the whole house in which he lived.[949] At her death, an odor of sweetness pervaded the place to where St. Colette died as well as the adjoining rooms.[950] Her worn body began to transform and become a beautiful and fragrant white.[951] St. Peregrine Laziosi's lifeless body gave off the most fragrant odor immediately after his death.[952]

A celestial fragrance surrounded the body of St. Rita of Cascia at death and her body has been fragrant ever since her death with a sweet odor of sanctity.[953] Shortly after his death, a heavenly perfume arose from the body of St. Louis Bertrand. Likewise, when the body of St. Catherine of Genoa was exhumed to be placed in a marble sepulcher, it was found to be almost perfectly preserved and a sweet fragrance emanated from it.[954]

The sepulcher of St. Cuthbert was opened 418 years after his death and his body found

---

[940] Cruz, MMM, op.cit., p. 52.
[941] Freze, TBWC, op.cit., p. 188.
[942] Cruz, MMM, op.cit., p. 51.
[943] Thurston, op.cit., p. 231.
[944] Cruz, MMM, op.cit., p. 54; Gallick, op.cit., p. 62.
[945] Cruz, MMM, op.cit., p. 52.
[946] Freze, TBWC, op.cit., p. 188.

[947] Gallick, op.cit., p. 297.
[948] Cruz, MMM, op.cit., pp. 50, 59.
[949] Cruz, Inc, op.cit., p. 169.
[950] Cruz, MMM, op.cit., p. 386.
[951] Guiley, op.cit., p. 79.
[952] *The Wanderer*, January 23, 2003, p. 2.
[953] Cruz, MMM, op.cit., p. 387; Cruz, Inc., op.cit., p. 132.
[954] Cruz, Inc. op.cit., pp. 160, 184.

perfectly preserved, flexible, and exhaling a heavenly fragrance.[955] Similar heavenly perfume exuded from the dead bodies of Sts. Frances of Rome, Francis Xavier (1506–1552), Francis Solanus (1549–1610),[956] Paul of the Cross,[957] Angela Merici, Paschal Baylon,[958] Colette, Clare of Montefalco, Angela of Foligno, Blessed Jane of Orvieto, Blessed Margaret of Castello,[959] and Venerable Dominica of Paradiso.[960] Upon the exhumation of Sts. Guthlac[961] and Stanislaus Kostka's remains, fragrance said to be more exquisite than that of the sweetest flower emanated from them.[962]

Blessed Lucy of Narni's body had the scent of violets when exhumed.[963] Sweet fragrances are also said to have emanated from the gravesite of St. Catherine of Bologna.[964] As soon as the lid of the casket of St. Martin de Porres was opened during exhumation, a sweet perfume having the odor of roses issued from it.[965] Eighteen months after her death, the incorrupt body of St. Rose of Lima was found exuding a delightful perfume.[966] The ashes of Blessed Alexandrina da Costa, the victim soul and stigmatic from Portugal, continues to emit a heavenly perfume to visitors to her grave.[967]

Venerable Maria of Jesus also died in the odor of sanctity at Toledo and her body was found to be incorrupt. A mysterious oil and heavenly scent surrounded her body when it was exhumed in 1929 and a sweet perfume having the odor of roses and jasmines issued from it. The garments of her body were found saturated with this perfumed oil which coated the flesh of the entire body. It was noted that everything that Maria had touched during her lifetime such as books and manuscripts bore this same flowery fragrance. This was mystifying since the venerable had touched these things hundreds of years ago.[968] Her incorrupt body is presently enclosed in a marble sarcophagus at the Carmelite Convent of San Jose in Toledo, Spain.[969]

Linen stained with the stigmata blood of St. Francis of Assisi, still preserved at Assisi, on certain occasions, reportedly gives out sweet odors. A hundred years after the death of St. Lydwine, the linen with which her stigmata was enveloped was still said to be filled with perfume.

Blessed Helen of Veszprim, Hungary (d.c.1270), the first Dominican stigmatic, had been dead for some time when it was decided to translate her body to a more convenient place. Her body was found to be incorrupt and reportedly gave out a celestial odor. Her stigmata, closed towards the end of her life, was reopened in the tomb. The chaplain placed his two fingers into the wound of the side. When he withdrew them, they were bathed in pure blood having a most fragrant odor.[970]

The tomb of St. Gerard Majella was opened one hundred years after his death for the process of beatification. Official statements ascertained that a mysterious perfumed oil that gave off a sweet odor flowed from his bones and his head. The oil filled a basin.[971] This liquid was said to be "beyond

---

[955] Ibid., p. 54.
[956] Miracles, op.cit., p. 4.
[957] Cruz, MMM, op.cit., p. 58.
[958] Thurston, op.cit., p. 248.
[959] Farges, op.cit., p. 557.
[960] Cruz, MMM, op.cit., p. 53.
[961] Thurston, op.cit., p. 224.
[962] Johnson, op.cit., p. 136; Cruz, Inc., op.cit., p. 180 ; Cruz, MMM, op.cit., p. 294; Thurston, op.cit., p. 248.
[963] Cruz, MMM, op.cit., p. 389.
[964] Cruz, Inc., op.cit., p. 143.
[965] Cruz, MMM, op.cit., p. 392.
[966] Cruz, Inc., op.cit., p. 225.
[967] Freze, TBWC, op.cit., p. 280; Thurston, op.cit., p. 249.

[968] Cruz, MMM, op.cit., pp. 392–93
[969] Cruz, Inc. op.cit., p. 236.
[970] Farges, op.cit., p. 556.
[971] Guiley, op.cit., p. 131.

the natural order."[972] A fragrant oily liquid more odoriferous than balm also exuded from the body of St. Maria Maddalena de' Pazzi some sixty years after her death.[973] This balsam was used for a sanctuary lamp as a posthumous act of homage to God in the Holy Eucharist.[974]

Likewise, when the body of St. Camillus of Lellis was exhumed eleven years after his death, a flow of pure fragrant liquid proceeded from an incision formed on his body. The faithful soaked their clothes in this liquid and it was said to have effected many cures.[975] The same was said of Marie Marguerite of the Angels, a Carmelite born at Antwerp in 1605, of the Valckenissen family, who also had gifts of bilocation and prophecy. After her death, her body gave off a fragrant oil which cured the sick.[976]

Odor of Sin

It would seem only proper that if sanctity has a perceptible fragrance, sin would have the opposite effect; that is, sanctity emitting a perfume, sin emitting an unpleasant odor. Because of these scents, a number of saints have had the ability to detect the difference between a person in the state of grace and another in need of confession.[977] The stench of sin can be a very terrible thing. In some cases, it has caused a saint uncontrollable vomiting or fainting because of the overwhelming foul odor.[978]

St. Christina the Astonishing, for example, could not stand the odor of other people because she could smell the sin in them. She would climb trees or buildings, hide in ovens or cupboards, jump into rivers or simply levitate to avoid contact with them.[979]

In his *Life of St. Hilarion*, St. Jerome (c.342–420) says that St. Hilarion (c.291–371) had the gift of knowing what sins or vices anyone was inclined to by simply smelling either the person or his garments.[980]

St. Catherine of Siena once revealed to her confessor Bl. Raymond of Capua (1330–1399) that the "stench of sin" was so overpowering in many of her callers that she could not endure it. She even told Pope Gregory XI in an audience with him in the Vatican that there was a "stench of all the vices of hell" in that holy city.[981]

St. Joseph of Cupertino could detect the stench of sin. Once he was so overcome by that he asked permission to go to town. There he went straight to a home wherein sorcerers dwelt. Furious, he is said to have broken all their vessels with a cane.[982] St. Pio of Pietrelcina (Padre Pio) could literally smell the stench of sin in others.[983]

Bl. Anna Maria Taigi had an olfactory aversion to sin in others. The stench of sin in people was a constant added torment for her.[984] Her sense of smell was violated by the horrible stench of sin she perceived in the world, which became more pungent when a sinner approached her.[985] She could tell the state of grace of individuals, living or dead. St. Paul of the Cross had the gift of perceiving a stench from souls infested with the sin of impurity.[986] St. Gemma Galgani could also "smell" the purity of a person's soul upon being introduced to them for the first time. If the person were

---

[972] Cruz, MMM, op.cit., p. 364.
[973] Cruz, Inc., op.cit., p. 217.
[974] Farges, op.cit., p. 557.
[975] Cruz, Inc., op.cit., p. 222.
[976] Biot, op.cit., p. 28.
[977] Cruz, MMM, op.cit., p. 62.
[978] Guiley, op.cit., p. 385.

[979] Delaney, op.cit., p. 117; Johnson, op.cit., p. 73.
[980] Michael Rose, *Heroes, Holiness and Mystical Phenomena*, http://www.4marks.com/articles/details.
[981] Cruz, MMM, op.cit., p. 62.
[982] Guiley, op.cit., p. 193.
[983] Miracles, op.cit., p. 5.
[984] Johnson, op.cit., p. 73.
[985] Lord, VMS, op.cit., p. 310.
[986] Miracles, op.cit., p. 5.

in the state of sin, the horrible stench emitted by that person would make her shudder and become physically ill.[987] St. John Bosco could detect an impure soul in a group just by its evil odor. Sts. Joseph of Cupertino, Philip Neri, and Anthony Marie Claret are likewise examples of saints who could perceive sinful persons by the horrible stench emanating from their bodies.[988] The French priest and mystic Pere Lamy (1855–1931) could smell sin even through a penitent's perfume.[989]

Prophecy

Scripture states the following: "Know this first of all, that there is no prophecy of scripture that is a matter of personal interpretation, for no prophecy ever came through human will, but rather human beings, moved by the Holy Spirit spoke under the influence of God" (2 Pt 1:20–21). Prophecy is a divinely inspired word or message given by God or His messenger (an angel or saint) to reveal a divine truth or mystery of faith, or in order to instruct, inspire, warn, correct, or praise. There are two types of prophecy: (1) those practical lessons of faith given for the benefit of a particular people in a specific circumstance and place; and (2) those pointing to future events in the overall plan of redemption and salvation. The latter is the most popularly known, which includes apocalyptic messages of warning of end times, divine retribution, the Second Coming of Christ, judgment, and the life hereafter. The former sense of prophecy is in reality the more common and the more accurate expression of scriptural prophecy, dealing with moral and ethical instructions for the people of God in times of change, challenge, or crisis. The majority of the prophecies and

The Prophet Agabus predicting St. Paul's suffering in Jerusalem, 1687, by Louis Cheron

prophets of the Old Testament fall under this category.[990]

We have numerous examples of prophecies of divine origin from Scripture to include scores of Old Testament prophecies about Jesus' birth, life and ministry, death and resurrection, titles and attributes. New Testament prophecies abound to include Christ's prediction of the destruction of the Temple (Lk 21:6), His own Passion and Resurrection (Lk 24:7; Mt 20:18–19), Peter's denial (Mt 26:34), the betrayal of Judas (Mt 14:18), the coming persecution (Lk 21:12–17), the great tribulation (Lk 21:20–14), the Coming of the Son of Man (Lk 21:25–28), and at the Presentation of the infant Jesus in the temple, Simeon's prophecy where, inspired by the Holy Spirit, he said: "Behold, this child is destined for the fall and rise of many in Israel, and to be a sign that that will be contradicted." This elderly prophet also foretold

---

[987] Guiley, op.cit., p. 129.

[988] Cruz, MMM, op.cit., pp. 63–65.

[989] See www.mysticsofthechurch.com/2009/11/pere–lamy.

[990] Freze, VVA, op.cit., pp. 313–14.

that a sword of sorrow would pierce Mary's soul (Lk 2:34–35).

A divine prophecy, however, differs from a vision of the future. When the Lord of the world and history, transcendent over time imparts information about the future, this is not a "vision" but a "word." As such, this "word" does not show a picture of part of the future, but communicates something about it together with an interpretation. There will always be men and women in the Church with charismatic gifts who will look into the future like the prophets of old and warn us to make the right decisions in the present.[991]

The gifts of prophecy like the reading of hearts are given for the benefit of others.[992] Prophecy in this section has nothing to do with matters of faith or the prediction of future world events, but simply tells how the saints and holy people, inspired by the Holy Spirit, have been able to reveal things concerning people with whom they come into contact or those people who were suggested to them. These prophecies might take the form of a saint or holy person predicting the time and place of a person's death, warnings or consolations. Some might even concern events that would take place in years to come such as St. Benedict's prophecy of (the destruction of) Monte Cassino centuries later.[993] St. Godric had knowledge of events occurring hundreds of thousands miles away.[994] Venerable Gertrude van de Oosten had knowledge, at the actual time, of what took place at a distance as well as what was about to happen in the future.[995]

St. Rose of Viterbo foretold the imminent death of Emperor Frederick II weeks before it happened.[996] Saints and beati prophesized the elevation of certain religious figures to the papacy long before their election to that post. Such was the prediction of St. Bardo (981–1051) who, before his death, stated that Gebhard of Eichstatt would be the next pope known as Pope Victor II (1055–1057).[997] Blessed Conrad of Ascoli (1234–1289) predicted the election of his childhood friend Jerome to the papacy (Pope Nicholas IV) years before the actual event.[998] Blessed Elizabeth von Reute foretold the election of Martin V (1417–1431) to the papal throne and the end of the Western Schism.[999] The same could be said for St. Francis of Paola who predicted the election of Cardinal Giuliano della Rovere as Pope Julius II (1503–1513) and Giovanni de Medici as Pope Leo X (1513–1521) long in advance of their elevation to that post.[1000]

St. Joseph of Cupertino not only foresaw the deaths of Pope Urban VIII (1623–1644) and Pope Innocent X (1644–1655) but predicted the time and day when they would and did die. He also foretold the ascension of King John Casimir to the throne of Poland.[1001] St. Paul of the Cross, founder of the Passionist Order, prophesized shortly after the election of Pope Pius VI in 1775 that the pope would have a long and glorious pontificate but would suffer many calamities and would be forced to leave Rome. The pope reigned for twenty-five years, had great difficulties with Emperor Joseph II, and was taken captive by Napoleon who took him to France where he later died.[1002] St. Maria

---

[991] Rahner, VAP, op.cit., pp. 95, 102.

[992] Cruz, MMM, op.cit., p. xv.

[993] Ibid., p. 186.

[994] Freze, VVA, op.cit., p. 220; see also http://saints.sqpn.com/saintg6t.htm.

[995] http://www.newadvent.org/cathen/06535a.htm.

[996] Cowan, op.cit., p. 396.

[997] Miracles, op.cit., p. 11.

[998] Cruz, MMM, op.cit., p. 189.

[999] http://www.newadvent.org/cathen/05391b.htm.

[1000] Cruz, MMM, op.cit., p. 192.

[1001] Lord, VMS, op.cit., p. 150.

[1002] Cruz, MMM, op.cit., p. 196.

Maddalena de' Pazzi astonished Cardinal Alexander dei Medici with her prediction that he would be elevated to the papacy as Leo XI but would only enjoy a short reign. As a matter of fact, he only survived his election by twenty-eight days.[1003] Two years prior to the event, Bl. Anna Maria Taigi predicted the exact date that Pope Pius VII (1800–1823), the second pope taken prisoner by Napoleon, would return to the Vatican. Anna Maria also predicted the imminent death of Pope Pius VII and later on told of the short pontificate and death of Pope Pius VIII (1829–1830).[1004] Marie-Julie Jahenny also had many prophetic insights. For instance, she foretold the two World Wars, the election of Pope Saint Pius X (1903–1914) and the various persecutions of the Church.[1005]

St. Louis Marie Grignion de Montfort's most impressive faculty was his gift of prophecy. He could tell the future careers of people in the crowds, predicted happy deaths for the converted, and miserable deaths for the unrepentant. His most remarkable prophecy of all was his prediction of the whole course and substance of Marian apparitions that began a hundred and fourteen years after his death, beginning with the apparitions of St. Catherine Laboure in 1830.[1006]

St. Paul of the Cross, mentioned above, also predicted the imminent death of people who appeared to be in robust health, and also made predictions about many persons who would recover from what appeared to be life-threatening situations. St. Joseph of Cupertino had visions of the future whereby he revealed those persons who, though looking healthy, nevertheless were to die unexpectedly. St. Gerard of Majella

also predicted the death of certain persons, even giving the exact date when their death would take place. St. John Bosco accurately predicted the untimely death of a number of his young students.[1007]

More recently, Saint Andre of Montreal who also possessed the mystical gift of prophecy foretold when certain people would die. St. Padre Pio obliged three priests in accurately predicting the order in which they would pass from this world.[1008] St. Bernard of Clairvaux, knowing that King Louis VI of France remained obstinate in his dispute with the pope, mournfully predicted that his oldest son Philip would die an early death and this came to happen. Other servants of God such as Blessed Margaret of Castello and St. Frances of Rome predicted the admittance of certain women to religious life. St. Colette coming out of an ecstasy told her good friend St. Vincent Ferrer that he would die in France not his native Spain within two years. This turned out to be true.[1009] Some other saints known to have the gift of prophecy or the ability to predict future events were: Sts. Bardo (981–1051), John Gualbert (993–1073), Hildegard of Bingen, Bridget of Sweden, Louis Bertrand, Pacifico of San Severino, Gemma Galgani,[1010] and Marianna de Jesus Paredes y Flores, Anthony of Padua, and Maria Maddalena de' Pazzi.[1011]

At the age of thirty-two, St. Angela Merici was favored with a prophetic vision in which she saw, on a staircase which reached into the heavens, a number of young women and some angels. One of the young ladies detached herself from this celestial group and advanced to where Angela knelt in ecstasy and delivered this message: "Know, Angela, that our Divine

[1003] Farges, op.cit., p. 29.
[1004] Cruz, MMM, op.cit., p. 198.
[1005] http://www.communityofhopeinc.org/prayer%20pages/saints/marie%20julie.html.
[1006] Johnson, op.cit., p. 94.

[1007] Cruz, MMM, op.cit., pp. 194–97, 200.
[1008] Ibid., pp. 203–4.
[1009] Ibid., pp. 187, 190–91.
[1010] Miracles, op.cit., p. 12.
[1011] Cruz, MMM, op.cit., pp. 189, 194.

Lord has sent you this vision to teach you that before you die you are to establish in Brescia a company of young virgins like these. This is His will for you." Around 1535, a group of some twenty–eight young ladies began helping Angela in her catechetical work with young children. This group came to be known as the Company of St. Ursula.[1012]

A number of saints knew and predicted the time of their own death and the circumstances of their torment or that of their companions. Such, for instance, were the prophetic visions of St. Perpetua (d. 203) in her prison cell. Several days before her death, she was warned that she and her brother, St. Saturus (d. 203) would be exposed to wild beasts. The event confirmed her visions. Similar visions were accorded to Sts. Cyprian (c. 200–258), Pionius (d.c. 250), Marianus (d. 260, James (d. 44), and many others of whom there is an endless list. St. Lawrence (d. 258), when stretched on his gridiron, in an ecstasy which illumined his face, foretold to his brethren the future of Christianity in Rome, and the reign of a Christian emperor who would bring to a close the era of persecutions and give peace to the Church. This prediction made a century in advance of the famous victory of Constantine and the edict of Milan, cannot be explained naturally.[1013]

St. Benedict, (c. 480–543) died on March 21, 543, on the Saturday preceding Passion Sunday, the day he had predicted. St. Dominic claimed he would die before the feast of the Assumption (August 15). He died on August 6, being fifty–one years of age. St. Rose of Lima not only knew the exact date of her death but that she would painfully die of consumption, although she was at the time in perfect health. St. Gerard Majella even foretold the exact day

The Martyrdom of St. Lawrence, 1614, by Peter Paul Rubens

and hour of his death some six months in advance. St. Catherine Laboure predicted she would never see the year 1877. She died during the evening of December 31, 1876.[1014] St. Aloysius Gonzaga (1568–1591) received a vision telling him he had not long to live, a revelation that filled him with joy. Aloysius revealed he would die on the octave of Corpus Christi. He took his last breath about June 20–21, 1591.[1015] St. Padre Pio predicted the time of his own death on many occasions.[1016] He also predicted that,

[1012] Cruz, Inc., op.cit., p. 164
[1013] Farges, op.cit., p. 22.

[1014] Cruz, MMM, op.cit., pp. 211–15.
[1015] Guiley, op.cit., p. 11.
[1016] Rega, op.cit., p. 249.

upon his death, his stigmata wounds of fifty years would completely heal.[1017] St. Veronica Giuliani prophesized that her stigmata would last three years and it did, and Marie-Julie Jahenny similarly predicted when her various wounds and blemishes would appear and disappear.[1018] St. Joseph of Cupertino predicted he would die on the day he would not receive the Eucharist.[1019] Blessed Stephanie de Quinzanis predicted the day of her death and the place of her burial. St. Peter of Verona (1206–1252) predicted that he would be murdered by heretics who indeed waylaid him on the road between Como and Milan.[1020]

Blessed Villana de Botti was warned in a vision that her time on earth was drawing to an end and she expired a short time afterwards. Before her death, however, she prophesized that she would send her friends flowers from heaven, and this was accomplished when a friend, a Franciscan tertiary, bent over the beata's body to view her beautiful face. It was then that great armloads of flowers fell from the sky, fulfilling Villana's prophecy.[1021]

Other holy servants of God who predicted the exact day and even the hour of their death include: Sts. Columba (521–597), Bardo (981–1051), Godric of Finchale, Malachy O'Morgair, Isidore the Laborer (1070–1130), Margaret of Scotland Queen (1045–1083), Peter Gonzalez (1190–1246), Martin de Porres, Collette, Aloysius Gonzaga (1568–1591), Joseph Mary Tommasi (1649–1713), Lucy Filippini (1672–1732), Louis Bertrand, Faustina Kowalska, Blessed Anna Maria Taigi,[1022] Sts. Joseph of Leonissa (1556–1612), Madeline Sophie Barat (1779–1865), Blessed Gerard of

Villamagna (1174–1242), Blessed James of Bevagna (1220–1301), Blessed Francis Patrizzi (1266–1328), Blessed Bernard Scammacca (1430–1487), and many, many others.[1023]

Rapture

The mystical phenomenon known as rapture (also referred to as mystical flight, mystical swoon, or transport) is often difficult to separate from the state of ecstasy, primarily because this spiritual flight takes place within the ecstatic state. It is really a peak moment within the state of ecstasy, a kind of momentary mystical height that draws the soul closer to God. Frequently when the soul is suspended from the normal senses and caught up in the state of rapture, it loses all sense of time and reality, as if transported to another dimension. Furthermore, the condition is impetuous and sudden and often uncontrollable, an irresistible urge from the divine impulse to lose oneself in the bosom of the Lord. The experience of rapture can totally overwhelm the soul, even making it "swoon and fall to the ground as if dead."[1024] An experience of rapture can literally separate one's soul from the physical body while in the presence of the divine. In this rare state, one may receive extraordinary visions (intellectual, imaginative, or physical) of such things as the Three Persons of the Trinity, or of heaven, hell, and purgatory.[1025]

St. Teresa of Avila notes that in ecstasy, as in all spiritual phenomena, there is a greater and lesser, with all degrees of intensity in between. An ecstasy of significantly greater intensity and longer duration is often called rapture (which cannot be resisted) or, as she preferred to call it, suspension. In suspension, she says, the

[1017] Guiley, op.cit., p. 266.
[1018] Wilson, op cit., p. 70.
[1019] Cruz, MMM, op.cit., p. 213.
[1020] Miracles, op.cit., p. 11.
[1021] Cruz, MMM, op.cit., p. 43; see also Patron Saints Index.
[1022] Miracles, op.cit., pp. 11–12.

[1023] Cruz, MMM, op.cit., p. 215.
[1024] Freze, TBWC, op.cit. ,pp. 153–55.
[1025] Freze, VVA, op.cit., p. 316.

The Rapture of Saint Paul, 17th century (oil on canvas), Domenichino (Domenico Zampieri) (1581-1641) (after) / Pinacoteca Ambrosiana, Milan, Italy / © Veneranda Biblioteca Ambrosiana/Paolo Manusardi/Mondadori Portfolio / Bridgeman Images

union lasts longer, and the body shows different symptoms; the senses of the body stop working and the senses of the soul take over. The soul is so transfixed with joy at the union, she says, that it seems to forget all about the body. Suspension that comes more quickly is called transport. St. Teresa states that in transport, the soul leaves the body completely. It surrenders itself into the arms of the Lord to go wherever He may want to bring it. Beyond transport, she defines the flight of the spirit.[1026] She describes this phenomenon as transport that is virtually instantaneous and of an unimaginable intensity. It throws the mind into a stupor and thrill of wonderment. It was such a rapture which raised St. Paul to the third heaven, where he heard secrets which no mortal tongue could express.[1027]

St. Thomas Aquinas writes that "rapture involves something more than ecstasy, for ecstasy precisely speaking implies a transport out of and beyond oneself, so that a man is removed from his normal well-ordered condition, but rapture entails something of violence."[1028]

The Cistercian Cardinal Bona (1609–1674) in his great work *De Discretione Spirituum* (On the Discerning of Spirits), states that "this is the essential difference between ecstasy and rapture. The former state withdraws the mind from the senses more gently and (as it were) more persuasively. The latter is more powerful and not without violence of a kind. Rapture adds this (force) to ecstasy, namely it catches up the resistless soul with power and might, most rapidly and with divine compulsion sweeping upwards and onwards away from the senses and all things appertaining, so that the soul is swiftly carried and borne aloft to the enjoyment of the intellectual vision and aflame with the ardent love of heavenly things."[1029]

As already stated, a rapture cannot be resisted. St. Philip Neri had to lean against the altar during the consecration at Mass to keep from collapsing in rapture.[1030] When St. Michaelde Sanctis fell into rapture, often during prayer, he ran through the cloisters at wonderful speed uttering cries of joy, and darting hither and thither with such celerity that nobody could stay him.

In the Bull of Canonization of St. Maria Maddalena de' Pazzi it is related that when the rapture overwhelmed her, she rushed to and fro, up and down the stairs and along the corridors, through the nuns' quarters with inconceivable rapidity, often tearing her habit in her haste, and throwing to one side anything that came in her way.

Gianbattista Scaramelli in his great work *Il Direttorio Mistico* divides rapture into three classes: 1) Those raptures in which the exterior senses are suspended, while the interior senses are retained, which is not, strictly speaking, a rapture at all, yet is (as it were) a promise of a rapture to come; 2) Those raptures in which both the exterior and interior senses are suspended which he terms "perfect rapture," and; 3) Those raptures when both exterior and interior senses are suspended in the contemplation of the beatific vision. Scaramelli opines that a state of rapture may last for several hours or even for days, but that there will be fluctuations in its intensity. What he means to say is that rapture must and will ebb back to ecstasy. He adds that, at its highest point, rapture will scarcely exceed

thirty minutes. This is consistent with what Cardinal Bona says above.[1031]

[1026] Johnson, op.cit. p. 47.
[1027] Farges, op.cit., p. 169.
[1028] See Thomas, Saint Aquinas. *Summa Theologica*, translated by Dominican Fathers. NY: Benzinger Brothers, 1948. Section, II, 2dae, q. 175, art. 2.

[1029] Summers, op.cit., p. 103.
[1030] Johnson, op.cit., p. 47.
[1031] Summer, op.cit., p. 104.

Extraordinary phenomena accompany divine rapture. On October 18, 1501, Venerable Dominica of Paradiso fell into an ecstasy, which increased with a violent spasm to rapture, whereupon she saw the Mother of God attended by St. Gabriel and her own guardian angel. At Mary's command, the two celestial beings led Dominica to heaven and there, by a special privilege of Our Lady, she was permitted a clear understanding of the humanity of Jesus and the Divine Essence. Blessed Elisabetta Canori-Mora passed into rapture on October 23, 1816 and had a vision of the Madonna holding the infant Jesus surrounded by St. Joseph, the three Magi, St. John de Matha (1160–1213), St. Felix of Valois (1126–1212), and an infinite host of angels.[1032] St. Gemma Galgani experienced a rapture whereby she had a vision of her guardian angel in the company of the Blessed Virgin Mary.[1033] St. Teresa of Avila while enraptured was overcome by divine love, resulting in a wound to her heart caused by a fiery arrow that pierced her soul and united her to the Sacred Heart of the Savior.[1034] The stigmatic St. Gertrude (1256–1302) experienced profound moments of rapture, especially when contemplating on Our Lord's Passion. On one Good Friday, Gertrude's union with God became so engaging that she could not attend to anything exterior or sensible. She remained in rapture the whole day and throughout the next day (Holy Saturday).[1035]

Stigmatization (Stigmata)

This mystical phenomenon is the spontaneous appearance upon the bodies of God's most chosen souls of wounds and bleeding that resemble the physical wounds that Christ suffered during His Passion and Crucifixion.[1036]

The stigmata is not given to the stigmatic for his or her own benefit but for the benefit of others. The stigmatic represents the Crucified Christ to a world continually in need of a loving sacrifice that atones for our sin. The stigmatic is this loving sacrifice, one who is transformed into a living crucifix who shares in the Lord's Passion for the redemption of the world. There are other Christs among us as signs of God's mercy and love for unbelievers and channels for His grace to those who need healing, renewal, and conversion.[1037] These are extraordinary souls, holy and pure, who, by imitating Christ so intensely, have been invited to become one with Him. They are role models for all of us on our journey toward perfection and salvation.[1038] It should be noted that a saint may be a stigmatic, but a stigmatic is by no means necessarily a saint.[1039]

It is claimed that St. Paul was the first stigmatic. He says: "I have been crucified with Christ" (Gal 2:19). "I bear the marks of Jesus on my body" (Gal 6:17). This is about as explicit as you can get on the matter.

St. Francis of Assisi, however, is recognized as the first documented case of stigmatization although a case could be made for Blessed Dodo of Hascha (d.1231) whose stigmata might have predated that of St. Francis of Assisi.

[1032] Ibid., pp. 105–6.
[1033] Johnson, op.cit., p. 192.
[1034] St. Teresa, *Life*, op.cit., p. 244.
[1035] From *The Life and Revelations of St. Gertrude*, op.cit., p. 390; Freze, TBWC, op.cit., p. 155.

[1036] Aumann, op.cit., p. 432.
[1037] Freze, TBWC, op.cit., p. 8.
[1038] Ibid., p. 12.
[1039] Wilson, op.cit., p. 124.

Stigmatization of Saint Francis, 1297–1299, by Giotto di Bondone

Thomas of Celano, the biographer of St. Francis of Assisi, relates that while praying in his cell on Mount Alverna (La Verna) on September 14, 1224, the Feast of the Exaltation of the Cross, St. Francis saw in the vision of God a man standing above him like a seraph with six wings, his hands extended and his feet joined together and fixed to a cross which had between its wings the figure of a man crucified nailed to a cross. Two of the wings were extended above his head, two were extended as if for flight, and two were wrapped around the whole body. While St. Francis was trying to understand what the vision could mean, the marks of the nails began to appear on his hands and his feet, just as he had seen them a little before in the crucified man above him.[1040] The nails were said to protrude beyond the skin on both sides of his palms. This was the climax of a series of supernatural events he had experienced throughout his life.[1041]

As the outward reflection of the Lord's Passion imprinted upon the soul, the stigmatic's wounds usually appear during the rapture of ecstasy. As a general rule, the wounds do not become inflamed or infected. Some of the wounds never bleed. Others bled on Fridays or at other times.[1042] While most stigmatics have their nail wounds in the middle of their palms, the form of these wounds vary markedly. Some have slits in their palms, others mere round indentations, others almost unbroken skin. Likewise the wounds on the backs of the hands have varied, with some such as those of Therese Neumann, ever

changing from round to rectangular.[1043] The wounds can appear in a variety of ways. The victim need not have all the marks of the crucifixion in order to be considered a stigmatic. If a soul has received one or several of the wounds of the Passion, he or she is considered to have a partial or incomplete stigmata; nevertheless, they are still considered true stigmatics.

When only one wound is present, it is known as a stigma. Sometimes the entire body of the stigmatic is covered with wounds, as if from a scourging, or the forehead is punctured as if by thorns. The marking with the "Five Wounds," (side, two hands, and both feet) accompanied or unaccompanied by the crown of thorns has been designated by some as the "Complete Stigmatization."[1044] Yet there are other stigmatic imprints that have been recorded. Such are the wheals of the scourging; the wounds from carrying the cross either on the right or left shoulder, wounds of the heart, the side wound (see wound of love, the ferita), wounds on the wrists, the livid bruising of the cords, and, on the mouth, the hyssop mark of the sponge sopped with vinegar which was set upon a reed[1045] as well as the tears and sweats of blood.[1046]

Each wound of the stigmata does not always appear at the same time, nor do they bleed in exactly the same manner among the stigmatists. In the many cases where all of the Five Wounds appeared in these victim souls, most of them occurred simultaneously. Such is the case, for instance, of St. Francis of Assisi, whose wounds appeared all at once.[1047] Yet with others it is quite different. Delicia di Giovanni (1550–1622) received each of the Five Wounds, one in each succeeding year: the first year, the

---

[1040] Cruz, MMM, op.cit., pp. 218–19.

[1041] Johnson, op.cit., p. 159; see also Thomas of Celano, St. Francis of Assisi. *First and second life of St. Francis with selection from the treatise on Blessed Francis.* Translated from Latin with introduction and footnotes by Placid Hermann. Chicago, Illinois: Franciscan Herald Press, 1988, ch. 3, 84–86.

[1042] Cruz, MMM, op.cit., p. 216; Summers, op.cit., p. 61.

[1043] Wilson, op. cit., pp. 63–64.

[1044] Freze, TBWC, op.cit., p. 198.

[1045] Summers, op.cit., p. 118.

[1046] Freze, TBWC, op.cit., p. 198.

[1047] Ibid., p. 200.

right hand, and in the second, the left; the third year saw the right foot wound, and with the fourth came the left; in the fifth year, Delicia received the wound of the heart; in her sixth year, she experienced the scourge marks; finally, in the seventh year, she received the crown of thorn wounds, thus completing her stigmatization.[1048] No one has ever carried the entire suffering of the Passion in his or her body. A few stigmatics, however, have come close to suffering all of the physical torments of the Passion, such as Therese Neumann of Konnersreuth, West Germany (1898–1962) and, reportedly, Mary Rose Ferron of Woonsocket, Rhode Island (1902–1936).[1049]

As already mentioned, some of the wounds never bleed. Others bleed on Fridays or at other times. There is also a wide variety of experience in just how long the bleeding and suffering lasts in these victim souls. For instance, every Thursday, the thirty-two puncture wounds from the crown of thorns Jesus had bestowed on the Dominican nun Maria de la Visitacion (1556–1598) bled at the hour of the Ave Maria.[1050] When St. Francis of Assisi received his Five Wounds all at once, they were permanently fixed in his body. St. Padre Pio's wounds continually bled without any interruption the entire time he had the stigmata (1918–1968). St. Francis had wounds for only two years (1224–1226), whereas St. Padre Pio's wounds lasted for fifty years. The Belgian mystic Louise Lateau had the stigmata for sixteen years, but her wounds only bled on certain days each week (nevertheless it is believed that she hemorrhaged some eight hundred times in her life!). This was also the case with Blessed Stephanie de Quinzanis, St. Catherine of Ricci, and Therese Neumann.[1051]

St. Gemma Galgani, known as "The Passion Flower of Lucca," received the holy stigmata on June 8, 1899 and then experienced a rapture in which she had a vision of her guardian angel in the company of the Blessed Virgin Mary. Her stigmata gradually appeared during her ecstasies, first as red marks on her hands and feet that progressively tore open and bled copiously and then the nails themselves formed out of flesh, hard and dark, just like St. Francis's. However, they would disappear after her torments subsided, leaving her with only whitish marks on her skin.[1052] For two years afterwards, every Thursday evening at eight o'clock, she would be caught up in ecstasy and the wounds would open up. Finally, on Friday at 3 o'clock, the wounds would close, leaving only a small white scar and the pain.[1053] A flowery perfume emanated from her wounds day and night, winter and summer, although they continued to putrefy and resist any kind of medication.[1054]

Some of these souls only bled from their wounds once each year during Holy Week of Lent. Such was the case of Domitilla Calucci (d. 1671), a Capuchin nun of unusual sanctity.[1055] The stigmata of Blessed Elizabeth Von Reute appeared only now and again, but her pains never ceased.[1056] The Dominican nun Blessed Emily Bicchier of Vercelli (1238–1314) was stigmatized with only the crown of thorns and suffered only three days of unbearable pain during which time she was visited by several of the saints associated with Christ's Passion. At the end of three days, the pain went away.[1057]

[1048] Biot, op.cit., pp. 42–43.
[1049] Freze, TBWC, op.cit., p. 199.
[1050] Summers, op.cit., pp. 219–20.
[1051] Freze, TWBC, op.cit., p. 200.

[1052] Johnson, op.cit., pp. 159–60.
[1053] Ibid., pp. 192–93.
[1054] Ibid., p. 136.
[1055] Freze, TWBC, op.cit., p. 200.
[1056] Agnes B. C.Dunbar, *A Dictionary of Saintly Women.* 2v. London: G. Bell & Co. 1905, v. 1, p. 266.
[1057] Dorcy, op.cit., p. 126.

Saint Rita of Cascia, 16th-century Portuguese school

There is considerable variety in the combinations of the sacred wounds. For example, there are the marks of one foot alone in the case of Catherine Perez of Carvalho, the Cistercian, while Mary of the Crown, a Dominican of the Seveda monastery who died in 1554, had the marks on both feet, but no other wound. So had Jean Gray and Marie Marguerite of the Angels, a Carmelite born at Antwerp in 1605, of the Valckenissen family, who had gifts of bilocation and prophecy. After Marie Marguerite's death, her body gave out a fragrant oil which cured the sick.[1058] Others were stigmatized just in the hands or feet.[1059]

There are those stigmatics who only bore the crown of thorns. Such was the case with St. Margaret Mary Alacoque,[1060] Blessed Christina d'Aquila, an Augustinian nun (d. 1543), Ursula Aguir (1554–1608),

a Dominican Tertiary of Valencia. A Franciscan tertiary Caterina Ciaulina (d. 1619) only felt the crown of thorns. Hippolita of Jesus (1553–1624), an enclosed contemplative in the Dominican convent of the Holy Angels in Barcelona, was crowned by the Hands of Our Lord in a mystic vision. Louise de Jesus, a Carmelite of Dole, received the crown of thorns six months before her death.[1061] In 1441, in response to a prayer to suffer as Christ, St. Rita of Cascia received a thorn-induced wound in the middle of her forehead which bled for fifteen years. This single stigmatic wound had little worms in it and smelled so supernaturally foul that her sister nuns made her live isolated from them for fifteen years. At the time of her death, a great light emanated from the wound on her forehead while the little worms were transformed into sparks of light. The wound can still be seen on her forehead, since her body remains marvelously incorrupt.[1062]

Some who bore the Five Wounds and the crown of thorns include: Blessed Christina of Stommeln,[1063] Blessed Ida of Louvain, Blessed Stephanie de Quinzanis,[1064] Blessed Osanna d'Andreasi, Venerable Giovanna Maria of the Cross (1603–1673),[1065] Venerable Passitea Crogi,[1066] Marthe Robin, Mary Rose Ferron, and Theresa Neumann.[1067] Maria Dominica Lazzari is of particular interest since the crown of thorns was bestowed on her not by Jesus but by the Blessed Virgin Mary.[1068] Likewise, the crown of thorns was placed on Berthe Petit's head during an ecstasy by St. Catherine of Siena.[1069]

[1058] Biot, op.cit., p. 28.

[1059] See appendix 1 for more information.

[1060] Johnson. op.cit., p. 267.

[1061] Summers, op.cit., p. 169.

[1062] Cruz, MMM ,op.cit., pp. 222–23; Freze, TBWC, op.cit., p. 261.

[1063] Wilson, op. cit., p. 132.

[1064] Cruz, MMM, op.cit., pp. 52, 148.

[1065] Summers, op.cit., p. 154.

[1066] Cruz, MMM, op.cit., p. 223.

[1067] Freze, TWBC, op.cit., pp. 286, 275, 280.

[1068] Summers, op.cit., p. 165.

[1069] Freze, TWBC, op.cit., p. 278.

Those having all Five Wounds, the crown of thorns plus the marks of the scourging include: St. Catherine de' Ricci whose stigmata wounds were located in her hands, feet, shoulder, and side. Those wounds along with those inflicted by the crown of thorns and injuries produced by the whips and cords of the scourging were variously described by people who viewed them. Some declared that her hands were pierced through and bleeding; others perceived a brilliant light that dazzled their eyes; and still others saw the wounds as being healed but red and swollen.[1070] Blessed Catherine of Racconigi received the Five Wounds, the crown of thorns, and the shoulder wound. One day Christ appeared to her carrying His cross, and she offered to help. He let the cross rest for a moment on her shoulder and it inflicted a wound that lasted for the rest of her life.[1071]

Sts. Clare of Montefalco, Veronica Giuliani, Padre Pio, and Blessed Elizabeth Von Reute, Louise Lateau, Therese Neumann, Mary Rose Ferron, and Marie-Julie Jahenny all had the five stigmata wounds along with the shoulder wound. Aside from wounds in the hands and feet, St. Gemma Galgani, mentioned above, experienced other physical phenomena of Christ's passion, such as the sweat of blood, scourging, and the crowning with thorns.[1072] Blessed Anne Catherine Emmerich received the complete stigmatization along with a cross-shaped wound on her breast. Berthe Petit received all the sacred wounds plus bleeding from the lips and tongue, along with tremendous thirst.[1073]

On September 6, 1934, Jesus appeared to Blessed Alexandrina Maria da Costa and offered her a share of His Cross. She

Saint Catherine of Siena by Agostino Carracci

bravely accepted, and from then on this servant of God felt the pains of Christ's wounds in her hands, feet, and side as well as the crown of thorn wounds and the scourging. These Passion ecstasies would continue weekly for the rest of her life, although her stigmata never appeared outwardly. She was called to bear the invisible stigmata.[1074] For a period of three-and-a-half years she received the mystical gift of experiencing each Friday the pains of Christ on the cross, from Friday October 3, 1938 to March 24, 1942. On one hundred and eighty-two Fridays, she lived out the sufferings of the Passion. Alexandrina reproduced the various movements of the Via Crucis for three-and-a-half hours. Her passion ecstasies included the agony, the scourging, the crowning of thorns, and the vision of Mother Mary at the foot of the Cross.[1075]

[1070] Cruz, Inc., op.cit., p. 197, see also Cruz, MMM, op.cit., p. 222; NCE, v. 14, 1912, p. 295.

[1071] Dorcy, op.cit., p. 272.

[1072] Johnson, op.cit., p. 192.

[1073] Freze, TWBC, op.cit., pp. 270, 278.

[1074] Ibid., p. 279.

[1075] Ibid.; see also Andrew Rabel, "Alexandrina Maria da Costa," in *Inside the Vatican*, May 2004, pp. 60–64.

The stigmata may be partial or, as mentioned above, invisible (concealed stigmata). The stigmata may occur only during ecstasy or remain more or less permanently.[1076] The stigmatics reach the highest mystical state, the divine union, because of their profound love for God as for themselves, and not for the favors they receive from Him.[1077]

In some cases, the wounds were visible at first, but were rendered invisible by the Lord when the saint asked this grace out of humility. This is a condition whereby a stigmatic bears all or a part of the Lord's sufferings and wounds intensely, though invisibly, in his or her body or soul. In fact, the suffering can be as great as or greater in these souls than in those who have visible, exterior stigmata. St. Catherine of Siena received the stigmata during an ecstasy in 1375 while in a church in Pisa. Although the wounds were only visible to her, she asked for them to be made invisible as an act of humility and to avoid publicity. The Lord granted her this request. She continued to have the same intense pains of these invisible wounds as she had when they were visible. It was clearly apparent, however, at the time of her death, that the marks were quite pronounced.[1078]

On February 24, 1476, being mystically espoused to Christ, Blessed Osanna of Mantua received from the Lord the crown of thorns. The wound in her side next appeared on June 5, 1477[1079] while she was wrapped in ecstasy and she was raised up into the seventh heaven where she saw the Lord in exceeding great glory. A year later, during a Friday in Passion Week, Christ appeared to her and rays from the wounds in His hands and feet pierced through her flesh.[1080] For the rest of her life, Osanna experienced the Passion in a more intense way on Wednesdays and Fridays.[1081] In her case, the stigmata did not seem to have bled, but simply to have appeared as small black, intensely painful swellings, full of blood.[1082] After the beata's death, the stigmata which were scarcely visible during life became quite pronounced.[1083]

The invisible stigmata was also granted to St. Maria Madeline de' Pazzi in 1585 and to St. Mary Frances of the Five Wounds of Jesus.[1084] In all cases, the stigmata's wounds are a matter of careful study by medical personnel and representatives of the Church. Berthe Petit experienced the pain of the invisible stigmata in her hands, feet, and side. She begged Jesus to keep her wounds hidden and He did, except for occasional moments. On many Fridays of the year (especially Good Friday), friends have related how the wounds in her hands and feet bled and caused her tremendous pain.[1085]

St. Pio of Pietrelcina (Padre Pio), a Capuchin-Franciscan priest, visionary, and stigmatic, exhibited a spiritual sensitivity from early childhood. By the time he was five, he was already having mystical experiences, including ecstasies, visions of the Madonna, and occasional harassment from diabolical forces.[1086] Ordained in 1910, he is said to have requested his spiritual adviser for permission to ask Our Lord to accept him as a victim soul to alleviate the sufferings of souls in purgatory and to win souls for heaven. God apparently accepted the offer and he received

---

[1076] Johnson, op.cit., p. 365; see appendix for more information.
[1077] Freze, TWBC, op.cit., p. 93.
[1078] Ibid., pp. 197–98, 258; Cruz, Inc.,op.cit., p. 15.
[1079] Cruz, MMM, op.cit., p. 226.
[1080] Summers, op.cit., p. 154.
[1081] Dorcy, op.cit., p. 239.
[1082] Thurston, op.cit., p. 62, Cruz, MMM, op.cit., p. 226.
[1083] Cruz, Inc, op.cit., p. 157.
[1084] Cruz, MMM, op.cit., pp. 233–34.
[1085] Freze, TWBC, op.cit., p. 278.
[1086] Rega, op.cit., p. 3.

the invisible stigmata later on that year.[1087] In 1916, St. Padre Pio was assigned to the friary at San Giovanni Rotundo where he remained until the end of his life. On August 5, 1918, like St. Teresa of Avila, he experienced the mystical gift of trans-verberation, a spiritual wound of love that transfixed his heart.[1088] Then, on September 20, 1918, while immersed in prayer before Our Lord's crucifix, a heavenly visitor came and pierced his body with the Five Sacred Wounds of Christ.[1089] His were the full wounds of Christ in the feet, hands and side. Physicians who examined the wounds declared that "they pierced the palms of the hands completely so that one could see light through them. Witnesses attest that the wound in the side was shaped like a cross, a slash about three inches long that cut parallel to the ribs.[1090] These wounds were to last some fifty years until close to his death in 1968. Miraculously, Padre Pio's wounds completely disappeared during the last few days of his life. It was as if God had taken away his wounds because his mission had finally ended. Perhaps the disappearance of the wounds was also another extraordinary sign from God that they were genuine.[1091]

Other stigmata that disappeared in answer to prayers include that of Venerable Gertrude van de Oosten of Delft who begged the Lord that her stigmata might be withdrawn. Her prayer was granted. The blood ceased to flow but the marks of the stigmata remained visible.[1092] Venerable Dominica of Paradiso's stigmata also disappeared in answer to her prayers as did Clare de Bugny's.[1093]

Blessed Giovanna Maria Bonomo (1606–1670) prayed to have her stigmata kept invisible.[1094] Likewise, Venerable Teresa Helena Higginson[1095] pleaded with the Lord to remove all outward signs of the stigmata and He agreed. Adrienne von Speyr prayed fervently for her stigmata wounds to disappear, and later, they did become less visible, appearing only on the days of her Passion ecstasies. When the wounds became hidden, Adrienne still felt as much pain as she had when they were visible. Her crown of thorn wounds remained invisible, but she could still feel the sensation of blood oozing out of them.[1096]

Some of the other stigmatics who bore the invisible stigmata include: The Blessed Virgin Mary (Lk 2:35), Sts. Teresa of Avila, Francis de Sales,[1097] Margaret Mary Alacoque, Faustina Kowalska,[1098] Anna Schaffer (1882–1925),[1099] Blessed Anne Catherine Emmerich, Blessed Alexandrina da Costa,[1100] Blessed Giovanna Maria Bonomo,[1101] Mary Rose Ferron, Berthe Petit, and Adrienne Von Speyr.[1102] As in the case of St. Catherine of Siena and Blessed Osanna of Mantua, the stigmata of Blessed Lucy of Narni which was scarcely visible during her lifetime became quite pronounced after her death. Upon the demise of Clare de Bugny, her stigmata shone with a radiant glow.[1103] The visible appearance of these mysterious markings, after all apparent signs of life had left the body, completely refutes the opinion of those who attribute the stigmata to autosuggestion, since quite

---

[1087] Ibid., pp. 21–22; see also Cruz, MMM, op.cit., p. 229.

[1088] Ibid., pp. 40, 51.

[1089] Freze, TWBC, op.cit., p. 284.

[1090] Cruz, MMM, op.cit., pp. 231.

[1091] Freze, VVA, op.cit., p. 42.

[1092] Cruz, MMM, op.cit., p. 232.

[1093] Summers, op.cit., p. 158; see also "Stigmatization" 1902 Catholic Encyclopedia.

[1094] http://nouvl.evangelization.free.fr.giovanna.

[1095] Paul Hafner, *Inside the Vatican*, March, 2005, p. 61.

[1096] Freze, TWBC, op.cit., p. 282.

[1097] Farges, op.cit., p. 535.

[1098] Freze, TWBC, op.cit., pp. 267, 277.

[1099] http://www.DenKatolskeKirke–Densalige AnnaSchaffer.

[1100] Freze, TWBC, op.cit., pp. 270, 279.

[1101] http//nouvl.evangelization.free.fr.Giovanna.

[1102] Freze, TWBC, op.cit., pp. 275, 278, 282.

[1103] Summers, op.cit., pp. 78, 158.

A young Padre Pio bearing the Stigmata

understandably, a dead body has no control over what happens to it.[1104]

One of the most common wounds experienced in the stigmatic is that of the side wound or ferita (see also transverberation). Close to a hundred stigmatics have been known to have it alone or with several other wounds. There have been marked variations in the location of the side wound. According to Dr. Imbert-Goubeyre's census, twenty-two have had the wound on the left side of the body, while only the following six have had it on the right side: St. Francis of Assisi (1182–1226), Blessed Dodo of Hascha, Blessed Ugolino of Mantua (d. 1471), Onofrio of Fiamenga (1566–1639), Angela della Pace (1610–1662), and Maria Osk (1622–1684). Some bore it over their heart or opposite the heart, while others sported it almost under the arm. There have been equally marked disparities

in the shape of the side-wound. St. Francis' was reported to have resembled "an unhealed lance wound." The eighteenth-century Swiss nun Maria-Josepha Kumi as well as St. Padre Pio are reliably reported to have had side-wounds in the form of a cross. Therese Neumann's was apparently crescent-shaped. Catherine Emmerich's was in the form of a Y, while others have featured a straight cut or even a triangle.[1105]

Other stigmatics mentioned as having the side wound (ferita) include: Venerable Francesca dal Serrone (1557–1600), a Franciscan Tertiary who received the ferita at the age of fourteen. Every Friday the wound gushed blood and was fragrant with the odor of sweet violets. Clare de Bugny, while in ecstasy, is said to have received the ferita wound. Large quantities of deliciously fragrant gurgling blood poured out from this wound which amazed and baffled doctors. The Dominican ascetic Blessed Matteo (d. 1470) received the ferita the year before he died. Seventy years after the entombment of the Augustinian monk Blessed Ugolino Zefirini of Mantua, his body was found to be not only incorrupt but the ferita was welling with blood. Blessed Jane of Orvieto, a Dominican nun of the Third Order,[1106] Venerable Mary Martha Chambon, Maria de Moerl, and the Dominican nun Maria-Josefa Kumi also had wounds in their side.[1107]

Stigmatics are particularly prone to the "dark night of the soul," and the severest attacks from the evil one. This is because their vocation calls them to represent Christ to a broken world, and to help win back souls from the clutches of Satan.[1108] Robert C. Broderick's article in *The Catholic Encyclopedia*[1109] has described the "dark

---

[1104] Cruz, Inc., op.cit., p. 157.

[1105] Freze, TWBC, op.cit., p. 199; Wilson, op.cit., p. 6.

[1106] Summers, op.cit., pp. 158, 169–170.

[1107] Summers, op.cit., pp. 158, 167.

[1108] Freze, TWBC, op.cit., p. 107.

[1109] *Catholic Encyclopedia*. Thomas Nelson Publishers,

night of the soul" as "the time when the soul seeks God by pure faith and is given no assistance from the senses, when it may be difficult to make acts of prayer, when nature rebels against self-scrutiny and the effort demanded to draw close to God. This dark period may be accompanied by actual suffering of the spirit, as though scruples and temptations against faith, or physical suffering in the form of sickness, permitted by God as a trial."[1110]

The test for stigmatization being of divine origin is that it is usually found in persons who practice virtue to a heroic degree and have a tender love of Christ's Passion. It usually occurs during periods of ecstasy and prayer. In addition, the authentic stigmatic remains sound in character and is well balanced mentally and emotionally. The appearance of the true stigmata is usually instantaneous, whereas in pathological cases, it often appears gradually.[1111]

Even with all the known authenticated cases of stigmata, there have been many cases of "false stigmata," normally associated with a series of possible causes such as diabolical origins, mental disease or sickness, hysteria, self-hypnotic suggestion, and nervous conditions that can cause the skin to redden, break, and even bleed.[1112] There is the famous case of Magdalena of the Cross, a Spanish abbess, who was under the oppression of the evil one for more than fifty years. She inflicted herself with stigmata wounds, not letting them heal, opening them up again and again for thirty-eight years. She made a deathbed confession stating she had been under the influence of Satan. After which the wounds disappeared never to be seen again.[1113]

That the divine stigmata could be produced through the force of the emotions acting upon a lively subject is altogether impossible. In true stigmatization, the wounds are spontaneous—that is to say, not caused by any external or physical injury or accident—and, as imprinted upon the bodily members of the stigmatic, they are very definitely restricted to the wounds of the Passion of which they are the replica.[1114] Usually the wounds of the true stigmatic bleed on days or at times when the Passion of Christ is commemorated. The flow of blood is often so great at times that it cannot be explained naturally. Moreover, the blood of the true stigmata never discharges pus and the blood is always clean and pure. The wounds cannot be healed by natural medication.[1115] Aside from the foul smell emitted by the stigma of St. Rita of Cascia, at times the stigmata sends out incomparable perfume and light, as happened with St. Francis of Assisi, St. John of the Cross, Blessed Lucy of Narni, and many others.[1116]

According to Gianbattista Scaramelli in his 1574 work entitled *Il Direttorio Mistico*, other tests of true stigmatization are that a notable spiritual progress along the mystic path should have been made, and hence the subject should have endured the purgation of the senses and a supernatural detachment from the world. Also, some degree of infused contemplation must have been attained. True stigmatization is inevitably accompanied by great physical pain. The pain and the heavenly joy, as constantly as they recur, must result in interior recollection and an extraordinary elevation of the mind to God, which gives a supernatural strength enabling the stigmatic to endure the physical anguish and to partake fully in the gladness of God.[1117] It is surprising

Nashville, TN, 1976.

[1110] Freze, TWBC, op.cit., p. 106.

[1111] Aumann, op.cit., pp. 432–33.

[1112] NCE, 1st ed., v. 10, op.cit., p. 173; Freze, TWBC, op.cit., p. 13.

[1113] Freze, TWBC, op.cit., p. 216; Summers, op.cit., pp. 216–18; Thurston, op.cit., 83, 89–90,

96,142; Johnson, op.cit., pp. 323–24.

[1114] Summers, op.cit., pp. 127–28.

[1115] Aumann, op.cit., p. 433.

[1116] Farges, op.cit., p. 533.

[1117] Summers, op.cit., p. 208.

that Scaramelli omits another test of a true stigmatic, a test which encompasses everything; namely, humility.

An 1894 study conducted by renowned Parisian scholar Dr. Imbert-Gourbeyre found there had been 321 genuine stigmatics up until that time. Since then, many others have joined the list of authentic stigmatics. He found 41 to be males and 280 to be females.[1118] It is no accident that most known stigmatics in Church history have been women. St. Teresa of Avila (1515–1582) once said that the Holy Spirit generally selects the weaker sex for extraordinary graces. They have also been more humble and obedient to God and their superiors.[1119]

Of the several hundred stigmatics whose lives had been studied by Doctor Imbert-Gourbeyre since the thirteenth century, only about sixty-two, or a fifth of this group, had so far been either canonized or beatified.[1120] At the time of publication of his monumental two-volume work entitled *La Stigmatization*,[1121] the author identified all of the stigmatics to be Roman Catholics with the majority being female and Italian. He found the proportion to be seven females for every male.[1122] Since that time, numerous others have borne the stigmata, such as Sts. Padre Pio, Faustina Kowalska, Gemma Galgani, Anna Schaeffer, Mariam Baouardy, Blesseds Alexandrina da Costa, Therese Neumann, Anna Rosa Gatorno, Dina Belanger, venerables Mary Martha Chambon, and Elena Aiello, just to name a few.

Dr. Imbert-Gourbeyere calculated, at the time, that of the stigmatics regarded as being genuine, 229 were from Italy; Sicily claimed 10; France 70; Spain 47; Germany 33; Belgium 15; Portugal 13; 5 each from Switzerland and Holland; 3 from Hungary; and 1 from Peru.[1123] With regard to religious affiliation, Dr. Imbert-Gourbeyere relates that well over two-thirds of the stigmatics had taken religious vows: 109 stigmatics were from the Dominican Order; the Franciscans numbered 102, of which a quarter were Poor Clares; Carmelites, 14; Ursulines, 14; Visitation nuns, 12; Augustinians, 8; Jesuits, 3.[1124] What seems to emerge from the study is that stigmatics tend to come from those orders laying their greatest focus on personal austerity and the contemplative life.[1125] Lay stigmatics are much less common than religious ones. Only two out of eighteen were recognized in the eighteenth century and ten out of a total of twenty-nine cases in the nineteenth century. Again it should be pointed out that Dr. Imbert-Gourbeyere's studies do not include any cases after 1894.[1126]

The stigmata comes to a wide variety of ages and types of people. Madeleine Morice (1736–1769) was a dressmaker who lived in poverty. She first received the stigmata when she was only eight years old. These wounds eventually disappeared over a period of time, but they reappeared when she was thirty-two. Another very young stigmatic was Angela della Pace, who was only nine when she had the sacred wounds imprinted on her body. She was even marked with the sponge and hyssop on the mouth. Angela's side wound issued forth both blood and hot water.[1127]

[1118] Biot, op.cit., p. 19.

[1119] St. Teresa, op.cit., *Life*, p. xl.

[1120] Cruz, MMM, op.cit., p. 235; Biot, op.cit., p. 23.

[1121] Antoine Imbert–Goubeyre, *La Stigmatisation, l'exstase divine et les miracles de Lourdes, Reponse aux libre – spenseurs*, 2 vols., Clermont–Ferrand Bellet, 1984.

[1122] Cruz, MMM, op.cit., p. 235; Biot, op.cit., p. 19.

[1123] Biot, op.cit., p. 19–20; Freze, TWBC, op.cit., p. 200.

[1124] Cruz, MMM, op.cit., p. 236.

[1125] Wilson, op. cit., p. 72.

[1126] Freze, TWBC, op.cit., p. 201.

[1127] Ibid., p. 199; see also Biot, op.cit., pp. 25, 50; 1902 *Catholic Encyclopedia*.

Many stigmatics have received the wounds while in the tender years of puberty: Blessed Agnes of Jesus, the Dominican from Le Puy who was known for her ecstasies and visions as well as her odor of sanctity, received the wounds at age twelve. Venerable Marguerite Parigot, known as Marguerite of the Blessed Sacrament, a Carmelite nun from Beaune, received the stigmata at the age of thirteen.[1128] At the age of fourteen, Venerable Francesca dal Serrone was given the Sacred Wounds. At fifteen, they were imprinted on Blessed Stephanie de Quinzanis. Louise Lateau received them at eighteen. St. Maria Magdalena de Pazzi, Maria Dominic Lazzari, Crescentia Nierklutsch, and Jeanne de-Jesus Marie were stigmatized at age nineteen while St. Catherine of Ricci, Blessed Lucy of Narni, Blessed Mary of Jesus Crucified, Maria-Josefa Kumi, Etienne Guyot, Sister Bernard of the Cross,[1129] and Marie-Julie Jahenny[1130] received these wounds when they were twenty. After the age of twenty, many have received the stigmata, but rarely has it been given after the age of forty. Unusual cases of older stigmatics do include, however, the following: the widow Joanna of Jesus and Mary at Burgos, a poor Clare nun who was marked in her sixtieth year;[1131] Christina Mary of the Cross of Strumbele (1242–1312), a Franciscan Poor Clare, and Prudenziana Zagnoni (1583–1650) received the wounds when they were sixty-five; Venerable Ursula Benincasa (1547–1618) received the Sacred Wounds at the age of sixty-nine. Delicia di Giovanni (1550–1622), a Dominican from Palermo, Italy, had the stigmata imprinted on her between the ages of sixty-five and seventy-two.[1132] Blessed Bernard of Offida

(1604–1694) is said to have received the stigmata when he was seventy-two.[1133] St. Padre Pio probably has the record of bearing the stigmata for the longest period of time, from 1918 to 1968. They finally disappeared just prior to his death in 1968.[1134]

Supernatural Empery Over Nature and Creatures

Miracles over nature may be referred to as supernatural empery over nature. Jesus calming the storm on the Sea of Galilee is a good example of this. St. Dominic likewise was said to calm a storm at sea by his prayers when the galley he was aboard was caught in a fierce tempest.[1135] St. Joseph of Cupertino reportedly could also control the elements and stop storms.[1136] St. Francis Xavier, while on his way to Cochin-China on a Portuguese ship, allegedly calmed a storm at sea.[1137] At the prayers of St. Peter Gonzalez, storms reportedly ceased and droughts were ended. St. Vincent Ferrer stilled a storm so he could be heard preaching. St. Agricolus (Agricola) of Avignon (630–700) was said to produce rain and fine weather by his prayers. St. Germaine (1579–1601) reportedly made the Sign of the Cross to part the raging waters of a river so she could cross it to go to Mass.[1138] St. Genevieve's (422–500) prayers were said to be instrumental in bringing rain and ending a drought as well as ending a plague that took many lives in Paris.[1139] The wonder-worker St. Francis of Paola seemed to exert direct authority over nature just like Christ. With a command "in the name of charity," stories say that he moved boulders, opened springs from

---

[1128] Biot, op.cit., p. 25.
[1129] Freze, TWBC, op.cit., p. 200.
[1130] Wilson, op.cit., p. 62.
[1131] See 1902 *Catholic Encyclopedia*.
[1132] Biot, op.cit., p. 26; Freze, TWBC, op.cit., p. 200.

[1133] http//www.capuchinfriars.org.au/saints/bernardo.
[1134] Freze, TWBC, op.cit., p. 200.
[1135] Summers, op.cit., p. 68.
[1136] Guiley, op.cit., p. 193.
[1137] Farges, op.cit., p. 567.
[1138] Miracles, op.cit., p. 9.
[1139] Cowan, op.cit., pp. 180–81.

St. Francis Preaching to the Birds by Antonio Carnicero

rocks, healed the lame, blind and deaf, and raised the dead.[1140] The Franciscan mystic St. Peter of Alcantara, an ascetic of surprising holiness, was said to have walked like Jesus on the waves of the sea as though it were dry land. St. Peter Nolasco, (c. 1189–1258), Father of the Mercedarians, St. Mary de Cervellon of the same Order, and the Dominican St. Peter Gonzalez are also reported to have walked on water.[1141]

Often saints have been said to make abundant springs burst out in barren and

desolate places, which have transformed the soil. This is the reason why so many springs and fountains bear their names or are consecrated to them. Such, for instance, are the fountains of St. Clement (d.c. 100), St. Venantius (c. 530–610), St. Julian of Le Mans (4th c.), Sts. Primus and Felician, (d.c. 297), St. Ethelburga (d. 675), Blessed Agnes of Jesus, etc.[1142]

Other saints and beati with stories of having exercised control over the forces of nature include St. Alphonsus Marie Liguori who stopped a possible eruption of Mt.

[1140] Ghezzi, VOS, op.cit., p. 448.
[1141] Summers, op.cit., p. 68.

[1142] Farges, op.cit., p. 568.

Vesuvius;[1143] St. Anthony Mary Claret, the Archbishop of Cuba, who calmed an earthquake; St. Francis of Paola who appeared to control the wind and tides; St. Joseph of Cupertino who commanded a hurricane to cease; St. Dominic who saved his vineyard from a storm; St. Frediano, Bishop of Lucca (d.5 88), who diverted a river; Blessed Francis Xavier Bianchi (d. 1815); and Blessed Peter Geremia (d. 1452) who stopped lava flow through their prayers. The following saints caused heavy rainfalls: Sts. Scholastica (d. 543), Dominic, and John Bosco; others such as Sts. Paul of the Cross, Anthony of Padua, and Gasper del Bufalo caused rain to cease or not fall on the crowd while preaching outdoors.[1144]

Then there are saints who have been said to have astonishing power of control over creatures. The Fathers of the desert often enjoyed a wonderful dominion over all the forces of nature. Serpents and the most savage and ferocious animals allegedly became docile to their voices and, far from harming them, would often render them services, as is related of St. Didymus (c. 313–399), St. Hilarion (c. 291–371), St. Pachomius (d. 346), and many others.[1145] St. Francis of Assisi is well known for chatting familiarly with all the animals, calling them his brethren.[1146] He had remarkable influence over birds, fish, and wildlife. There are many stories of his rapport with birds and animals, who tamely gathered around him to listen to him preach.[1147] So too was his friend Conrad of Offida (1241–1306) who inherited the Franciscan power over animals.[1148] Blessed Bernard Scammacca (d. 1486) was likewise said to have had great power over birds and animals. When he walked outside in the garden praying, the

birds would flutter down around him singing, but as soon as he went into ecstasy, they kept still, for fear they would disturb him.[1149] Legend has it that St. Blaise (c. 316) talked and interacted with wild beasts and had animals approach him when they were ill or injured for his healing touch. St. Kevin's (d.c. 618) rapport with nature was so strong that it seems his own spirit found kinship and fellowship with the birds and the animals. Stories abound of how animals and Kevin assisted each other and shared their environment.[1150]

While observing a very penitential life, the hermit St. Godric was noted for his special power over wild creatures. It is said that in snow and ice he would bring rabbits and field mice to his hut, warm them by the fire, and then set them free. St. Seraphim of Sarov lived as a hermit in the depths of a Russian forest where he cared for wild animals such as foxes, hares, wolves, and bears.[1151] St. Maedoc's (d.c. 626) love of wild animals was unlimited. Wolves were his special companions.[1152] St. Gall (550–635), like many forest-dwelling saints, enjoyed personal relationships with wild animals. He is said to have once befriended a bear by removing a thorn from its paw. Sts. Cosmas and Damian (4 c.) had a special rapport with animals and included veterinary services in their ministry.[1153] Likewise, St. Bernard of Corleone (1605–1647) healed animals through prayer.[1154] Others who had supernatural empery over animals include: Sts. Jerome (c. 342–420), Sylvester Gozzolini (1177–1267),[1155] Herve (6th c.), Columba (521–597),[1156] Anthony

---

[1143] Cruz, MMM, op.cit., p. 399.
[1144] Ibid., pp. 400–9.
[1145] Farges, op.cit., p. 24.
[1146] Ibid., p. 569.
[1147] Guiley, op.cit., p. 116.
[1148] Underhill, *Mystics*, op.cit., p. 94.

[1149] Dorcy, op.cit., p. 221.
[1150] Cowan, op.cit., pp. 78, 271.
[1151] Farmer, op.cit., pp. 227, 472.
[1152] Cowan, op.cit., pp. 286–87.
[1153] Ibid., pp. 178, 126.
[1154] see http://saints.sqpn.com/
[1155] Summers, op.cit., p. 68.
[1156] Cowan, op.cit., p. 120.

of Padua (1195–1231),[1157] Francis Solanus (1549–1610), Martin de Porres, Gerard Majella,[1158] Guthlac,[1159] and the Russian forest hermit Sergius of Radonezh (1314–1392); the latter reportedly had mastery over birds, fish, and wildlife that rivaled that of St. Francis.[1160] St. Joseph of Cupertino is said to have had special powers over animals that even surpassed those of St. Francis.[1161]

Telekenesis

The Oxford English Dictionary describes telekinesis as "a movement of or in a body, alleged to occur at a distance from, and without material connection with, the motive cause or agent." That is the movement of objects (at a distance) by scientifically inexplicable means. What first comes to mind is the transference of the Host from the altar or from the hands of an officiating priest through the air by some unexplained agency to the lips of the expectant communicant.

The reception of the Sacred Species from a distance or in a state of spiritual ecstasy is also sometimes referred to as supernatural or mystical Communion. Dr. Imbert-Gourbeyre, in his 1894 study of 321 stigmatists, identified 27 of them who had miraculous Communions only once, but 14 who had this experience many times, and 27 frequently. This type of miraculous reception of Communion usually happens in one of two ways. Sometimes the stigmatic receives the Communion directly from the Lord, a saint, or an angel, always during the state of ecstasy; or the Host has been seen to suddenly disappear from the priest's hands, where it was instantly transported to the tongue of the stigmatic without the aid of the priest placing it there.

Aside from stigmatists, extraordinary cases of these spiritual Communions have been observed in the lives of other pious souls, such as St. Angela of the Cross who reportedly received a hundred of these Communions.[1162]

The saintly John Vianney, the Curé of Ars, testified to the fact that a Host detached itself from his fingers when he was a good distance away from a communicant and placed itself on that communicant's tongue.[1163] Sts. Gertrude the Great and Catherine of Siena frequently received the Sacred Host from Christ Himself, as well as from angels, during their states of ecstasy.[1164] Blessed Raymund of Capua (1330–1399), the confessor of St. Catherine, states that the Host would sometimes depart out of his hands and, like an arrow, shoot into her mouth when she communicated. Blessed Anna Maria Taigi had the sacred consecrated Host on more than one occasion leave the celebrant's hands, glide through the air, and then come to rest on her lips. The same is also true of the French stigmatic and ecstatica Venerable Marie de Jesus du Bourg (Anna Rose Joseph du Bourg, 1788–1862).[1165] Others who drew the Host through the air to themselves include: Sts. Margaret of Hungary (1242–1271), Catherine of Sienna, Teresa of Avila, Gemma Galgani, Veronica Giuliani,[1166] Lydwina of Schiedam, Stanislaus Kostka, Francis di Girolamo, Gerard Majella,[1167] Blessed Veronica of Binasco, Blessed Ida of Louvain, Blessed Ivetta of Huy (1158–1228), Venerable Dominica of Paradiso,[1168] and Madeleine Morice, a lay stigmatic who

---

[1157] Farges, op.cit., p. 25.
[1158] Guiley, op.cit., pp. 119, 227, 131.
[1159] Cruz, Inc., op.cit., p. 58.
[1160] Fanning, op.cit., p. 46.
[1161] Guiley, op.cit., p. 193.

[1162] Freze, TWBC, op.cit., pp. 172–73.
[1163] Thurston, op.cit., p. 14.
[1164] Freze, TWBC, op.cit., p. 174.
[1165] Thurston, op.cit., pp. 145, 155.
[1166] Summers, op.cit., p. 60.
[1167] Biot, op.cit., pp. 66–67.
[1168] Summers, op.cit., p. 60.

The Miraculous Communion of Saint Catherine of Siena by Domenico di Pace Beccafumi

several times experienced the phenomenon of Communion from a distance.[1169]

Aside from receiving Communion from a distance, St. Mary Frances of the Five Wounds of Jesus also reportedly had the chalice mysteriously move from the altar to her lips and then return back to the altar.[1170] Usually, at the sight of the Sacred Host, Therese Neumann went into an ecstatic repose. When the Host was placed on her tongue, It immediately disappeared without any effort of swallowing; the Species spontaneously entered her body as fast as It was placed in her mouth.[1171]

Communion was reportedly brought to Belgian mystic Louise Lateau daily when the stigmata wound in her feet prevented her from attending Mass. She would often

experience the reception of Communion from a distance, whereby the Host miraculously leapt onto her tongue from places far away or beyond her reach. Occasionally the ecstatic "with a quick movement of her tongue," took the Host from a distance of several centimeters before it could be placed on her tongue. But it also happened that the sacred Host moved by itself toward her, especially when her tongue was paralyzed by illness.[1172]

There is also the strange case of St. Juliana Falconieri, a nun of the Third Order of the Servants of Mary (Servite order), who was given to a severe stomach disorder throughout her life and could not retain food, nor could she walk to the communion rail. At the end of her life, because of constant vomiting, she was refused the

---

[1169] Biot, op.cit., p. 67.
[1170] Summers, op.cit., p. 60.
[1171] Freze, TWBC, op.cit., p. 174.

[1172] Biot, op.cit., p. 67–68; Freze, TWBC, op.cit., p. 173–74, 271.

St. Juliana Falconieri statue in Chiesa di Santa Maria dei Servi

Eucharist. However, on one occasion, she requested the priest spread a corporal upon her breast and lay the Host on it. Soon afterwards the Host could not be seen. After Juliana's death, the figure of Christ nailed to the Cross was found impressed on her flesh within a circle like a Host.[1173]

Telekinesis (see Prophecy) also may include the knowledge of events which are happening or which have just happened at a considerable, sometimes very great distance away. Saints and mystics have also had an extraordinary knowledge of what was going on elsewhere, although it may have occurred very far away and there could be no normal channel through which the information could be so immediately transmitted. One of the

most striking examples of divinely supernatural telekinesis was when Pope St. Pius V (1566–1572), on October 7, 1571, was informed of the outcome of the Battle of Lepanto and the victory of Don Juan.[1174] St. Alphonsus Mary de Liguori,[1175] Blessed Mary of Oignies, Blessed Ivetta of Huy, and Venerable Gertrude van de Oosten also had knowledge of distant events.

Mention should also be made here of Blessed Anna Maria Taigi's "mysterious sun" which she first saw in 1790 or 1791, shortly after her marriage. The luminous disc, somewhat like a miniature sun, maintained a constant position before her. Above the upper rays was a large crown of interwoven thorns with two rather lengthy thorns on either side, curved downward so that they crossed each other under the solar disc, their points emerging on either side of the rays. In the center of the disc, Anna Maria saw a beautiful woman seated majestically, her face raised toward heaven in ecstatic contemplation. In this globe the beata saw things of the natural, moral, and divine order and could see present or future events anywhere in the world, as well as the state of grace of living individuals and the fate of those departed.[1176]

St. Catherine dei Ricci possessed one of the rarely mentioned mystical gifts noted in the lives of the saints. This gift consisted in the privilege of conversing frequently with other saints such as St. Philip Neri while he was in Rome and St. Maria Maddalena de Pazzi while she was in Florence. These conversations were said to take place while Catherine remained in her convent at Prato. Although they had exchanged a number of letters, these saints never actually met one another, except through these mystical visits.[1177]

[1173] Aradi, op.cit., p. 86; Cruz, MMM, op.cit., pp. 533–34; Thurston, op.cit., pp. 156, 161; Gallick, op.cit., p. 184.

[1174] Summers, op.cit., p. 6.
[1175] Guiley, op.cit., p. 13.
[1176] Cruz, Inc., op.cit., pp. 264–65.
[1177] Cruz, MMM, op.cit., pp. 6, 529.

Victim Souls

A victim soul may be defined as an innocent person asked by God to suffer torments or reparation for the sins of the world, for sinners, or for the benefit of the Church.[1178] This is a chosen soul who freely sacrifices oneself, one's health, material goods, happiness, etc. as an offering to divine justice. These generous souls, after the example of the crucified Christ, are needed to "balance the scales" for the expiation of sin in the world. He or she is one called upon to emulate the mission of Christ Himself. For at the end of His brief life, Jesus became a stigmatic—a prototype for all victim souls who would follow His way throughout the history of the Church. He is the precursor of all of God's suffering servants, a model that needs no other. The Church understands the victim's role in the example of Christ as the ultimate victim. With this in mind, one can understand the co-redemptive work the victims have undertaken in union with Christ for the sake of saving others from their sins.[1179]

The whole concept of victim is nothing new but has been in practice since ancient times. The Jewish priests would make burnt offerings or prepare victims (animals) for sacrifice to God for expiation of sin (Lv 16:27). However, this was a mere prefigurement of the ultimate victim, Jesus Christ, Who, of course, is the king of victim souls, the perfect and unblemished offering Who redeemed and restored fallen humanity to its original state of justice in which it was created.

Nevertheless, in the mysterious design of the Eternal Father, a certain reparation must still be made for sin so that our sufferings and trials may "fill up those things that are wanting of the sufferings of Christ" (Col 1:24).

All victim souls have several things in common: 1) they are chosen by God for this way of life because it is His will for them; 2) they are free to reject the role of victim. Once the soul consents, however, God is free to do whatever He wills with the person who will be His redemptive helper; 3) sometimes one becomes a victim first without realizing his or her lot; usually, however, the chosen ones freely offer their sufferings up to God with the specific intentions of making atonement or expiation for their own sins or for the sins of others. This offering is a voluntary and unconditional surrender to God's holy will.[1180] It must be emphasized again that these desires are not aimed at suffering for its own sake since that would be pathetic and even pathological. Rather, they are impulses for a share in Christ's Passion: their redemptive and purifying values are what is at stake. We must hold in awe the victim soul's mission of self-sacrifice through suffering out of love for God and His people.[1181]

Theresa Neumann was such a victim soul. On April 23, 1923, Theresa experienced an inner voice which appeared to be that of St. Therese of the Little Flower[1182] who told her that "more souls have been saved through suffering than by the finest sermons."[1183] During the Lent of 1926, Theresa began to have "Friday ecstasies" in which she saw in a vision the Passion of Christ, with many details not mentioned in the Gospel. Her Friday ecstasies were associated with the stigmata on her hands, feet, and left side. By November of 1926, Theresa had received the wounds of the crown of thorns, making her stigmata complete. From that time on, she relived the Passion of Christ on the Fridays of Lent and Advent, as well as on those days within the

---

[1178] Aumann, op.cit., p. 175.
[1179] Freze, TWBC, op.cit., pp. 28–29, 60.
[1180] Ibid., p. 59.
[1181] Ibid., p. 196.
[1182] Hebert, op.cit., p. 236.
[1183] Aradi, op.cit., p. 10.

St. Lydwina de Schiedam falling on ice by Jan Dunselman

octaves of those seasons, about twenty-six to twenty-eight times a year for thirty-six years.[1184]

Another such victim soul was St. Lydwina de Schiedam born at Schiedam, Holland. Lydwina was injured during the winter of 1395 while ice skating. Gangrene appeared in the wound caused by her injury and spread over her entire body. From that time on, she became a lifelong invalid suffering pain as reparation for others. She was later scarred by smallpox, suffered the buboes of the Black Death which devoured her flesh and bones until her right arm was only attached by a single tendon. Her body was later also ravaged by the "burning illness," an indescribable plague that consumed skin and muscle with an unremitting fire until the bones themselves burst. This disease split her face from her hairline to her nose. She became epileptic, lost all sight in her right eye, and, in fact, her left eye bled at the least light. Lydwina lost blood through her mouth, ears, and nose so copiously that the doctors wondered how she could lose more blood than her body could possibly hold. At one point, her lungs and liver decayed, her stomach, swollen on her skeletal frame, burst, and her intestines spilled forth.[1185]

No matter how horribly she suffered, she never lost her sense of humor. During the last nineteen years of her life, this victim soul experienced the mystic gift of inedia whereby she ate virtually nothing or absolutely nothing year after year. Over that time, she only took the small communion wafer once a week for the remaining years of her life. Lydwina, in fact, could not even keep water down.[1186] She slept very little (insomnia), if at all, during the last seven years of her life,[1187] and also became almost completely blind. On the morning of Easter-day 1433, Lydwina was in deep contemplation and beheld, during a vision, Christ coming toward her to administer the sacrament of Extreme Unction. She soon after died in the odor of great sanctity.[1188] At death, her body was made whole again, taking on the fresh and beautiful appearance that it had before she even had gotten smallpox.[1189] An ecclesiastical commission appointed to investigate her life declared her experiences to be valid.[1190]

Twentieth-century victim souls include: St. Faustina Kowalska who battled illness after illness and ultimately died of tuberculosis. She was told by Christ that other souls would greatly profit from her sufferings.[1191] Sts. Gemma Galgani, Therese of Lisieux, Saint Elizabeth of the Trinity,[1192] St. Padre Pio, Marie-Julie Jahenny, Sister Josefa Menendez, Mary Rose Ferron, Alexandrina da Costa, Berthe Petit, and Marthe Robin are other examples of modern day victim souls.[1193]

[1184] Johnson, op.cit., p. 161.
[1185] Ibid., pp. 88–89; see also Freze, TWBC, op.cit., pp. 259–60.
[1186] Ibid., pp. 90, 147.
[1187] Freze, TWBC, op.cit., p. 260.
[1188] Vie de Sainte Lidvine; http://www.newadvent.org/cathen.
[1189] Johnson, op.cit., p. 90.
[1190] Delaney, op.cit., p. 325.
[1191] Michalenko, op.cit., p. 41.
[1192] Aumann, op.cit., p. 175.
[1193] Freze, TWBC, op.cit., pp. 70, 148, 186, 275, 277, 279, 285.

Pope Saint Pius V had vision of Battle of Lepanto on 7th October, 1571

Vision Through Opaque Bodies

This charism may be also associated with the phenomenon of telepathy and second sight. Ezekiel tells us that, while seated in his house, he saw in spirit the scenes of abomination that were being committed in the temple of Jerusalem (Ez 8:1–6). Pope Pius V, from his window in the Vatican, saw the naval battle of Lepanto and Don Juan's victory over the Turks.[1194] One of the most extraordinary examples of a person upon whom this gift was conferred is the Trinitarian Blessed Anna Maria Taigi. She saw the bottom of seas and lakes, and of the fathomless ocean. She is said to have penetrated the heights of heaven, and saw into the abyss of the earth as clearly as she discerned the four walls of a room.[1195]

Wounds of the Heart (Transverberation)

Transverberation has been described as a type of mystical wound of the soul that pierces the depth of one's being, bringing about a spiritual delight through the experience of God's loving presence. Transverberation of the heart refers to the wound caused by an arrow (dart, lance, spear, steel blade, or sword) hurled by a seraph, cherub, another celestial being, a saint, or even the Lord Himself which results in a fire of divine love that inflames the soul and unites it to the heavenly spouse.[1196] This piercing of the spiritual heart by the love of God (Lk 2:35), accompanied by the intensified sorrow for one's own sins and the sins of others, is sometimes known as the ferita (see side wound) or called the stigma of the heart, the heart wound, or transverberation of the heart.[1197] A mystical arrow (dart, lance, spear, steel blade, or sword) is said to pierce the heart or soul, leaving the victim consumed in the fire of divine love. The soul is then transported to an intensely intimate relationship with God.[1198] This wound is parallel to the same lance wound inflicted on Christ by a Roman centurion when the Savior's Heart was opened on the Cross.[1199] Dr. Imbert-Gourbeyre, in his nineteenth-century study of stigmatics, reported fourteen cases of heart wounds up to that time, testified to by autopsy.[1200]

A seraph is usually seen as the one who inflicts the soul with this arrow. The resulting wounds are normally given in the higher mystical states of ecstasy or rapture. Transverberation is often a prelude to the visible or invisible stigmata upon the body or soul. Many holy souls, however, receive this wound without receiving the stigmata later. Once received, it is usually a permanent wound of the heart or soul, either invisible or, in some cases, visible as a wound directly in the heart or above it on the exterior body of the victim.[1201] Under such a condition the subject would normally die, since the wound (humanly speaking) ought to be mortal.[1202]

[1194] Farges, op.cit., p. 408.
[1195] Summers, op.cit., p. 66.

[1196] Freze, VVA, op.cit., p. 322.
[1197] Summers, op.cit., p. 118.
[1198] Freze, TWBC, op.cit., p. 193.
[1199] Johnson, op.cit., p. 48.
[1200] Farges, op.cit., p. 535.
[1201] Freze, TWBC, op.cit., p. 303.
[1202] Summers, op.cit., p. 118.

Statue of the Transverberation of St. Teresa of Jesus by Heinrich Meyring

Saint Angela of Foligno expresses this state in the following manner:

> When the soul is elevated above itself, and, illuminated by the presence of God, (it) enters into intimate communication with Him; it knows, enjoys and rests in a divine happiness which it cannot express, for it surpasses every word and every concept. Each ecstasy is a new ecstasy and all the ecstasies together are one inexpressible thing.

After this victim experiences this level of mystical ecstasy, a heavenly being sent by God, or even the Lord Himself, may pay a visit to this victim and impart a permanent wound in the heart or soul by means of a spear, dart, or arrow.[1203]

St. John of the Cross, in his work entitled *Living Flame of Love*, explains transverberation as the spiritual wounding of the heart. He says: "It will happen when the soul is inflamed with the love of God and it will feel as if a seraphim is assailing it by means of an arrow or a dart, [thus making the heart] all afire with love."[1204]

This is why transverberation or wound of the heart is sometimes referred to as the "seraph's assault," because as St. John reminds us above, the soul is interiorly attacked by a seraph who pierces the heart with a fiery dart (or spear) piercing it permanently but with a sweet delight.[1205] He specifically describes the phenomenon of transverberation as follows: "The soul being inflamed with the love of God is interiorly attacked by a seraph, who pierces it through with a fiery dart. This leaves the soul wounded, which causes it to suffer from the overflowing of divine love."[1206]

What might be the first case of transverberation occurred to St. Lutgard, a Cistercian mystic who, while in prayer, saw a vision of Jesus in His glory and was wounded with a wound like the spear wound in Jesus' heart. She carried the scar from this wound to her death.[1207]

The best known case of a heart mystically wounded by an arrow of love is that of St. Teresa of Avila. In her *Autobiography*, the saint describes how this transverberation took place. In a vision, she was aware of a cherub holding a long spear with a shaft of gleaming gold, which was tipped with a red-hot iron. Time after time, the angel thrust her with this celestial lance piercing her heart and causing excruciating pain. Although she said the pain was sharp, it was sweet and left her afire with a great love for God.[1208] During an exhumation of St. Teresa's body, the heart was removed and placed in a crystal reliquary.[1209] Upon medical examination, it was noted that the heart seemed to have been perforated by a keen blade, the wound being about an inch and a half across. The edges of the wound are burned and charred as if by a red-hot iron.[1210] Moreover, the preservation of this organ could not be credited to any natural or chemical means.[1211]

The same type of a celestial visitor described by St. Teresa of Avila visited St. Padre Pio who also received a mystical wounding of love, but unlike St. Teresa, he received the wound during a vision while he was in the confessional. The event took place on August 5, 1918 and, as the saint describes it, "A heavenly being appeared with a sharp-pointed steel blade which seemed to spew out fire and he hurled it with all his might into his soul."[1212] In a deposition

---

1203 Freze, TWBC, op.cit., p. 194.
1204 Cruz, MMM, op.cit., p. 66.
1205 Freze, TWBC, op.cit., pp. 195–96.
1206 Ryan Gerhold "The Second St. Francis," *The Angelus*: 12–18.

1207 Cruz, MMM, op.cit., p. 71.
1208 See Teresa, *Life* [Kavanaugh], ch. 29, pp. 193–94, 244; Summers, op.cit., p. 192.
1209 Cruz, MMM, op.cit., p. 67.
1210 Summers, op.cit., p. 192.
1211 Cruz, MMM, op.cit., p. 67.
1212 Freze, TWBC, op.cit., pp. 194–95; Rega, op.cit., pp. 51–52; Guiley, op.cit., p. 266.

made in February 1967, Padre Pio's biographer attested that a visible, physical wound in his side resulted from the experience which was identified as a transverberation or piercing of the heart.[1213]

Saint Gertrude the Great experienced the wound of divine love (transverberation) once after taking communion when her soul was pierced by a triple-pointed golden arrow, leaving her more than ever consumed by the love of God. The two favors which Gertrude received, the impressions of the wounds of Christ in her heart and the piercing with the arrow of divine love, gave her such joy, she says, that even if she were to live for a thousand years in complete desolation, she would find solace, light, and gratitude in the remembrance of these graces.[1214]

Sometime in 1895, St. Therese of Lisieux had begun the stations of the cross when she felt herself wounded by a flaming dart and thought she would die from the intensity of the fire of divine love. The experience was similar to the transverberation, or piercing of the heart with fiery arrows and blades, as experienced by Sts. Teresa of Avila and Padre Pio.[1215]

St. Francis of Assisi also received his wounds from the appearance of a majestic, celestial being described as a seraph with six resplendent and flaming wings.[1216] Although many a stigmatic received the transverberation wounds from the hands of a heavenly figure, nevertheless, sometimes it was the Lord Himself who visited the soul to wound the heart with His divine love. St. Gertrude the Great is one example of this.[1217] Another is St. Veronica Giuliani who had an arrow sent deep into her heart by the infant Jesus.[1218]

On May 30, 1664, while living at home, Venerable Beatrice Mary of Jesus was wounded with a dart that pierced her heart by St. Francis of Assisi. It was discovered after her death that she bore a crescent-shaped wound on her left breast.[1219] Other saints have had almost similar experiences but not all in a vision of an angel. The Little Flower, St. Therese of Lisieux, related on her deathbed that she was wounded by a dart of fire which consumed her with burning love.[1220]

Venerable Maria Villani was a Dominican nun from Naples. Her biographer, Fr. Francis Marchese O.P., reveals that she believed she was wounded in the heart and side by a fiery spear of love. This wound was attested to by three of her confessors. The fire of love sparked by the flaming arrow produced such heat that Maria was forced to drink an excessive amount of water each day. The surgeon who made an incision in her heart during an autopsy was, along with other witnesses, amazed to see "smoke and heat exhaled from her heart, a veritable furnace of divine love." The heat was so intense that the surgeon had to wait for the body to cool down before extracting the heart, but even then the heart was hot enough to burn his hands. Upon examination of Maria's heart, an open wound was found which indicated that it was likely made by a spear of fire.[1221]

On May 24, 1868, while in ecstasy, Mariam Baouardy (Saint Mary of Jesus Crucified, 1846–1878), the little Arab cried out to St. Teresa that Jesus had pierced her heart as if by a sword. The transverberation of her heart was discovered later after her death. The surgeon who removed her heart at death perceived a deep wound, triangular in shape, and appearing as though it had been inflicted by a broad sword.[1222]

[1213] Rega, op.cit., p. 53.

[1214] Mary Jeremy Finnigan. *Scholars and mystics.* Chicago: H. Regnery Co., 1962, pp. 82–83.

[1215] Guiley, op.cit., p. 324.

[1216] Freze, TWBC, op.cit., p. 150.

[1217] Ibid., p. 195.

[1218] Lord, VMS, op.cit., p. 270.

[1219] Thurston, op.cit., p. 118.

[1220] Cruz, MMM, op.cit., p. 68.

[1221] Ibid., pp. 70–71, 179.

[1222] Summers, op.cit., pp. 237–38.

During a vision, Blessed Maria of the Passion of Our Lord Jesus Christ (1866–1912) felt the piercing pains of the crucifixion and Jesus Himself piercing her heart with a lance. It was this wound of love that bound her to Jesus, her spouse. From that moment on, this servant of God received the stigmata which she bore until her death. The heart of the saintly Augustinian Blessed Cherubin of Avigliani was found after death to have been pierced by a lance.[1223]

Maria Dominica Lazzari was a stigmatic whose side was gashed as if by a spear.[1224] Leonardo da Lettere, a Dominican monk, while in ecstasy, was favored with a mystic vision of Our Lord Who was said to have pierced his heart with a gold spear tipped with a flame.[1225]

The heart of Venerable Serafina di Dio was allegedly pierced through by a golden dart received during a vision of the Divine Child.[1226] When she was rapt in prayer after Holy Communion, her sister nuns would see Serafina with her face glowing like a red flame and her eyes sparkling fire. "It burned them if they but touched her." Her sister religious repeatedly had heard her say that she was consumed with a living fire and that her blood was boiling as if there was molten lead in her veins.[1227]

On July 2, 1823, upon the Feast of the Visitation, Blessed Elisabetta Canori-Mora fell into a rapture during which time she beheld a vision of the Mother of God and endured the mystery of the transverberation of her heart. From that day until her death, her life was one long, almost uninterrupted, series of ecstasies and raptures.[1228]

In 1648, while adoring the Holy Eucharist, St. Charles of Sezze, a Franciscan lay brother, experienced the so-called transverberation.[1229] A visible wound was opened in his side by a piercing ray of light that came from an elevated Host during Mass at the Church of Saint Joseph in Capo le Case. After his death, it was shown that this stigmatic had a deep scar on his side and his heart had a wound, a crucifix, and a hard fleshy nail, perfectly formed and four or five inches long, straight through it.[1230] Maria-Josefa Kumi, visionary, ecstatic, and stigmatic Dominican nun, received the wound of love in 1803. At that time, her heart was pierced in the form of a cross.[1231]

A fiery dart also figures in the life of Venerable Mary Martha Chambon (1841–1907) who had a visit from the Holy Trinity while she was ill in her cell. The Holy Spirit is said to have hurled a fiery dart into her heart and the Father called her to be a victim soul.[1232]

Others who have experienced transverberation or the wound of the heart include Sts. Lutgard, Charles of Sezze, Veronica Giuliani, Clare of Montefalco,[1233] Terese of Lisieux, and, most recently, Blessed Mariam Thresia Chiramel Mankidiyan who is said to have incurred transverberation five times starting on 10 February 1906. An angel came and thrust a spear into her left side which she felt pierced her heart.[1234]

[1223] Ibid., p. 170.
[1224] Ibid., p. 165.
[1225] Ibid., p. 170.
[1226] Ibid., p. 196.
[1227] Ibid., p. 71.
[1228] Ibid., p. 106.

[1229] Ibid., p. 170.
[1230] Thurston, op.cit., p. 69; Johnson, op.cit., p. 50.
[1231] Summers, op.cit., p. 158.
[1232] Cruz, MMM, op.cit., p. 70.
[1233] Ibid., pp. 71–73.
[1234] http://www.mariamthresis.org?p=206.

Mystical Experiences of the Saints and Others

There are four steps toward sainthood which may begin when an individual after having been dead for at least five years before he or she could even be considered for recognition of his or her heroic virtue. This process is usually initiated by the bishop of his or her local diocese and the individual is then called a Servant of God. His or her life and writings are closely examined until the investigators conclude that he or she practiced the theological virtues of faith, hope, and charity as well as the cardinal virtues of prudence, justice, temperance, and fortitude to a heroic degree. At that point, with the help of postulator, a *positio*, a lengthy document attesting to the potential saint's life of virtue, reputation for sancity and cultus (established veneration by the faithful), is composed and submitted to the Congregation for the Causes of Saints which is based in the Vatican. If it is confirmed by decree that the individual has lived a life of heroic virtue, then they are declared Venerable and the process begins for his or her beatification and eventual canonization. An investigation begins into miracles attributed to the candidate's intercession. Today these miracles are usually healings and cures. Such cures must involve a serious medical condition and be instantaneous, complete and lasting without medical treatment received effecting the healing. When a miracle is approved by the congregation's medical review board, the congregation can review the case and choose to recommend that the candidate be beatified. The pope can then choose to declare him or her Blessed, which means that he or she can be venerated on a local level and by his or her religious order. Even after an individual is declared Blessed, the investigation continues, while supporters await the discovery and validation of a second miracle. This miracle must occur after beatification. Once canonized, an individual is declared worthy of veneration by the Universal Church. A new saint is usually given a specific feast day in the Church's Universal Calendar. On that day, the saint is remembered at Mass and in the Church's Divine Office. It should be noted that Pope Benedict XVI waived this five-year waiting period so that Pope John Paul II's own cause for sainthood could be launched immediately.[1235]

For purposes of this work, "Ven." is a short form for "Venerable," a title given to a person at the stage before beatification in a process toward sainthood. It means that a person has practiced Christian virtue to an heroic degree and is worthy of respect and emulation. "Bl." is the abbreviation

[1235] Gallick, op.cit., pp. 3–4.

for "Blessed," the proper title of a person who's been formally beatified; that is, declared to be with God after a formal process. Such a person stands as a worthy example of Christian virtue, is established to be in heaven with God as seen by an authenticated intercessory miracle and is commemorated in a local or regional feast day, but not with one in the Church's Universal Calendar. After receiving the sequential titles of Venerable and Blessed, a person can be advanced, after more investigations and procedures, to full canonization, being enrolled in the Church's universal "canon" or calendar of commemorations and given the title "Saint" (St.).

Saints

Agnes of Montepulciano, St. (1268–1317)

Dominican nun, mystic, visionary, and ecstatica born as Agnes de Segni in Tuscany, Italy to wealthy parents. Legends about her birth say that great lights surrounded the house where she was born and, from her childhood, she was one specially favored for her dedication to God. Due to her holiness and intelligence, Agnes was anxious to enter religious life, and eventually she was allowed to join a group of nuns in Montepulciano when she was only fifteen years old. Soon thereafter, she was elected prioress. This servant of God led an austere existence, fasting on only bread and water for fifteen years and sleeping on the floor with a stone as a pillow. In a vision, the Mother of God is said to have placed in her arms the Infant Jesus. She was allowed to hold Him and caress Him. When Agnes awoke from this ecstasy, she was reportedly clutching a gold cross which the Child Jesus wore

Saint Agnes of Montepulciano, photo by Sailko

around His neck. Several times, while in ecstasy, Agnes was said to have been privileged to receive Holy Communion from angels. She was reported to be often seen levitating. In these levitations, the sisters of the Convent del Sacco would often witness her levitating five or more feet off the ground. On one occasion, she was seen rising in the air to venerate a crucifix on a high wall. One of the most extraordinary occurrences recorded in her mystic life was the formation of white cross-shaped particles, described as manna, which frequently fell on her and the area where she was kneeling in prayer. She possessed the gift of prophecy and reading hearts as well as the ability to perform many miracles including raising a drowned child from the dead. She was said to be able to cast out devils by just using the Sign of the Cross. Agnes is also known to have mysteriously supplied food for her convent. Although never embalmed, the body of St. Agnes remained whole and incorrupt for over two hundred years, until the sixteenth century. A precious liquid, similar in color to balm, dripped from her hands and feet at her death. She was canonized in 1726.[1236]

[1236] NCE, 1st ed., v. 1, 204; NCE, 2nd ed., v. 1, 179; Cruz, Inc., pp. 106–8; Hebert, pp. 133–34; Galick, p. 122; Cruz, MMM, pp. 30, 367; Farmer, 9; Dorcy, 126–29; Paul O'Sullivan, Fr.

Aldobrandesca, St. (1245–1310) (aka Alda, Auda, Blanca, Bruna)

Lay mystic, visionary, and ecstatica born in Siena, Italy. As a young woman, she had reluctantly agreed to an arranged marriage but seemed to have grown to love her husband. When her spouse died at a young age, this childless widow decided to remain celibate and dedicate herself to a life of prayer. Aldobrandesca became a tertiary of the Holy Humility of Mary (the Humiliati), an order of penitents who served the poor and the sick. For a while she lived in Siena but later sought solitude on a small farm outside the town. She was a popular curiosity in this area because of her many visions, ecstasies, and miracles. She cured people, includin cancer victims, with the sign of the cross. Her biographer says she had to fight persistent sexual temptations. Erotic memories of relations with her husband bothered her, and she tried to fight them off by wearing a hair shirt. In her old age, Aldobrandesca moved to a hospital, where she could care for the sick and the poor. She also comforted widows and orphans and evangelized prostitutes. This medieval mystic had an astonishing vision of the Blessed Mother not long before she died. In it "she saw the Blessed Virgin, dressed in the most glowing white linen and adorned with the most precious jewels, with a gold crown of marvelous beauty. And, the following Sunday, she again saw Our Lady in a golden robe, having on her head a crown of twelve stars, with the moon beneath her feet, and a tablet in her hand, on which was written: 'Daughter, be obedient to the law of the Mother.'"[1237]

O.P. *All about the Angels.* Rockford, Ill., TAN Books and Publishers, Inc., 1990, 124.

[1237] Ghezzi, VOS, pp. 406–7; Carol Lee Flinders, *Enduring Grace: living portraits of seven women mystics*, San Francisco, CA: Harper's San Francisco, c. 1993, 4–5.

Alexis Falconieri, St. (1200–1310)

Servite brother, mystic, and visionary born the son of a wealthy Florentine merchant. In 1225, along with six other young Florentines, he joined the Confraternity of the Blessed Virgin in Florence. On the Feast of the Assumption in 1233, the seven experienced a mutual mystical vision that changed their lives. A supernaturally bright light appeared and in the center was Mary surrounded by a host of angels. She told them, "Leave the world and retire together in solitude in order to fight yourselves. Live wholly for God. You will thus experience heavenly consolations. My protection and assistance will never fail you." The men sold their possessions, gave the money to the poor, and left their families to lead a life of prayer and solitude as hermits. They founded a house at La Camarzia on the outskirts of Florence and then moved to nearby Monte Senario, and in 1240, as a result of another vision of Mary, founded the Servants of Mary (the Servites). They were all ordained except Alexis who did not consider himself worthy enough to become a priest. St. Juliana (1270–1341), his niece, was trained in sanctity under his personal direction. At his death, recorded at the age of 110, he was visited by the infant Jesus in visible form, as was attested to by eye-witnesses. His body rests near the Church of the Annunciation in Florence.[1238]

[1238] Guiley, 303; NCE, 2nd ed., v. 5, 610; Delaney, 80.

St. Alphonsus, Popular Graphic Arts, Schile, H.

Alphonsus Marie Liguori, St. (1696–1787)

Doctor of the Church, Redemptorist founder, mystic, visionary, and ecstatic born at Marianelli, near Naples, Italy, the son of a captain of the royal galleys. Alphonsus received his doctorate in both canon and civil law from the University of Naples when only sixteen. He practiced law successfully for eight years. While visiting the sick in a hospital for incurables on August 28, 1723, he suddenly saw a dazzling light around him while a voice sounded in his ears: "Leave the world and give thyself to me." When the voice repeated the same thing a second time, Alphonsus replied, "Lord Jesus, too long have I resisted your grace; do with me what you will." From the hospital, he walked over to the Church of Our Lady of Ransom (in Foggia). While kneeling before the altar of Our Lady, he saw a bright light around him and was favored with a vision of the Blessed Virgin Mary. Alphonsus promised her to become a priest. He then abandoned his law practice, joined the Oratorians, and was ordained a priest in 1726.

During a nun's retreat, he met Ven. Sister Celeste Crosta Rosa (1696–1755) who had a vision of a new religious order. She reorganized her convent according to the rule she was given in the 1731 vision thus founding the Redemptoristines. Father Liguori moved to Scala in 1732 and organized the Congregation of the Most Holy Redeemer (the Redemptionists), devoted to mission work. The rule of the order was approved by Pope Benedict XIV in 1749 and Alphonsus was elected the first Superior of this new order. He and his men set out to preach missions in rural areas and small villages. Trouble later broke out in the order and a new superior was appointed. Fourteen years after his encounter with Our Lady, Alphonsus was preaching about Mary in the very same Church in Foggia during the 1745 Christmas season. At that time, the people there reportedly saw the picture of the Virgin Mary become animated and move, as though she were alive. As she moved within the frame of her portrait, the faithful in the pews gazed in wonder and were startled when a ray of heavenly light left the Virgin's face and rested on that of Alphonsus, giving it a marvelous glow. After asking the vision, "My Lady, is it your pleasure to play with me?" the Redemptorist founder fell into a profound ecstasy and was allegedly raised bodily in the air several inches from the floor.

During the last few years of his life, Alphonsus suffered bouts of ill health, experienced temptations, dreadful apparitions, deep spiritual depression, and went through "a dark night of the soul." This period, however, was later replaced by a time of peace and light when he experienced visions, ecstasies, bilocations, and knowledge of people's secrets and hidden thoughts. He also had the ability to foresee events in distant locations, to make prophecies that were later fulfilled, to control nature and the elements, and to perform miracles. Credible witnesses on a number of occasions saw him preaching in a distant location while at the same time being in the confessional. Another time, during September 22, 1774, while being in a prolonged ecstasy at his church, he was reportedly seen attending to a dying Pope Clement XIV (1769–1774) in Rome. This servant of God also wrote prolifically on moral, theological, and ascetical subjects (notably his *Moral Theology*) and was constantly engaged in combating anti-clericalism, Jansenism, as well as being involved in several controversies on the subject of probabilism. Alphonsus was beatified in 1816 by Pope Pius VII and canonized in 1839 by Pope Gregory XVI. He was declared a Doctor of the Church by Pope Pius IX in 1871.[1239]

Alphonsus Rodriguez, St. (1532–1617) (aka Alonso Rodriguez)

Jesuit mystic, visionary, ecstatic, and stigmatic born in Segovia, Spain. Alphonsus married Mary Francisco Suarez at the age of twenty-six. His wife died in childbirth three years later. Within a few years, his mother and son had also died. After this, in 1571, Alphonsus gained admittance into the Society of Jesus as a lay brother. For the next forty-six years he served as a porter at the Jesuit College in Majorca, Spain. This humble lay brother was favored by God with remarkable mystical graces to include ecstasies and visions of Our Lady and Christ resplendent in glory along with other saints, including St. Francis (1182–1226). In his old age, Alphonsus experienced no

---

[1239] Delaney, 317–18; Cruz, MMM, 1–2, 24, 170, 548; NCE, 1st ed., v. 1, 336ff; Guiley, 11, 13; Frederick M. Jones, *Alphonsus De Liguori: Saint of Bourbon Naples, 1696–1787, Founder of the Redemptorists*. Liguori, Mo.: Liguori Publications, 1999; Farges, 31–32; Ghezzi, VOS, 610.

The Vision of Saint Alphonsus Rodriguez by Francisco de Zurbarán, 1630

Andre of Montreal, St. (1845–1937) (aka Brother Andre Bessette; Miracle Worker of Montreal)

Religious brother and mystic born as Alfred Bessette in a small town near Montreal, Canada. He was orphaned at age nine. Six years later, he entered the Congregation of the Holy Cross as a working brother and took the name Andre. As the doorkeeper of Notre Dame College for forty years, he counseled thousands of poor, suffering, and despondent in his little Montreal office and prayed for them. Brother Andre kept a hectic schedule but throughout most of his life ate nothing but a wheat-like flour softened in hot water and seasoned with salt (inedia). From an early age, he had a deep devotion to St. Joseph and a primary love for the Passion of Christ. As a great devotee of St. Joseph, Andre was known as a miracle worker who healed many people during his lifetime. He always credited the cures to the intercession of Saint Joseph his patron. Brother Andre never spoke of ecstasies, visions, or inner locutions; he referred to them as dreams. It is said that because of his ministry to the sick and the poor, this angel of mercy was frequently attacked by the devil who is said to have taken the form of a cat. He spent many sleepless nights being disturbed by strange sounds and the clanking of chains caused by the evil one. He also prophesized his own death. His tomb lies within the Oratory of St. Joseph which he built in honor of his patron saint. Some two million people of all faiths from all over the world come to Montreal each year to pray for his intercession. Brother Andre's heart is on

relief from his trials. The more he mortified himself, the more he seemed to be subject to spiritual dryness, vigorous temptations, and even diabolical assaults. In 1605, he met St. Peter Claver, then a young man, who wanted to serve God but didn't know how. Alphonsus had a vision in which he was told that Peter would do great things in South America. He urged him to go as a missionary to Cartagena, Columbia, where he did indeed do great things. Alphonsus had his final ecstasy on October 31, 1617, the night before he died. He was beatified in 1825 by Pope Leo XII and canonized in 1888 by Pope Leo XIII.[1240]

[1240] NCE, 1st ed., v. 12, 547; NCE 2nd ed., v. 12, 280; Wiebe, 19; William Thomas Walsh, *St. Teresa of Avila, complete works*, 3v. ed.; William J. Walsh, *The Apparitions and Shrines of Heaven's Bright Queen*. Four volumes. New York: Cary–Stafford

Co., (1904), 61; www.newadvent.org; Ghezzi, VOS, 502–3; Guiley, 13–14; Joseph N. Tylenda. *Jesuit saints and martyrs: short biographies of the saints, blesseds, venerable and servants of God of the Society of Jesus*, Chicago: Loyola Press, 1998, 359–62.

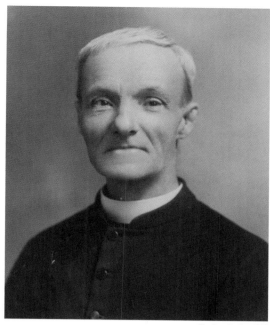

Brother Andre, 1912

view as a relic, encased in a clear glass container in the oratory. This servant of God is the source of the devotion to St. Joseph for those looking to buy or sell a home. Pope John Paul II beatified him on May 23, 1987, and Pope Benedict XVI canonized him on October 17, 2010.[1241]

Angela Merici, St. (1474–1540) (aka Angela of Brescia; Angela de Marici)

Ursuline Order foundress, mystic, visionary, and ecstatica born into wealth at Desenzano, a town in Brescia, Lombardy in Northern Italy. She was orphaned at ten and raised by her uncle. Angela's older sister died suddenly when she was thirteen,

---

[1241] Ann Ball, *Modern Saints, Their Lives and Faces*, Rockford, Ill., TAN Books and Publishers, Inc. 1983; Patron Saints Index; H.P Bergeron,. *Brother Andre: The Wonder Man of Mount Royal*, Montreal: St. Joseph's Oratory, 1997; Cruz, MMM, 255–56; Lord, VMS, 397; Guiley, ix, 57–58; http://www.wau.org/saints/saintarchive/besette.htm; Cruz, A&D,180, 210; http://www.catholic–forum.com/saints.

without the benefit of the last rites. Angela prayed and suffered on her sister's behalf until she received a vision of the Blessed Mother accompanied by her sister—confirmation to Angela that her sister was in heaven. The vision revealed that she would found an order of virgins devoted to teaching Catholicism to young ladies. In gratitude, Angela consecrated herself to God, becoming a Franciscan tertiary at age fifteen and began a life of great austerity. This servant of God experienced many visions during her lifetime. At the age of thirty-two she was favored with two remarkable supernatural visions. The first of these was seeing the skies open up and St. Ursula (d.c. 453) and companions descend to earth. In the middle of the company stood Angela's older sister. Angela was reportedly so transported by her ecstasy that she apparently levitated. Not long after that, Angela had a prophetic vision in which she saw a number of young women, all wearing crowns, being led by angels up a staircase which reached to heaven. One of the young ladies detached herself from this celestial group and advanced to where Angela knelt in ecstasy and delivered this message: "Know, Angela, that our Divine Lord has sent you this vision to teach you that before you die you are to establish in Brescia a company of young virgins like these. This is His will for you." Years would pass, however, before Angela could accomplish her goal.

She was nearly sixty when she had still another vision in which Christ rebuked her for neglecting her designated mission. She knew that she could delay no longer. Around 1535, she gathered a group of some twenty-eight young ladies from all of Brescia's social classes. This group came to be known as the Company of St. Ursula. These women pledged to lead a chaste life. They began helping Angela in her catechetical work with young children as well as ministering to the poor and those in prisons and hospitals. After Angela's death, these women were reorganized by St. Charles Borromeo (1538–1584), Bishop of Milan, and became known as the Ursulines, the first female teaching order of the Church dedicated to the education of young women. Pope Paul III formally recognized the Ursulines in 1544. The incorrupt body of St. Angela Merici now rests in a glass case in the Casa St. Angela in Brescia, Italy. At her disinterment in 1672, her body had a sweet scent, and as of 1876 it was still intact. Angela was beatified by Pope Clement XIII in 1768 and canonized by Pope Pius VII in 1807.[1242]

Angela of Foligno, St. (c. 1248–1309) (aka the Swooning Saint, Teacher of Theologians)

Franciscan tertiary, mystic, visionary, ecstatica, stigmatic, and mystical writer born a non-Christian at Foligno, Umbria, Italy. Angela married a man of substantial means while still young and had several children with him. She lived a wild, adulterous, and sacrilegious life until her late thirties. In 1285, following a vision of St. Francis of Assisi in a dream, she had an interior conversion and returned to the sacraments. In 1288, her whole family, mother, husband, and children died in short succession from the plague. After this, she sold everything she owned, gave the money to the poor, and joined the

Third Order of St. Francis. Angela then spent the rest of her days in prayer and penance. She is said to have seen Our Lady and been given the infant Jesus to hold in her arms. This servant of God also experienced vivid visions of Christ's Passion and crucifixion. She saw how Christ comes in the sacrament of the altar accompanied by a mighty thong or host of angels. In her book entitled *Book of Visions and Instructions*, Angela traced the twenty steps of penitence by which she was led to the threshold of the mystical life. Upon entering into the mystical life proper, she then describes a sequence of seven steps which culminates in her vision of seeing herself in God. This beata is said to have experienced the mystical marriage with the Lord and to have borne on her body the wounds of the stigmata. Angela also received revelations on the inner life of the Divine Trinity, on the extension of the Incarnation in the Eucharist, and on the greatness and power of God. The flood of intellectual visions she received so quickly was followed by eight days of ecstasy, during which time she laid motionless and was unable to speak. At Christmas 1308, Angela told her companions she would die shortly. A few days later, Christ appeared to her, promising to come personally to take her to heaven. At that time, Jesus is said to have shown her the royal robe of light with which a soul is clothed at death. She died in her sleep on January 3, 1309.

Saints such as Teresa of Avila, Francis de Sales, and Alphonsus Liguori as well as the visionary theologian Pierre Teilhard de Chardin (1881–1955) were influenced by her writings. Although often referred to as a saint, Angela has never been canonized. This mystic reportedly was also tormented by countless demonic afflictions. She was likewise said to have had the ability to go without food (inedia) for long periods of time. Allegedly, Angela

---

[1242] Delaney, 353–54; NCE, 1st ed., v. 9, 681; NCE 2nd ed., v. 9, 508; Cruz, Inc., 164; Ebenezer Cobham Brewer, *A dictionary of miracles, imitative, realistic and dogmatic*, London: Chatto & Windus, 1884, 367; Wiebe, 18; Gallick, 35; Guiley, 20–21; Bernard, L.D. O'Reilly, *St. Angela Merici and the Ursulines*, NY: D & J Sadlier, 1880; Thurston, 248; Cruz, A&D, 73; Catholic Wonderworkers.

lived for twelve years without taking any nourishment except for Communion said to have been brought to her by the hands of angels. She is the Patroness of the death of children and the author of another work entitled *The Little Treatise on Love*. In her book of visions, she describes the divine transformation as able to occur in three different ways: The first unites the soul to the will of God (the conforming union); the second unites the soul with God Himself (the mystical union and espousal); the third unites the soul in God and God in the soul (the spiritual marriage). Angela was beatified by Pope Innocent XII in 1693.[1243]

Angela of the Cross, St. (1846–1932) (aka Maria de los Angeles Guerrero Gonzalez)

Foundress of the Institute of Sisters of the Company of the Cross, mystic, and visionary born in Seville, Spain, and given the baptismal name of "Maria of the Angels." She was one of fourteen children, only six of whom reached adulthood. As a child, she was affectionately known as "Angelita." In 1868, this holy soul entered the Daughters of Charity of Seville, but ill health caused her to leave during the novitiate. While in prayer at home, Angela had a vision of an empty cross in front of a cross on which Jesus was hanging. She took this to mean that God was asking her to hang from the empty cross, to be "poor for the poor in order to bring them to Christ." On August

Angela of the Cross, Iglesia de Santa Ana, Spain, photo by CarlosVdeHabsburgo

2, 1875, along with three other women, she began a community whose purpose was to give assistance to the poor and dying, day and night. Known as the Sisters of the Company of the Cross, these holy women lived a recluse, contemplative life under the guidance of "Mother Angela of the Cross." They dedicated themselves to prayer and silence when not working among the poor and the dying. While alive, Mother Angela established twenty-three convents dedicated to this work. Mother Angela reportedly made a hundred spiritual Communions every day, and then a hundred more each night (see telekinesis). By the time of her death at age eighty-six, the Company of the Cross had spread throughout Spain, Italy, and Argentina. They continue their ministry today. Angela was beatified on October 3, 1982 and canonized in 2003 both times by Pope John Paul II.[1244]

[1243] Cruz, SS, 37–38; Visions, ch. 24; Freze, TBWC, 206; NCE, v. 1, 501–2; NCE 2nd ed., v. 1, 411–13; Gallick, 19; www.newadvent.org/cathen; Johnson, 108; Biot, 59; Wiebe, 19; Walsh, v. 2, 167; Ghezzi, VOS, 408–9; Hebert, 242; http://www.catholic-forum.com/saints; Angela of Foligno, *Complete Works*, translated with an introduction by Paul Lachance, preface by Romana Guarnieri, NY: Paulist Press, c1993; Wilson, 132; Cruz, A&D, 15, 131; DeVinck, rev., 41–57; Fanning, 87–90.

[1244] Gallick, 72, 413.

Angelo of Acri, St. (1669–1739) (aka Angelus of Acri)

Capuchin mystic, visionary, ecstatic, and stigmatic born as the son of a manual worker in Acri, Italy. Ordained as a Capuchin, he went on to become a famous preacher. However, after failing miserably in his first homilies, he prayed to God for assistance. In a locution, the Lord told him, "I am He who is. Do not be afraid. I will give you the gift of words and your works will not be futile." Angelo went on after this to convert thousands of souls in Calabria and Naples as well as perform many miracles of healing. As a priest, his fervor at Holy Mass was sometimes so great that he was rapt in ecstasy. He was reputed to have the gifts of prophecy and bilocation. He also would travel long distances in a miraculously short period of time to hear the confessions of the sick and dying. Angelo also experienced visions and ecstasies and was a much sought-after confessor who had the ability to see into men's souls. Pope Leo XII beatified him in 1825.[1245]

Anna Schaeffer, St. (1882–1925)

Franciscan tertiary, mystic, visionary, ecstatica, stigmatic, and victim soul born into a devout Catholic family in Mindelstetten, Bavaria in Southern Germany. As a child, Anna dedicated herself to God with the expectation of joining a religious community. However, when she was fourteen, her father unexpectedly died and she had to work to help support her now impoverished family. At age sixteen, she had a vision of St. Francis of Assisi who revealed that she would experience great suffering before the age of twenty and counseled her

to remain faithful to the Rosary. In 1901, she suffered an industrial accident at work. She fell into a vat of lye up to her knees. She underwent some thirty operations on her legs, but they proved to be unsuccessful. For the rest of her life, Anna was bedridden with her legs wrapped in bandages. She joyfully embraced her "bed-cross," as she called it, and devoted herself to catechizing the village children and praying for others. She offered her suffering in reparation for sins. Eventually she became a Franciscan tertiary.

On October 4, 1910, Anna received the visible stigmata but asked the Lord to make it invisible so that she could suffer in secret, and He agreed. This victim soul also experienced visions, which she referred to as "dreams." She was in constant pain. By the end of her life, her legs became paralyzed and she developed cancer of the rectum. Five weeks before she died, she fell out of bed and suffered a brain injury which resulted in the loss of her voice. Pope John Paul II beatified her on March 8, 1999 and Pope Benedict XVI declared her a saint on October 21, 2012.

Anthony Mary Claret, St. (1807–1870)

Born in Sallent, Spain. He founded a congregation of preachers called the Sons of the Immaculate Heart of Mary [the Claretians]. Anthony was appointed the first Archbishop of Santiago, Cuba. His holiness was manifested by extraordinary signs. Among these was the resplendent light that surrounded him while he celebrated Mass. He possessed many supernatural gifts to include the discernment of conscience. There were occasions in which, without having seen the persons, he knew the state of their conscience. Many persons knew that Father Claret had the particular gift of penetrating into the secrets of

---

[1245] Delaney, 41; NCE 2nd ed., v. 1, 414; http://www.traditioninaction.org.; http://www.roman-catholic-saints.com.

Saint Anthony Mary Claret, 1860

Convent of the Sisters of Perpetual Adoration where he went into ecstasy upon seeing a vision of the BVM holding the infant Jesus. Like St. Anthony of Padua, he was given the privilege of holding the child Jesus in his arms. This servant of God was persecuted terribly by demons. Satan would sometimes afflict him with terrible maladies. He acknowledged, however, that he experienced the visible protection of the Blessed Virgin and of the angels and saints, who guided him through unknown paths, freed him from thieves and murderers, and brought him to a place of safety without him ever knowing how. It is said that his body was incorrupt years after his death. In 1899, Pope Leo XIII declared him venerable. In 1934, Pope Pius XI pronounced him blessed and on May 7, 1950, Pope Pius XII declared Anthony Mary Claret a saint.

Anthony of Egypt, St. (c. 251–356) (aka Antony of Egypt, Anthony the Abbot, St. Antony of the Desert)

Monk, abbot, mystic, visionary, and ecstatic born at Coma, near Memphis, in Upper Egypt. After his parents death around 271, this future ascetic father of monasticism heard the gospel text "Go sell what thou hast, give it to the poor and thou shalt have treasure in heaven" (Mt 19:21). Anthony then sold his inheritance, put his sister in a convent, and in 272, became a hermit and lived for fifteen years in huts and tombs near the village of Koman. His life was one of prayer, penance, and the strictest austerity, taking only bread and water once a day. At any time, a visitor might find him rapt in mystical ecstasies. St. Anthony is said to have been favored with frequent divine visions, the ability to know the future, clairvoyance, discernment between good and evil spirits, the ability to distinguish good from

consciences, and for that reason they tried to place themselves under his authority and direction. The BVM once commanded him, saying "Anthony, write!" and he did, publishing 120 written works to include a Spanish Catechism and a Manual for Seminarians. Five times he heard Jesus and Mary tell him he had written well. Anthony has related that he was given the great grace of retaining the Blessed Sacrament in his breast. He thus preserved in his bosom uncorrupted, from one Communion to the other, the sacramental species, from August 26th, 1861 until the date of his death on October 24th, 1870, Thus he was day and night a living tabernacle of Jesus Christ. This was a most singular favor which has scarcely ever occurred in the lives of the Saints. The other spiritual consolation granted to this Fr. Claret occurred in Madrid on Christmas night 1864 in the

Saint Anthony Abbot Shunning the Mass of Gold, Fra Angelico

bad visions, and the gift of healing. When this mystic wished to know something of which he was ignorant, he simply had to pray to God, who, by symbolic and often prophetic visions, immediately gave him the knowledge he needed.

It is claimed that Anthony once had a vision of Elias and St. John the Baptist. It is also claimed that he saw the soul of his friend St. Paul the Hermit (d. 342) ascend to heaven in the company of a choir of angels. He also saw prophets and various saints. This holy ascetic would get caught up into trances and ecstasies like that of St. Paul. He related that these were for the benefit of his disciples so that "they would learn that discipline yields good fruit and that the visions frequently take place as an assuagement of trials." While Anthony

viewed visions, voices, and apparitions to be among the divine charisms and the reward for an ascetic life, he also recognized that some visions were of demonic origin sent to tempt the monks into sin. He warned his disciples that demons were capable of taking on various shapes and of sending visions, which should be ignored even if they foretold the future or urged the monks to pray or to fast. Anthony related his own demonic visions that came "having the appearance of light." While living in solitude for some twelve to fifteen years, he engaged in struggles with and was severely beaten and abused by the devil and experienced torments and temptations that are legendary. Demons appeared to him as different beasts and reptiles as well as a comely woman who came to tempt him. When he later moved to the desert, Anthony was known to have possessed power over demons. He is said to have rebuked them by remarking that they must be very weak to come in such numbers against one little old man. About the year 355, Anthony went to Alexandria to join those combating Arianism. While there, he worked with his close friend St. Athanasius (c. 297–373) whose *Vita Antonii* is the chief source of information about his life. Anthony was the founder of Christian monasticism and was famous all over the civilized world for his holiness, asceticism, wisdom, and miraculous cures. He was consulted by people of all walks of life from Emperor Constantine to the humblest monk.[1246]

Anthony of Padua, St. (1195–1231) (aka The Wonder-Worker of Padua, The Evangelical Doctor, and The Hammer of Heretics)

Doctor of the Church, Franciscan priest, mystic, and visionary born Fernando de Bouillon in a palace in Lisbon, Portugal. Originally an Augustinian, he later transferred to the Franciscans and took the name of Anthony when he entered the Friars Minor. As a new Franciscan, he proved to be very erudite. His preaching and miracles drew thousands of people wherever he went in Europe. His sermons were noted for their eloquence, fire, and persuasiveness. Anthony's contemporaries called him "Hammer of Heretics" and the

Saint Anthony and the Infant, 17th-century, by Alonso Miguel de Tovar

"Living Ark of the Covenant." He healed the sick and is credited with a dozen resuscitations of people from the dead.

St. Anthony also possessed unusual spiritual gifts such as exorcizing demons, reading hearts, the ability to predict the future, bilocation, and the quality of agility, the mystic ability to transcend time and space. One of the best documented cases of this latter phenomenon was when he once took a trip from Padua, Italy to his home town of Lisbon in Portugal within a day's time-frame. His father had been arrested and accused of murdering a young nobleman in Lisbon, Portugal. When the matter was made supernaturally known to St. Anthony, he asked his superior's permission to leave the monastery in Padua where he lived to travel on foot to Lisbon.

[1246] NCE, 1st ed., v. 1, 594–95; NCE 2nd ed., v. 1, 505–6; Delaney, 48–49; Athanasius, *St. Antony of the Desert (251–356)*, Rockford, TAN, 1995; Athanasius, *St. The Life of St. Anthony and the Letter to Mercellinus*, Robert C. Craig (trans.), NY, Ramsey and Toronto, Paulist Press, 1980; Guiley, 26; Johnson, 325; Fanning, 28; Freeze, VVA, 221; Fargas, 24; Ghezzi, MM, 45–47; Cruz, A&D, 169, 195–96.

While enroute, he found himself miraculously transported to Lisbon in time to speak in defense of his father. He convinced the authorities to travel to the victim's grave and is said to have commanded the corpse, in the name of God, to speak out. According to the story, the corpse sat up and declared his father guiltless. When Anthony reappeared in Padua, he had been absent two nights and a single day.

On one occasion, a visitor saw Anthony enraptured and holding the infant Jesus in his arms. The two seemed to be surrounded by a heavenly mist. The report of this vision inspired many depictions of the saint after his death. He is often shown in art holding the infant Jesus in his arm because of this famous apparition with the Christ child. At the actual time of his death, the saint was described as being wasted, his face haggard by continuous fasting and unceasing labors, and he was "enfeebled to the verge of decrepitude." However, after death his body assumed the incomparable beauty of youth. And, like the tongue of St. John Nepomucene (c. 1340–1393), this great preacher's tongue was found to be incorrupt and still red in color It is also interesting to note that after his death and up until the time of the Protestant Reformation, apparitions of St. Anthony of Padua were reported more frequently than those of any other saint, except the Virgin Mary. St. Anthony is often implored to find various lost objects. He was canonized in 1232 by Pope Gregory IX and declared a Doctor of the Church in 1946 by Pope Pius XII.[1247]

Saint Augustine, by Philippe de Champaigne

Augustine, St. (354–430) (aka Doctor of Grace, Augustine of Hippo)

Doctor of the Church, Augustinian founder, mystic, visionary, and ecstatic born in Tagaste, Northern Africa, located about sixty miles outside of Carthage near modern-day Tunis in Algeria. His father, Patricius, was a hot-tempered pagan and his mother, Monica, a devout Christian. Brought up a Christian by his mother, St. Monica (c. 336–387), he abandoned the Christian faith for Manichaeism, lived a wayward life, and took a mistress for fifteen years who bore him a son, Adeodatus. While praying in a garden in Milan, he heard a voice which repeated the refrain "take and read, take and read." He took this as an invitation to open his book of Scripture and read the first passage on which his eyes fell. This turned out to be the passage from Romans 13:13–14 which said: "Let us conduct ourselves properly as in the day, not in orgies and drunkenness,

_____
[1247] Delaney, 46–47; Charles Stoddard, *St. Anthony, the Wonder-Worker of Padua*, Rockford, Ill.: TAN Books and Publishers, 1992; NCE 2nd ed., v. 1, 506–7; Cruz, MMM, 90, 300; Johnson, 130–1, 155, 273–79; Guiley, 31; Cowan, 4; Ghezzi, MM, 100–6.

not in promiscuity and licentiousness, not in rivalry and jealousy. But put on the Lord Jesus Christ, and make no provision for the desires of the flesh." This event, along with the influence of the sermons of St. Ambrose (c. 339–397), the Bishop of Milan, resulted in Augustine's return to the Christian faith. He was baptized along with his son by St. Ambrose in 387. Augustine then came to live a community life of prayer and meditation. Before his mother died, they both shared a great vision of the Trinity, the Godhead, in Ostia, Italy. After this ecstasy, St. Monica said she found no joy in things of this world. She soon after fell ill and died a few days later. This was in 387. Adeodatus, his seventeen-year-old son, died a few years later. In 396, Augustine became bishop of Hippo and led bitter fights against the heresies of Manichaeism, Donatism, and Pelagianism. Among his best known works are his *Confessions* and *City of God*.[1248]

Beatrice of Silva, St. (1424–1492) (aka Beatrice da Silva Meneses, O.I.C., sometimes called "Brites")

Foundress of the Order of the Immaculate Conception, mystic, and visionary born in Ceuta, Kingdom of Portugal, as one of eleven children to nobleman Rui Gomes da Silva and Isabel de Menezes. Raised in the household of Princess Isabel of Portugal, Beatrice accompanied her mistress to Spain in 1447 where the princess married King John of Castile. Out of irrational jealousy, the new Queen had Beatrice

imprisoned in a tiny cell. During this incarceration, Beatrice experienced an apparition of the Blessed Virgin Mary in which she was instructed to found a new order in Mary's honor. Upon escaping her imprisonment, Beatrice took refuge in the Dominican Second Order monastery of nuns in Toledo. Here this servant of God lived a life of holiness for forty years without becoming a member of that order. In 1484, Beatrice, with some companions, took possession of a monastery in Toledo. Here she adapted the Cistercian rule and founded the congregation of the Immaculate Conception of the Blessed Virgin Mary. The order spread through Portugal, Spain, Italy, and France as well as to Brazil. Beatrice is also the sister of Saint Amadeus of Portugal, O.F.M., and a noted reformer of the Order of Friars Minor. Beatrice was beatified on July 28, 1926 by Pope Pius XI and canonized on October 3, 1976 by Pope Paul VI.[1249]

Benedict Joseph Labre, St. (1748–1783)

Lay mystic, visionary, and ecstatic born at Amettes, near Boulogne, France, the eldest of eighteen children. Benedict was refused entry into several religious orders either because he was too young, too eccentric, too physically weak, or it was felt that he could not abide by their religious rule. After being rejected, he set himself to wander. During his wanderings, Benedict received a vision that enlightened him about his future life. The inner illumination he received revealed that it was God's will that he should leave his country and family and all that is pleasant in life and live a life of penance like St. Alexis who lived in the fifth century.

Benedict resumed his wanderings and his life thenceforth was spent on the highways

[1248] Delaney, 57–58; Johnson, 168ff; Peter Brown, *Augustine of Hippo,* Berkeley: University of California Press, 1967; NCE 2nd ed., v. 1, 850–68; *Book of Augustinian Saints* edited by John Rotelle, Villanova, PA, Augustinian Press, 2000, 17, Saint Augustine, *The Confessions of Saint Augustine,* translated by Edward B. Pusey, NY, P.F.Collier & sons, (c 1909), ch. 8, 136–37.

[1249] http://en.wikipedia.org/wiki/Beatrix_da_Silva.

Saint Anthony and the Infant, 17th-century, by Alonso Miguel de Tovar

and byways of Europe. During the day, he visited churches that were open, and at night, looked for Churches in which perpetual adoration was observed. This vagabond saint is said to have spent whole days praying in church and was so frequently lost in prayer that he was unaware of his surroundings. He would quench his thirst at public wells and slake his hunger with leftovers and refuse he found on the streets. He slept under bridges and gateways. Most of the time he was unkempt, unclean, and infested with vermin.

In 1774, he came to Rome and lived in the Coliseum, becoming known as the "Beggar of Rome" or "the poor man of the Coliseum" for his poverty and sanctity. He was also noted for his attendance at and dedication to the Forty Hours' devotion. Benedict Joseph was often overwhelmed by Divine ecstasies and raptures. He

likewise reportedly experienced mystical favors such as levitation and bilocation. One account says the he was once seen levitating in a kneeling position while he prayed at the Church of Gesu in Rome. His funeral drew such crowds as were seen during the funeral of St. Philip Neri (1515–1595). After death, reportedly his body remained warm for many days, his limbs were supple and his hand grasped onto a bench with the natural gesture of a living person. He was also reported to have perspired. Some 136 miracles attributed to him were reported to have occurred in fewer than two months following his death. Benedict was canonized in 1883 by Pope Leo XIII.[1250]

Bernadette Soubirous, St. (1844–1879)

Visionary and victim soul born at Lourdes, France, the oldest child of a miller. On February 11, 1858, the Blessed Virgin Mary appeared to her as she was gathering firewood along the banks of the river Gave. Mary appeared as a beautiful young woman in a long white dress surrounded by a bright light and holding a rosary with large white beads. In the space of the next few months, Bernadette experienced a series of eighteen visions of the Blessed Mother at the rock of Massabielle, Lourdes. Bernadette's daily visions of Our Lady extended from February 18 to March 4, 1858 and drew large crowds of people. Despite great hostility from the civil authorities, Bernadette persisted in her claims of seeing the Blessed Mother. As a sign of this, during a vision on February 25, the Virgin asked Bernadette to dig in the ground beneath a rock. Water from an underground spring flowed up on a site where none had been

1250 Cruz, SS, 81–84; Delaney, 299; Thurston, 280; Summers, 101–2; Aradi, 177–78, Ghezzi, 606–7; Guiley, 45; Farmer, 308; NCE, 2nd ed., v. 8, 267–68.

Bernadette Soubirous, 1861

stupid. Although never having actually had a vision of hell, this saintly soul did experience the sounds of hell during one of the times Our Lady appeared to her. This occurred during the fourth apparition, which took place on Friday, February 19, 1858. Our Lady had no sooner appeared to Bernadette when the child heard the most horrible roaring sounds, much like screaming and raving very low and guttural at first and very angry. These sounds started off with a low rumble and then graduated to loud yells. After painstaking investigation, the apparitions were ecclesiastically approved.

Bernadette suffered for years from tuberculosis of the bone in her right knee which was normalized after her death. In her later years in the Convent of Nevers, Bernadette would be harassed by the devil until the end of her life. When her body was exhumed thirty years after her death, it bore the least trace of corruption. It now lies in the Chapel of St. Bernadette in the mother house of her order in Nevers, France. She was beatified in 1925 and canonized in 1933 by Pope Pius XI.[1251]

Bernardine of Siena, St. (1380–1444) (aka Bernardino of Siena, Bernardine Albizzeschi)

Franciscan preacher and propagator of the devotion to the Holy Name, mystic, visionary, and ecstatic born in Massa Marittina in the territory of Siena, Italy. Bernadine was orphaned at the age of six and raised by paternal relatives in Siena.

before. Mary directed Bernadette to build a chapel on this site. Lourdes soon became one of the great pilgrimage centers of modern Christianity. The water continues to flow, and thousands of visitors come yearly to bathe, drink, and take the water home. Miracles were reported at the Shrine and in the waters of the spring. Its curative powers have healed people with all kinds of illnesses and afflictions.

On March 25, 1858, the Blessed Virgin appeared and identified herself as the Immaculate Conception. With these words the Mother of God confirmed the pious belief which Pope Pius IX (1846–1878) four years earlier had raised to the dignity of a dogma of the infallible Church. In 1866, this pious visionary became a Sister of Notre Dame in Nevers, France and remained there until her death. When someone asked her why God would pick her for the message, Bernadette thought for a minute and answered that it must be because He could not find anybody more

[1251] Cowan, 73; Johnson, 97, 157, 229; Delaney, 461; Gallick, 118; Cruz, Inc., 288–90; Trochu, *Saint Bernadette Soubirous*; Ann Ball, *Modern Saints, Their Lives and Faces*; Guiley, 47; Farmer, 56; NCE 2nd ed., v. 13, 331–32; Francisco Sanchez–Ventera y Pascual, *Stigmatises et apparitions*, Paris, Nouvelles editas latines, 1967, 175–89.

Saint Bernardino Curing a Young Girl by Pietro Perugino

He was devoted to Mary and had visions of her. In one of these visions, she appeared to him and showed him a farm near Bergamo where a friary could be built. Three years later when Bernardine returned to dedicate the friary, Mary with the infant Jesus appeared in a brilliant light. This was said to be witnessed by many. The Virgin Mary also reportedly sent a globe of fire from heaven down to cure him of a chronic speech defect. This servant of God then went on to become one of the greatest popular preachers of his time. His eloquence and fiery sermons reached large audiences, sometimes numbering as many as thirty thousand, throughout central and northern Italy. Bernardine is especially remembered for his zeal in promoting devotion to the name of Jesus and for popularizing, with the help of St. John Capistrano (1386–1456), a symbol representing the Holy Name. The Gothic letters for the name of Jesus "IHS" (a monogram for the name of Jesus using the first three letters of the word written in Greek), were set in a blazing sun to whose tongues of fire and spreading rays he attributed mystical significance.

Many miracles were attributed to Bernardine after his death. He resuscitated four people from the dead to include Blasio Massei, an eleven-year-old boy from Cascia, near Naples, who came back to life to relate what he had seen in heaven, hell, and purgatory. After being restored to life, the youth related how he witnessed great horrors and various tortures suffered by the impure, avaricious, and other sinners. In speaking of heaven, Blasio told, in particular, of the great multitude of angels around the throne of God, and of the Blessed Virgin Mary's great beauty and glory. On the twenty-fourth day after Bernardine's death, a flow of blood issued from his nose and saturated his habit and pillow. He was canonized by Pope Nicholas V in 1450.[1252]

Bernardine Realino, St. (1530–1616) (aka Bernardineo Realino)

Jesuit mystic, visionary, and ecstatic born at Carpi, near Modena, Italy into a devout academic family. He had married but his much-loved wife died young. During a retreat, Bernardine had a vision of Our Lady who commanded him to join the Jesuit Order. He, in turn, renounced a successful career as a lawyer, was ordained on May 24, 1567, and spent most of his Jesuit life as a humble parish priest. While rapt in ecstasy, the future saint reportedly levitated about two and a half feet off the ground. Those testifying before his beatification also reported seeing sparks of fire coming from all over his body. Others acknowledged that, while alive, they witnessed an extraordinary radiance coming from his countenance which dazzled them on numerous occasions. Quite a few miraculous cures and prophecies were also attributed to him. Bernardine is said to have experienced several visions of the Blessed Virgin and Christ crucified. Just before the Jesuit's death, the blood from an unhealed leg wound that he had

sustained six years earlier was collected in vials. Reputable witnesses over the next 250 years testified that they had seen the blood in these vials, which had remained in a liquid state, bubble and boil. The blood also appeared to increase and decrease in volume. This phenomenon however ceased in 1895 when he was beatified by Pope Leo XIII. Bernardino was canonized in 1947 by Pope Pius XII.[1253]

Bridget of Sweden, St. (1303–1373) (aka Birgitta)

Patron Saint of Sweden, Bridgettines foundress, mystic, visionary, and ecstatica born in Finista, in the Province of Uppland, about fifty miles north of Stockholm, to the governor of that province. Bridget was the cousin of the Swedish King Magnus. Legend has it that Bridget's mother was shipwrecked while pregnant with her but was brought safely to shore. The next night, a person in shining garments appeared to her and told her she was saved because of the special child she had within her body. At Bridget's birth, a priest saw a bright shining cloud and a woman holding a book in her hand. The woman spoke saying, "This child's voice will be heard throughout the whole world. It will be a voice of gladness and health in the tabernacles of just men" (Ps 118:15). At the age of seven, after her mother had died, Bridget had her first earthly vision. A beautiful lady appeared and offered her a precious crown. When the youngster accepted it, it was placed on her head so that she felt its touch. When she was ten years old, Bridget had another supernatural vision, a vision of Christ crucified on Mount Calvary, naked and scourged with blood flowing from His wounds. From that time on, she began to meditate on the

---

[1252] Schouppe, 84–86; NCE 2nd ed., v. 2, 320–21; Cruz, Inc., 127; Delaney, 75; *The Preacher's Demons: Bernardino of Siena and the Social Underworld of early Renaissance Italy* (Chicago, 1999); Hebert, 113; Ghezzi, 435; Guiley, 49; R. Brown, *Saints*, 77–85; Stavinskas, 399.

[1253] NCE, 1st ed., v. 12, 109–10, photo; NCE 2nd ed., v. 11, 941; Cruz, MMM, 22, 166–67, 336; Thurston, 22ff, 164; Delaney, 428; Farmer, 452.

Saint Bridget of Sweden. Line engraving after M. de Vos.

and His Blessed Mother during which she received over 650 revelations on a multitude of important subjects. In 1344, Bridget founded a monastery in Alvastra which marked the beginning of the Order of the Most Holy Trinity (the Brigettines). She wrote Pope Clement VI (1242–1352) at Avignon telling him about a vision she had whereby the Lord demanded that he return the papacy to Rome and that he mediate peace between England and France. In 1349, at the command of our Lord, Bridget made a pilgrimage to Rome. At that time, the Lord is said to have dictated to her the famous "Fifteen Prayers of St. Bridget" in honor of His Passion. While in Rome, Bridget impressed the whole city with her austerity, holiness, concern for the poor and pilgrims, and her unceasing efforts to get the pope to return to Rome.

This servant of God wrote down her experiences in a work entitled *Revelations.* In it, she claimed to have once received visions of Mary's visitation to her cousin Elizabeth, the birth of Jesus, and Our Lord's agony in the Garden of Gethsemane. In her vision of the nativity of Jesus, she says: "The virgin knelt down with great veneration in an attitude of prayer, and her back was turned to the manger . . . and while she was in prayer, I saw the child in her womb move and suddenly in a moment, she gave birth to her Son, from whom radiated such an ineffable light and splendor that the sun was not comparable to it. I saw the glorious infant lying on the ground naked and shining. His body was pure from any kind of soil and impurity. Then I heard the singing of angels, which was of miraculous sweetness and great beauty." Also, after praying to Jesus to inquire how many blows He received during His Passion, He appeared to her and said, "I received 5,475 blows upon My Body. If you wish to honor them in some way, recite fifteen Our Fathers and fifteen Hail Marys with the following

mysteries of the Passion. In obedience to her father, Bridget was married at the age of fourteen to Ulf Gudmarsson. She bore him eight children, one of whom was St. Catherine of Sweden (1331–1381). Upon the death of her husband in 1344, Bridget spent the next four years at the Cistercian monastery in Alvastra.

The saint-to-be lived a life of great austerity and experienced numerous remarkable visions and sublime revelations. Fearing she was deluded or being duped by the devil, she sought advice from her confessor. He assured her that her visions were from God and authentic. They were all recorded by Prior Peter of Alvastra and are still available today. Bridget is said to have had frequent intimate talks with Jesus

prayers, which I myself will teach you, for an entire year. When the year is finished, you will have honored each of my wounds." In book six of her work, she saw herself transported in spirit into purgatory. She was given knowledge of the souls of the dead, whether they were in purgatory, the nature of their punishment, and in what way prayers and alms on earth could free them from their suffering.

It is related of St. Bridget that she often, in one single instant of time, saw all the inhabitants of heaven, earth, and hell, and perceived what each was saying to the other. Bridget is credited with having brought two or three persons back to life who had been pronounced dead. Prompted by a revelation, Bridget made a pilgrimage to Jerusalem in 1371. On her return, she paid her prophetic visit to Naples. This mystic died in Rome on July 23, 1373. Her heart was found to be incorrupt after her death. Her visions influenced the work of such artists as Fra Angelico and Michelangelo. She was canonized in 1391 by Pope Boniface IX for her virtue, not her revelations.[1254]

Camilla Battista Varano, St. (1458–1524) (aka Baptista Varano/Varani)

Poor Clare Mystic, visionary, ecstatica, stigmatic, and victim soul born as Camilla Varani to a noble family in Camerino, Macerata, Italy. Her early years were a mixture of piety and worldliness. As a young woman, she was mostly concerned with dancing and similar amusements. Her life turned around however after a Good Friday service when the priest urged worshippers to take a few minutes every Friday to meditate on Christ's sufferings and His love for His people. Camilla considered this meditation the beginning of her spiritual life. Her commitment grew and she entered a Poor Clare convent at Urbino, taking the name Battista in honor of St. John the Baptist. Her virtue increased and she was blessed with extraordinary mystical gifts such as interior illumination, ecstasies, and visions of angels, saints, and Our Lord Himself. Christ is said to have appeared to her on numerous occasions. She held a special devotion to His Passion. Once two angels were said to have carried her to the foot of the Cross on Calvary. Camilla Battista is said to have remained there in spirit for two months. When she asked Christ how great was the sorrow in His heart, He replied from the Cross, "As great as the love which I bear toward my creatures." Before the Poor Clare nun left, Christ decorated her soul with three lilies, and she believed the fragrance stayed with her for the rest of her life. After receiving the stigmata, this servant of God suffered the Passions of Christ. She also endured violent temptations and went through a period of spiritual aridity. Upon her death, her manuscript entitled *My Spiritual Life* was published. It remains today a classical description of the mystical life. Camilla Battista was beatified in 1843 and canonized in 2010 by Pope Benedict XVI.[1255]

[1254] Johnson, 155; R. Brown, 60; Cowan, 89; Fanning, 133; Freze, VVA, 214, 217, 226–27; Poulain, 17, 81; Delaney, 91–92; Hebert, 188; *Revelations of St. Bridget on the Life and Passion of Our Lord and the Life of His Blessed Mother*, Rockford, Illinois, TAN Books and Publishers, 1984; Paul Hafner, Fr. "St. Bridget of Sweden," in *Inside the Vatican*, June/July 2008, 58; Ghezzi, VOS, 422–23; Gallick, 220, 425; Guiley, 55; Farmer, 78; NCE 2nd ed., v. 2, 914–16; Schouppe, Purg. 119; Dunbar, 1: 137–39; Catholic wonderworkers, 14th century.

[1255] Gallick, 164; Battista Varani, *My Spiritual Life*, trans. Joseph R. Berrigan, Toronto, Peregrina, 1989.

Ecstasy of Saint Camillus de Lellis, by Cristóbal Lozano

Camillus De Lellis, St. (1550–1614)

Mystic and founder of the Order of Ministers of the Sick, also known as the Camellians, born at Bocchiavico near Naples, Italy. In his early life, Camillus fought for the Venetians against the Turks at Lepanto. He later became addicted to gambling and, in 1574, after losing all his money, became homeless and was forced to beg on the streets of Naples. As he bottomed out, this six-foot-six giant of a man found work on a construction project commissioned by the Capuchin monks. Camillus desired to join these friars but was rejected because of a leg wound he received in battle. The former soldier then went off to Rome where he met St. Philip Neri (1515–1595). The latter became his advisor, priest, and confessor and gave permission for him to be ordained. After his ordination on May 23, 1584, Camillus remained in Rome for medical treatment on his leg. He entered

San Giacomo Hospital for the Incurable for treatment and eventually became its administrator. It was here that he founded the Congregation of the Servants of the Sick (the Camellians) who cared for the sick both in the hospital and at home. The saint's mother is said to have had a vision in which she saw a child with a red cross on his chest and a standard in his hand leading other children who bore the same symbol. The Camellians later came to wear the symbol of the red cross on the front of their black habits. Camillus was also reported to have the gifts of miraculous healing and prophecy. He is the patron of the sick, of nurses, and of hospitals. When his body was exhumed eleven years after his death, a flow of pure fragrant liquid proceeded from an incision made on his body. The faithful soaked their clothes in this liquid and it was said to have effected many cures. He was canonized in 1746 by Pope Benedict XIV.[1256]

Catherine de' Ricci, St. (1522–1590) (aka Catherine of Ricci)

Dominican contemplative nun, mystic, visionary, ecstatica, stigmatic, and victim soul born in a palace in Florence, Italy as Alessandra Lucrezia Romola. She lost her mother in infancy and was raised by a stepmother. Legend has it that she spoke to her guardian angel and learned to pray the rosary from him. The angel is also said to have instructed her in the practice of virtue. From her earliest years, Alessandra had ecstasies, raptures, and visions. At age thirteen, she entered the Dominican convent of San Vincenzio at Prato, Italy and was given the name Catherine. Lost in celestial visions and ecstasies, the new nun seemed merely sleepy and at times

---

[1256] Patron Saints Index; Delaney, 308–9; Cruz, MMM, 372–73, 534; NCE, 1st ed., v. 2, 1108c; NCE, 2nd ed., v. 2, 914–16; Guiley, 61–62.

Ecstasy of Santa Catherine de' Ricci, by Jacopo Vignali, Church of Ss. Stefano and Caterina a Pozzolatico

extremely stupid to her community. She was on the verge of being sent home until her confessor insisted she tell her superiors of the heavenly favors she was receiving. As she matured, Catherine's dedication and humility won the respect of her entire community. During Holy Week of 1542, she began to experience the weekly ecstasies of the Passion. She underwent the entire events of Our Lord's suffering and Crucifixion in a series of scenes that started each Thursday at noon. These mysterious sufferings were repeated every week for the next twelve years. They began at midday every Thursday and ended on Friday at 4 p.m., lasting exactly twenty-eight hours. During these raptures, Catherine's body would move in conformity with the movements of Our Lord and she would occasionally address exhortations to those witnessing her suffering.

As Catherine relived Christ's journey to Calvary mentioned above, the wounds of the stigmata would appear on her body. They were located in her hands, feet, right shoulder, and side. These wounds, as well as those inflicted by the crown of thorns and injuries produced by the whips and cords of the scourging, were variously described by people who viewed them. Some declared that Catherine's hands were pierced through and bleeding while others perceived a brilliant light that dazzled their eyes, and still others saw the wounds as being healed but red and swollen. The head of the Dominican order and a cardinal sent by Pope Paul III investigated and declared Catherine's experiences to be authentic.

Our Lady reportedly appeared to Catherine on Christmas Day 1540 with Baby Jesus in her arms and allowed her to hold Him. On Easter Sunday of 1542, Our Lord Himself appeared to her clothed in glory, carrying a resplendent cross on His shoulder, and wearing a magnificent crown on His head. He was accompanied by the glorious

Virgin Mary, Sts. Maria Maddalena, and Thomas Aquinas and another blessed one of her order. Mary begged her divine son to take Catherine for His bride. Jesus consented and took a shining ring from His finger and placed it on the forefinger of her left hand in commemoration of their spiritual marriage. After the ecstasy, some of her sister nuns described the ring on her finger as being of gold and set with a large, brilliant diamond in it. Others saw it only as a swelling and reddening circlet around her finger which various experiments could neither duplicate nor erase. Catherine reportedly bore one of the best-documented mystic rings.

Catherine also had the gift of bilocation and is known to have slept only one hour per week. This servant of God also possessed one of the rarely mentioned mystical gifts noted in the lives of the saints. This gift consisted in the privilege of conversing frequently with other saints such as St. Philip Neri (1515–1595) while he was in Rome and St. Maria Maddalena de' Pazzi (1566–1607) while she was in Florence. These conversations took place while Catherine remained in her convent at Prato. Although they had exchanged a number of letters, these saints never physically met one another, except through these so-called mystical visits.

This contemplative is said to have descended in spirit into purgatory every Sunday night. Her devotion to the souls in purgatory was so great that she often suffered in their place on earth that which they had to endure in the other world. Catherine also received the grace of exchange of heart. A radiant light is said to have surrounded her when she fell into ecstasy, and, at the same time, a sweet smelling fragrance filled the room. More than twenty nuns attested to the celestial fragrance that clung to her and lingered in the room where she died. Some compared this "odor of sanctity" to violets,

but most could not liken it to anything on earth. St. Catherine of Ricci purportedly was also influenced by preconceived ideas. Her devotion to the excommunicated Dominican preacher Girolamo Savonarola (1452–1498) who had cured her of a serious illness, was an obstacle at first to her canonization. Pope Benedict XIII (1724–1730) resolved the issue by separating the saint's virtues from her visions. This led to the principle that when a servant of God is canonized, it is his or her virtue that is canonized and not his or her visions. She was beatified in 1732 by Pope Clement XII and canonized in 1746 by Pope Benedict XIV. Her incorrupt remains are exposed for public veneration at the Basilica of Prato.[1257]

Catherine Laboure, St. (1806–1876) (aka Zoe Laboure, Catherine Labore)

Vincentian mystic, visionary, and inaugurator of the "Miraculous Medal Devotion" born to a farmer at Fain-les-Moutiers, Cote d'Or, Burgundy, France and named Zoe. Pious from early childhood, Zoe joined the Daughters of Charity of St. Vincent de Paul taking the name Catherine. As a young postulant at the novitiate in Rue de Bac, Paris, she frequently had visions of Jesus in front of the Blessed Sacrament during Mass. On three separate occasions, she also reportedly saw mystical, symbolic visions of St. Vincent de Paul (c. 1580–1660) above the reliquary containing his

---

[1257] Johnson, 69; Poulain, 45–46, F. M. Capes, *St. Catherine de' Ricci, her Life, her letters, her community*, Burns, Oates and Washburn, London, 1911, 54, 57, 79, 270–71; G. Di Agresti, *St. Caterina de' Ricci*, Fonti (Florence, 1963); Cruz, MMM, 6, 222, 529; Cruz, Inc.,197–98; Hebert, 243; Aradi, 172; Freze, TBWC, 264; Cowan, 97; Guiley, 62–63; NCE, 1st ed., v. 14, 1912, 295; NCE 2nd ed., v. 3, 259, 267; Procter, 28, 30; Gallick, 62; Schouppe, Purgatory, xxxviii, 175; Dorcy, 325–26; Wilson, 135; Farges, 178–79.

Stained glass window depicting Mary appearing to Saint Catherine Laboure

she had for her. In a second apparition which took place on November 27, 1830, this mission was revealed when the novice beheld a picture of Mary standing on a luminous globe of the world with streams of light coming from her hands. Her feet crush the serpent to proclaim that Satan and all his followers are helpless before her. Around the Virgin were the words in French: "O Mary, conceived without sin, pray for us who have recourse to thee." The visionary picture revolved so that Catherine could see the back of it. Here was the letter "M" with a cross and two hearts surrounded by twelve stars. One of the hearts was crowned with thorns, the other was pierced by a sword. These two hearts tell us that Mary is not only Queen and intercessor, but also our mother who knows our sorrows and mother of Our Redeemer. The twelve stars may represent the twelve apostles. They may also be reminders of the stars in the vision of St. John, in which "a great sign appeared in heaven, a woman clothed with the sun, and the moon under her feet, and on her head a crown of twelve stars." After manifesting the miraculous medal, Mary asked Catherine "to have a medal struck from this model." The Blessed Virgin entrusted to Catherine the inauguration of the devotion to her Immaculate Conception.

The third and last vision of Mary occurred in September of 1831. Catherine saw Mary standing above and in the rear of the tabernacle on the altar. Under Mary's feet was a green serpent with yellow spots. When she noticed that some of the jewels on Mary's hands did not shine, Catherine was told, "Those stones which remain dark symbolize the graces that people have forgotten to request." Catherine was again shown the design for the medal and instructed to have it made. Mary told Catherine she would not appear again but would speak to her in her prayers. Catherine confided her

incorrupt heart. The latter informed her that God wanted her to work with the sick.

Catherine's most extraordinary visions, however, were those concerned with Our Blessed Mother. According to Catherine, at 11:30 on the night of July, 18, 1830, she was awakened by her guardian angel, who appeared as a child of about five years of age, dressed in white, and surrounded with a supernatural radiance. He, in turn, led her to the chapel where she met and conversed with the Blessed Virgin Mary for over two hours. Kneeling before the apparition, Our Lady told her about the mission

experience only to her superior and her spiritual adviser and confessor, Father M. Aladel. The latter, in 1832, obtained permission from Archbishop Quelen of Paris to have fifteen hundred medals struck. Eventually millions would be produced and distributed worldwide. It was known as the "miraculous medal," and Catherine was told by Our Lady that wearers of the Miraculous Medal would receive great graces and would enjoy special devotionals in the modern Church. In 1836, an archdiocesan commission canonically approved the authenticity of Catherine's visions and her mystical experiences continued.

In 1847, she had a mysterious vision of the cross and made remarkable prophecies. This virtuous soul always predicted that she would not live to see the year 1877. Catherine died during the evening of December 31, 1876. When her body was exhumed nearly fifty years after her death, it was found to be in a perfect state. The incorrupt body of this saint lies in the chapel of the motherhouse on Rue de Bac, Paris where she experienced the visions of the Blessed Mother. Her incorrupt hands that were allowed to touch Our Lady had not been allowed to decay. Both her hands and heart are kept in special reliquaries. Catherine had never gone to school as her mother died when she was eight. She could neither read nor write. She could not figure out why God picked her for the message. She once made the comment, "I have always been so stupid that I do not know how I shall explain myself in heaven." Catherine was beatified in 1933 by Pope Pius XI and canonized on 27 July 1947 by Pope Pius XII.[1258]

[1258] Johnson, 97, 213ff; Delaney, 299; Rene Laurentin, *Catherine Laboure; visionary of the miraculous medal,* translated by Paul Inwood, Boston, MA., Pauline Books, 2006; Cruz, MMM, 215; Cruz, Inc., 281–85; Cruz, A&E, 20; Cowan, 99; Ball, book 2, 132–43; NCE 2nd ed., v. 8, 266–67; http://www.catholic–forum.com/saints;

Catherine of Bologna, St. (1413–1463) (aka Caterina de'Vigri)

Poor Clare mystic, visionary, ecstatica, and abbess of St. Clare convent born as Caterina de'Vigri in Bologna, Italy, the daughter of a lawyer and diplomat. She grew up in the court of the Prince of Ferrara as a lady in waiting for his young daughter. In 1427, after the princess married and the death of her father, Catherine joined a group of Franciscan tertiaries at Ferrara who adopted the Rule of St. Clare. Desiring to punish a presumptuous feeling in her at the outset of her religious life, God permitted that she should not detect a diabolic action in her for some length of time, in spite of the disquiet that accompanied it. Feeling herself favored with great graces, she had said audaciously to the devil: "Know that you could send me no temptation without my perceiving it?" After this imprudent challenge, Catherine had false apparitions of Our Lord and the Blessed Virgin for five years, from ages fifteen to twenty.

She then fell into a dreadful period of spiritual aridity until God finally enlightened her completely with regard to this temptation. Soon after, she began to have creditable visions of Christ and Satan, and wrote of these experiences. During one of her ecstasies, God gave her a glimpse of the Final Judgment. It was so terrifying that it was imprinted in her mind forever. Catherine was then favored with a number of remarkable visions. One of these occurred on Christmas Eve when she was visited by Our Lady who is said to have placed the newborn Christ in her arms. This vision has often been reproduced in art (see picture). In fact, she is the patron saint of artists. On another occasion, the Franciscan tertiary was permitted to hear the angelic chorus singing after the Elevation of the

---

Gallick, 358, 445; Guiley, 70–71; Aradi, 217ff.

Mass and from that time on was relieved of the constant temptation to slumber during religious exercises. Like many true mystics, Catherine abhorred external publicity for her visions. She also had a most tender devotion toward the holy souls in purgatory. She authored an important treatise entitled *The Seven Spiritual Weapons*, which reflects the mystical quality of her spiritual life. An incredibly sweet fragrance emanated from her gravesite and miracles also began to happen there. The incurably sick were healed. Catherine is said to have appeared to one of her sister nuns, Leonora Poggi, at the end of the year 1500, and requested that her body be placed in a special chapel, the location and layout being specified by the saint herself. She further requested that her incorrupt body be kept in a sitting position. Catherine was beatified in 1592 by Pope Clement VIII and canonized by Pope Clement XI on May 22, 1712.[1259]

Catherine of Genoa, St. (1447–1510) (aka Caterinetta Fieschi Adorna and The Theologian of Purgatory)

Lay mystic, visionary, invisible stigmatic, and ecstatica born in Genoa, Italy, as Caterinetta Fieschi, the youngest of five children to an aristocratic Genoese family that claimed popes, cardinals, and bishops among its members. At age sixteen, Catherine was married to Giuliano Adorno, a wayward, hot-tempered, dissolute, self-indulgent and unfaithful man, to the point of having fathered his mistress's

Vision of St. Catherine of Genoa, 1747, by Marco Benefial

child. The first ten years of her married life were marked by neglect from her husband and a great deal of emotional distress. After ten years of marriage, her husband's extravagance reduced them to poverty. After enduring years of intense unhappiness, sometime in mid-March of 1473, Catherine was rewarded by experiencing an overwhelming flow of grace and love of God, followed by a vision of the Crucified Christ. After making a full confession of her sins, she became a daily communicant. Through Catherine's prayers and heroic patience, Giuliano later converted and became a Franciscan Tertiary. The couple also both agreed to live together celibately. Catherine chose to live a most unusual and intensive spiritual life while she and her husband devoted themselves to working in the Pammetone Hospital among the sick poor. In 1499, after her spouse died, Don Cattaneo Marabotto became her spiritual director. Over the last twenty-five years of her life, Catherine is said to have received personal spiritual direction from Our Lord Himself by means of visions, ecstasies, and mystical experiences. This mystic is reported to have had a vision of Jesus Christ incarnate crucified, all bloody from head to foot. This vision moved her to greater contrition. In yet another vision,

[1259] NCE, 2nd ed., v. 3, 269; Schouppe, 338–39; Delaney, 497–98; Cruz, Inc., 142–43; Lord, 17; Bolland, March 9, *Second Life*, No. 10ff; J. R. Berrigan, "Saint Catherine of Bologna: mystic," in *Woman Writers of the Renaissance and Reformation*, K. N. Wilson, ed. (Athens, Ga. 1987), pp. 81–95; Gallick, 141; Guiley, 64–66; Thurston, 233, 285–86; R. Brown, 136–45.

Catherine saw the evil in the human soul and the purity of God's love. She maintained that the real and permanent enemy of the soul is self-love.

Catherine's life was marked by frequent ecstatic absorptions and by long, mysterious fasts (inedia) during which she was unable to take food. It is claimed that for twenty-three Lents and as many Advents, the saint took no solid food at all but occasionally drank a glassful of a beverage made up of water, vinegar, and pounded salt. Exceptional heat was reported from her stigmatic blood, and elongation of her arm during agonies preceding her death. When her body was exhumed to be placed in a marble sepulcher, it was found to be almost perfectly preserved and a sweet fragrance emanated from it. Her incorrupt body is presently exposed in a glass reliquary high above the altar of a church built in her honor in Genoa, Italy. After her death, many cures began to occur attributed to her intercession. Her two works, *Dialogue between the Soul and the Body* and *Treatise on Purgatory*, are outstanding classics in the field of mystical literature. The latter is considered one of the finest works we have on the subject. In a vision of purgatory that the Lord revealed to her, Catherine describes the suffering, disposition, and happiness of the souls bathed in the purgatorial fire of divine love. She was beatified by Pope Clement V in 1675 and canonized by Pope Clement XII in 1737.[1260]

[1260] Delaney, 109–10; Cruz, Inc., 159; Catherine of Genoa; *Purgation and Purgatory, The Spiritual Dialogue*, trans. and with notes by Serge Hughes, Macwah, NJ, Paulist Press, 1979 (Western Spirituality Series); *Life and Doctrine of St. Catherine of Genoa*, translated from the Italian, NY, 1874; Fanning, 134–35; Gallick, 278, 437; Guiley, 66; Dunbar, 1:161–62; NCE, 2nd ed., v. 3, 269–72; Thurston, 213; Cruz, SS, 115–18, Cruz, MMM, 253, 284; Wilson, 133; Underhill, *Mystics*, 162–64; Garrigou–Lagrange, 190–94; Flinders, 129–54.

Saint Catherine of Siena, 1665, by Carlo Dolci

Catherine of Siena, St. (1347–1380) (aka Catherine Benincasa)

Doctor of the Church, Dominican tertiary, mystic, visionary, ecstatica, invisible stigmatic, victim soul, and copatron saint of Europe, born in Siena, Italy as Catherine Benincasa, the youngest of twenty-five children. In 1970, Catherine was declared a Doctor of the Church, only the second woman to have received such an illustrious title. A pious child, Catherine was always favored with the visible presence of her guardian angel. She began having lifelong mystical experiences starting when she was only six years old. At that time, during one of her first mystical experiences, she reportedly had her first vision of Christ in glory above the church of St. Dominic where He was clothed in pontifical robes, a tiara upon His head, and seated upon a throne around which stood Sts. Peter, Paul, and John the Evangelist.

Although illiterate early in her religious life, Catherine emerged from one of her ecstasies with the ability to read and write. This servant of God increasingly experienced ecstasies and visions of Christ, Mary, and the saints, interspersed with diabolical visions and spiritual aridity. Diabolic visions tormented her as much as ecstasies ravished her. She experienced the extremes of the glory of God and the terrible punishments of sinners, especially of those who defiled the sanctity of marriage. Like all great mystics, she suffered the painful dark night of the soul during the course of her early life.

Most likely, in the spring of 1368, Catherine had another vision whereby Christ had accepted her as His "bride." She was said to have experienced the spiritual marriage in which Our Lord gave her a mystic golden ring adorned with four precious stones, in the center of which blazed a superb diamond. The ring was visible only to Catherine during her lifetime. The finger bearing this ring was kept as a separate relic. Present at the mystical espousal was the Virgin Mary and Sts. John the Evangelist, Paul the apostle, and Dominic (1170–1221) as well as the prophet David playing the harp.

During the summer of 1370, Catherine received a series of special manifestations of Divine mysteries, which culminated in a prolonged trance, a kind of mystical death. She had a vision of hell, purgatory, and heaven, and heard a Divine command to leave her cell and enter the public life of the world. From this trance Catherine produced her great mystical work *The Dialogue of the Seraphic Virgin Catherine of Siena.*

On the fourth Sunday of Lent in 1375, this holy soul was praying before a crucifix in a Church in Pisa. In her ecstasy, she saw five rays of blood come from the points of Christ's wounds onto her. Catherine received the marks of the stigmata in this vision. Although the wounds were only visible to herself, she prayed that the marks would not be visible to others as long as she lived. The Lord granted her wish, although it was clearly apparent at the time of her death that the marks were quite pronounced, as verified by her incorrupt hands and feet. She said the five wounds did not pain her but strengthened her. Catherine experienced possibly all of the mystical gifts. She is known to have delivered many souls from diabolical possession (exorcisms) and to have performed many miracles of healing to include having raised her mother Lapa Benincasa from the dead through her prayers and pious tears. Lapa lived to the ripe old age of eighty-nine. Catherine is said to have levitated for as long as it would take to say the Miserere (Ps. 50), but only high enough so that people could pass their hands under her. She enjoyed an extraordinary intimacy with Our Lord and His Mother, experiencing heavenly apparitions almost on a daily basis. On one occasion, during a deeply moving vision, the Virgin Mary allowed Catherine to hold the infant Jesus in her arms for a moment.

It is claimed that Catherine also possessed the gifts of luminosity, hierognosis (the ability to recognize holiness or evil in any person place or thing), and the ability to multiply food. She was said to perceive secret sins in people and could smell the stench of sin in them. Catherine would confront these people, urging them to repent. Like St. Thomas Aquinas, this mystic reportedly received the cord of purity from angels. Catherine is also said to have frequently received the Sacred Host from Christ Himself, as well as from angels, during her states of ecstasy. Blessed Raymond of Capua (1330–1399), her confessor, states that the Host would sometimes depart out of his hands and like an arrow shoot into the mouth of the holy virgin when she communicated. At the age of twenty, this favored soul experienced the mystic gift of inedia. After a vision of the Sacred Heart, she promised the Lord to become a victim soul—to suffer and fast for the salvation of souls and to contribute to the world's redemption. Catherine then declined all food, except for the Eucharist. Whenever she was forced to eat anything, she was sick with violent retching pains. The future saint also experienced mystical insomnia by which she slept very little.

Catherine also was said to experience the grace of an exchange of heart with the Lord. While in ecstasy, Jesus opened the left side of her chest and placed His heart within it saying, "As I took your heart away, now, you see, I am giving you Mine, so that you can go on living with it forever." He closed the opening He had made but, as a sign of the miracle, a scar remained.

To spare her father the pains of purgatory, Catherine is said to have suffered them in his stead. Blessed Raymond of Capua, her spiritual director and close friend, later became her biographer. Her mystical experiences were published as the *Dialogue of St. Catherine*. In addition to this work, nearly four hundred of her letters to people of every class in society are still extant. She was canonized in 1461 by Pope Pius II and declared a Doctor of the Church in 1970 by Pope Paul VI. Relics of her body including her severed head are to be found in locations in Siena, Rome, Florence, Venice, and in Bow, England.[1261]

Catherine of Sweden, St. (1331–1381) (aka St. Karen of Vadstena, St. Katherine)

Bridgettine nun, mystic, and visionary and first abbess of the Order of the Most Holy Savior (now commonly called the Bridgettines) born in Vadstena, Sweden. Catherine was said to be the favorite daughter of St. Bridget (1301–1373). She was married to the nobleman Eggard von Kurnen at age fourteen but persuaded her husband to join her in taking a vow of perpetual chastity. She became a friend of St. Catherine of Siena (1347–1380). Though never formally canonized, St. Bridget's daughter is listed in the Roman martyrology. She had an apparition of the soul of her sister-in-law Gida, who was in purgatory and asked for her prayers. Catherine herself is credited with raising two men from the dead. She is alleged to have simply touched them and restored them to life and health. Pope Innocent VIII gave permission in 1484 to venerate her as a saint.[1262]

Catherine Thomas, St. (1533–1574) (aka Catalina Tomas, Catherine of Palma)

Augustinian mystic, visionary, ecstatica born in Valdemuzza, Majorca, Spain. Catherine was so religious as a child that several convents offered to accept her. At age three, she could say the rosary, and at four, she knew her entire catechism. At

[1261] Delaney, 110–11; Wiebe, 19; Brewer, 323; NCE 2nd ed., v. 3, 272–74; Catherine of Siena, *the Dialogue*, trans. Suzanne Noffke O.P. The classics of Western Spirituality. Mahwah, NJ, Paulist Press, 1980; Freze, TBWC, 174, 258; Gallick, 131, 417; Guiley, 66–68; Sabine Baring–Gould, Rev. *The Lives of the Saints: with introduction and additional lives of English martyrs, Cornish, Scottish and Welsh saints , and a full index to the entire work*, New and revised edition illustrated by 473 engravings. Edinburgh: John Grant, 1914, 4: 377–381;Cruz, MMM, 121 148,155, 163, 174,232, 236,248, 259,282, 520, 543; Cruz,

Inc.,119–123; R. Brown, 76; Johnson, 70, 128,162; Dorcy, 177–178; Thurston, 145; Underhill, Mystics, 156; Farges, 179; Ghezzl, MM, 32; Cruz, A&D, 143,198; Flinders, 103–127.

[1262] NCE, 2nd ed., v. 3, 274; Schouppe, 121–23; Hebert, 86, 188; Gallick, 94, 414; Guiley, 69; Bridget of Sweden, Saint. *Life and selected revelations/Birgitta of Sweden,* edited with a preface by Marguerite Tjader Harris, translation and notes by Albert Ryle Kezel, introduction by Tore Nyberg, NY, Paulist Press, c 1990 (Classics of Western Spirituality).

seven, she became an orphan and worked as a shepherdess for an uncle who beat and starved her. At age sixteen, she entered the convent of St. Mary Magdalen in Palma as a lay nun consigned to menial tasks. From the day she arrived at the convent, Catherine experienced profound ecstasies, especially after receiving Holy Communion. Some of her ecstasies reportedly lasted as long as three weeks. She is also said to have conversed with angels and to have experienced severe temptations and assaults from demons that left her bruised and pained. The devils that tormented Catherine were said to have terrified her convent. They filled the cloisters with fearful shrieks, and one time, the sisters watched in horror as an invisible devil lifted Catherine in the air and tossed her down a well. This holy mystic is alleged to have talked with souls in purgatory, to have prophesized the future, and to have performed miracles. Catherine foretold the day of her own death at age forty-one. Forty years after her demise, her body was exhumed and found to be incorrupt.[1263]

Charles of Sezze, St. (1616–1670) (aka Carlo of Sezze, Giancarlo Marchioni, John Charles Marchionni, Karl von Sezze, Karl av Sezze)

Franciscan mystic, stigmatic, spiritual writer, and victim soul born as John Charles Marchioni to a poor family in Sezze, Italy. Challenged as a student, Charles did, however succeed in becoming a Franciscan lay brother at the age of twenty-two in Naziano, Italy. In this capacity, he served primarily in menial positions. His pious nature led him to strong devotions to the Eucharist and the Passion. In 1648, while adoring the Holy Eucharist,

Saint Charles from Sezze by Antonio Sicurezza

Charles was said to have experienced the so-called transverberation. A visible wound was opened in his side by a piercing ray of light that came from an elevated Host during Mass at the Church of Saint Joseph in Capo le Case. After his death, it was shown that the stigmatic had a deep scar on his side and that his heart had been wounded. His heart was said to have been marked with a crucifix. There was also a four- or five-inch-long hard fleshy nail, perfectly formed, going straight through it. This saint may have shared internally the pains of Christ's wounds in his hands and feet but he displayed no visible signs of them during his lifetime. Charles had a special gift for reading souls, and people often consulted him on the authenticity of

[1263] NCE, 2nd ed., v. 3, 274; Gallick, 103; Cruz, A&D, 200.

their religious experiences. This servant of God managed to write several mystical works on the spiritual life such as *The Three Ways of Meditation, Interior Journey of the Soul,* and his autobiography entitled *The Grandeurs of the Mercies of God.* Charles was canonized in 1959 by Pope John XXIII.[1264]

Christina the Astonishing, St. (c. 1150–1224) (aka Christina the Admirable, Christina Mirabilis, Saint Christina, Blessed Christina)

Belgian lay mystic, visionary, ecstatica, stigmatic, and victim soul born in the village of Brustem near Liege, Belgium to a peasant family. Christina was thought to have died at age twenty-one from a severe seizure that made her cataleptic. Supposedly, during the Requiem Mass for her, she suddenly sat up in her coffin, levitated in the air, and flew to the top of the church ceiling. Ordered down by the priest, she landed on the altar and related that during this ecstatic rapture, she had indeed died, visited heaven, hell, and purgatory, and recognized the souls of many people she knew in all three places. It is said God offered her a choice to remain in heaven for all eternity or to return to earth and suffer. She chose to return to earth with a ministry to pray for the suffering souls in purgatory. By her reparational sufferings, she would convert many sinners from their road to hell. From then on, Christina fled from human contact. She is said to have exhibited some bizarre and unusual traits and abilities which were cataloged by Thomas de Cantimpre, a Dominican professor of theology at Louvain, and by

Saint Christina the Astonishing (Mirabilis) prayer card from 1892

Cardinal Jacques de Vitny, who knew her personally. For example, she could not stand the odor of other people because she could smell the sin in them. She would reportedly climb dangerously high into tall trees and towers, hide in fiery ovens or cupboards, or simply levitate to avoid contact with others. She would roll in fire or handle it without harm, stand in freezing water in winter for hours at a time, spend long periods in tombs of the dead, or allow herself to be dragged under water by a mill wheel, though she never sustained any injury. Christina also required very little sleep and possessed the gift of prophecy and infused knowledge. She was credited with predicting the fall of Jerusalem to the Muslims in 1187. This victim soul was given to ecstasies, during which she is said to have led the souls of the recently

---

[1264] Johnson, 50; Thurston, 69–70; NCE 2nd ed., v. 3, 435; Cruz, MMM, 71–72 Guiley, 74–75; Delaney, 333; Ghezzi, VOS, 560–61; http://www.catholic–forum.com/saints,photo;www.newadvent.org/cathen.

dead to purgatory, and those in purgatory to heaven. People were divided in their opinions of her: viewing her either as a holy woman, one tormented by devils, or simply insane. Although sometimes listed as St. Christina or Blessed Christina, she was never formally beatified or canonized. Among those who sought her advice were St. Lutgard of Aywieres. This servant of God spent the last years of her life in St. Catherine Convent at Saint Trond.[1265]

Clare of Assisi, St. (1194–1253)

Franciscan mystic, visionary, and ecstatica born in Assisi, Italy as the eldest daughter of a noble family. Legend has it that while pregnant with Clare, her mother prayed before a crucifix for her child and heard a voice saying to her, "Woman have thou no doubt, nor without peril, thou shalt be delivered of a daughter which shall by her doctrine illumine the world." From her childhood, young Clare was a virtuous soul devoted to prayer, mortification, and a great pity for the poor. As she passed into adolescence, she exhibited a distaste for the world and a yearning for a more spiritual life. Clare was converted under the influence of St. Francis of Assisi and in 1212 received the habit from him in the church of Portiuncula. Soon joined by others to include her mother, sisters, and nieces, she and her followers were set up by St.

Saint Clare of Assisi, 1548, by Giovanni Battista Moroni

[1265] Schouppe, *Purgatory*, 46–47; Delaney, 117; Gallick, 222, 430; Hebert, 243; Fanning, 97–98; http://www.catholic–forum.com/saints; Patron Saints Index; Johnson, 73; Dunbar, 1:176–78; Thomas de Cantimpe, *The Life of Christina the Astonishing*, Toronto: Pergrina, 1999; Thomas de Cantimpe, *Thomas of Cantimpre: The collected saints' lives: Abbot John of Cantimpre, Christina the Astonishing, Margaret of Ypes and Lutgard of Aywieres*, edited and with an introduction by Barbara Newman, translated by Margot H. King and Barbara Newman, Turnhout, Brepols, c2008, 127–57; http://www.mirabilis.ca/.

Francis in the convent of San Damiano near Assisi. Here she established an order of contemplative nuns known as the Poor Clares. They adopted Francis' ideal of poverty and devoted themselves to the Divine Office, contemplative prayer, and mental and manual labor. Clare remained abbess of this order until her death. She was especially devoted to the Holy Eucharist and used the Blessed Sacrament and prayer to twice intercede with God to save the convent and town of Assisi from invading soldiers. Clare was known to experience ecstasies and was alleged to have her heart pierced by divine love. This mystic was also said to have been visited by Jesus and Mary on occasion and to have been buffeted by the evil one. Clare is said to have experienced her own "Multiplication of the

Loaves" when, on one occasion, she fed fifty sisters and all of the Franciscan friars with a single loaf of bread. Olive jars were also filled after she blessed them. The sick were cured after she made the Sign of the Cross over them. At times, when she meditated, the sisters reported seeing a rainbow aura surrounding her. Clare was canonized by Pope Alexander III in 1255 and her body was said to be incorruptible.[1266]

Clare of Montefalco, St. (c. 1268–1308) (aka Clare of the Cross)

Mystic, visionary, ecstatica, stigmatic, and member of the Third Order of Franciscans and the Third Order of Augustinians, born Chiara di Damiani at Montefalco (province of Perugia), Italy. From early childhood, Clare was called "the little nun" at home and displayed signs of infused knowledge and an unusual sanctity. Her spirituality centered on the Passion of Christ, and she was often favored with revelations and mystical visions. By the mid-1290s she had become a nun in the Monastery of the Holy Cross in Montefalco. Later on she became its abbess. There was an eleven-year period in her life, however, when she was tormented by scruples, fatigue, and demonic temptations. She feared that God had abandoned her. After this, thanks to the prayers of her community, her visions and revelations returned. Christ, in fact, came to her during this period in an apparition and informed her: "I have been searching the whole world over for a strong place to plant My Cross in and have found no better site than your heart." From then on, Clare suffered great pain, and during her final illness, she repeatedly told the nuns that they would find the cross of Christ imprinted on her larger-than-normal heart. Upon

Saint Clare of Montefalco, Line engraving by H. Weyen

autopsy, her heart was found to bear tiny but distinct images of the scourge, the column and the cord of the flagellation, the Crown of Thorns, three nails, the lance, the sponge, and a thumb-sized crucifix. All this was in fine detail and made out of nerves and cardiac tissue. In addition, three mysterious pellets were found in her gallbladder. The pellets were about the size of hazel nuts and were judged by theologians to be symbols of the trinity. It was reported that any one of them was as heavy as the other two, while at other times any one of them equaled the weight of all three together.

Clare's heavenly visions often occurred during Christmas time. During one of her ecstasies, she saw the heavenly court of saints inviting her into heaven with a bridal party of saints and angels, awaiting her. Her Bridegroom was standing at the High Altar and God the Father was presiding. On another occasion, on the Feast of the Epiphany, she felt herself being drawn up again into the celestial surroundings. She went into such an ecstasy that she was lost to the entire world for thirty days. During

[1266] www.stclareseeds.com; Flinders, 15–23; http://www.poorclares.ie.users/clarissenklooster; NCE, 1st ed., v. 3, 913.

this ecstasy, she witnessed God's judgment of souls and was graced with a vision of the Blessed Trinity. The "little nun" was to behold her triune God in three distinct Persons, yet in one substance, equal. St. Clare wrote that even should God come to her and ask what gift He could give her, there would be nothing she could desire that would equal this vision of her Lord in His glorious Trinity. Clare's life was distinguished also by the performance of miracles and the gift of prophecy. This holy soul also describes a vision in which she could see her own sins: defects which she would have never seen as wrong before all of a sudden taking on grave significance calling for severe consequences. She also saw thousands and thousands of demons in front of her. During the last ecstasy before her death, Clare joined the saints exclaiming: "Behold the Virgin Mary; here is St. Augustine; here is Saint Francis." Her incorrupt body can be seen in her shrine in the Church of the Holy Cross in Montefalco.

Clare's canonization process began in 1318 but dragged on for more than five hundred years. Scholar Katherine Park writes that the process "was the first in the Church's history to attempt to authenticate systematically the visions and revelations of a holy person, and her advocates [promoted her cause] in the face of an unprecedented level of skepticism and suspicion." She was beatified in 1737 by Pope Clement XII and canonized in 1881 by Pope Leo XIII.[1267]

[1267] NCE, 2nd ed., v. 3, 760–61; Edward A. Foran, *Life of St. Clare of the Cross*, Oconomowoc, Wisconsin, 1954; Johnson , 50; Cruz, Inc., 103–4; Gallick, 247, 433, Guiley, 76–77; Lord, VHHP, 103–11; *Book of Augustinian Saints*, 30–33; photo, 31; Fargas, 26; *The Miracle Hunter: Marian Apparitions*; Katherine Park, "Relics of a Fertile Heart: The Autopsy of St. Clare of Montefalco," in *The Material Culture of Sex, Procreation and Marriage in Premodern Europe*, ed. Anne L. McClanan and Karen Rosoff Encarnacion, Hampshire, England: Palgrave, 2002.

Clelia Marie Rachel Barbieri, St. (1847–1870)

Religious sister and mystic born in Le Budrie (diocese of Bologna), Italy to poor hemp workers. Clelia was devout as a child and spent much of her time in contemplative prayer. At the age of twenty-one, she founded the order known as Suore Minime Dell'Addolorata (Sisters Minims of Our Lady of Sorrows), which ministered to the poor and sick in the community. The order took St. Francis of Paola (c. 1416–1507) as their patron. As the youngest founder of a religious community in the Catholic Church, Clelia was blessed with mystical favors such as the reading of hearts, prophesy, and miraculous cures. Her voice was heard praying with her nuns one year after her death. It is described as "unlike any on this earth." Many attest to hearing her voice periodically in houses of the order in Tanzania singing in Swahili and in India in Malayalam. She was beatified in 1968 by Pope Paul VI and canonized by Pope John Paul II on April 9, 1989.[1268]

Colette, St. (1381–1447) (aka Colette of Corbie)

Poor Clare mystic, visionary, ecstatica, stigmatic, victim soul, and abbess general of the Second Order of St. Francis born Nicolette Boylet (or Boellet) in Picardy, France. This future saint was a miracle baby born to a mother who was more than sixty years old. Baptized Nicolette, she was always known by her nickname, Colette. During her childhood in Corbie, she was said to have seen the devil who was later to torment her, appearing in various animal and reptile forms such as a roaring black

[1268] NCE 2nd ed., v. 2, 95–96; Cruz, MMM, 347–50, 509; Gallick, 209, 430; NCE Jubilee, 474–75; Cesare Zappulli, *The Power of Goodness: The Life of Blessed Clelia Barbieri*, trans. David Giddings, Boston, Daughters of St. Paul, 1980.

lion or a huge dragon and sometimes in "loathsome human forms." She dismissed Satan and his demons with her crucifix and holy water. Upon growing into a tall, striking woman, Colette entered and left several religious orders while struggling to find her vocation. After receiving a vision of St. Francis of Assisi and St. Clare, she joined the Poor Clares. Again, in 1406, in response to a vision of Sts. Francis and Clare, she was charged with reforming the Poor Clare nuns and bringing them back to their original strict rule of life. Colette is the foundress of the Coletinne Poor Clares. Pope Benedict XIII (1394–1417) authorized the reformation of the Poor Clare order and appointed her as superior over all of the houses which she reformed. Colette was renowned for her sanctity, ecstasies, and visions. She reportedly once saw souls falling from grace in great numbers, like flakes in a snowstorm. Afterwards she prayed daily for the conversion of sinners. Her friend, the illustrious St. Vincent Ferrer, more than once saw her with her face streaming with light during ecstasies. Nuns and friars of her order testified that after receiving Holy Communion, "she was all enraptured and transfigured, and remained in this state as if in a trance. And when she returned to herself, sometimes her face was like an angel's, so beautiful and bright." Collette's visions included those of Our Lord's Passion on Fridays as well as visions of people falling from grace in appalling numbers. During her Holy Week ecstasies, she is said to have participated in the sufferings, so much so that she was left with visible marks on her body (stigmata). This holy abbess is also said to have had an espousal ring placed on her finger by St. John the Evangelist on behalf of Our Lord. In one of her ecstasies, she allegedly received a small golden crucifix. On one side were said to be five precious stones: a blue stone on each extension, and a red stone in the middle. Surrounding

this red stone were four pearls with a fifth pearl added at the foot of the cross. On the other side was a figure of the crucified Jesus. Known as the "Cross from Heaven" this reliquary is housed at the Monastery de Ste. Claire in Besancon, France. St. Colette is also credited with raising many souls back to life. She purportedly brought back to life more than a hundred still-born infants. Hers was a special devotion to the souls in purgatory. This servant of God is said to have required very little sleep, had the ability to bilocate, and to have prophesied her own death in her convent at Ghent. At her death, an odor of sweetness pervaded the place where her body laid as well as in the adjoining rooms. Collette was beatified in 1740 by Pope Clement XII and canonized in 1807 by Pope Pius VII.[1269]

Crescentia Hoess, St. (1682–1744) (aka Maria Crescentia Hoss, Crescentia of Kaufbeuren)

Franciscan tertiary, mystic, visionary, ecstatica, and stigmatic born in Kaufbeuren, Bavaria. From her childhood, she exhibited a beautiful voice and unusual spiritual maturity. As a Franciscan nun, she was appointed mistress of novices and then Mother Superior. Crescentia gained a reputation for her visions on the mystical suffering of Christ, as well as for her ecstasies and prophecies. Her mystical experiences frequently occurred after receiving Holy Communion. In one of her ecstasies, she had a vision of the scourging of Our Lord, and at her Superior's request, she described to her the kind of implements that were employed. There were, according to her accounts, bundles of thorny

[1269] NCE, v. 3, 833; Butler, 36, 56; www.newadvent.org/cathen; Thurston, 139; Delaney, 123–24; Hebert, 88, 243; Cruz, MMM, 149, 164, 235, 302, 386, 506; Ghezzi, 438–39; Gallick, 46; Guiley, 78–79; Cruz, A&D 172–73.

boughs and also whips formed of a number of cords which had small metal sickles attached to their extremities. Her Superior commanded her to draw a sketch of these implements while she stood by watching. Crescentia, who had never learned to draw, was said to have produced two sketches which, from the point of view of draftsmanship, were astounding for their delicacy and firmness of every line.

This mystic was said to have frequently seen the Holy Spirit and other saints in her visions. Although these visions troubled her, she eventually came to see them as a grace from God. She had a special devotion to the Holy Spirit and envisioned this divine entity as neither man nor woman, but as a youth dressed in a flowing white gown. Her vision of the Holy Spirit was painted by Joseph Ruffini in 1728. This Servant of God was beatified in 1900 by Pope Leo XIII and canonized on November 25, 2001 by Pope John Paul II.

Cuthbert of Lindisfarne, St. (c. 634–687) (aka the British Thaumaturge)

Monk, mystic, visionary, and Northumbrian-born wonder-worker of early Britain. Orphaned as a child, Cuthbert supposedly had a vision while tending sheep when he was sixteen. The vision convinced him that he should dedicate his life to God. In this vision he saw choirs of angels descending from heaven. He later went on to became a monk at Melrose Abbey and was ultimately consecrated a bishop. He was to hold various administrative posts in monasteries at Ripon, Melrose, and Lindisfarne. In 676, however, he became a hermit on a tiny island nine miles from Lindisfarne. It was said that angels frequently appeared here to him, conversed with him, and brought him food. This holy man of God was also purportedly, at times, tormented by devils,

Athelstan, c. 895-939, Illuminated manuscript from Bede's Life of St Cuthbert

many of whom he put to flight, both from his own person and from others who were obsessed. He also had gifts of prophecy and healing in addition to reportedly performing many miracles to include obtaining food miraculously, resuscitating a dead boy, and healing a girl left dying in terrible pain. So many miracles occurred in his ministry that he became known in his lifetime as the "Wonder-Worker of Britain." He healed people with sprinklings of holy water, anointments with oil, and consecrated bread. He healed others simply by the laying on of hands, and also at a distance with prayer. Cuthbert's sepulcher was opened 418 years after his death and his body was found to be perfectly preserved, flexible, and exhaling a heavenly fragrance.[1270]

[1270] Delaney, 132–33; Cruz, Inc., 53–54; Hebert, 327; Cowan, 128, Cruz, MMM, 503; Ghezzi, VOS, 274; Guiley, 84–85; Edward C. Sellner,

Saint Dominic of Guzmán, 1685, by Claudio Coello

Dominic, St. (1170–1221) (aka Dominic de Guzman)

Mystic, visionary, ecstatic, and founder of the Order of Preachers, the Dominicans, born in Calaruega, Spain. Dominic was born to Felix Guzman and the pious Blessed Joan of Aza (c. 1140–1203). Before his birth, his mother prayed to St. Dominic of Silos (d. 1073), known as a protector of women in labor, for a son. In the seventh day of her novena, Dominic of Silos appeared to Joan in a vision and declared she would bear a son who would become a light unto the world and a successful opponent of heresies. In a later vision, Joan saw her future son Dominic in a symbolic form representing a black and white dog holding in its mouth a torch illuminating the whole world. This dog became a symbol of the Dominican Order and later gave rise to the pun "Domini Canes" ("the watchdogs of the Lord"). Grateful that her prayers had been answered, Joan named her son after St. Dominic of Silos. Just before her son's baptism, Joan had a prophetic dream where she saw a bright star that enlightened the world on Dominic's forehead. Granted many mothers have big dreams for their children, but Joan's visions and dreams were revelations that came true.

When Dominic reached adulthood, he preached against the Albigensians who denied the humanity of Christ and helped reform the Cistercians. One night in July 1206, Dominic was resting on a hill near Fanjeux overlooking the little village of Prouille. As he watched, a fiery globe seemed to descend from the heavens and settle over a chapel dedicated to Mary. Dominic interpreted this vision as a sign from God that he was to establish a community of women at the church of Our Lady of Prouille. The first sisters to take up residence in this community were nine former Albigensians who were converted by his preaching.

As recorded in the Golden Legend, Dominic had another vision in 1217 while praying in St. Peter's Basilica in Rome. Here he saw an angry Christ in the sky above Rome brandishing three lances, one in retribution for each of the vices predominant at the time (pride, lust, and avarice). In this vision, Mary showed Jesus two figures whose work would spare the world from God's wrath. Dominic related that it was only through Mary's intercession for mercy that the city was spared. Mary told Jesus that she "had a Faithful son and valiant warrior who would go throughout the world and conquer it for Him," and I, she said, "will give you another servant who will be his rival in zeal and valor." Our Lady had in mind both St. Dominic and St. Francis of Assisi. Between them, two of the greatest founders of orders of the Church, the tide was turned, faith renewed, and the hand of God held back from just retribution.

Dominic was said to levitate in ecstasy during Mass. He also possessed the gift of miraculous transport, not only for himself, but others as well. This servant of God reportedly could multiply food and is said to have had the gift of tongues as well as to have had empery over nature. It is claimed that an angel was sent to guard him while he was in Rome and, on another occasion, two angels lit the way at night for him to say his divine office at a church in Faenza, Italy. In a dream, Dominic reportedly saw two ladders, one with the Blessed Virgin Mary at the top and the other with Jesus at the top with angels going up and down. He once commanded a youngster, the nephew of Cardinal Stefano of Fossanova, who had

Wisdom of the Celtic Saints, illustrated by Susan McLean–Keeney, Notre Dame, Ind.: Ave Maria Press, 1993; Farmer, 127–28; NCE 2nd ed., v. 4, 448.

died after having fallen off a horse to come back to life. (See above depiction). Dominic later also raised two others from the dead. The tradition that the Virgin Mary revealed the Rosary to St. Dominic is supported by thirteen popes. Our Lady promised her protection to those who prayed the Rosary regularly. Dominic foresaw his own death and claimed he would die before the next feast of the Assumption (August 15). He died on August 6, being fifty-one years of age. During an exhumation of his body, it was found to be incorrupt and a sweet fragrance exuded from it. Dominic was canonized in 1234 by Pope Gregory IX. By 2010, there were 5,906 Dominican friars including 4,456 priests active in the world.[1271]

Dorothy of Montau, St. (1347–1394) (aka Dorothea von Montau)

Mystic and visionary born in Gross Montau, Prussia. At the age of seventeen, she married a wealthy swordsman named Albrecht of Danzig, an ill-tempered man in his forties. The couple produced nine children, eight of whom died, four in infancy and four during the plague of 1383. The surviving daughter Gertrud joined the Benedictines. Almost immediately after marrying, Dorothy began to experience visions. Her husband had little patience with her spiritual experiences and abused her. In 1391, upon the death of her spouse, she moved to Marienwerder and, two years later, established her hermitage there. Dorothy was noted for her visions and her devotion to the Blessed Sacrament. Her

confessor, the deacon Johannes of Marienwerder, a learned theologian, wrote down her communications in seven books entitled *Septililium*.[1272]

Saint Elizabeth of Portugal, 1635, by Francisco de Zurbarán

Elizabeth of Portugal, St. (c. 1270–1336) (aka Isabella of Portugal)

Franciscan tertiary, mystic, and visionary Queen of Portugal born in Zaragoza, Spain. She was the daughter of Pedro III and Constance of Aragon and the grandniece of St. Elizabeth of Hungary (1207–1231). Elizabeth married King Dinis of Portugal at age twelve. She bore his infidelity with loving patience and raised his illegitimate children as her own. Elizabeth was known for her piety, charity, and concern for the poor. She founded convents, hospitals, foundling homes, and shelters for wayward girls. She had a church dedicated to the Holy Spirit, after God told her in a dream that this is what He wanted her to do. Widowed in 1325, she took the habit of the Franciscan Third Order. Elizabeth had Masses said for

---

[1271] Cruz, SS, 352; Delaney, 147–48; Hebert, 188ff; Cruz, MMM, 384–85; Freze, VVA, 292; Gallick, 236, 303; Guiley, 92–93; Johnson, 92, 145; Sister Mary Jean Dorcy, *Saint Dominic*, Rockford, Ill.: TAN Books and Publishers, 1993; NCE 2nd ed., v. 4, 828; Ghezzi, MM, 87–93; Cruz, A&D, 23, 74.

[1272] Delaney, 149.

her daughter Constance after she found out in a vision that she was languishing in the depths of purgatory.[1273]

Elizabeth of Schonau, St. (c. 1129–1165)

Benedictine abbess, mystic, visionary, and ecstatica born to a prominent family in Schonau, near present-day Bonn, Germany. In 1152, after a serious illness, Elizabeth began to experience extraordinary visions, ecstasies, prophecies, and often diabolical assaults that left her bruised and beaten. The devil frequently appeared in her cell as monks or priests who mocked and threatened her, but the most impressive apparition of the devil was the time that he appeared as a great black bull. The bull was then said to dissolve into a midst of fire from which emerged a herd of loathsome goats. Elizabeth also had a problem with an angel who had ordered her to warn certain sinners about the woes that would befall them if they did not repent. When she was reluctant to do this, the angel allegedly took a whip and beat her so badly that her back ached for three days. This mystic had many dark and terrifying visions. She prophesized that Satan would receive power to create violent havoc on earth, that the sun would appear blood red and streaked with shadows, and that Christians would cry out in tribulation.

This visionary is said to have seen displayed before her eyes not only scenes of the Passion but those of the Incarnation, the Nativity, the Epiphany, and the holy childhood of the Savior. Elizabeth described her visions, especially of the Lord's Passion, Resurrection, and Ascension into heaven in three books entitled *Visiones*. Her visions were first recorded by her brother Eckbert, who became a monk at Schonau

and later was its abbot. Some of the visions described in her books are inaccurate and have been questioned by scholars, but her sincerity was never questioned and she was held in the highest esteem. Her most controversial revelation concerns Ursula and her Companions, but modern scholars blame its fantastic content on her editor, Eckbert, who may have manipulated Elizabeth's original vision. He edited and published her complete works after her death. Elizabeth's visionary writings were never sanctioned by the Church. She has never been formally beatified or canonized, although she is referred to as St. Elizabeth in the Roman Martyrology in 1584. Elizabeth was a protégé and very close friend of St. Hildergard of Bingen.[1274]

Elizabeth of the Trinity, St. (1880–1906) (aka Elizabeth Catez)

Discalced Carmelite nun, mystic, ecstatica, and victim soul born in Dijon, France to a military family. Elizabeth had an early reverence for God and, at the age of fourteen, made a vow of virginity. She was said to be always in the presence of God. It is claimed that this devout soul twice received the grace of transforming union, first on the Feast of the Ascension in 1906, and again a little later. She wrote a spiritual work entitled *The Praise of Glory*. Elizabeth, devoted to the divine indwelling, became an apostle of the praise of the glory of the Trinity. Her spiritual legacy includes a prayer to the Trinity that is now part of the Catholic catechism. This servant of God died of Addison's disease at age twenty-six. She was a victim soul offering up all

---

[1273] Schouppe, *Purgatory*, 205–6; Delaney, 159; NCE 2nd ed., v. 5, 166.

[1274] NCE 2nd ed., v. 5, 166; Delaney, 160; Freze, VVA, 214; Gallick, 183; Kathleen Jones, *Women Saints: Lives of Faith and Courage*, 9; Dunbar, 1:258–59; Elisabeth of Schonau, *Complete Works*, trans. and ed. Anne L. Clark, NY: Paulist Press, 2000; Farges, 87; Cruz, A&D, 180.

her suffering as an opportunity of grace for others. Pope John Paul II beatified her on November 25, 1984.[1275]

Eustochia Smeralda Calafato, St. (1434–1486) (aka Eustochia of Messina, Eustochia Montevergine)

Poor Clare abbess, mystic, visionary, and stigmatic born as Smerelda Colonna to Sicilian nobles in Annunziata, Messina, Sicily. From the beginning of her life, this holy soul was special. She was born in a stable on Good Friday because her mother had received a vision directing her to go there. Smeralda later on received her own vision, the image of Christ crucified. This experience led her to join the Poor Clare Convent of Santa Maria di Basico, taking the religious name Eustochia. Her convent, however, drifted away from the "holy poverty" of Clare of Assisi. As a result of this, she received permission in 1463 to found the Santa Maria Accomandata convent. She was elected its abbess in 1464. The nuns soon outgrew this facility and moved to Montevergine, near Messina in Northern Sicily, where the convent still stands. This holy soul is said to have borne the stigmatic wounds of the Lord's Passion in her flesh. Many miracles are attributed to her, the most dramatic of which was the protection of her city from the damaging earthquakes of 1615. Her sister nuns removed her perfectly preserved body and charged the saint to pray for the protection of the city. Eustochia's lips were said to have opened and she was heard chanting the first verse of the night office. Her incorrupt body rests in the Sanctuary of Montevergine in Messina. She was beatified in 1782 and declared a saint by Pope John Paul II on June 11, 1988.[1276]

Faustina Kowalska, St. (1905–1938) (aka Maria Faustyna, God's Messenger of Divine Mercy)

Mystic, visionary, invisible stigmatic, victim soul, apostle of Divine Mercy, and virgin of the Congregation of the Blessed Virgin Mary of Mercy born at Glogowiec near Lodz, Poland as Helenka Kowalska, the third of ten children in a poor, religious Polish peasant family.

Throughout her entire life, this servant of God reported a number of inner locutions and visions of Jesus which she wrote about in her diary entitled *Divine Mercy in my Soul*. In this work, she says she first felt called to religious service while attending the exposition of the Blessed Sacrament at the age of seven. It was at that time she claims to have first heard Jesus in an inner locution (voice) inviting her to strive for perfection. Then just prior to her twentieth birthday, Helenka had a vision of a suffering Christ who chastised her for her spiritual sloth and ordered her to enter a convent. After being rejected for being penniless and lacking enough education by several religious orders, she ultimately joined the Congregation of the Sisters of Our Lady of Mercy in Warsaw on August 1, 1925. When she was professed, Helenka took the name of Maria Faustina of the Blessed Sacrament. The name Faustina means "the fortunate, happy or blessed one."

Things in religious life did not go smoothly for Sister Faustina at first. By 1927 she started to experience the "dark night of the soul". However, on Good Friday of 1928, Jesus' divine flame of love suddenly filled

---

[1275] Gallick, 338; NCE Jubilee, 475; NCE 2nd ed., v. 5, 167; Fanning, 202.

[1276] Cruz, MMM, 344; Gallick, 28; Patron Saints Index; Rudolf M Bell, *Holy Anorexia*, Chicago: Univ. of Chicago Press, 1985, 141–45; NCE Jubilee, 453–54; NCE 2nd ed., v. 2, 856–57.

her entire soul, giving her some strength and inspiration during those years to come of trial and torment. On February 22, 1931 in Plock, Faustina wrote in her diary that while she was in her cell at Plock, Jesus appeared to her as the "King of Divine Mercy," wearing a white garment with rays of white and red light emanating from near His heart. In this and subsequent visions, Christ directed the humble sister to propagate devotion to His Divine Mercy.

The many visions of Jesus that Faustina was receiving reassured her of her mission; namely, to remind the world of God's merciful love for every human being; to spread devotion to the Divine Mercy through veneration of the image, instituting a feast of the Divine Mercy, reciting the chaplet of Divine Mercy, praying at the Hour of Mercy (3 p.m.), proclaiming and entreating God's mercy for the world, and an attitude of mercy toward one's neighbor. The Lord instructed her to have a sketch artist render a painting of His image with the streams of red and white light shining from His heart. He further promised that anyone who honored it would be saved. Moreover, He told Faustina that He wanted the whole Church to celebrate the first Sunday after Easter as the Feast of Divine Mercy. It was His wish that this devotion depicting Him as a merciful savior spread throughout the whole world. Faustina's first efforts to carry out Jesus' message were met with ridicule, doubt, and lukewarm support. However, in 1933, after having undergone a complete psychiatric examination at the insistence of her spiritual director, Father Michael Sopocko, she was declared of sound mind. Fr. Sopocko then began to have confidence in her and supported her efforts. He directed Faustina to keep a journal of her mystical experiences, to record her conversations and messages from Jesus, and to have a painting of the

Saint Faustina

Divine Mercy image made. On Good Friday, April 19, 1935, Jesus told Faustina that he wanted the Divine Mercy image publicly honored. The following Friday, with Faustina in attendance, Fr. Sopocko delivered the first sermon ever on Divine Mercy. On April 28, 1935, the second Sunday after Easter, the Divine Mercy image was displayed. From that time on, the Divine Mercy devotion made good but slow progress. By late 1935, thousands in Poland were participating in promoting the message of Divine Mercy.

Only a few of Faustina's superiors, her confessor, and spiritual director knew of Faustina's visions, interior locutions, revelations, invisible stigmata, gifts of ubiquity, reading of souls, prophecies, and her spiritual marriage. It was only later revealed in her diary for instance that during Lent of 1933, she began to feel the pains of the Passion in her body. She claims that while deeply immersed in prayer, brilliant rays of light completely enveloped her; suddenly she felt intense pain in her feet, hands, and side, then the sting of thorns around her head. She would continue to experience the Passion of Our Lord every Friday, but the wounds would never appear outwardly. Faustina would bear the invisible stigmata until the end of her life. She also agreed to become a "victim soul" and battled illness after illness, and ultimately succumbed to tuberculosis. Christ told her that other souls would profit greatly from her sufferings.

This apostle of Divine Mercy was also given unusual heavenly graces, including visions of heaven and hell as well as of souls doing penance in purgatory. On October 20, 1936, Faustina went on an eight-day retreat. During that time, accompanied and protected by an angel, she was said to have made a mystical journey to the abysses of hell so that she might tell souls about it and testify to its existence. Faustina also relates in her diary the sublime happiness she experienced in the vision of heaven she had on November 27, 1936 as well as the appearance of Our Lady to her with the infant Jesus in her arms.

This victim soul also reportedly saw her guardian angel a number of times as well as had visits from and visions of St. Michael the Archangel and St. Barbara, a virgin and martyr who lived in the fourth century. In addition, as mentioned in her diary, Faustina had to contend with spiritual struggles with Satan who raged in anger and hatred against her and tempted her on many occasions. She also recounts all the Lord's instructions and describes the encounters experienced between her soul and God. Her diary published under the title *Divine Mercy in My Soul* is ranked as a spiritual classic alongside the works of St. Teresa of Avila and St. Therese of Lisieux. It is also interesting to note that Faustina's description of "Prevenient Grace," or "Final Grace," whereby the mercy of God "exerts itself without any cooperation of the soul" has become church dogma. By this, she claimed that only if even this grace is refused does the soul pass into eternal separation from God.

As her health deteriorated by the end of 1937, Faustina's reported visions intensified and she was looking forward to the end of her life. In September 1938, Fr. Sopocko visited her at her sanatorium and found her very ill, but in ecstasy as she was praying. On October 25, 1938, Faustina made her final confession and died. This mystic, visionary, and victim soul who bore the invisible stigmata is today venerated in the Catholic Church as God's Messenger of Divine Mercy. Pope John Paul II beatified Faustina on April 18, 1993 and canonized her on April 30, 2000.[1277]

Flora of Beaulieu, St. (1309–1347)

Mystic, visionary, ecstatica, and stigmatic born in Maurs, Saint Flour, France. Flora was a devout child. She later resisted all attempts by her parents to marry and joined the Hospitaliers Nuns of the Order of St. John of Jerusalem at a young age. Beset with many trials, Flora fell into a depressed state and was ridiculed by many of her religious sisters. However, she never ceased to find favor with God and was granted many unusual and mystical gifts. One year at the feast of All Saints, she went into an ecstasy that lasted for three weeks. During this entire time, she was said to have taken no nourishment. On another occasion, it was said that while meditating on the Holy Spirit, she was raised four feet from the ground and hung in the air in full view of many onlookers. Still, another time, an angel reportedly brought her a piece of consecrated Host from a church eight miles away. Flora also seemed to be pierced with the arms of Our Lord's cross, causing blood to flow freely at times from her side and her mouth. Other instances of God's favoring of His servant were also reported. She had prophetic knowledge of matters of which she could not naturally know. Flora's confessor believed that she had never committed a mortal sin, yet she suffered from endless sexual temptations. The devil tried to seduce Flora, and when

1277 Sophia Michalenko, Sr. *The Life of Faustina Kowalska: the Authorized Biography,* Ann Arbor, Mich.: Charis Books, 1999; NCE 2nd ed., v. 8, 243–45; FrezeTBWC, 276–77; Freze, VVA, 262; Gallick, 301; Guiley, 107; Farmer, 306; NCE Jubilee, 528; Ghezzi, VOS, 716; Sullivan, 425; Cruz, A&D, 148; Treece, App., 126–28.

flattery failed, he used Satanic logic. An angel is said to have given her a symbolic sword to drive the devil away from her heart. Flora died in the odor of sanctity surrounded by the fragrance of roses and lilies. These aromas were also noted around her tomb, which became the site of many miracles. She was beatified in 1746 and canonized in 1852.[1278]

Frances of Rome, St. (1384–1440) (aka Francesca de Ponziani)

Foundress of the Oblates of St. Frances, mystic, visionary, ecstatica, and stigmatic born in Trastevere, Rome, Italy to a wealthy noble couple. Frances married Lorenzo dei Ponziani at age thirteen and bore him three children, two of whom later died in the plague. She herself was deathly sick for the first two years of her marriage. It is claimed that St. Alexis of Rome (5th c.), patron saint of beggars and the sick, appeared to her one night during this period and healed her, saying the Lord wished her to remain in the world to glorify Him. For forty years Frances was a model Christian wife and mother in an ideal marriage. During that time, she ministered to the poor of Rome and led a life of great holiness. In fact, she organized the Oblates of Mary, a society of women living in the world not bound by vows, but dedicated to helping the poor. It was affiliated with the Benedictines of Mount Oliveto.

Later, Frances was to experience numerous other visions and ecstasies. During Christmas of 1432, she spent forty-eight hours in ecstasy after Mary gave her the infant Jesus to hold in her arms. This virtuous soul is said to have seen the Mother of God frequently in visions "more clearly," she said,

Vision of St Francesca Romana by Carlo Maratta

"than her Oblates saw one another." She once revealed that she had been invited by Mary to attend various feast day ceremonies with the Blessed in heaven. The Oblate founder also claimed to her confessor that the words of the Oblate rule were dictated to her by St. Paul in the presence of the Blessed Virgin, St. Benedict, and St. Maria Magdalena de' Piazzi, who were the heavenly patrons of the new community. Frances performed many miracles of healing and possessed the gift of prophecy. She once had a vision in which she saw her dead son, Evangelista, accompanied by an angel. This angel was to become her constant, visible companion who followed her wherever she went. He was to remain with her for twenty-four years until she founded her religious order. In 1436, Frances joined her own community and was granted a vision in which she saw God seated on a high throne and surrounded by a myriad of angels. At this time, God is said to have appointed one of the high-ranking archangels to guide her in the last years of her life. This resplendent being was only visible to her. He was said to have shown her whatever she needed to know and to exhibit such great power and courage that he could put demons to flight by his very

[1278] Gallick, 297; Cruz, MMM, 36; Dunbar, *Saintly Woman*, I: 319–20; http://www.smom–za.org/smom/.

Carlos the V receives a visit from Saint Francis Borgia, 1862, by Joaquín María Herrer y Rodríguez

glance. This Holy soul also possessed the ability to recognize holiness or evil in any person, place, or thing (Hierognosis).

Frances is said to also have had visions of the various torments of hell and purgatory and even reportedly visited these places. Her vision of hell was so horrendous that she could not even speak of it without sobbing uncontrollably. This vision of hell and its horror, the excruciating agony of its tenants, tormented her more than any of the sufferings she had endured on earth. Frances underwent frequent painful persecution by devils. It is said that six demons presented themselves to her one day in the form of six beautiful doves. The saint saw this deception and they then changed into crows and tried to injure her. On another occasion, seven demons appeared to her in the form of seven lambs declaring that they symbolized the seven gifts of the Holy Spirit. She again recognized them and they changed into wolves and tried to attack her. Frances fended off all her encounters with demons with holy water, the Sign of the Cross or calling on the name of Jesus. Several months after her death, her tomb

was opened and her corpse found to be in a perfect state of preservation and emitting the same fragrance which had been noted before her death. She was canonized by Pope Paul V in 1608.[1279]

Francis Borgia, St. (1510–1572)

Jesuit mystic and oldest son of the Third Duke of Gandia born in Gandia, Spain. His paternal grandfather was Pope Alexander VI (1431–1503) and his mother's grandfather was King Ferdinand, the Catholic. In 1529, Francis married Leonor de Castro and they had eight sons together. After

---

[1279] Johnson, 25, 325; Ghezzi, VOS, 437; NCE, 2nd ed., v. 5, 863–64; Cruz, Inc., 125; Delaney, 194–95; Freze, VVA, 220; R. Brown, 86, 92–93; Gallick, 79; Guiley, 110–11; Hebert, 91, 239; Lord, VHHP, 131; Poulain, 87; Schouppe, Purg., xxxviii, 15; Lady Georgiana Fullerton, *The life of St. Frances of Rome, of Blessed Lucy of Narni, of Dominica of Paradiso and of Anne De Montmorecy,* NY: Routledge, 2001; F. P. Keyes, *Foundress of the Oblates, Three Ways of Love,* NY, Hawthorne Books, (1963); Bolland, March 9; *First Life,* Book III, 33, 37; O'Sullivan, 29, 131–36; Cruz, A&D, 22, 31–33, 143, 188.

the sudden death of his wife in 1546, he took his first vows to become a Jesuit. He received a doctorate in theology on August 20, 1550 and was ordained on May 23, 1551. On July 2, 1565 Francis was elected the third Superior General of the Society of Jesus and started new missions in the Americas. This Spanish Jesuit is noted for his interior mystical life and his ability to recognize consecrated from unconsecrated hosts.[1280]

Francis De Sales, St. (1567–1622)

Doctor of the Universal Church, mystic, visionary, ecstatic, invisible stigmatic, and founder of the Order of the Visitation born to a distinguished family in Thorens in the Duchy of Savoy as the eldest of thirteen children. Francis received a doctorate in Civil and Canon Law from the University of Padua at the age of twenty-four. During his time in Italy, while at the shrine of the Holy Family in Loretto, he experienced the first of his many mystical experiences, falling into rapture as his face transfigured, shining "in an unearthly manner." Ordained in 1593, Francis proved to be an outstanding preacher and confessor, having preached over four thousand sermons throughout his lifetime. During his consecration ceremony as bishop of Geneva, he again became entranced and transfigured, during which the Trinity placed their hands on him.

His saintly friends included Sts. Vincent de Paul (c. 1580–1660) and Philip Neri. He was also the spiritual advisor to Bl. Marie Acarie (aka Marie of the Incarnation) and St. Jane Frances de Chantal. Along with St. Jane, he founded the Order of the Visitation, which now boasts about three thousand sisters and 168 monasteries

Saint Francis of Sales. Line engraving by L. Visscher after C. Maratta.

around the world. St. John Bosco, the miracle worker of the nineteenth century, was so attracted to St. Francis that the religious order he founded, the Salesians, was named in honor of this saintly bishop. Despite repeated attacks on him by assassins and mobs of Calvinists, Francis was most successful in attracting thousands back to Catholicism and making new converts. He was also renowned as a healer, being especially effective in cases of possession. Francis was said to have cured over four hundred people with this affliction. He had marvelous powers to convert heretics whom he exorcized before evangelizing them. Francis also possessed the gift of tears, had astonishing visions of the future, and predicted his own death.

This servant of God was said to bear the invisible stigmata. Francis' entrance into heaven was made known supernaturally to many of his friends and relatives, especially to St. Jane Frances de Chantal mentioned above, who was informed of his death by an interior voice. During Francis' autopsy, his heart was removed and placed in a silver coffer in the Church of the Visitation in Lyons. A clear oil has exuded from the relic at intervals throughout the years. His incorrupt heart was imbued with his blood almost three hundred years after his death. Francis was beatified in 1661, canonized in 1665 by Pope Alexander VII, and declared a Doctor of the Church in 1877 by Pope Pius IX. His two works published during his lifetime entitled *Introduction to the Devout Life* and *Treatise on the Love of God* are regarded as classics in the field of spiritual literature.[1281]

Francis of Assisi, St. (1182–1226)

Founder of the Franciscan Order, mystic, visionary, ecstatic, stigmatic, victim soul, and the patron saint of Italy born in Assisi, Umbria, Italy to Pietro Bernadone, a wealthy silk merchant. Francis' youth was spent in extravagant living and pleasure seeking. He went cheerfully off to war and was taken prisoner in 1202. He languished for a year in a prison in Perugia before being ransomed. On his release, he resumed his carefree ways, became seriously ill for a time, and returned to the wars in 1205. The first step in Francis' conversion occurred after a vision of Christ he experienced at Spoleto. God told him what he was doing was wrong and that he should "serve the master, and not the man." However, it was not until the Lord spoke to him again in the Church of San Damiano that Francis turned his life around. One day, while praying in the ancient church located on

the outskirts of Assisi, Jesus spoke to him through the crucifix of San Damiano, telling him three times the following: "Francis, go and repair my house, which you see is falling down." Francis shook with terror and, at that moment, was profoundly changed. The former soldier then went on a pilgrimage to Rome in 1206 and upon his return devoted himself to a life of poverty and the care of the sick and the poor. Although it appears he was never ordained, Francis attracted numerous disciples to his way of life and, on April 16, 1209, founded the Franciscan Order (Friars Minor). In 1210, the Order received the blessing of Pope Innocent III (1198–1216) who commissioned the Friars Minor to preach repentance. In 1212, St. Clare formed a Second Order of St. Francis for religious women known as the Poor Clares. In 1219, Francis sent his first missionaries to Tunis and Morocco while he himself went off to Egypt to evangelize the Moslems in that country.

Thomas of Celano, his biographer, relates that while praying in his cell on Mount Alverna (La Verna) on September 14, 1224, Francis had a deep mystical experience. He had a vision of a man standing above him like a seraph with six luminous wings, his hands extended and his feet joined together and fixed to a cross. Two of the wings were extended above his head, two were extended as if for flight, and two were wrapped around the whole body. While St. Francis was trying to understand what the vision could mean, the marks of the nails began to appear on his hands and his feet, just as he had seen them a little before in the crucified man above him. Moreover, a gaping wound opened on his right side, as if he had been pierced with a lance. The nails of the stigmata were said to protrude beyond the skin on both sides of his palms. This was the climax of a series of supernatural events which he experienced

---

[1281] Francis de Sales, *Philothea or An Introduction to a Devout Life*, Rockford, Ill.: TAN Books and Publishers, 1994; Delaney, 197–98; Fanning, 159–62; NCE, 1st ed., v. 6, 34–36; Farges, 30; Cruz, MMM, 79; Cruz, Inc., 230–31; Summers, 58, 62, 69.

Saint Francis of Assisi in Ecstasy, 1594, by Caravaggio

throughout his life, to include talking to dead saints such as Peter, Paul, and John. St. Francis' stigmata, which appeared all at once, was the first documented case of stigmatization (although St. Paul said he bore the marks of Christ). St. Bonaventure (1221–1274) notes in his *Life of St. Francis* that Francis spoke about his stigmata only under compulsion, although he related that the one who had appeared to him had told him some things that he would never tell any man as long as he lived.

Besides ecstatic visions of Jesus, Mary, and a multitude of angels, St. Francis possessed other mystical gifts such as healing, inedia, luminosity, and the ability to levitate and bilocate. This saint had several confrontations with the devil and was said to be able to see the devil within others. At times, people suffering diabolical obsession or possession were brought to him for deliverance. Although he did not always see a physical manifestation of the devil, Francis often spoke to the evil spirits and they at times spoke back. He himself was attacked by demons. Once they seized him with great violence and fury and dragged him around the church. On another occasion, while in Rome, devils came and severely beat him for a long time, leaving him half-dead. Frances performed many miracles during his lifetime, curing many people of various illnesses, diseases, and deformities. One time he healed a man of his leprosy after washing him and rubbing sweet herbs on him with his holy hands. He is also attributed with miraculous healings after his death.

There are many stories about Francis' rapport with birds and animals, who tamely gathered around him to hear him preach. Thus, Francis is honored as the patron saint of animal lovers. Aside from having empery over nature, this servant of God also reportedly multiplied food on several occasions. The Franciscan family today, to include all three orders, number about 1.2 million Christians. Francis was canonized in 1228 by his old friend Pope Gregory IX, formerly Cardinal Ugolino.[1282]

Francis of Paola, St. (c. 1416–1507)

Founder of the Hermits of St. Francis of Assisi ("Minims" or "the Least"), mystic, visionary, and ecstatic born at Paola in the province of Cosenza, Calabria, Italy. Francis' future sanctity was indicated nine months before his birth when tongues of fire were said to have danced above the humble home of his parents, Giacomo and Vienna d'Alessio, a deeply religious couple who were childless after fifteen years of marriage. On March 27, 1429, St. Francis of Assisi appeared at his bedside and told him to join the Friars Minor. His parents took him to the Franciscan friary at San Marco where he received his education. However, he was never ordained a priest. At age fifteen he became a hermit near Paola. In 1436, he and two companions began a community that is considered the foundation of the Minim Friars. They set a rule for their followers emphasizing penance, charity, and humility, and added to these the monastic vows of fasting and

Saint Francis of Paola, 1652, by Jusepe de Ribera

abstinence from meat. Francis was said to possess the gifts of casting out demons, prophecy, clairvoyance, control over the elements, invisibility, insight into men's hearts, and the ability to bilocate. As regards the latter, he was seen at the same time in prayer in the chapel as well as out on the street talking to people, or working in the kitchens while he also attended the altar. A story from 1483 relates that King Ferdinand of Naples witnessed the future saint floating in midair, his whole body glowing with light, his hands clasped while in profound ecstasy. However, later, because of his opposition to the King, Francis was arrested. Although the king's soldiers searched the church and many times passed by him, Francis remained invisible to them. This servant of God was likewise known for his many mystical experiences to include visions of Jesus, Mary, the angels, and the saints.

Francis also seemed to exert direct authority over nature just like Christ Himself. With a command "in the name of charity," it is said that he moved boulders, opened

[1282] Cruz, MMM, 218–19; Freze, VVA, 289; Freze, TBWC,182, 255–56; Guiley, 114–16; www.thestigmata.com; Delaney, 195–96; Johnson, 92, 159; NCE, v. 6, 28–31; NCE 2nd ed., v. 5, 870–71; Wiebe, 20; William Thomas Walsh, *Saints in action*, Garden City, NY: Hanover House, 1961, v. 2, 286; Biot, 42; Thomas of Celano, *St. Francis of Assisi*, ch. 3, 94, 144; Treece, 15; James Martin, S.J., *My life with the saints*, Loyola Press, Chicago, 2006, 292; Ghezzi, MM, 117–23; Cruz, A&D, 39, 175, 197; Fanning, 86–87.

springs from rocks, passed through fire, healed the lame, the blind, the mute, the deaf, and raised the dead. This wonder-worker was credited with raising his dead nephew and at least five other people to life. He predicted the election of Cardinal Giuliano della Rovere (Pope Julius II, 1503–1513) and Giovanni de Medici (Pope Leo X, 1513–1521) to the papacy, long in advance of their elevation to that post. Francis also had the gift of miraculous transport. He took companions great distances across water by using his cloak for a boat. Because so many of his miracles were connected with the sea, Francis was declared the patron saint of seafarers. He was canonized in 1519 by Pope Leo X.[1283]

Gabriel Francis Possenti, St. (1838–1862) (aka Gabriel of Our Lady of Sorrows)

Mystic and ecstatic Passionist seminarian born in Assisi, Italy, the eleventh of thirteen children. In his youth, Gabriel was very vain. He was a ladies' man, with a passion for dancing, fine clothes, and attending the theatre. In 1856, he entered the Congregation of the Passionists taking the name of Brother Gabriel of Our Mother of Sorrows. Here Gabriel developed a special devotion to the Blessed Virgin and would become enraptured when meditating on her sorrows and joys. He was stricken with tuberculosis a year before being ordained a priest. Through his intercession after death, miraculous cures were obtained, leading to his canonization in 1920 by Pope Benedict XV.[1284]

Gaspar Del Bufalo, St. (1786–1837) (aka Gaspare del Bufalo)

Apostle of the devotion to the Precious Blood of Christ, mystic, and ecstatic born in Rome. This servant of God spent four years in exile and prison for refusing to swear allegiance to Napoleon I who had gained control of the Papal States. He was exiled along with other "intractable priests" to a remote part of the Italian peninsula. After four years of exile, part of which he was imprisoned, he returned to Rome in 1815 and founded the Congregation of the Missionaries of the Precious Blood. Gaspar counted among his friends Sts. Vincent Palloti (1795–1850) and Vincenso Strambi (1745–1824). Witnesses saw a luminous cross upon his head and said his ecstasies were often accompanied by levitation. Furthermore, he was favored with the gift of discerning the secrets of the heart and could predict the future. Numerous miraculous cures were also attributed to him. This founder of the Congregation of the Precious Blood was also alleged to have stopped rainfall and to have turned stones into money. Gaspar died in ecstasy and was canonized on January 2, 1954 by Pope Pius XII.[1285]

Gemma Galgani, St. (1878–1903) (aka "The Passion Flower of Lucca")

Italian lay mystic, visionary, ecstatica, invisible stigmatic, and victim soul born at Borgo Nuovo di Camigliano near Lucca, Italy as one of seven children. Gemma was a favored soul since early childhood. With a deep love for prayer and an intense

[1283] Hebert, 114, 188, 241; NCE, 2nd ed., v. 5, 872–74; Butler, 4/2, 11; Delaney, 197, Freze, VVA, 248; Guiley, 117; Cruz, MMM, 5, 30, 192; Ghezzi, VOS, 448–49; Gino J. Simi, *Saint Francis of Paola, God's miracle worker supreme*, Rockford, Illinois: TAN Books, 1977; Ghezzi, MM, 131–37.

[1284] Delaney, 417; Summers, 10; NCE, 1st ed., v. 11, 626; NCE 2nd ed., v. 11, 548; Ghezzi, VOS,

652–53; Farmer, 442.

[1285] Cruz, MMM, 106, 409; NCE, v. 2, 858; NCE 2nd ed., v. 2, 674–75; Farmer, 141–42; Treece, MB, 100–2; Delaney, 142.

La seraphique Gemma Galgani, 1916, photo by Jules Ernest Livernois

devotion to the Cross, this mystic had an unusual reputation for piety before her First Communion at age nine. She was favored with extraordinary graces and heavenly revelations. During the early years of her youth, Gemma had visions of Christ, the Blessed Virgin, and her guardian angel. She was shown all of her life's sins and all of the pains Christ had suffered because of them and was invited by the Lord to a life of sacrificial atonement for the sake of others. Upon agreeing to become a victim soul, she was plagued by illnesses and soon came down with meningitis, lost her hearing, and was totally paralyzed for a year. Doctors despaired over her condition; however, St. Gabriel Francis Possenti, a Passionist to whom Gemma was devoted, was said to appear to her, after which she was instantly cured. Even her healing caused some dissension because some attributed it to autosuggestion.

On June 8, 1899, this servant of God experienced a rapture in which she had a vision of her guardian angel in the company of Jesus and the Blessed Virgin Mary. Our Lady drew her close, then wrapped her inside her mantle whereupon the Crucified Savior approached her and gave her the sacred stigmata. She saw flames of fire issuing from Our Lord's wounds which suddenly leapt forth from them and pierced her hands, feet, and side. Blood flowed from Gemma's mysterious affliction, and she realized that Jesus had given her the visible stigmata. Aside from wounds in her hands and feet, Gemma experienced other physical phenomena of Christ's Passion, such as a wound on her left shoulder, the sweat of blood, scourging, and the crown of thorns. Gemma's stigmata gradually appeared during her ecstasies, first as red marks on her hands and feet that gradually tore open and bled copiously and then the nails themselves formed out of flesh, hard and dark, just like those of St. Francis of Assisi. For two years afterwards, every Thursday evening at 8 p.m., she would be caught up in ecstasy and the wounds would open up. Finally on Friday at 3 p.m., the wounds would close, leaving only a small white scar and the pain. A flowery perfume emanated from her wounds, day and night, winter and summer, although the wounds continued to putrefy and to resist any kind of medication. Out of obedience to her spiritual director, Gemma asked the Lord to remove the visible wounds. Her request was granted but not until the last three years of her life. Even then she continued to have the invisible stigmata which lasted until her death.

Aside from the pains of the stigmata, Gemma suffered from tuberculosis of the spine. She bore her illness with great fortitude and to a heroic degree. She likewise endured the scorn and ridicule of her relatives and townsfolk who jeered at her visions. She was an inediac, partaking of no food of any kind, except the Blessed Sacrament, from Whit Sunday in June 1902 until her death on April 11, 1903. Many of her conversations, while in ecstasy, were recorded. She related her visions and other spiritual favors to her spiritual director because, she said, Jesus commanded her to do so.

At times Gemma was disturbed by diabolical assaults and manifestations. She was so hateful to Satan that he waged a continual war against her, trying to fill her head with unclean thoughts to get her to despair. The "evil one" tortured her by bruises and blows, attempting the most abominable deceits to entrap her. She once wrote that the devil smeared the pages (of her diary) with black hoof-prints, of black ink and carbon from the fires of hell. These marks can still be seen on the pages of her writings. However, her guardian angel with whom she had daily visions and conversations, was constantly at her side to protect her in the dreadful battles she had with Satan. Her angel would counsel her and even scold her at times. According to her spiritual director, Father Germanus, whenever she saw or listened to her angel, she entered into an ecstatic state of consciousness, as though lost in another world. As soon as she turned her eyes away, she resumed her usual personality. One of the most remarkable trademark of Gemma's angel was his use as a messenger. Gemma would send him off on errands to deliver verbal messages or letters to her spiritual director and people in distant places. He would then return with their replies. Gemma was reportedly favored with other unusual phenomena such as numerous levitations, knowledge of future events, and the ability to see and smell the condition of some people's souls. She was beatified in 1933 by Pope Pius XI and canonized in 1940 by Pope Pius XII.[1286]

Genevieve of Paris, St. (c. 422–500) (aka Genovefa)

Mystic and visionary born at Nanterre, near Paris. After meeting St. Germanus of Auxerre (c. 378–448) at age seven, Genevieve dedicated herself to God. When her parents died, she moved to Paris and became a nun at age fifteen. She had frequent communications with the other world in the form of visions. These visions along with her prophecies evoked hostility from the inhabitants of Paris. They accused her of being a hypocrite. Many say that her mystical experiences were a pretense and deceit. An attempt was even made on her life. However, the support of St. Germanus and the accuracy of her predictions changed their attitude. By the frequent use of fasting and prayer, Genevieve is credited with saving Paris from many catastrophes to include an imminent invasion by Attila the Hun in 451. It is also believed that an epidemic that swept through the city in 1129 was said to have ended through her intercessions. She reportedly had encounters with the devil who allegedly blew her candles out when she went to pray at night in church. This holy nun also exorcized many people during her lifetime using holy oil blessed by the bishop.[1287]

[1286] Cruz, MMM, 227–29, 255; Delaney, 204; Freze, VVA, 169; Freze, TBWC, 272; Hebert, 236; Johnson, 136, 159–60, 187ff; NCE, 2nd ed., v. 6, 58; Rahner, 10; Rudolf M. Bell and Christina Mazzoni, *The Voices of Gemma Galgani: The Life and Afterlife of a Modern Saint*, Chicago: Univ. of Chicago Press, 2003; Ball, *Modern Saints*,174–81; Lord, VOS, 319–46; Guiley, 128–29; Gallick, 113; Wilson, 143; Paul O'Sullivan, O.P., *All About the Angels*, Rockford, Ill.: TAN Books and Publishers, Inc., 1990, 16–18; Treece, MB, 183; Cruz, A&D, 37, 56, 125.

[1287] Delaney, 207; Gallick, 11; Farmer, 212–13; NCE 2nd ed., v. 6, 134–35; Bernard Bangley, *Butler's Lives of the Saints: concise, modernized edition*, Brewster, Massachusetts: Paraclete Press, 2005, 3; Dubois, Jacques, O.S.B., *Sainte Genevieve de Paris: La Vie*, La Culte, L'Art, Paris: Beauchesne, 1982.

Gerard Majella, St. (1726–1755)

Redemptorist lay brother, mystic, ecstatic, stigmatic, and visionary born in Muro Lucano (Potenza), a small town south of Naples, Italy to a tailor. When Gerard was about five years old, his sister Elizabeth claimed to witness him kneeling before a statue of the Blessed Mother holding the Child Jesus. She claimed the Child Jesus left His mother's arms to play with her brother. The Child Jesus then gave Gerard a loaf of bread and returned to His Mother's arms. At the age of eight, it is said that St. Michael the Archangel brought him his first Holy Communion. Gerard joined the Redemptorist Fathers in 1748 and was professed as a lay brother in 1752 by its founder St. Alphonsus Liguori. Brother Gerard became known for his extraordinary mystical experiences and supernatural gifts such as bilocation, clairvoyance, prophecy, reading of hearts, levitation, infused knowledge, invisibility, and the multiplication of food. He also experienced ecstasies, raptures, and visions. On one occasion, Gerard reportedly started to levitate while speaking to a prioress through the iron grill of the convent parlor. He took hold of the grill, bending it like wax as he rose into the air. On another occasion, he was said to have flown rapidly for about one-quarter of a mile.

This favored soul also had the ability to discern spirits, read consciences, and control the forces of nature. Gerard read souls, hearts, and thoughts so frequently that he is said to have sent many sinners back to the confessional to confess sins that they had deliberately withheld. The Redemptorist also had countless confrontations with demons. He was a special object of the devil's fury and was assaulted by demons on many occasions. These attacks were witnessed by many of his brothers in religion.

After being physically attacked and bruised all over with demonic blows, he would use a few drops of holy water to instantly cure his wounds. His many miracles, to include restoring two dead infants back to life and his many conversions, earned him the title of a wonder-worker. This saintly brother was most successful, however, in converting sinners. He was also widely known for his charity and holiness. Gerard foretold the exact day and hour of his death some six months in advance when he related to Dr. Santorelli that he would die of consumption, although he was then in perfect health. His tomb was opened a hundred years after his death for the process of beatification. Official statements ascertained that a mysterious perfumed oil that gave off a sweet odor flowed from his bones and his brain and that it filled a basin. This liquid was said to be "beyond the natural order." In 1893 Pope Leo III beatified him, and on December 11 1904, Pope Pius X canonized him as a saint.[1288]

Germaine of Pibrac, St. (1579–1601) (aka St. Germaine Cousin)

Born at Pribac near Toulouse, France to a poor laborer. Her mother died when she was eight and she was raised by a cruel and hateful stepmother who forced her to sleep in the stable with the sheep. Germaine was born with a crippled right hand and was sickly as a child with a scrofulous condition that deformed her appearance. She was a daily communicant who shared her

---

[1288] Guiley, 131; NCE 2nd ed., v. 9, 61–62; Johnson, 128; Delaney, 209–10; Farmer, 340; http://www.catholic–forum.com/saints; Hebert, 153, 284; Aradi,184; Cruz, MMM, 214, 364, 515; Ghezzi, VOS, 598–99; Edward Saint–Omer, *St. Gerard Majella,* Rockford, Ill.: TAN Books and Publishers, 1999; Thomas Tobin, E., C.SS.R., *St. Gerard Majella, The Mother's Saint,* MO, Liguori Press, nd., 4–12; Cruz, A&D, 175–76.

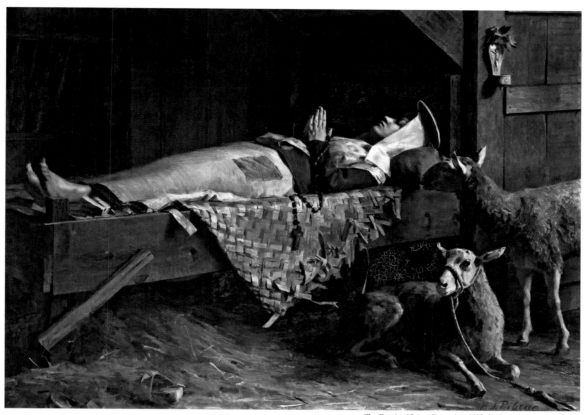

The Death of Saint-Germaine, 1910, by Raoul Du faur de Pibrac

meager rations with the poor. In one story witnesses claimed to see an overflowing stream part at her crossing. On other occasions she was said to be able to pass through waters without getting her garments wet. Her body was incorrupt after two hundred years and even bled. Many miracles were attributed to her after her demise.[1289]

Gertrude the Great, St. (c. 1256–1302)

Benedictine nun, mystic, visionary, ecstatica, stigmatic, and victim soul born in the small town of Eisleben in the county of Manfield, Germany of unknown parentage. Gertrude was placed in the care of the Benedictine nuns at Helfta in Saxony,

Germany when she was orphaned at the age of five. While there, she became a pupil and close friend of St. Mechtilde of Hackeborn. She showed early signs of being extraordinarily gifted and favored by God. When older, Gertrude herself would become a Benedictine nun and experience profound moments of rapture, especially when contemplating on Our Lord's Passion. At the age of twenty-five, this mystic began to enjoy the first of her many visions of Christ and the interior graces that she was to receive throughout her lifetime. She was said to have been favored with mystical visions in which Jesus appeared and spoke to her personally. During her ecstatic states, she reportedly was often given the Sacred Host from Christ Himself, as well as from angels.

Her first mystical experience took place on January 27, 1281 when she had a living

---

[1289] Cruz, MMM, 93, 334, 409, 429, 485; NCE, v. 6, 385; NCE 2nd ed., v. 6, 168–69; Cruz, SS, 262; Thurston, 390.

encounter with Christ and the revelation of a bond of love between Him and herself. He revealed His heart to her and placed seven golden circlets in the form of rings on her hand, one on each finger and three on the signet finger. She was the forerunner of St. Margaret Mary Alacoque in her devotion to the Sacred Heart of Jesus. Because of her profound devotion to the Sacred Heart, it was said that Our Lord favored her by imprinting His five Sacred Wounds in her heart, permanently wounding her with His seal of predilection. Gertrude experienced the Infant Jesus lying close to her bosom during one of her many ecstatic states; another time she claimed to have seen Christ face-to-face during the celebration of the Mass. It is said that, except for a period of eleven days (when she indulged in "worldly conversation"), Christ appeared to her at least once a day for a period of twenty years. So close was Gertrude to Our Lord that she often felt the imprint of the Trinity within the depths of her soul. This Benedictine experienced the wound of divine love (transverberation). Once, after taking communion, her soul was pierced by a triple-pointed golden arrow leaving her more than ever consumed by the love of God. These two favors which Gertrude received, the impressions of the wounds of Christ in her heart and the piercing with the arrow of divine love gave her such joy, she says, that even if she were to live for a thousand years in complete desolation, she would find solace, light, and gratitude in the remembrance of these graces.

This favored soul was also blessed with many visions and conversations with the saints to include: St. Agnes (d.c. 304), St. Benedict (c. 480–547), and St. John the Evangelist. Once Gertrude prayed to Mary, asking her to fill her heart with virtues. The Mother of God appeared to this holy nun and is said to have planted in her

Saint Gertrude the Great, engraving by G. Foschi

heart various symbolic flowers: the rose of chastity, the lily of purity, the violet of humility, and the sunflower of obedience. Gertrude also became versed in the Bible and the writings of St. Augustine (354–430), St. Gregory (c. 1021–1085), and St. Bernard (1090–1153).

Three Latin works are attributed to St. Gertrude. (1) The *Exercitia spiritualia* which includes seven effective meditations that tend to renew in the soul a consciousness of the work of holiness accomplished by grace from baptism up to the preparation for death. (2) *Insinuations* (called also *Revelationes* or *Legatus divina pietatis*) composed of five books. Her visions and supernatural experiences are recorded in this work. (3) *Preces Gertrudianae.* This is the book by which most people know her; however this book is not really authentic. Only some of the passages represent a faithful reproduction of her actual texts. She also wrote a *Book of Extraordinary Grace* which include St. Mechtilde's mystical experiences in *Liber Specialis Gratiae* which St. Gertrude recorded. Also, in collaboration with St. Mechtilde, Gertrude wrote a series of prayers that became very popular. Through their writings, they helped spread devotion to the Sacred Heart.

Gertrude is especially invoked for living sinners and souls in purgatory. In a vision, Jesus had told her that a certain prayer would release one thousand souls from purgatory each time it is said. The prayer was extended to include living sinners as well: "Eternal Father, I offer Thee the Most Precious Blood of Thy Divine Son, Jesus, in union with the Masses said throughout the world today, for all the Holy Souls in Purgatory, for sinners everywhere, for sinners in the universal church, those in my own home and within my family. Amen."

Although never formally canonized, Pope Innocent XI (1676–1689) in 1677 added her name to the Roman Martyrology and Pope Clement XII (1730–1740) established her feast day throughout the Western Church. She is the only female saint to attain the title of "great." This pure soul also had visions of liturgies celebrated in heaven on major feast days, such as Christmas and the Exaltation of the Holy Cross as well as on major saints' feast days such as that of St. Augustine. On Gaudete Sunday, the third Sunday of Advent, for example, Gertrude was not feeling well, and complained to Jesus that she could not attend Mass. So Jesus offered to celebrate Mass for her, bringing her into the celestial court. It is also said that on still another occasion, while assisting at holy Mass, she became rapt in ecstasy. While in this state, Gertrude saw her guardian angel bearing her prayers to the throne of the Divine Majesty presenting them to the three Divine Persons and imploring them to hear her petitions. The prayers of the guardian angels were accepted and Gertrude was said to be blessed by each person of the Godhead. Gertrude is usually regarded as one of the most important medieval mystics.[1290]

Godric, St. (1069–1170) (aka Godric of Finchale)

Hermit, mystic, visionary, and ecstatic born at Walpole, Norfolk, England. Godric was the oldest of three children of an Anglo-Saxon farmer. He spent his youth as a sailor (some say a pirate), peddler, and prosperous trader. He was known to drink, fight, chase women, and con customers. After a pilgrimage to the Holy Land and Rome, the former profligate became a hermit to make amends for his earlier indiscretions. Godric spent his life as a hermit, first in a cave in Finchale and later in a more formal hermitage to which he was led by a vision of St. Cuthbert. He spent sixty years of his life at Durham in his hermitage at Finchdale. While observing a very penitential life there, he was noted for his special power over wild creatures. It is said that in snow and ice, Godric would bring rabbits and field mice to his hut, warm them by the fire and set them free. He was also venerated for his austerity, gift of prophecy, knowledge of events occurring hundreds or thousands of miles away, and his supernatural ecstatic visions. Although described as ignorant

---

[1290] *The Life and Revelations of St. Gertrude the Great*, Christian Classics Inc., Westminster, Md. 1983; *Gertrude of Helfta: The Herald of Divine Love*, Margaret Winkworth, ed. Mahwah, N.J.: Paulist Press, 1993; Delaney, 211–12; Freze, VVA, 248; Freze, TBWC, 155, 167, 174, 257; NCE, 2nd ed., v. 6, 190–91; tradition.org/angels/guardian; Cruz, MMM, 148; Gallick, 345; Guiley, 132–34; Farmer, 219; R. Brown, 55, 58; O'Sullivan, 45; Mary Jeremy Finnigan, *Scholars and mystics,* Chicago: H. Regnery Co., 1962, 73–85; Ghezzi, MM, 67–70.

about music, he composed hymns which he said were taught him during visions of the Blessed Virgin Mary. He also counseled St. Aelred, (1110–1167), St. Robert of Newminister (d. 1159), St. Thomas à Becket (1118–1170), and Pope Alexander III (1159–1181). Toward the end of his life, Godric experienced preternatural phenomena believed to be of diabolic origin. These were said to be remarkably similar to those recorded of St. Jean Vianney (Cure d'Ars) seven centuries later.[1291]

Guthlac, St. (667–714) (aka St. Guthlac of Crowland)

Hermit, mystic, and visionary born in Lincolnshire, England. His biographer, a monk named Felix, reports that at Guthlac's birth, a shining hand surrounded with a golden-red brightness descended from Heaven, blessed the house where he was being born, and then disappeared into the heavens. It is said that all present at this holy apparition fell on the ground and praised the Lord. Guthlac entered the monastery at Repton but left after two years to become a hermit on a desolate island. St. Bartholomew the Apostle appeared to him many times and assisted him when he was tempted and attacked by devils. Besides his many miracles of healing, Guthlac prophesized the future, cast out demons, and, like St. Francis of Assisi, had remarkable influence over the birds, fish, and wildlife. On his death bed, the saint told for the first time of an angel sent by God to be his companion. He said the angel revealed many mysteries to him but he declined to talk about them. Just as his birth was heralded by a miracle, so his death saw his hut surrounded by an unearthly light and a scent of "honey-laden flowers" which filled the whole house. St. Guthlac is alleged to have appeared in a vision to King Aethelbald, a close friend, who had a tomb built for him. His body was said to be incorrupt.[1292]

Herman Joseph of Steinfeld, St. (1150–1241) (aka Herman of Cologne)

Premonstatensian mystic, visionary, and ecstatic born in Cologne, Germany. From an early age Herman had a tender devotion to the Blessed Virgin and was often found rapt in prayer before her altar. It has been alleged that around the year 1160, the infant Jesus came to be his playmate. Herman joined the Premonstratensians when he was but twelve years old. After he was ordained a priest, he continued to have ecstatic visions of Mary and composed wonderful prayers and hymns in her honor. Mary, in turn, favored him by calling him her chaplain and her spouse, being betrothed to him in mystical marriage. She also confirmed his surname "Joseph" given him by his brothers in religion. His cult was approved in 1958 in an action equivalent to canonization.[1293]

Hildegard of Bingen, St. (1098–1179) (aka Hildegarde of Bingen)

Doctor of the Church, Benedictine abbess, mystic, visionary, ecstatica, and prophetess born in Bockelheim on the Nahe, Germany to noble parents. Hildegard was never formally canonized but her name appears in the Roman Martyrology. She was called the Sybil of the Rhine for her powers as a seer and prophetess. St. Elizabeth of Schonau was her intimate friend and frequent visitor. From her earliest years, Hildegard was favored

---

[1291] Cruz, MMM, 480, Delaney, 217; NCE, 1st ed., v. 10, 180b; Freze, VVA, 220; Farmer, 227.

[1292] Cruz, Inc., 58–59; NCE 2nd ed., v. 6, 586.

[1293] Summers,158; NCE, 1st ed., v. 6, 1072; NCE 2nd ed., v. 6, 782–83; Wiebe, 20; Walsh, v. 1, 313.

The Vision of the Saint Herman Joseph, 1629, by Anton van Dyck

with supernatural experiences, visions, prophecies, and revelations. Her mystical life began with an ecstasy and vision when she was five. Although illiterate, she could write perfectly well what she saw in her visions and could read the necessary Latin books just by looking at the pages. It is said, however, that she mingled her human thoughts with the messages that came through in her visions. Detractors claim she subconsciously included in her writing many theological facts that she had picked up from sermons and from her talks with theologians and scholars, in addition to other things. In 1141, a flaming light of marvelous brightness coming from a rift of heaven is said to have penetrated her brain and heart. This light is said to have given her a divine intuition into the spiritual meaning of the Scripture, and commanded her to give her revelations to the world.

Hildegard related these mystical experiences to her spiritual adviser, a monk named Godfrey. He, in turn, ordered a monk named Volmar to copy them down. They were approved as coming from God by Archbishop Henry of Mainz. Her best known work is called *Scivias* or *Know God's Ways* written between 1141 and 1151. In the introduction, she describes the nature of the twenty-six visions she had over ten years about the hidden mysteries of God. Her visions were cerebral, unaccompanied by emotions except those of weariness and infirmity. Her account of her visions is un-sensational and exact. They were pictures, she says, seen within the mind, "neither in dream, sleep, nor any frenzy," involving no hallucination and never interfering with her outward sight. "I did not see these things with the bodily eyes or hear them with outward ears, but I beheld them according to God's will, openly and fully awake, considering them in the full light of the mind, eyes and ears of the inner mind." She visualized the whole

theology of creation and redemption and then reported her apocalyptic vision. Like St. John the Evangelist, she says, "And I heard a voice from heaven saying . . ." and insists repeatedly, "These things are true." Her first book contains six visions, the second, seven visions, and the third, thirteen visions. Many miracles are said to have been wrought by St. Hildegard's intercession. She was beatified in 1324 by Pope John XXII. Her name was inserted in the Roman martyrology in the fifteenth century. Pope Benedict XVI declared her a Doctor of the Church on October 7, 2012.[1294]

Hyacinth, St. (1185–1257) (Apostle of the Slavs)

Dominican priest, Bishop of Krakow, mystic, and visionary born of noble parents at Oppeln, Poland. Hyacinth preached in Scandinavia, Prussia, Lithuania, Russia, Tartary, Tibet, and even up to the borders of China. He is known as the "Polish St. Dominic" because he established the Dominican Order in Poland. He is also credited with traveling twenty-five thousand miles on foot during his evangelizing journeys which, as previously mentioned, took him from Denmark and Prussia to Greece, White Russia, Tartary, and Tibet. He worked many miracles along the way to include restoring sight to two boys born without eyes and bringing back to life a child who had drowned. In all he is reputed to have restored at least fifty people back to life in Krakow alone as well as restoring

---

[1294] Sabina Flanagan, *Hildegard of Bingen: A Visionary Life*, London, Routledge, 1989; Johnson, 33, 308; Delaney, 239–40; Guiley, 146–47; Gallick, 280, 438; Cowan, 198, Ghezzi, VOS, 350; NCE 2nd ed., v.6, 831–32; Farmer, 250; http://www.newadvent.org/cathen/07351a.htm; K. Jones, 6–8; Fanning, 83; Underhill, Mystics, 77–78.

seventy-two dying persons to perfect health. Many miracles were, likewise, claimed by his intercession after his death.

Hyacinth received the special help of the Blessed Virgin to whom he was devoted in much of his work. At the beginning of his apostolate, he had a vision of Mary in which she promised him that he would obtain all he asked for through her intercession. On one occasion, St. Hyacinth rushed into a burning convent chapel set afire by invading Tartars. His purpose was only to remove the Blessed Sacrament and hide it as a protection from desecration. Our Lady told him to take her statue out of the chapel also. Her statue was large and heavy but Mary lightened it so he could carry both items. St. Hyacinth then crossed the Dnieper River on his cloak carrying the Blessed Sacrament and the statue of Our Lady. He saved them both from desecration at the hands of the invading Tartars. On three occasions, the Dominican was reportedly witnessed walking on water or using his cloak to sail great distances over water. This occurred once in Moravia, another time in Russia, and the third time mentioned above. At the altar, the day before he died, this servant of God had a magnificent vision of the Blessed Virgin who is said to have given him a crown from her own head.[1295]

Ignatius Loyola, St. (1491–1556)

Founder of the Society of Jesus (Jesuits), mystic, visionary and ecstatic born in the castle of Loyola near the town of Azpeitia in the Basque province of Guipuzcoa, Spain, the last of thirteen children. Ignatius' early life was spent in dancing, dueling, gambling, carrying out passionate love affairs

---

[1295] Delaney, 248–49; Hebert, 162–63, 174, 241, 284; Wiebe, 20; Walsh, v. 2, 27; Guiley, 150; NCE 2nd ed., v. 7, 236; Dorcy, 56–57.

Saint Ignatius of Loyola's Vision of Christ and God the Father at La Storta, 1622, by Domenichino

and getting into all kinds of trouble. At that time, he was definitely a rake and may be the only canonized saint with a notarized police record for night time brawling with intent to inflict serious harm. Ignatius entered the military and in 1521, during the siege of Pamplona, was wounded by a cannon ball which shattered his right leg and badly injured the other. While recuperating, the former soldier had a religious conversion and decided to devote his life to Christ. He spent the years 1522–1523 on a retreat at Manresa where he underwent various spiritual trials and experienced mystical phenomena to include visions. It was here that the reformed profligate probably wrote most of his *Spiritual Exercises.* These spiritual exercises are methods of preparing and disposing the soul to free itself of all inordinate attachments, and, after accomplishing this, of seeking and discovering the Divine Will regarding the disposition of one's life, thus ensuring the salvation of the soul. One of Ignatius' visions was of Our Lady with the holy child Jesus. After seeing this vision, the saint-to-be never again gave the slightest consent to sins of the flesh. In 1540, on a voyage to Rome to offer his services to the pope, Ignatius had the famous vision of La Storta, (seen above) in which Christ promised everything would go well in Rome. In this vision, Ignatius saw God the Father standing behind Christ bearing His Cross. He heard the Father saying to Christ, "I want you to accept this person as your servant." Jesus then accepted Ignatius, saying, "I want you to serve us, in Rome, I will be propitious to you." In Rome, things indeed did turn out well, as Christ had promised. Pope Paul III (1534–1549) gave his approval for the establishment of the Society of Jesus.

St. Ignatius developed his own theory of Christian education and by the time he died in 1556, he had opened thirty-three colleges around the globe and had approved six others, the world's first systematic education organization on such a scale. In 1710, there were more than six hundred Jesuit universities and nearly two hundred seminaries. By 2012, there were close to twenty-thousand Jesuit priests in the world, serving in 112 nations on six continents.

Sometimes when he was celebrating Mass, it is said that the heartbeats of St. Ignatius could be heard throughout the Church. Moreover, some one hundred or so miracles have been attributed to this Jesuit founder, including bringing back to life a man named Lessani who had hanged himself after losing a lawsuit. Ignatius also had many supernatural visitations, and was accomplished in discerning spirits and fighting the devil who once tried to suffocate him as he slept. This faithful servant of God was reportedly witnessed in rapture, levitating in a kneeling position while in prayer. On other occasions, while in prayer, he was seen to be surrounded by a brilliant supernatural light and once, during an ecstasy, a flame of fire appeared hovering over his head. Ignatius was beatified in 1609 by Pope Paul V and canonized in 1622 by Pope Gregory XV.[1296]

Ildefonso, St. (607–667) (aka Ildephonsus)

Born in Toledo. He was perhaps a pupil of St. Isidore of Serville. Ildefonso had a strong Marian devotion and was a staunch defender of the true Christian faith. In 657, he became archbishop of Toledo. On the feast day of the Assumption of the Virgin Mary, in the early morning Ildefonso came in with some priests in the Cathedral of Toledo, and found it was, surprisingly, lit up. On the gate of the chapel, Mary praised the religious fervor of the bishop and handed him a golden chasuble [see above] that had been especially woven for him in heaven as a symbol of his protection. For a long time in the diocese of Toledo a special celebration was held to commemorate this apparition. There are those who say the present location of this chasuble of Saint Ildephonsus is not known, or that the story is only legend, but neither of these assertions is correct. This celestial gift is still preserved and is now kept at Oviedo. Alphonsus, the chaste King of Castile, transferred it to the church of Saint Savior which he had built.

1296 Hebert, 122, 188; Delaney, 251–52; Johnson, 55, 59–61, 75, 149; Guiley, 154–56; William W. Meissner, *Ignatius of Loyola: The Psychology of a Saint,* New Haven, Conn.: Yale University Press, 1994; NCE 2nd ed., v. 7, 312–14; Martin, 75–76; Ghezzi, MM, 162–67; Tylenda, 232–40; Cruz, A&D, 178, 201.

Saint Ildefonso by El Greco

It, along with the Sudarium of Jesus Christ, and many other relics, is contained in the Holy Chest of Oviedo. The Spanish hero Rodrigo Diaz, better known as El Cid, was a living witness when the chest was opened in his presence.

Ita of Killeedy, St. (c. 475–570) (aka St. Ita of Limmerick, Brigid of Munster, Deidre, Mida)

Irish mystic and visionary born in the present county of Waterford. From a young age Deidre, as she was known then, had visions and intimations that she was called to lead a saintly life. One night, she dreamed that an angel gave her three precious stones. The next day she wondered what they meant, and then the angel appeared and told her that the stones represented the three aspects of the Blessed Trinity that would come into her life in a remarkable way. The angel also said that her dreams and night vigils would be occasions for angels and God to appear to her. Deidre refused to marry, and her father, a powerful chieftain, resisted her desire for a monastic life until an angel assured him that she would become an advocate for many souls on Judgment Day. Deidre would eventually receive her father's blessing to live a celibate life. On making her religious vows, she took the name Ita, which means "thirsting for divine love." According to the story, angels then led Ita to the foot of a mountain on the Cork-Kerry border where she founded her monastery. She called it Cluain Creedal ("Holy Meadow"), but it became known as Killeedy ("Church of Ita"). Ita's monastery drew men and women from all over Ireland. She also supervised a boys' school in Killeedy where she molded several future saints, most famously St. Brendan the Navigator (c. 486–578) who sailed to the New World long before Columbus. Young Brendan once asked St. Ita what three things pleased God the most. She replied: true faith in God with a pure heart, a simple life with a religious spirit, and generosity inspired by charity. Brendan went on to ask what three things displeased God the most. Her answer: a mouth that hates people, a heart harboring resentments, and confidence in wealth. Her austerities are told by St. Cuimin of Down (d. 662) and many extravagant miracles have become associated with her, including healing a man who had been decapitated, and living solely off food delivered from heaven.[1297]

[1297] Cowan, 214–15; Delaney, 259; Gallick, 23; Farmer, 265; NCE, 2nd ed., v. 7, 648.

Jane Frances De Chantal, St. (1572–1641) (aka Jane Frances Fremyot, Jeanne Francoise de Chantal, Madame de Chantal)

Foundress of the Visitation nuns, mystic, and visionary born in Dijon, France. Jane was well-born, attractive, and naturally pious. In 1592, she married Baron Christopher de Chantal and bore him six children. In 1601, her spouse was killed in a hunting accident. For many years she had been receiving feelings that God was within her as a burning fire. She had received visions as well. In 1610, after making provisions for her children, the holy widow founded the Order of the Visitation of Holy Mary. From that date until her death, she participated in founding eighty-six monasteries of that Order. In a vision or dream, it was revealed to her that she would meet St. Francis de Sales and that he was to become her spiritual adviser. The meeting of the two saints at Dijon is well known. They recognized one another and each became conscious of the intentions of the other, although they had never before met or corresponded. During the last years of her life, Jane experienced spiritual aridity and the "dark night of the soul". Like St. Francis de Sales, her heart was also extracted at her death. It is said to swell at times like a heart under the pressure of sorrow. Jane was beatified in 1751 by Pope Benedict XIV and canonized in 1767 by Pope Clement XIII.[1298]

Jean-Baptiste Marie Vianney, St. (1786–1859) (aka as the Curé of Ars)

Mystic, visionary, ecstatic, victim soul, and patron saint of parish priests, born in the small village of Dardilly, near Lyons, France. Although beset by difficulties with his studies especially with Latin, Jean-Baptiste was ordained in 1813. Five years later, he was appointed Curé of Ars and remained there for the rest of his life. His greatest fame came as a confessor. This simple parish priest had great insight into the minds and hearts of his penitents. Father Vianney would often spend from twelve to sixteen hours in a cramped, stifling confessional seeing on average three hundred visitors a day. He assisted many of these penitents in the revelation of their sins which he was aware of through Divine inspiration. It is said that a few minutes in his confessional was enough to turn hardened sinners into saints. Due to the long lines, some waited for days to confess. The Curé of Ars, however, often invited certain persons to confess before others because of an interior insight telling him that these individuals should speak to him without further delay. While in this dark setting, several penitents reportedly witnessed a transparent and unearthly radiance emanating from their confessor's face.

For thirty years, after 1824, his few hours of nocturnal sleep were said to be interrupted and disturbed by diabolical attacks. These took the form of strange phenomena such as deafening nocturnal noises like nails being driven into the floor, sounds of horses prancing around his room, insulting conversation, cruel beatings, and, once, a fire in his bed. On December 4, 1826, this simple priest claimed that the devil took form in his room and vomited in front of him. Another time, this saintly soul witnessed the devil in the form of a serpent at

[1298] Delaney, 116–17; NCE, 1st ed., v. 3, 452; NCE 2nd ed., v. 3, 381–82; Cruz, 239; Cowan, 218; Ghezzi, 540–41; Gallick, 233, 434; Jones, 201–2; Fanning, 162; Underhill, Mystics, 197; Farges, 30.

a sick parishioner's home. On still another occasion, the Curé of Ars described seeing Satan in the form of a black dog at 3 a.m. These onslaughts continued to torment this servant of God for the remainder of his life.

Jean-Baptiste reportedly once levitated during a homily so that his feet were said to be above the top of the pulpit. It is believed that he also experienced mystical espousal sometime before 1856 and that he bore a golden ring of extraordinary brilliance. During the year of his beatification, his perfectly preserved heart was removed and enclosed in a beautiful reliquary. It is presently housed along with his incorrupt body in the Basilica at Ars in France. The Curé of Ars was declared venerable in 1874 by Pope Pius IX, beatified in 1905 by Pope Pius X, and canonized in 1925 by Pope Pius XI.[1299]

Joan Marie of the Cross, St. (1603–1673) (aka Giovanna/ Joanna Maria della Croce, Bernardina Maffeotta Floriani, The Mystic of Roverto)

Poor Clare mystic, visionary, ecstatica stigmatic, and abbess of the Poor Clares' Convent of St. Charles born in Roverto in the Italian Tyrol. Joan received the stigmata in 1638. She bore the markings of all Five Wounds of Jesus along with the Crown of Thorns which she is said to have concealed beneath her veil. It is also reported that she had an especially deep spear wound from the transverberation which she allegedly received on September 17, 1642.

When her body was exhumed many years after her death, it was discovered that not only was it incorrupt but that the wound in the side was fresh and blood issued from it. In 1644 this favored soul is said to have received from Our Lord an espousal ring with five diamonds.[1300]

Joan of Arc at the Coronation of Charles VI, 1854, by Jean Auguste Dominique Ingres

Joan of Arc, St. (1412–1431) (aka Maid of Orleans, Jeanne la Pucelle)

Lay mystic, visionary, and patron saint of France born as the youngest of five children to a peasant farmer at Domremy, in Lorraine, France. A pious child, Joan was only thirteen when she experienced the first of her supernatural visions, which she described as voices accompanied by great

---

1299 Abbe Francis Trochu, *The Cure D'Ars: St. Jean–Marie–Baptiste Vianney,* Rockford, Ill.: TAN Books and Publishers, 1977; NCE 2nd ed., v. 14, 469–70; Johnson, 128; Delaney, 495–96; Cruz, MMM, 171, 272; Cowan, 256; Freze, VVA, 289, Ghezzi, VOS, 634–35; Guiley, 174–76; Farges, 347; Cruz, A&D, 188, 204.

1300 Thurston, 59, 139, 395, 229; NCE, 1st ed., v. 6, 496; Summers, 154; Cruz, MMM, 235; "Stigmatization," in the 1912 *Classic Encyclopedia*; Wilson, 138.

blazes of light. As time went on, Joan identified the voices she heard as those of Sts. Michael the Archangel, Catherine of Alexandria (d.c. 310), Margaret of Antioch (d.c. 304), and others. These saints reportedly spoke to her and visited her often. Not only could she see and hear her heavenly messengers, but it was said that she could also touch and smell them. Soon they began to give her commands. Joan claimed they urged her to take up arms as a warrior and lead French troops against the English invaders and place Charles, the Dauphin (the uncrowned prince of France), on the French throne. She kept this secret for almost five years before revealing that it was her God-given mission to deliver the French Kingdom from English control. At first, laughed at by the French commander at Vaucouleurs, his skepticism was soon overcome when her prophecies came true and the French were defeated in the Battle of Herrings outside Orleans in February of 1429.

Joan was then sent to see the Dauphin who was kept from the French throne by the British. By recognizing him, despite a disguise he had assumed, she then communicated a secret sign to him which the voices had given her. The Dauphin became convinced of Joan's authenticity and allowed her to fulfill her divinely appointed task to lead an expedition to relieve besieged Orleans. Joan led her forces to victory followed by another victory over the British on June 18 and the capture of Troyes shortly after. Finally, on July 17, 1429 the Dauphin was crowned as King Charles VII at Rheims, with Joan at his side. The coronation rallied the people of France and marked the end of English victories. After carrying out her mission, the voices warned her that she would not live very long. Her attempt to seize Paris failed and Joan was captured at Compiegne by Burgundians (England's allies) and sold to the British. She was charged with witchcraft and heresy before the court of bishop Pierre Cauchon.

Joan's visions were declared to be false and of diabolical origin. She was condemned as a witch and lapsed heretic by the church court in a decision approved of by the University of Paris. The Maid of Orleans was burned to death at the stake at Rouen on May 30, 1431 and her ashes thrown into the Seine River. This servant of God was exonerated some twenty-five years later by a court appointed by Pope Callistus III (1455–1458). She was found innocent of all charges and eventually canonized in 1920. Although the process of canonization does not consider the question of the authenticity of visions and revelations, Joan's acceptance as a saint certainly dismisses the charge that her visions were satanic and evil. One gets some real credibility from canonization although, as we have seen in the earlier part of this work, a saint may be wrong about a vision. When Joan was in prison, she asked her locutionary saints if she was going to be burned. They said things like "Trust in the Lord," "He will aid you," "You will receive support," or "You will be delivered by a great victory." Moved by wishful thinking, she at first thought this meant that she would not be burned. But then the voices told her not to fear on account of her martyrdom for, they said, "it will bring you at last into Paradise." Joan was beatified in 1909 by Pope Saint Pius X and canonized in 1920 by Pope Benedict XV.[1301]

[1301] Delaney, 269–70; Johnson, 306; Cowan, 225; Gallick, 163; Guiley, 169–70, 217; Groeschel, AASV, 41; Farmer, 273; NCE, 1st ed., v. 7, 992–93; NCE 2nd ed., v. 7, 878–79; Siobhan Nash–Marshall, *Joan of Arc: A Spiritual Biography*, NY: Crossroad Publishing Co., 1999; Martin, 18; Ghezzi, MM, 148–53.

Saint John Bosco in 1880

John Bosco, St.
(1815–1888) (aka Don Bosco)

Founder of the Salesian Order, mystic, visionary, and ecstatic born at Becchi, near Turin, in Piedmont, Italy of poor parents. Before his birth, John's mother reportedly had a vision of a large dog bearing a lighted torch in its mouth. This was meant to indicate the future greatness of her son who would set fire to the world and kindle and illuminate men's hearts through the ministry of his words. It is also said that a large and ferocious Alsatian-like dog named "Grigio" (whom he later referred to as his guardian angel) would often appear at times to this holy man to furnish him providential protection from the many dangers he faced in his lifetime. After a life-shaping, mysterious dream of Our Lord and Our Lady at age nine, John Bosco was determined to become a priest. It was in that dream that the Blessed Virgin told him to "care for her flock of sheep." From this moment on, God spoke to him in dreams. Many of his dreams were prophetic and concerned the Salesian Order. In 1871–1872 he dreamt about Argentina and the individual Indians of Patagonia whom he later evangelized. It was said that Don Bosco oftentimes had an angel or saint as a dream interpreter. At the request of Pope Pius IX (1846–1878), he kept detailed records of all his dreams.

Upon being ordained, John opened a hospice in Turin, Italy to catechize and train homeless street youths in trades. This hospice grew into what became known as the Oratory of St. Francis de Sales. Father Bosco's reputation as a preacher became widespread and miracles were attributed to his intercession. So numerous and extraordinary were his miracles that one of his biographers described his life as "an astonishing invasion of the supernatural." It is said that hardly a day passed without his precipitating some supernatural intervention—a revelation, a prophecy, a mysterious appearance, a multiplication of food, a healing. Witnesses have attested that he levitated several times while in ecstasy during the celebration of Mass. It has likewise been reported that this saint possessed mystical knowledge, that is the ability to know "the mystery of hearts, the secrets of conscience, and men's innermost thoughts." With a glance it was said that he could look into people's souls and read their spiritual state.

In his dreams, this mystic foresaw the exact revelation of events (including deaths) that were to occur. At least 150 of the saint's revelatory dreams are a matter of record. He also sometimes saw in these prophetic dreams the state of the souls of his boys in the Oratory. A vision of fiery tongues over a boy's head would tell him that the young man was called to the priesthood. On November 11, 1873, John Bosco had a vision of several of his boys with their sins written upon their foreheads. On many occasions a dream would reveal to him a colleague's life span or a boy's approaching death. One of his boys named Dominic Savio (1842–1857), preceded John Bosco in death and was later raised to sainthood. In 1876, St. Dominic Savio accompanied by many holy souls, appeared before Father John in a vision and revealed that he was in heaven. On April 19, 1868, began a series of dreams in which this servant of God was led by a heavenly guide (possibly his guardian angel) on a journey to hell. His lengthy and vivid description of this dark realm and its horrors is frightening. It is said that the putrid smell of evil remained after he awakened. In 1861, over a period of three nights Don Bosco had a vision of heaven. Each night the vision continued where it had left off the night before.

Dreams and visions also guided John Bosco's work. He foresaw that he would assemble a large company of priests who would extend his ministry to the far ends of the earth. St. Francis de Sales, a Doctor of the Church, was allegedly seen in one of his visions. St. Francis told Father Bosco in this vision that he had been sent to speak of future things and presented him with a book of advice for rules and acceptable behavior for those in his new-found order. In 1854, true to the vision's words, John Bosco went on to found the Salesian Order, whose apostolate came to include work on the missions as well as the education of boys. Together with St. Maria Mazzarello (1837–1881), he also founded the Salesian Sisters for a similar apostolate among girls. By the time Father Bosco died, there were eight hundred Salesian priests and some fifty-seven houses in Italy, Spain, France, England, Argentina, Uruguay, and Brazil. Today Salesians are in 120 countries and number 17,000 members. They are one of the largest communities in the Catholic Church.

On still another occasion, on February 13, 1884, the Salesian founder received a vision of Sts. Peter and Paul who encouraged him to reprint the *Life of Saint Peter* and the *Life of Saint Paul.* John Bosco is also credited with restoring at least two boys back to life from the dead. Charles, one of these boys, related that he had found himself in hell surrounded by a mob of demons who were about to throw him into a huge furnace when a beautiful Lady intervened and offered him a second chance. St. Dominic Savio, mentioned above, appeared to him and told him how the Virgin Mary would console him at the point of his death. John Bosco was canonized in 1934 by Pope Pius XI.[1302]

John Joseph of the Cross, St. (1654–1739)

Alcantarine mystic, visionary, and ecstatic born as Carlo Gaetano on the island of Ischia in the Gulf of Naples to wealthy parents. From his earliest years, Carlo was given to prayer and virtue. He had a great devotion to the Blessed Mother and set up an altar to her in a secluded place in his home. At the age of sixteen, he was the first Italian to join the Alcantarines, a strict reform group within the Franciscan Order newly introduced in Italy by friars from Spain. Throughout his life, Carlo (now called John Joseph after his ordination) was given to the greatest austerity. He hated sin and fasted constantly, slept but three hours

[1302] Ann Ball, *Modern Saints: Their Lives and Faces,* 102–6; NCE, 2nd ed., v. 2, 543–44, Delaney, 87–88; Freze, VVA, 217, 233; Edna Beyer Phelan, *Don Bosco: A Spiritual Portrait,* Garden City, NY: 1963; Pietro Stella, *Don Bosco: religious outlook and spirituality,* translated by John Drury, New Rochelle, NY: Salesian Publishers, 1996; Pietro Stella, *Don Bosco Life and Work,* trans. J. Drury, New Rochelle, NY, 1985; Hebert, 129–30, 236; Guiley, 176–77; Aradi, 197–98; Cruz, MMM, 258, 482–85; Cruz, SS, 170–71; Lord, VHHP, 240; *Forty Dreams of John Bosco,* Rockford, Ill.: TAN books, 1996; O'Sullivan, 18–21; Ghezzi, MM, 138–43; http://www.thermaturges.blogspot.com.

Saint John Joseph of the Cross. Engraving by Alessandri after P.A. Novelli.

John of God, St. (1495–1550)

Founder of the Brothers Hospitallers, mystic, visionary, and stigmatic born as John Ciudad at Montemoro Novo, Portugal. Tradition holds that at the time of his birth, the church bells in the town rang of their own accord, heralding the arrival of a saint. As a young man, John joined the Spanish army and took part in wars between France and Spain and against the Turks in Hungary. Military life completely undermined his morals and he pursued an immoral life until his military discharge at the age of forty. At this time, the former sinner started to change his ways, after having become remorseful and guilt-ridden over his sinful life. In 1538, after hearing a sermon by St. John of Avila (1500–1569), he became so extreme in his fervor and behavior that he was confined for a time in a mental institution. Through the counseling of St. John of Avila, however, the former soldier returned to normalcy and devoted himself to the care of the sick. In a legendary visit from the child Jesus, he was given the name of John of God and told, "Thou wilt find thy cross in Grenada." John made a pilgrimage to the Spanish Shrine of Our Lady of Guadalupe, where he had a vision of what he was to do with his life. The new convert returned to Grenada, rented a house, and devoted himself to helping the abandoned sick and poor there. He was reportedly aided in this work not only by charitable people but also by angels, including the archangel Raphael. John did not intend to found an order, but one grew up around his work. It became known as the Order of Brothers Hospitalers, also known as the Brothers of St. John of God. St. John of God is the patron saint of the sick, nurses, and hospitals.

This servant of God bore the stigmata in the form of the crown of thorns. A heavenly fragrance was claimed to pervade his sickroom and the whole house in which he had

each night and scourged himself daily. For the last thirty years of his life, he abstained from all liquids. It was usual for him to be seen rapt in heavenly ecstasies and visions. During prayer, a halo of light reportedly often surrounded his head, and during Mass, a supernatural brightness came over his face. John allegedly was once found in the chapel in ecstasy raised far above the floor. Besides levitation, this servant of God was said to be favored with the gifts of miracles, prophecies, and mystical transport whereby his walking stick moved through the air. He is said to have had the ability to read the thoughts of those who came to consult him as clearly as though they had been written words.[1303]

[1303] Cruz, MMM, 30, 95, 279; NCE, 1st ed., v. 7, 1057; NCE 2nd ed., v. 7, 959; Thurston, 24; Farmer, 282; *The Lives or the Fathers, Martyrs and Other Principal Saints,* Rev. Alban Butler, vol. 1, (1864 edition), published by D. & J. Sadlier & Company.

lived for nine days before his death. The Blessed Virgin was said to have appeared to him just before his death to lead him to Paradise. His incorrupt remains are enshrined in the Basilica of St. John of God in Grenada. John was beatified in 1638 by Pope Urban VIII and canonized in 1690 by Pope Alexander VIII.[1304]

John of Sahagun, St. (1429–1479) (aka John of St. Facundo, John of Saint Fagondez)

Augustinian mystic and visionary born at Sahagun, Leon, Spain as Juan Gonzales de Catrillo, the oldest of seven children to a pious, well-to-do family. As a young boy, John studied under the Benedictines. He was ordained in 1454 and by mid-1463 had become an Augustinian canon at Salamanca. John was noted for his devotion to the Blessed Sacrament. During Mass, he reported that he often saw the Host surrounded by light and sometimes had visions of the bodily form of Jesus at the moment of consecration. Father John's devotion and his visions often led to some very lengthy Masses. He was also reported to levitate during his prayers. Moreover, his ability to read hearts during confession made him a much sought-after spiritual director. He had an uncanny ability to discern the secrets of conscience much like that of St. Pio of Pietrelcina (Padre Pio). In 1479, this servant of God prophesized his own death which took place later that same year. Miracles were attributed to his intervention, both before and after his death. He was beatified in 1601 and canonized in 1690.[1305]

St. John of the Cross, 1701 (engraving), Spanish School, (18th century) / Private Collection / Index Fototeca / Bridgeman Images

John of the Cross, St. (1542–1591) (aka John of St. Matthias, San Juan de la Cruz)

Doctor of the Church, Carmelite mystic, ecstatic, visionary, stigmatic, and founder of the first Reformed Carmelite House for Men born at Fontiveros, Old Castile, Spain as Juan de Yepes y Alvarez. John was especially devoted to the Blessed Virgin and credited her for having saved his life on several separate occasions, once at the age of five and another time at the age of twelve when her intervention saved him from drowning. On February 24, 1563, he joined the Carmelites at Medina, taking the name Fray Juan de Santo Maria. He was ordained in September of 1567. Upon meeting St. Teresa of Avila, Father John was persuaded by her to join in her efforts to reform the Carmelite Order. As such, on November 28, 1568, he, along with

---

[1304] www.newadvent.org/cathen; Delaney, 281–82;Cruz, Inc., 168–69; Cruz, MMM, 235, 389; NCE, 1st ed.,v. 7, 1052; NCE 2nd ed., v. 7, 968–69; 1912 *Catholic Encyclopedia*; Ghezzi, VOS, 478–79; Guiley, 186–87; *The Miracle Hunter: Marian Apparition.*

[1305] NCE 1st ed., v. 12, 850; NCE 2nd ed., v. 1, 888;

Farmer, 284; *Book of Augustinian Saints*, 38–39.

four others, founded the first men's house of Discalced Carmelites. It is at this point that he took the name of John of the Cross.

In 1577, this Discalced Carmelite priest was ordered by the Calced Carmelites to abandon the reform of the Order. When he refused, he was imprisoned by his own religious superiors and the representatives of the Inquisition. He was scourged twice and locked up in a tiny, dark cell in the monastery of Toledo. After nine months of incarceration, Our Lady appeared to him in a radiant vision and helped him escape. For the next two years, John headed the Discalced college in Baeza. His writings are among the world's greatest spiritual classics. He is the author of *The Ascent of Mount Carmel*, *The Spiritual Canticle*, and *The Living Flame of Love*. The latter two books are based upon memories of the ecstatic spiritual states through which he had passed in the course of his development. His most famous work, however, entitled *The Dark Night of the Soul*, was written while he was in prison. It recounts the depression, dryness, lack of enthusiasm, and severe discouragement that most people experience now and then when pursuing a deep spiritual life. During his imprisonment, he experienced intense raptures and transient ecstasies which he calls the "spiritual betrothal' of the soul to God. This holy Carmelite was one of the true great mystics to draw one of his visions: a little pen-and-ink sketch that he gave to sister Ann Marie of Jesus. It shows Christ crucified from a perspective unprecedented in contemporary art. It is alleged that John once held the infant Jesus in his arms.

While serving as the spiritual director at the convent where St. Teresa of Avila was prioress, it was reported that many of the sisters living there came to witness his levitations during ecstatic prayer. Once, when walking and talking about Jesus with St. Teresa, both went into ecstasy and levitated at the same time. In his writings, John views the soul's struggle to unite with God as a long, dark night. He talks about the transition from active to passive purgation, the mystic gift in which God takes over and does all the work of purification. He goes on to say that mystic phenomena like apparitions, locutions and levitation can happen at this point, because they are by nature concomitant phenomena, attendant events that may accompany this level of spiritual activity. It was claimed that John was seen to sometimes have an actual halo, a celestial brightness, radiating from his head. He also possessed the mystical ability to forego sleep for long periods of time. Friars who witnessed his body at death said a triple crown seemed to encircle his head and his face shone with a brilliant pallor. His expression was said to be one of peace and joy. At his exhumation, St. John's incorrupt body was found still perfectly preserved under a layer of lime, which had been previously applied to it. It was found to be pleasingly fragrant nine months after death. Moreover, a finger cut off his body (as a relic) was reported to have bled. John was beatified in 1675 by Pope Clement X and canonized in 1726 by Pope Benedict XIII. He was declared a Doctor of the Church in 1926 by Pope Pius XI.[1306]

[1306] Delaney, 278–79; Johnson, 65, 67, 78–79, 134, 147; Cruz, Inc., 199–200; Cruz, MMM, 319, 391; Aradi, 170; Guiley, 181–83; Bede Frost, *Saint John of the Cross: Doctor of Divine Love, an Introduction to his Philosophy, Theology and Spirituality*, NY: Vantage, 1980; NCE, 1st ed., v. 7, 1045–56; NCE, 2nd ed., v. 7, 986–89; Wiebe, 20; R. Brown, 126; Cowan, 247; Ebenezer Cobham Brewer, *A Dictionary of Miracles*, London: Chatto & Windus, 1884, 20; Underhill, *Mystics*, 184–85.

Saint John the Evangelist in Patmos by Juan Bautista Mayno

John the Evangelist, St. (c. 6–104) (aka "the seer of Patmos," John of the "Apocalypse," John the Divine)

Apostle, mystic, visionary, and ecstatic born in Galilee, the son of Zebedee and Salome and younger brother of James the Greater. John was a fisherman on Lake Genesareth until, with James, he was called by Christ to follow Him (Mt 4:21–22; Mk 1:19–20). At the time, he was the youngest of the apostles. James the Greater and John were called "Sons of Thunder" by the Lord because of their volatile temperaments (Mk 3:17), but John would become the Lord's beloved disciple (Jn 13:23; 19:26; 20:2ff; 21:7; 21:24). That he was one of those closest to Christ was attested to by the fact that only he, Peter, and James were present at such events as the Transfiguration (Mt 17:1; Mk 9:2; Lk

9:28), the healing of Peter's mother-in-law (Mk 1:29–31), the raising of Jairus' daughter from the dead (Mk 5:22–43; Lk 8:40–56), and the agony in the garden of Gethsemane (Mt 26:37ff; Mk 14:33ff). He was the first apostle at the tomb of the risen Christ and the only apostle at the crucifixion, where Jesus placed Mary in his care (Jn 19:25–27). He was best known as the apostle "who Jesus loved." John was imprisoned with Peter and appeared before the Sanhedrin (Act 4:1–21). He accompanied Peter to preach to the Parthians in Samaria (borders of what is now Russia and Iran) and was at the Council of Jerusalem in the year AD 49. According to tradition, John went to Rome during the reign of Emperor Domitian. He miraculously escaped martyrdom there. He was, however, exiled to the island of Patmos, a penal colony off the coast of Turkey, where he wrote the book of Revelation.

On the death of Domitian in AD 96, John returned to the city of Ephesus in Western

Turkey where he wrote the fourth Gospel and three epistles. He died in Ephesus at a very old age, the only one of the apostles who did not suffer martyrdom. John is also referred to as the "seer of Patmos." For it was on the island of Patmos itself "on the Lord's Day that he was caught up in ecstasy" (Rv 1:10), had a grandiose vision, and heard extraordinary messages that were to have a strong influence on the history of the Church and of entire Western culture. The vision is revealed to him by an angel sent from God. The heavenly scene described in the apostle John's vision is filled with images commonly associated with the Temple, a place regarded by the Jews as a microcosm of creation. In his book of the Apocalypse or Revelation, John has a vision of a Lamb that is slain, yet standing (Rv 5:6), and is placed before the throne on which God Himself is already seated.

In this fundamental vision, Jesus (the Lamb of God) is depicted as having been raised up to fully share in the kingship and saving power of the Father. The subject of one of the most important visions in this book of Revelation is this lamb in the act of opening a scroll with seven seals that no one has been able to break open (Rv 5:4). Only the sacrificed Lamb can open the sealed scroll and reveal its contents. At the heart of the visions in this work is the vision of a Woman bringing forth a male child and the complementary one of the dragon, already thrown down from Heaven but still very powerful. John also has a vision of the New Jerusalem (Rv 22:1–5). The elaborate nature of the visions of Revelation shows that John had seen things which he only partly understood and which he could not express except by symbols. The apocalyptic vision of the book of Revelation uses Old Testament symbols or images to show the spiritual significance of historical events. In this work, John also frequently uses allegory, as in the visions of the seven seals and the seven bowls, weaves in fragments of Old Testament prophecy

and Jewish apocalypse and includes his own thoughts upon his ecstatic experiences. This beloved apostle was also said to have experienced apparitions of the Blessed Mother after her dormition.[1307]

Retrato do Padre José de Anchieta, 1902, by Benedito Calixto

Joseph of Anchieta, St. (1534–1597) (aka Apostle of Brazil, Jose Anchieta)

Jesuit mystic born to a wealthy and prominent family in San Cristobal de la Laguna on Tenerife in the Canary Islands. Joseph was possibly related to St. Ignatius of Loyola. He joined the Jesuits in 1551 and was sent to Brazil in 1553 where he labored among the colonists and savage natives for forty-four years. This servant of God was ordained a priest by the first bishop

[1307] NCE 2nd ed., v. 7, 895–913; Delaney, 280–81; Pope Benedict XVI, *The Apostles*, Illustrated edition, Huntington, Indiana: Our Sunday Visitor Publishing Division, 2008, 111–16; Connell, 39.

of Brazil. Joseph is said to have possessed supernatural powers such as the gift of prophecy, insomnia, and some control over nature. He was called the wonderworker and Apostle of Brazil because he restored many sick people back to health. He had a great devotion to the Blessed Mother as well as to the souls in purgatory. It is said that a dazzling light frequently surrounded this holy priest. Pope John Paul II beatified him on June 22, 1980.[1308]

Joseph of Cupertino, St. (1603–1663) (aka Joseph of Copertino, Joseph Desa, the "Flying Friar")

Conventual Franciscan friar, mystic, visionary, and ecstatic born as Joseph Desa of poor parents in Cupertino, near Naples, Italy. Joseph is said to have been born in a stable and had deformed feet. As a child he was known in his village as "Bocca Apertura" ("the Gaper") because he often walked around in a stupor with his mouth hanging open. As a youngster he was forgetful, clumsy, distracted, slovenly, lazy, and had an irascible temper. The only thing he had going for him was a deep interest in religion and spiritual practices. At the age of eight, he is said to have had his first ecstatic vision.

Joseph initially became a Capuchin lay brother but was dismissed after eight months for clumsiness and low intelligence. He later was grudgingly accepted as a servant and Franciscan tertiary by the Conventual Franciscans at La Grottela, where he remained for the next seventeen years. Though a poor scholar, he was ordained March 18, 1628 and his life of miracles began and his ecstasies became more frequent. Almost anything holy would

Saint Joseph of Cupertino by Ludovico Mazzanti

trigger an ecstatic experience: the name of God, Mary, or a saint, church music, sacred images, etc. He became famous for his supernatural gifts, particularly the gift of his ecstatic levitations and aerial flights. He is reputed to have experienced these some seventy or more times in his lifetime. All of these events were recorded and usually took place before reputable eyewitnesses. This holy friar levitated at will so frequently and so forcefully that he often took with him the brothers that he grabbed to steady himself. On one occasion, he flew some seventy yards, scooped up a heavy thirty-six foot high cross that ten men could not lift, and planted it in its prescribed spot. Whenever he rose into the air, he would give out a shriek of ecstasy.

While he was in a state of ecstasy, blows, burning, and pinpricks failed to awaken him. Once, while in Rome to visit the Holy Father, Joseph went into ecstasy at the sight of Pope Urban VIII (1623–1644). He rose from the ground until the head of his order called him to his senses. The pope marveled at this phenomenon and told the

---

[1308] Schouppe, *Purgatory*, 227; Butler, 6/9, 81; NCE, 2nd ed., v. 7, 1044; Patron Saints Index; Tylenda, 163–65.

Father General that he himself would bear witness to this occurrence should Joseph die during his pontificate.

At his last monastery in Osimo, the Franciscan flew eight feet into the air to kiss a statue of Jesus, and then carried it to his cell, where he floated about with it. Joseph's ecstatic flights earned him the title the "flying friar." He is invoked as the patron saint of air travelers and pilots.

In 1639, Joseph was sent to Assisi and, for a time, experienced the desolation of spiritual aridity. At the same time, he encountered relentless attacks by the devil. The "evil one" tried to drown him, strangle him, kill him by running him through with a sword, and by destroying his reputation by gossip. Ironically, Joseph was, later on, ordered by his superior to exorcise demons. Joseph gradually regained great spiritual joy and happiness and experienced visions of Christ and daily supernatural manifestations until his death. He recognized his own guardian angel and was familiar with other angels who appeared to him in visible form to bring him heavenly comfort. He once saw angels ascending and descending from heaven much like Jacob's ladder.

As a confessor he also knew the consciences and sins of those with whom he came into contact. He would often approach people to remind them to confess hidden sins. When they replied that they were not conscious of any hidden sins, the saint would reveal the time, place, and circumstances of the offenses against God. Joseph predicted that he would die on the day on which he would not receive the Holy Eucharist. For five days before his death, he was unable to rise and say Mass because of a ferocious fever. However, during these days he reportedly experienced miraculous ecstasies and levitations.

On his deathbed, the "flying friar" asked the Lord to take his heart, burn, and rive it. When his heart was examined after death, it was found that the tissue around the heart was shriveled, the ventricles were without blood, and the heart itself withered and dry. It would seem that his deathbed request that his heart be taken and burned had actually been realized long ago. The condition of his heart seemed to be the effects of a burning love of God. Joseph was also said to bilocate. He reportedly came to the assistance of dying souls on their deathbed. He even appeard to assist his mother at the time of her death. He was likewise said to have special powers over animals surpassing even those of St. Francis of Assisi. Joseph also had the ability to detect the stench of sin in others. He was beatified in 1753 by Pope Benedict XIV and canonized in 1767 by Pope Clement XIII.[1309]

Juan Masias, St. (1585–1645) (aka John Masias, John de Massias or Macias)

Dominican mystic, visionary, and ecstatic born at Rivera del Fresno, Estremadura, Spain. Juan was an intense, spiritually-minded youngster who preferred to pray and to go to church rather than play with other children. Both his parents died when he was young and he was adopted by an uncle who gave him the job of tending sheep. Our Lady and the Christ Child are said to have appeared to him several times and he was often visited by his patron saint, St. John the Evangelist. The latter once showed him a vision of heaven, telling him: "This is my country." Moreover,

---

[1309] Johnson, 128; NCE, 1st ed., v. 7, 1116; Angelo Pastrovicchi, *St. Joseph of Copertino*, Tr. Francis S. Laing, Rockford, Ill.: TAN Books and Publishers, 1994; Cowan, 264; Delaney, 287–88; Cruz, MMM, 32, 54, 77, 213–14, 481; Ghezzi, VOS, 558–59; Guiley, 192–93; Farmer, 291; NCE 2nd ed., v. 7, 1044; Lord, VMS, 130, 135, 140, 151; Johnson, 128–29; Farges, 452.

the Evangelist encouraged Juan to leave Spain and go to the New World. So, taking his advice, Juan left his uncle and emigrated to Peru where he worked on a cattle ranch for two years and then joined the Convent of St. Mary Magdalene in Lima, Peru. In 1622, Juan became a Dominican lay brother. On the night of his profession, demons are said to have appeared to tempt and reproach him as well as bodily attack him. This type of torture and torment by devils was to continue over a period of fourteen years. Juan became known for his austerities, miracles and visions. He also reportedly levitated while rapt in ecstasy.

The poor and sick in Lima were drawn to him. He ministered to them spiritually and physically. Rays of light are said to have streamed from his face as he taught the catechism to the poor or prayed by himself. This lay brother purportedly liberated over a million souls from purgatory by his many daily rosaries and visits to the Blessed Sacrament. Many of these souls were said to come back to him when he was at prayer to thank him for his help. Juan was also a friend of St. Martin de Porres. At the time of John's death, the Blessed Virgin Mary, Sts. Dominic, John the Evangelist, and many other saints came to accompany him into heaven. These figures were allegedly seen by some of his brother religious. Juan was beatified in 1837 by Pope Gregory XVI and canonized in 1975 by Pope Paul VI.[1310]

Juliana Falconieri, St. (1270–1341) (aka Giulani Falconieri)

Juliana was a Servite mystic whose life began and ended with miracles. She was born to elderly parents who were long past hoping for a child. In gratitude for her birth, her parents built the church of the Annunciation in Florence. Her saintly uncle, St. Alexis Falconieri, became her spiritual director. Juliana founded the Third Order of the Servants of Mary (Servite order) when she was merely fourteen years old. The women of this order were called the Mantellate because they wore a short black cape (mantella) that freed their hands for working with the sick. This servant of God took the habit of her Order from another spiritual director, St. Philip Benizi (1233–1285). She governed the Mantellate for some forty years.

Juliana's death was marked by a Eucharistic miracle. Throughout her life, she was given to chronic gastric problems and could not retain food. At the end of her life, because of her constant vomiting and being too weak to swallow, the priests refused to give her the Eucharist. However, on one occasion, she requested the priest spread a corporal upon her breast and lay the host on it. In that moment, Juliana breathed her last and the host vanished, leaving witnesses convinced that she had miraculously absorbed it. After a few moments of stunned silence, the sisters began preparing her body for burial. When they removed her habit, they reportedly discovered the figure of Christ nailed to the Cross impressed on her flesh within a circle similar to a Host. Juliana was beatified in 1698 and canonized in 1737 by Pope Benedict XIII.[1311]

[1310] NCE 2nd ed., v. 9, 303; Johnson, 128; Thurston, 26; Delaney, 346; Guiley, 188; Dominican Saints; Procter, 271–73; http://willingshepherds.net/lives; Cowan, 243; Dorcy, 406–7; Farmer, 334–35.

[1311] NCE, 1st ed., v. 5, 813; NCE 2nd ed., v. 5, 610; v. 13, 24; Cruz, MMM, 533; Thurston, 156, 161; Gallick, 184, 426, Sabine Baring-Gould, Rev.,

Saint Louis Bertrand, 1640, by Francisco de Zurbarán

Louis Bertrand, St. (1526–1581)

Dominican missionary, mystic, and visionary born in Valencia, Spain. Louis is purported to be a relative of St. Vincent Ferrer. Exceptionally pious as a child, Louis entered the Dominicans at age nineteen and was ordained three years later. In 1562, Father Bertrand was sent to South America and lived among the native Indians of Panama. While there, several attempts were made on his life. Louis prayed for the gift of tongues, and this favor was granted him. He often spoke in languages with which he was naturally unfamiliar. In his seven years in New Granada, this servant of God is said to have baptized nearly twenty-five thousand Indians. The fame of his teaching brought him to the attention of St.

Teresa of Avila who sought his counsel in matters of reforming her order. Remarkable miracles accompanied his preaching during his lifetime as well as after his death. This holy Dominican was afforded other extraordinary graces including the gift of prophecy and the ability to raise the dead back to life. As regards his resuscitation gift, Louis is credited with raising at least thirteen people from the dead. One of them, a young girl, was allegedly brought back to life simply by the application of a Rosary. Souls released from purgatory, among them deceased religious, were said to often appear to thank him for his intercession for them. This Dominican often attributed the miraculous powers he manifested to the intercession of Our Lady. He prophesized the day on which he would die. Shortly after his death a heavenly perfume arose from his body and a reportedly a light which glowed for several minutes proceeded from his mouth and illuminated his whole cell. Seraphic music was also purportedly heard in the Church before his funeral. Louis' body remained incorrupt for over 350 years until it was maliciously destroyed during the 1936 Spanish Revolution.[1312]

Louis Marie Grignion De Montfort, St. (1673–1716)

Dominican Tertiary, mystic, and visionary born at Montfort-la-Canne, France, as the oldest of eight children. Louis founded two new congregations: the Missionaries of the Company of Mary (Montfort Fathers) for men and the Daughters of Wisdom for women. This influential "Apostolic Missionary" and Marian author was ordained on June 5, 1700 and spent the greater part of his priestly years as a traveling missionary, preaching retreats and missions

---

The Lives of the Saints: With Introduction and Additional Lives of English Martyrs, Cornish, Scottish and Welsh Saints and a Full Index to the Entire Work, Edinburgh: John Grant, 1914 6:267–68.

[1312] NCE, 2nd ed., v. 2, 336; Schouppe, Purgatory, 13–14; Cruz, Inc., 184; Hebert, 235; Cruz, MMM, 166, 215, 395; Dorcy, 316–17.

throughout western France, especially in Brittany and Vendee. Louis had a very special relationship with Our Lady. She appeared to him many times and it is said she communicated with him often through apparitions and inner locutions. His sermons were successful in fostering devotion to Mary and the rosary and in battling the Jansenism heresy. Father Louis cured the sick, made the blind see, triggered the gift of tears in those who came to jeer or stone him, and stirred whole cities to rebuild their ruined churches and to make use of them. His most impressive faculty was his gift of prophecy. The most remarkable prophecy of all was his prediction of the whole course and substance of Marian apparitions that began 114 years after his death, beginning with the apparition of St. Catherine of Laboure in 1830.

This servant of God converted thousands through the rosary, through his preaching and through his books. His writings include many works about Mary such as the *Secret of Mary*, *Admirable Secret of the Rosary*, *Little Crown of the Blessed Virgin*, and *True Devotion to the Blessed Virgin Mary*. In *The Love of the Eternal Wisdom*, Montfort advocates the surrender to Christ, through Mary. Pope John Paul II commented that reading *The True Devotion to the Blessed Virgin Mary* was a decisive turning point in his life. From it he took his motto: "Totus tuus" (I am all thine). Louis was also said to have been pounded and beaten by devils frequently during his lifetime. He was beatified in 1888 and canonized on July 20, 1947.[1313]

Saint Lutgard, 1787, by Francisco Goya

Lutgard of Aywieres, St. (1182–1246) (aka St. Lutgardis of Aywieres, Lutgarde of Tongres)

Cistercian mystic, visionary, ecstatica, stigmatic, and victim soul, born in Tongeren, Brabant (Belgium). In her early years, Lutgard had no true religious feeling. At age twelve, she was put into the Benedictine Convent of St. Catherine near Saint-Trond by her mother after her father had lost her dowry money in a failed business deal. Lutgard had a fondness for nice clothes, jewelry, and fun. She came and went in the convent as if she were a border and even entertained men and women inside the convent itself. In brief, she led an interesting but unorthodox social life. Then one day while Lutgard was entertaining a visitor, Jesus appeared to her in a vision and instructed her to reform her life. After seeing His wounds and hearing His request, she took Jesus to be her bridegroom and gave over her affections to no one but Him. This vision of Christ caused a change in her outlook on life and she became a Benedictine nun at age twenty. During the next twelve years Lutgard experienced numerous ecstasies, during which she had visions of Our Lord, Our Lady, and a multitude of saints to include Sts. John the Baptist, John the Evangelist (seen as an eagle), and Catherine. Following a vision of the Blessed Mother, the ecstatica began the first of her three-year fasts of reparation for sinners. During these years she lived on nothing but bread and weak beer.

While meditating on the Passion of Christ, it was said that Lutgard would often fall into ecstasy, levitate, and suffer the bloody sweat of Gethsemane. When rapt in ecstasy as she meditated on the Passion, her body became bathed in blood which then flowed from her hands and face. In her apparitions of Christ, He was usually represented as showing her His heart, and she was perhaps the first saint in whom the mystical "exchange of hearts" was effected. In her twenty-ninth year, Lutgard received the spear wound (transverberation) and carried the scar from this wound to her death. In a quest for a stricter rule, Lutgard moved from the Order of St. Benedict to become a Cistercian nun at the convent at Aywieres. She lived there the thirty remaining years of her life, being totally blind until her death eleven years later. As a Cistercian sister, she was renowned for her spiritual wisdom, miracles, and prophecies which even included predicting the day of her own death five years in advance. Souls in purgatory would often appear to her. On July 16, 1216, Pope Innocent III (1198–1216), enveloped in flames, reportedly appeared to her seeking her help in expiating three of his own faults. Demons

likewise appeared to her. She spat at them and drove them off by the sign of the cross. Lutgard is said to have exorcized nuns from their indwelling demons. Her title to sanctity was officially recognized by Rome without judicial process in 1584.[1314]

Lydwina De Schiedam, St. (1380–1433) (aka Lydwina, Lydwine of Schiedam, Lidwine de Schiedam)

Lay mystic, visionary, invisible stigmatic, ecstatica, and victim soul born at Schiedam, Holland, the only girl in a family of nine children. During the winter of 1395, Lydwina (from the Dutch word *lijden* meaning "to suffer") fell and broke a rib while ice skating. Gangrene soon set into the wound caused by her injury and spread over her entire body. The putrefaction bred worms that developed in three large ulcers. From this time on, Lydwina became a lifelong invalid suffering pain as reparation for others. She was later scarred by smallpox, suffered through the buboes of the Black Death which devoured her flesh and bones until her right arm was only attached by a single tendon. Her body was later also ravaged by the so-called "burning illness," an indescribable plague that consumed skin and muscle with an unremitting fire until the bones themselves burst. This disease split her face from her hairline to her nose. She became epileptic, lost all sight in her right eye, and, in fact, her left eye bled at

[1314] Schouppe, *Purgatory*, 93–95; Butler, 8, 877; 6/16, 122; Cowan, 284; Cruz, MMM, 220, 248; Delaney, 324; Ghezzi, VOS, 372–73; Gallick, 180, 427; Farmer, 330; Freze, VVA, 227; NCE 2nd ed., v. 8, 877; Biot, 56; Wilson, 131–32; Thomas de Cantimpe, *Thomas of Cantimpre: The collected saints' lives: Abbot John of Cantimpre, Christina the Astonishing; Margaret of Ypes and Lutgard of Aywieres,* edited and with an introduction by Barbara Newman, translated by Margot H. King and Barbara Newman, Turnhout, Brepols, c 2008, 207–96; Ghezzi, MM, 39–41.

the least light. Lydwina lost blood through her mouth, ears, and nose too, so copiously that the doctors wondered how she could lose more blood than her body could possibly hold. At one point, her lungs and liver decayed, her stomach, swollen on her skeletal frame, burst, and her intestines spilled out. This once beautiful girl became a pitiful sight to behold. If these afflictions had been natural, one alone would have been enough to kill her.

Like many great mystics, Lydwina was plunged into the purifying "dark night of the soul". Beginning in 1407, she began to experience supernatural gifts—ecstasies and visions in which she participated in the Passion of Christ, saw and visited purgatory, hell, and heaven, constantly saw angels including her guardian angel, and visited with saints such as St. Paul and St. Francis of Assisi. It is said that every night for twenty-eight years, this victim soul had an ecstasy, lasting an hour, during which time she was conveyed to heaven, to purgatory, to hell, or to a great variety of places, such as the Holy Land, Rome, etc. While at these places, Lydwina venerated the relics of the saints and visited a great many churches and monasteries, the situations of which she knew about as well as the names of the inhabitants. Once, enraptured by a vision of heaven and the veneration paid to the Blessed Virgin's maternity, she was said to have seen a Seraphim ministering to the Holy Child. During another ecstasy in which she was admitted to heaven, she saw its beauty and those of its inhabitants as well as heard heavenly music and the voices of angels.

During her ecstasies, this suffering servant of God is said to have entered purgatory, being led into the subterranean dungeons by her guardian angel. Here she saw dwellings, prisons, diverse dungeons, one more dismal than the other. She is said to have visited many poor tormented souls who were enveloped in flames. In one special case where she had helped a soul through purgatory, she saw the heavens opening for him as he went into glory. Lydwina once had a vision of hell during an ecstasy. Hell appeared to her like a great dark abyss, frightening to the sight and filling one with horror. Heart-rending screams and curses issued forth from this abyss, the sounds of the suffering souls who were damned. Confused with this vision at first, Lydwina's guardian angel appeared to her and revealed that it indeed was a true vision of hell. During another vision, Our Lord first appeared to her as a child and then was transformed into a man whose Face was disfigured and scarred. During this vision, luminous rays darted from Christ's wounds and pierced Lydwina's hands, her feet, and her heart. Upon receiving the stigmata, her body began to smell like that of fresh roses, violets, and lilies.

This servant of God was also the object of violent diabolical beatings and mocking throughout her virtuous life, as is so often the case with God's chosen victim souls. Frequently harassed and beaten by evil spirits, she courageously looked to the cross for her liberation. Lydwina also gave evidence of discernment and a vast and sophisticated theological knowledge. No matter how horribly she suffered, she never lost her sense of humor. During the last nineteen years of her life, Lydwina experienced the mystical gift of inedia whereby she ate virtually nothing or absolutely nothing year after year. Over that time, she only took the small communion wafer once a week for the remaining years of her life. She, in fact, could not even keep water down. This victim soul also slept very little (insomnia), if at all, over the last seven years of her life. To top it off, she became almost completely blind. On the morning of Easter-day, 1433, Lydwina was in deep contemplation and beheld, in a vision, Christ coming toward her to administer the sacrament of Extreme Unction. Soon after, Lydwina died in the odor of great sanctity. At death, her body was miraculously transformed, taking on the fresh and beautiful appearance that it had had before she even contracted smallpox. She seemed as lovely as a girl of seventeen. An ecclesiastical commission appointed to investigate, declared her experiences to be valid. She was canonized in 1890 by Pope Leo XIII.[1315]

Malachy O'Morgair, St. (c. 1094–1148)

Mystic, visionary, and Archbishop of Armagh, Ireland, born as Malachy O'Mara (Mael Maedoc Ua Morgair) in Armagh, Ireland. Malachy was ordained by St. Celsus (1079–1129) when he was twenty-five. In 1142, he founded the Mellifont Abbey. As one of the great saints of Irish history, Malachy was responsible for the unification of the Irish Clergy, the restoration of discipline, the revival of religious fervor, and the restoration of morality. In these undertakings, he proved to be determined, humble, and lacking any desire for self-aggrandizement. He is reputed to have performed many miracles, among them curing Henry, son of King David of Scotland, of a grave disease as well as to have exorcized demons from many people.

Malachy reportedly received many visions about future events from the time of Pope Celestine II (1143–1144) until the end of the world. A collection of 112 mystical mottoes believed to have been written by

Stained glass window depicting Saint Malachy by Lucien-Leopold Lobin, Cathedral of the Immaculate Conception, Ireland

St. Malachy was discovered in 1590 in the Roman archives. They purport to be brief descriptions of all future popes, although in symbolic fashion, from the time of his vision to the end of the world. Each pope is described by a phrase, symbol, or an image. Sometimes the description refers to the pope's background, his family's coat of arms, or key world events taking place during the individual pope's reign. It is said that all his prophecies about future popes were fairly accurate up to 1590, but a bit vague after that. According to the many scholars who have studied St. Malachy's prophecies, only two or three popes are now left before the last pope, who will be named Peter II. Then the end will come, Rome will be destroyed and Christ will return to earth. It should be noted, however, that a debate has raged among scholars ever since the discovery of this work as to whether these prophecies are forgeries or genuine predictions of St. Malachy. One theory is that these so-called prophecies are not by St. Malachy but are a late-sixteenth-century compilation published by Dom Arnold de Wyon in 1595.

Malachy's sister is claimed to have once appeared to him from purgatory and requested his prayers and the Holy Sacrifice of the Mass for her release. St. Bernard of Clairvaux (1090–1153), in whose arms Malachy died, highly praised this prelate for his devotion to the souls in purgatory. He proclaimed Malachy a saint in his requiem Mass, in 1148; an action that was formally confirmed by Pope Innocent III (1198–1216).[1316]

Margaret Fontana, St. (1440–1513)

Dominican mystic born at Modena, Italy. Margaret was a pious youth and became a Dominican tertiary. She was devoted to the sick and poor, spending whole nights praying over the sick in her care. She was said to be frequently visited by various demons who sought to turn her away from the faith. Margaret successfully drove them away with the Sign of the Cross. In time, she would be invoked by many who suffered from demonic oppression or possession. Besides her mystical gifts, Margaret was blessed with the gift of healing. She is also invoked by those women who suffer in childbirth.[1317]

Staind glass window depicting Sacred Heart and Saint Margaret Mary, detail, Saint Julie Billiart Catholic Church (Hamilton, Ohio)

Margaret Mary Alacoque, St. (1647–1690) (aka Margaret Mary of the Visitation)

Visitandine mystic, visionary, ecstatica, invisible stigmatic, and victim soul born at L'Hauthecour, Burgundy, France. Margaret became a contemplative nun of the Visitation Order in Paray-le-Monial and apostle to the devotion of the Sacred Heart of Jesus. Her baptismal name was Margaret, and the name Mary was added at her confirmation in 1669. As a young child, she was extremely devoted to the Blessed Virgin Mary and to the Blessed Sacrament. When she turned nine, she was stricken with rheumatic fever which kept her bedridden for four years. As a teenager, Margaret had recovered and engaged in worldly activities. One night after returning home from a carnival ball, she had a vision of Christ being scourged. During this vision, the Lord reproached her for her infidelity to Him. After this, she spent the rest of her life regretting going to the ball and wearing a mask at the carnival to please her brothers.

1316 Schouppe, *Purgatory*, 223–24; Cowan, 292–93; Delaney, 329–31.; Farmer, 340–41; Freze, VVA, 219; NCE 2nd ed., v. 9, 65.

1317 Cruz, SS, 484; Freze, VVA, 288.

After being professed at the Visitation Convent in Paray on November 16, 1672, Margaret had the first of a series of revelations. The Risen Christ is said to have appeared to her in an apparition while she was in the state of rapture praying before the Blessed Sacrament. Jesus showed her His Sacred Heart in flames. He told her that men and women must honor His heart, and that they were to perceive His heart as (real) flesh. For the next eighteen months, Margaret Mary's visions filled out the program that Jesus was asking of her. This contemplative nun also experienced many interior locutions of Our Lord. She had apparitions of Christ not only as the God-Man but even as an infant. Jesus usually appeared to her on the first Friday of the month during which He gave instructions for the implementation of the devotion to His Sacred Heart. In her autobiography, Margaret Mary writes that Our Lord "asked me for my heart, which I begged Him to take. He did so and placed it in His own adorable heart, where He showed it to her as a little atom which was being consumed in this great furnace, and withdrawing it hence as a burning flame in the form of a heart."

Christ requested that a special feast day devoted to His Sacred Heart be celebrated in the universal Church. He called for a Nine-Fridays devotion and a Holy Hour every Thursday to be set aside in honor of His Sacred Heart. "Communion on the first Friday for nine consecutive months," he said, "will find that My Heart shall be their assured refuge at that last hour." This Feast of the Sacred Heart of Jesus was to be celebrated on the first Friday after the feast of Corpus Christi, the feast honoring the body of Christ in the Eucharist. At first, Margaret Mary's efforts to establish such a devotion met only resistance and ridicule. Her prioress dismissed her as an over enthusiastic novice or worse. It was not until St. Claude la Colombiere (1641–1682)

declared her experience to be genuine that she began to be accepted. In 1794, Pope Pius VI (1775–1799) formally approved the devotion to the Sacred Heart for the whole Church, but it was not until 1856 that the Feast of the Sacred Heart was listed in the Church's universal calendar.

There is evidence from Margaret Mary's letters to her superiors and friends that she experienced the sufferings of Our Lord's Passion continuously, bearing the invisible stigmata which included the crown of thorn wounds. In fact, her *Autobiography* mentions the words from Our Lord: "Receive this crown, my daughter, as a sign of that which will soon be given thee in order to make thee conformable to Me." This servant of God also suffered from misunderstandings caused by some of her close relatives, and her soul was plunged into darkness. Satan was not long in seizing the chance to drive her to despair, and he attacked her spirit relentlessly, suggesting to her that her devotions were wrong and bringing to mind her past sins.

Margaret Mary, however, also experienced numerous ecstatic states and mystical graces. Like St. Teresa of Avila, she witnessed an apparition of the Blessed Virgin Mary concerning the dogma of her Assumption into heaven. She also mystically visited purgatory on a number of occasions where she witnessed souls with hands raised to heaven imploring God's mercy. All the while, the guardian angels of these souls were at their side consoling and encouraging them. Numerous souls from purgatory would reportedly appear to her asking for her intercession. This victim soul also rightly predicted the day of her death. Sts. Margaret Mary, John Eudes (1601–1670), and Blessed Claude La Colombiere are called the "Saints of the Sacred Heart," a devotion officially recognized and approved by Pope Clement XIII in 1765. Margaret Mary was declared venerable in 1824 by Pope Leo XII. She was beatified in 1864 by Pope Pius IX and canonized in 1920 by Pope Benedict XV.[1318]

Margaret of Cortona, St. (1247–1297) (aka Margherita di Laviano)

Franciscan tertiary, mystic, visionary, ecstatica, and stigmatic born at Laviano in Tuscany, Italy to a poor farmer. Due to harsh treatment by an unsympathetic and abusive stepmother, Margaret ran away from home at the age of sixteen. She was seduced by nobleman Arsenio del Monte from Montepulciano who took her to his castle with the promise of love, luxury, and marriage. For nine years she lived scandalously as this man's mistress and eventually bore him a son. They all lived together ostentatiously in great luxury. However, after her lover was assassinated for political motives, Margaret returned to her father's house dressed as a penitent where her stepmother refused to receive her. At that point in her life, Margaret resolved to change her lifestyle and made a public confession of her sins in the church at Cortona. She and her son were then befriended and taken in by two ladies living in Cortona. Margaret went on to become a Franciscan tertiary and suffered through three years of spiritual despair and aridity. Her

spiritual advisers helped her through this rough period, frequently admonishing her to moderate the severity of the penances and mortifications she imposed on herself. After a brief period as a recluse, Margaret then devoted herself to caring for the poor and the sick.

This repentant sinner next began to experience ecstasies and visions of Christ. In 1277 she had the first of her mystical experiences. While praying in the church of the Franciscan Friars, she heard these words: "What is thy wish, poverella (poor one)?" She responded, "I neither seek nor wish for aught but thee, my Lord Jesus." From then on she experienced a continuing and intense communion with Christ. Initially, He called her "poverella" ("poor one") and then "my child." In her frequent ecstasies, Margaret received many messages from the Lord, some for her and some she delivered to others. She acted as a peacemaker and often admonished worldly prelates. Some of her visions were concerned with reforming the lax practices of religious and ecclesiastical life, others with averting political strife. In 1286, Margaret received permission to form a community of woman nurses to care for the sick and the poor called Le Poverelle ("poor ones"). This servant of God was favored with exceptional mystical graces and converted great numbers of sinners. She was sought after by people from all over Italy, France and Spain for spiritual advice and for her miraculous healing powers. Margaret is also credited with restoring a dead boy back to life. These miracles continued on after her death. Many departed souls in purgatory are said to have appeared before her to implore her prayers and assistance for their release. She was able to secure the release for many of these souls through her prayers, mortifications, vigils, sufferings, communions, and Masses for them.

[1318] Schouppe, *Purgatory*, xxxviii, 76–77, 149, 381; Patron Saint index, http://www.catholicforum. com; NCE, 1st ed., v. 1, 203; Johnson, 12, 325; http://www.newadvent.org/cathen; Emile Bougaud, *The Life of Saint Margaret Mary Alacoque*, Rockford, Ill.: TAN Books and Publishers,1994; Alacoque, Margaret Mary, Saint, *The Autobiography of Saint Margaret Mary Alacoque*, Rockford, Ill.: TAN Books and Publishers, 1995; *Saint Margaret Mary Alacoque and the Promises of the Sacred Heart*, tr. M.A Bouchard, Boston, Mass., 1975; Cowan, 299; Cruz, MMM, 75; Freze, TBWC, 267; Ghezzi, VOS, 578–79; Gallick, 313; Guiley, 219–20;, Lord, VMS, 221, 223, NCE 2nd ed., v. 1, 203, 67–68; Dunbar, 1:29–30; Cruz, A&D, 87, 124, 175, 202; Connell, 60–66.

Saint Margaret of Cortona by Gaspare Traversi

Margaret also had confrontations with demons. Once, when an evil spirit appeared to her seeking to terrify her, her guardian angel appeared to comfort her. The angel told her that he was the guardian of her soul which is an exalted abode of God and revealed to her the degrees or stages of the interior life she was called to enter. A holy person in the city of Castello, Italy, who was rapt in ecstasy at the moment when this mystic died, related that she saw a multitude of souls that the saint had delivered from purgatory form a procession to escort her to Paradise. Margaret's incorrupt body is venerated in her Church at Cortona, Italy. She was canonized in 1728 by Pope Benedict XIII.[1319]

[1319] NCE 2nd ed,v.9, 148–149; A.M Hiral, The Revelation of Margaret of Cortona, tr. R. Brown, St. Bonaventura, NY, 1952; Delaney, 334–335; Hebert, 156; Cruz, ss, 475–78; Freeze, VVA, 168; Gallick, 148, 422; Guiley, 218–219; Schouppe, 148, 309; Cowan, 30; L'Osservatore Romano, Spanish ed.June 4, 1993

Marguerite Bays, St. (1815–1879)

Franciscan tertiary, mystic, visionary, ecstatica, stigmatic, and victim soul born in La Pierraz, Fribourg, Switzerland. Marguerite worked as a dressmaker and, at the age of thirty-five, developed intestinal cancer. Being very devoted to the Blessed Mother, she asked Our Lady during an apparition to intercede with her Son to exchange her suffering for a different pain that would enable her to share more directly in His Passion. Marguerite was said to have been miraculously cured of her cancer on December 8, 1854, at the very moment that Pope Pius IX pronounced the dogma of the Immaculate Conception. After her miraculous recovery, Marguerite was given a "mysterious affliction" and asked to suffer as a victim soul for the sins of the world. Every Friday, she was said to go into ecstasy and reenact the phases of Jesus' Passion, from the Agony in the Garden to His Crucifixion and death. From the time she became a Third Order Franciscan, this victim soul began to show signs of the stigmata. Like most authentic stigmatics, she went to great lengths to hide these wounds and avoided the world's attention until her death. Marguerite was beatified by Pope John Paul II in 1995[1320] and canonized by Pope Francis in 2019.

Maria Maddalena De' Pazzi, St. (1566–1607) (aka Maria Magdalen de' Pazzi and "The Ecstatic Saint")

Carmelite mystic, visionary, ecstatica, invisible stigmatic, and victim soul born in Florence, Italy to a distinguished Florentine family and given the baptized name of Catherine. This future saint was strikingly beautiful. As a child she was spiritually

[1320] Gallick, 191; NCE 2nd ed., v. 2, 166.

Ecstasy of St Mary Magdalene de' Pazzi by Alessandro Rosi

precocious and had a devout prayer life. In 1582, she joined the Carmelites at St. Mary of the Angels Convent in her native city, taking the name of Maria Maddalena as a postulant. Trinity Sunday, May 27, 1584 marked the beginning of her extraordinary ecstatic experiences whose number, intensity, and variety were to gain her the title of the "Ecstatic Saint." For immediately after the profession of her vows, Maria fell into an ecstasy that lasted about two hours and was repeated after Holy Communion on the following forty mornings. These ecstasies were rich experiences of union with God and marvelous insights into divine truths. Besides remarkable visions and locutions of Our Lord and the Blessed Virgin, Maria also experienced visions of a number of saints. She practiced great mortifications, and is said to have spent some years in the depths of spiritual depression and aridity. Maria Maddalena has been called a mystic for mystical souls. On many occasions she experienced the phenomenon of levitation and performed miracles of healing. This holy Carmelite also possessed other symbolic mystical graces, such as abstinence

from food (inedia), the gifts of prophecy, the ability to read people's minds, and the exchange of hearts.

In a vision that occurred on March 24, 1585, St. Augustine of Hippo appeared to her. He is said to have written upon her heart in crimson and gold letters: *Verbum caro factum est* ("The Word was made flesh"). On April 11, 1585, while participating in the sufferings on Calvary, Maria received the invisible stigmata, the pains of which she suffered at various intervals. A few days later, she beheld in a supernatural way, all the sins of the world and the malice of them. She became drowned in tears (gift of tears) and could not stop crying until Sts. Augustine and Catherine of Siena appeared and turned her sorrow into joy. On May 4, 1585, the Lord together with His mother, the aforementioned saints and St. Angelo the Carmelite (1642–1720) appeared and crowned her with the crown of thorns. Thenceforth, on every Friday, Maria Maddalena suffered the agony of the crown of thorns. On the following May 7 while praying, this servant of God was instantly rapt in an ecstasy where she saw Our Lord and Our Lady and experienced the supreme mystery of exchange of hearts. Our Lord was said to have taken His Sacred Heart from His breast and placed it within the bosom of the Carmelite, thus exchanging her heart for His own.

Maria's life was, in fact, one long ecstasy. In one such ecstasy, she allegedly levitated to a height of about thirty feet. Her utterances while in ecstasy and descriptions of her revelations were copied down by some of the sisters in the convent and were later published. These ecstasies are covered in detail in her five-volume work. Maria reportedly talked so inhumanly fast while in ecstasy that it required as many as six scribes to record everything she said. During her luminous ecstasy, the saint's face was said to become transparent as crystal and her cheeks a fiery red. This victim soul wanted nothing more than to share in the salvation of human beings. In another of her ecstasies, she offered God the Father the Passion of His Son for the souls in purgatory. Maria Maddalena was granted the privilege of seeing a large number of souls being delivered from purgatory. She even saw souls of persons she had known while alive. Once she witnessed a sister nun who had just died still being held captive in the dungeons of purgatory. She herself was allowed to descend into purgatory and was granted the privilege of visiting the dungeons and prisons there. The Carmelite was also allowed by God to see the soul of her mother as well as one of her fellow sisters in the glory of heaven.

Maria Maddalena is also said to have been tormented by temptations of lust and gluttony and to have had encounters with demons. Demons are said to have shown themselves to her in the form of the Eternal Father, Our Lord and at other times as the Holy Spirit or one of Maria's own angelic protectors. In all these disguises, the devil eventually betrayed himself. These demons are said to have tried to distract her by screaming in her ear, pushing her down stairs, and wrapping themselves around her body like snakes, frequently causing her great pain by biting her. She threw some out a window and ultimately overcame them all. Today, Maria's incorrupt body lies in the Carmelite Church in Florence, Italy. It was still intact and fresh some sixty years after her death with a fragrant oily liquid more odoriferous than balm exuding from it. She was beatified in 1626 by Pope Urban VIII and canonized in 1669 by Pope Clement IX.[1321]

[1321] Schouppe, *Purgatory*, 14, 18, 136, 171, 222, 254–55, 346, 361; http://www.thestigmata.com; Gallick, 158, 423; Aradi, 175; Delaney, 397; http://www.newadvent.org/cathen; Johnson, 125, 134, 325; Summers, 193ff; NCE 2nd ed., v.

Mariam Baouardy, St. (1846–1878) (aka Al Qiddisa "The Holy one", Marie of Pau, Marie of Jesus Crucified, Mary Baouardy, The Little Arab)

Carmelite mystic, visionary, ecstatica, and stigmatic born at Ibillin, located in the hill country of upper Galilee, Palestine to a poor Greek Melchite Catholic family. Mariam's parents died when she was only two. She was raised by a paternal uncle. Around 1854, the family moved to Alexandria, Egypt. Mariam refused to agree to an arranged marriage at age thirteen and so her uncle hired her out as a domestic servant. She found work alongside a Muslim servant who tried to get her to convert to Islam. When she told him she would never abandon her faith, he slit her throat and dumped her in an alley. At that moment, the Virgin Mary appeared to her in an apparition and treated her wound. Once fully recovered, she left her uncle's house forever. The "Little Arab," as she was later called, then went to work for a Christian family and, in 1860, moved in with the Sisters of St. Joseph.

Supernatural events, however, began to occur around her and the Sisters of St. Joseph refused to let her join their community. One of the most terrible spiritual trials she endured at that time was that of diabolical possession which she fought off for a period of forty days. Miriam persevered in her simple child-like faith in God the Father, Our Lord, and His Mother as well as her great devotion to the Holy Spirit. In 1865, she entered the Sisters of

11, 47–48; NCE 1st ed., v. 11, 36; Cruz, MMM, 234, 371–72; Freze, TBWC, 265; Ghezzi, VOS, 528–29; Farmer, 418–19; *Maria Maddalena de'Pazzi: Selected Revelations*, trans. with an introduction by Armando Maggi, NY: Paulist Press, 2000; Cruz, A&D, 147, 177–78, 200.

Compassion but was forced to leave there due to ill health. For the next two years (May 1865 to June 1867) Mariam was a postulant of the Sisters of St. Joseph of the Apparition until she was judged unsuited for the cloister. This was due to the mystical phenomena she experienced which included levitation, ecstasies, and stigmatization. When the "Little Arab" did indeed receive the stigmata, her Superior accused her of self-inflicted knife wounds. This accusation caused her shame and ridicule among her peers. She was exorcised, refused Holy Communion, and prevented from attending choir. In 1867, Miriam was taken in by the Discalced Carmelites at Pau, France. She became a lay sister and was later professed on November 21, 1871, taking the name of Sister Mary of Jesus Crucified. Her rewards were those reserved for the most privileged of humans. She continued to experience supernatural events from 1867 to 1876.

On May 24, 1868, while in ecstasy, the "Little Arab" cried out to St. Teresa that Jesus had pierced her heart. The transverberation of her heart was discovered later after her death. Dr. Carpani, the surgeon who removed her heart at death, perceived a deep wound, triangular in shape, and appearing as though it had been inflicted by a broad sword. This beata permitted her guardian angel to speak through her. She was also seen to levitate to the top of a lime tree and hop like a bird from branch to branch, had the gift of prophecy, bilocation, knowledge of hearts, and facial radiance. Her sayings while rapt in ecstasy were carefully written down. In 1870, Sister Mary of Jesus was sent with a group of founding sisters to Mangalore, India. Her spiritual adviser there, believing her mystical experiences were a sign of demonic obsession, obliged her to return to Pau, France in 1872. She was beatified by Pope John Paul II on November 13, 1983, at Rome[1322] and canonized by Pope Francis on May 17, 2015.

Mariam Thresia Chiramel Mankidiyan, St. (1876–1926)

Mystic, visionary, ecstatica, stigmatic, and victim soul born in the village of Puthchira, Trichur District, Keralia, India as the third of five children to Thoma and Thanda Chiramel Mankidiyan. Thresia grew up in piety and holiness under the loving guidance of her saintly mother. From early childhood she was moved by an intense desire to love God. For this purpose she fasted four times a week and prayed the rosary several times a day. She consecrated her virginity to Christ when she was about ten years of age. The death of her mother when she was twelve ended her education, but she came to lead an eremitical life of prayer and penance in the solitude of the far away woodhills. She visited the poor and nursed the sick, even those with leprosy and smallpox who were often abandoned by relatives. Upon the death of their parents, she took care of their orphaned children. Thresia received guidance in her apostolate from the Holy Family whom she frequently saw in visions.

Thresia also was granted several mystical gifts such as prophecy, healing, aura of light, and an odor of sanctity. Like St. Teresa of Avila, she had frequent ecstasies and levitations. On Fridays, people used to gather to see her lifted high and hanging in the form of a crucifix on the wall of her room. And, like St. Padre Pio, she bore the stigmata, carefully hiding it from public view. Perhaps to help keep her humble amidst such mystical favors, the Lord let

---

[1322] Summers, 237ff; Thurston, 29; http://www.catholic–forum.com/saints; Freze, TBWC, 124; Biot, 26; Gallick, 251, 435; NCE Jubilee, 440; NCE 2nd ed., v. 2, 55–56; Wilson, 142; Treece, MB, 178–79; http://mytbaytel.net/nitesky/christian/miracles.htm.

her be tormented by diabolical attacks and vexations almost all through her life. She was once hoisted to the attic in her house and tied and fastened with ropes from neck to feet by devils. Under orders of her bishop who wondered if she was simply a play thing of the devils, this servant of God was repeatedly submitted to exorcisms between 1902 and 1905 by her parish priest. She submitted to these exorcisms with exemplary humility. Mariam Thresia also had to fight against temptations against faith and chastity as she passed through the dark night of the soul. On February 10, 1906, Jesus appeared before her with a heavy cross and in great suffering. He asked her to bear the cross for her and she agreed to become a victim soul. Soon afterwards, an angel came and thrust a spear into her left side. She was said to experience this trans-verberation of the heart a total of five times. It is also reported that she underwent an exchange of hearts and spiritual espousal to Jesus. Mother Mariam Thresia went on to found the Congregation of the Holy Family (CHF). By the time of her death, the Congregation consisted of fifty-five sisters, three convents, two schools, two hostels, a study house, and an orphanage. By the year 2000, CHF had 1,584 professed sisters, serving in Kerala, in the mission areas of North India, in Germany, Italy, and Ghana, with a total of 176 houses in seven provinces and 119 novices. This heroic soul was declared venerable by Pope John Paul II on June 28, 1999, blessed on January 27, 2000 and canonized in 2019. She is the fourth Indian to be beatified.[1323]

[1323] http://mariamthresia.org/cat+14; http://www.vatican.va.news_service/liturgy/saints/ns_lit_doc_20000409_beata-Mankidyan; http://mariamthresia.org/?p+206.

Mariana De Jesus by Sylverio de Sotomayor

Mariana De Jesus Paredes Y Flores, St. (1618–1645) (aka Mary Ann de Paredes, Mariana de Paredes y Flores, Marianne de Jesus of Quito, Marianna of Jesus, Marianna of Quito, "The Lily of Quito")

Franciscan tertiary, mystic, visionary, ecstatica, and victim soul born in Quito, Ecuador of noble Spanish parents. Many sources speak of a phenomenon displayed in the sky at her birth which signaled the type of faith life she would lead. Orphaned as a child, Mariana was raised by an older sister and her husband, where she later lived as a hermit. Almost from infancy, she showed signs of an extraordinary attraction to prayer and mortification as well as of love of God and devotion to the Blessed Virgin Mary. Mariana is said to have been miraculously saved from death several times. She practiced unheard of corporal austerities, ate hardly anything, except the Eucharistic bread (inedia), and slept for only three hours a night for years (insomnia).

Mariana offered herself up as a victim soul for the sins of the world. This so-called "Lily of Quito" was given to ecstasies, saw symbols of God's indulgences, predicted the future, read the secrets of hearts, and cured diseases. Mariana also brought back to life her niece whose skull had been fractured by a mule as well as a woman who had been strangled and then thrown over a cliff by her jealous husband. This mystical child of God performed many miracles while alive as well as after her death for those who invoked her intercession. She publicly offered her life to spare Quito from a serious plague that hit the city. She died shortly afterwards. Mariana is the patron saint of Ecuador. She was beatified by Pope Pius IX in 1853 and canonized by Pope Pius XII in 1950.[1324]

Marie of the Incarnation Guyart, St. (1599–1672) (aka Marie Guyard, Marie Guyart of the Incarnation, Marie de l' Incarnation Martin, Marie of the Ursulines, Mother of New France)

Ursuline mystic, visionary, and ecstatica born to a baker at Tours, France. A pious and sometimes mystical child, Marie is said to have had a dream-vision of Jesus at the age of seven whereby He asked her to be His spouse and she agreed. However, Marie was forced into an arranged marriage at the age of seventeen and soon became the mother of a son. Widowed after two years of marriage, she moved back in with her family.

On March 25, 1620, Marie experienced a vision in which she was shown all her faults and human frailties, then was immersed in Christ's blood. In May 1625, Marie had the first of her visions of the Trinity. She was reportedly shown the persons of the Trinity, how they operated, as well as received an understanding of the gradation of angels. This vision was said to have lasted the duration of several Masses. About two years later, Marie had her second Trinitarian vision. This vision is said to have culminated in the summit of all mystical experiences, her spiritual marriage to Christ. In January 1631, Marie asked her sister to take care of her son Claude and joined the Ursulines at Tours. She took her final vows in 1633 as Marie de l'Incarnation. A few years later this future beata received yet another vision in which she was told to move to Canada to build a house there for Christ. Marie arrived in Quebec on 1 August 1639 as the first superior of the Ursulines in Canada. She worked as a missionary to the natives and even wrote prayers and a catechism in the Algonquin, Huron, and Iroquois languages. In 1641, her son Claude became a Benedictine priest as well as her biographer. A full account of her mystical life can be found in her works entitled *Relation of 1633* and *Relation of 1654*. Marie was beatified by Pope John Paul II on June 22, 1980.[1325]

[1324] Schouppe, 252; Delaney, 388; Freze, VVA, 221; Gallick, 159, 423; Guiley, 222–23; Hebert, 144; http://www.Catholicity.com; NCE, 1st ed., v. 10, 999; NCE 2nd ed., v. 10, 880–81; Cruz, MMM, 248; Patron Saints Index; Baring–Gould, 392–93; Farmer, 411; Daily Reflections, March 28, 2010; Dunbar, 2:30.

[1325] NCE, 1st ed., v. 9, 219; Patron Saints Index; Fanning, 164–65; Marie de l' Incarnation, *The Autobiography of Venerable Marie of the Incarnation, O.S.U. Mystic and Missionary*, Chicago: Loyola University Press, 1964; Ghezzi, VOS, 564; Gallick, 132; Guiley, 223; NCE, Jubilee, 540; Underhill, Mystics, 202.

Saint Martin De Porres, Peru

Martin De Porres, St. (1579–1639) (aka Saint of the Slaves, Patron of the Negroes)

Dominican mystic, visionary, and ecstatic born in Lima, Peru as an illegitimate son of a Spanish grandee and a free black woman. In 1594, Martin became a Dominican lay brother at Rosary convent in Lima. Here he ministered to African slaves that were brought into Peru. He was a close friend of Sts. Rose of Lima, Juan Masias, and Toribio de Mangrove (1538–1606), the latter of whom baptized Rose. Martin was said to have experienced visions and ecstasies. On such occasions, brilliant celestial rays of light are said to have converged on him. The Blessed Mother, Sts. Dominic, Vincent Ferrer, and many other saints and angels reportedly visited him during his lifetime. The Virgin Mary was said to often send angels to light his way from his dormitory to the choir. This was witnessed by many of Martin's fellow religious. The saint was also very devoted to his guardian angel to whom he often turned in prayerful petition and for supernatural assistance.

Brother Martin is reputed to have been gifted with such supernatural gifts as bilocation, aerial flights, reading men's minds, as well as the multiplication of food. Moreover, this Dominican lay brother possessed infused theological knowledge, an astonishing control over animals, as well as the gift of mystical transport. On more than one occasion, Martin was said to have entered rooms through locked doors by some means known only to himself and God. He appeared at the bedside of sufferers without being asked. Two other times, witnesses attest that while darkness was falling and being at a considerable distance from the monastery, Martin bade his companions join hands and before they knew it were suddenly transported to the doors of the monastery in the brief space of a moment. They had covered several miles in but a few seconds. Also, once when enemies arrived in his room to harm him, he was made invisible to them. He also helped others by cloaking them with invisibility. Once two escaped prisoners took refuge in his monastery cell. He had them kneel and pray. When authorities came to search the monastery, including Martin's cell, the criminals could not be found. Martin later advised them to mend their ways.

This servant of God was thrice visited by the "evil one" who tried to deflect him from the path of his faith, but each time he managed to defeat him. The first time the devil took the form of a man who accosted him at the bottom of a flight of stairs. The second time the devil and other demons appeared in his cell one night. They hit and shook him and set his cell on fire. The third time was shortly before Martin's death. This time the devil's tactic was to tell him how saintly he was, trying to make Martin suffer by tempting him to feel vain and

Saint Martin of Tours and the Beggar, 1918, Wilfred Thompson

superior. On this last occasion, the Virgin Mary, Sts. Dominic, and Vincent Ferrer joined him, and together they pushed the devil away. Instances of the saint being raised three of four feet from the ground while rapt in a profound ecstasy before a crucifix were numerous. Several priests who had witnessed these levitations gave depositions to this effect for the process of his beatification.

Although he spent all of his religious life at the Monastery of the Holy Rosary in Lima, Peru, Martin was seen to appear, according to reliable witnesses, at different times in Mexico, Central America, China, Japan, Turkey, Africa, the Philippine Islands, and perhaps even in France. The saint often offered detailed descriptions of places he had visited abroad. He is also said to have performed miraculous cures. Martin was known to dispense food that miraculously multiplied to meet the demand, to have been visibly helped by angels, and to have brought a dead fellow monk back to life. Martin knew when someone was going to die and even predicted the day and time of his own death. While waiting for heaven to claim him, this mystic experienced visions of various saints to include Sts. Dominic and Vincent Ferrer as well as the Blessed Virgin. As soon as the lid of his casket was opened during exhumation, a sweet perfume having the odor of roses issued from it. This first black South American saint and patron saint of racial harmony was beatified in 1837 by Pope Gregory XVI and canonized in 1962 by Pope John XXIII.[1326]

Martin of Tours, St. (c. 316–397)

Mystic and visionary monk, Bishop of Tours, and Patron Saint of France born in Sabaria, Pannonia (now Hungary), the son of a pagan army officer. His family later moved from Hungary to Pavia, Italy where the youngster was raised. At age fifteen, Martin was inducted into the army against his will. Around 337, the famous incident at Amiens occurred where he was stationed. It is said that he cut his cloak in half and gave half of it to a poorly clad beggar who was freezing to death. That evening, Martin had a vision of Christ coming down from heaven and surrounded by angels, clad in his half cloak. So moved by the vision was the young soldier that he went immediately and asked to be baptized into the Christian faith. From that time on, Martin refused to fight and was discharged from the army. He proceeded to ask for and was granted land at Liguge from St. Hilary (d. 468), Bishop of Poitiers, and became a hermit there. Others joined him and the first monastic community in Gaul was founded. In 371, despite his objections, Martin was named Bishop of Tours. In this capacity, he worked ceaselessly to spread the faith and convert pagans, ruthlessly destroyed pagan temples, and was often saved from harm by seemingly miraculous means.

Martin is reputed to have experienced other visions and revelations and was gifted with the ability of prophesy. He reportedly also had colloquies with angels and visible encounters with devils, sometimes on the occasion of exorcisms. Satan once appeared to him as an "angel of light," saying he was Christ. The "evil one" was clad in a royal garment with his head encircled with a diadem. Martin said that he would not recognize him as the savior unless he saw him with the stigmata and the cross, whereupon the diabolical phantom vanished, leaving behind an intolerable odor. The future saint worked many wonders in his lifetime including raising three people from the dead. It is claimed that he healed St. Paulinus of Nola's (c. 354–431) diseased eye by simply touching it lightly with a fine paintbrush. Martin is also credited with many posthumous miracles and is regarded as one of the great saints of Gaul and the outstanding pioneer of Western monasticism before St. Benedict (c. 480–547). A radiant globe, supernatural light of the aureole, is said to have appeared often over his head while he celebrated Mass.[1327]

Mary De Cervellon, St. (1230–1290) (aka Maria de Cervellione, Sor Maria del Socors)

Mercedarian Order foundress, mystic, and ecstatica born in Barcelona, Spain to a noble family. After her parents died, Mary established the second order of Mercedarians, devoted to an active apostolate toward the sick and poor. She reputedly enjoyed gifts of counsel and prophecy and foretold the outcome of battles as well as the date of

[1326] Giuliani Cavallini, *St. Martin de Porres–Apostle of Charity*, translated by Caroline Holland, Rockford, Ill.: TAN Books and Publishers, 1999; Johnson, 145; Delaney, 416–17; Dorcy, 398–99; NCE, 1st ed., v. 11, 595; NCE 2nd ed., v. 11, 522–23; Hebert, 141, 284; Lord, 110, 124; Cruz, MMM, 4, 26, 94–95, 168, 213, 392; Ghezzi, 544–45; Guiley,226–28; Cowan, 315; Cruz, A&D, 25, 217; *Columbia Magazine*, Nov. 2012, 5.

[1327] Ghezzi, VOS, 129; Johnson, 133; Delaney, 340–41; Hebert, 53; Guiley, 228–29; NCE 1st ed., v. 9, 303–4; NCE 2nd ed., v. 9, 220; Edward Watkin, *Neglected saints*, NY: Sheed and Ward, 1955, 13–31; Cruz, A&D, 170.

her own death. Mary also had thaumaturgic (wonder-working) and bilocation powers especially regarding seamen in danger. They called her Sor Maria del Socors. These seamen frequently claimed they saw her (at the time she was in deep ecstasy in her convent) walking on the waters or hovering over their stricken ships. She is invoked especially against shipwreck and is generally represented with a ship in her hand. After her death, Mary's body was found to be incorrupt.[1328]

Mary Frances of the Five Wounds of Jesus, St. (1715–1791) (aka Anna Maria Rosa Gallo, Maria Francesca of the Five Wounds, Anna Maria Rosa Nicoletta)

Franciscan Tertiary, mystic, ecstatica, invisible stigmatic, and victim soul born in Naples, Italy as Anna Maria Rosa Gallo. This servant of God grew up to become one of the most thoroughly documented stigmatists in history. Before her birth, Sts. John Joseph of the Cross, and Francis de Geronimo (1642–1716) are said to have predicted her future sanctity. At a very early age, Anna Maria began to practice penances and to meditate on Christ's Passion. As young as the age of two, she had an intense yearning for the Holy Eucharist. Anna Maria claimed that her guardian angel instructed her in spiritual matters when she was very little. Her angel is also said to have helped her through the terrible period in her life when she refused to marry and her ill-tempered father beat her and locked her in her room as punishment. At her reception among the Franciscan tertiaries on September 8, 1731, Anna Maria took the name of "Mary Frances of the Five Wounds of Jesus" out of devotion

to the Blessed Virgin, St. Francis, and the Sacred Passion.

This holy soul came to be favored with extraordinary mystical graces and was reputed to be endowed with the gift of prophecy. Moreover, every year during her (adult) life, the Franciscan Tertiary had ecstasies on the Passion. On Fridays, she would experience, in a physical manner, the agonies of the Passion and invisible stigmatization. Her special devotion to the Passion of Christ and to making the Stations of the Cross resulted in her receiving Christ's five wounds on her own body. While making the Stations of the Cross on Fridays, especially the Fridays during Lent, Mary Frances would experience pains corresponding to the Agony in the Garden, the Scourging, the Crowning with Thorns, and those other pains experienced by Our Lord during His Passion.

Her deep devotion to the Infant Jesus, the Blessed Virgin, the Holy Eucharist and sufferings of Christ helped her to endure serious illness, misunderstandings by her relatives and spiritual directors, and spiritual aridity. She became a counselor to priests, sisters, and pious laymen. Mary Frances willingly asked God to be a victim soul and to transfer to her the sufferings of the souls waiting in purgatory so that they would gain admittance to heaven more quickly. Her spiritual advisor once remarked that there should be no souls left in purgatory because of her vicarious help. Recently deceased spirits often appeared to her to ask for particular prayers and spiritual help.

This virtuous soul spent the last thirty-eight years of her life as a recluse in the home of Father Giovanni Pessiri. While there, she experienced the Host miraculously transported to her from various distant places. The archangel Raphael once reportedly brought her the Blood of Christ from the altar while the Mass was still in progress.

[1328] NCE, 1st ed., v. 9, 387; NCE, 2nd ed., v. 9, 285.

A local priest testified that after he consecrated the bread and wine, the archangel took the chalice from the altar, carried it to Mary Frances's home, and allowed her to drink a portion of it. On several other occasions, she also received the sacred bread in her mouth in miraculous ways that defy any physical explanation. Mary Frances was said to have lived for many years on nothing but the Holy Eucharist. This victim soul was declared venerable by Pope Pius VII in 1803, beatified in 1843 by Pope Gregory XVI, and canonized in 1867 by Pope Pius IX.[1329]

Mechtild of Hackeborn (c. 1240–1298) (aka Mechtilde of Heldelfs, Mechtild von Hackenborn-Wippa, "The Nightingale of Christ")

Benedictine mystic, visionary, and stigmatic born Matilda von Hackeborn-Wippa to one of the noblest and most powerful Thuringian families. Mechtild's sister was the illustrious Abbess Gertrude of Hackeborn. She, herself, was the protégé of Mechthilde of Magdeburg (1210–1285). At her birth, the priest said, "She will become a saintly religious in whom God will work many wonders." Mechtild was to become later the teacher and spiritual mother of St. Gertrude the Great who, as a child of five years, came under her care. This Benedictine sister began to experience apparitions and locutions around the year 1290. St. Albert the Great (c. 1206–1280) was one of the saints who appeared to her. During a Mass, around 1293, she also reportedly saw Jesus with many angels and on the

Statue of Saint Mechtildis of Hackeborn by Johann Georg Üblhör.

Feast of the Assumption had a vision of the Blessed Virgin Mary.

In 1292, Mechtild began to confide the secrets of her interior life to Gertrude and another nun, and for seven years, without her knowledge, these revelations were committed to writing. At first deeply disturbed by this, Mechtild, at last, allowed St. Gertrude the Great to edit the secrets of her extraordinary graces in what is now known as *Liber specialis gratiae*, the *Book of Special Grace*, more popularly known as *Revelations of St. Mechtild*. Like St. Catherine of Siena, Mechtild had a special devotion to the Sacred Heart of Jesus and was asked to make a dwelling for Him within her heart. When she asked Christ how to greet Mary, He told her to hail Mary's "virginal heart." Our lady appeared numerous times to the saint, including one time when she revealed her heart inscribed with letters of gold bearing the words "Hail Mary, full of grace! The Lord is with thee!"[1330]

[1329] Cowan, 320–21; Summers, 60; Thurston, 55, 153, 230; Biot, 67; Freze, TBWC, 174, 269; Gallick, 302, 443; Cruz, MMM, 234; www.newadvent.org/cathen; Patron Saints Index; http://www.catholic–forum.com/saints; NCE, 1st ed., v. 6, 269.

[1330] Guiley, 245; Johnson, 182, NCE, 1st ed., v. 9, 545; Hebert, 235; NCE 2nd ed., v. 9, 422; R.

Michael De Sanctis, St. (1591–1625) (aka Miguel Argemir; Miguel de los Santos, Michael of the Saints and cancer patron)

Trinitarian mystic, ecstatic, and stigmatic born in the town of Vich in Catalonia, Spain. Michael practiced austerities of fasting in early childhood and, at the age of eight, made a vow of chastity. He had a special devotion to the rosary and the Little Office of the Blessed Virgin. At age sixteen, he entered the Discalced Trinitarians which had been founded by the royal hermit St. Felix de Valois (1126–1212) and St. John de Matha (1160–1213). He was ordained in Portugal. This holy soul experienced unique mystical phenomena. In fact, He is said to be one of the most amazing ecstatics in the whole range of mysticism. It was said that Michael was frequently caught up in phenomenal ecstasies and raptures and often levitated. In Cordova, while meditating on paradise, he was said to have soared out of the choir, across a field, and to have come to rest on a church tower. When preaching in Salamanca, he reportedly was raised in the air in sight of all. It has been truly said of him that throughout all his days he seemed never to have passed out of the state of rapture. In these raptures, often during prayer, this servant of God ran through the cloisters at wonderful speed uttering cries of joy, and darting hither and thither with such celerity that nobody could stay with him. He appeared as an angel not a man. One day while Michael was in ecstasy, Our Lord deigned to make the mystical exchange of His Most Sacred Heart with the heart of the saint. Pope Benedict XIV (1740–1758) gave the most plausible theological explanation of the exchange of hearts phenomenon when he stated in his eulogy of St. Michael de Sanctis that the exchange of hearts was a mystical and spiritual exchange. This Trinitarian mystic was beatified in 1779 by Pope Pius VI, and canonized by Pope Pius IX in 1862.[1331]

Nicholas of Flue, St. (1417–1487) (aka Nicholas von Flue, "Brother Klaus")

Hermit, mystic, and visionary born to a peasant farmer family near Sachseln, Canton Obwalden, Switzerland. Nicholas took his surname from the river Flueli nearby. As a boy, this Swiss youngster was drawn to a life of self-denial and prayer. When he became an adult, he married Dorothy Wissling and during their happily married life she bore him ten children. The family prospered and Nicholas was widely respected. He served as a soldier and was elected to public office. He became a magistrate and counselor, but declined several times to serve as governor. In 1465, Nicholas had a vision in which he was visited by three strangers who told him he would die at the age of seventy and that he was to persevere in his devotion to God until then.

Nicolas felt the strangers were representatives of the Blessed Trinity and that he had been summoned to devote the rest of his life to God. For the next two years, he spent much time meditating on the Passion of Christ. More visions confirmed his conviction. On October 16, 1467, with his wife and childrens' consent, Nicholas resigned his offices and left his family, which by that time was able to support itself. He left home as a pilgrim wearing only a robe, with no hat or shoes, and carrying no money. He took only a staff

---

Brown, 52; Walsh, v. 2, 138; Wiebe, 20; Mary Jeremy Finnigan, *Scholars and mystics*, 31–53.

[1331] Aumann, 434; Summers, 104, 147, 195; Thurston, 31; NCE 2nd ed., v. 9, 599; Cruz, MMM, 75.

and a rosary, and set out toward Alsace. A vision convinced him to remain close to home, and he went into the woods to pray and fast and live as a hermit. He came to be known as Brother Klaus and "the living saint." Nicholas was revered by many and had frequent visitors. He was called upon to settle political disputes and played an instrumental role in preventing civil war in 1481.

According to legend, Nicholas did not eat, but subsisted only on the Holy Eucharist. This mystical fast was said to last for nearly twenty years. His neighbors built him a hut and a chapel at Ranft, near Sachseln which he dedicated to the Virgin Mary, his special patron. Our Lady is said to have often appeared to him and had conversations with him. Toward the end of his life, Nicholas had a glorious vision in which he was in a castle with people dressed in white robes. In this vision, he saw the Holy Trinity. Each person of the Trinity thanked him personally for his love and devotion, and for teaching others to love and serve God. Nicholas died on his seventieth birthday. His beatification and canonization were championed by Sts. Charles Borromeo, Peter Canisius, and Robert Bellarmine. He was beatified in 1669 by Pope Clement IX and canonized in 1947 by Pope Pius XII.[1332]

Nicholas of Tolentino, St. (1245–1305) (aka Nicholas of Tolentine)

Augustinian friar, mystic, and visionary born at Sant'Angelo in Pontano, Italy to an infertile, older couple who prayed at the shrine of St. Nicolas of Myra for a child. From the age of seven, Nicholas showed unusual signs of saintliness. He would hide in caves and pray like a hermit. At the age of eighteen, he joined the

Saint Nicholas of Tolentino, 1604, by Luis de Carvajal

Augustinian monastery in his birth city and was ordained in 1271 in Cinguli. In 1274, Nicholas had a vision of an angel who urged him to go to Tolentino. It was here that he was to became famous as an eloquent preacher and confessor who converted hardened sinners. As a newly ordained priest, the Augustinian had great success as a street-corner preacher and minister to the poor, sick, criminals, and the needy. He was blessed with healing powers and cured the blind and the sick. Father Nicholas was likewise favored by God with visions and abilities to work miracles and combat demons. As regards the latter, this saintly man was said to have been beaten frequently by devils. One time, he was assaulted so viciously as to be left half-dead resulting in him being lame for the rest of his life.

In the latter years of his life, Nicholas endured a prolonged illness. The Blessed

Virgin accompanied by Sts. Augustine and Monica (c. 331–387) appeared to him one night and instructed him to take a small piece of bread signed with the Cross, dip it in water, and then eat it, promising that he would be cured by his obedience. This cure worked for him and in grateful memory of his immediate restoration to health, the Augustinian friar began blessing similar pieces of bread and distributing them to the sick. This practice produced numerous favors and marvels of healing. In commemoration of these miracles, the shrine of the saint continues to distribute worldwide the "Bread of St. Nicholas," with stories of many favors and graces. Nicholas is the first member of the Augustinians to be canonized. He is venerated for the many miracles he performed as well as revered as the patron saint of the souls in purgatory. Nicholas' great devotion to the souls in purgatory is well known. In fact, it is said that he was transported to this realm and delivered many departed souls from there to heaven by offering the Holy Sacrifice of the Mass for them.

An interesting anecdote of Nicholas' life recounts that a year before his death a star, usually depicted as the sun, started to precede him wherever he went and that this star continues to appear on the anniversary of his death. At the time of his death, Jesus appeared to him along with Mary, His mother, and St. Augustine. His body is considered among the incorruptibles. Forty years after his death, his incorrupt body was disinterred and exposed to the faithful. It is alleged that at this time a German monk secretly detached Nicholas' arms from his body and took them to his native country. This amputation began the strange, almost four hundred year history of the bleeding arms. The arms were later assigned to the tomb with the incorrupt body but a hundred years later during another exhumation, the arms

remained perfectly incorrupt and imbued with blood. The Basilica of St. Nicholas of Tolentino contains the Chapel of the Holy Arms, where relics of the blood are kept in ornate vessels. Concerning his miracles, Nicholas is reported to have resuscitated over a hundred dead children, including several who had been under water for days. He also allegedly appeared over a sinking ship and calmed a storm, thereby saving nine people. Nicholas was canonized in 1446 by Pope Eugene IV. In 1884, he was proclaimed "Patron of the Souls in Purgatory" by Pope Leo XIII.[1333]

Odilia, St. (c. 660–720) (aka Adilia, Othilia, Ottilia, Odilia of Alsace, Odile)

Benedictine abbess, mystic, and visionary who, according to legend, was born at Obernheim in the Vosges mountains, the blind daughter of Adaric, an Alsatian lord. Legend further states that when Odilia was twelve, she was put in a convent at Baume, where she was baptized by the saintly Bishop St. Erhard of Regensburg (7th c.). The bishop was purportedly told in a dream that he was to go to the monastery and baptize a young blind girl, giving her the name of Odilia. When the bishop touched the girl's eyes with chrism during the baptism ceremony, the child miraculously recovered her sight. Odilia went on to be venerated for her visions and the miracles attributed to her. She is said to have

---

[1333] Schouppe, 207–8; A. P. Metzger, "The Great Patron: Saint Nicholas and the Suffering Souls," *The Tagastan* 15 (1952), pp. 8–11, 49; Cowan, 345; Delaney, 372; Guiley, 258–59; Cruz, Inc., 96; Cruz, MMM, 330; Walsh, v. 2, 172; Johnson, 325; Wiebe, 19; Lucy Gorden, "He Raised 100 Children from the Dead," in *Inside the Vatican*, July 2005, 42–43; NCE 2nd ed., v. 10, 378–79; *Book of Augustinian Saints*, 48–50; Cruz, A&D, 207; Catholic wonderworker, 14c.

Saint Odilia Healing a Young Blind Child, 1914, by Carl Jordan

resurrected her brother, who was accidentally killed by her father. Odilia is the patron saint of the blind and of Alsace. She was canonized in 1807 by Pope Pius VII.[1334]

Pacifico of San Severino, St. (1653–1721) (aka Pacificus di San Severino)

Franciscan mystic, ecstatic, and victim soul born to a distinguished family in San Severino in the Marches. Pacifico was orphaned at an early age and brought up by an uncle who mistreated him. He was ordained a Franciscan priest in 1678 and worked among the poor in the Apennine villages. At age thirty-five, Pacifico contracted an illness which left him deaf, blind, and crippled. He bore these infirmities for more

than thirty years but they did not prevent him from ably performing his priestly duties. This victim soul offered up his sufferings for the conversion of sinners. The Franciscan frequently experienced prolonged ecstasies while celebrating Mass. He was favored with the gift of reading souls, displayed the gift of prophecy, and many times miraculously cured the sick. Four years after his death, Pacifico's body was found to be incorrupt and emitted sweet perfume. When his body was being moved sometime after his death, his head detached from his trunk and blood flowed freely from the neck. He was canonized in 1839 by Pope Gregory XVI.[1335]

Paschal Baylon, St. (1540–1592) (aka "Seraph of the Eucharist")

Franciscan brother, mystic, visionary, and ecstatic born at Torre-Hermosa, Aragon, Spain. Paschal worked first as a shepherd and taught himself to read and write. He had an intense devotion to the Blessed Eucharist from youth. Popular belief tells us that he saw the chalice with a host suspended over it. Likewise, he evidently received a vision of St. Francis and St. Clare urging him to join the Order of Friars Minor. In 1564, he became a Franciscan lay brother. Paschal had frequent ecstasies and visions and was reputed to possess supernatural powers, such as being able to hear the Blessed Sacrament. Once while travelling in France, he defended the Real Presence against the blasphemies of a Calvinist preacher and narrowly escaped death by a Huguenot mob. Paschal also had marvelous insights into the mysteries of religion. His counsel was sought by learned and saintly persons. At his death, his body was covered with a thick layer

[1334] NCE 2nd ed., v. 10, 551; Butler 12/13, 16; Delaney, 376; Gallick, 369, 452; Dunbar 2:114–16; Baring–Gould, 15:174–75; Farmer, 393–94; Jones, WS, 173.

[1335] Cruz, MMM, 337; NCE, 1st ed., v. 10, 854; NCE 2nd ed., v. 10, 744.

Saint Paschal Baylon worshiping the Holy Eucharist, 1811,
by Bernardo López Piquer

of quicklime so as to quickly consume his flesh. He, however, was found to be incorrupt nine months later and his body exuded a marvelous fragrance. There was perspiration on his brow and his limbs remained supple. A miraculous crystalline liquid-like balm was distilled from his hands and face. It has also been reported that he opened his eyes after death. A great number of healing miracles were worked through his intercession. He was canonized in 1690 by Pope Alexander VIII.[1336]

[1336] Thurston, 248, 280; NCE,1st. ed., v. 10, 1049; Cruz, MMM, 293, 316, 370; Summers, 60; Delaney, 65, Ghezzi, VOS, 504–5; Carole Breslin, "St.Pascal Babylon," *The Wanderer*, May 23, 2013, 5B.

Paul, St.
(c. 1–67) (aka The Apostle to the Gentiles, Saul of Tarsus)

Mystic, visionary, ecstatic, and stigmatic born of Jewish parents from the tribe of Benjamin sometime around AD 1–5 in Tarsus in what is now Southeast Turkey. Apart from being a Jew, Saul (his birth name) was also a citizen of Rome suggesting that his family came from a very high station. He studied under the most famous Jewish rabbi of the time, Gamaliel of Jerusalem. A tentmaker by trade, Saul became a rigid Pharisee and a rabid persecutor of Christians whom he viewed as the mortal enemy of the Jewish legalistic tradition. He was reportedly present at the stoning of St. Stephen (d.c. 35) but only as a spectator. Paul never knew Jesus in the flesh.

Around AD 34, Saul set out on the road to Damascus to arrest some Christians and bring them back to Jerusalem. On the outskirts of this city, he experienced his famous mystical encounter with the risen Christ, one of the most dramatic visionary experiences recorded in religious journals. It led to his dramatic conversion. In his writings, Saul (later called Paul) was suddenly surrounded by a bright light, knocked to the ground, and heard a voice that spoke in Hebrew saying, "Saul, Saul why are you persecuting me?" When he asked who spoke, he was told, "I am Jesus whom you are persecuting." He was directed to go into the city of Damascus and await further instructions. Upon getting up from the ground, Saul discovered that he was blind. His companions led him by the hand into Damascus. For three days he was unable to see and he neither ate nor drank (Acts 9:3–5, 8–9). Finally, a Christian disciple named Ananias, acting on directions given him by Jesus in a vision, baptized him and his sight was restored and he was filled with the Holy Spirit.

St Paul by Jan Lievens

(Acts 9:10–19; Acts 22:6–16; 26:12–16). Several other Christic experiences of a visual character are attributed to Paul. Jesus told him that He would appear to him more times in the future and in the book of Acts, Paul records two additional visions of Jesus. One took place while praying in the Temple of Jerusalem immediately following his conversion. Here he experienced an ecstasy in which Jesus revealed to him his peculiar vocation to preach to the Gentiles. In yet another vision of Jesus, Paul was instructed to carry out his work in Rome (Acts 22:17ff).

St. Paul's vision on the road to Damascus is considered to be at once, corporeal, imaginative, and intellectual. He beheld with his eyes blinding light; he saw with his imagination the personal traits of Ananias; and his mind understood God's will. Saul interpreted this experience as a call to preach the risen Christ to the Gentiles. It was this actual vision of Christ which engendered Paul's faith. The transformation of his soul and his conversion to Christ after this divine revelation is absolute. He had another vision of Christ while in Corinth (Acts 18:9) and, most likely, another mentioned in Acts 23:11 where Jesus comforted him. Paul also laid claim to a full ecstatic experience that he mentioned to the congregation in Corinth. He told them that "whether in the body or out of the body he did not know, God knows, [he] was caught up to the third heaven and then [passed even beyond it] to paradise where he heard ineffable things, which no one may utter" (2 Cor 12:1–5).

After his conversion, his baptism, and his miraculous cure, Paul set out to traverse the civilized world as the apostle to the nations. Commanded by the Holy Spirit to evangelize the Gentiles, the twelve-year period from AD 45–57 was to prove to be the most active and fruitful of Paul's life. It comprised three great Apostolic expeditions, of which Antioch was, in each instance, the starting point and which invariably ended in a visit to Jerusalem. The full story of his missionary works and his name change to Paul is to be found in the Acts of the Apostles. St. Paul is credited with restoring the youth Eutychus back to life (Acts 20:12). He likewise comforted passengers and a crew about to be shipwrecked by telling them that an angel of God revealed to him that they all would be saved (Acts 27:23–24).

It is also claimed that St. Paul was the first stigmatic: "I have been crucified with Christ," he says, "I bear the marks of Jesus on my body." This is about as explicit as you can get on the matter (Gal 2:19; 6:17). St. Paul was also frequently beaten by demons. He mentions that the Lord kept him humble by giving him a thorn in the flesh, a messenger of Satan to torment him (2 Cor 12:7–9). This Apostle to the Gentiles suffered chronic ill-health and was subjected to scourging, stoning, shipwreck, and imprisonments, all for the love of Christ. He was ultimately beheaded in Rome in the year AD 67 during the reign of Nero.[1337]

St Paul of the Cross

Paul of the Cross, St. (1694–1775)

Founder of the Passionist Fathers, mystic, ecstatic, and visionary born as Paolo Francesco Danei at Ovada, Italy, the oldest son of impoverished noble parents. As a young man, Paul fought in the Venetian army against the Turks. Upon his discharge, he resumed his life of prayer and penitence. In 1720, this former soldier had a vision of Our Lady wearing a black habit with the name Jesus and a cross in white on the chest. Mary directed him to establish a religious order devoted to preaching on the

[1337] Johnson, 325; Delaney, 391–93; Fanning, 18; Guiley, 272; Tanquery, 702; NCE 2nd ed., v. 11, 1–12; Underhill, *Mystics*, 45.

Passion of Christ. Paul received permission to proceed to do this from the bishop of Alessandria, who decided the visions were authentic. In 1741, this servant of God received approval from Pope Benedict XIV (1740–1758) and the Barefooted Clerks of the Holy Cross and Passion (Passionists) began to spread throughout Italy. They garbed themselves in the habit Mary had worn in Paul's vision. Paul was elected the first superior general and held that position until the end of his life. He also opened the first house of the Passionist nuns in Corneto, Italy. The archangel Michael was said to have visibly appeared at times to defend the new Passionist congregation order and its blessed founder.

This spiritual giant was one of the most celebrated preachers of his time. He often succeeded in bringing the most hardened sinners and criminals back to the faith. Paul was blessed with supernatural gifts such as prophecy, levitation, miraculous healings, and reading the secrets of hearts. Once, while giving a mission on the island of Elba, the Passionist was reported to have walked off the platform during the most fervent part of his sermon, levitated through the air and over the heads of the people, and then returned to the platform as if nothing had happened. Another time, during a rapture, he reportedly rose in a chair to a height of five or six feet. Paul also once brought a child back to life who had been instantly killed after having fallen out of a building window. This mystic also received the gift of bilocation and the ability to appear to people in visions in distant places. He likewise had visions of souls in purgatory. Many of these souls which he saw there were allowed to come into his cell and tell him about their sufferings. Devils reportedly appeared to him in the form of cats, enormous dogs, or hateful-looking birds. These devils were said to attack him so fiercely that bruises on his

body were observed by his fellow religious. Once, while aboard a ship at sea, a storm nearly caused the ship to sink. Paul told the crew that the storm was caused by devils that were persecuting him. Paul blessed the sea, called on Jesus to quell the storm and the ship arrived safely in port. At times rays of light were reportedly seen by others shining around Paul's head. After his death, his body remained flexible and he had an odor of sanctity about him.[1338]

Peregrine Laziosi, St. (1260–1345) (aka "The Cancer Saint")

Servite mystic and visionary known throughout the world as "The Cancer Saint," born in Forli, Italy of well-to-do parents. As a youth, Peregrine was active in the antipapal party in Romagna and lived a dissolute lifestyle. He underwent a conversion experience after striking the face of the future St. Philip Benizi (1233–1285) who turned the other cheek and forgave him. In a vision, the Blessed Mother told Peregrine that she wished to direct his steps along the way of salvation and reportedly requested he join the Servite Order. Accompanied by his guardian angel, the future saint traveled to Siena and entered the Servites. Upon ordination, Father Laziosi became famous for his preaching, austerities, holiness, and being a confessor. He is known to have cured many who were afflicted with various diseases, to have frequently multiplied wheat and wine for the poor during a famine, and, on more than one occasion, raised the dead to life.

One of the special penances he decided on was to stand whenever it was not necessary to sit. It is claimed that Peregrine did

---

[1338] Cruz, MMM, 27; Cruz, A&D, 54, 113, 176, 202; Delaney, 393–94; Hebert, 127; Thurston, 247, 251; Ghezzi, VOS, 604–5; Farmer, 415–16; NCE 2nd ed., v. 11, 34–36.

Saint Peregrine Laziosi by Giacomo Zampa

said that during the thirty-two years prior to his canonization in 1726 by Pope Benedict XIII, there were over three hundred miracles attributed to him and authenticated by Church officials. His body was found to be incorrupt after death.[1339]

St Peter-Celestine by Philippe Sauvan

not sit for thirty years, which caused him to develop varicose veins and then cancer on his leg and foot. The sores became painful and doctors prepared to amputate his foot. However, the night before the surgery was scheduled to take place, Peregrine dragged himself to the foot of a crucifix and spent many hours in prayer. When he fell asleep, he received a vision of Christ descending from the Cross and reaching out His hand to touch his cancerous foot. The next morning he was found perfectly cured, with no trace of the former disease. Because of this miracle and those which followed after his death, he became known as the "Universal Patron of Cancer Victims." When he died, it is said that the Blessed Virgin Mary along with St. Philip Benizi (1233–1285) and Blessed Francis of Siena (1266–1328), both of the Servite Order, conducted his soul to the heavenly kingdom. Immediately after his death, to the amazement of all present, his lifeless body gave off the most fragrant odor. It is

Peter Celestine, St. (1221–1296) (aka Pope Celestine V)

Benedictine mystic, visionary, and future pope born in Isernia in the Abruzzi, Italy, the eleventh of twelve children to peasant parents. As a child Peter had visions of the Blessed Virgin Mary, angels, and saints. At the age of twenty, he left his home in Apulia to live as a hermit in a mountain solitude. Here he passed three years, assaulted by evil spirits and beset with temptations

---

[1339] Cruz, Inc.,115–16; Servite saints; Farmer, 420; *The Wanderer*, January 23, 2003, 2.

of the flesh, but consoled by angels' visits. Peter was ordained a Benedictine priest and returned to the monastic life as abbot of the Celestine Order he founded. When the papacy stayed vacant after the death of Pope Nicolas IV (1288–1292) due to political bickering, the then eighty-four-year-old Benedictine was elected as Pope Celestine V on August 29, 1294. After a reign of four months, Peter was overwhelmed by the burden of the office and the scheming of King Charles of Naples and abdicated. On December 12, 1294, he returned back to monastic life where he enjoyed his loving intimacy with the saints and angels. Peter was canonized in 1313 by Pope Clement V.[1340]

Peter Claver, St. (1580–1654)

Jesuit mystic, visionary, victim soul, and Apostle of the Negroes of Cartagena born at Verdu, near Barcelona, Spain. Peter joined the Jesuits at the age of twenty. During his studies at Montesione College in Palma, Majorca, he was influenced by St. Alphonsus Rodriguez whom he met there and who encouraged his desire for missionary work in the New World. After further study at Barcelona, Peter was sent out as a missionary to the New Kingdom of Granada in 1610. He was ordained in 1615 at Cartagena, in present-day Colombia. Cartagena was an important center of the slave trade and Peter joined Father Alfonse de Sandovel, his Jesuit mentor and inspiration, in trying to alleviate the horrendous conditions of the slaves that poured into that city. He worked in the yards where the slaves were penned after being brought from West Africa. Peter ministered to them with food and medicine, instructed them in the faith, and baptized them. He reportedly converted some 300,000 of them in

the forty years he labored among them. This servant of God also ministered to the lepers in St. Lazarus Hospital and to condemned prisoners. He always made himself available to these people as a confessor.

Father Claver preached in the main plaza of the city, practiced great austerities, and became known as one blessed with supernatural gifts such as prophecy, miracle-working, and the ability to read men's hearts. It is claimed that his person was sometimes illuminated with rays as he passed through the hospital wards of the city. His cloak was used for many purposes such as a covering for lepers and the putrescent, a pillow for the sick, and a pall for the dead. It was reported that many souls of slaves who went to purgatory after death came to ask for his intercessory prayers. Peter suffered greatly from Parkinson's disease for several years before he died and was confined to his room. He offered his suffering up for his sins. Father Peter Claver was canonized in 1888 by Pope Leo XIII and declared patron of all missionary work among the Negroes.[1341]

Peter Damian, St. (1007–1072)

Doctor of the Church, Benedictine cardinal, mystic, and visionary born in Ravenna, Italy as the youngest child in a large family. After being orphaned at an early age, Peter was sent to live with a brother who mistreated him. He was educated in Parma, became a professor, and basically lived an austere life. In 1035, he joined the Benedictines at Fonte Avellana. After ordination, he went on to found five hermitages and worked toward ecclesiastical reform. In 1057, Peter, against his will, was elevated to be the Cardinal Bishop of

---

[1340] Delaney, 113–14, Catholic saints; Farmer, 425–26; NCE 2nd ed., v. 3, 316–18.

[1341] Schouppe, *Purgatory*, 357–58; Delaney, 121–22; Ghezzi, 546–47; Guiley, 279; Farmer, 110; NCE 2nd ed., v. 3, 770–71; Tylenda, 294–97.

Ostia. This Benedictine wrote prolifically on purgatory, the Eucharist, and clerical celibacy. He denounced immorality and simony. Peter revealed that on the feast day of the Assumption, the Blessed Virgin Mary delivers several thousand souls from purgatory. He once claimed that he knew a man who lived a life of worldly amusement, then died in his sin. Later, this mystic reported seeing a vision of this poor man's soul in hell where he was immersed in a fiery pool with others who were howling and screaming in pain. Peter Damian was never formally canonized. He was declared a Doctor of the Church in 1828 by Pope Leo XII.[1342]

Peter Nolasco, St. (c. 1182–1256)

Founder of the Mercedarian Order, mystic, and visionary born into a noble family at Mas-des-Saintes-Puellesnear, Castel Nauday, France. Peter was noted for his piety as a youth. According to pious tradition, the Blessed Virgin Mary appeared to him on August 10, 1218. After mature deliberation and moved by this heavenly vision, he resolved to found a religious order. In this, he was encouraged by his confessor, St. Raymond of Penafort (1175–1275), and King James I of Aragon who, it seems, had been favored with the same inspiration (vision or dream). The institute that resulted from this vision or dream was called Mercedarians or the Order for the Redemption of Captives. Its members were bound by a special vow to employ all their means and wealth for the redemption of captive Christians, and if necessary, to remain in captivity in their stead. Peter himself twice served as a captive in Africa ensuring the release of over four hundred captives. Supposedly hundreds of Christians were ransomed from Muslims

Apparition of the Virgin to Saint Peter Nolasco

in Valencia and Grenada. Mary is called Our Lady of Ransom because of her protection from foreign invaders in Spain and for her intercession against religious error throughout the country. Many today ask Our Lady of Ransom to "free us" from the bondage of sin.[1343]

Peter of Atroa, St. (773–837)

Abbot, mystic, and visionary born the eldest of three children near Ephesus, Asia Minor (Modern Turkey) and christened Theophylact. Following a message from the Blessed Virgin Mary, he became the spiritual student of St. Paul the Hesychast (d. 805) who named him Peter. On the day of his ordination in Zygos, Greece, Peter exorcized a possessed man at the door of the church. This was the beginning of a ministry of healing. This servant of God was also a well sought-after confessor who could read the souls of his parishioners. He set out on a pilgrimage with his teacher Paul to Jerusalem, but they did not make it there. A mystical vision from God turned them around and sent them to Mount Olympus where Paul founded a monastery near Atroa. Peter succeeded Paul as abbot but was forced to close the monastery years later due to the iconoclastic persecution under Emperor Leo the Armenian. Peter then went off to Ephesus and Crete. When he returned back to Atroa, he found he was a wanted man. He escaped imperial troops by miraculously becoming invisible. Peter settled at Kalonaros near the Hellespoint, but his fame as a healer forced him to move on. His wonder-working caused an accusation of practicing magic and invoking devils but he was completely cleared by St. Theodore the Studite (759–826).[1344]

Philip Romolo Neri, St. (1515–1595) (aka The Apostle of Rome)

Dominican mystic, visionary, and ecstatic, Founder of the Congregation of the Oratory, and co-founder of the Confraternity of the Most Holy Trinity (40-hours devotion), born in Florence, Italy. At the age of eighteen, Philip had a mystical experience that turned him to the religious life. He received word in a vision that he had an apostolate in Rome. After this, Philip cut himself off from his family and went to that great city to study philosophy and theology.

The day before Pentecost in 1544, while praying in the catacomb of Saint Sebastian, Philip felt, in an extraordinary way, "filled with God." At that time, he received a vision of a great globe of fire that appeared and entered through his mouth and lodged in his heart, setting it aflame.

During this ecstasy, Philip felt that his heart in his chest was as large as his fist. At once he began to experience loud palpitations of the heart and an unbelievable sensation of heat and fire. His body then began to shake violently. A swelling about the size of his fist arose at the side of his heart and remained there for the rest of his life. After his death, an autopsy revealed that the swelling that had existed from that experience was caused by two broken ribs which were raised to form an arch over his enlarged heart. The pulmonary artery was very large but the other organs appeared normal. The doctors attested that the cause was supernatural and could not explain how Philip had lived without experiencing extreme pain. On the contrary, the future saint seemed to glow visibly with the flames of love. He kept his windows open and never wore a coat, even in the winter, because the heat of his ardors was so intense.

This servant of God entered the priesthood late in life. He was ordained in 1551 at the age of thirty-six. A man of advanced spirituality, Philip evangelized thousands of people in Rome, from the poor to popes. He numbered among his friends such saints as Ignatius of Loyola, Camillus de Lellis, Charles Borromeo (1538–1584), Catherine dei Ricci, and Francis de Sales.

Father Neri often had to hurry through Mass to avoid levitating. It is said that many times he had to lean against the altar to keep from collapsing in rapture at the consecration. The Dominican heard confessions for hours at a time. He possessed the mystic gift of cardiognosis whereby he knew one's secret thoughts and could tell penitents their sins before they even confessed them. He also possessed the gift of conferring visions. Philip once converted a nobleman by showing him a vision of hell. Aside from experiencing ecstasies and multiple visions, this Apostle of Rome

---

[1344] Delaney, 402–3; Saint.sqpn.com.

Apparition of the Virgin to Saint Peter Nolasco

had the gift of bilocation, prophecy, and was credited with performing miracles. In fact, he was said to cure many people with just the touch of his hand. Philip is likewise credited with raising the dead both during his life and through his intercession after death. This great mystic had a tender devotion towards the holy souls in purgatory and confessed that many of those under his spiritual direction appeared to him after death, either to ask his prayers or to thank him for what he had already done for them. Philip is also said to have had unusually strong powers over demons. His cell was often radiant with light that emanated from his body. When enraptured his face glowed with unearthly radiance. He was beatified in 1615 by Pope Paul V and canonized in 1622 by Pope Gregory XV.[1345]

Pio of Pietrelcina, St. (1887–1968) (aka Francesco Forgione, St. Pio of Pietrelcina)

Capuchin-Franciscan priest, mystic, visionary, ecstatic, stigmatic, and victim soul born Francesco Forgione in Pietrelcina in the Province of Benevento, Italy. From early childhood, little Francesco exhibited a spiritual sensitivity bordering on mysticism. By the time he was five, he was already having mystical experiences, including ecstasies, visions of the Madonna, and occasional harassment from diabolical forces. Being extremely pious and prayerful, he preferred being alone with God to the company of others. Young Francesco was on fire with the love of God, particularly evident was his devotion to Mary.

[1345] Schouppe, *Purgatory*, 318–19; Johnson, 39, 149, 319, 326; Cruz, Inc., 211; NCE 2nd ed., v. 10, 248–49; Aradi, 172; Hebert, 123; Guiley, 283–84; Delaney, 364–65 http://www.catholic-forum.com/saints; Paul Turks, *Philip Neri: The Fire of Joy,* tr. Daniel Utrecht of the Oratory, NY: Alba House, 1995.

Photograph of Padre Pio performing Mass / TAN Books

Francesco claimed to have experienced heavenly visions and ecstasies, and his mother attested to the fact that he spoke with Jesus, Mary, and his guardian angel as a child. He joined the ascetic Capuchin order in 1902 and was ordained on August 10, 1910 taking the name of "Pio". Later, on September 7, 1910, Padre Pio was given the first transitory signs of the visible stigmata. He felt burning pains and, at times, red and swollen patches would appear, then they would disappear. His superiors had seen these patches themselves, which he tried to conceal from everyone else. From 1910 to 1918, the friar suffered the invisible stigmata continually during the pre-stage of the permanent crucifixion.

By 1916, Padre Pio was assigned to Our Lady of Grace friary in San Giovanni Rotondo, Italy where he remained until the end of his life, except for about a six-month stint in military service during WWI. Due to his frail condition, he was later discharged after having developed double bronchial pneumonia. The newly ordained friar is said to have asked his spiritual adviser at the time for permission to beseech Our Lord to accept him as a victim soul to alleviate the sufferings of souls in purgatory and to win souls for heaven. God apparently accepted the offer as Padre Pio began to suffer a number of mysterious illnesses that left him wracked in pain. He was to come down with prolonged influenza, tuberculosis, intestinal problems, excruciating headaches, failing eyesight, asthma attacks, and high fevers. His temperature during his sufferings at times reportedly reached 120–125 degrees Fahrenheit, resulting in several broken thermometers.

On August 5, 1918, like St. Teresa of Avila, Padre Pio had an intellectual vision in which an angel hurled with all its might a long sharp-pointed steel blade that seemed to spew out fire into his soul. The pain was so intense that he thought he was dying. He felt as if his interior organs had ruptured. The wound remained open and caused him continual agony. This is known as the mystical gift of transverberation—a spiritual wound of love that transfixed his heart.

Then, on September 20, 1918, immersed in prayer while sitting in the monastery choir before an ancient crucifix, a heavenly visitor come and pierced his body with the Five Sacred Wounds of Christ. Suddenly Padre Pio collapsed and the wounds of the visible stigmata appeared on his body. His were the full wounds of Christ in the feet, hands, and side. Physicians who examined the wounds declared that "they pierced the palms of the hands completely so that one could see light through them." Witnesses attest that the wound in the side was shaped like a cross, a slash about three inches long that cut parallel to the ribs. He was the first priest in history to receive the five wounds of Christ. The wounds of his stigmata are also the longest lasting ones on record. They were to last some fifty years until his death in 1968 whereupon they disappeared

completely without even leaving a scar. It was said that the blood from these wounds gave forth a perfume which did not resemble any man-made perfume. It reportedly had a scent somewhere between roses and violets. This numinous odor was associated with his earthly visits after death.

It is purported that Padre Pio had daily communications with his guardian angel. He believed that God used the angel to make it possible for him to understand foreign languages that he had not learned and to have clairvoyant knowledge of secrets within the heart. He became a marked target of the "evil one" because he had helped save countless souls from ruin and damnation. This victim soul was frequently plagued with encounters with demons, being attacked by them spiritually, mentally, and physically. In fact, he was reportedly often beaten by them and even seriously injured. His bouts with the devil sometimes lasted entire nights. The enemy would throw things at him, curse him with filthy words, pull him out of bed, and beat him unmercifully, leaving him with cuts and bruises over his entire body. He was once found in his room on the floor in a pool of blood. His face was swollen and blood was pouring from his nose and cuts above his eyebrows. A pillow was said to have been placed under his head by the Blessed Virgin. This bloodstained pillow is still shown at his cell in Our Lady of Grace Friary in San Giovanni Rotondo.

Padre Pio declared that the devil appeared to him "in the most abominable form." At times as a black cat; another time as a naked woman who danced lasciviously in his room. The devil is also said to have used diabolical tricks to increase Padre Pio's torment. He would appear to him in the form of various friends, colleagues, his confessor and superiors, even in the form of the reigning pontiff and of Jesus, Mary, St. Francis, and his guardian angel. These were also said

Colorized photograph of Padre Pio / TAN Books

Masses would last up to four hours. This servant of God also possessed miraculous healing powers. He had a long history of miraculous cures. Just a small sampling of these types of cures include curing Gemma Di Giorg, the daughter of Count Marzotta of blindness. The girl was born with no pupils. After the friar's intercession, she was able to see. Likewise, Father Pio healed the Marchioness Giovanna Rizzani Boschi of an incurable disease. He also cured others of such illnesses as extreme pneumonia, tongue diseases, kidney failure, heart and thyroid disease, etc. It is claimed that this favored soul once brought a boy killed in an auto accident as well as a six-month-old baby back to life.

Although he never left his friary in San Giovanni Rotondo after 1918, Padre Pio freely contradicted inviolable laws of nature by appearing in two places at the same time in order to help people in trouble. Witnesses from all over Italy and as far as Hawaii and even Uruguay reported that he appeared to them for several minutes, solid and alive. He would comfort them and then disappear. The purpose of his bilocations were to perform miraculous healings, in response to the many prayers made to him for his intercessions. He was also visited by many deceased people who needed his prayers to help them with their after-death growth so they could attain the development necessary for heaven. This favored soul also had the ability to read hearts, had the gift of tongues, the gift of conversions, the odor of sanctity, and the extraordinary abstinence of need for much sleep and nourishment. He was also known to have the gift of prophecy. On numerous occasions, he even predicted the time of his own death. Pio of Pietrelcina was beatified on May 2, 1999 and canonized in the summer of 2002 by Pope John Paul II. He is the patron saint of adolescents.[1346]

to include apparitions such as an "angel of light." However, this holy Capuchin had the gift of discernment of spirits and was able to distinguish between real apparitions of Jesus, Mary, and the saints and the illusions created by the devil by carefully analyzing his state of his mind and the feelings produced in him during the apparitions. He recognized the diabolical ruse by a certain feeling of apprehension and disgust, and to prove the true identity of the apparitions, he insisted that the demon utter words of praise to Jesus Christ. An order the "evil one" always refused. Whereas diabolical visions gave Padre Pio an uneasy and unholy feeling, actual visions of holy persons gave him a feeling of love, exhilaration, and contentment.

Padre Pio was frequently enraptured while celebrating his holy Mass. His face took on a radiant glow, especially during the consecration of the Eucharist. Some of his

1346 Johnson, 132, 158–59, 301; NCE 2nd ed., v.

Rafqa De Himlaya, St. (1832–1914) (aka Rafqa Petronilla Shabaq Ar-Reyes, Rafka, The Little Flower of Lebanon, the Purple Rose, Boutrosiya)

Maronite nun, mystic, visionary, and victim soul born into the El-Choboq family in Himlaya, Lebanon (near Bikfaya Mten). Her mother died when she was six years old, and from 1843–1847, she had to work as a house maid. Rafqa allegedly heard a voice telling her, "You will become a nun." In 1853, she entered the Marian Order of the Immaculate Conception at the Convent of Our Lady of Rescue in Bikfaya, Lebanon taking the name of Anissa (Agnes). In 1860, this religious order was reorganized into the Sacred Heart of Jesus and Mary. Throughout her life, Rafqa was gifted with extraordinary revelations as well as locutions, dreams, and visions. In 1871, her religious order was united with another to form the Order of the Sacred Heart of Jesus and Mary. Each sister was given the choice of staying or leaving. Rafqa claimed she dreamt that St. Anthony the Hermit (251–356) told her to become a nun in the ascetic Baladiya Order of the Maronites. At the age of thirty-nine, the "Little Flower of Lebanon" responded to this dream by joining the cloistered Saint Simon Convent located in El-Qarn where she was known as Boutrosiya from Himlaya. It was there on August 25, 1873 that she made her perpetual vows taking the name of Rafqa (Rebecca) after her saintly mother. As a member of this ascetic order, Rafqa asked Our Lord to share in His suffering as a victim soul. From that time on her health began to deteriorate. She soon became blind, crippled, and eventually paralyzed. She suffered these afflictions joyfully to the end of her life. It was noted that a few nights after Rafqa's funeral a radiant light appeared around her tomb. Her grave site still draws thousands of Christian and Muslim pilgrims. The light is said to reappear whenever a cure occurs there. This Lebanese Maronite nun was declared venerable in 1982, beatified in 1985 and canonized on June 10, 2001 by Pope John Paul II

Rita of Cascia, St. (1381–1457) (aka Margherita of Cascia, Rita La Abogada de Imposibles, Saint of the Impossible and Desperate Cases, Miracle Worker of Cascia)

Augustinian mystic, visionary, stigmatic, and victim soul born at Roccaporena, near Spoleto, Italy to elderly parents. This so-called Saint of the Impossible was a miracle baby. Legend has it that an angel appeared to Amata Ferri and told her that after twelve years of a childless marriage, she would bear a daughter and name her Margherita. Later her name was shortened to Rita. When Rita was only a few months old, her parents left her in a basket under a shady tree while they cut wheat in nearby fields. A peasant who had cut his hand was looking for help when he saw bees swarming around the baby's mouth. He brushed them away and his wound was suddenly

10, 750–51; Charles Carty, Rev., *Padre Pio–The Stigmatist*, Rockford, Ill.: TAN Books and Publishers, 1973; Ann Ball, *Modern Saints, Their Lives and Faces*, 415–25; Bernard C. Ruffin, *Padre Pio: The True Story*, Huntington, Ind.: Our Sunday Visitor, 1995; Rega, 3, 40, 249, 264; Hebert, 154, 241; Guiley, 266–67; Farmer, 437; Freze, TBWC, 148–49, 167–68, 194–97, 209–10, 283; Freze, VVA, 285–87; Cruz, MMM, 229–31; Biot, 40–42; Treece, APP, 36; Wilson, 144; Francisco Sanchez-Ventera y Pascual, 43–71; Ghezzi, MM, 73–80; Cruz, A&D, 182, 192, 206–7.

healed. This miracle of the bees was the first of many in Rita's life.

Rita married the wealthy Paolo Mancini against her will at age sixteen and bore him twin sons. After enduring eighteen years of an unhappy, abusive marriage, her unfaithful, violent husband who had treated her cruelly, was stabbed to death in a brawl. Her two sons had vowed to avenge their father's death, but they themselves died during an epidemic before they could carry out their threat. In 1413, after the death of her sons, Rita applied to enter the Augustinian Convent of St. Mary Magdalen at Cascia but was refused entry because of a stipulation against accepting widows. Then, one night, three great saints appeared to Rita in a dream: Sts. Augustine of Hippo, Nicholas of Tolentino, and John the Baptist. They led Rita to the Augustinian Convent where bolted gates and locked doors miraculously opened. The next morning, the astonished sisters found the widow praying in their chapel. Needless to say, this future saint was admitted to the order and lived in this convent for the next forty years.

Rita became known for her austerities, penances, and concern for others. She is said to have brought many souls back to religion through her prayers. Once, she is said to have exorcised a demon from a woman who had been possessed for many years. This saintly soul was devoted to the Passion of Christ and experienced many visions. One such vision was that of a ladder with God at the top and angels ascending and descending. In 1441, in response to a prayer to suffer as Christ, she received a thorn-induced wound in the middle of her forehead which bled for fifteen years. This single stigma wound became infected and had little worms in it. It emitted such a supernaturally putrid odor that her sister nuns made her live isolated from them. Many claimed that they saw a powerful

Saint Rita (TAN Books)

light coming from this mysterious wound, a sign of God's intervention in the life of this holy victim soul.

Confined to her bed the last four years of her life, Rita ate little more than the Eucharist (inedia). Three days before her death at age seventy-six, this servant of God was blessed with a vision of Our Lord and His Holy Mother. St. Rita's life exhibited heroic virtue and sanctity beyond question, stigmata or no stigmata. When she died, the bells of the city were said to have been joyously pealed by angels. In addition, the sweet odor of sanctity filled her cell and an astounding light emanated from the stigma wound on her forehead. It was said that the wound shone and glistened like a jewel and the little worms were transformed into sparks of light. Rita's body has remained fragrant ever since her death with this sweet odor of sanctity. Numerous miracles have been attributed to her after death.

Her intact and incorrupt body which is displayed in a glass case in the Basilica of St. Rita in Cascia, Italy has shifted positions several times since her death in 1457. The eyes of her body reportedly have said to have opened and closed unaided. Moreover, her dead body has been seen to rise to the top of her reliquary on several occasions. St. Rita of Cascia is venerated as the patron saint of desperate, seemingly impossible causes and situations. She was beatified in 1627 by Pope Urban VIII and canonized in 1900 by Pope Leo XIII.[1347]

Rose of Lima, St. (1586–1617) (aka Rosa de Santa Maria; Patroness of the Americas)

Dominican tertiary, mystic, visionary, ecstatica, stigmatic, and victim soul born Isabel de Santa Maria de Flores in Lima, Peru, the eleventh child of Spanish-Indian parents. Isabel took the name Rose at her confirmation. This future saint exhibited unusual sanctity. She practiced great austerities. While still a child, she undertook fasts and other mortifications. During a good part of her life, Rose lived on nothing but a bread soup (inedia). She took St. Catherine of Siena as her model and built for herself a small chapel in the family garden. From the time of her childhood, she reportedly had beautiful visions of Our Lord, His Mother, angels and saints, and especially of her mentor, St. Catherine of Siena. She is said to have received instruction from her visions. Rose especially was to experience many apparitions, inner locutions,

Saint Rose of Lima, 1670, by Bartolomé Esteban Murillo

and conversations with Our Lady. She once saw Mary appear to her as the Queen of the Most Holy Rosary, dressed in a Dominican habit. It was a reaffirmation that Rose was called to live the life of a Dominican tertiary.

On another occasion, the Blessed Virgin appeared to her with the infant Jesus on her knee. Mary gave Him over to her who she called "Rose of St. Mary." Rose then embraced Him sweetly in her arms. This favored soul reportedly saw Jesus as a child many times and her heroic penances and gift of contemplation ultimately culminated in her mystical marriage to Our Lord. The Lord said to her, "Rose of My Heart, be my bride." God let it be known to her that she was so favored in this mystical state that she would never have to suffer the pains of purgatory.

[1347] Joseph A. Sicardo, *St. Rita of Cascia,* tr. Dan J. Murphy, Rockford, Ill.: TAN Books and Publishers, 1993; Johnson, 136, 158, 319–20; Delaney, 432; Freze, TBWC, 261; Guiley, 294–96; Gallick, 154; www.newadvent.org/cathen; www.catholic-forum.com; NCE, v. 12, 514; NCE 2nd ed., v. 12, 255; Cruz, Inc.,130–34; Cruz, MMM, 223, 386–87; Farmer, 456; Dunbar, 2:189–90; *Book of Augustinian Saints*, 53–56; Cruz, A&D, 73, 208–9.

Rose experienced mystical gifts and visions of such an extraordinary nature that a commission of priests and doctors was appointed to examine her. They ultimately decided that these gifts were of a supernatural origin. When earthquakes struck the city of Lima, Rose was credited through her prayers with sparing the city. Through the blessings of the Child Jesus, Rose is said to have been instrumental, while alive, in the cures of many souls who were afflicted with chronic diseases. Along with St. Martin de Porres, she ministered to the poor black slaves from Africa.

Like many of the great mystics and stigmatists, Rose was plunged into the purifying "dark night of the soul". She suffered extreme anguish in this state for many years. Her bouts with the devil are well known. Satan frequently threatened and assaulted this childlike saint in an attempt to take her from God. Rose once saw her guardian angel before the throne of God, pleading with Him for help during her torment and trials.

This servant of God possessed the gift of bilocation and the odor of sanctity. Because of Rose's profound devotion to the Passion of Our Lord and her heroic efforts to associate herself with those who suffered, Jesus gave her a share of His Cross by imprinting the Five Sacred Wounds (stigmata) in her heart. Rose may have received the crown of thorn wounds from Our Lord as well. This future saint apparently had prophesized the exact date of her death as well as the pains she would suffer, a prophecy which she received during a vision of the Sacred Heart. In death, her body was simply beautiful, supple, and fragrant. Eighteen months after her death, her incorrupt body was found exuding a delightful perfume. Through her intercession after death, two people were claimed to have been raised to life and many sick people were cured. Rose was beatified in 1668 by Pope Clement IX and canonized in 1671 by Pope Clement

X. She has been named "Patroness of the Americas" and the first American saint.[1348]

Rose of Viterbo, St. (1235–1252) (aka Rosa of Viterbo)

Poor Clare mystic, visionary, and ecstatica born of poor and pious parents in Viterbo, Italy, some forty miles north of Rome. During a serious illness at age eight, the Blessed Virgin Mary appeared and miraculously healed Rose and instructed her to join the Third Order of St. Francis of Assisi. Our Lady wanted her to continue to live at home in Viterbo to preach penance and to witness to the blessings of God in her own neighborhood. Later on, Rose had a vision of a wounded and bloody Christ who told her to fight without ceasing for God and the Church. For at that time, Emperor Frederick II (1194–1250) was at war with the pope and had conquered northern Italy. When Frederick marched into Viterbo and was welcomed by local princes, twelve-year-old Rose could not accept this. She began preaching in the streets, urging her neighbors to remain loyal to the Holy Father. Rose rallied so much opposition that the governor of Viterbo banished her and her parents for two years to Soriano for being a threat to imperial power. Rose prophesied that the emperor would soon die. This prophecy was realized a week after she made it. When papal power was restored, Rose returned to Viterbo in triumph.

Rose had hoped to join the local Poor Clares but the abbess was reluctant to

[1348] *The Rose and the Lily*, NY: 1961; Mary Alphonsus, *St. Rose of Lima*, Rockford, Ill.: TAN Books and Publishers, 1993; Delaney, 438; Hebert, 140, 284; Cruz, MMM, 212, 254, 395; Dorcy, 364–66; Wiebe, 20; Lord, VMS, 69, 82, 84; Walsh, v. 3, 126; Freze, TBWC, 166, 171, 207, 266; Gallick, 253, 436; Guiley, 298–300; Dunbar 2:196–98; NCE, 1st ed., v. 12, 673–74; NCE, 2nd ed., v. 12, 378–79.

Communion of St. Rose of Viterbo, 1667, by Juan Antonio de Frías y Escalante

admit her because of her celebrity status and because she had no dowry. This pious youngster had yet another vision of Our Lord, who appeared before her suspended on His cross, nailed by His hands and feet, and crowned with thorns. His body bore many marks of torture and abuse. At the sight of this vision, Rose fainted. When she regained consciousness, Christ told her that "the sins of men have done this to me." Rose died at age seventeen and was buried in her parish graveyard. Seven years later, she appeared to Pope Alexander IV (1254–1261) three times in dreams, telling him that it was God's will that she be placed with the Poor Clares. Alexander ordered her body moved to the convent that had rejected her. Her incorrupt heart was extracted and placed in a reliquary. Her incorrupt body is enshrined in the Monastero Clarisse S. Rosa in Viterbo. She was canonized in 1457 by Pope Callistus III.[1349]

Salvator of Horta, St. (1520–1567) (aka Salvatore of Horta; Salvador d'Horta)

Franciscan brother, mystic, and visionary born to a poor family at Santa Coloma de Farnes near Girona (Catalonia), Spain. Salvator worked as a shepherd and shoemaker until he became a Franciscan lay brother at Barcelona. As a lay brother, he worked as a cook and a porter at the friary in Horta. He acquired a reputation as a healer and his cell became a destination for the sick especially the blind, lame, and deaf, many of whom he cured. Salvator was devoted to the Blessed Virgin Mary and to St. Paul, the latter of whom appeared to him on several occasions and most notably on his death bed. He was canonized by Pius XI on April 17, 1938.[1350]

Seraphim of Sarov, St. (1759–1833)

Russian mystic, visionary, and ecstatic born Prokhor Moshnin at Kursk. As a boy, he was said to have been healed by a wonder-working icon of Our Lady of Kursk. In 1780, Seraphim fell ill and remained bedridden for three years. During this time, he was consoled by visions of the Blessed Virgin and the Apostles. Ordained a priest in 1793, he celebrated the Eucharist every

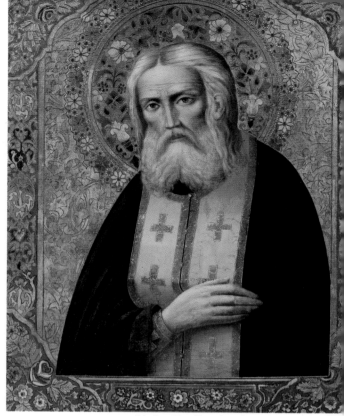
Saint Seraphim of Sarov, by anonymous

day, then a rare practice in Russia. During the liturgy on one Holy Thursday, it is said that Father Seraphim saw angels who were serving and singing in church. He also saw Jesus Christ Almighty in the form of the Son of Man. This mystic's face was observed to be brighter than the sun and he reportedly exuded an odor of sanctity. It is also claimed that Seraphim often had to abandon celebrating Mass because he would lose consciousness of his surroundings during the raptures which frequently came upon him. In 1794, with the blessings of his superior, Seraphim became a hermit living in the depths of the forest and caring for wild animals such as foxes, hares, wolves, and bears. In 1804, this servant of God was attacked by robbers who beat him and left him for dead. In this dire state, Seraphm was said to have had a four-hour visitation from the Blessed Virgin Mary, along with the apostles Peter and John. After being healed, he shut himself up in a cell at the Sarov Monastery,

[1349] Cruz, SS, 658–59; Cruz, MMM, 39–40; NCE, lst ed., v. 12, 674; NCE 2nd ed., v. 12, 379–80; Brewer, 20; Cowan, 396; Gallick, 265, 439; Guiley, 300; Baring-Gould 9:57–65; Dunbar 2:195–96.
[1350] NCE 2nd ed., v. 12, 630.

Vision of the Youth Bartholomew (Saint Sergius of Radonezh), by Mikhail Nesterov

near Moscow, in western Russia where he maintained complete silence. Seraphim lived the last twenty-five years of his life as a hermit. His silent seclusion is said to have brought him a number of visions of celestial life. This Russian mystic was purportedly favored with many spiritual gifts to include reading the thoughts of those who came to see him, clairvoyant powers, and the ability to heal physical illnesses. He was also reportedly observed levitating, walking through the air above ground. After some opposition, the former hermit was canonized by the Council of the Russian Church in 1903. Seraphim of Sarov was referred to as a saint by Pope John Paul II in his work entitled *Crossing the Threshold of Hope*.[1351]

[1351] George P. Fedotov (ed.), *Treasury of Russian Spirituality*, Gloucester, MA: Peter Smith, 1969,

Sergius of Radonezh, St. (1314–1392)

Russian mystic, visionary, and ecstatic born with the name of Bartholomew to a noble family of Rostov. While in his mother's womb, Sergius was said to have thrice cried out in church. After his birth, the family moved to Radonezh, about forty miles northwest of Moscow. He apparently had great difficulty learning how to read. Legend has it that an angel gave him "blessed bread" (prosphora) and from that time forward he was able to read. Sergius is most renowned as one of the early Russian forest saints. Following the "voice of God," he set out to a place deep in the

---

242–79; Catholic Wonderworkers; Ghezzi, 624–25; Farmer, 472; NCE 2nd ed., v. 13, 5–6; Fanning, 54–55.

forest to live a life of solitude and secret meditation. Other monks joined him and he soon became an abbot of a small collection of hermits. He was later ordained a priest and organized the monks into a monastery.

Sergius was a miracle worker, an exorcist, and lived in harmony with the wild animals of the forest, even feeding a wild bear by hand. He was granted wondrous visions, the first recorded for a Russian saint. On one occasion, while in prayer, he was favored by a visit from the Virgin Mary and the apostles Peter and John radiant with an ineffable glory. The Mother of God touched him and told him she would bless and protect his monastery and reassured him that after his passing, he would remain the patron of the monastery he founded in Rostov. As the vision ended, Sergius "in ecstasy, stood in trembling awe and wonder," and he was in such ecstasy that his face glowed. Sergius reportedly was assisted in the celebration of Mass by an angel. It is said that fire descended into the chalice after the consecration. This servant of God is famous in Russian history for having a clairvoyant vision whereby he saw Prince Dmitriy of Moscow victorious over the Mongols at the battle of Kulikovo. Allegedly often assaulted by demons, he used prayer to chase them away. Sergius was canonized before 1449, and his cult has been approved by Rome.[1352]

Sharbel Makhluf, St. (1828–1898) (aka Charbel Makhlouf, Sharbel the Maronite)

Maronite Monk and mystic born of religious but poor parents in Beqaa-Kafra (Lebanon) and given the name Joseph Zaroun Makhlouf at baptism. Upon entry into the monastery of St. Maroun at Anaya, Lebanon, Joseph's name was changed to Sharbel, the name of an early martyr in the Church. Ordained in 1859, Sharbel spent twenty-three years as a Maronite Monk in the Hermitage of Sts. Peter and Paul near the monastery. He had a reputation for holiness and practiced severe mortifications. Sharbel was very devoted to the Holy Eucharist and was known to levitate during his prayers. While saying Mass just before his death, the monk was stricken with a fatal illness. His body was not embalmed but consigned to the grave without a coffin. Because of a mysterious bright, divine light that surrounded his tomb for forty-five nights, his body was exhumed. It was found to be incorrupt and in perfect condition, perfectly flexible and lifelike. From the pores of the body a liquid exuded described as "manna-like." An exhumation in 1950 revealed that the fluid constantly exuded from the body and collected, at times, to a depth of three inches in his casket. Many miracles of healing were attributed to this saint after his death. He was beatified in 1965 and canonized in 1977 by Pope Paul VI.[1353]

[1352] The Miracle Hunter, Marian Apparitions; *Treasury of Russian Spirituality*, 50–83; Farmer, 473; Fanning, 47; http://thermaturges.blogspot.com; NCE, 2nd ed., v. 13, 15–16.

[1353] Catholice Wonderworkers; Cruz, MMM, 287, 375; Patron Saints Index; Farmer, 476; NCE, 2nd ed., v. 13, 69.

Madonna Extradites the scapular to St Simeon Stock by Sebestyén Stettner

Simon Stock, St. (1165–1265) (aka Simon Anglus)

Carmelite mystic and visionary born at Aylesford, Kent, England. As a child, Simon had an intense devotion to Mary. While still in his teens, he became a hermit and lived in the hollow of a great tree. Mary is said to have often appeared to him in many visions and advised him to join the Carmelites. In 1247, he was elected Sixth Superior General of the Order of Mt. Carmel. This servant of God is best known for the controversial vision of the Blessed Virgin Mary he had in Cambridge, England, on July 16, 1251. In this vision, the Mother of God is said to have appeared to him with the infant Jesus in her arms and promised salvation to all Carmelites who wore the brown scapular that she displayed to him. At that time, Mary specifically told Simon, "Whoever shall be clothed in this habit shall not suffer the eternal fires."

Speaking of this revelation, Pope Benedict XIV (1740–1758) says, "She [The Blessed Virgin] does not say that those who have worn the scapular will be preserved from eternal fire by this means alone, without having done anything else. Good works and perseverance in well-doing are still necessary for eternal salvation." The revelation of the brown scapular led to the widespread devotion to Mary over the next centuries by those wearing this scapular in her honor. Simon Stock was never formally canonized but is venerated as a saint by the Carmelites and is recognized in some dioceses.[1354]

Stanislaus Kostka St. (1550–1568)

Mystic and visionary born in Rostkono, Poland into high Polish nobility, the second of seven children. Stanislaus was the recipient of some unusual spiritual favors during his short life. On one occasion, while seriously sick, he saw two angels attended by St. Barbara (4th c.), patron of his sodality at school, bringing him Holy Communion. He also reportedly took "Communion from a distance." This young Pole is said to have beheld the Blessed Virgin in a vision holding the Christ Child. In this vision, Mary encouraged him to join the Society of Jesus. Once, while in the middle of saying the Rosary, a woman from purgatory appeared to him in a vision. This departed soul told Stanislaus that the sufferings on earth were nothing compared to those in purgatory. To prove her point, she asked Stanislaus to put out his hand. Suddenly a drop of sweat from the visitor fell upon his skin. Stanislaus screamed with agony as the liquid burned a hole in his hand. This suffering soul claimed this was only

[1354] Schouppe, *Purgatory*, 370; Delaney, 457; Poulain, 37; http://www.newadvent.forgather; Hebert, 43; Guiley, 305–6; NCE, 2nd ed., v. 13, 134; Connell, 46–47.

Saint Stanislaus Kostka Receiving the Holy Communion from the Hands of Angels by Jan van Cleve

a portion of the pain she continuously felt in the depths of purgatory. Moved with compassion, Stanislaus continued to offer his prayers and penances for these suffering souls in their state of purification. It is claimed that this saintly teenager foresaw his imminent death. Early in the morning on the feast of the Assumption, 1568, he told a priest that he saw Mary surrounded by many angels. Shortly afterwards he died. At his death, Stanislaus' face is said to have shone with a most serene light. Upon exhumation of the young man's remains, a fragrance, said to be more exquisite than that of the sweetest flower emanated from them.[1355]

[1355] NCE, lst ed.,v. 8, 258; NCE 2nd ed., v. 8, 242–43; Cruz, MMM, 390; Freze, VVA, 230; Biot, 66; Ghezzi, 518–19; Tylenda, 382–84; Cruz, A&D, 179.

Teresa of Avila, St. (1515–1582) (aka St. Teresa of Jesus)

Carmelite mystic, visionary, ecstatica, invisible stigmatic, and Doctor of the Church born Teresa de Cepeda y Ahumada in Avila, Spain, the third of nine children. As the first woman to be declared a Doctor of the Church, Teresa enjoyed the seraphic heights of mystical union as no other saint did. In her early years, she was torn between the vanities of the world and a spiritual life. A typical upper-class girl, she enjoyed reading romances, dancing, and having nice clothes and good food. Her mother died when she was twelve and she turned to the Blessed Mother for maternal care. Mary often appeared to her to reassure her of her love and to bestow mystical favors upon her. Teresa entered the lax Carmelite Convent of the Incarnation just outside of Avila when she was twenty years of age. She said she was a "gadabout" nun maintaining an active social life for twenty years, not getting serious about her spirituality until she was forty.

One day while praying, Teresa was caught up for the first time in ecstasy. She heard within her these words: "I will not have you hold conversations with men but with angels." Thereafter, the trickle of Teresa's mystical experiences drastically increased. One of her visions was a terrifying revelation of the horrors of hell that galvanized her faith and her commitment. Once again, while praying, she is said to have found herself in the middle of hell. She went on to describe in detail what she saw (see *Book of Her Life* 32, 1–5,). In this vision, the Carmelite was shown the place in hell that would be hers one day if she did not change her ways. From 1555–1556, she experienced a series of heavenly visions which disturbed her and caused her great anguish. Ecstasies and states of rapturous

Saint Teresa of Avila, 1827, by François Gérard

absorption would come upon her, even in public, to her great distress. St. Peter of Alcantara (1499–1562), who became her spiritual director in 1557, convinced her that her visions (and ecstasies) were genuine. Over the next several decades, Teresa had transitory mystical experiences to include ecstasies, visions, apparitions, levitations, deep raptures, and receipt of an invisible stigmata.

Around 1558, this holy soul began to hear interior locutions which her confessors then ordered her to reject. At the age of forty-five, she was favored with visions of Our Lord. These visions were, at first, intellectual and lasted continually for thirty months. Teresa saw Our Savior walking continually on her right side and Sts. Peter and Paul on her left side. Sometime after the first of these visions, she experienced imaginative visions. On the first occasion, she saw Our Lord's hand, a few days later His divine Face, and finally she saw His whole Person. Teresa almost always saw Him as He was after the Resurrection, in His glorified Body. She never

had any exterior visions, nor heard auricular words. God the Father spoke to her at times, the Holy Spirit never, the Word very often, but always by means of His sacred humanity.

The Carmelite also saw her departed friends being taken up to heaven. In a vision of heaven, Teresa saw a particular religious surrounded by angels, standing very close to God. On many occasions, in her visions, she saw all the Jesuits, Franciscans, Carmelites, Dominicans, and Augustinians "together in heaven with white banners in their hands." She had many visions of angels and once saw the Blessed Virgin Mary descend with a multitude of angels at the beginning of the recitation of the "Salve." She immediately fell into ecstasy at the sight. This vision she classified as intellectual.

This holy soul reported in her writings that she physically levitated from time to time. She was extremely embarrassed by these levitations and made efforts to stop them by holding on to the altar rail or ordering her sister nuns to hold her down. Sometime around 1559, God comforted her when others told her these were signs of the devil by granting her the favor of transverberation of the heart (the Wound of Love). It is said that a cherub pierced her heart several times with a long golden spear, which set her on fire for the love of God. Her contemporary and friend St. John of the Cross described Teresa's experience as the "cauterization of her soul." Teresa herself referred to it as "an imaginary vision seen by the eyes of the soul." The pain was very real, however, and lasted several days. At her death, her heart was said to have been found with a fissure consistent with such a wound.

One Christmas vigil, this mystic saw St. Joseph, her beloved patron, in a vision along with the Blessed Virgin praying to Jesus for the reform of the Carmelite Order.

First miracle of Saint Teresa of Jesus. Resurrection of her nephew Don Gonzalo Ovalle by Luis de Madrazo

This vision assured Teresa that God wanted her to establish new reformed communities. This servant of God went on to found fourteen Carmelite reformed convents and fourteen Carmelite reformed monasteries for men throughout Spain. Teresa is also widely acclaimed for her three spiritual masterpieces—her *Autobiography*, which was written at the request of her spiritual directors and largely dealt with her mystical experiences, *The Way of Perfection* (1566), and the *Interior Castle* (1577). In her works, she describes the mystical experience in three stages or phases: the purgative, in which the soul reaches out to God through ascetic practices; the illuminative, in which God reaches back mystically; and the unitive, in which the two draw together intimately. She is best known for the four very different contemplative states which

she calls Mansions of the Interior Castle of the soul. She calls these four spiritual mansions: 1. Prayer of passive recollection and quiet; 2. Prayer of union; 3. Prayer of ecstatic union; 4. Prayer of perfect union, or spiritual marriage. This last mystical state is when the soul receives the blessings of a spiritual marriage with the heavenly Spouse as a sign of its total union with God. This state is also referred to as mystic marriage, mystic union, and exchange of hearts. On November 18, 1572, at the age of fifty-seven, while receiving communion from the hands of St. John of the Cross, she herself received the favor of the spiritual marriage.

By her prayers and good works, St. Teresa helped deliver many souls from purgatory. God often showed her the souls for whom she prayed as they were released from purgatory into paradise. She is also said to have raised her six-year-old nephew Gonzalo from a premature death. Teresa claims to have rarely seen Satan in a bodily form although she knew of his presence through a vision. She did, however, see other demons in most hideous forms. The saintly nun reported experiences in which diabolic agents sought her undoing. She said she would use holy water to put them to flight. One time, when she was sixty-two years old, the Carmelite is said to have broken her arm when she was thrown down a flight of stairs by demonic forces.

Teresa was privileged to die on the feast of St. Francis of Assisi, October 4, 1582 during a prolonged ecstasy. It is believed that at her death, the Lord came personally with His Mother, St. Joseph, and many other saints to gather her soul. Her incorrupt body exuded a powerful scent of supernatural roses known as the odor of sanctity. Her body was not embalmed but found to be incorrupt nine months later. It still remains so today. An examination of her heart after death revealed that it still bore the wound of the angel, a deep horizontal wound almost dividing the heart in two. At her exhumation, the provincial ordered that her left hand be removed as a relic. As it was removed, oil issued out from it. Not only her left hand but the left arm was also amputated. They were given to the convent at Alba de Tormes when the body was removed to the saint's native Avila. Teresa was beatified in 1614 by Pope Paul V and canonized in 1622 by Pope Gregory XV. She was declared Doctor of the Church in 1970 by Pope Paul VI for her teaching on prayer.[1356]

[1356] NCE , 1st ed., v. 13, 1013–17; NCE 2nd ed., v. 13, 826–30; Cruz, Inc., 186–90; MMM, 36, 515; A&D, 33, 43, 81, 173–74; *Collected work of St. Teresa of Avila*, 414; Hebert, 188, 239; Freze, TBWC, 181, 202, 262; Fanning, 155; Ghezzi, VOS, 486–87; MM, 125–29; 187; Gallick, 311, 444; Guiley, 317–20; Johnson, 29ff, 68, 128,

Portrait of Saint Therese of the Child Jesus, Carmelite religious / Photo © Gusman / Photo © Patrice Cartier / Bridgeman Images

Therese of Lisieux, St. (1873–1897) (aka Therese of the Child Jesus and of the Holy Face, "The Little Flower")

Carmelite mystic, visionary, ecstatica, victim soul, Doctor of the Church (1997), and co-patroness of France born as Marie-Francoise Therese Martin at Alencon, France, the youngest of nine children. Pope Pius XI (1922–1939) called her "the star of my pontificate." At the age of ten, Therese fell seriously ill. She blamed the illness on the devil who was angry at the family because her older sister had entered

---

136, 250, 325; Lord, VHHP, 153, 160; Wiebe, 17; Poulain, 5–6, 24; R. Brown, 122, 125; Schouppe, *Purgatory*, 11; Underhill, *Mystics*, 175; Fargas, 28, 117–19; Connell, 55–60; Flinders, 155–90.

the convent. Her illness brought fits of delirium and strange behavior as well as great suffering. She was cured one day when she had a vision in which a statue of the Blessed Virgin Mary came to life and smiled at her. On Christmas Eve of 1886, Therese had yet another mystical experience which she later called "my conversion." On that night, she had a vision of the infant Jesus which she claimed filled her soul with light.

Therese was admitted to the Carmelites at Lisieux at the age of fifteen and was professed two years later, taking the name of Therese of the Child Jesus and of the Holy Face. During her novitiate, she reportedly had transports of love, or raptures, in which she felt far removed from the earth. In 1895, while in prayer, she offered herself as a victim soul to "God's merciful love." Once, upon beginning the stations of the cross, Therese felt herself wounded by a flaming dart and thought she would die from the intensity of the fire of divine love. The experience was similar to the transverberation, or piercing of the heart with fiery arrows and blades, as experienced by Sts. Teresa of Avila and Padre Pio.

Therese is the author of *The Story of a Soul*, which became one of the most widely read modern spiritual autobiographies. As one of the Church's most influential mystics, she reported having only one apparition and never had any spectacular mystic gifts but said she never wanted any. "To ecstasy," she said, "I prefer the monotony of sacrifice." This is ironic because in more than one hundred years since her agonizing death from tuberculosis, "The Little Flower" has appeared in more creditable apparitions and healings than any other saint, except perhaps Our Lady, St. Francis, and her namesake St. Teresa of Avila, all of whom had long head starts. Therese's countenance was beautiful in death and she was said to have worn a mysterious smile on her lips. Moreover, upon exhumation in 1910, her body exuded a strong scent of violets. Therese was beatified in 1923 and canonized in 1925 by Pope Pius XI. She was declared a Doctor of the Church in 1997 by Pope John Paul II.[1357]

Thomas Aquinas, St. (c. 1225–1272) (aka The Angelic Doctor).

Dominican mystic, visionary, ecstatic, and Doctor of the Church born as Tomasso Aquino at the family castle of Roccasecca near Aquino, Italy. A hermetic prophet once told his mother Theodora that her son would be extremely holy and learned and would enter the Order of Friars Preachers. In 1244, Thomas joined the Dominicans and studied in Paris from 1245–48 under St. Albert the Great (c. 1206–1280). He was ordained at Cologne around 1250. Gifted with infused knowledge, Aquinas is probably the greatest theological master of Christianity. His magnum opus, the unfinished *Summa Theologiae*, is unquestionably the greatest exposition of theological thought ever written and has become the accepted basis of modern Christian theology. Thomas is said to have had life changing dreams or visionary experiences that altered the course of his work. During his composition of the *Summa Theologicae*, he struggled with deciphering a theological passage in Isaiah. The next morning he suddenly deciphered it with ease. He told his scribe that he had a dream in which he dialogued with the apostles Peter and Paul

---

[1357] Johnson, 79; Delaney, 379–80; Cruz, MMM, 306, 394; John Fink, *The Doctors of the Church: an introduction to the church's great teachers*, NY: Alba House, c2000, 213; Gallick, 295; Guiley, 323–24; NCE 2nd ed., v. 13, 938–39; Saint Therese, *Autobiography of St. Therese of Lisieux: The story of a soul*, a new translation from the original manuscript by John Clarke, Washington, D.C.: ICS Publications, 1975, 66–67, 97ff, 190; Treece, 219; Flinders, 191–19.

Saint Thomas Aquinas, 1476, by Carlo Crivelli

and they told him what to say. In addition to his towering intellect, Aquinas was a man of great humility and holiness. He had heroic resistance to temptation against purity and was said to have been girded by an angel with a miraculous invisible cincture, a cord of purity, which preserved him from temptations of the flesh for the rest of his life. Asked by Pope Urban IV (1261–1264) to write a proper Mass for the feast of Corpus Christi, the Dominican not only wrote the Mass but the great hymns "O Salutaris Hostia" (O Saving Victim) and "Tantum Ergo." The Angelic Doctor allegedly experienced visions, locutions, ecstasies, and revelations during his lifetime.

One day at Mass, kneeling before the Blessed Sacrament, Thomas heard Christ say to him in a vision, "You have written well of the sacrament of My Body." Struck with ecstasy, the Dominican is said to have levitated and remained suspended off the floor long enough for the phenomenon to be witnessed by everyone present. This gifted theologian left the *Summa Theologiae*, his greatest work, unfinished. It was completed only as far as the ninetieth question of the third part. On December 6, 1272, while saying Mass, Thomas experienced a supernatural vision in an unusually long ecstasy. What was revealed to him we can only surmise from his reply to Father Reginald who urged him to continue his writings (and finish his work): "I can do no more," St. Thomas said, "such secrets have been revealed to me that all I have written seems like straw to me." After that experience, Thomas put his pen aside and would write no more. In time, of course, the Summa was completed by the Dominican theologian Reginald of Piperno (c. 1230–1290) who compiled the remaining materials from earlier writings of Thomas that had yet to be inserted in the Summa. It is said that Thomas' sister, the Abbess

of St. Mary's Convent in Capua, appeared to him in an apparition after her death to thank him for his help in her deliverance from purgatory and to announce to him the fate of his other deceased siblings. Thomas was canonized in 1323 by Pope John XXII and declared a Doctor of the Church and Doctor Angelicus in 1567 by Pope Pius V.[1358]

Saint Thomas of Villanova by Francisco Camilo

Thomas of Villanova, St. (1488–1555) (aka Thomas the almsgiver, God's almoner)

Augustinian mystic, visionary, and ecstatic born as Thomas Garcia Martinez in Fuenllana, Castile, Spain. Thomas joined the Augustinians and was ordained to the priesthood in 1518. He became chaplain to Emperor Charles V (1500–1558) and, on January 1, 1545, reluctantly accepted an appointment as Archbishop of Valencia.

[1358] Schouppe, *Purgatory*, 347–49; Delaney, 480–81; Fink, 79; Freze, VVA, 239; Hebert, 243; Johnson, 107; Dorcy, 75; Catholic Wonderworkers; http://thermatuges.blogspot.com; NCE, 1st ed., v. 14, 132; NCE 2nd ed., v. 14, 13–22; Guiley, 326–28.

This Spanish almsgiver was known for his austerity, poverty of life, and generosity to the poor and needy. He possessed supernatural gifts of healing the sick, multiplication of food, and redressing grievances. He once is said to have fallen into a twelve-hour rapture and levitated. Thomas frequently experienced mystical ecstasies during Mass. On one occasion, when preaching in the Cathedral of Valladolid before the Emperor and a large congregation, he was ravished in ecstasy in the pulpit. Twenty-three years after his burial, his body was still found to be incorrupt. Soon after this, however, it dissolved into dust but remained fragrant. He was beatified in 1618 by Pope Paul V and canonized in 1658 by Pope Alexander VII.[1359]

Tikhon of Zadonsk, St. (1724–1783)

Russian Orthodox bishop, mystic, visionary, and ecstatic born Timothy Sokolovsky in Korotsk to a poor village reader. His inclination to become a monk was said to be reinforced by a vision in which he was directed to live a life of solitude. He did, however, serve as the Bishop of Voronezh for seven years before retiring to the monastery in Zadonsk. Tikhon was reportedly given to ecstasies and visions in his meditations. He is said to have heard the singing of angels and to have engaged in conversations with the Virgin Mary and the apostles Peter and Paul. During one of his meditations, he allegedly beheld Christ descending from the cross, walking toward him, his tortured body covered with wounds and blood. Besides clairvoyance, Tikhon was also favored with the gift of tears. At times during the saying of Mass, he would weep and sob audibly even though many were in attendance. He is known as the author of a work entitled *A Spiritual Treasure Gathered from the World.*[1360]

Tommaso Da Cori, St. (1655–1729) (aka Tommaso Placidi da Cori, OSF, Thomas of Cori)

Franciscan mystic, visionary, and ecstatic born in Cori, Latina, Italy. Orphaned at the age of fourteen, Tommaso was left to take care of his two sisters. After his sisters were married, he became a Franciscan priest. Most of his life was spent in the friary of Civitella (today Bellagra). It is said that Father Cori had apparitions of the child Jesus several times while celebrating Mass. He also was said to fall into ecstasy while distributing communion. Tommaso is said to have experienced apparitions of the Virgin Mary and St. Francis during his lifetime. Once, it is said that he levitated to the roof so rapidly that the congregation thought he had broken his neck against the rafters. He was also raised up horizontally from his bed into the air during his last sickness. Tommaso was favored with the spiritual gifts of miracles, healing and the multiplication of food. This holy soul was beatified in 1785 by Pope Pius VI and canonized by Pope John Paul II on November 21, 1999.[1361]

[1359] Thurston, 238, 250, 391; Ghezzi, VOS, 468; Farmer, 434–35; NCE 2nd ed., v. 14, 38; *Book of Augustinian Saints*, 57–61; Farges, 171; Edward Watkin, *Neglected saints*, NY: Sheed and Ward, 1955, 161–99.

[1360] *Treasury of Russian Spirituality*, 210; http://www.roca.org; Fanning, 50–51.

[1361] NCE, v. 14, 72, 119; NCE Jubilee, 615; Bernard Bangley, *Butler's Lives of the Saints: concise, modernized edition*, Brewster, Massachusetts: Paraclete Press, 2005, 8; Cruz, MMM, 28; http://www.santiebeati.it.

Veronica Giuliani, St. (1660–1727).

Capuchin Poor Clare abbess, mystic, visionary, stigmatic, ecstatica, and victim soul born as Ursula Giuliani in Mercatello, Duchy of Urbino, Italy. This holy soul is considered one of the most extraordinary mystics of the eighteenth century, being favored with revelations, visions, ecstasies, and other graces. Ursula, as she was known then, had a great devotion to the Eucharist and the Sacred Heart of Jesus. She first received visions as a child. When she was four years of age, her dying mother, Benedetta, entrusted each of her five daughters to one of the sacred wounds of Christ. Ursula, the youngest, was assigned to the wound in the side. At the age of ten, Ursula heard God order her "To War! To War!" She at first misunderstood what this meant but later understood it to mean war on the world, the flesh, and the devil. As a teenager, Ursula was inclined to be dictatorial. In her sixteenth year, this imperfection of character was brought home to her in a vision in which she saw her own heart as a heart of steel. In 1677, Ursula was accepted into the Convent of the Capuchin Poor Clares in Citta di Castello taking the name Veronica in memory of Christ's Passion. During the first year of her religious life, sister Veronica suffered the slings and arrows of the devil through her sister novices. The "evil one" took on the identity of some of her fellow sisters accusing her of vile misconduct. When that was not enough to destroy her, he abused her physically, inflicting wounds and bruising her body mercilessly. The Lord gave her the strength not only to withstand these assaults but to infuriate the devil as she laughed at his stupid antics.

Veronica's mystical experiences continued, and she began receiving visions of Christ accompanied by the pain of the

The Blessed Veronica Giuliani Receiving the Stigmata, 1832 (canvas) / Mondadori Portfolio/Electa/Giuliano Ghiraldini / Bridgeman Images

wounds of the Passion. On April 3, 1697, in the presence of her guardian angel, Christ impressed the crown of thorns upon her head. Two days later while in rapture, she beheld a glorious vision of the Risen Lord and Our Lady along with angels. In this vision, Christ told her, "Thou shalt be wounded as I am, wounded with five wounds." The saint prayed for the wounds to disappear but was told during another vision that they were to remain visible for three years. They did, in fact, disappear on April 5, 1700, exactly three years later. After that date, they reappeared intermittently. The wound in the side, however, remained and bled profusely. There was much skepticism concerning her stigmata. She underwent many examinations, but it was never disproven. In 1700, Veronica drew a picture of the instruments of the Passion that, she said, were imprinted on her heart during a vision. Her sketch was confirmed at her autopsy by Prof. Gentili and Dr. Bordiga thirty hours after she died. A post-mortem examination performed in the presence of a bishop and many witnesses showed that her heart bore a number of the figures corresponding to those she had drawn. In fact, the marks on her heart were quite similar to those on the heart of St. Clare of Montefalco.

Veronica also bore a ring of mystical espousal. This union was said to have taken place on April 11, 1694. At that time, Jesus and His Mother accompanied by Sts. Catherine of Siena and Rose of Lima appeared to her. Jesus placed a mystical wedding ring embossed with His name on her finger. Veronica called it her Ring of Love or her Ring of the Cross—warning her of approaching sufferings. The ring consisted of a raised stone as large as a pea and red in color. It was periodically seen by witnesses. As a bride of Christ, this pure soul was to also experience visions of the Blessed Virgin Mary and the Holy Trinity.

Veronica received many other supernatural gifts during her lifetime to include levitation and the multiplication of food. Having been shown and felt the pains of both purgatory and hell, Veronica devoted her life to keeping souls from ending up there by offering herself as a victim soul to hold back the hand of the God of Justice.

At her confessor's command, this Poor Clare sister kept a daily diary of her mystical experiences. These were contained in a ten-volume work entitled *Diary of the Passion* published during her canonization process. Written at the direction of her confessor, these tomes are the best-documented examples of extraordinary mystical experiences. Veronica's body remained incorrupt for many years until it was destroyed during an inundation of the Tiber River. Her incorrupt heart which was extracted after her death is kept in a special reliquary and is said to still be well-preserved. Veronica was beatified in 1804 by Pope Pius VII and canonized in 1839 by Pope Gregory XVI.[1362]

Vincent Ferrer, St. (1350–1419) (aka the "Angel of Judgment")

Dominican missionary, mystic, visionary, stigmatic, and Doctor of Theology born in Valencia, Spain. While preparing to take his vows at the Dominican convent in Valencia, Vincent heard a voice saying, "We are all called to chastity." Confused, he asked the Virgin Mary to help him understand the meaning of these words. Our Lady appeared to him saying, "These words mean that Satan will attempt to weaken or steal your crown of chastity. Trust in me and God, so that the attacks of Satan will be turned against himself." So, supported and reassured by the Mother of God, Vincent was able to overcome temptation. He was ordained a priest in 1378 and later became the confessor of the antipope Benedict XIII (1394–1417). The latter tried to make him a cardinal, but Vincent refused the offer. This celebrated bona fide miracle worker of the order of St. Dominic performed his first miracle when he was still in his mother's womb. A blind woman is said to have pressed against his mother's stomach and was instantly healed. In all, St. Vincent is credited with working thousands of dazzling miracles as well as raising a total of twenty-eight persons from the dead. Once asked how many miracles he had worked, Vincent modestly estimated 3,000. The church had carefully documented 873 of these when it declared him a saint.

[1362] NCE, 2nd ed., v. 6, 234; Aradi, 164, 176; Gallick, 206, 433; www.newadvent.org/cathen; Johnson, 50, 69; Lord, VMS, 257–85, 277–78; Delaney, 215; Farmer, 224; Cruz, MMM, 150; Cruz, Inc., 252–53; Summers,.152–53; Cruz, MMM, 224–26; Freze, TBWC, 268, Ghezzi, VOS, 590–91; 1902 *Catholic Encyclopedia*; Dunbar 2:288; Wilson, 139.

Das Zelebrationswunder des heiligen Vinzenz Ferrer, 1694, by Filippo Lauri

Vincent was also favored with the gift of tongues. Although his native tongue was Limousin, reliable writers attest that all his hearers—French, Greeks, Germans, Sardinians, Hungarians, and Italians—understood every word he spoke.

In 1398, this servant of God became deathly ill and prayed for recovery so that he might continue preaching. Christ, accompanied by Sts. Dominic and Francis of Assisi, appeared to him in a vision and healed him. Jesus allegedly touched Vincent tenderly on the cheek and commanded him to get up. It is said that, in so doing, Jesus left permanent finger marks on his face. The Lord then directed Vincent to preach repentance for sin throughout the whole world in preparation for the Last Judgment. The future saint was told in a very clear and unconditional vision that the end of the world would come in his lifetime, unless people amended their sinful lives. Vincent then went on to spend the last twenty-one years of his life announcing that the judgment of God was at hand, in the everyday sense of the word. He was given ecclesial authority to preach anywhere, but preached mainly throughout Western Europe—mostly in Spain, southern Germany, France, and northern Italy.

Wherever he went, he attracted enormous crowds. Everyone in the crowd could hear him plainly in their own language, no matter how far they stood away from him.

This so-called "Angel of Judgment" enjoyed tremendous success making converts by the tens of thousands. In the Bull of his canonization, it is recorded that he converted approximately 80,000 Jews, 70,000 Moslems, and an incredible number of the most hardened sinners. In Spain alone, he is said to have converted 25,000 Jews and 8,000 Moors. Among his converts were St. Bernadine of Siena and Blessed Margaret of Savoy. In 1412, at Salamanca, preaching before a crowd of 30,000, Vincent brought to life, for the duration of fifteen minutes, a dead woman who was being carried to the cemetery, and who, in turn, confirmed his prediction that the end of the world would come in his lifetime. However, the thousands of conversions he made across Christendom evidently averted God's judgment.

Vincent is often depicted with wings. Multitudes of people have witnessed that in the middle of preaching, reportedly he would suddenly assume wings and fly off to help some suffering person (transport). His hagiographers claim that he delivered seventy people from diabolical possession. Vincent reportedly had such power over demons that it was often simply enough for him to just touch a possessed person for him to be freed. His sister once appeared to him after her death. She said she was condemned to suffer the torments of purgatory until the day of the Last Judgment and asked for his assistance. Vincent was canonized in 1455 by Pope Callistus III.[1363]

[1363] Schouppe, *Purgatory*, 96–97; NCE 2nd ed., v. 14, 520–21; Cruz, MMM, 529; Delaney, 498–99; Dorcy, 187–88; http://www.Catholic-forum.com/saints; Hebert, 166; Ghezzi, VOS, 430–31; Guiley, 343–44; Johnson, 306; Poulain, 36; Andrew Pradel, *St. Vincent Ferrer: Angel of the Judgment*, Rockford, Ill.: TAN Books

Blesseds

Agnes of Jesus, Bl. (1602–1634) (aka Agnes Galand, Agnes of Jesus Joanna Galand, Agnes of Jesus of Langeac, Agnes de Langeac)

Dominican mystic, visionary, ecstatica, and stigmatic born in Le Puy, Haute-Loire France (near Langeac) as Agnes Galand. From the age of seven, this precocious child is said to have had visions and ecstasies. It was claimed that she heard a voice telling her at this time that if she wished to be delivered from the great spiritual anguish she was suffering and protected against all her enemies, she should make herself a servant of Our Lord and His Blessed Mother. Agnes followed this advice and found great peace of soul. The youngster was purported to have been favored with a sensible presence of her guardian angel. At the age of twelve, this future beata was reportedly marked with the stigmata, the wounds of Christ.

When she was nineteen, Agnes received the habit of a Dominican tertiary. She entered the convent at the age of twenty-one and was elected abbess four years later. However, false charges and jealousy were to result in her removal from the convent.

Later on in her life, the Blessed Virgin appeared to her accompanied by St. Cecilia (2nd c.). Mary put a gold chain around her neck to show how happy she was that Agnes had taken their advice to become a servant of both her and her Son. During yet another mystical experience, this young visionary was reportedly transported in

---

and Publishers, 2001; Ghezzi, MM, 108–11; The Miracle Hunter: Marian Apparitions; Paul O'Sullivan, Fr., *The Holy Ghost Our Greatest Friend*, Rockford, Ill.: TAN, 1991.

spirit to a place of expiation where she saw many souls in the midst of flames.

This servant of God was said to have received another visit from the Blessed Mother who asked her to pray for a troubled priest who was living a carefree and irresponsible life. She never met this priest but prayed over the course of three years for him. Agnes is said to have later bilocated to the church where this priest was praying during a retreat given under the direction of St. Vincent de Paul. The priest later turned out to be Father Jean Jacques Olier (1608–1657) who needed prayers at the time to overcome a spiritual crisis in his life. He later founded the Sulpician Order.

When Agnes became bedridden just before her death, Father Olier reportedly came to see her and recognized her from a dream as the Dominican nun who had been praying for him. Agnes died in the odor of sanctity a few months afterwards. Upon her death, this servant of God diffused a "celestial perfume" and obtained startling cures. Agnes was beatified by Pope John Paul II on November 20, 1994.[1364]

Alexandrina Maria Da Costa, Bl. (1904–1955) (aka "The Little Saint of Balasar," Alexandrina of Balasar, Alexandrina of Portugal)

Lay mystic, visionary, ecstatica, invisible stigmatic, and victim soul born in Balasar in the province of Oporto, archdiocese of Braga in Portugal. Alexandrina is considered one of the most important mystics of the twentieth century. As a child, she was a lively tomboy, gifted with a happy and communicative disposition. She was

[1364] Schouppe, *Purgatory*, 229; Butler, 6, 50; Patron Saints Index; http://www.catholic-forum.com/saints; Biot, 25; Gallick , 316, 440; Dunbar 1:38; Dorcy, 386–87; Thurston, 144–45ff; NCE 2nd ed., v. 6, 50; NCE Jubilee, 497; Farges, 31.

Portrait from prayer-card of Blessed Alexandrina placed in the public domain by her Shrine in Balazar.

devoted to the Blessed Sacrament, the Mass, Our Lady of the Rosary, and St. Joseph. At the age of twelve, Alexandrina fell ill with a serious infection that brought her to the brink of death. She overcame this illness but was to remain an invalid. Two years later on Holy Saturday of 1918, three men broke into her house and threatened to violate her chastity. She fled by jumping out a window. The thirteen-foot plunge to the ground permanently damaged her spine and crippled her for life. At the age of twenty-one, Alexandrina became totally paralyzed and permanently bedridden. She accepted this affliction as God's will for her and an opportunity to offer herself totally as a "victim soul" for the conversion of sinners and the sanctification of young people.

Alexandrina experienced her first ecstasy in 1931 when she heard Jesus say to her, "Love, suffer and make reparation." He asked her to use her sufferings with acts of reparation for the sins of the world, sins against sexual innocence in particular, especially those committed by priests.

On other occasions, Alexandrina had visions of Jesus, Our Lady, the angels, and some of the saints. By 1934, this servant of God would begin to experience the Passion of Our Lord through her many ecstatic visions. On September 6, 1934, Jesus appeared to her and said He wanted her to assist Him in the redemption of mankind by sharing the suffering of His crucifixion. This victim soul bravely accepted, and from then on she felt the pains of Christ's wounds in her hands, feet and side, as well as the crown of thorn wounds and the scourging. These "passion ecstasies" would continue weekly for the rest of her life, although her stigmata never appeared outwardly. She was called to bear the invisible stigmata. Every Friday, for a period of three and a half years, from October 3, 1938 to March 24, 1942, Alexandrina would experience the pains of Christ on the cross. On 182 occasions, this servant of God was to live the sufferings of the Passion. She would reproduce the various movements of the Via Crucis for three and a half hours. Her Passion ecstasies included the agony, the scourging, the crowning of thorns, and the vision of Mother Mary at the foot of the Cross. These events were filmed and the pictures were an important part of her case for beatification. During her ecstasies, many have witnessed her various sufferings: vomiting, the twisting of bodily limbs, groans of excruciating pain, bleeding, and swellings of her facial area.

After eighteen years of invalidism, on Good Friday 1942, the now thirty-eight year old ecstatic visionary believed Christ said to her: "You will not take food again on earth. Your food will be my flesh; your blood will be my divine blood, your life will be my life. You receive it from me when I unite my heart to your heart." So for the last thirteen years of her life, she was imbued with the mystical phenomenon of being nourished solely by the Eucharist (inedia).

One of her charisms was the gift of prophecy. She predicted difficult times ahead for the Church and foretold 1955 as the year of her death. Seeing Alexandrina was beginning to save sinners with her sacrificial reparations, the devil began to assault and torment her with suggestions and horrendous temptations against the faith. Later on, the devil progressed to outright threats, then physical beatings. He continued his attacks on her for a ten-year period. Her body was allegedly covered with purplish bruises from the blows received by the "evil one." Although in apparent physical discomfort, Alexandrina was always outwardly joyful and smiling, transmitting to all a profound peace. Visions of the Holy Family and her guardian angel gave her fleeting relief from her appalling suffering. As she had earlier predicted, her body would not remain incorruptible, but would turn to ashes without any signs of decomposition. Her ashes have been known to emit a heavenly perfume. She was declared Blessed in 2004 by Pope John Paul II.[1365]

Alpais of Cudot, Bl. (1156–1211) (aka Alpais of Sens)

Mystic and visionary born in Trigueres, France. Alpais was about twelve when she moved with her widowed mother and brothers to the town of Cudot. She was said to suffer from a hideous, disfiguring disease that was probably leprosy. When she became covered with festering sores and nearly paralyzed, her disgusted family abandoned her. Alpais was almost dead of starvation and

---

[1365] Andrew Rabel, "Alexandrina Maria da Costa," in *Inside the Vatican*, May 2004, 60–64; Catholic Saints online; Francis Johnston, *Alexandrina: The Agony and the Glory*, Rockford, Ill.: TAN Books and Publishers,1982; www.ewtn.com/, Index of the Biographies of the Blesseds 1993–2007; Gallick, 310; Freeze, TBWC, 152, 278–79; Sullivan, 37–40; Treece, MB 130–31.

thirst when she had a vision in which the Blessed Mother appeared to her and healed her sores. Although she remained paralyzed and confined to bed, Alpais continued to have visions of heaven, hell, and purgatory. She described what she saw so vividly that royalty, clergy, and ordinary people came to seek her counsel. Alpais refused to make any claims about her visions. She only reported what she saw. The Blessed Mother assured Alpais that because she bore her suffering with humility and patience she would thrive on celestial food alone. Until her death, Alpais appeared to live solely on the Eucharist. Some skeptics suspected demonic possession, but the Cistercian priests became her strong supporters and built a church to accommodate the thousands of pilgrims who came to see her. Her tomb is to be found in the church at Cudot. Alpais was beatified by Pope Pius IX in 1874.[1366]

Anna Maria Taigi drawing (TAN Books)

Ana of the Angels, Bl. (c. 1602–1686) (aka Ana de los Angeles Monteagudo)

Dominican mystic, visionary and victim soul born in Arequipa, Peru. Ana became a Dominican nun in 1618. The bishop of Arequipa encouraged the nuns to elect her their new prioress. Ana, however, felt incapable of this position, but when the voice of God commanded her, she obeyed. Her strict reforms were not received well and she survived several assaults and three poisoning attempts. Remaining serene, Ana blamed all these episodes on Satan. She allegedly experienced a vision of Mary with a host of angels surrounding her. It was also claimed that she became a victim soul and was called to suffer and pray for the poor souls in purgatory. This holy nun was frequently comforted by angels during her times of trial. Ana was beatified by Pope John Paul II on February 2, 1985.[1367]

Anna Maria Taigi, Bl. (1769–1837) (aka Anne Marie Taigi)

Trinitarian tertiary, mystic, visionary, ecstatica, stigmatic, and victim soul born in Siena, Italy. Reported to have been ill-treated by her father, this future beata married Domenico Taigi in 1790. She was a devoted spouse for forty-eight years and bore seven children within a twelve-year period. Three of these children were to die in infancy. Anna attained her position among the blessed in heaven by being an exemplary wife and mother amid poor and trying circumstances. Her husband caused her considerable anguish during her lifetime because of his exacting, jealous, and temperamental attitude. She patiently endured aridity of spirit, nursed her argumentative mother through a long illness, faithfully performed her duties as a

---

1366 Gallick, 333.
1367 Freze, VVA, 280–81; Gallick, 27; NCE Jubilee, 553–54; Blanca Gomez Cano O.P., *Sor Ana de los Angeles Monteagudo y Ponce de Leon*, Lima, Peru: *Monasterio de Santa Catalina de Sena*, 1984.

housewife and mother, saw to the needs of her quarrelsome husband, and struggled to maintain peace among family members in their overcrowded house amid an almost-steady stream of visitors.

In spite of this seemingly uncongenial atmosphere, Anna was frequently in ecstasy, worked miracles of healing, foretold deaths and future events, read hearts, slept very little (insomnia), and as a tertiary of the Third Order of the Most Holy Trinity, fulfilled perfectly the obligations of the rule. Both her daughters-in-law and her husband Domenico, then aged ninety-two, were to give evidence of her heroic virtue at her beatification. She was particularly devoted to St. Joseph who frequently appeared to her. This servant of God is said to have possessed the gift of healing and to have cured hundreds and even thousands of their afflictions, like a neighbor child of diphtheria and her own granddaughter's torn eyeball, at a touch. She experienced ecstasies while engaged in household chores and was known to have occasionally levitated. It is even alleged that she used to tie up traffic by slipping into ecstasies in the middle of the street if she happened to see a cross or an image of Jesus or Mary. This blessed layperson possessed an olfactory aversion to sin in others. The stench of sin in people was a constant added torment for her. On the other hand, she recognized souls in a state of grace by their sweet fragrance.

Mention should also be made here of the beata's "mysterious sun" which she first saw in 1790 or 1791, shortly after the birth of her first child. The luminous disc, somewhat like a miniature sun, was visible only to her and maintained a constant position before her. Above the upper rays of this sun was a large crown of interwoven thorns with two rather lengthy thorns on either side, curved downward so that they crossed each other under the solar disc,

their points emerging on either side of the rays. In the center of the disc, Anna Maria saw a beautiful woman seated majestically, her face raised toward heaven in ecstatic contemplation. In this globe, the beata saw things of the natural, moral, and divine order and could see present or future events anywhere in the world, as well as the state of grace of living individuals and the fate of those departed. She is said to have penetrated the depths of hell and soared to the heights of heaven. It was purported that Anna entered prisons in China and Arabia where priests were being held and suffered along with them. She predicted the return to the Vatican of Pope Pius VII, the second pope taken prisoner by Napoleon, as well as the pope's imminent death and the short pontificate and death of Pope Pius VIII.

Anna Maria could also discern the secret thoughts of persons who were present or far off. Among her friends could be counted St. Vincent Pallotti (1795–1850), St. Gaspar del Bufalo, and St. Mary Euphrasia Pelletier (1796–1868). One of her closest friends was Blessed Elizabeth Canori-Mora who also was a wife and mother. They helped and supported each other in their marriages and difficulties and grew together in holiness and sanctity in their married vocation. Demons are said to have frequently assaulted Anna in ways that are reminiscent of the diabolical attacks experienced by St. John Vianney. They punched, kicked, and beat this holy housewife over the head and shoulders and tried to strangle her. These entities were said to often appear in frightful shapes like wild beasts out of the Apocalypse. They frequently disturbed her prayers and tried to break down her purity by sensual apparitions, suggesting unclean imaginings and doubts against the faith. Anna Marie foretold her own death. She suffered an increase in bodily ailments during the months before she died but remained at peace. After a vision of Our Lord, and upon delivering a message to each of her children and her husband, Anna passed away on June 9, 1837. She was beatified in 1920 by Pope Benedict XV. The *Degree of Beatification* speaks of this "mysterious sun" as "a prodigy unique in the annals of sanctity." Her body remained incorrupt for a time after her death.[1368]

Anne Catherine Emmerich, Bl. (1774–1824) (aka Anna Katharina Emmerick, "The Living Crucifix")

Lay mystic, visionary, invisible stigmatic, ecstatica, victim soul, and Augustinian nun born at Flamske in the Diocese of Munster, Westphalia, in Germany. It is said that this holy soul had the use of reason from birth and, as a child, saw visions even of her guardian angel. God is said to have allowed her to entrust her will to this angelic creature who, in turn, enlightened her to God's designs upon her soul. Anne later revealed that during her ecstatic moments, her angel often took her to various places throughout all of Europe and even to the Holy Land. Endowed with extraordinary spiritual graces, Anne Catherine became an Augustinian nun at the Convent of Agnetenberg at Dulmen in 1802. During her lifetime, she experienced the mystical phenomenon of the full stigmata, the wounds of Christ, to include the crown of thorns. It is claimed that the stigma in her side was three inches long. A study ordered by her bishop by a panel of physicians and clergy determined these wounds to be authentic. The complete stigmatization, which she tried to hide, occurred on December 29,

Anne Catherine Emmerich

1812. It also included a double cross on her breast. Because of the great trouble caused by her visible stigmata, Anne implored the Lord to remove them, a prayer that was granted, at least partially. The stigmata disappeared on Christmas Day 1819 leaving white scars, but the pain remained. At certain times, particularly on feast days or during Lent until her death, the stigmata would reappear with blood gushing out of the marks of the wounds. Anne was never without the stigmata, but for the rest of the time they were invisible, and equally as painful.

Almost from infancy, Anne Catherine is said to have also possessed hierognosis: the ability to recognize holiness or evil in any person, place, or thing. She likewise exhibited the mystic gift of inedia and soon stopped eating altogether. For the last twelve years of her life, she subsisted only on Holy Communion. In addition, this servant of God experienced mystical visions. Many have considered her to be the greatest visionary in Church history. The content of these visions came to be written down by the popular Romantic poet Clemens Brentano, a man who served as her secretary in this regard. The nun only agreed to communicate her visions on the repeated commands of her spiritual directors. From 1818 to her death in 1824, Brentano wrote down everything Anne Catherine told him. She reportedly said she felt in her body whatever the saints or Christ felt in her vision: the heat, the cold, the distress, everything (called mystic sensitivity). All in all, she dictated to Brentano a truly stunning account of the day-to-day lives of Christ, Mary, and their family and friends. Her visions were given in bits and pieces, so Brentano had to rearrange a lot of the details. He may even have embellished or refined her language a little. In any event, under Brentano's influence, the beata's visions were said to have become much more elaborate than they had been before.

Among the most famous of the beata's works are *The Dolorous Passion of Our Lord and Savior Jesus Christ* and the *Life of the Blessed Virgin Mary*. The written reports of the visions themselves contain long descriptions not only of biblical events but also of apocryphal stories. They also include many historical and topographical details, some of which are correct, others quite mistaken. This unlettered peasant woman sees in her imaginative visions the travels of the Savior through Palestine. She describes the area's geography with exactitude, along with its rivers, mountains, forests, and towns, inhabitants and their manners and customs. All these images are evidently transcendental and supernatural. It is interesting to note, however, that some of the locations and descriptions of buildings and artifacts

she presents in her visions have been confirmed by scholars since her time. For instance, the exact house that the Blessed Virgin Mary lived in after Christ's crucifixion and Ascension has been identified through her visions. She placed the house to be firmly in Ephesus (in present-day Turkey).

Anne Catherine's other visions include those of heaven, hell, and purgatory. She once saw in heaven a dome that was surrounded by three of the nine angelic choirs. The three archangels Michael, Gabriel, and Raphael stood over part of the dome. There were many seraphim and cherubim standing around the throne of God hymning incessant praise. The beata also had visions of a host of saints, to include intimate details of their lives and many prophecies of future events. Some of the saints she is said to have encountered through her almost continuous ecstatic visions include: St. Agnes (d.c. 304); St. Agatha (n.d); St. Paula (347–404); St. Dorothea; St. Apollonia (d. 249); St. Benedict (c. 480–547); St. Scholastica (d. 543); St. Paschal (d. 824); St. Cyprian (3rd c.); St. Isidore (1070–1130); St. Stephen (d.c. 35); St. Lawrence (d. 258); St. Nicodemus (1st c.); St. Clare (1194–1253); St. Thomas Aquinas; St. Perpetua (d. 203); St. Felicity (d.c. 165); St. Justina (d.c. 305); St. Denis (d.c. 258); St. Ursula (5th c.); St. Hubert (d. 727); St. Gertrude; St. Cecilia (2nd c.); St. Catherine of Siena; St. Augustine; St. Francis de Sales; and St. Jane Frances de Chantal. This is far from being a complete list. Often, this favored soul would communicate with the poor souls in purgatory via her angel, who led her safely through this place of purification in order that she might visit those who implored her aid. In turn, Anne would pray and suffer in order to help free them from their pain and to help gain their entrance into their heavenly kingdom.

This victim soul allegedly once received blows to the face from the devil who appeared to her in the form of a great, black dog. Another time, the "evil one" tried to hurl her down a ladder. She even experienced icy-cold hands grabbing at her feet, with the intention of throwing her to the ground. The cause for her beatification was suspended in 1928 by the Congregation for the Causes of the Saints when it was suspected that Brentano fabricated materials attributed to her. The Holy See re-opened her cause forty-five years later on the sole basis of her life, without reference to the possibly doctored writings. On July 2, 2003, a decree of miracle was promulgated by the Congregation of the Causes of the Saints. She was beatified by Pope John Paul II on October 3, 2004.[1369]

Anne of St. Bartholomew, Bl. (1549–1626)

Carmelite mystic, visionary, and stigmatic born as Anne Garcia Manzanas in Almendral, Spain. When she was ten, Anne lost both her parents to a plague that swept across Spain. She led an extraordinary spiritual existence, being graced with mystical experiences such as visions and revelations throughout her entire life. Our Lord first revealed Himself to Anne in a divine ray of light when she was only three years old. He kept on appearing to her as a child, seeming to grow along with her. From these encounters, the future beata experienced a lifelong awareness of God's sanctity and greatness. As a teenager, one night, after having fallen asleep with her rosary in her hands, the Blessed Virgin appeared to her and pressed her to become a nun. Our Lord later appeared and seconded His Mother's words. He directed her to enter the first monastery of Discalced Carmelites in Avila, Spain. Anne's family opposed her vocation, whereupon she became very sick. Her health miraculously returned, however, after making a pilgrimage to the hermitage of St. Bartholomew on August 24, 1570. That same year, Anne entered the Carmelite Monastery taking the habit as Sister Anne of St. Bartholomew in gratitude for her cure. Anne was to become the inseparable companion and secretary of St. Teresa of Avila. She nursed Teresa during her last illness and the saint died in her arms. When the widowed Jane Frances de Chantal tried to enter the Discalced Carmelites, Anne discouraged her, saying that Teresa would not accept Jane as a daughter because God had other plans for her. Jane later founded the Visitation Order. On the other hand, Anne worked closely with Barbe Acarie (Bl. Marie of the Incarnation) who played a key role in bringing Anne and the Carmelites to France. This servant of God is said to have mystically experienced events in the Lord's life, such as His Passion. In 1671, Anne moved to Belgium. It is believed that her prayers saved the city of Antwerp when it was under siege by the prince of Orange. Soon after Anne's death, miracles were attributed to her intercession. It is claimed that by 1632, over 150 miracles attributed to her had been approved. In 1735, Pope Clement XII declared the heroicity of her virtues and she was later beatified by Pope Benedict XV in 1917.[1370]

[1369] *L'Osservatore Romano*, no. 29, 16 July 2003, 2; Hebert, 234; 284; Summers, 159ff; Freze, TBWC, 139, 166, 270–71; Gallick, 55; Johnson, 260–64; Biot, 31; NCE 2nd ed., v. 5, 193; Karl, E. Schmoger, C.S.S.R., *The Life of Anne Catherine Emmerich*, Rockford, Ill.: TAN Books, Inc., 1976; Farges, 333; Cruz, A&D, 120, 145, 168.

[1370] http://www.catholic.org/saints; Gallick, 171, Cruz, MMM, 542; www.theCarmelite.ca/saint_anne.aspx.

Anthony Della Chiesa, Bl. (1395–1459)

Dominican mystic, visionary, and ecstatic born in San Germano, near Vercelli in the Piedmont region of Italy to a noble family. For many years, Anthony was the companion of St. Bernardine of Siena (1380–1344) and traveled with him throughout Italy preaching to the people. He had a special gift for consoling the afflicted and for converting obstinate sinners. Blessed Anthony had an ardent devotion to Our Lady, from whom he received many favors. He is said to have conversed with the Blessed Virgin on several occasions while in ecstasy. On one occasion, while rapt in ecstasy when conversing familiarly with the Queen of Heaven, his room was seen flooded with light and his own countenance radiant with celestial splendor. Anthony was also endowed with the gifts of reading hearts and healing the sick. He was beatified in 1819.[1371]

Archangela Girlani, Bl. (1460–1494)

Carmelite abbess, mystic, and ecstatica who founded a convent in Mantua born in Trino, Northern Italy. She was baptized as Eleanora but took the name Archangela as a postulant. She had a special devotion to the Holy trinity. This saintly Carmelite prioress at Mantua was the recipient of extraordinary mystical favors. On many occasions she was found by her sister religious enraptured in ecstasy and in a levitated position several feet above the floor. One of her more notable ecstasies was said to have lasted more than twenty-four hours. Many miracles took place through this beata's intercession after her death. Blessed Archangela's body remains incorrupt. It is viewed by countless devotees in the Church of St. Lorenzo in Trino

Vercellese, Italy. She was beatified in 1864 by Pope Pius IX.[1372]

Augustine of Biella, Bl. (1430–1493) (aka Augustine Fangi)

Dominican mystic and ecstatic born of noble parents in Biella, near Fangi, in the Piedmont region of Italy. His parents had a secular life planned for him but Augustine opted to join the Dominicans. In 1464, he was made prior of the Soncino Convent. This servant of God possessed the gift of tears and was often seen levitating in ecstasy. He worked numerous miracles and was especially able to cast out demons. Augustine was said to have once raised to life a deformed infant who had died without baptism long enough for the child to be baptized. The Dominican's body was found incorruptible forty years after his death despite having been buried in a damp place and his coffin found floating in water. He was beatified in 1878 by Pope Leo XIII.[1373]

Beatrice of Nazareth, Bl. (1200–1268) (aka Beatrijs van Nazareth)

Cistercian mystic, visionary, and stigmatic born in Tienen (Tirlemont), Belgium to a wealthy family. At the age of seven, her mother died and she went to live with the Benguines. Ten years later, Beatrice joined the Cistercian nuns at Bloemendaal. She was sent from there to Nazareth, Belgium where she founded and became the first abbess of Our Lady of Nazareth near Lier in Brabant. This Flemish mystic is renowned for her work entitled the *Seven Ways of Holy Love*. She reportedly practiced

[1371] Procter, 210–12; Dorcy, 207–8.

[1372] Cruz, Inc., 154–55; http://calendar.jtm.blogspot.com; NCE 2nd ed., v. 1,631; Cruz, MMM, 423.

[1373] Hebert, 136; Dorcy, 224–25; *Dominican saints*.

severe austerities to include wearing a girdle of thorns. Beatrice had her first mystical experience in early January 1217. At that time, the Holy Spirit revealed to her that she would become espoused to Christ and this took place. Beatrice had a special devotion to the Sacred Heart of Jesus. Her Spouse is said to have appeared to her in a vision and to have pierced her heart with a fiery dart (transverberation). It is claimed that this servant of God once saw the heavenly Jerusalem while enraptured. She was also said to have had an intellectual vision where she witnessed heavenly beings gazing unceasingly on the Godhead. After the town of Nazareth was abandoned by a disturbance, Beatrice's body was believed to have been transferred by angels to Lier.[1374]

Beatrix D'Ornacieux, Bl. (c. 1260–1309)

Carthusian nun, mystic, and stigmatic born at the Chateau d'Ornacieu, Dauphine, France. Beatrix's life was distinguished by humility, obedience, charity, and above all, by a fervent devotion to the Passion of Christ. For many years, she had remarkable mystical experiences as well as diabolical persecutions. While praying for her captive brother, she experienced a vision of Jesus bearing His five wounds. It is reported that she later was stigmatized with these Five Wounds but only endured the pain of the stigmata with no visible wounds. On certain feast days, Beatrix is said to have had intense pain in her hands, feet, and side. Some say, however, that she may have driven a nail through her left hand to help realize the sufferings of the crucifixion.[1375]

Benevenuta Bojani, Bl. (1254–1292)

Dominican tertiary, mystic, visionary, and stigmatic born the last of seven daughters in Vividale del Friuli, Italy. As a young girl, she refused to play childhood games that smacked of worldliness or vanity. At age twelve, Benevenuta voluntarily wore hair shirts and a rope belt. As she grew, the rope began to cut into her. It had to be removed but was too embedded to be untied. She prayed over it and it fell to her feet. As a Dominican tertiary, Benevenuta practiced extreme austerities. Confined to her bed with a serious illness, she had to be carried to daily Mass. During a Mass on the feast day of St. Dominic, the saint is claimed to have appeared to her along with St. Peter Martyr and she was miraculously healed. Benevenuta is also said to have had a vision of Our Lady holding the infant Jesus and to have had visits from both angels and demons. The devil reportedly often attacked her, appearing to her in horrifying forms. She could, however, banish the "evil one" by mentioning the name of the Blessed Virgin Mary. This servant of God was beatified by Pope Clement V in 1763.[1376]

Catherine of Racconigi, Bl. (1486–1547) (aka Caterina, Catherine de Mattei)

Dominican nun, mystic, visionary, invisible stigmatic, and ecstatica born in Racconigi, province of Cuneo, Piedmont, a village south of Turin, Italy, to a poor manual worker. She was a contemporary of both St. Teresa of Avila (1515–1582) and St. Catherine of Ricci (1522–1590) and is known to have been favored with prophecies and many mystical graces

[1374] http://www.cns.bu.edu; NCE, 1st ed., v. 2, 197–98.

[1375] Summers, 147, 196; Cruz, MMM, 235; NCE 2nd ed., v. 3, 192.

[1376] http://www.ingplants.com; "Blessed Benevenuta Bojani" Saints, SQPN.

Engraving of Catherine of Racconigi

starting from the age of five. As a child of ten, Catherine saw Christ in a vision. He offered her either a garland of flowers or a crown of thorns. When she offered to take the latter, a smiling Christ said He could not lay that on a child but deferred it until she was twenty-four. We are told that the Blessed Virgin appeared to her one time while she was praying and told her that the Child Jesus wanted to take her as His spouse. Her first betrothal to Christ took place in the presence of angels and saints to include St. Catherine of Siena and St. Peter Martyr (c. 1205–1252). Jesus appeared at the time as a child of Catherine's own age and Our Lady placed the ring of espousal on her finger. A second mystical espousal took place when Catherine professed her vow of virginity. At that time, a mark of a ring appeared upon her finger.

Catherine was favored with frequent ecstasies. Our Lord always appeared to her as if He were her own age. He conversed with her, taught her to pray, and several times took her heart away to cleanse and purify it. One day, He appeared to her carrying His cross, and she offered to help. He let

the cross rest for a moment on her shoulder and it inflicted a wound on her that lasted for the rest of her life. On Easter Sunday in 1510, she did, in fact, receive the stigmata, the Five Wounds and the crown of thorns, but they disappeared in answer to her prayers. Before their disappearance, however, her garments were always soaked with her blood. The Dominican mystic also experienced the mystical fast (inedia). She was sustained only by the Eucharist for ten years. The devil, who feared the beata's influence over souls, persecuted and tortured her. He is said to have appeared to her in many forms, such as being disguised as men, beasts, birds, and corpses. She was defended against him by saints and angels. Her best weapon against him, however, was the aspiration "Jesus, my hope!" Catherine purportedly was taken to heaven, hell, and purgatory. She is said to have recognized friends in all three places. Upon visiting purgatory one time, she reportedly brought back an agonizing wound from a mere spark that had fallen on her cheek. Angels are said to have carried Catherine over great distances. Blessed Lucy of Narni was among those who reported her miraculous visits. Catherine was beatified in 1808 by Pope Pius VII.[1377]

Cherubin of Avigliana, Bl. (1451–1479) (aka Cherubino of Avigliana)

Augustinian friar, mystic, and stigmatic born as Cherubin Testa, an only son, in Avigliana in Piedmont. At the age of twenty, Cherubin entered the Augustinian Order and was ordained in 1479. This saintly priest was devoted to the Passion of Christ. At his death, he was found to have

[1377] Schouppe, *Purgatory*, 61; Butler, 9/4, 36; www. newadvent.org; NCE, 1st ed., v. 3, 258; Hebert, 240; Summers, 164; Cruz, MMM, 147, 255; Dorcy, 272–73; Biot, 56; Gallick, 274, 437; NCE 2nd ed., v. 3, 272; Wilson, 135.

been wounded with the lance. A deeply spiritual man, it is said that church bells rang unaided by human hands at his death. His body continued to give off a sweet fragrance long after he had died.[1378]

Christina D'aquila, Bl. (1480–1543) (aka Christine d'Aquila)

Augustinian mystic, visionary, ecstatica, and stigmatic born Mattia Ciccarelli at Colle de Lucoli, Italy. Mattia entered the Augustinian monastery of Saint Lucy in Aquila in 1505 taking the religious name Christina. She was elected abbess several times. This servant of God had a particular devotion to the Eucharist and to the Passion and death of Christ. Bl. Vincent of Aquila (d. 1504) was her spiritual adviser. It is said that Christina once had a vision of Christ on the feast of Corpus Christi. She was also said to have been stigmatized, but only with the crown of thorns.[1379]

Christina of Stommeln, Bl. (1242–1312) (aka Christina von Stommeln, Christina Bruso and Christina Bruzo)

Beguine nun, mystic, visionary, ecstatica, and stigmatic born at Stommeln northwest of Cologne, Germany. As a five-year-old, she had visions of the Christ Child and reportedly became mystically married to him by the age of ten. Christina entered the Convent of the Beguines at Cologne when she was twelve. She lived a life of severe penance here spending much of her time in prayer and often falling into convulsions. While in ecstasy, Christina never gave any sign of life. Her body was

rigid like that of a corpse or of a cataleptic, but marvelous wonders accompanied her ecstasies. In her fifteenth year, she manifested the stigmata on her hands and feet and the marks of the crown of thorns on her head. Every year, at Passiontide and Holy Week, her wounds dripped with blood. Some scholars conjecture that her mystical experiences were hallucinations and hysteria. Christina is said to have suffered many assaults by the devil. On three occasions, according to her parish priest, Satan dragged her from her bed and took her to the roof of her house. Another time she was left bound to a tree in her garden. The devil is also said to have tormented her by fixing hot stones to her body which people could see and touch. Other diabolic activity against her included invisible teeth bites, resulting in bits of flesh being torn from her arms. Christina endured many trials to her faith and was even tempted to commit suicide. The Beguines thought her crazy and treated her with contempt, leading her to return to her home village in 1267, where she was first taken in by the parish priest and then moved into a small cloister in Stommeln. In 1288, the torments which Christina suffered from the devil ceased, and she lived out the rest of her life peacefully, wearing always the dress of the Beguines. Although she lived a pure life, there is some doubt about how much literal truth exists concerning her visions and apparitions of purgatory.[1380]

Clara Isabella Fornari, Bl. (1697–1744) (aka Chiari Fornari)

Poor Clare nun, mystic, visionary, ecstatica, and stigmatic born at Rome, Italy as Anna Felicia Fornari. She joined the Poor Clares of Todi, Italy at the age

---

[1378] Summers, 170; NCE, 1st ed., v. 3, 551; NCE 2nd ed., v. 3, 467–68; *Book of Augustinian Saints*, 96.
[1379] Summers, 169; Cruz, MMM, 235; NCE 2nd ed., v. 3, 350; *Book of Augustinian Saints*, 98.

[1380] Summers, 155; NCE, 1st ed., v. 3, 655; NCE 2nd ed., v. 3, 550; Cruz, MMM, 235; Wilson, 132; Farges, 452; Cruz, A&D, 199.

of fifteen, and a year later took her vows under the name of Clara Isabella. Clara was given to long and frequent ecstatic visions of Jesus, Our Lady, St. Clare of Assisi, and St. Catherine of Siena. During one of these ecstasies, Jesus placed a ring on her finger and pronounced her His "spouse of sorrow." She received the stigmata with constant marks and periodic bleeding. Her head was weighed with a mystical crown of thorns that invisibly, but painfully grew through the skin until the thorns popped through and fell, leaving bleeding open wounds. Clara was driven to depression and despair from the pain and was tempted toward apostasy and suicide. Toward the end of her short life, she lost the memories of her earlier, consoling visits from heaven. However, not long before she died, the memories of those earlier, ecstatic times came back to her. Her joy in God returned, and she went happily into the next life.[1381]

Clare of Rimini, Bl. (1282–1346) (aka Chiari Agolanti da Rimini "Clarissa")

Poor Clare nun, mystic, visionary, and stigmatic born Chiara Agolanti da Rimini. This beautiful, frivolous, self-indulgent young woman inherited a fortune from her first husband, married again, and lost herself in worldly pleasures. She lead a life of sinful dissipation. At the age of thirty-four, while attending Mass, she heard a voice that bade her to pray with fervor and attention. Clare immediately began to feel a deep sense of remorse for her life. Shortly after this, she experienced a vision of the Blessed Mother that gave her the strength to turn her life around. She converted her second husband, and after his death, devoted herself to charity work. Clare went on to became a

Franciscan tertiary and resolved to expiate her sins by living a life of extreme penance. She later entered the Order of Poor Clares and became abbess of the Convent of Our Lady of the Angels at Rimini. This penitent servant of God is said to have had a vision of Jesus in 1346, seated on His throne of glory, surrounded by St. John the Baptist (c. 1–32) and the apostles. In this vision, the Lord showed her the wound in His side. Clare reportedly worked numerous miracles toward the end of her life and was granted an extraordinary gift of contemplation. She is said to have converted many women from immoral lives and endowed dowries for many poor girls.[1382]

Columba of Rieti, Bl. (1467–1501) (aka Angiola Guardagnoli)

Dominican mystic, visionary, and ecstatica born in Rieti, Umbria, Italy as Angelella Guardagnoli to a poor family. Legend has it that when she was born, angels gathered around her house singing and that during her Baptism, a white dove flew down and settled on her head. After this incident, her parents decided to change her name to Columba ("Dove"). Reluctantly accepting her refusal to marry, her parents allowed her to live at home. This holy soul developed an intense devotion to the Blessed Sacrament and is said to have had a vision of Christ on a golden throne surrounded by Sts. Dominic, Jerome, and Peter Martyr. Columba took this vision as a sign to dedicate herself to God. One day, at the age of nineteen, she beheld a vision of the three holy founders—Sts. Benedict, Francis, and Dominic—each inviting her to assume the habit of the Dominican Order. She became a Dominican tertiary and settled down to live the life of a recluse in her

---

[1381] http://saints.sqpn.com/blessed-clara-Isabella-fornari/; Omer Englebert, *Lives of the Saints.*

[1382] Wiebe, 19; Brewer, 19; Gallick, 54; NCE, 1st ed., v. 3, 914; Baring-Gould, 2:256–59; NCE 2nd ed., v. 3, 761.

The Vision of the Blessed Clare of Rimini / Francesco da Rimini (Master of the Blessed Clare). ca. 1333-1340.

parent's house where she began experiencing ecstasies and mystical phenomena. During one such ecstasy, her spirit is said to have toured the Holy Land.

The Dominican mystic is said to have had a vision which led her to leave Rieti and head north on foot. A series of miraculous adventures brought her to the city of Perugia, where she was welcomed with great fanfare and was credited with saving the people there from a bloody civil war. She spent eleven years as the Dominican prioress in Perugia. In the summer of 1498, Pope Alexander VI visited Perugia and

Columba was brought before him. As she touched the hem of his garment, she fell into ecstasy. During an illness late in her life, Columba was tormented by diabolical visions of food and naked bodies. She was purportedly consoled, however, by a vision of St. Dominic who brought her a garland of flowers and assured her that she would soon join him in heaven. At the moment of her death, her soul appeared radiant in glory to her spiritual friend and contemporary Blessed Osanna of Mantua (1449–1505). During her funeral, a white dove was said to have flown into the church, settled on her coffin, and remained there until the Mass ended. Columba was beatified in 1697 by Pope Innocent XII.[1383]

Dina Belanger, Bl. (1897–1929) (aka Marie Sainte-Cecile de Rome or Sister Cecilia)

Catholic nun, mystic, visionary, ecstatica, stigmatic, victim soul, and religious of the Sisters of Jesus-Marie born in Sillery, Quebec, Canada to religious parents. Dina was a pampered only child and, even as a toddler, was determined to become a saint. She was devoted to the Blessed Sacrament and the Blessed Mother. As a youngster, she had dreams of Jesus as a Child as well as of being in Paradise. In 1908, after having made her first Holy Communion, Dina began to experience inner locutions. She is said to have heard the voice of Jesus speaking to her. Later on, Jesus would pierce her heart with the Cross and surround it with a crown of thorns. As a teenager, she had the stirrings of a religious vocation, but she was also a gifted pianist and she trained for a career in music. After briefly pursuing a career as a concert pianist, Dina gave this up and, in 1923, entered the Convent of Jesus-Marie in Quebec. She took her final vows five years later. Sister Marie of St. Cecilia of Rome, as she was now known, was said to have been spiritually guided by St. Cecilia (2nd c.), her namesake, and St. Therese (1873–1897). On January 22, 1927, this victim soul received the gift of the stigmata in her hands, feet, and side. Upon begging the Lord not to let her wounds show, Jesus agreed to make them invisible. In May of 1927, this Canadian mystic claimed to have seen a vision of Christ. The voice that spoke to her said the following:

"My heart sheds tears of blood in Gethsemane over many of these consecrated souls." Jesus then showed her an image of the Agony in the Garden. According to the mystic, Jesus told her that there is a need for victim souls to suffer for the sins of the world. This beata described her spiritual journey in a compelling autobiography published after her death entitled the *Canticle of Love*. She was beatified in Rome by Pope John Paul II on March 20, 1993.[1384]

Dodo of Hascha, Bl. (d.1231) (aka Dodo van Bakkeveen, Dodo de Hascha)

Premonstratensian mystic and stigmatic. Reluctantly married, Dodo later became a monk in the Premonstratensian order at Hascha in Frisia and his wife entered a convent. As a hermit at various places, he was known for his austerities and wonderworking. At his death, it was discovered that his hands, feet, and right side were marked with the Five Sacred Wounds of Christ. His stigmata may have even predated that of St. Francis of Assisi (1182–1226). Dodo died in 1231 when a wall of his cell fell on top of him and crushed him.[1385]

Elena Aiello, Bl. (1895–1961) (aka Elena Emilia Santa Aiello)

Foundress of a religious order, mystic, visionary, stigmatic, and victim soul born at Montalto, Uffugo, Italy to a tailor. Elena became a religious nun later in her life and founded the contemplative religious order the Sisters Minims of the Passion of Our

---

[1383] Gallick, 152; Wiebe, 17; Procter, 135–36; NCE 2nd ed., v. 3, 863; Dorcy, 233–35; Dunbar, *Saintly Women*, I, 199–200.

[1384] NCE, v. 2, 211; Lord, VMS, 354, 357, 365, 367, 372; Freze, VVA, 253; Gallick, 271, 437; NCE Jubilee, 444; Ann Ball, *Faces of Holiness II: Modern Saints in Photos and Words*, Huntington, IN: Our Sunday Visitor, 2001.

[1385] NCE, v. 4, 947; NCE 2nd ed., v. 4, 810; Wilson, 131.

Lord Jesus Christ. She then presided over this order as its Mother Superior. After a vision of our Lord, sister Elena began suffering the full stigmata every Good Friday from March 1923 until her death in 1961. During this time, her stigmata wounds bled profusely. She also experienced apparitions of the Blessed Virgin Mary from 1947 until her death. These visions provided her with the gift of prophecy as the Blessed Virgin showed her visions of the future and warned her of a coming chastisement over the world if people did not amend their sinful ways. Sister Elena also had apparitions of Jesus, Sts. Francis of Paola, Rita of Cascia, and other saints. On Good Friday, April 16, 1954, Jesus allegedly appeared to Mother Elena covered with wounds that were bleeding. In 1959, Our Lord again appeared to her in the same manner, speaking of a coming destruction for a world that had turned its back on God. Jesus appealed to Elena to let the world know that His apparitions and messages are serious and real. He also told Mother Elena of His disappointment in all the priests and bishops who will not believe in His appearances and messages. Pope John Paul II declared Elena venerable in 1992 and Benedict XVI beatified her in 2011.[1386]

Elizabeth Von Reute, Bl. (1386–1420) (aka Elizabeth Achler, Elizabeth the Good, "the good Betha")

Franciscan tertiary, mystic, visionary, ecstatica, and stigmatic born at Waldsee in Swabia, Germany. Elizabeth showed a rare piety from her earliest days. At age

[1386] Freze, VVA, 247; http://www.MontaltoUffugo.net; http://www.catholicrevelations.org; Anna Maria Turi, *Stigmate e stigmatizzati; segni del cielo:soria e attalita*, Roma: Edizioni Mediterranean, c1990, 98–106; Francisco Sanchez-Ventera y Pascual, 102.

Elizabeth Von Reute by anonymous

fourteen, she received the habit of the Third Order of St. Francis but continued to live at home. She later entered a house for tertiaries at Reuter on the outskirts of Waldsee. Here, "the good Betha" was to suffer much from attacks by an evil spirit, suspicions of her sisters in religion, from leprosy, and other sicknesses. She endured all this patiently. In consequence, God permitted her to bear the marks of the Passion on her body. Her head often showed the marks of the thorns, and her body those of the scourging. The stigmata appeared only now and again, but her pains never ceased. To the five wounds and the crown of thorns were added those marks resembling the stripes and marks of the scourging. These, her biographer Rev. Conrad Kugelin relates, bled copiously on Fridays and in Lent. The pain continued with few respites until the end of her life. Elizabeth received many mystical favors and visions of heaven, hell, and purgatory. She was shown the happiness of the blessed and the souls in the state of purgation. The secrets of hearts and of the future were likewise unveiled to her. Elizabeth foretold the election of Martin V (1417–1431) to the papacy and the end of the Western Schism. Although more than 112 witnesses testified to miracles attributed to her intercession, her case for beatification stalled for three hundred years. In about 1757, a cardinal on his way to Vienna learned about the local devotion to Elizabeth and reopened her cause. She was finally beatified in 1766 by Pope Clement XIII.[1387]

Elizabetta Canori-Mora, Bl. (1774–1825) (aka Maria Elisabetta Cecilia Gertrude Canori)

Married mystic, visionary, ecstatica, stigmatic, and Tertiary of the Discalced Trinitarians born to a wealthy Christian family in Rome. As a child, Elizabetta showed an extraordinary knowledge of mystical things far beyond her years. She related to her spiritual director that she was taught these things by Jesus Himself. On January 10, 1796, Elizabetta married Cristoforo Mora, a lawyer and son of a wealthy physician. After their first child died at birth, her husband became very cold and detached. He neglected her and took a mistress. A second daughter was also to die in childbirth but a third and fourth daughter lived. Cristoforo let his law practice fall apart and Elizabetta took up sewing to support her children. In 1801, a mysterious illness brought her to death's door. She was cured in an inexplicable way and had her first mystical experience. On October 23, 1816, this servant of God passed into a rapture during which she had a vision of the Madonna holding the Infant Jesus in her arms. Also appearing in this vision were St. Joseph, the three Holy Magi, the two Patriarchs of the Trinitarians, St. John of Matha (1160–1213) and the royal hermit St. Felix of Valois (1126–1212) along with an infinite host of angels. In this vision, the Divine Child placed upon the finger of the ecstatica, whose hand He took in His, a ring brilliant with heavenly jewels. Elizabetta thus experienced the supreme mystical experience of the spiritual marriage. Such was the effect of this rapture that the ecstatica remained in ecstasy for a full fortnight. On July 2, 1823, upon the Feast of the Visitation, Elizabetta again fell into a rapture during which time she beheld a vision of the Mother of God and endured the mystery of the transverbation of her heart. From that day until her death, her life was one long, almost-uninterrupted, series of ecstasies and raptures. Elizabetta Canori Mora is an example of a mystic who was compelled by circumstances to live in the world, to mix in Roman society, to marry, and to endure the martyrdom of an unhappy domestic life rather than to live in a cloister which she would have preferred. She was the wife of a bad husband, a reckless and disloyal profligate. She was also the tender mother of two daughters. Like Blessed Anna Maria Taigi, this mystic has a marvelous message for ordinary people, for those who are weighed down by the dull burden of domestic care. They showed the way for lay people how to maintain their interior life on the highest plane. Shortly after her death, as she had predicted, her husband converted, joined the Trinitarian Third Order, and later became a priest of the Conventual Franciscans. He died on September 9, 1845. Pope John Paul II beatified Elizabetta on April 24, 1994.[1388]

[1387] Thurston, 148–49, 341; Gallick, 353, 446; Dunbar 1:266; Catholic wonderworkers.

[1388] Summers,106, 235ff; Gallick, 59; www.ewtn. com/Index of Biographies of Blesseds 1993–2007; Paolo Redi, *Elisabetta Canori Mora: Un Amore Fedele tra le Mura de Casa,* Rome: Citta Nueva, c1994.

Emily Bicchieri, Bl. (1238–1314) (aka Emilia of Vercelli, Emilia Bicchieri of Vercelli)

Dominican tertiary, mystic, visionary, ecstatica, and stigmatic born at Vercelli, Italy, the fourth of seven daughters. Her mother was said to have seen in a dream something of her daughter's future work. She related this dream to a Dominican priest who told her that the child she was bringing into the world would become a saint. Overly conscientious about her small faults, Emily rarely received Communion until our Lord Himself appeared to her to relieve her of her doubts and feelings of unworthiness. He told her that it was more pleasing to receive Him through Holy Communion than to abstain from receiving through fear of unworthiness. Emily was then noted for her frequent communion which was uncommon in those days. The beata refused her father's plans for her to marry and convinced him to build a convent. The first Convent for Dominican regular tertiaries was then built outside Vercelli and dedicated to St. Margaret. Emily became its first abbess at the age of twenty.

Emily had a special devotion to Christ's Crown of Thorns. She asked the Lord to let her share His pain, and He granted her the stigmata in the form of a crown of thorns. This wound would only last three days, however it was three days of unbearable pain during which time she was said to have been visited by several of the saints associated with the Lord's Passion. At the end of the three days, the pain went away but this servant of God retained her devotion to the crown of thorns all her life. Twice the Blessed Virgin appeared to Emily, both times to teach her how to pray. Many miraculous cures were attributed to her by her prayers. She was beatified in 1767 by Pope Clement XIII.[1389]

Francis of Posadas, Bl. (1643–1713) (aka Francisco Martin Fernandez de Posadas)

Dominican mystic born in Cordova, Spain. Francis was remarkably pious as a child. While still an infant, the name of Mary was found miraculously imprinted over his heart, and Mary's name was the first word he uttered. It is said that twice during his childhood he was miraculously saved from death. He became a noted Dominican preacher and confessor in southern Spain known for reading the hearts of his penitents and visitors. He would also reveal to them in the confessional sins that had been deliberately concealed. Francis experienced many levitations which he tried to resist, but without success. On one occasion his body remained suspended in the air during the consecration. On several other occasions, while celebrating Mass, observers saw a brilliant light emanate from his body which illuminated the whole altar. This saintly Dominican was also able to bilocate by being led interiorly to the bedside of the dying who were in need of the Last Sacraments. He also underwent terrible encounters with the "evil one" from which he emerged victorious. In addition, Francis was endowed with the gifts of prophecy, discernment of spirits, and other supernatural favors. He was beatified by Pope Pius VII in 1818.[1390]

[1389] Delaney, 78; Summers, 169; Cruz, MMM, 235; Gallick, 249, 434; Dorcy, 123–26; "Stigmatization," in 1911 *Classic Encyclopedia*; *Dominican Saints*; Dunbar 1:268; Procter, 232–33; Wilson, 132.

[1390] Cruz, MMM, 30, 169, 181, 278; Dorcy, 470–71; Procter, STL, *Short Life of the Dominican Saints,* London: Kegan, Paul, Trench, Trubner & Co. ltd., 1901, 263–65.

Gandolf of Binasco, Bl. (c.1200–1260) (aka Gandulphus of Binasco)

Franciscan mystic and ecstatic born in the little town of Binasco in Lombardy, Italy. Gandolf lived a life of continual penance and abstinence. He had a great zeal for the salvation of souls and was known for his long hours of prayer. He was often seen rapt in ecstasy. On Wednesday of Holy Week in 1260, while in perfect health, he announced that this would be his last sermon since he would soon die. Not too long after, he experienced a violent fever and on Holy Saturday he announced he would not see the dawn of the next day. Gandolf died as he had predicted. Legend has it that birds gathered to sing in the church where his body was laid out. Many miracles occurred through his intercession after his passing. His body was found to be incorrupt sixty years after his death.[1391]

Giovanna Maria Bonomo, Bl.(1606–1670) (aka Joanna of Jesus, Jane Mary Bonomo, Joanna Maria Bonomo)

Benedictine abbess, mystic, visionary, ecstatica, and stigmatic born in Asiago, Lombardy region in Northern Italy. Giovanna was only two when her father killed a man in a jealous rage and was sent to prison. She was educated by the Poor Clare nuns at Trent and, in 1622, became a Benedictine nun at Bassano, Italy. During the profession of her vows, Giovanna fell into ecstasy for the first time. She later was to experience ecstasies and visions of Christ's Passion. This blessed nun also received the stigmata but prayed to have it kept invisible. The flesh of her hands was said to have stood out like the head of a nail.

Giovanna reportedly also received a ring of mystical espousal from Christ. This servant of God was also said to be able to bilocate. Giovanna was persecuted by members of her own community for her dedication and mystical experiences. Many thought her supernatural phenomena to be heretical or a play for attention. She was beatified on June 9, 1783 by Pope Pius VI.[1392]

Helen of Veszprim, Hungary, Bl. (c. 1270) (aka St. Ilona of Hungary)

Dominican nun, mystic, ecstatica, and stigmatic born as Countess Olympiade. She entered the Dominican convent in Veszprim, Hungary and took the religious name Ilona (Helen). As the novice mistress at the convent, she trained the future St. Margaret of Hungary (c. 1242–1270) in the ways of holiness. Helen was known for her gift of contemplative prayer that frequently led to ecstasy. Once, as she prayed, a sister religious witnessed the corpus of the crucifix take her hand in His. Helen was to remain in ecstasy for twenty-four hours during which time her fellow sisters tried to pry her hand loose from the hand of the corpus on the crucifix. No one succeeded. On another occasion, the large cross from the altar came down and suspended itself over her head. It remained suspended in the air over her head until, at the completion of her prayer, she replaced it herself back on the altar. It is claimed that Helen was the first Dominican to be marked with the stigmata. Before 1237, while in a state of ecstasy, she received the stigma on the right hand. Later on, she received the mark on the left hand. At some point later, she received the wounds in the side and the feet. The nuns later testified that they saw and even touched the

---

1391 Cruz, MMM, 212; NCE, 1st ed., v. 6, 279; NCE 2nd ed.,v. 6, 88.

1392 http://www.catholic-forum.com/saints; http://www.nouvlevangelization.fre.fr.giovanna; Butler, 3/1, 7; Gallick, 71; Wilson, 138.

wounds. Sister Helen also was known to levitate and perform miraculous healings. Her hands reportedly shone with a soft radiant glow and a mysterious and lovely heavenly light accompanied her. Candles on the altar would suddenly light themselves whenever she appeared, but would never burn out. It was also said that flowers sprung up from the ground wherever she stepped. At the moment of her death, in 1270, Helen was rapt in ecstasy and so radiant at the prospect of seeing God that the sisters could hardly tell that she was dead. When her tomb was opened seventeen years after her death, her body was found to be incorrupt and gave out a celestial fragrance. The wounds of the stigmata, which closed near the end of her life, had reopened in the tomb. A priest placed two fingers into the wound on her side. When he withdrew them, they were covered in blood having a most fragrant odor.[1393]

Henry Suso, Bl. (c. 1295–1365)

German Dominican monk, prior, visionary, ecstatic, and mystical writer born at Bihlmeyer, near Constance, Switzerland as Henrich von Berg. Henry took his mother's family name Suso instead of his father's von Berg. He entered the Dominican convent at Constance where he was professed at age fourteen. He then went on to study in Cologne under the great and controversial German mystic Johann Eckhart (1324–1328). In his *Little Book of Truth*, he ardently defended Eckhart against charges of heresy. Henry's mystical life began at eighteen when he had a mystical experience that propelled him to become "the Servant of the Eternal Wisdom." At that time, he was flooded with divine light and joy and felt transported out of the world. This experience changed his thinking and

Henry Suso Kneeling before Eternal Wisdom by Abraham van Diepenbeeck

opened the way for frequent visions and ecstasies throughout his life. Angels in visible form often appeared to him when he offered the holy sacrifice of the Mass.

Henry initiated a practice of severe austerities. He had a great veneration for the Holy Name of Jesus. He went so far as to cut the Lord's name into his flesh in the form of IHS above his heart with a pointed stiletto so that at every beat of his heart, Jesus' Holy Name moved with it. Henry is also one of the first responsible for devotion to Mary's sorrows. Once, while in ecstasy, it is said that a light streamed from his heart. For ten years this holy Dominican inflicted the most rigorous mortifications and penances on himself. He endured

[1393] Summers, 155–57; Saints index; Gallick, 339; Dorcy, 72–74; Wilson, 132; Farges, 556.

arid periods of spirituality and experienced visions of Christ, Our Lady, and the saints. Henry wore a hair shirt with 150 brass nails pointed inward as his night shirt for sixteen years. An angel is said to have appeared to him on Pentecost Sunday and whispered that God wanted him to discontinue this practice. When he was forty, Henry began preaching and was tremendously successful in making converts and in causing sinners to repent. He was a much sought-after spiritual director in Dominican convents. During his lifetime, this holy monk suffered innumerable slanders. He was accused of theft, sacrilege, heresy, adultery, and even poisoning, but he was completely exonerated of all charges. Henry wrote mystical treatises, notably *The Little Book of Eternal Wisdom* which contains most of his many mystical experiences. In it are contained descriptions of his many revelations and apparitions of the Blessed Virgin and an autobiography purportedly pieced together by Elsbeth Stagel from material he gave her. Henry was beatified in 1831 by Pope Gregory XVI.[1394]

Hosanna of Kotor, Bl. (1493–1565) (aka Catherine Cosie, Katarina Kosic, Ozana of Kotor, Osanna of Cattaro)

Dominican tertiary, virgin, mystic, visionary, anchoress, and convert from Greek Orthodoxy born as Katerina Kosic at Kumano, Montenegro. Her father was an orthodox priest and her brother later became a monk and the Orthodox bishop of Zeta. Hosanna was a shepherdess in her youth and spent her solitary hours in prayer. She began to have visions of the Christ Child and Christ Crucified. Such visions continued throughout her life. When she was twelve years old, the visions were followed by an odd desire to travel to the town of Kotor (Cattaro) where she felt she could pray better. Her mother arranged a position in this town for her as a servant with a wealthy Catholic family. After a period of time, she converted to Roman Catholicism. She then went on to become a Dominican tertiary taking the name Hosanna in memory of Blessed Osanna of Mantau. Over the next fifty-two years, this servant of God lived in a tiny cell at St. Paul's Church and followed the Dominican rule. She spent her time in prayer and penitence and experienced a mystical union with Christ. In her tiny cell, she is said to have received many visions to include Christ as a baby, the Blessed Virgin Mary, several saints, and demons who opposed her prayer life. Satan allegedly once appeared to her in the guise of the Blessed Virgin Mary. She knew it was the "evil one" when the vision tried to get her to modify her penances and give up her religious life. Hosanna is credited through her prayers of saving her city from the plague as well as from attacks by the Turks. She was beatified in 1934 by Pope Pius XI.[1395]

Ida of Louvain, Bl. (d. 1300)

Cistercian mystic, ecstatica, and stigmatic born at Louvain, Belgium. Ida became a Cistercian nun at Roosendael near Mechelen. She exhibited many supernatural charisms. She was especially known for her fealty to the Blessed Virgin Mary and the Holy Eucharist. Her devotion to the Sacred Passion was eventually rewarded with the stigmata in her hands, feet, and side, with the additional wounds of the

[1394] Butler, 1/25, 173, 185; Cruz, MMM, 163; Delaney, 467; Dorcy, 164–67; Freze, TBWC, 34; Fanning, 107; Ghezzi, VOS, 418–19; Guiley, 143–44; Procter, 60; NCE 2nd ed., v. 13, 453, 468, 765; Underhill, 142; Cruz, A&D, 40; The Miracle Hunter: Marian Apparitions; Catholic wonderworkers 14c.

[1395] Gallick, 117; Patron Saints Index; Dorcy, 295–96.

crown of thorns. These marks are said to have appeared as colored circles. Her ecstasies were frequent and her miracles numerous. Witnesses attested to the fact that she was often radiant with light and that a fragrant perfume was perceived by many who approached her.[1396]

James of Bitetto, Bl. (d. 1485) (aka Giacomo of Bitetto, James of Dalmatia, James the Slav, Jakov Varingez)

James was an ecstatic and one of the greatest mystics of the Franciscan Observance. His levitations, prophecies miracles and mystical gifts were attested to by his fellow religious during his beatification process. Employed as a cook for his order at the friary in Bitetto, this lay brother was often rapt in ecstasy and seen to levitate while preparing meals. His incorrupt body is located in Bitetto, Italy. James was beatified by Pope Clement XI in 1700.[1397]

Jane of Orvieto, Bl. (c. 1264–1306) (aka Vanna of Orvieto, Giovanna of Orvieto)

Dominican tertiary, mystic, visionary, ecstatica, and stigmatic born in Carnaiola, Italy to a peasant family. Jane was a pious and intelligent child who spent much time in prayer. She was orphaned at the age of five and grew up with a special reliance on her guardian angel. Jane later became a Dominican nun of the Third Order at Orvieto, Italy. This future beata was witnessed in ecstasy and suspended in air for one hour. Mere mention of the love of Jesus, the material goodness of Mary, or

Blessed Giovanna of Orvieto by Andrea di Bartolo

the suffering of a martyr was enough to send her into ecstasy. She lived a life of deep prayer and was said to have been a prophet and miracle worker. During the last ten years of her life, Jane experienced the terrible agony of the Passion every Good Friday. She would go into ecstasy and be outstretched on the floor in the position of Christ Crucified. Witnesses could hear her bones crack and see her bloody sweat. Jane is also reported to have received the stigmata wound in the side but it was not always visible. Once she was allegedly cured of a serious illness by the miraculous appearance of Our Lord on the Cross. He is said to have appeared to her in the midst of a bright light and offered her a cup of wine to drink. Upon drinking it, she was instantly cured. Another time when she was too ill to go to church to receive Communion, Our Lady came and brought the Holy Child to her. The whole town came to know of her ecstasies. She also experienced frequent levitation and bilocations. People asked for her blessing but she was embarrassed by all the attention and sought out her privacy. Jane was beatified in 1754 by Pope Benedict XIV.[1398]

[1396] Cruz, MMM, 52; "Stigmatization," in the *Catholic Encyclopedia*; NCE, 1st ed., v. 7, 335a; NCE 2nd ed., v. 7, 288.

[1397] Patron Saints Index; NCE 2nd ed., v. 7, 208–9; Cruz, MMM, 423.

[1398] Summers,169; Cruz, MMM, 23; Patron Saints Index; Procter, 175–76; Dorcy, 136–37; Wilson,

John of Alvernia, Bl. (1259–1322)

Mystic, ecstatic, and visionary born at Fermo, Italy. John was a part-time hermit, part-time evangelist and spiritual advisor in the area around Mount Alvernia and in central and northern Italy. He had the gifts of infused knowledge and mind-reading. John also experienced ecstasies and visions of Christ. He was often rapt in ecstasy. One of these ecstasies is said to have set his heart aflame for three years. On another occasion, while celebrating Mass on All Souls day, he is said to have seen purgatory open and many souls liberated. This virtuous soul reportedly had his guardian angel present with him for three months before his death.[1399]

Julian of Norwich, Bl. (c. 1342–1423) (aka Mother or Dame Julian of Norwich)

Julian was a mystic, visionary, and ecstatica. She was not a member of a religious community but an "anchoress"; that is, a woman living alone in a state of poverty and chastity, similar to that of a religious, and devoting her life to prayer and meditation. Nothing is known of her early life before she became an anchoress outside the walls of St. Julian Church in the village of Conisford in Norwich, England. Her actual name is unknown. She is called "Julian" because of her connection to St. Julian Church in Norwich. Though Julian is often called blessed, she was never formally beatified by the Church. Some Benedictine calendars even give her the title of "saint." On May 8, 1373, the anchoress experienced a series of fifteen revelations

Statue of Julian of Norwich by David Holgate, west front, Norwich Cathedral, photo by Poliphilo

and a sixteenth on the following day, while in a state of ecstasy. The "showings," as she called them, were mostly visions related to Jesus' Passion. Other revelations concerned spiritual truths and the indwelling of the Blessed Trinity in the soul and of Mary. Christ Himself told her these were no hallucinations, to accept them, and believe and to hold firmly to them. Her visions took three forms: "Corporal," which probably meant perceived with the physical senses; "Corporal and yet more spiritual" (imaginative), which probably meant a combination of sensory and inner perception; and "spiritual" (intellectual), which probably referred to an inner visioning seen with the spiritual eye only. The visions filled her with peace and joy. Although she did not at first completely understand the significance of the revelations, she meditated on them and the suffering she had endured just prior to

---

132; Catholic wonderworkers, 14c.

[1399] Patron Saints index; http://www.franciscanfriars.com; Schouppe, *Purgatory*, 221; Franciscan Friars, T.O.R; www.catholictradition.org/angels/guardian.

the revelations for the next twenty years. Then one day she heard a "ghostly" voice explain the meaning to her. The meaning of Jesus' sufferings was nothing more than divine love and her revelations were said to be given for the benefit of all fellow Christians.

Julian kept her mystic life a secret while she lived but wrote it all down. The result was her classic work in Christian mysticism entitled *Sixteen Revelations of Divine Love*, on the love of God, the Incarnation, redemption, sin, penance, and divine consolation. Her writing is regularly punctuated by concern with the problem of sin and damnation. At the time of her death, Julian had a widespread reputation for sanctity. This attracted visitors from all over Europe to her cell.[1400]

Juliana of Cornillon, Bl. (1192–1258) (aka Juliana of Liege, Juliana of Mont-Cornillon)

Augustinian mystic and visionary born at Retinnes, near Liege, Belgium. Juliana was orphaned at age five and placed in the care of the nuns of Mont-Cornillon. She later became an Augustinian nun and Cistercian Prioress of the Convent at Mont-Cornillon near Liege. At the age of fourteen, Juliana began having dreams about a full moon marred by a dark stain. She came to understand what this meant as early as 1209. It was during this time that she also received persistent apparitions of Christ whereby the Lord pointed out to her that there

was no feast in honor of the Blessed Sacrament. The moon she came to recognize was Christ's Church and the dark stain signified the absence of a feast commemorating the gift of Himself in the Eucharist. Juliana thus became one of the earliest proponents for a feast of the Blessed Sacrament. Based on this, Sister Juliana promoted what became known as the feast of Corpus Christi. Quiet about her visions for over twenty years, the beata eventually told three prominent church leaders, including the aged Archdeacon of Liege who later became Pope Urban IV (1261–1264). This resulted in the feast of Corpus Christi being celebrated for the first time locally in Liege in 1246. The struggle to establish the feast for all Christendom was carried on by Juliana's friend Bl. Eva of Liege (13 c.) and was sanctioned by Pope Urban IV in the Bull of 1264. The feast of Corpus Christi for the entire Church is celebrated in the United States on the first Sunday after Trinity Sunday. Blessed Julianna is often depicted holding a monstrance. She was beatified in 1869 by Pope Pius IX.[1401]

Lucy of Narni, Bl. (1476–1544) (aka Lucy Brocadelli, Lucy de Alessio, Lucia Broccadelli, Lucia of Narnia)

Dominican tertiary, mystic, visionary, ecstatica, stigmatic, and victim soul born in Narni, Umbria, Italy as Lucy Brocadelli, the eldest of eleven children. A pious child, Lucy, at age five, received a vision of Our Lady. Two years later, she had a heavenly vision of our Divine Lord, accompanied by His Blessed Mother, Sts. Dominic Guzman, Catherine of Siena, and a glorious troop of angels and saints. During this

[1400] NCE lst ed., v. 8, 48–49; Delaney, 290; Johnson, 182ff; Fanning, 124ff; Cowan, 268; Ghezzi, VOS, 426–27; Gallick, 145, 422; Guiley, 197–98; DeVinck, 61–76; Paul Molinari, SJ, *Julian of Norwich: The Teaching of a Fourteenth Century English Mystic*, NY: Longmans Green and Co., NY, 1958; M. L. Del Mastro, *Julian of Norwich, Revelations of Divine Love*, NY: Image Books, 1977; Flinders, 77–101.

[1401] www.Catholic-forum.com/saints; NCE, 2nd ed., v. 8, 51; Johnson, 195; Jones, 11–14; Delaney, 289–90; Poulain, 75–76; Gallick, 108, 418.

vision, Jesus espoused her to Himself, placing a precious ring on her finger, and St. Dominic and St. Catherine took her under their special protection. St. Dominic bestowed on her the scapular of his Order. Many other heavenly favors, together with the gift of prophecy, were granted to Lucy during her childhood. She was reportedly thrice miraculously restored to health by St. Catherine of Siena and St. Peter Martyr (1205–1252).

This young visionary reluctantly agreed to marry Count Pietro de Alessio of Milan with the understanding that they would live as brother and sister. When he demanded his marital rights three years later, Lucy ran off to a Dominican convent in Rome to consecrate herself entirely to her Heavenly Spouse. Pietro, who would eventually become a Franciscan and noted preacher, burned the convent down. In 1496, Lucy accepted an invitation to become a prioress in Viterbo, Italy and joined a group of Dominican Tertiaries. She still continued to be graced with many miraculous visions. She began to fall more and more into ecstasy during prayer and at the age of twenty received the visible mark of the stigmata by which she suffered Christ's Passion every Wednesday and Friday. This virtuous soul was ultimately referred to the Inquisition by her bishop. Three successive papal commissions composed of doctors and theologians examined Lucy closely and declared her wounds authentic and unexplainable. The inquisitors referred her case to the Vatican. Pope Alexander VI (1492–1503) had her stigmata wounds rigorously examined by his own physician, Bernardo de Recanati, and others. Her wounds were pronounced genuine and were noted for their sweet-smelling perfume. The Pope decided her mystical signs were from God and asked Lucy to pray for him.

Lucy later served as prioress of the Convent of St. Catherine of Siena in Narni.

However, in 1505, she was replaced as prioress. The new superior had her confined at the convent for the remaining thirty-nine years of her life in some of the lowest positions in the community. The future beata lived out her years in silence, completely obedient, spending all her free time in prayer, frequently going into ecstasies and receiving visions. During this time, she is said to have received miraculous visits via bilocation from another contemporary Dominican mystic and stigmatic, Blessed Catherine of Racconigi (1486–1547).

At the time of Sister Lucy's entrance into heaven, angelic voices were heard singing in her cell and the whole house was filled with an extraordinary perfume. The wound in her side was examined at this time and was found dripping with fresh blood. After her death, miracles were reported at her tomb. Her body remained incorrupt. When exhumed, it was found to be in excellent condition with the marks of the stigmata still visible and having the scent of violets. Lucy left behind a written account of her spiritual journey that was later widely circulated as Seven Revelations. She was beatified in 1710 by Pope Clement XI.[1402]

[1402] Cruz, Inc., 166–67; Cruz, MMM, 389; Gallick, 344, 448; Dorcy, 267–70; Dunbar, 1:473; Procter, 327–29; Benedict M Ashley, O.P., *Blessed Osanna d'Andreasi and Other Italian Dominican Woman Mystics*, read online at www.op.org/domcentral/study/ashley/osanna.htm; Georgiana Fullerton, Lady, *The Life of St. Frances of Rome, of Blessed Lucy of Narni, of Dominica of Paradiso and of Anne De Montmorecy,* NY: Routledge, 2001; http://www.catholic-forum.com/saint; www.newadvent.org/cathen; Patron Saints Index; Wilson, 135.

Margaret of Castello by Andrea di Bartolo

Margaret of Castello, Bl. (1287–1320) (aka Margaret of Metola, Margaret of Citta Di Castello)

Dominican tertiary, mystic, visionary, and stigmatic born deformed in Metola, near Florence Italy to a noble family. Margaret was blind, hunchbacked, dwarfed, and lame as her right leg was much shorter than the left. She was described quite candidly as "ugly." Imprisoned by her parents and deprived of parental love when she was six years old, this poor creature was eventually abandoned by these same parents in a church in Metola at age twenty. For several years, Margaret was handed over from one family to another. Due to her extreme piety, the cloistered nuns of St. Margaret's Monastery invited her to join them. Later on she joined the Mantellate sisters and became a Dominican Tertiary. Despite her miseries, Margaret was serene, cheerful, and courageous. She was never bitter, never complained, never reproached others nor lost heart. She found strength in prayer, daily Mass, and Holy Communion. Margaret once confided to her confessor that every time she attended Mass she saw Christ Incarnate on the altar. Her mind was often described as "luminous." This beata was one of the pioneers in the devotion to St. Joseph. During periods of intense prayer, she was known to levitate up to twenty inches off the floor and remain suspended for a long time. It is likewise recorded that although completely blind all her life, she was nevertheless the recipient of many visions of Our Lord. She was often heard to exclaim, "Oh, if you only knew what I have in my heart!" Upon death, her heart was examined and in it were discovered three pellets or pearls on which were carved images which some perceived as being the religious depictions of Our Lord, the Blessed Mother, and St. Joseph. More than two hundred miracles have been attributed to her intercession after death. Her incorrupt body can be seen in a glass sarcophagus in the Chapel of the School for the Blind in Citta di Castello, Italy. Margaret is an inspiration to those tempted to self-pity. She is the patron saint of the unwanted, especially nowadays, of aborted babies. She was beatified in 1609 by Pope Paul V.[1403]

[1403] Fr. William R. Bonniwell, O.P., *The Life of Blessed Margaret of Castello 1287–1320*, Rockford, Ill.: TAN Books, 1983; Cruz, SS, 456–63; Cruz, MMM, 76; Gallick, 115, 419; Guiley, 218.

Margaret of Savoy being offered three arrows by Christ

Margaret of Savoy, Bl. (1390–1464)

Dominican tertiary, abbess, mystic, visionary, and ecstatica born in Pinerolo, Piedmont, Italy to an illustrious family. In 1403 Margaret married the Marquis of Montferrat, a widower with two children. After her husband's death in 1418, she vowed to remain a widow and devoted herself to caring for her stepchildren. Through the influence of St. Vincent Ferrer, she took the habit of the Third Order of St. Dominic. Later, Margaret founded the Monastery of St. Mary Magdalen, made solemn vows as a nun of the Second Order, and served the community as abbess until her death. The future beata was favored during her life with many ecstasies and numerous miracles. During one of her visions, she beheld Our Lord offering her three arrows, each of which was marked by a word: Sickness, Slander, Persecution. She generously accepted all three. This vision is frequently depicted in her iconography. It has been established that at one time or another during her life she had been wounded by all three of these arrows. This favored soul died on November 23, 1464, having been strengthened by a vision of St. Catherine of Siena which was seen by all those assisting at her deathbed. Her incorrupt body which still retains its softness and flexibility, after some five hundred years, lies in a glass reliquary in the Church of St. Magdalen in Alba, Italy.[1404]

Margaretha Ebner, Bl. (1291–1351) (aka Margaret Ebner, Margrete Ebner, Mystic of Medingen)

Dominican nun, mystic, visionary, ecstatica, stigmatic, and victim soul born at Donauworth, Bavaria, Germany into a rich and influential Swabian family. At age fifteen, she followed a family tradition and entered the Dominican convent at Maria-Medingen. However, Margaret became extremely ill from 1312 to 1322 and remained at her home to recover. During that time she offered her sufferings for the victims of Louis of Bavaria's war. Her life was to become one of expiation for the sins of others. While at home, she began to experience visions, raptures, revelations, and prophecies. Her mystical experiences began when souls from purgatory, many of whom were deceased sisters of her community, appeared to her to thank her for her prayers. In time, Margaret also had visionary encounters with the Infant Jesus,

---

[1404] Cruz, 146; Dorcy, 208–9; NCE, 1st ed.,v. 9, 203; NCE 2nd ed., v. 9, 150.

the Virgin Mary, and her favorite apostle, St. John the Evangelist. She was also given revelations of truth of hidden things and experienced raptures that caused her to levitate. She also prayed to receive the stigmata as St. Francis had. Fr. Henry of Nordlingen was her spiritual adviser and commanded she write a full account of her mystical experiences. She did this in a work entitled *Revelations*. Margaret's writings are still regarded as classics of Western spirituality. She was beatified by Pope John Paul II (1978–2005) on February 24, 1979, the first beatification of his pontificate.[1405]

Maria Mancini, Bl. (1355–1431) (aka Catherine Mancini of Pisa)

Dominican tertiary, mystic, visionary, and ecstatica born Catherine Mancini in Pisa, Italy of noble parentage. This beata enjoyed miraculous favors from childhood to include being able to see her guardian angel. At the age of three, she was warned by some heavenly agency that the porch her nurse had placed her on was unsafe. Catherine's cries alerted her nurse to remove her from the porch which then collapsed just after her removal from it. At the age of five, while in ecstasy, she had a vision of a citizen of Pisa named Peter Gambacorta (who later became her benefactor) about to be hanged. Her prayers for him allegedly caused the rope to break and Peter was released and his death sentence commuted.

Despite her early mystical experiences, Catherine was married at twelve and bore two children. Her husband died four years later and she was pressured to marry again. She did and bore her second husband five children. Her second husband died eight years later. Of her seven children, only one survived the death of her second husband. Catherine learned through a vision that this child too was soon to be taken from her. The twenty-five-year-old widow refused to marry a third time and turned her house into a hospital. Our Lord approved of her works by appearing to her as a sick man in need of food and medicine. She became a Dominican tertiary and forged a holy friendship with St. Catherine of Siena. On the advice of the saint, Catherine Mancini retired to an enclosed convent of the Second Order and took the name of Maria. She was favored with many visions and was in almost constant prayer. It is said that sometimes she would go into an ecstasy while walking along the street. This future beata became prioress of her convent of Santa Croce in Pisa upon the death of her friend Blessed Clare Gambacorta (1362–1419). She was beatified by Pope Pius IX in 1855.[1406]

Maria of the Passion of Our Lord Jesus Christ, Bl. (1866–1912) (aka Maria della Passione)

Mystic, visionary, stigmatic, and victim soul born in Barra, Naples, Italy as Maria Grazia Tarallo. Maria was raised in a pious family and, at the age of five before a statue of the Blessed Mother, made a private vow of virginity. When she was seven years old, the Infant Jesus appeared to her on the day of her first Holy Communion. His hands were wounded and bloody. He told her that "His wounds were caused by the sins of mankind." From that time on, Maria consecrated her life to the Eucharist and the salvation of souls. In 1891, she entered the monastery of the Sisters Crucified Adorers of the Eucharist taking the name Sister Maria of the Passion. This servant

---

[1405] NCE 2nd ed., v. 5, 32; Gallick, 165; Dorcy, 157–58; Fanning, 108–9; http://saints.sqpn.com/saintm2y.htm; Margaret Ebner, *Major Works*, NY: Paulist Press, 1993.

[1406] Dorcy, 195.

of God desired to became a victim soul for sinners. During another apparition, Jesus confided in Maria, saying, "I am in the Eucharist to dispense pardon and mercy, but I receive ungratefulness, irreverence, and sacrilege. The Eucharist is abused and no one seems to care. My beloved, remedy this with adoration for my Real Presence." Among the many mystical gifts Maria received were bilocation and inedia, in which she is said to have subsisted during the last years of her life only on the Eucharist. Maria is also said to have experienced the exchange of hearts. As with all mystics, this beata likewise experienced torment by demons because she was snatching souls of sinners away from Satan. In this regard, souls in purgatory are said to have appeared to Maria to thank her for her prayers for them. During yet another vision, the beata felt the piercing pains of the crucifixion and Jesus Himself piercing her heart with a lance. It was this wound of love, the so-called transverberation, that bound her to Jesus, her spouse. From Holy Week 1903 on, this servant of God received the stigmata which she bore until her death. She was beatified by Pope Benedict XVI on May 14, 2006.[1407]

Mariana of Jesus, Bl. (1565–1624) (aka Mary Ann of Jesus Navarro, Mariana Navarra de Guevara, "Lily of Madrid")

Discalced Mercedarian tertiary, mystic, and stigmatic born in Madrid to Luis Navarro and Juana Romero. From early childhood, Marianna showed an extraordinary maturity of judgment. The Lord is said to have graced her with many heavenly gifts and miraculous interventions.

She was noted for her life of penance, devotion to the Eucharist, and intense prayer. She had the gifts of prophecy and discernment of spirits and showed a great devotion to the Sacred Heart of Jesus, even before the devotion became common in the church. This servant of God manifested a tender love for the Blessed Virgin and for the Blessed Sacrament. Her body is incorrupt. Mariana is also the author of a spiritual autobiography. She was beatified in 1783 by Pope Pius VI.[1408]

Marie of the Incarnation, Bl. (1566–1618) (Barbara Aurillot, Barbara Avrillot, Barbe Aurillot, Madame Acarie, Barbara Acarie, Marie de l'Incarnarcion)

Carmelite lay sister, mystic, visionary, ecstatica, and stigmatic born in Paris, France as Barbe Aurillot. She married Viscount Pierre Acarie at the age of sixteen and bore him six children, three of whom became Carmelites, and one a priest. She was known as "La Belle Acarie," in Parisian society of that time as well as "the conscience of Paris." Barbe was widowed at the age of forty-seven and became a Carmelite lay sister in 1613 at Amiens, France taking the name Marie of the Incarnation. After reading the autobiography of St. Teresa of Avila, the Carmelite reformer appeared to Barbe in a dream telling her it was God's will for her to introduce the Discalced Carmelite Order in France. Madame Acarie considered the idea ridiculous, but when St. Teresa visited again, she could not ignore her wishes. She won permission from the French king and the Order took root in France.

[1407] Thurston, 63, 272, 347–48; Patron Saints Index; Maria della Passione; www.ewtn.com, Index of the Biographies of the Blesseds from 1993–2007; Wilson, 143.

[1408] Summers, 107; Cruz, MMM, 235; Patron Saints Index; NCE, 2nd ed., v. 2, 858; 1913 Catholic Encyclopedia; http://www.orderofmercedarians.org.

This beata is best known for her visions, ecstasies, and supernatural gifts, one of which was cardiognosis. She was just twenty-two when she had the first of her many ecstatic experiences. In the late summer of 1590, she went to High Mass at her parish church, Saint-Gervais, and during the Sursum Corda was transported into a state of ecstasy. It is said that Madame Acarie was so prone to ecstasy that her confessors could not give her the usual penances to say. She sometimes played her spinet to distract herself and get through the requisite prayers, but she usually fell into ecstasy before she got through a Hail Mary. While in her ecstatic trances, she sometimes received the stigmata. As she advanced spiritually, she became better able to control her reveries, though she still continued to receive the stigmata. It is interesting to note here that this visionary perceived the supposed seventeenth-century mystic Nicole of Rheum's outstanding acts of piety as the products of pride, stimulated by the devil. Nobody, however, listened to her for, during this time, as a purported mystic herself, she was under investigation and not an admissible witness. All Madame Acarie's three daughters became Carmelite nuns. Pope Pius VI beatified her in 1791.[1409]

Mary Magdalen of the Incarnation, Bl. (1770–1824) (aka Caterina Sordini)

Franciscan mystic, visionary, ecstatica, stigmatic, and foundress of the Perpetual Order of the Blessed Sacrament born as Caterini Sordini at Grosseto, Italy, the fourth of nine children to a deeply Catholic family. Caterina's father arranged for her marriage. However, before the ceremony was to take place, Caterina stood before a mirror in her jewelry and finery and saw the image of a crucified Jesus. The Lord allegedly spoke to her saying: "Do you want to leave me for another?" To the shock of her father, Caterina left and entered the Franciscan monastery in Ischia di Castro in February, 1788 taking the name of Sister Mary Magdalene of the Incarnation. On February 19, 1789, this newly professed nun fell into ecstasy and saw a vision of "Jesus seated on a throne of grace in the Blessed Sacrament, surrounded by virgins adoring Him." She heard Him tell her: "I have chosen you to establish the work of perpetual adorers who, day and night, will offer me their humble adoration." This servant of God was thus called to become a foundress of the Perpetual Order of the Blessed Sacrament. She spent the remainder of her life adoring Jesus in the Eucharist. Marie was elected abbess on April 20, 1802. The period of her governance was accompanied by extraordinary phenomena and an increasingly fervent spiritual life, and the abbey thrived. The Napoleonic laws, however, suppressed her Order and she was exiled to Tuscany. There she formed a new group of adorers. On March 19, 1814, she returned to Rome and settled in Sant'Anna al Quirinale. Pope Pius VII (1800–1823) approved the Institute dedicated to perpetual, solemn, public exposition of the Most Blessed Sacrament on February 13, 1818. Blessed Mary Magdalen's remains are located in the Church of Santa Maria Maddalena, the new generalate of the Perpetual Adorers in Rome. Pope John Paul II decreed her heroic virtues in 2001, and in 2007, Pope Benedict XVI recognized a miracle attributed to her intercession. She was beatified by him in 2008.[1410]

[1409] Johnson, 76, 299, 322; Jones, 129; Gallick, 109, 416; Guiley, 239–40; Jones, 128–36; Underhill, Mystics, 191–96; http://www.catholic-forum,com/saints; NCE, 1st ed., v. 9, 219 c.; NCE 2nd ed., v. 9, 164–65; www.newadvent.org; Patron Saints Index.

[1410] See http://www.Vatican.va/news_services/liturgy/saints/2008.

Mary of Oignies, Bl. (1167–1213) (aka Marie d'Oignies)

Mystic, visionary, ecstatic, stigmatic, and victim soul born in Nivelles, a diocese of Liège, Belgium. Mary married against her will at age fourteen. She convinced her husband to live a celibate life and to turn their home into a leper hospice. Because of the gossip this caused, Mary left Nivelles, joined the Beguine community and moved to a hermit's cell near the Augustinian house at Oignies. This Belgian Beguine developed a great devotion to St. John the Evangelist (c. 6–104) as well as had a high regard for her contemporary, St. Christina the Astonishing.

Mary is noted for her visions of the infant Jesus, St. John the Evangelist, and her guardian angel. She also experienced other mystical phenomena such as ecstasies, the gift of tears, as well as clairvoyance, prophecy, and knowledge of events taking place at a distance. Mary was devoted to the Eucharist. She frequently experienced the taste of honey in her mouth upon receiving the Host and her face transfigured. She often saw Jesus as a baby surrounded by angels or in the form of a lamb or dove at the elevation of the Host. When the priest celebrant received communion, Mary saw Jesus descend into his soul and fill it with uncreated light. Her biographer also reported that she experienced the mystical "fire of love," with her body radiating discernible heat while her clothing gave off the odor of incense. This servant of God spent the rest of her life at Oignies praying for the souls in purgatory. She dressed exclusively in white and is said to have received the stigmata in 1212. Mary reportedly cut off pieces of her flesh to rid herself of desire for the world. Food repulsed her (inedia) and she is said to have once gone thirty-five days without eating. She also possessed the odor of sanctity while praying.[1411]

[1411] Cruz, MMM, 51, 176, 247, 275; NCE, 1st ed.,

Mechthild von Magdeburg , 1896, by Peter Paul Metz

Mechtild of Magdeburg, Bl. (c. 1209–1294)

Dominican tertiary, mystic, stigmatic, and visionary born to noble parents in Lower Saxony, Germany. According to Mechtild's own testimony, her first mystical experience occurred when, at the age of twelve, she was greeted by a mystical vision of the Holy Spirit. Thus would begin a series of visions of "Godly Greetings" that would continue on a regular basis throughout her life. Desiring to live wholly for God, Mechtild became a Beguine at Magdeburg

---

v. 9, 389b; NCE 2nd ed., v. 9, 288–90; Patron Saints Index; Fanning, 95–96; *Two Lives of Marie d' Ognies*, trans. Margot H. King and Hugh Feiss, O.S.B., Toronto: Pegrina, 2000, 53–56; Gallick, 190, 428; Baring-Gould 6:319–22; Dunbar 2:54–55; Catholic Wonderworkers; http://thermatuges.blogspot.com.

in 1230 and, under the direction of the Dominicans, led a life of intense prayer and austerity for forty years. The hostility aroused by her extraordinary mystical experiences and by her severe criticism of the clergy forced her, in 1270, to leave Magdeburg. Ailing and partially blind, she sought refuge in the Cistercian convent at Helfta, where she was warmly received by Sts. Mechtild of Helfta and Gertrude the Great. There she would remain in a congenial atmosphere until her death. Although regarded as a saint by her contemporaries, Mechtild has never been formally canonized. Since childhood, this Beguine began writing down the revelations she had been receiving from the Holy Spirit. These revelations were recorded in her work entitled *The Flowing Light of the Godhead* which was circulated all over Europe. This manuscript is basically a trail of her inner spiritual journey. Her book combines a number of genres—mystical love poems describing the soul's communion with God, dialogues with Christ, as well as vivid accounts of her visions of heaven, purgatory, and hell and the destiny of all creatures. At the moment of her death, Our Lord and His Blessed Mother came to conduct her to heaven. St. Gertrude is said to have witnessed Our Lord bend over and give her the kiss of peace as she lay dying.[1412]

Blessed Osanna Andreasi, Bonsignori, Francesco (c.1455-1519) / Palazzo Ducale & Museo, Mantua, Lombardy, Italy / Bridgeman Images

Osanna of Mantua, Bl. (1449–1505) (aka Osanna d'Andreasi, Hossana of Mantua, Hosanna Andreasi)

Dominican tertiary, mystic, visionary, ecstatica, stigmatic, and victim soul born in Mantua, Italy, the eldest child of aristocratic parents. As a youngster, this extremely pious child shared Christ's Passion and experienced ecstasies and raptures. She reportedly also had visions of the nine choirs of angels, paradise, the Trinity, and of Jesus her own age carrying a cross. It is said that Osanna was taught to read and write by the Blessed Mother herself. At fourteen years of age, she became a Dominican tertiary but remained in her own home. Called by some an "ecstatic saint," this servant of God is claimed to have had ecstasies lasting for hours or even days whenever anything reminded her of

[1412] Robert Ellsberg, *All Saints: Daily Reflections on Saints, Prophets, and Witnesses for Our Time*, NY: The Crossroad Publishing Company, 1997, 320, Gallick, 330, 443; NCE, 1st ed., v .9, 546; NCE 2nd ed., v. 9, 423; Dorcy, 106; Mechtilde of Magdeburg, *The Flowering Light of the Godhead*, trans. with an introduction by Frank Tobin, Mahwah, N.J.: Paulist Press, 1997 (Classics of Western Spirituality Series); De Vinck, 3–25; Flinders, 43–75; Fanning, 99–100.

the blood of Christ or whenever she began to speak of God. During one Lent, she is alleged to have fallen into an ecstasy which lasted three whole days.

When Osanna was eighteen, the Blessed Virgin Mary appeared to her with Sts. Catherine of Alexandria and Catherine of Siena and told her she was to be her Son's bride. Christ, in turn, placed an invisible wedding ring on her finger. On February 24, 1476, being mystically espoused to Christ, the beata received from Him a crown of thorns. A wound in her side next appeared on June 5, 1477 while she was rapt in ecstasy. At that time, it is claimed that she was also raised up into the Seventh Heaven where she saw the Lord in exceeding great glory. A year later, during the Friday of Passion Week, Christ is said to have appeared to her and rays from the wounds in His hands and feet pierced through her flesh. For the rest of her life, Osanna experienced the Passion in a more intense way on Wednesdays and Fridays and during Holy Week. In her case, the stigmata did not seem to have bled, but simply to have appeared as red, intensely painful swellings. They were noticeable to other people only on Wednesdays and Fridays and during Holy Week, but they were always visible to her, as a source of great pain and spiritual joy. On still another occasion, the Lord purportedly removed her heart and replaced it flaming with love.

After this beata's death, the stigmata which were scarcely visible during life became quite pronounced, as also occurred in the case of St. Catherine of Siena. The visible appearance of these mysterious markings, after all apparent signs of life had left the body, completely refutes the opinion of those who attribute the stigmata to auto-suggestion, since quite understandably, a dead body has no control over what happens to it.

This bride of Christ later had a vision in which her heart was transformed and divided into four parts. The agonies Osanna endured never satisfied this victim soul's insatiable thirst to suffer for sinners and for the souls in purgatory. She also lived on virtually no food at all (inedia). Many revelations were given to her and she was said to have been led by her guardian angel through purgatory as well as given a glimpse of heaven by him. Her guardian angel showed her that heaven was to be her preoccupation and happiness even while on earth. From early childhood until her death, Osanna enjoyed loving companionship with the angels.

In the last years of her life, the monk Father Jerome of Mantua became her spiritual son and intimate confidant. His conversations with Osanna have resulted in a remarkable biography of her life. Like other visionaries, Osanna was known for her prophetic judgment, for her competence in human affairs, and for her charity. She often spoke out against the rampant moral corruption of state and church in Italy. Before her death, the soul of another Dominican tertiary, Blessed Columba of Rieti, appeared to her and told her to prepare for death. Osanna's incorrupt body, still showing the marks of the holy stigmata, is to be found in the Cathedral of Mantua. She was beatified in 1694 by Pope Innocent XII.[1413]

[1413] Schouppe, Purgatory, xxxviii; www.newadvent.com/cathen; Patron Saint Index; Butler, 6/20, 148; Cruz, Inc., 156–57; Dorcy, 238–40; Wiebe, 20; Walsh, v. 2, 321; Gallick, 185, 428; Ghezzi, VOS, 450–51; http://www.domcentral.org; Freze, TWBC, 262; Wilson, 134; http://www.catholic-forum.com/saints; Procter, 175–76; Summers, 78, 100, 105, 154; Edward Watkin, *Neglected saints*, NY: Sheed and Ward, 1955, 139–59.

Engraving of Ramon Llull

Raymond Lull, Bl. (1232–1316) (aka Raymundis or Ramon Lluyl, Luyl, Lullus, Lullius)

Franciscan tertiary, mystic, and visionary born in the city of Palma on the island of Majorca. Despite his marriage and two children, Raymond led a dissolute, playboy life. He had mistresses both before and during his marriage. One night around 1266 while composing a poem, he had an apparition of Christ crucified beside him, with both the Cross and the Redeemer hanging in midair. This same vision would appear to him five separate times, each in more hideous detail. The former playboy immediately converted from his past sins and inclinations and became a Franciscan tertiary. He provided for his family, left home for a period of seclusion and prayer, and devoted the rest of his life to converting Moslems. Raymond spent the next nine years of his life studying Arabic and Moslem culture and philosophy. The future blessed saw Islam not so much as a

false religion but as an incomplete religion, a heresy of Christianity. He believed that Islam replaced the tribe scattered idolatry of Middle Eastern paganism with basic ideas like a single, invisible, all-powerful God, an individual afterlife and account-ability for one's actions, but that it left out the rest of Judeo-Christian revelation. Blessed Raymond wrote voluminously— more than three hundred treatises (many in Arabic) on philosophy, theology, etc. Chief among his writings were *Blanquerna* (1283), a long moral tale and the first novel in any Romance language; *Arbre de philoso-phia de armor* (Work on the Philosophy of Love), *Ars compendiosa inveniendi veritatem* (The Brief Art of Finding Truth). Raymond was later to experience another vision which he described as a mystic illumina-tion in which he saw the whole world in relationship to the attributes of God. In a flash, he understood that all human wis-dom pales before knowledge of God, and that human wisdom and human memory had to be used, just as the emotions and the heart, in the soul's ascent to God. On his third visit to Africa, this Islamophile was stoned by the Saracens in Tunis and died of his injuries. Being a martyr for his faith, he is revered as a saint in Majorca although he has not yet been canonized. The Francis-cans honor him as Doctor Illuminatus, the Enlightened Teacher. He was beatified by Pope Pius IX in 1847.[1414]

Sibyllina Biscossi, Bl. (1287–1367)

Mystic, visionary, and ecstatica born of humble parents in Pavia, Italy. Sibyllina became orphaned at an early age and, as a result of a severe illness, was rendered completely blind. This pious girl was taken in by a community of Dominican tertia-ries. While praying that her sight might

---

[1414] Cruz, SS, 645–46; Delaney, 426; Johnson, 173ff; NCE 2nd ed., v. 8, 866–67.

be restored, Sibyllina knelt before a statue of St. Dominic (1170–1221) and, rapt in ecstasy, saw this saint come out of the darkness to take her by the hand and lead her through an area of darkness where she sensed the presence of evil creatures. She was then brought into an area of radiant light and peace. After awakening, this future beata came to realize that her blindness in this world would be rewarded by the sight of heavenly wonders.

Sibyllina lived as a holy recluse, a contemplative who was favored with many heavenly visions and revelations. She had a reputation for holiness and was especially devoted to the Holy Spirit. She was also blessed with great gifts of discernment. A singular gift possessed by this servant of God was the ability to sense the Real Presence in the Blessed Sacrament. Legend has it that, on one occasion, she warned a priest that the Host he was carrying for a sick call was unconsecrated. He checked it out and discovered that she was right. He had taken the Host from the wrong container. Sibyllina's body was found to be incorrupt and is enshrined in the cathedral in Pavia. Many favors and miracles have been reported through her intercession. Sibyllina was beatified by Pope Pius IX in 1853.[1415]

Stephanie Quinzani, Bl. (1457–1530) (aka Stephana Quinzanis, Stephanie de Quinzanis)

Dominican tertiary, mystic, visionary, ecstatica, and stigmatic born to pious parents in Brescia, Italy. Stephanie was taught her catechism by the stigmatic Blessed Matthew Carrieri (d. 1470), the heroic Dominican friar of Mantua, who once

offered himself to be sold into slavery to ransom others from Muslims. Her mystical experiences began at age seven when she took vows of poverty, chastity, and obedience. At that time, little Stephanie continually heard an inner voice repeating to her the words, "Charity, Charity, Charity." At age twelve, St. Andrew appeared to her in a vision holding a large cross and addressed her in the following words: "Behold, my daughter, the way to heaven. Love God, fear God, honor God; flee from the world and embrace the Cross." Stepahnie then went on to become a Dominican tertiary at Soncino, near Bergamo, Italy when she was fifteen. This future beata was to be later favored with visitations from Our Lord, the Blessed Virgin Mary, Sts. Dominic, Thomas Aquinas, and Catherine of Siena. Other Dominican saints were also said to appear to her, including Blessed Matthew Carrieri, mentioned above, allegedly in a vision shortly after he died. It was not long after this vision of Matthew that Stephanie herself received the stigmata at age fifteen. Her confessor testified to having seen the marks of her stigmata on her hands and feet and the crown of thorns on her head.

Stephanie reportedly experienced ecstasies, including participation in various stages of Christ's Passion. This was attested to by some twenty-one witnesses in 1497 in an account that is still extant. Every Friday for forty years, this servant of God experienced the agony of the sweat of blood in Gethsemane and the pains of the crown of thorns which was often plainly seen encircling her head. Also seen was the elongation of her left arm as accompaniment of apparent nailing to the cross. During one of Our Lord's visits, Stephanie was said to have been given a beautiful ring as a token of her espousal to Christ. This ring was purportedly seen by a great many people. This beata led a life of constant penance, was devoted to the Holy Eucharist and

---

[1415] Cruz, SS, 672–73; Gallick, 94; NCE, 1st. ed., v. 13, 190; Procter, 72–74; Dorcy, 172–74; Catholic Wonderworkers, 14 c.

heroically bore the wounds of the sacred stigmata.

Like St. Thomas Aquinas, she was also girded by angels with a cord of purity. She was said to be also gifted with profound theological understanding, the gift of prophecy, and was credited with performing numerous miracles of healing. Stephanie also had the power to read the hearts of the many who came to consult her, among whom were Blessed Osanna d'Andreasi (1449–1505), Blessed Augustine of Biella (1430–1493), and St. Angela Merici, the foundress of the Ursulines. This virtuous soul lived in a nearly continuous fast, and inflicted severe penances on herself. Stephanie also had the gift of being able to multiply wine, flour, and even money for the poor. She also predicted the day of her death and the place of her burial. Stephanie was beatified in 1740 by Pope Benedict XIV.[1416]

Ugolino Zefiriniof Mantua, Bl.(1320–1367)

Augustinian mystic and stigmatic born in Cortono, Italy. As an infant, his family was banished from his birth place and forced to flee to Mantua. In 1336, at the age of sixteen, Ugolino entered the Augustinian Order in the monastery of Saint Agnes in Mantua. He spent the last years of his life, however, in his native city in solitude as a hermit. Upon opening his tomb in Cortona about seventy years after his death, his body was found to be not only incorrupt but his ferita (side wound) was welling with blood. When his body was exhumed, the wound found on the right side of his breast was said to have flowed with fresh and fragrant blood, which healed the sick.[1417]

Ulrika Franziska Nisch, Bl. (1882–1913) (aka Franziska Nisch)

Mystic and visionary born out of wedlock in the village of Mittelbiberach-Oberndorf in the state of Wurtermberg, Germany. Franciska left school at the age of twelve. Ten years later, she began working as a nanny in Switzerland for four children. After recovery from a serious infection, she longed to become a nun. At this time, she also reportedly began to experience frequent visits from angels and saints. She confided these things to her pastor and he arranged for her to be admitted to the Holy Cross convent, despite her illegitimate birth and lack of a dowry. Taking the religious name Ulrika, this virtuous soul tried to hide her mystical experiences, but they were observed by the other sisters. An associate explained that, when questioned, she would quietly report visions of Christ as an infant, but especially as a Bridegroom. Ulrika had frequent special knowledge of the future, including World War I, and she possessed an odor of sanctity. Since her death, she has interceded for thousands, and the number of pilgrims who visit her tomb in Hegne has grown to more than 100,000 a year. She has also been credited with miracles. She was beatified on November 1, 1987 by Pope John Paul II.[1418]

[1416] Cruz, MMM, 147, 214; Delaney, 422; Dorcy, 251–52; Wiebe, 20; Biot, 26; Freze, VVA, 227; Gallick, 10; Thurston, 291, 216; www.op.org/domcentral/study/ashley/osanna.htm; Procter, 4; Summers, 147, 154; Wilson, 134; http://www.Miraclehunter.com/marian_apparitions/visionaries/index.html.

[1417] Summers, 170; Biot, 27; Book of Augustinian Saints, 149.

[1418] Gallick, 149; NCE, 2nd ed., v. 10, 399–400.

Veronica of Milan, Church of Turago Bordone, Fresco by Luigi Migliavacca

Veronica of Binasco, Bl. (1445–1497) (aka Veronica of Milan)

Augustinian mystic, visionary, stigmatic, and ecstatica born Giovanna Negroni to a poor family in Binasco, near Milan, Italy. From early childhood, Giovanna enjoyed the gift of contemplation. She attempted to enter a convent but was turned away from several of them because she was illiterate. Giovanna struggled to read and write until the Blessed Mother appeared to her in a dream and assured her that there were only three lessons she needed to learn: purity of heart, patience, and the Passion of Christ. After three years of studying these lessons, she was received into the Augustinian Convent of St. Martha in Milan. When professed, she took the religious name of Veronica.

This holy nun was favored with innumerable ecstasies and visions as well as blessed with wondrous revelations. In 1495, she journeyed to Rome in order to give Pope Alexander VI (1492–1503) a secret message from Christ. It was also said that she was shown the entire life of Jesus in a series of visions. Veronica likewise possessed the gifts of prophecy and discernment. She was devoted to the Eucharist and to the

Passion of Christ. On one occasion, it was reported that this servant of God drew the Blessed Sacrament from the altar through the air to herself. Veronica also had a zeal for the salvation of souls and experienced visions of purgatory and Christ's sufferings. It was also claimed that she experienced mistreatment by the devil, but that her guardian angel always stood by to help her. With her angel's assistance, she is alleged to have learned to sing the Divine Office. Veronica was beatified by Pope Benedict XIV in 1749.[1419]

Villana De Botti, Bl. (1332–1361)

Dominican tertiary, mystic, visionary, ecstatica, and stigmatic born in Florence to a merchant family. Although a very pious child, Villana reputedly ran away from home at the age of thirteen to join a convent, but was refused admittance due to her age. She was then forced to marry a wealthy merchant against her will. For a while, she led a carefree, frivolous, and worldly life, losing herself in a whirl of clothes, jewels, and parties. One night, while dressing for an evening's entertainment with friends, she looked into a mirror to fix her hair and saw the deformity of her soul. What she saw was a horrible demon, a hideous monster with hair of coiled serpents. She ran from room to room, but every mirror in her palace reflected the same horrible face. Grace touched her and she came to realize that her soul had been corrupted by her decadent and sinful lifestyle. In the days that followed, Villana made a sincere confession and began distributing food and

[1419] Schouppe, Purgatory, xxxviii; Butler, 1/13, 93; Gallick, 21; Summers, 60; Wiebe, 20; Walsh, v. 2, 286;. Book of Augustinian Saints, John E. Rotelle, O.S.A., ed Villanova, PA: Augustinian Press, 2000, 150–51; www.catholic tradition. org/angels/guardian; Book of Augustinian Saints, 150, 151; Cruz, A&D, 143.

clothing to the poor and visiting the sick in a nearby hospital.

As a married woman, Villana converted and became a Dominican tertiary. After being widowed, the future beata grew rich in virtue and was often found in ecstasy, especially during Holy Mass. Because of this, she was often subjected to ridicule and slander. Villana's health began to suffer but this servant of God came to be favored with wonderful visions and colloquies with the Blessed Virgin Mary and other saints. Even her fiercest opponents eventually came to view her as a living saint. Villana is said to also have had the ability to read the hearts of those who visited her. The devil caused her great mental sufferings and fierce temptations. Once when she was being tempted by the devil, St. Catherine of Alexandria (292–310) appeared to her with a beautiful crown in her hand, saying, "Be constant, my daughter, and behold the magnificent reward that awaits you in heaven." By this vision, Villana understood that her time on earth was drawing to an end. She expired a short time afterwards. Before her death, however, she prophesized that she would send her friends flowers from heaven. This was accomplished when a friend, a Franciscan tertiary, bent over the beata's body to view her beautiful face and great armloads of flowers fell on her, fulfilling Villana's prophecy. Villana was beatified in 1829 by Pope Leo XII.[1420]

Venerables

Antonio Margil, Ven. (1657–1726) (aka Antonio Margilian, Antonio Margil of Jesus, Apostle of New Spain and Texas)

Franciscan missionary, mystic, ecstatic, and stigmatic born in Valencia Spain. Antonio was ordained to the priesthood at the age of twenty-five and assigned to Queretaro, Mexico, located about two hundred miles north of Mexico City. He was a promoter of missionary colleges in Spanish America and a powerful preacher to the Indians. Known as the "Barefoot Friar," Antonio was famous in his time for his miracles and sanctity. He converted hundreds of thousands of Indians, an estimated 80,000 in Guatemala alone. He was also called the "Flying Father" because he could cover so many miles in such a short period of time. It was nothing short of a miracle for him to cover forty or fifty miles a day over rough terrain. Testimonies from his brother and soldier companions attest to the fact that he literally walked on water as he crossed swollen streams and rivers on his apostolic journey. This capacity to pass from place to place with great speed is known as the gift of agility. God also granted him the mystical gifts of bilocation and subtility which enabled him to enter dwellings through closed doors. Along his travels, he also cured the sick, read souls, and prophesized the future. This Franciscan mystic experienced great raptures. He was witnessed floating in the air brought about by ecstasies of love. It was also claimed that Antonio would appear radiant with a celestial glory as well as wearing a crown of thorns. Although an ocean apart, this faithful son fulfilled a promise he made to be at the bedside of his dying mother in Spain to console her at her hour of death.

[1420] Cruz, SS, 723–24; Cruz, MMM, 301, 432; Gallick, 68, 413; Patron Saints Index; Dorcy, 160–62; Procter, 50.

Sculpture of Friar Antonio Margil de Jesus located at the atrium of Holy Cross Church in Queretaro, photo by Mizael Contreras

Many witnesses attest to his presence there at that moment. Pope Gregory XVI issued the decree that his virtues were heroic in 1836.[1421]

Beatrice Mary of Jesus, Ven. (1632–1702) (aka Beatrice of Grenada)

Poor Clare mystic, ecstatic, and invisible stigmatic born in Grenada, the daughter of Don Lorenco de Enciso y Navarette, a devout Catholic. Beatrice lived as a Franciscan tertiary in her parents' home until the age of thirty-five. On certain feast days, she had intense suffering in her hands, feet, and side, without any external indication that would reveal her condition. On May 30, 1664, while living at home, she was reportedly wounded by a dart by

St. Francis of Assisi that pierced her heart. It was later discovered after her death that she bore a crescent-shaped wound on her left breast. Beatrice often fell into trances and ecstasies that sometimes would last an entire day. On March 1, 1665, after experiencing certain ecstasies of rather unusual duration, she fell "into an extraordinary condition in which she exhibited all the external characteristics of a little four-year-old child." This puerile condition continued, with interruptions, for about ten days. In 1667, this heroic soul was accepted as a postulant in the Poor Clare Convent in Grenada. She would eventually became the abbess there. Beatrice was also observed to levitate. It is claimed that she would fall into convulsions when she smelled food. She underwent many fasts to include one that was observed to last fifty-one days.[1422]

Benoite Rencurel, Ven. (1647–1718) (aka Benedicta Rencurel, shepherdess of Laus)

Dominican tertiary, mystic, visionary, and stigmatic born in Saint-Etienne d'Avancon (Laus) in the Southern French Alps. In May of 1664, the Blessed Virgin appeared to her every day for four months. Our Lady told Benoite that her name was Mary and urged her to "pray continuously for sinners." Benoite informed the woman who owned the flocks she shepherded about the visions, but the woman did not believe her. One day, however, her employer secretly followed her and, although she did not see the vision, heard Mary's voice tell the little shepherdess that her own soul was in danger. The woman was deeply moved by the message and turned her life around.

[1421] NCE, 1st ed., v. 9, 203; NCE, 2nd ed., v. 9, 151; Thurston, 19ff, 220; Eduardo Enrique Rios, *Life of Fray Antonio Margil, O.F.M.,* translated and revised by Benedict Leutenegger, Washington: Acad. of American Franciscan History, 1959.

[1422] Thurston, 91, 115–18; NCE 2nd ed., v. 2, 180.

Benoite received the stigmata on her hands and feet during a Friday in July of 1673, before she had become a Dominican tertiary, under the name of Sister Benedicta. This shepherdess of Laus continued to have apparitions of Mary for more than fifty years. Hers were probably the longest single series of apparitions in history. She saw Jesus as both a child and as an adult. Sister Benedicta received five visions of the suffering Jesus. In these visions, the Lord showed her His wounds so that she could participate in His Passion.

Our Lady asked that a house be built in Laus for priests, with the intention of drawing people to greater conversion. This holy site still exists in Laus and draws 120,000 pilgrims annually. Numerous physical healings have been associated with this site, especially when oil from the sanctuary lamp is applied according to the directives which the Virgin Mary gave to Benedicta. During a Mass celebrated in the Basilica of Notre Dame in Laus, France on May 4, 2008, Bishop Jean-Michel de Falco of Gap officially approved these apparitions. He noted that these were the first Marian apparitions to be approved in the twenty-first century by the Vatican and the Church in France. After death, her body was still preserved. Benoite was declared venerable on April 3, 2009 by Pope Benedict XVI. Her cause has been proposed for beatification.[1423]

Catherine Paluzzi, Ven. (1571–1645)

Dominican mystic, ecstatica, stigmatic, and victim soul born as Frances Paluzzi in Morluppo, just north of Rome. The oldest of seven children, young Frances started having visions at the age of four. It took several years before she attempted to explain her visions and ecstasies to her father. Both he and her mother ended up scolding her for what they thought to be fantasies. Frances would receive a revelation that she would become a Dominican and found a community. She would later put on the habit of the Third Order and found a Dominican Convent in Nepi, Italy. During one of her ecstasies, she is said to have witnessed the Blessed Virgin Mary's descent into purgatory to console souls devoted to her. She also claimed to have seen her religious sister Bernardine there in purgatory. This servant of God continued to offer fervent prayers for the soul of her deceased father and assumed that he was in heaven. She became especially grieved one day when Our Lord in the company of St. Catherine of Sienna, her patroness, led her in spirit to purgatory. Here she saw her father in torment. Imploring his daughter's assistance, she immediately begged the Lord to intercede for him, even offering to take on his indebtedness. Christ granted her request and released her father from purgatory. This victim soul, in turn, suffered in his stead while on earth. She also bore the stigmata in her hands, feet, and side. The devil often tried to keep her from praying, sometimes pushing or hitting her. She once is said to have suffered a broken knee at his hands. This virtuous soul was favored with the gift of prophecy. She also purportedly told her community exactly when she would die.[1424]

[1423] The Miracle Hunter: Marian Apparitions: Laus; Dorcy, 475–76; Biot, 21; Wiebe, 20; see Appendix IV.

[1424] Dorcy, 407–8; Schouppe, 108, 180–81.

Concepcion Cabrera De Armida, Ven. (1862–1937) (aka Maria Concepcion de Cabrera de Armida and La Grande Cochita)

Mystic, visionary, and victim soul born in San Luis Potosi, Mexico. Conchita, as she was later called, had a special devotion to the Holy Eucharist from an early age. In 1884, she married Francisco Armida and gave birth to nine children. Widowed in 1901, Conchita had to care for these children, the youngest of which was only two years old. During this time, Jesus is said to have appeared to her. He revealed that He gave the exterior stigmata to some souls who agreed to become His victims and suffer for the sins of the world. This Mexican mother agreed to become a victim soul for priests. Jesus also revealed to her that His Mother possessed the invisible stigmata, that she suffered His Passion interiorly in the perfect image of her son. Conchita is also said to have reached the state of the mystical spiritual marriage. She related that she spoke to Jesus and Mary through her prayers and meditations. Aside from reporting that she heard Jesus ask her to lead a life of suffering, Conchita said the Lord also requested she write everything down. To that end, she went on to write over 60,000 handwritten pages. These religious writings were widely distributed and inspired the establishment of the five apostolates of the 'works of the Cross' in Mexico. Some of her books include: *To My Priests*, *Holy Hours*, *Before the Altar*, and *Irresistibly Drawn to the Eucharist*. Pope John Paul II (1978–2005) declared this heroic soul venerable on January 20, 1999. She is currently in the process of beatification.[1425]

Dominica of Paradiso, Ven. (1473–1553) (aka Dominica dal Paradiso)

Dominican tertiary, mystic, visionary, ecstatica, and invisible stigmatic born in Paradiso, a little village near Florence, Italy. While still a very small child, Dominica was already associating with angels and saints, who reportedly came to her in visions. Our Lady is said to have appeared to her when she was six years old, surrounded by a troupe of angels, and advised her: "Love God, avoid sin, and do good." At the age of seven Dominica took a vow of virginity. Upon the refusal of her mother to instruct her for her First Communion, Our Lady came and prepared her for this sacrament. The Lord Himself appeared to her the day before her First Communion. This resulted in an ecstasy which lasted until Mass the next day. The anecdote that is most frequently remembered about Dominica is the apparition of Our Lady with the Holy Child when Dominica was still very young.

On New Year's Day of 1485, Dominica was favored with mystical espousal with Christ. Angels clothed her with white robes and pearls and great numbers of saints and angels filled her drab cottage as Our Lord placed a ring on Dominica's finger. She also experienced the mystical exchange of hearts with the Lord. In a vision, Jesus extracted her heart from her chest and submitted one of burning fire. She was ill before this vision, but after it, regained her health. She also received infused knowledge which enlightened her mind.

Dominica had tried to enter different religious communities for ten years but was rejected by each. Finally she had a vision of Blessed Columba of Rieti and Our Lord who encouraged her to found an order of Dominican tertiaries. She did this and remained prioress of her Order for forty

---

[1425] Freze, VVA, 128, 246; De Vinck, 111–25.

years. Dominica's spirituality attracted a number of young ladies who placed themselves under her direction. Dominica bore the stigmata. It purportedly featured what looked like nails penetrating her hands and feet. It was said to be always highly visible on Fridays, although not at other times. However, as in the case of St. Catherine of Siena, it disappeared in answer to her prayers. This servant of God also suffered from diabolical attacks with burns and blows, one of which resulted in blindness in her right eye. Dominica was reportedly taken in spirit to Palestine, hell, purgatory, the Indies, and to all the major basilicas of Europe. She remained twenty years in complete abstinence from food, living only on the Blessed Sacrament. Her body was found to be incorrupt some sixty years after her death.[1426]

Francesca Dal Serrone, Ven. (1557–1600)

Franciscan tertiary, mystic, ecstatica, and stigmatic born in San Severino della Marche, six miles northwest of Tolentino, Italy. At the age of fourteen, Francesca received the ferita or wound in the side. At that time, she had already become a Franciscan tertiary. Francesca later joined an enclosed convent. Every Friday she is said to have bled bucketfuls of blood. Her blood had a fragrant smell like the odor of sweet violets and was so hot that it burst the vessels in which it was collected. This holy soul also experienced inedia and was often seen rapt in ecstasy.[1427]

Gertrude Van De Oosten (c. 1300–1358) (aka Gertrude of Delft)

Beguine lay mystic, visionary, and stigmatic born in Delft, Holland. Gertrude was remarkable from childhood for her piety and prudence. Beguines were not members of religious orders. They sprung up in Europe in the Middle Ages and flourished in the Netherlands and Belgium. They offered unattached women the chance to lead a spiritual life without taking permanent vows or enduring the rigors of a monastery. Gertrude, one of the most famous Beguines, worked as a maid. She evinced great devotion to the mysteries of the Incarnation, especially to the Sacred Passion. On Good Friday, in the year 1340, while meditating on the Passion, Gertrude experienced the sacred stigmata on her hands, feet, and side. Witnesses attested that blood flowed freely from these wounds seven times a day, at each of the canonical hours. Word of Gertrude's stigmata spread throughout the country. Distressed and alarmed at the multitude that flocked to see such a wonder, she begged that the favor be withdrawn. Her prayer was so far granted in that the blood ceased to flow, but the pain remained as did the marks of the sacred stigmata (as colored scars) for the rest of her life. This favored soul was blessed with other mystical gifts such as the consolation of others, prophecy, the ability to see in real time events taking place at a distance as well as of what was about to happen in the future. Gertrude also wrote forty-five meditations as well as a number of hymns.[1428]

[1426] Wilson, 135; Cruz, MMM, 53, 74–75; "Stigmatization," in the 1912 Classic Encyclopedia; Biot, 31; Dorcy, 284–85; Thurston, 150; Summers, 60; Georgiana Fullerton, Lady, *The Life of St. Frances of Rome*, London, D & J Sadler & Co., 1855.

[1427] Summers, 169–70; Cruz, MMM, 180; Wilson, 136.

[1428] NCE 2nd ed., v. 6; 1912 Catholic Encyclopedia, 535; Cruz, MMM, 231–32; Ghezzi, VOS, 416–17; Gallick, 24, 407.

John of Saint Samson, Ven. (1571–1636) (aka Jean du Moulin)

Carmelite lay brother, extraordinary mystic, and ecstatic born of wealthy parents in Sens, France. John was blinded from age three by the mishandling of an eye disease. He entered the Carmelite Monastery at Rennes in 1612 and died there in 1636. He was known to be very pious. He would allegedly fall into ecstasy whenever a religious work was read to him. John was also seen to exhibit a special radiance.[1429]

Margaret of the Blessed Sacrament, Ven. (1619–1648) (aka Marguerite Parigot, Little Spouse of the Infant Jesus)

Carmelite nun, mystic, visionary, victim soul, ecstatica, and stigmatic born in Beaune, Cote-d'Or, in the Burgundy region of France. From earliest childhood, Margaret gave proof of external virtue as an ecstatica of the Blessed Sacrament. At the age of five, she received her first vision of the Child Jesus. She went on to enter the Carmelite order at the age of eleven and was professed on June 24, 1634, taking the name of Margaret of the Blessed Sacrament. This holy soul was said to have received the stigmata at the age of thirteen. After joining the Carmelites, Margaret was afflicted with convulsions, rigidity in her limbs, and a constant feeling of fear and oppression. Doctors called to perform a useless operation that left her with lifelong head pain. Her mother superior decided she was under demonic attack and cured her by prayer. Soon after this, Margaret started to have visions and to fall into ecstasies during prayers. She began to relive the mysteries of the life of Our Lord as each came up in the liturgical calendar. This servant of God also agreed to become a victim soul for the sins of humanity, especially for the sins of priests and religious. Anne of Austria maintained that it was through Margaret's intercession that she became the mother of Louis XIV. Jesus revealed to Margaret His early years as a child. She was chosen by God to honor His infancy. On March 24, 1636, she founded the Family of the Child Jesus, an association to honor the Holy Childhood of Jesus. The association continues today with the name Archconfraternity of the Infant Jesus. Following a request by Christ in a vision, she also helped build a chapel in the nearby monastery of St. Etienne. Margaret is best known for the revelation of the Chaplet of the Holy Infant Jesus. Our Lord revealed to her that He would grant special graces to those who practice this devotion. The Congregation of Rites decreed the herocity of her virtues on December 10, 1905. This is the first step to her eventual beatification, which is still under consideration.[1430]

Maria of Jesus, Ven. (1579–1637) (aka Maria di Gesu, Maria de Jesus de Tomelin, Mother Maria of Jesus, "El Lirio de Puebla")

Carmelite abbess, mystic, visionary, and ecstatica born in Valladaid, Spain to Sebastian de Tomelin and Francizca de Campo. Maria entered Discalced Carmelite Order at the age of seventeen and took her final vows in 1599. Her piety was recognized by St. Teresa of Avila herself. Maria had a special devotion to and made sacrifices for the

---

[1429] NCE, 1st ed., v. 7, 1070; NCE 2nd ed., v. 7, 982–83; Cruz, MMM, 167; http://www.santiebeati.it/dettaglio/92397.

[1430] Biot, 25–26; Patron Saints Index; Cruz, Prayers, 42; NCE, 2nd ed., v. 9, 150–51; Wilson, 138; Francisco Sanchez-Ventera y Pascual, 91; Farges, 31.

souls in purgatory. She had visions of Our Lady and Christ, as well as had colloquies with Mary, her guardian angel, Sts. John the Baptist, Theresa, and Gertrude. Maria experienced many other mystical phenomena reported to include clairvoyance, telekinesis, bilocation, and levitation. "El Lirio de Puebla," as she was called, was witnessed in ecstasy by her sister nuns on many occasions. She died in the odor of sanctity at Toledo and her body was found to be incorrupt. A mysterious oil and heavenly scent surrounded her body when it was exhumed in 1929 and a sweet perfume having the odor of roses and jasmine issued from it. The garments of her body were found saturated with this perfumed oil which coated the flesh of the entire body. It was noted that everything that Maria had touched in her lifetime such as books and manuscripts bore this same flowery fragrance. This was mystifying since the Carmelite mystic had touched these things hundreds of years ago. Her incorrupt body is presently enclosed in a marble sarcophagus at the Carmelite Convent of San Jose in Toledo, Spain.[1431]

Maria Villani, Ven. (1584–1670)

Dominican mystic, ecstatica, and stigmatic born in Naples, Italy. Maria's mother died when she was three years old. At the age of six, Maria hovered near death due to a serious illness. One day, during this sickness, her deceased mother is said to have appeared to her in the company of the Blessed Virgin Mary and St. Catherine Martyr. She was cured by them and encouraged to pursue a religious life. Maria did and was elected prioress of her order. However, she begged her sisters to change their minds. The Lord then appeared to her and seemingly told her to accept this position. Once,

while in an ecstatic state, Maria was taken to purgatory where she begged a soul there to allow her to feel something of what the soul was suffering. Immediately she felt as though a finger of fire had touched her forehead. The pain which she experienced instantly caused her ecstasy to cease. The mark remained, and so deep and painful was it that two months afterwards it was still seen. It caused her terrible suffering. Maria's biographer, Fr. Francis Marchese, O.P., also reveals that she believed she was wounded in the heart and side by a fiery spear of love. This wound was witnessed by three of her confessors in signed depositions, dated November 12 and 19, 1620 and March 29, 1621. They attested that they had seen and touched the wound in her side. The fire of love sparked by the flaming arrow produced such heat that Maria was forced to drink an excessive amount of water each day. She became a furnace of love, consumed by an almost unstoppable flame of love which dominated all her thoughts. A surgeon who made an incision in her heart during her autopsy was, along with other witnesses, amazed to see "smoke and heat exhaled from her heart, a veritable furnace of divine love." The heat was so intense that the surgeon had to wait for the body to cool down before extracting her heart, but even then the heart was hot enough to burn his hands. After her death, the impressions of the spear, sponge, and reed were reported to be found on her heart.[1432]

[1431] Thurston, 288; Cruz, MMM, 373–74, 392–93; Farges, 557.

[1432] Cruz, MMM, 21, 70, 179; Dorcy, 446–47; Stigmatization, 1911 Catholic Encyclopedia; Schouppe, 120–21; 289; Thurston, 219ff; Wilson, 137.

Vision of Christ as a Jesuit by the venerable Marina de Escobar
by Diego Valentin Diaz

Marina De Escobar, Ven. (1554–1633)

Mystic, visionary, stigmatic, and foundress of the Brigittines in Spain born in Valladolid, Spain. Marina's adolescence was disturbed somewhat by alterations of fervor, dryness, and scruples. During the Lent of 1587, she offered herself totally to God. Bedridden for the last thirty years of her life, Marina is said to have conversed with God, angels, and saints. All this is described in her autobiography entitled *Vida Maravillosa de la Venerable Virgen Dona Marina de Escobar*. In this work, she gives an account of her own mystical experiences such as participation in the mysteries of the humanity of Christ, her internal stigmata, her experience of the divine attributes, the wonderful ways in which God communicates Himself to the soul, her sufferings of purification, etc. Marina is said to have experienced mystical marriage with Christ

twice, once at the age of forty-eight and again at the age of fifty-seven. She had been given an espousal ring by Our Lord. St. Joseph was said to have assisted at one of these ceremonies.[1433]

Mary Martha Chambon, Ven. (1841–1907) (aka Marie-Marthe Chambon, Francoise Chambon)

Mystic, visionary, stigmatic, victim soul, and lay nun of the Monastery of the Visitation Order in Chambery, France. As a youngster, she allegedly first saw Christ in the crypt of the Church of Lemenc. Later, she claimed to see Him every time she took communion. Francoise, as she was named, entered the Visitandines of Chambery on April 29, 1863 taking the name of Mary-Martha. While seriously ill in September 1867, the light of the Holy Trinity is said to have illuminated her cell. She watched with great joy as God the Father placed a Host on her tongue. Next He revealed to her the mysteries of Bethlehem and the Cross, filling her soul with special insights into these mysteries. Then He bestowed on her the Holy Spirit as a fiery dart. Soon afterwards, this servant of God started having more visions of Jesus. She said He appeared to her to teach her specific prayers and meditations on His wounds. He revealed to her the devotion of the Holy Wounds with the accompanying chaplet, which bears numerous promises for the good of souls. Our Lord asked her to champion this devotion to His most Sacred Wounds. Mary Martha is best known for introducing to the world the Rosary of the Holy Wounds. Jesus also asked her to unite her sufferings with His as a form of reparation for the sins of the world. He told her His Holy Wounds are the treasure of

---

[1433] NCE, 1st ed., v. 5, 538; Thurston, 140; Biot, 72; Freze, TBWC, 205.

treasures for the souls in purgatory. This saintly nun received the stigmata on June 12, 1874. In one of her visions of Our Lord, He called her attention to a group of angelic spirits pressing around the altar during Holy Mass. Mary Martha died in the odor of sanctity. The cause for her beatification was introduced in 1937.[1434]

Mary of Agreda, Ven. (1602–1665) (aka Maria de Agreda, "Blue Lady," "Lady in Blue," Mother of the Sky, Mary of Jesus)

Mystic, visionary, ecstatica, and stigmatic Spanish discalced Franciscan nun, born one of eleven children to a wealthy family in Agreda, province of Burgos, Spain. Hers was a pious family. The entire family eventually entered religious life in 1618. Her father and brothers became Franciscan brothers. Mary and her mother and sister became Franciscan nuns. Their castle was converted into a convent and all the family's wealth was given to the poor. Chosen abbess of this convent in 1627, Mary held this position the remaining thirty-eight years of her life. During her lifetime, she also experienced mystical phenomena, numerous ecstasies, levitations, bilocations, locutions, visions, and apparitions of the Blessed Virgin Mary. During her ecstasies, her body was reportedly raised off the ground and could be moved as weightlessly as a feather. Her face was enraptured in beauty. She would remain in trances for two to three hours at a time. The sisters of her convent would often open the shutters of the choir so that she could be seen levitating after communion. This Spanish

Mary of Agreda (TAN Books)

nun was reportedly said to have bilocated and traveled mystically throughout Spain and Portugal. She is also said to have bilocated to America more than five hundred times between 1620 and 1631. Our Lord commanded that she go there to teach the natives about the Catholic faith. In some of her ecstasies, Mary said she was teaching Christianity to people in foreign lands. A vision of her, known as the "Lady in Blue," was simultaneously reported teaching the native Tiguas and Caddoes Indians in the areas of what are now New Mexico and Texas.

Mary's ecstasies led to many private revelations. From 1627 to 1637 she received many graces from the Blessed Virgin, who appeared to her while she was in ecstasy. Commanded by Our Lady to write about her life, the Franciscan initially resisted. It was not until 1637, when she began to set down what became the four-volume work entitled *The Mystical City of God: Divine History of the Virgin, Mother of God*. This work contains revealed details about the life of the Blessed Virgin Mary, the "hidden life"

[1434] Freze, VVA, 252; Cruz, A&D, 57; Cruz, MMM, 70; http://www.miraclehunter.com/marian_apparitions/approved; Fr. Paul O'Sullivan, *Read me or Rue it*, Rockford, Ill.: TAN Books and Publishers, Inc., 1992, 34; Biot, 18.

of Jesus, intimate accounts of the Lord's public life, St. Joseph, heaven, hell, creation, the meaning of the apocalypse, and other Christian topics. Because of certain historical questions in these works, however, there remains concern about possible editorial changes after Mary of Agreda's death. These matters may never be adequately resolved. For instance, the Franciscan claimed to know precisely that the Blessed Virgin Mary lived twenty-one years, four months, and nineteen days after the Crucifixion. Other saints, however, have given different times which disagree with hers. Eusebius Amort (1692–1775), a German Jesuit theologian, quotes twenty-one points on which Mary of Agreda contradicts other revelations.

The "Blue Lady" considered it a sin for people not to believe in her. According to Mary, God declared to her: "I desire that these revelations should be regarded not as opinions, or simple visions, but as certain truths." This violates Church doctrine, for no private revelation has a right to impose belief on the faithful at large. Theologians have pointed out that these are probably the result of illusion. Mary's imagination may have led her to go astray. It is also alleged that her confessors tampered with the text of her works. There is no question, however, about Mary's heroic virtue and real union with God.

Mary reportedly received terrible bodily sufferings inflicted by Satan, who also tempted her with vile words and images. These assaults were occasionally interrupted by visions of the Blessed Virgin and Our Lord, which greatly inspired and encouraged her. Her body remains incorrupt. She was declared venerable by Pope Innocent XI in 1689.[1435]

Passitea Crogi, Ven. (1564–1615)

Mystic, visionary, ecstatica, stigmatic, and Sienese Capuchin abbess who founded several Capuchin convents. On Palm Sunday in 1589, Passitea experienced an ecstasy which lasted four days. On the following Good Friday, between two and three o'clock, a dazzling ray-like lightning flashed in the room she was in accompanied by a loud noise like thunder. The abbess cried out in pain and collapsed. Those who came to assist her saw blood gush out of her hands, feet, and head. A priest was called and he soon recognized she had received the sacred stigmata. Passitea told the priest she had a vision of Christ crucified, livid and bruised and covered with wounds streaming with red blood. She said she heard the words: "Daughter, drink of My Chalice," after which rays of transparent glory struck her hands, feet, side, and encircled her head. The wounds in her hands and feet did not pierce through, but four years later in 1593, while Passitea was in deep contemplation, a seraph encircled in light, crucified, and covered with wounds, appeared to her. As the vision approached, there was another loud noise like thunder. Passieta fainted and once again was found covered in blood. Whereas the first stigmatic wounds did not pierce through, this second event produced wounds that bore completely through her hands and feet. On certain days, especially during Holy Week, the wounds bled profusely and caused excruciating pain. At other times, the flow and pain were less. The wounds reportedly were visible right up until her death.

[1435] Venerable Mary of Agreda, *The Mystical City of God,* tr. Rev. George J. Blatter, Abridged version, Rockford, Ill.: TAN Books and Publishers, 1978; Guiley, 238; NCE, 1st ed.,v. 1, 212–13; NCE 2nd

ed.,v. 1, 187; Poulain, 46, 77; Cruz, A&D, 26, 200; http://www.catholic-forum.com/saints; Patron Saints Index; Johnson, 128, 308; Freze, VVA, 252–53.

Christ appeared to her in a vision on another occasion and asked for her heart. She agreed and lived as if her heart had disappeared. While in her ecstasies, Passitea's blood was gathered in vials of various shapes. These were hermetically fastened and sealed. The blood in the vials has been known to change into a rosy-hued fluid that increases in size until it fills almost the entire vial. Passieta was also known for her extraordinary levitations. She was often seen by witnesses lifted six feet off the ground while in rapture.[1436]

Serafina Di Dio, Ven. (1621–1699) (aka Serafina of God)

Carmelite mystic, visionary, ecstatica, and stigmatic born Prudenza Pisa into a wealthy family in Naples, Italy. Prudenza rejected a suitor chosen for her by her father, and he, in turn, threw her out of his house. She ended up cutting her hair and living in a chicken coup type structure in the back yard with her mother sneaking her food. Prudenza went on to become a Carmelite nun in the Capri convent taking the name of Sister Serafina of God. This heroic soul was later to receive the stigmata wounds on her hands and feet. These wounds were clearly seen by many. During a vision of the Divine Child, Serafina's heart was said to have been pierced through by a golden dart. While rapt in prayer after Holy Communion, her sister nuns would often see her with her face glowing like a red flame and her eyes sparkling fire. They attested, "It burned them if they but touched her." Her sister religious repeatedly had heard her say that she was consumed with a living fire and that her blood was boiling as if there was molten lead in her veins. She was

declared venerable in 1723 by Pope Innocent XIII. The cause for her beatification was introduced in 1742.[1437]

Teresa Helena Higginson, Ven. (1844–1905) (aka "The Little Apostle")

Lay mystic, visionary, ecstatica, and invisible stigmatic born in Holywell, Flintshire, Wales in the archdiocese of Liverpool. She was named after the Spanish mystic St. Teresa of Avila and St. Helena, reputedly the discoverer of the True Cross. At age four, Teresa offered herself to the Holy Trinity. From her childhood onwards, she felt a deep longing to share in Jesus' sufferings and had a burning love for Him. The "Little Apostle" desired to teach the Catholic faith and spent three of her earlier adult years as an elementary school teacher at St. Mary's School in Wigam. While here, Teresa was favored with visions of Our Lady, Jesus as a child and adult, her guardian angel, and several saints to include St. Joseph and St. Peter. This lay teacher experienced many ecstasies where, especially during Lent, she participated in Our Lord's Passion. During Holy Week in the year 1874, Teresa was marked with Christ's Sacred Wounds to include the crown of thorns. She attempted to hide the stigmata and begged the Lord to remove all outward signs of it. He agreed and allowed her to bear the invisible stigmata throughout the rest of her life.

This servant of God was also favored with the spiritual or mystical marriage to Christ which occurred in the presence of the whole court of heaven on October 23, 1887. In one of the many visions of the Lord, He requested Teresa promote public devotion to His Sacred Head which was to

---

[1436] Thurston, 29; Cruz, MMM, 28, 223, 337; Summers, 137–38; Wilson, 136; Francisco Sanchez-Ventera y Pascual, 86.

[1437] See http://www.santiebeati.it/dettaglio/91388; Summers, 71, 196; Thurston, 218, 220; Cruz, MMM, 181.

be especially adored as the Seat of Divine Wisdom. This devotion was meant to be the antidote to the sins of pride and rationalism current in our age. Teresa was continually tormented by the devil who tried to get her to doubt the truth of her revelation regarding the devotion to the Sacred Head of Jesus. She related to her confessor that the devil would hurl filthy stuff at her, beat, drag, and choke her, rouse her when asleep, and throw her out of bed and around the room. Satan was said to have used every type of temptation against her to include coming to her as an "angel of light" to comfort and console her. He also came to her pretending to be Our Lord with the Blessed Sacrament. At times he would take horrible forms and follow her about with a serpent, fox, bird, or pig's head.

This heroic soul was also favored with the mystical gifts of prophecy, levitation, and bilocation. As regards bilocation, she recalled how she found herself mysteriously transported to some country, which she supposed to be Africa, among aborigines whose peculiar habits and dispositions she described very fully. She was able to instruct them and help them in many ways. It was reported, however, that after her mystical marriage to the Lord, all the outward marvels that she experienced became less and less rare.[1438]

Ursula Benincasa, Ven. (1547–1618) (aka Orsola Benincasa)

Mystic, visionary, ecstatica, and stigmatic foundress of the Theatine Sisters as well as the Oblates of the Immaculate Conception and the Contemplative Hermit Sisters, born in Naples, Italy. By the age of ten,

Ursula is said to have possessed mystical gifts. Her ecstasies were so frequent as to almost be uninterrupted. These childhood ecstasies caused her to be maltreated by those who did not understand what she was going through. Her life was described as one long ecstasy of divine love. When in rapture, Ursula was observed to levitate. On February 2, 1581 Ursula received a vision of Mary and the Infant Jesus. Christ asked that she build a convent for cloistered sisters to pray for conversions and to dress as Mary in a white gown and blue veil. Ursula was sent to Rome to have her vision investigated. She was questioned by Pope Gregory XIII and Saint Philip Neri, who were greatly impressed by her piety.

In 1617, in Naples, Italy, on the Feast of the Presentation of the Lord, Ursula, having received Holy Communion, had another vision of the Blessed Mother clothed in a white garment over which she wore another garment of azure blue. In her arms, Mary held the Infant Jesus. Our Lady was surrounded by many persons, all similarly attired. The Blessed Mother spoke to Ursula with these words: "Cease weeping, Ursula, and turn your sighs into heartfelt joy. Listen closely to what Jesus, whom I am holding in my lap, will say to you." Then Jesus revealed to Ursula that she would found a convent where thirty-three nuns, dressed in the same attire as the Most Blessed Virgin Mary of her vision, would live a life of solitude and seclusion. The Savior promised special graces and many spiritual gifts to those who would zealously follow this way of life. The Venerable Servant of God besought the Lord to extend these favors also to such people who, living in the world, would have a special devotion to the mystery of the Immaculate Conception, observe chastity according to their station in life, and wear a small blue scapular. This vision is attributed to the origin of the Blue Scapular of the Immaculate Conception.

[1438] Summers,155; Cecil Kerr, Fr. Paul Hafner, *Inside the Vatican*, March 2005, 60–61; Wilson, 142; Cruz, A&D, 179, 206, 218.

As a sign that her prayer had been heard, Jesus showed Ursula in a vision a multitude of angels distributing scapulars over the earth. This scene is artistically captured in a fresco at the Theatine Sisters' Convent in Naples.

Ursula went on to establish the Theatine Hermit Sisters in 1617. She took thirty-three companions as Christ had revealed and retired with them to a hermitage. Overwhelmed with joy, the sisters personally made scapulars similar to the ones seen in Ursula's visions, had them blessed, and distributed them among the faithful. The practice of wearing the Blue Scapular began to spread quickly during Ursula's lifetime. After her death, her spiritual daughters undertook the promotion of this scapular as their Order's special mission.

Several years later, Clement XI granted specific indulgences for the wearing of this scapular and succeeding popes increased the number of such indulgences. The summary of the indulgences was approved by the Congregation of Indulgences first in 1845. Ursula had a great devotion to souls in purgatory and, at times, took upon herself their penalties. She was also said to have received the stigmata at the age of sixty-nine. When assailed as an impostor and threatened to be burnt at the stake, this holy ecstatica resigned herself to this fate in perfect obedience and humility. She did, however, end up dying a natural death. On August 7, 1793, Pope Pius VI recognized the heroic virtues of Ursula and proclaimed her a Venerable Servant of God.[1439]

[1439] Summers, 106, 208–9; NCE, 1st ed., v. 2, 311; NCE 2nd ed., v. 2, 282; Biot, 26; saints.sqpn.com/saintu22.htm; http://www.padrimarian.org.

Bibliography

A Kempis, Thomas. *Imitation of Christ.* Translated by Leo Sherley-Price. Baltimore, MD: Penguin Books, 1956.

Acta Sanctorum (January to October), 54 volumes, Paris and Rome, 1868.

Agresti, G. Di. *St. Caterina de' Ricci.* Florence: Fonti, 1963.

Alacoque, Margaret Mary. *The Autobiography of Saint Margaret Mary Alacoque.* Rockford, IL: TAN Books and Publishers, 1995.

Albertson, Clinton, ed. *Anglo-Saxon Saints and Heroes.* NY: Fordham Univ. Press, 1967.

Alphonsus, Mary. *St. Rose of Lima.* Rockford, IL: TAN Books and Publishers, 1993.

Amorth, Gabriele. *An Exorcist: More Stories.* Ignatius Press: San Francisco, 2002.

Angela of Foligno. *Complete Works/Angela of Foligno.* Translated with an introduction by Paul Lachance. Preface by Romana Guarnieri. NY: Paulist Press, 1993.

Aquinas, Thomas. *Summa Theologica.* Translated by Dominican Fathers. NY: Benzinger Brothers, 1948.

Aradi, Zsolt. *The Book of Miracles.* NY: The Farrar, Straus and Cudahy Co., 1956.

Ashley, Benedict M. *Blessed Osanna d'Andreasi and Other Italian Dominican Woman Mystics.* www.op.org/ domcentral/study/ashley/osanna. htm.

Athanasius. *St. Antony of the Desert (251–356).* Rockford, IL: TAN Books and Publishers, Inc. 1995.

———. *The Life of St. Anthony and the Letter to Mercellinus.* Translated by Robert C. Craig. NY: Ramsey and Toronto, Paulist Press, 1980.

Augustine. *The Confessions of Saint Augustine.* Translated by Edward B. Pusey. NY: P. F.Collier & sons, 1909.

———. *The Confessions of Saint Augustine.* Translated by F. J. Sheed. NY: Sheed and Ward, 1943.

———. *The literal meaning of genesis.* (Ancient Christian Writers) Translated and annotated by John Hammond Taylor. NY: Newman Press, 1982.

Aumann, Jordan. "Private Revelation," in *Our Sunday Visitor's Encyclopedia of Catholic Doctrine by Russell Shaw.* Huntington, IN: Our Sunday Visitor, 1997.

Aumann, Jordan. *Spiritual Theology.* London: Contiuum, 1980.

Bacchiarello, J., ed. *Forty Dreams of St. John Bosco; The Apostle of Youth.* Rockford IL: TAN Books and Publishers, Inc. 1996.

Baker, H. A. *Visions beyond the veil.* Monroeville, PA: Whitaker Books, 1973.

Ball, Ann. *Faces of Holiness: Modern Saints in Photos and Words.* Huntington, IN:

Our Sunday Visitor, 2001.

———. *Modern Saints: Their Lives and Faces*. Rockford, IL: TAN Books and Publishers, Inc. 1983.

Bangley, Bernard. *Butler's lives of the saints: concise, modernized edition*. Brewster, MA: Paraclete Press, 2005.

Baring-Gould, Sabine. *The Lives of the Saints: with introduction and additional lives of English martyrs, Cornish, Scottish and Welsh saints , and a full index to the entire work*. New and revised edition illustrated by 473 engravings. Edinburgh: John Grant, 1914.

Battista Varani. *My Spiritual Life*. Translated by Joseph R. Berrigan. Toronto: Peregrina, 1989.

Beer, Frances. *Women and mystical experiences in the middle ages*. Woodbridge, Suffolk, England: Boydell Press, 1992.

Bell, Rudolf M. *Holy Anorexia*. Epilogue by William W. Davis. Chicago: Univ. of Chicago Press, 1985.

———. and Christina Mazzoni. *The voices of Gemma Galgani: the life and afterlife of a modern saint*. Chicago: Univ. of Chicago Press, 2003.

Benedict XIV. *Heroic virtue, a portion of the treatise of Benedict XIV*. London: T. Richardson & Sons, 1850–52.

———. *On the Beatification and Canonization of the servants of God*. De Canon., Book III, ch. Liii, no. 15; Book II, ch. xxxii, no.ll. Eng. trans. Benedict XIV on Heroic Virtue, vol. III, ch. Xiv, NY:Edward Dunigan and Brother, 1850.

———. *The Apostles*. Illustrated edition. Huntington, IN: Our Sunday Visitor, 2008.

Bergeron, Henry Paul. *Brother Andre: The wonder man of Mount Royal*. Montreal: St. Joseph's Oratory, 1997.

Berrigan, J. R. "Saint Catherine of Bologna: Franciscan mystic," in *Woman Writers of the Renaissance and Reformation*. K. N. Wilson, ed. Athens, GA: 1987.

Biot, Rene. *The enigma of the stigmata*. Translated from the French by P. J. Hepburne-Scott. New York: Hawthorne Books, 1962.

Biver, Paul. *Pere Lamy*. Dublin: Clonmore & Reynolds Ltd., 1951.

Boadt, Lawrence. *Reading the Old Testament: an introduction*. New York: Paulist Press, 1984.

Bonniwell, William R. *The Life of Blessed Margaret of Castello 1287–1320*. Rockford, IL: TAN Books, 1983.

Bore. *Les Stigmatises du Tyrol*. Paris, 1846.

Bosco, John. *Dreams, Visions and Prophecies*. Edited by Eugene Brown. New Rochelle, NY: Don Bosco Publishers, 1986.

Boudreau, F. J. *The happiness of heaven: The joys and rewards of eternal glory*. Rockford: TAN Books, 1984.

Bougaud, Emile. *The Life of Saint Margaret Mary Alacoque*. Rockford, IL: TAN Books and Publishers, 1994.

Brewer, Ebenezer Cobham. *A dictionary of miracles, imitative, realistic and dogmatic*. London: Chatto & Windus, 1884.

Bridget of Sweden. *Life and selected revelations/Birgitta of Sweden*. Edited by Marguerite Tjader Harris. Translation and notes by Albert Ryle Kezel. NY: Paulist Press, 1990.

———. *The revelations of St. Birgitta of*

Sweden. Translated by Denis Searby with introduction and notes by Bridget Morris. Oxford, NY: Oxford University Press, 2006–2008.

Brown, Michael Harold. *Secrets of the Eucharist.* Milford, OH: Faith Publishing Co., 1996.

Brown, Peter. *Augustine of Hippo: A biography.* Berkeley: University of California Press, 1967.

Brown, Raphael. *The little flower of St. Francis.* Garden City, NY: Image Books, 1958.

———. *Saints Who Saw Mary.* Rockford, IL: TAN Books and Publishers, 1994.

Butler, Alban. *Butler's lives of the saints; supplement of new saints and blesseds.* Collegeville, MN Liturgical Press, 2005.

———. *Lives of the saints; for every day in the year.* Rockford, IL: TAN Books and Publishers, 1995.

———. *Lives of the saints: new concise edition.* Edited by Michael Walsh. Turnbridge Wells Kent: Burnes and Oates, 1997.

———. *The lives of the saints; originally compiled by Albin Butler, now edited, revised & copiously supplemented by Herbert Thurston*; 12 Vols. London: Burns, Oates & Washbourne, 1926–1938.

———. *The Lives of the Fathers, Martyrs and Other Principal Saints,* vol. 1. D. & J. Sadlier, & Company, 1864.

Callahan, Sidney. *Women who hear voices; the challenges of religious experience.* Mahwah, NJ: Paulist Press, 2003.

Cantimpe, Thomas de. *Thomas of Cantimpre: The collected saints' lives: Abbot John of Cantimpre, Christina the Astonishing; Margaret of Ypes and Lutgard of Aywieres.* Edited and with an introduction by Barbara Newman. Translated by Margot H. King and Barbara Newman. Turnhout, Brepols, 2008.

———. *The Life of Christina the Astonishing.* Toronto: Peregrina,1999.

———. *The Life of Lutgard of Aywieres by Thomas of Cantipre.* Translated by M. H. King. Toronto: Peregrina, 1991.

Capes, F. M. *St. Catherine de' Ricci, her Life, her letters, her community.* London: Burns, Oates and Washburn, 1911.

Carrera, Elena. *Teresa of Avila's Autobiography. Authority, power and the self in mid–sixteenth century Spain.* London: Legenda/Modern Humanities Research Assn. and Maney Pub., 2005.

Carty, Charles. *Padre Pio–The Stigmatist.* Rockford, IL: TAN Books and Publishers, 1973.

———. *The Stigmata and Modern Science.* Rockford, IL: TAN Books and Publishers, 1974.

———. *The Two Stigmatists Padre Pio and Teresa Neuman.* St. Paul, MN: The Radio Replies Press Society, 1956.

Catechism of the Catholic Church. Liguori, MO: Libreria Editrice Vaticana, 1994.

Catherine of Genoa. *Purgation and Purgatory, The spiritual dialogue.* Translated and notes by Serge Hughes. Introduction by Benedict Groeschel. NY: Paulist Press, 1979.

———. *A Treatise on purgatory.* Translated by Charlotte Balfour & Helen Douglas Irvine. London: Sheed & Ward, 1946.

Catherine of Siena. *The dialogue.* Translated and introduction by Suzanne Noffke O.P. NY: Paulist Press, 1980.

Catholic Encyclopedia. NY: Robert Appleton, Co., 1902.

Catholic Encyclopedia. NY: The Encyclopedia Press Inc., 1912.

Catholic Encyclopedia. Nashville: Thomas Nelson Publishers, 1976.

Cavallini, Giuliani. *St. Martin de Porres, apostle of charity.* Translated by Caroline Holland. Rockford, IL: TAN Books and Publishers, 1999.

Cioran, E. M. *Tears and Saints.* Chicago, IL: U. of Chicago Press, 1995.

Connell, Janice T. *Meeting with Mary; Visions of the Blessed Mother.* NY: Ballantine Books, 1995.

Conte, Ronald L. "Discernment of Apparition Claims," Sept. 14, 2005, Catholic Planet, http://www.catholicplanet.com/articles/instructionOO7.htm; http://www.miraclehunter.com/marian_apparitions/discernment/conte.html.

Coulson, John, ed. *An Angelus Book of Saints.* NY: Guild Press, 1957.

Cowan, Tomas Dale. *The way of the saints: prayers, practices and meditations.* NY: Putnam, 1998.

Crean, Thomas. *God is no delusion; A refutation of Richard Dawkins.* San Francisco: Ignatius Press, 2007.

Cristani, Leon. *Saint Margaret Mary Alacoque and the promises of the Sacred Heart.* Translated from the French by. M. Angeline Bouchard. Boston: St. Paul Editions, 1975.

Cruz, Joan Carroll. *Angels & Devils.* Rockford, IL: TAN Books and Publishers, Inc., 1999.

———. *The incorruptibles; A study of the incorruption of the bodies of various Catholic saints and beati.* Rockford, IL: TAN Books and Publishers, Inc., 1977.

———. *Mysteries, Marvels, Miracles in the Lives of the Saints.* Rockford, IL: TAN Books and Publishers, Inc., 1997.

———. *Prayers and Heavenly Promises.* Rockford, IL: TAN Books and Publishers Inc., 1990.

———. *Secular saints, 250 canonized and beatified lay men, women and children.* Rockford, IL: TAN Books and Publishers, 1989.

Culleton, Richard Gerald. *The Prophets and Our Times.* Rockford, IL: TAN Books and Publishers, Inc., 1974.

———. *The reign of antichrist.* Rockford, IL: TAN Books and Publishers, 1974.

De Capoa, Chiara. *Old Testament figures in art.* Edited by Stefano Zuffi. Translated by Thomas Michael Hartmann. Los Angeles: The J. Paul Getty Trust, 2003.

De' Pazzi, Maria Maddalena. *1566–1607: Maria Maddalena De'Pazzi, Selected Revelations.* Translated and introduced by Armando Maggi. NY: Paulist Press, 2000.

De Rosweyde aux Acta Sanctorum: la recherché hagiographiques des Blandishes a travers quatre siecles: acts du colloque international. Bruxelles: Societe de Bollandistes, 2009.

De Vinck, Jose. *Revelations of woman mystics; from the Middle Ages to modern times.* NY: Alba House, 1985.

———. *The works of Bonaventure; cardinal, seraphic doctor and saint.* Paterson, NJ: St. Anthony Guild Press, 1960–1970.

Delaney, John J. *Pocket dictionary of saints.* Abridged ed. Golden City, NY: Image Books, 1983.

Del Mastro, M. L. *Julian of Norwich, Revelations of Divine Love.* NY: Image Books, 1977.

Denison, Henry. *Visions of God.* London: Robert Scott, 1914.

Di Agresti, Domenico Guglellmo. *St. Caterina de' Ricci: l'esperienza spirituale della santa di Prato.* Prato: Liberia Cattolica, 2001.

Dorcy, Mary Jean. *Saint Dominic.* Rockford, IL: TAN Books and Publishers, 1993.

———. *Saint Dominic's Family: The Lives of Over 300 Famous Dominicans.* Rockford, IL: TAN Books, 1983.

Drane, Augusta Theodosia. *The history of St. Catherine of Siena and her companions.* London: Burnes & Oates, 1880.

Drummey, James J. *Catholic Replies.* Volume 1. Norwood, MA: C. R. Publications Inc., 1995.

———. *Catholic Replies.* Volume 2. Norwood, MA: C. R. Publications Inc., 2003.

Dubois, Jacques. *Sainte Genevieve de Paris: La vie, la Culte, l'art.* Paris: Beauchesne, 1982.

Dulles, Avery. *Models of Revelation.* Garden City, NY: Doubleday Books, 1983.

Dunbar, Agnes B. C. *A Dictionary of Saintly Women.* 2 Vols. London: G. Bell & Co., 1905.

Ebner, Margaret. *Margaret Ebner major works.* Translated and edited by Leonard P. Hindsley. NY: Paulist Press, 1993.

Elisabeth of Schonau. *Elisabeth of Schonau; the complete works.* Translated and introduced by Anne L. Clark. NY: Paulist Press, 2000.

Elizabeth of the Trinity. *Elizabeth of the Trinity: Always Believe in Love.* Edited by Martin Murphey. Hyde Park, NY: New City Press, 2009.

Ellsberg, Robert. *All saints: daily reflections on saints, prophets, and witnesses for our time.* NY: Crossroad Pub. Company, 1997.

Englebert, Omer. *The lives of the saints.* NY: D. Makay Co., 1951.

Euteneuer, Thomas J. *Exorcism and the Church Militant.* Front Royal, VA: Human Life International, 2010.

Faber, F. W., ed. *The Lives of Rose of Lima, the Blessed Colomba of Rieti and of St. Juliana Falconieri.* NY: Edward Dunigan, 1847.

Fanning, Stephen. *Mystics of the Christian Tradition.* London: Routledge, 2001.

Farges, Albert. *Mystical phenomena compared with their human and diabolical counterparts; a treatise on mystical theology in agreement with the principles of St. Teresa set forth by the Carmelite Conference of 1923 at Madrid by Msgr. Albert Farges.* Translated from the French by S.P. Jacques. London: Burns, Oates & Washbourne, Ltd. 1926.

Farmer, David Hugh. *The Oxford Dictionary of Saints.* Oxford: Oxford University Press, 2004.

Fedotov, Georgii Petrovich. *Treasury of Russian Spirituality.* Gloucester, MA: Peter Smith, 1969.

Finnegan, Mary Jeremy. *Scholars and mystics.* Chicago: H. Regnery Co., 1962.

Fink, John F. *The Doctors of the church; an introduction to the church's great teachers.* NY: Alba House, 2000.

Flanagan, Sabina. *Hildegard of Bingen, A visionary life.* London: Routledge, 1989.

Flinders, Carol Lee. *Enduring Grace: living portraits of seven women mystics.* San Francisco: Harper's San Francisco, 1993.

Floyd, E. Randall. *In the realm of miracles and visions.* Augusta, GA: Harbor House Books, 2006.

Foran, Edward A. *Life of St. Clare of the Cross.* Oconomewoc, WI: 1954.

Francis, de Sales. *An introduction to the devout life.* Rockford, IL: TAN Books and Publishers, 1994.

Freze, Michael. *They bore the wounds of Christ: the mystery of the sacred stigmata.* Huntington, IN: Our Sunday Visitor, 1989.

———. *Voices, visions and apparitions.* Huntington, IN: Our Sunday Visitor, 1993.

Frost, Bede. *Saint John of the Cross (1542–1591), doctor of divine love, an introduction to his philosophy, theology and spirituality.* NY: Gordon Press, 1981.

Fullerton, Georgiana. *The life of St. Frances of Rome.* London; D & J Sadler & Co., 1855.

———. *The life of St. Frances of Rome, of Blessed Lucy of Narni, of Dominica of Paradiso and of Anne De Montmorecy.* NY: Routledge, 2001.

Furlong, Monica. *Visions and Longings; Medieval women mystics.* Boston, MA: Shambhala, 1997.

Gallick, Sarah. *The big book of women saints.* San Francisco: Harper San Francisco, 2007.

Garrigou-Lagrange, Reginald. *Life Everlasting and the Immensity of the Soul; A theological treatise on the four last things: death, judgment, heaven and hell.* Translated by Patrick Cummins. Rockford, IL: TAN Books and Publishers, Inc. 1991.

Gertrude the Great. *The herald of divine love, Gertrude of Helfta.* Translated and edited by Margaret Winkworth. NY: Paulist Press, 1993.

———. *The life and revelations of St. Gertrude the Great.* Westminster, MD: Christian Classics Inc., 1983.

Ghezzi, Bert. *Mystics and miracles; true stories of lives touched by God.* Chicago: Loyola Press, 2002.

———. *Voices of the saints. A 365-Day Journey with our Spiritual Companions.* Chicago: Loyola Press, 2000.

Giorgi, Rosa. *Saints, a year in faith and art.* NY: Harry N. Abrams, Inc., 2006.

———. *Saints in Art.* Edited by Stefano Zuffi. Translated by Thomas Michael Hartmann. Los Angeles: Getty Publications, 2003.

Glenn, Paul Joseph. *A tour of the Summa.* Rockford, IL: TAN Books and Publishers, 1978.

Gomez Cano, Blanca. *Sor Ana de los Angeles Monteagudo y Ponce de Leon.* Lima, Peru: Monasterio de Santa Catalina de Sena, 1984.

Godding, Robert et al. *Bollandistes, saints et legendes:quatre siecles de recherché.* Bruxelles: Societedes bollandistes, 2007.

Gorden, Lucy. "He Raised 100 Children from the Dead," in *Inside the Vatican,* July 2005.

Grey, E. Howard. *Visions, previsions and miracles in modern times.* London: L. N. Fowler & Co., 1915.

Groeschel, Benedict J. *A still, small voice; a practical guide on reported revelations.*

San Francisco: Ignatius Press, 1993.

———. *Spiritual passages; the psychology of spiritual development: "For those who seek."* NY: Crossroad, 1983.

Guiley, Rosemary. *The encyclopedia of saints.* NY: Facts on File, 2001.

Hafner, Paul. "St. Bridget of Sweden," in *Inside the Vatican*, June/July 2008.

———. "Teresa Helena Higginson" in *Inside the Vatican*, March 2005.

———. "The Spouse of Christ," in *Inside the Vatican*, March, 2005.

Harrison, Ted. *Stigmata: a medieval mystery in a modern age.* NY: St. Martin's Press, 1994.

Hebert, Albert J. *Saints Who raised the dead; true stories of 400 resurrection miracles.* Rockford, IL: TAN Books, 1986.

———. *The discernment of visionaries and apparitions today.* Paulina, LA: 1994.

Hiral, A. M. *The Revelation of Margaret of Cortona.* Translated by R. Brown: St. Bonaventura, NY: 1952.

Horvat, Miriam. *Venerable Antonio Margil of Jesus, Apostle of New Spain.* http://www.traditioninaction.org/Margil.

Hospers, John, "Is the Notion of Disembodied Existence Intelligible?" in *Immortality.* Edited by Paul Edwards. New York: Macmillan, 1992.

Hurndall, Bernadette F. G. *By God's Command: the Amazing Supernatural Life of Teresa Higginson, Stigmatic, Servant of God....I Saw the Lord.* Compiled by Chester and Lucille Huyssen. Tarrytown, NY: Chosen Books, 1992.

Imbert-Goubeyre, Antoine. *La Stigmatisation, l'exstase divine et les miracles de Lourdes, Reponse aux librespenseurs.* 2 vols. Clermont-Ferrand Bellet, 1984.

John of the Cross. *Spiritual canticle.* Translated by E. Allison Peers. 3rd rev. ed. Garden City, NY: Image Books, 1961.

———. *The Collected Works of St. John of the Cross.* Translated by Kieran Kavanaugh and Otilio Rodriguez. Washington, DC: ICS Publications, 1991.

———. *The Complete works of St. John of the Cross, doctor of the church.* 3 vols. Translated and edited by E. Allison Peers. Westminster, MD: Newman, 1964.

Johnson, Kevin Orlin. *Apparitions: mystic phenomena and what they mean.* Dallas, TX: Pangaeus Press, 1995.

———. *The ten most common misconceptions about apparitions.* http://www.catholicculture.org/culture/library/view.cfm?id–1093&CFID–455311494&CFT.

Johnston, Francis. *Alexandrina: the agony and the glory.* Rockford, IL: TAN Books and Publishers, 1982.

Jones, Frederick M. *Alphonsus De Liguori: saint of Bourbon Naples, 1696–1787, founder of the Redemptorists.* Liguori, MO: Liguori, 1999.

Jones, Kathleen. *Women saints: lives of faith and courage.* Maryknoll, NY: Orbis Books, 1999.

Julian of Norwich. *Revelations of Divine Love.* Garden City, NY: Image Books, 1977.

Kaczmarek, Louis. *The Eucharist and the Rosary; The Power to Change the World.* Plattsburgh, NY: M.B.S., 2000.

Keating, Karl. *Catholicism and Fundamentalism: the attack on "Romanism" by "Bible Christians."* San Francisco: Ignatius Press, 1988.

Kelly, J. N. D. *The Oxford Dictionary of*

Popes. NY: Oxford University Press, 1988.

Kelsey, Morton. *Discernment: A study in ecstasy and evil.* NY: Paulist Press, 1978.

Kerr, Cecil. *Teresa Helena Higginson, servante de Dieu, epouse du crucifie, 1844–1905.* Paris: Desclee, de Brouwer, & Cie, 1935.

Keyes, Frances Parkinson. *Three Ways of Love.* NY: Hawthorne Books, 1963.

———. *The Rose and the Lily, the lives and times of two South American saints.* NY: Hawthorn Books, 1961.

Kik, Jacob Marcelles. *Voices from heaven and hell.* Philadelphia: Presbyterian Reformed Publishing Co., 1955.

King, Ursula. *Christian mystics. The spiritual heart of the Christian tradition.* NY: Simon & Schuster, 1998.

Klein, Peter. *The Catholic Source Book.* Edited by Peter Klein. 3rd ed. Dubuque: Brown-Roa, 2000.

Koenig-Bricker, Woodeene. *365 Saints: your daily guide to the wisdom and wonder of their lives.* San Francisco: Harper San Francisco, 1995.

Languet, Jean Joseph. *The life of the Venerable Mother Margaret Mary Alacoque, religious of the Order of the Visitation.* London: T. Richardson & Sons, 1850.

Laurentin, Rene. *Catherine Laboure; visionary of the miraculous medal.* Translated by Paul Inwood. Boston, MA: Pauline Books, 2006.

Life and Doctrine of St. Catherine of Genoa. NY: 1874.

Likoudis, Paul. "German Mystic; A Guide to a Eucharistic Jesus," in *The Wanderer,* November 17, 2005.

Lord, Bob and Penny. *Visionaries, mystics and stigmatics down through the Ages.* Westlake village, CA: Journeys of Faith, 1995.

———. *Visions of heaven, hell and purgatory.* NP, 1996.

Lucia of Fatima. *Fatima in Lucia's Own Words.* Edited by L. Kondor. Fatima, Portugal: Postulation Centre, 1976.

———. *Her own words to the nuclear age: The memoirs of Sr. Lucia.* By John Haffert. Asbury Park, NJ:101 Foundation, 1993.

MacKenzie, Andrew. *The Seen and the Unseen.* London, Whitefield & Nicolson, 1987.

MacKenzie, Janet P. *Saint John Masias, Marvelous Dominican Gatekeeper of Lima, Peru.* Study guide.

Mahoney, Denis. *Marie of the Incarnation, mystic and missionary.* Garden City, NY: Doubleday, 1964.

Manual of Indulgences, Norms and Grants. Apostolic Penitentiary. Washington, DC, USCCB, 2006.

Marechal, Joseph. *Studies in the psychology of the Mystics.* Translated by Algar Thorold. London: Burns, Oates and Washbourne Ltd., 1927.

Maria de Jesus, de Agreda. *The mystical city of God.* Translated by George J. Blatter. Abridged version. Rockford, IL: TAN Books and Publishers, 1978.

Maria Maddalena de'Pazzi: Selected Revelations. Translated by Armando Maggi. NY: Paulist Press, 2000.

Marie de l' Incarnation. *The Autobiography of Venerable Marie of the Incarnation, O.S.U. Mystic and Missionary.* Translated by John. J. Sullivan. Chicago: Loyola University Press, 1964.

Marie de Saint Pierre de la Sainte Famille. *The golden arrow; the autobiography and revelations of Sister Mary of St. Peter on Devotion to the Holy Face of Jesus.* Edited and translated by Emeric B. Scallan. NY: William Fredech Press, 1954.

Martin, James. *My life with the saints.* Chicago: Loyola Press, 2006.

Mechtilde of Magdeburg. *The Flowering Light of the Godhead.* Translated by Frank Tobin. Mahwah, NJ: Paulist Press, 1997.

Medieval women mystics Gertrude the Great, Algela of Foligno, Brigitta of Sweden and Julian of Norwich; selected spiritual writings. Edited by Elizabeth Ruth Obbard. Hyde Park, NY: New City Press, 2002.

Meissner, William W. *Ignatius of Loyola: the psychology of a saint.* New Haven, CT: Yale University Press, 1992.

Melton, J. Gordon. *The encyclopedia of religious phenomena.* Detroit, MI: Visible Ink Press, 2008.

Menendez, Josefa. *The Way of Divine Love; the meaning of the Sacred Heart to the world and a short biography of His messenger Sister Josefa Menendez, coadjutrix sister of the Society of the Sacred Heart of Jesus.* Rockford, IL: TAN Books, 1973.

Metzger, A. P. "The Great Patron: Saint Nicholas and the Suffering Souls." *The Tagastan* 15, 1952.

Michalenko, Sophia. *The life of Faustina Kowalska; the authorized biography.* Ann Arbor, MI: Charis Books, 1999.

Miller, Frederick L. *The Message of Our Lady of Fatima.* New Haven, CT: Knights of Columbus Supreme Council, 2001.

Miracles Will Follow the True Church. http://my.tbaytel.net/nitesky/christian/miracles.htm.

Molinari, Paolo. *Julian of Norwich: The Teaching of a 14c English mystic.* Norwood, PA: Norwood editas, 1976.

Monden, Louis. *Signs and wonders; a study of the miraculous element in religion.* NY: Desclee Co., 1966.

Mormando, Franco. *The preacher's demons: Bernardino of Siena and the social underworld of early renaissance Italy.* Chicago: University of Chicago Press, 1999.

Nash-Marshall, Siobhan. *Joan of Arc: a spiritual biography.* NY: Crossroad, 1999.

Niebuhr, H. Richard. *The meaning of revelation.* NY: The Macmillan Company, 1941.

New Catholic Encyclopedia. Prepared by the editorial staff of Catholic University of America. 1st ed. 18 vols. NY: McGraw Hill Book Company, 1967.

New Catholic Encyclopedia. Catholic University of America. 2nd ed. 15 vols. Detroit, MI: Thomson-Gale 2003.

New Catholic Encyclopedia. Jubilee volume. The Wojtyla years. Detroit, MI: Gale Group in association with the Catholic University of America, 2001.

Noort, Gerardus Van. *Dogmatic Theology.* Vol. 3, *The Sources of Revelation.* Translated and revised by John J. Castelot and William R. Murphy. Westminster, MD: Newman Press, 1955.

O'Reilly, Bernard. *St. Angela Merici, and the Ursulines.* NY: D & J Sadlier, 1880.

O'Sullivan, Paul. *All about the Angels.* Rockford, IL: TAN Books and Publishers, Inc., 1990.

———. *Read me or Rue it.* Rockford, IL: TAN Books and Publishers, Inc., 1992.

———. *The Holy Ghost Our Greatest Friend.* Rockford, IL: TAN, 1991.

Our Sunday visitor's encyclopedia of Catholic doctrine. Edited by Russell Shaw. Huntington, IN:Our Sunday visitor, 1997.

Overman, Dean L. *A case for the existence of God.* Lanham, MD: Rowman & Littlefield, 2009.

Oxford English Dictionary. Oxford: Clarendon Press, 1971.

Park, Katherine. "Relics of a Fertile Heart: The Autopsy of St.Clare of Montefalco," in *The Material Culture of Sex, Procreation and Marriage in Premodern Europe.* Edited by Anne L. McClanan and Karen Rosoff Encarnacion. Hampshire, England: Palgrave, 2002.

Pastrovicchi, Angelo. *St. Joseph of Copertino.* Translated by Francis S. Laing. Rockford, IL: TAN Books and Publishers, 1994.

Peyret, Raymond. *Marthe Robin: the cross and the joy.* Translated by Clare Will Faulhaber. NY: Alba House, 1983.

Phelan, Edna Beyer. *Don Bosco, A spiritual portrait.* Garden City, NY: 1963.

Pilch, John J. *Visions and healings in the Acts of the Apostles: how the early believers experienced God.* Collegeville, MN: Liturgical Press, 2004.

Poernbacher, Karl. *Crescentia Hoess: A Saint for Our Time.* Translated by Sister Clara Brill, F.S.P.A. and Ursula-Blank Chiu. La Crosse, WI: Franciscan Sisters of Perpetual Adoration, 2003.

Poulain, Augustin. *The graces of interior prayer.* Translated by Leonora L. Yorke Smith. St. Louis, MO: B. Herder Book Co., 1950.

———. *Revelations and visions: discerning the true and the certain from the false or the doubtful.* Translated by Leonora L. Yorke Smith. Edited by Frank Sadowski. NY: Alba House, 1998.

Powers-Waters, Alma. *Saint Catherine Laboure and the Miraculous Medal.* San Francisco: Ignatius Press, 2000.

Pradel, Andrew. *St. Vincent Ferrer: Angel of the Judgment.* Rockford, IL: TAN Books and Publishers, 2001.

Procter. *Short Life of the Dominican Saints.* London: Kegan, Paul, Trench, Trubner & Co. ltd., 1901.

Rabel, Andrew. "Alexandrina Maria da Costa," in *Inside the Vatican,* May 2004.

Rahner, Karl. *Visions and Prophecies.* Translated by Charles Henkeyand Richard Strachan. Freiburg: Herder, 1963.

Rayek, Francis M. *Rafka, the blind mystic of Lebanon.* Still River, MA: St. Bede's Publications, 1980.

Raymond of Capua. *The life of St. Catherine of Siena.* NY: P. J. Kennedy & sons, 1960.

Redi, Paolo. *Elisabetta Canori Mora: un amore fedele tra le mura di casa.* Roma: Citta Nuova, 1994.

Rega, Frank M. *Padre Pio and America.* Rockford, IL: TAN Books and Publishers, 2005.

Rengers, Christopher. *The Youngest Prophet.* NY; Alba House, 1986.

Revelations of St. Bridget on the Life and Passion of Our Lord and the Life of His Blessed Mother. Rockford, IL: TAN Book and Publishers, 1984.

Rios, Eduardo Enrique. *Life of Fray Antonio Margil, O.F.M.* Translated and revised by Benedict Leutenegger. Washington,

Acad. of American Franciscan History, 1959.

Robin, Marthe. *The Cross and the Joy.* NY: Alba House, 1983.

Robinson, Edward. *The original vision: A study of the religious experience of childhood.* NY: Seabury Press, 1983.

Roschini, Gabriele. *Teresa Musco: Crucified with the Crucified.* 1979

Rose, Devin. *If Protestantism is true; The Reformation meets Rome.* Lexington, KY: Unitas Books, 2011.

Rose, Michael. *Heroes, Holiness and Mystical Phenomena.* http://www.4marks,com/articles/details.

Rossetti, Stephen. *When the Lion Roars: a primer for the unsuspecting mystic.* Notre Dame, IN: Ave Maria Press, 2003.

Rotelle, John E., ed. *Book of Augustinian Saints.* Villanova, PA: Augustinian Press, 2000.

Ruffin, C. Bernard. *Padre Pio: the true story.* Huntington, IN: Our Sunday Visitor, 1991.

Sadlier, J. *Purgatory: Doctrinal, historical and poetical.* NY: D & J Sadlier & Co., 1886.

Saint Catherine Laboure of the Miraculous Medal. Rockford, IL: TAN Books.

Saint Gerard Majella; his writings and spirituality. Edited by Noel Londono. Liguori, MO: Liguori Press, 2002.

Saint Margaret Mary Alacoque and the Promises of the Sacred Heart. Translated by M. A. Bouchard. Boston, MA: 1975.

Saint-Omer, Edward. *St. Gerard Majella.* Rockford, IL:TAN Books and Publishers, 1999.

Sanchez-Ventera y Pascual, Francisco.

Stigmatises et apparitions. Paris: Nouvelles editas latines, 1967.

Saunders, William P. *Straight Answers II; answers to 100 more questions about the Catholic faith.* Baltimore, MD: Cathedral Foundation Press, 2003.

Scaramelli, Giovanni Battista. *A handbook of mystical theology.* Translated by D. H. S. Nicholson. Berwick, ME: Ibis Press, 2005.

Schmoger, Karl Erhard. *Life of Anne Catherine Emmerich.* 2 vols. NY: F. Pustet & Co., 1885.

———. *The Life of Anne Catherine Emmerich.* Rockford, IL: TAN Books, Inc., 1976.

Schouppe, Francis Xavier. *Hell and How to Avoid Hell.* Rockford, IL: TAN Books and Publishers, Inc., 1989.

———. *Purgatory: explained by the lives and legends of the saints.* Rockford, IL: TAN Books, 1986.

Sellner, Edward Cletus. *Wisdom of the Celtic saints.* Notre Dame, IN: Ave Maria Press, 1993.

Sheppard, Lambert B. *Barbe Acarie, wife and mystic: A biography by Lambert B. Sheppard.* NY: David McKay Co., Inc., 1953.

Sicardo, Jose. *Life of sister St. Rita of Cascia of the order of St. Augustine, advocate of the impossible; model of maidens, wives, mothers, widows and nuns.* Translated by Dan J. Murphy. Chicago: D.bittansa, 1916.

Sicardo, Joseph A. *St. Rita of Cascia.* Translated by Dan J. Murphy. Rockford, IL: TAN Books and Publishers, 1993.

Simi, Gino J. *Saint Francis of Paola, God's miracle worker supreme.* Rockford, IL: TAN Books, 1977.

Singh, Sundar. *Visions of the spiritual world; a brief description of the spiritual life.* London: Macmillan, 1926.

Slatter, Mark. "Revelation," This Rock. Catholic Answers Inc. June 1998.

Society for Psychical Research. *Proceedings of the Society of Psychical Research.* Part 90, May 1924.

Sparrow, Gregory Scott. *I am with you always: true stories of encounters with Jesus.* New York: Bantam Books, 1995.

Stavinskas, Peter, ed. *Catholic Dictionary.* Huntington, IN: Our Sunday Visitor Publishing Division, 2002.

Steiner, Johannes. *Therese Neumann: A portrait, based on authentic accounts, journals and documents.* NY: Alba House, 1967.

Steiner, Johannes. *The visions of Therese Neumann.* NY; Alba House, 1976.

Stella, Pietro. *Don Bosco Life and Work.* Translated by J. Drury. New Rochelle, NY: 1985.

———. *Don Bosco: religious outlook and spirituality.* Translated by John Drury. New Rochelle, NY: Salesian Publishers, 1996.

Stoddard, Charles. *St. Anthony, the wonder-worker of Padua.* Rockford, IL: TAN Books and Publishers, 1992.

Stories about Purgatory and what they reveal; 30 days for the holy souls. Rockford, IL: TAN Books and Publishers, 2005.

Sullivan, Randall. *The miracle detector: an investigation of holy visions.* NY: Atlantic Monthly Press, 2004.

Summers, Montague. *The physical phenomena of mysticism, with especial reference to the stigmata, divine and diabolical.* London: Rider and Co., 1950.

Tanquery, Adolphe. *The spiritual life; a treatise on ascetical and mystical theology.* Translated by Herman Branderis. Rockford, IL: TAN Books and Publishers, Inc., 2000.

Teresa of Avila. *The Complete works of St. Teresa of Jesus.* 3 vols. Translated and edited by E. Allison Peers. London: Sheed and Ward, 1946.

———. *Collected works of St. Teresa of Avila.* Translated by Kieran Kavanaugh and Otilio Rodriguez. Washington, DC: Institute of Carmelite Studies, 1976 and 1980.

———. *Interior castle.* Translated and edited by E. Allison Peers. Garden City, NY: Doubleday, 1961.

———. *The Life of Teresa of Jesus; the autobiography of Teresa of Avila.* Translated and edited by E. Allison Peers. Garden City, NY: Doubleday, 2004.

———. *The way of perfection.* Translated by The Benedictines of Stanbrook. Rockford, IL: TAN Books and Publishers, 1997.

———. *The Life of St. Teresa of Avila by Herself.* Translated by J. M. Cohen. NY: Viking Penguin, 1957.

Thaisia. *Abbess Thaisia of Leushino, the autobiography of a spiritual daughter of St. John of Kronstadt.* Platina, CA: St. Herman of Alaska Brotherhood, 1989.

Therese of Lisieux. *The autobiography of St. Therese of Lisieux: the story of a soul.* Translated by John Beevers. Garden City, NY: Image Books, 1957.

———. *Story of a soul; the autobiography of St. Therese of Lisieux.* Translated by John Clarke. Washington, DC: ICS Publications, 1975.

The Catholic study Bible. New American Bible.

Donald Senior, General editor. New York: Oxford University Press, 1990.

"The Healer Fra Elia," *Inside the Vatican*, January 2006.

The New American Bible. South Bend, IN: Greenlawn Press, 1987.

The oxford dictionary of popes. NY: Oxford University Press, 1988.

The Pieta Prayer Book. Hickory Comers, MI: MLOR Corp, 2004.

The Preacher's Demons: Bernardino of Siena and the Social Under-world of early Renaissance Italy. Chicago: 1999.

The Random House College Dictionary. Laurence Urdang, editor in chief. NY: Random House, 1973.

The Saints; a concise biographical dictionary. Edited by John Coulson. NY: Hawthorne Books, 1958.

The secret of happiness; the fifteen prayers revealed by Our Lord to St. Bridget in the church of St. Paul at Rome. Stockbridge, MA: Marian Helpers Center Congregation of Marians, 1979.

The visions, revelations and teachings of Angela of Foligno; A member of the third order of St. Francis. Selected and modernized by Margaret Gauyon. Brighton, Portland: The Delphic Press, 2000.

The Wanderer. St. Paul, MN: National Catholic Weekly, selected issues.

Thomas Aquinas. *Summa Theologiae.* Translated by fathers of the English Dominican Province. 5 vols. Westminster, MD: Christian Classics, 1981.

Thomas of Celano. *St. Francis of Assisi. First and second life of St. Francis with selection from the treatise on Blessed Francis.* Translated by Placid Hermann. Chicago: Franciscan Herald Press, 1988.

Thurston, Herbert. *Ghosts and Poltergeists.* Chicago: Henry Regnery Co., 1954.

———. *The Physical Phenomena of Mysticism.* Edited by J. H.Crehan. Chicago: Henry Regnery Co., 1952.

Tobin, Thomas E. *St. Gerard Majella, The Mother's Saint.* Liguori, MO; Liguori Press, nd.

Treece, Patricia. *Apparitions of modern saints. Appearances of Therese of Lisieux, Padre Pio, Don Bosco, and others, messages from God to his people on earth.* Ann Arbor, MI: Charis, 2001.

———. *The mystical body; an investigation of supernatural phenomena.* NY: Crossroad, 2005.

Trochu, Francis. *Saint Bernadette Soubirous 1844–1879.* NY: Pantheon Books, Inc., 1958.

———. *Saint Bernadette Soubirous.* Rockford, IL: TAN Books and Publishers, 1993.

———. *The cure d'Ars: St. Jean-Marie-Baptiste Vianney (1786–1859).* Translated by Ernest Graf. Rockford, IL: TAN Books and Publishers, 1977.

Turi Anna Maria. *Stigmate e stigmatizzati; segni del cielo:soria e attalita.* Roma: Edizioni Mediterranean, 1990.

Turks, Paul. *Philip Neri: the fire of joy.* Translated by Daniel Utrecht. Edinburgh, T &T Clark, 1995.

Two Lives of Marie d' Ognies. Translated by Margot H. King and Hugh Feiss. Toronto: Pegrina, 2000.

Tylenda, Joseph N. *Jesuit saints and martyrs: short biographies of the saints, blesseds, venerable and servants of God of the Society of Jesus.* Chicago: Loyola Press, 1998.

Tyrrell, George Nugent Merle. *Apparitions*. London: Gerald Duckworth & Co., 1953.

Underhill, Evelyn. *The Mystics of the Church*. New York: Schocken Books, 1964.

Van Den Aardweg, Gerard J. M. *Hungry souls; supernatural visits, messages, and warnings from purgatory*. Rockford, IL: TAN Books and Publishers, 2009.

Van Noort, G. *Dogmatic Theology*, vol. 3, *The Sources of Revelation*. Westminster: Newman, 1963, no. 138.

Varano, Camilla Battista da. *My Spiritual Life*. Translated by Joseph R. Berrigan. Toronto: Peregrina, 1989.

Varghese, Roy Abraham. *There is life after death: compelling reports from those who have glimpsed the afterlife*. Franklin Lakes, NJ: Career Press, 2010.

Vatican Council 2nd (1962–1965): The Conciliar and Post Conciliar Documents. General editor Austin Flannery. Dublin: Dominican Publishers, 1975.

Vatican Council 2nd (1962–1965): Constitutions, Decrees, Declarations The Basic Sixteen Documents. General editor Austin Flannery. Northport, NY: Costello Publishing Co., 1975.

Mary of Agreda. *The Mystical City of God*. Translated by George J. Blatter. Rockford, IL: TAN Books and Publishers, 1978.

Visions of heaven and hell. Harrisburg, PA: The Christian Union, 1909.

Vogl, Adalbert Albert. *Theresa Neumann: Mystic and Stigmatist*. Rockford, IL: TAN Books and Publishers, 1987.

Walsh, William Thomas. *Saints in action*. Garden City, NY: Hanover House, 1961.

Walsh, William James. *The apparitions and shrines of heaven's bright queen in legend*. New York: Cary-Stafford Co., 1904.

Watkin, Edward. *Neglected saints*. NY: Sheed and Ward, 1955.

Weigl, A. M. *Voices from Heaven*. Kent, England: Pax christi Publications, 1983.

Wiebe, Phillip H. *Visions of Jesus; direct encounters from the New Testament today*. NY: Oxford University Press, 1997.

Wiesinger, Alois. *Occult Phenomena in light of theology*. Westminster, MD: Newman, 1957.

Wilson, Ian. *Stigmata: An investigation into the mysterious appearance of Christ's wounds in hundreds of people from medieval Italy to modern America*. San Francisco: Harper and Row, 1989.

Zaleski, Carol. *Otherworld Journeys; accounts of near death experience in medieval and modern times*. NY: Oxford University Press, 1987.

Zappulli, Cesare. *The Power of Goodness: The Life of Blessed Clelia Barbieri*. Translated by David Giddings. Boston, MA: Daughters of St. Paul, 1980.

Zuffi, Stefano. *Gospel figures in art*. Translated by Thomas Michael Hartmann. Los Angeles: The J. Paul Getty Museum, 2003.

Websites

http://en.wikipedia.org/wiki/Garabandal_apparitions.

http://en.wikipedia.org/wiki/Beatrix_da_Silva.

http://my.tbaytel.net/nitesky/christian/miracles.htm.

http://prophetesetmystiques.blogspot.com/2010/12stigmatises–et–stigmates.html.

http://saints.sqpn.com/.

http://www.bibleprobe.com/fatimvisionofhell.htm.

http//www.capuchinfriars.org.au/saints/bernardo.

http://www.Catholicwonderworkers.

http://www.Catholicity.com.

http://www.catholicplanet.com/articles/instructionOO7.htm.

http://www.catholicculture.org/culture/library/view.cfm?id=1093&CFID=455311494&CFT.

http://www.catholicdoors.com.

http://www.catholicplanet.com/articles/instructionOO7.htm.

http://www.miraclehunter.com/marianapparitions/discernment/conte.html.

http://www.Den Katolske Kirke – Den salige Anna Schaffer.

http://www.communityofhopeinc.org/prayer%20pages/saints/marie%20julie.html.

http://www.encyclopedia.com/topic/stigmata.aspx.

http://www.catholicforum.fisheaters.com.

http://www.eucharistadorationforpriests.com.

http:/www.kathpedia.com/index.php.Wundmale.

http://www.knocknovena.com.

http://www.catholicplanet.com/articles/instruction007.htm.

http://www.miraclehunter.com/marian_apparitions/visionaries/index.html.

http://www.miraclehunter.com/marian_apparitions/statements/index.html.

http://www.miraclehunter.com/marian_apparitions/approved apparitions /index.html.

http://www.miraclehunter.com/marian_apparitions/unapprovedapparitions/ index.html.

http://www.ewtn.com/Index of Biographies of the Blesseds 1993–2007.

http://www.mariamthresia.org/?p+206.

http://www.mariamthresia.org/cat+14),

http://www.mysticsofthechurch.com.

http://www.newmanchaplets.com.

http://saints.sqpn.com/saint.

http://www.newadvent.forgather.

http://www.new advent.org/cathen.

http://www.newadvent.org/cathen/03724a.htm.

http://www.new advent.org/cathen/05391b.htm.

http://www.newadvent.org/cathen/06535a.htm.

http://www.catholic-forum.com/saints.

http://www.nouvl.evangelization.fre.fr.giovanna.

http://www.padrimarian.org.

http://saints.sqpn.com/saintg6t.htm.

http://www.tearlove.com.

http://www.thermaturgs.blogspot.com.

http://www.tldm.org/News10/Akita.htm.

http://www.traditioninaction.org/Margil.

http://www.vatican.va/newsservices/liturgy/saints.

http://www.vatican.va.news_service/liturgy/saints/
ns_lit_doc_20000409_beata–Mankidyan.

http://www.wikitau.org/index.php5/WikiKto/Stigmates.

http://www.zenit.com.

http://www.1902encyclopedia.com/S/STI/stigmatization.html.

http://willingshepherds.net/lives.

"Fatima in Lucia's own words, Third and Fourth Memoir, the Vision of Hell, http://www.
concerned catholics.org/printable/pr-hell.htm.

Patron Saint Index, http://www.catholicforum.com/saints.

Santi Beati e testimony, http://www.santiebeati.it/index.html.

The Fatima Network, http://www.fatima.org/essentials/facts/hell.asp.

The Holy See, official site, http://www.vatican.va/.

Vie de Sainte Lidvine, http://www.advent.org/cathen.

www.newadvent.org/cathen.

APPENDIX I
Approved Apparition Claims

From MiracleHunter.com: As established in the Council of Trent (1545-1563), the local bishop is the first and main authority in the judgment of the authenticity of apparition claims. Vatican approval is not required for an apparition to be considered authentic. After an episcopal approval, the Vatican may officially release a statement or give less explicit forms of approval such as a papal visit or crowning of the associated icon, a papal gift such as a golden rose, the approval of the construction of a basilica, the establishment of a feast day, or the canonization of the associated visionary.

Positive judgments by the local bishop (but not yet by the Vatican) theoretically are able to be reversed by a subsequent bishop. Negative judgments (Non constat de supernaturalitate) and rulings of no evidence of supernaturality (Constat de non supernaturalitate) have later been changed to positive judgments on a few rare occasions with the ruling of a subsequent bishop.

If a Marian apparition is recognized by the bishop, it means that the message is not contrary to faith and morals and that Mary can be venerated in a special way at the site. But because belief in a private revelation is not required by the Church, Catholics are at liberty to decide how much personal spiritual emphasis to place on apparitions and the messages they deliver.

Traditionally Approved Apparitions

(No Formal investigation)

Zaragoza, Spain (40)

Our Lady of the Pillar

October 12

Investigated: N/A

Approved:

Visionaries: St. James the Greater

First Apparition: January 2, AD 40

Last Apparition: January 2, AD 40

Number of Apparitions: 1

Miracles & Signs: The chapel originally built by Saint James was later destroyed as were several subsequent chapels on the same site. The statue and pillar have been preserved however for almost two thousand years.

Summary: According to legend, in the early days of the Church on January 2, AD 40, the Apostle James the Greater was proclaiming the Gospel in Caesaraugusta (present day Zaragoza) by the river Ebro when he saw Mary miraculously appearing in the flesh on a pillar calling him to return to Jerusalem.

For more information, visit: http://www.miraclehunter.com/

Le Puy en Velay, France (250)

Our Lady of the Le Puy

July 11

Investigated: N/A

Approved: Traditional approval only

Visionaries: Villa, a convert woman

First Apparition: 250

Last Apparition: 250

Number of Apparitions: 1

Miracles & Signs: After seeing Our Lady, Villa was cured and built a small chapel on the site of the apparition. Throughout history, other miracles were performed there, which gained a certain popularity for the shrine.

Summary: Our Lady appeared in Le Puy (Haute-Loire, France), in a chapel built by the faithful a few years before on a high mountain, to a recent convert. She had been plagued by a serious illness and no doctor had been able to help. Our Lady, during her appearance, completely cured her.

For more information, visit: http://www.miraclehunter.com/

Rome, Italy (352)

Our Lady of the Snows

August 5

Investigated: N/A

Approved:

Visionaries: John of Rome, Pope Liberius

First Apparition: August 4, 352

Last Apparition: August 4, 352

Number of Apparitions: 1

Miracles & Signs: The Virgin Mary miraculously left snow in the middle of the hot month of August on Esquiline Hill on the precise area in which she wanted the church built.

Summary: A wealthy but childless Roman couple, John and his wife decided to leave their fortune to the Church. The Virgin appeared to them on the night of August 4 and told them that she wished a basilica to be constructed on the Esquiline Hill which would be outlined in snow. Pope Liberius also received the same message from the Virgin and ordered the construction of St. Mary Major Basilica.

For more information, visit: http://www.miraclehunter.com/

Covadonga, Spain (722)

Our Lady of Covadonga

September 7th

Investigated: N/A

Approved: A Basilica stands at the spot of the apparition to honor Our Lady of Covadonga.

Visionaries: Dom Pelayo, first King of the Asturias

First Apparition: 722

Last Apparition: 722

Number of Apparitions: 1

Miracles & Signs: The Christians defeated the Moors at the battle of Covadonga against incredible odds.

Summary: Dom Pelayo, first King of the Asturias led the first victory over the Moors in all the Iberian Peninsula in the year 722. Our Lady appeared to him and left behind a statue of Herself and the Christ Child.

For more information, visit: http://www.miraclehunter.com/

Walsingham, England (1061)

Our Lady of Walsingham

September 24th

Investigated: N/A

Approved: During Pope John Paul II's visit in 1982, he asked that the statue be placed on the altar for Mass. In 2000, he decreed that the feast of Our Lady of Walsingham would be cele-brated on September 24th in England.

Visionary: Richeldis de Faverches

First Apparition: 1061

Last Apparition: 1061

Number of Apparitions: 1

Summary: In 1061 Our Lady appeared to Richeldis de Faverches, a Catholic English noble-woman in the village of Walsingham in Norfolk, England. Our Lady of Walsingham presented her with the plans of the Holy House of the Holy Family in Nazareth and asked that she build the house as a shrine and place of pilgrimage.

For more information, visit: http://www.miraclehunter.com/

Barcelona, Spain (1218)

Our Lady of Ransom / Our Lady of Mercy

September 24th

Investigated: N/A

Approved: The Order of the Mercedarians was approved by Gregory IX on Jan 17, 1235

Visionaries: St. Peter Nolasco, St. Raymund of Pennafort, King James of Aragon

First Apparition: August 10, 1218

Last Apparition: August 10, 1218

Number of Apparitions: 1

Miracles & Signs: A plague of locusts was banished from Barcelona through the intercession of the Virgin of Mercy.

Summary: The Blessed Virgin appeared to three men who established the Mercedarian religious order for the redemption of Christian captives from Moorish imprisonment and offer themselves, if necessary, as an exchange.

For more information, visit: http://www.miraclehunter.com/

Aylesford, England (1251)

July 16th

Investigated: N/A

Approved: Confirmation of the Rule of the Order by Pope Honorius III, Gregory IX, and Pope Innocent IV

Visionaries: St. Simon Stock

First Apparition: July 16, 1251

Last Apparition: July 16, 1251

Number of Apparitions: 1

Summary: In answer to St. Simon Stock's appeal for help for his oppressed order, the Virgin Mary appeared to him with a scapular in her hand and the promise of safety from Hell. Soon after, he instituted the confraternity of the Brown Scapular.

For more information, visit: http://www.miraclehunter.com/

Cacerces, Spain (1326)

Our Lady of Guadalupe

Investigated: N/A

Approved: No official approval.

Visionaries: Gil Cordero

First Apparition: 1326

Last Apparition: 1326

Number of Apparitions: 1

Summary: Legend says that in 1326, near the Guadalupe river in Cacerces, Spain, cowherd Gil Cordero experienced an apparition of the Virgin Mary who directed him to a miraculous buried statue given to Spain from Pope Gregory the Great 600 years prior.

For more information, visit: http://www.miraclehunter.com/

Liguria, Italy (1490)

Our Lady of the Guard

Investigated: N/A

Approved: No official approval. The shrine was visited by Popes John Paul II and Benedict XVI.

Visionaries: Benedetto Pareto

First Apparition: August 29, 1490

Last Apparition: August 31, 1490

Number of Apparitions: 2

Summary: According to tradition, on August 29, 1490 the Virgin Mary appeared to a peasant called Benedetto Pareto and asked him to build a chapel on the mountain.

For more information, visit: http://www.miraclehunter.com/

Wesemlin, Lucerne (1513)

Our Lady of the Angels

Investigated: NA

Approved: Traditional approval only. A shrine was built on the location of the apparitions.

Visionaries: Maurice von Mettenwyl, city councilor

First Apparition: Pentecost 1513

Last Apparition: 1513

Number of Apparitions: 2

Summary: During the night of Pentecost of 1513, the city councilor, Maurice von Mettenwyl, saw the Virgin Mary surrounded by a heavenly light and surrounded by arrows and the moon was at her feet. Mary appeared crowned and carrying the Child Jesus on her left arm, while the right hand was a scepter. Faced with this majestic appearance of the man was shocked and fell on his knees, promising to rebuild the chapel and put the portrait of Mary in her place, as she had appeared.

Garaison, France (1515)

Notre Dame de Garaison

Investigated: NA

Approved: Traditional – Popes Urban VIII and Gregory XVI have issued indulgences for those who visit the Shrine built in honor of the apparitions.

Visionaries: Angleze Sagazan

First Apparition: 1515

Last Apparition: 1515

Number of Apparitions: 3

Miracles & Signs: Many cures are attested there. In the 17th century the young Louis XIV was cured, following a vow of his mother Ann of Austria to Our Lady of the "Cure."

Summary: In France, in the Pyrenees, the Virgin appeared to a shepherdess, Angleze Sagazan. Mary visited her three times near the source of the Cier. Mary made the request to her, "I want a chapel to be built here to me."

For more information, visit: http://www.miraclehunter.com/

Ocotlán, Tlaxcala, Mexico (1541)

Our Lady of Ocotlán

Second Sunday of July

Investigated: N/A

Approved: Pope Benedict XIV granted Indulgences, privileges and Apostolic indults to the faithful venerating the image of Our Lady of Ocotlan. Pope Clement XIII declared a feast day to be celebrated on a Sunday in July, in honor of this apparition.

Visionaries: Juan Diego Bernardino

First Apparition: Spring 1541

Last Apparition: Spring 1541

Number of Apparitions: 1

Summary: A young native Tlaxcalan man named Juan Diego Bernardino was going to draw water from a river believed at the time to have healing properties. Our Lady appeared to him and lead him to a special spring of water. She promised him that an image of herself could be found within a tree. The Franciscans discovered the image and placed it in the San Lorenzo monastery.

For more information, visit: http://www.miraclehunter.com/

Vailankanni, India (1580)

Our Lady of Good of Health

September 8th

Investigated: N/A

Approved: Nov 3, 1962 (Pope John the XXIII raises the Shrine to Basilica status)

Visionaries: A shepherd boy named Tamil Krishnannesti Sankaranaranayam and a crippled boy

First Apparition: 1580

Last Apparition: 1600

Number of Apparitions: 2

Miracles & Signs: A crippled boy is healed and a Portuguese trade ship is saved from a violent storm. Other miracles have been reported at the Shrine.

Summary: There are three major events associated with Our Lady of Good of Health in Vailankanni. The Virgin Mary is said by tradition to have appeared to a shephered boy named Tamil Krishnannesti Sankaranaranayamwho offered her child milk. She is subsequently said to have appeared to and healed a crippled boy selling buttermilk. A group of Portuguese sailors attribute being saved from a violent storm to her intercession. They constructed a larger chapel at their landing spot in Vailankanni.

For more information, visit: http://www.miraclehunter.com/

Coromoto, Portuguesa, Venezuela (1652)

Our Lady of Good of Coromoto

Februrary 2nd

Investigated: N/A

Approved: Traditional approval only. In 1950, Pope Pius XII declared Our Lady of Coromoto

Visionaries:Cospes Coromoto and his wife

First Apparition: 1652

Last Apparition: 1652

Number of Apparitions: 2

Summary: The first apparition of the Virgin Mary was in the forest where the Cospes had fled, on September 8, 1652, when the Virgin appeared to the Cacique (ruler) of the Cospes Coromoto and his wife, saying in his own language: "Go to the white house and ask them to pour water into their head to go to heaven"; then, the Virgin asked him and his tribe to be baptized.

Guáitara Canyon, Columbia (1754)

Title: Our Lady of Las Lajas

Feast Day: September 16th

Investigated: N/A

Approved: Traditional approval only. The Roman Catholic Church authorized the cult of Nuestra Señora de Las Lajas Virgin in 1951.

Visionaries: 2 (Maria Mueses de Quinones and her deaf–mute daughter Rosa)

First Apparition: 1754

Last Apparition: 1754

Number of Apparitions: 1

Summary: In 1754, Maria Mueses de Quinones, an Indian woman from the village of Potosi, Colombia and her deaf–mute daughter Rosa were caught in a very strong storm. They sought refuge in a canyon between the gigantic Lajas. To Maria's surprise, her mute daughter, Rosa exclaimed with her first words "the mestiza is calling me..." She did not see the figures of a woman and child that the girl described and fearfully ran back with her daughter to Ipiales and told the townspeople. After later returning to the spot, the woman saw an apparition of Our Lady and Child. Some months later, Rosa died and was returned to life when her mother prayed again at the cave. The townspeople came to see this place and encountered the miraculous image burned into the rocks.

For more information, visit: http://www.miraclehunter.com/

LaVang, Vietnam (1798)

Title: Our Lady of La Vang

Feast Day: November 22nd

Investigated: N/A

Approved: Traditional approval only. Pope John Paul II celebrated the 200th anniversary of the apparitions.

Visionaries: 100,000

First Apparition: 1798

Last Apparition: 1798

Number of Apparitions: 1

Summary: Many Christians took refuge in the jungle near Quang Tri where they prepared themselves for martyrdom. Many people died from the weather, wildlife, sickness and starvation. One night while praying the rosary they were visited by an apparition of Our Blessed Mother holding a child in her arms, with two angels at her sides. She comforted them and told them to boil the leaves from the surrounding trees to use as medicine. She also told them that all those who came to this place to pray, would get their prayers heard and answered. All those who were present, including Buddhists, witnessed this miracle.

For more information, visit: http://www.miraclehunter.com/

Lichen, Poland (1813, 1850)

Title: Our Lady of Lichen

Investigated: 1852

Approved: Traditional approval only. In 1967 the Primate of Poland crowned the image. Pope John Paul II consecrated the Sanctuary on June 7,1999.

Visionaries: Tomasz Klossowski (soldier) and Mikolaj Sikatka (63 – shepherd)

First Apparition: 1813

Last Apparition: 1850

Number of Apparitions: 2

Summary: According to legend, the Virgin Mary appeared in Lichen, Poland to Tomasz Klossowski, a wounded soldier, in 1813 who was healed and discovered a miraculous portrait of Our Lady. She then appeared to a poor shepherd, Mikolaj Sikatka, in 1850 who promoted her devotion. She foretold of a cholera epidemic and interceded for the healing of many who sought her help.

For more information, visit: http://www.miraclehunter.com/

Pompeii, Italy (1884)

Title: Our Lady of Pompeii

Feast Day: May 8

Investigated: N/A

Approved: Traditional approval only. Pope Paul VI crowned the image in 1965; John Paul II visited the shrine in 1979 and 2003.

Visionary: Fortuna Agrelli

First Apparition: March 3 , 1884

Last Apparition: May 8, 1884

Number of Apparitions: 2

Miracles & Signs: The miraculous cure of Fortuna

Summary: The Virgin appeared as the Queen of the Rosary on March 3, 1884 to Fortuna Agrelli after she and her parents had prayed for her recovery from an illness. The girl was healed on May 8 of that year.

For more information, visit: http://www.miraclehunter.com/

Dong Lu, China (1900)

Title: Our Lady of China

Feast Day: Vigil of Mothers Day (the second Sunday of May)

Investigated: N/A

Approved: 1932

(Pope Pius XI approved it as an official Marian Shrine)

Visionaries: Thousands

First Apparition: 1900

Last Apparition: 1900

Number of Apparitions: 1

Miracles & Signs: 300+ miraculous cures

Summary: The Virgin Mary appeared as a beautiful lady in the skies when Catholics implored Her to save them from their enemies and their city from destruction during the Boxer Rebellion. In thanksgiving for Our Lady's protection over the city of Donglu, a beautiful church was built in her honour. It was meant to serve as a constant reminder to the people of Mary's loving and motherly protection.

For more information, visit: http://www.miraclehunter.com/

APPENDIX III
Vatican Recognized Apparitions
(After Investigation and Approval by Local Bishop)

From MiracleHunter.com: As established in the Council of Trent (1545–63), the local bishop is the first and main authority in the judgement of the authenticity of apparition claims. Vatican recognition is not required for an apparition to be considered authentic. After an episcopal approval, the Vatican may officially release a statement or give less explicit forms of approval such as a papal visit crowning of the associated icon, a papal gift such as a golden rose, the approval of the construction of a basilica, the establishment of a feast day, or the canonization of the associated visionary.

Positive judgments by the local bishop (but not yet by the Vatican) theoretically are able to be reversed by a subsequent bishop—but this has never happened in the history of the Church. Negative judgements (*Non constat de supernaturalitate*) and rulings of no evidence of supernaturality (*Constat de non supernaturalitate*) have later been changed to positive judgments on a few rare occasions with the ruling of a subsequent bishop.

If a Marian apparition is recognized by the bishop, it means that the message is not contrary to faith and morals and that Mary can be venerated in a special way at the site. But, because belief in a private revelation is not required by the Church, Catholics are at liberty to decide how much personal spiritual emphasis to place on apparitions and the messages they deliver.

Guadalupe, Mexico (1531)

Title: Our Lady of Guadalupe

Feast Day: December 12th

Investigated: 1666, 1723

Approved: 1555 by Archbishop Alonso de Montúfar

Visionaries: St. Juan Diego (57), Juan Bernardino

First Apparition: Dec 9, 1531

Last Apparition: Dec 12, 1531

Number of Apparitions: 5

Miracles & Signs: Tilma of Juan Diego with imprint of image of Virgin; conversion of millions of indians.

Summary: Mary proclaimed herself "the Mother of the true God who gives life" and left her image permanently upon the tilma of Juan Diego, a recent convert to Christianity.

For more information, visit: http://www.miraclehunter.com/

Lezajsk, Poland (1578)

Investigated: Henryk Firlej, Bishop of Przemysl (1631–1635)

Approved: Maciej Pstrokonski, bishop of Bishop of Przemysl (1601–1608) built a larger church on the site of the apparition in 1606; Henryk Firlej, Bishop of Przemysl (1631–1635) confirms the supernatural origin of the miracle; On September 8, 1752, Pope Benedict XIV hinself crowned the image with Waclaw Hieronim Sierakowski, Bishop of Przemysl (1742–1760), after personally blessed the crown.

Visionaries: Thomas Michalek (woodcutter)

First Apparition: 1578

Last Apparition: 1578

Number of Apparitions: 2

Summary: A pious woodcutter saw a bright light in the forest. The Virgin asked him to alert the authorities to build a church. Thomas, scared, did nothing. The Virgin, then, appeared again, asking him to take action and ending his silence. Thomas went to the authorities but was not believed. After the death of the curate who was against the vision, a chapel was finally built by the parish priest.

For more information, visit: http://www.miraclehunter.com/

Siluva, Lithuania (1608)

Title: Our Lady of Siluva

Feast Day: September 8th

Investigated: 1612

Approved: Aug 17, 1775 by Pope Pius VI.

Visionaries: 4 children

First Apparition: 1608

Last Apparition: 1612

Number of Apparitions: Many over 4 years

Miracles & Signs: Complete conversion of Calvinist town; blind man cured.

Summary: One summer day, in 1608, a number of children were playing while tending their sheep in a field on the outskirts of the village of Siluva. They beheld a beautiful young woman standing on the rock holding a baby in her arms and weeping bitterly. The town which had lost its Catholic identity to the Calvinists over the course of 80 years was restored to the Faith.

For more information, visit: http://www.miraclehunter.com/

Laus, France (1664)

Title: Our Lady of Laus / Our Lady of Happy Meetings

Feast Day: September 27th

Investigated: 1665, 2007

Approved: May 4, 2008 Bishop Jean–Michel di Falco of the Diocese of Gap

Visionaries: Benoite (Benedicta) Rencurel (17)

First Apparition: 1664

Last Apparition: 1718

Number of Apparitions: Many (over 54 years)

Summary: Benoite Rencurel, a poor shepherdess, was born in 1647. The Virgin Mary started appearing to her in 1664 and continued visiting her throughout the rest of her life. The Blessed Mother told her to "pray continuously for sinners."

For more information, visit:

http://www.miraclehunter.com/marian_apparitions/approved_apparitions/laus/index. html

Rue du Bac, Paris, France (1830)

Title: Our Lady of the Miraculous Medal

Feast Day : November 27th

Investigated: 1836

Approved: 1836 by Archbishop de Quelen of Paris

Visionaries: St. Catherine Laboure (24)

First Apparition:

July 18, 1830

Last Apparition: Nov 27, 1830

Number of Apparitions: 2

Miracles & Signs: Miraculous Medal; Prediction of Paris Revolution (1871); incorruptible body of Catherine Laboure

Summary: In the chapel of the Daughters of Charity of St. Vincent de Paul, Mary showed herself three times to novice Catherine Laboure. Laboure said she was commissioned by the Virgin to have the medal of the Immaculate Conception or "Miraculous Medal" made in order to spread devotion to Our Lady.

For more information, visit: http://www.miraclehunter.com/marian_apparitions/approved_ apparitions/ruedubac/index.html

Rome, Italy (1842)

Title: Our Lady of Zion

Feast Day: November 17th

Investigated: Feb 1842

Approved: June 3, 1842 by the Vicar General of Pope Gregory XVI, Cardinal Patrizi

Visionaries: Marie Alphonse Ratisbonne (28)

First Apparition: Jan 20, 1842

Last Apparition: Jan 20, 1842

Number of Apparitions: 1

Summary: Marie Alphonse Ratisbonne, an anti–Catholic Jew, befriended a baron in Rome and began wearing the Miraculous Medal as a simple test. On Jan 20, 1842 while waiting for the baron in the church Sant Andrea delle Fratte, Ratisbonne encountered a vision of the Blessed Virgin Mary. He converted to Catholicism, joined the priesthood, and began a ministry for the conversion of Jews.

For more information, visit: http://www.miraclehunter.com/marian_apparitions/approved_apparitions/rome1842/index.html

La Salette, France (1846)

Title: Our Lady of La Salette

Feast Day : September 19th

Investigated: 1846

Approved: Nov 16th, 1851 by Mgr de Bruillard

First Apparition: Sept 19, 1846

Last Apparition: Sept 19, 1846

Visionaries: Maximin Giraud (11), Melanie Mathieu (14)

Number of Apparitions: 1

Summary: Six thousand feet up in the French Alps, Mary is believed to have come to Maximin and Melanie while they tended sheep. Her appearance in sorrow and tears called for conversion and penance for sins.

For more information, visit: http://www.miraclehunter.com/marian_apparitions/approved_apparitions/lasalette/index.html

Lourdes, France (1858)

Title: Our Lady of Lourdes

Feast Day: February 11th

Investigated: 1858

Approved: Jan 18, 1862 by Bertrand Severe Laurence, Bishop of Tarbes

Visionaries: St. Bernadette Soubirous (14)

First Apparition: Feb 11, 1858

Last Apparition: July 16, 1858

Number of Apparitions: 18

Miracles & Signs: Healings, Conversions, Incorruptible body of St. Bernadette.

Summary: At the Grotto of Massabielle, the Virgin showed herself 18 times to Bernadette Soubirous. Under the title "the Immaculate Conception," she called for penance and prayer for the conversion of sinners.

For more information, visit: http://www.miraclehunter.com/marian_apparitions/approved_apparitions/lourdes/index.html

Filippsdorf, Czech Republic (1866)

Title: Help of Christians

Feast Day: January 13th

Investigated: 1866

Approved: Bishop's commission examined the miraculous event and recognized the healing and supernatural character. Church was elevated to minor basilica and consecrated by Pope Leo XIII in 1885.

Visionaries: Magdalene Kade (31)

First Apparition: January 13, 1866

Last Apparition: January 13, 1866

Number of Apparitions: 1

Miracles & Signs: Cure of Magdalene and many others at the shrine.

Summary: Magdalene Kade, an orphaned 31 year woman bedridden due to many illnesses, received a vision of the Blessed Virgin Mary who immediately cured her. A bishop's commission examined the miraculous event and recognized the healing and supernatural character. In the period between 1870 and 1885 a neo–Romanesque church was built and was elevated to minor basilica by Pope Leo XIII, who officially consecrated it and dedicated to Mary, "Help of Christians."

For more information, visit: http://www.miraclehunter.com/marian_apparitions/approved_apparitions/filippsdorf/index.html

Pontmain, France (1871)

Title: Our Lady of Hope

Feast Day: January 17th

Investigated: 1875

Approved: Feb 1875 Bishop Laval

Visionaries: Eugene Barbadette (12), Francoise Richer (11), Jeanne–Marie Lebosse (9), Eugene Friteau (6)

First Apparition: Jan 17, 1871

Last Apparition: Jan 17, 1871

Number of Apparitions: 1

Miracles & Signs: Prussian army halts advances after soldiers see Virgin in the sky.

Summary: Mary appeared on a farm to students at the nearby convent school. Mary's message was written on a banner that unfurled from her feet: "But pray my children. God will hear you in a short time. My Son allows Himself to be moved by compassion."

For more information, visit: http://www.miraclehunter.com/marian_apparitions/approved_apparitions/pontmain/index.html

Gietrzwald, Poland (1877)

Title: Our Lady of Gietrzwald

Investigated: 1877

Approved: Bishop Filip Krementz 1878; Warmian Bishop, Jozef Drzazga Sept 11, 1977

Visionaries: Justyna Szafrynska (13), Barbara Samulowska (12)

First Apparition: June 27, 1877

Last Apparition: Sept 16, 1877

Number of Apparitions: 9

Miracles & Signs: Healing spring; return of piety and devotion to the villagers; Primate of Poland Cardinal Stefan Wyszynski is cured on 100th anniversary of apparitions.

Summary: In 1877, the Virgin Mary appeared to two girls over the course of 3 months and encouraged a return to prayer.

For more information, visit: http://www.miraclehunter.com/marian_apparitions/approved_apparitions/gietrzwald/index.html

Knock, Ireland (1879)

Title: Our Lady of Knock

Feast Day : August 21st

Investigated: 1879, 1936

Approved: In 1936 Archbishop of Tuam, Dr. Gilmartin's investigative commission returns a positive verdict.

Visionaries: 18

First Apparition: August 21, 1879

Last Apparition: August 21, 1879

Number of Apparitions: 1

Miracles & Signs: 300+ miraculous cures

Summary: During a pouring rain, the figures of Mary, Joseph, John the Apostle and a lamb on a plain altar appeared over the gable of the village chapel, enveloped in a bright light. None of them spoke. At least 15 people, between the ages of 5 and 75, saw the apparition.

For more information, visit: http://www.miraclehunter.com/marian_apparitions/approved_apparitions/knock/index.html

Fatima, Portugal (1917)

Title: Our Lady of Fatima / Our Lady of the Rosary

Feast Day: May 13th

Investigated: 1919

Approved: October 13, 1930 (Dom Jose Alves Correia da Silva, Bishop of the Diocese of Leiria-Fatima)

Visionaries: Lucia dos Santos (9), Jacinta Marto (8), Francisco Marto (7)

First Apparition: May 13, 1917

Last Apparition: October 13, 1917

Number of Apparitions: 6

Miracles & Signs: Dancing Sun, Healings, Conversion of Russia, Incorruptible body of Jacinta.

Summary: While tending sheep, Lucia de Santos and her two cousins, Francisco and Jacinta Marto, reported six apparitions of Mary, who identified herself as "Our Lady of the Rosary." Mary urged prayer of the rosary, penance for the conversion of sinners and consecration of Russia to her Immaculate Heart.

For more information, visit: http://www.miraclehunter.com/marian_apparitions/approved_apparitions/fatima/index.html

Beauraing, Belgium (1932)

Title: The Virgin with the Golden Heart

Feast Day: August 22nd

Investigated: 1949

Approved: July 2, 1949 by the Bishop of Namur

Visionaries: Fernande Voisin (15), Andree Degeimbre (14), Gilberte Voisin (11), Gilberte Degeimbre (9)

First Apparition: Nov 29, 1932

Last Apparition: Jan 3, 1933

Number of Apparitions: 33

Miracles & Signs: Miraculous cures, fireball

Summary: Mary is believed to have come 33 times to the playground of a conTvent school to five children. Identifying herself as "the Immaculate Virgin" and "Mother of God, Queen of Heaven," she called for prayer for the conversion of sinners.

For more information, visit: http://www.miraclehunter.com/marian_apparitions/approved_apparitions/beauraing/index.html

Banneux, Belgium (1933)

Title: The Virgin of the Poor

Feast Day : May 31st

Investigated: 1935–37

Approved: March 19th, 1942 Bishop Kerkhofs of Liege; Aug 22, 1949

Visionaries: Mariette Beco (11)

First Apparition: January 15, 1933

Last Apparition: March 2, 1933

Number of Apparitions: 8

Summary: In a garden behind the Beco family's cottage, the Blessed Mother is said to have appeared to Mariette Beco (age 11) eight times. Calling herself the "Virgin of the Poor," Mary promised to intercede for the poor, the sick and the suffering.

For more information, visit: http://www.miraclehunter.com/marian_apparitions/approved_apparitions/banneaux/index.html

Kibeho, Rwanda (1981)

Title: "Nyina wa Jambo" (Mother of the Word)

Investigated: April 1982

Approved: June 29, 2001 (Bishop Augustin Misago of Gikongoro)

Visionaries: Alphonsine Mumureke (17), Nathalie Mukamazimpaka (20), and Marie Claire Mukangango (21)

First Apparition: Nov 28, 1981

Last Apparition: Nov 28, 1989

Number of Apparitions: Many

Summary: The apparitions began in November 1981 when six young girls and one boy claimed to see the Blessed Virgin Mary and Jesus. But only the visions of the first three—17-year-old Alphonsine, 20-year-old Nathalie, and 21-year-old Marie Claire—have received Bishop Misago's solemn approval. Because there were reservations about the other four visionaries, and the supposed visions of Jesus, Bishop Misago didn't confirm the authenticity of either those visions or visionaries.

For more information, visit: http://www.miraclehunter.com/marian_apparitions/approved_apparitions/kibeho_rwanda/index.html

APPENDIX IV
Bishop Approved Apparitions

From MiracleHunter.com: As established in the Council of Trent (1545–1563), the local bishop is the first and main authority in the judgement of the authenticity of apparition claims. Vatican approval is not required for an apparition to be considered authentic. After an episcopal approval, the Vatican may officially release a statement or give less explicit forms of approval such as a papal visit or crowning of the associated icon, a papal gift such as a golden rose, the approval of the construction of a basilica, the establishment of a feast day, or the canonization of the associated visionary.

Positive judgments by the local bishop (but not yet by the Vatican) theoretically are able to be reversed by a subsequent bishop—but this has never happened in the history of the Church. Negative judgements (*Non constat de supernaturalitate*) and rulings of no evidence of supernaturality (*Constat de non supernaturalitate*) have later been changed to positive judgments on a few rare occasions with the ruling of a subsequent bishop.

If a Marian apparition is recognized by the bishop, it means that the message is not contrary to faith and morals and that Mary can be venerated in a special way at the site. But, because belief in a private revelation is not required by the Church, Catholics are at liberty to decide how much personal spiritual emphasis to place on apparitions and the messages they deliver.

Quito, Ecuador (1594)

Title: Our Lady of Good Success

Feast Day: February 2nd

Investigated:

Approved: Feb 2, 1611 – Bishop Salvador de Riber

Visionaries: Venerable Mother Mariana de Jesus Torres (31)

First Apparition: Feb 2, 1594

Last Apparition: Dec 8, 1634

Number of Apparitions: 4

Miracles & Signs: Blind girl cured at Mariana's wake; incorruptible body of Mariana

Summary: Our Lady of Good Success appeared to Spanish-born Mother Mariana de Jesus Torres at her Conceptionist Royal Convent in Quito, Ecuador. She requested that a statue be made in her likeness and warned of diminishing faith and vocations in the 20th century.

For more information, visit: http://www.miraclehunter.com/

Querrien, Bretania, France (1652)

Title: Our Lady of Eternal Aid

Investigated: 1652

Approved: Archbishop Denis de La Barde, bishop of Saint–Brieuc, authenticated the appearance in Sept 1652. The chapel was immediately built on site of the apparitions.

Visionaries: Jeanne Courtel (12), shepherdess

First Apparition: Aug 15, 1652

Last Apparition: Aug 20, 1652

Number of Apparitions: 15

Summary: The twelve-year-old Jeanne Courtel was born deaf and dumb. As she fed the sheep at her native village of La Prénessaye, the BVM appeared to her and healed her. She could now hear and speak normally. After this miracle Mary appeared again, This time the Virgin urged that a chapel be built. As evidence of her appearance, in addition to the miracle of healing, Mary showed her where a statue was buried of the image of "Our Lady of Eternal Aid." The statue was found and this place manifested fifteen apparitions of the Virgin which were considered and recognized as authentically supernatural by the Bishop of Saint-Brieuc. The chapel was immediately built on the site of the apparitions and the statue was unearthed on the inside.

For more information, visit: http://www.miraclehunter.com/

Montagnaga, Italy (1729)

Title: Madonna of Montagnaga

Feast Day: May 26

Investigated: 1730

Approved: Church of Sant'Anna expanded in 1740; Sanctuary enlarged in 1881; Image crowned on Aug 11, 1894; Feast day established as May 26.

Visionary: Domenica Targa, shepherdess

First Apparition: May 14, 1729

Last Apparition: May 26, 1730

Number of Apparitions: 5

Summary: The Virgin, dressed in white with a rosary in her hand, appeared to a shepherdess

For more information, visit: http://www.miraclehunter.com/

Robinsonville, WI (Champion), USA (1859)

Title: Our Lady of Good Help

Investigated: 2009

Approved: Dec 8, 2010 by Bishop David L. Ricken

Visionaries: Adele Brise (28)

First Apparition: October 9, 1859

Last Apparition: October 17, 1859

Number of Apparitions: 3

Miracles & Signs: On October 8th, 1871 (12 years from the first apparition), the greatest fire disaster in the history of the US destroyed 1.5 million acres of land in Wisconsin. The only place left untouched was the Chapel and Shrine property of Our Lady of Good Help. Many cures have been recorded at the Shrine.

Summary: Our Lady appeared 3 times to a 28-year-old Belgium farm woman and asked to pray for the conversion of sinners and encouraged her to evangelize and catechize the local people.

For more information, visit: http://www.miraclehunter.com/

Castelpetroso, Italy (1888)

Title: Our Lady of Sorrows

Feast Day: March 22

Investigated: 1889

Approved: 1889 (Mgr. Macarone–Palmieri, Bishop of the diocese of Bojano)

Visionaries: 2 shepherdesses - Fabiana Cecchino (35) and Serafina Giovanna Valentino (33)

First Apparition: March 22, 1888

Last Apparition: June 1890

Number of Apparitions: Many

Miracles & Signs: A healing spring appeared at the apparition site.

Summary: Two women, Fabiana Cecchino (35) and Serafina Giovanna Valentino (33), had a vision of Mary first as the Pieta and later as Our Lady of Sorrows in a cave at Castelpetroso, Italy.

Amsterdam, Netherlands (1945)

Title: Our Lady of All Nations

Investigated: 1956, 2002

Approved: May 31, 2002 by Bishop Jozef Marianus Punt of Haarlem

Visionaries: Ida Peederman

First Apparition: March 25, 1945

Last Apparition: May 31, 1959

Number of Apparitions: 56

Notes: Negative judgement was given by the bishop of Haarlem on May 7, 1956, confirmed in 1957 and 1972. Worship authorized by Mgr H. Bomers, bishop of Haarlem, on May 31, 1996.

Summary: During a series of 56 apparitions, lasting 14 years, prophecies were given to Ida Peederman along with an image of the Blessed Mother and a prayer. The revelations emphasize the importance of the Eucharist and portray in detail the events that will bring about the Triumph of the Immaculate Heart, most importantly the declaration of the final Marian dogma of Mary as The Lady of All Nations: Coredemptrix, Mediatrix, and Advocate.

For more information, visit: http://www.miraclehunter.com/

Betania, Venezuela (1976)

Title: Reconciler of People and Nations

Investigated: 1984

Approved: Nov 21, 1987 by Bishop Pio Bello Ricardo; Declared a sanctuary on May 26, 2009 by Bishop Freddy J. Fuenmayor.

Visionaries: Maria Esperanza

First Apparition: March 25, 1976

Last Apparition: Jan 5, 1990

Number of Apparitions: 31

Miracles & Signs: Many cures, bleeding Host, stigmata of Maria Esperanza

Summary: Maria Esperanza of Betania, Venezuela witnessed 31 apparitions of the Blessed Virgin Mary over the course of 15 years. The Virgin called herself the "Reconciler of People and Nations" and warned of impending war and suffering. Many visitors have come to the site, reporting numerous miracles and signs. On one occasion in 1984, over 100 people claimed to have witnessed a public apparition of the Virgin.

For more information, visit: http://www.miraclehunter.com/

Akita, Japan (1973)

Title: Our Lady of Akita

Investigated: 1973

Approved: April 22, 1984 approved by Bishop John Shoojiroo Ito of Niigata. In 1988, Joseph Cardinal Ratzinger allowed Ito's pastoral letter and its dissemination to the faithful.

Visionaries: Sr. Agnes Sasagawa (43)

First Apparition: July 6, 1973

Last Apparition: October 13, 1973

(The statue wept 101 times from July 6, 1973 to Sept 15, 1981)

Number of Apparitions: 3

Miracles & Signs: Bleeding Statue, Stigmata

Summary: Sister Agnes Sasagawa of the Handmaids of the Eucharist received 101 messages emanating from a bleeding wooden statue.

For more information, visit: http://www.miraclehunter.com/

Cuapa, Nicaragua (1980)

Title: Our Lady of Cuapa

Investigated: 1981

Approved: Nov 13, 1982 by Bishop Pablo Antonio Vega

Visionaries: Bernardo Martinez

First Apparition: April 15, 1980

Last Apparition: Oct 13, 1980

Number of Apparitions: 4+

Notes: After the initial 4 apparitions, the Virgin reportedly subsequently appeared in later years with messages of the destruction of atheistic communism and the whole world. She also requested the propagation of the devotion to the shoulder wounds of Christ.

Summary: Church sacristan Bernardo Martinez entered an old chapel and observed a supernatural light illuminating from a statue of the Blessed Virgin. The Virgin later appeared clothed in white and asked for the daily Rosary with Biblical citations and have the First Saturday Devotions renewed. She also warned of future sufferings for Nicaragua if the people didn't change.

For more information, visit: http://www.miraclehunter.com/

San Nicolas, Argentina (1983)

Title: Our Lady of the Rosary

Investigated: April 1985

Approved: Apparitions through Feb 11, 1990 approved Nov 14, 1990, by the Bishop of San Nicolas, Monsignor Domingo Castagna; Apparitions through 2016 approved by Bishop Hector Cardelli May 22, 2016

Visionaries: Gladys Quiroga de Motta

First Apparition: Sept 25, 1983

Last Apparition: Feb 11, 1990

Number of Apparitions: 1816

Notes: She reportedly additionally received 78 messages from Jesus Christ. Numerous healings, including the cure of a boy with a brain tumor, have been documented.

Summary: An ordinary housewife, a mother and grandmother who had no formal education and no knowledge off the Bible or theology claimed that she was visited by the Blessed Mother daily for a period of over 6 years.

For more information, visit: http://www.miraclehunter.com/

APPENDIX V
Coptic Approved Apparitions

Zeitun, Egypt (1968)

Title: Our Lady of Light

Investigated: 1968

Approved: May 4, 1968 by Pope of Coptic Orthodox Church and Local Catholic Bishop

Visionaries: Millions

First Apparition: April 2, 1968

Last Apparition: 1971

Number of Apparitions: Many

Miracles & Signs: Accompanying objects (Doves, Stars and Glowing Balls of Light, Cross, Incense, Clouds), Healings, Conversions

Summary: Our Lady reportedly appeared in Zeitoun, Egypt hovering above Saint Mark's Coptic Church for a span of three years. She appeared on many occasions especially at night, and sometimes she was accompanied by white doves. The apparitions attracted large crowds up to 250,000 people including Christians, Jews, and Moslems. The apparitions were photographed, filmed and broadcast on Egyptian TV. An estimated 40 million people witnessed the events.

For more information, visit: http://www.miraclehunter.com/

Edfu, Egypt (1982)

Investigated: 1982

Approved: 1982 HG Bishop Hedra of Aswan

Visionaries: Many people

First Apparition: Sat. Aug 21, 1982

Last Apparition: November 1982

Number of Apparitions: Many

Summary: The Blessed Holy Virgin Mary appeared on St. Mary's Coptic Orthodox Church located in El-Gomhourya (also known as El-Kenissa) street in the city of Edfu (Diocese of Aswan).

For more information, visit: http://www.miraclehunter.com/

Shoubra, Egypt (1986)

Investigated: April 9, 1986

Approved: June 21, 1986 H.H. Pope Shenouda III formally approved the apparitions

Visionaries: Many people

First Apparition: March 25, 1986

Last Apparition: 1991

Number of Apparitions: Many

Summary: The Holy Virgin Mary appeared on the church of Saint Demiana the Martyr in Papadouplo, near El-Teraa El-Boolakia street, in the overcrowded Shoubra quarter of Cairo, Egypt.

For more information, visit: http://www.miraclehunter.com/

Shentena Al–Hagger, Menoufiya, Egypt (1997)

Investigated: 1997

Approved: Unknown

Visionaries: Many people

First Apparition: 1997

Last Apparition:1997

Number of Apparitions: Many

Summary: In 1997, a small church in Shentena Al-Hagger in Menoufiya hosted thousands of Copts following news of an apparition.

For more information, visit: http://www.miraclehunter.com/

Assiut, Egypt (2000)

Title: Our Lady of Assiut

Investigated: 2000

Approved: Approved by H.H. Pope Shenouda III, Pope of Coptic Orthodox Church (2000)

Seen by: Millions

First Apparition: Aug 17, 2000

Last Apparition: Jan 2001

Number of Apparitions: Many

Summary: Apparition of Mary on top of St. Mark's Church accompanied by lights and doves.

For more information, visit: http://www.miraclehunter.com/

Gabal Dronka, Egypt (2001)

Investigated: 2001

Approved: Unknown

Visionaries: Many people

First Apparition: August 2001

Last Apparition:2001

Number of Apparitions: Many

Summary: Luminescent figure of Virgin Mary in Gabal Dronka, Egypt

For more information, visit: http://www.miraclehunter.com/

Warraq el-Hadar, Egypt (2009)

Investigated: 2009

Approved: Approved on December 14, 2010 by Anba Theodosius Bishop–General of Giza

Seen by: More than 200,000 (Christians and Muslims)

First Apparition: Dec 11, 2009

Last Apparition: 2010

Number of Apparitions: Many

Summary: Luminescent figure of Virgin Mary and Archangel Michael Coptic Orthodox Church in El-Warraq

For more information, visit: http://www.miraclehunter.com/

APPENDIX VI
No Decision
(APPROVED FOR FAITH EXPRESSION)

Mariahilfberg, Gutenstein, Austria (1661)

Title: Our Lady of Help

Investigated: 1661

Approved: Pope Clement IX authorized the cult of the veneration of the image and the construction of a church which was entrusted to a Marian religious order

Visionary: Sebastian Schmid Schlager

First Apparition: 1661

Last Apparition: 1661

Number of Apparitions: 6

Miracles & Signs: In front of the portrait that Sebastian painted, many noted miraculous healings and mystical phenomena occurred.

Summary: Holy Mary appeared to Sebastian Schmid Schlager, who was miraculously healed, to give him the initiative of the construction of a shrine in southern Gutenstein. The Most Holy Virgin had appeared to him six times and painted her image on a sheet and then put the portrait of the Madonna on a beech tree. The image of Mary, although painted rudimentarily, was similar to her apearance in the apparitions. Then pilgrimages began and a chapel was built of wood. The synod of Passau, as the agency of ecclesiastical authority, examined the case and informed Rome. Pope Clement IX authorized the cult of the veneration of the image. In addition, he also gave his consent for the construction of a church which was then entrusted to the care of servants, as a Marian religious order.

For more information, visit: http://www.miraclehunter.com/

Lescure, France (1717)

Title: Our Lady of the Visitation

Investigated: Msgr. D'Estaing du Saillans, Bishop of Saint.Flour

Approved: Msgr. D'Estaing du Saillans, bishop of Saint.Flour authorized the construction of a chapel, solemnly blessed on July 2, 1724. On July 2, 1869, a new larger church was inaugurated by Bishop De Pompignac. In 1934, the image of "Our Lady of the Visitation" wassolemnly crowned.

Visionaries: Jean Paillé (13) – shepherd

First Apparition: July 2, 1717

Last Apparition: July 4, 1717

Number of Apparitions: 3

Miracles & Signs: Discovery of a buried miraculous statue

Summary: The Virgin Mary appeared to a shepherd boy and called for the construction of a chapel on the site of the apparition.

For more information, visit: http://www.miraclehunter.com/

Saint Bauzille, France (1873)

Investigated: 1873 Bishop Cabrières

Approved: The commission recognized the authenticity of the apparitions. But the vicar general remained in opposition to this commission.

Visionaries: Auguste Arnaud (37)

First Apparition: June 8, 1873

Last Apparition: July 8, 1873

Number of Apparitions: 2

Miracles & Signs: Auguste was seen to miraculously run across a field at the speed of lightning to meet the Virgin.

Summary: At Saint Bauzille, the Virgin appeared twice to Auguste Arnaud, a non–practicing Catholic.

For more information, visit: http://www.miraclehunter.com/

Pellevoisin, France (1876)

Title: Our Lady of the Scapular of the Sacred Heart

Feast Day: February 14th

Investigated:

Approved: No official approval of supernatural event. May 1894 Pope Leo XIII approved the Archconfraternity of our Mother All Merciful of Pellevoisin. April 4, 1900 The Congregation of Rites granted approval to the Scapular of the Sacred Heart.

Visionaries: Estelle Fagguette (33)

First Apparition: Feb 10, 1876

Last Apparition: Dec 8, 1876

Number of Apparitions: 15

Miracles & Signs: Estelle is cured of her terminal disease after seeing the Blessed Mother.

Summary: In 1876 in the village of Pellevoisin, Estelle Faguette lay dying of pulmonary tuberculosis, acute peritonitis and an abdominal tumor. During the night of the February 14th, she claimed to witness the first of fifteen apparitions of the Blessed Virgin and was healed.

For more information, visit: http://www.miraclehunter.com/

Heede, Germany (1937)

Title: Queen of the Poor Souls in Purgatory

Investigated: 1945

Approved: for Faith Expression in 1945

Visionaries: Margaret Gansferth, Greta Gansferth, Anna Schulte, Susanna Bruns

First Apparition: October 1, 1937

Last Apparition: November 3, 1940

Number of Apparitions: 3 recorded

Summary: Mary appeared to four children near their homes, in a meadow, and at other places. She was holding the Divine Child in her arms when she first appeared. After the children were forbidden by the Gestapo (and briefly arrested) to go to the place of the original apparition, Mary appeared to them in secret. Prayer, conversion, and the rosary were the primary messages.

For more information, visit: http://www.miraclehunter.com/

Wigratzbad, Germany (1938)

Title: Our Beloved Lady of Victory

Investigated:

Approved:

Visionaries: Antonie Radler, Cecilia Geyer

First Apparition: 1919 (Antonie), Feb 22, 1938 (Cecilia)

Last Apparition: Feb 22, 1938

Number of Apparitions:2

Summary: In 1919, after Antonie Radler contracted the Spanish influenza, the Blessed Virgin appeared to her, laid her hands on her, and healed her. Later she was imprisoned and was freed through the intercession of Our Lady who appeared to Cecilia Geyer, who she asked that a chapel be built.

For more information, visit: http://www.miraclehunter.com/

Marienfried, Germany (1946)

Title: Mediatrix of all Grace

Investigated:

Approved: Bishop consecrated chapel July 13, 1972. Approved for Faith Expression by Bishop of Augsburg on March 20, 2000. New sanctuary consecrated Octo 23, 2011 by Bishop Konrad Zdarsa

Visionaries: Barbara Reuss (12)

First Apparition: April 25, 1946

Last Apparition: June 25, 1946

Number of Apparitions: 3

Notes: Mary identifies herself as Mediatrix of all Graces

For more information, visit:

http://www.miraclehunter.com/

La Codosera, Spain (1945)

Investigated:

Approved: The bishop of Badajoz authorized the construction of a chapel and, therefore, de facto, the cult.

Visionaries: Marcelina and Afra Brigida Blanco

First Apparition: May 27, 1945

Last Apparition:

Number of Apparitions:

Notes: The miracle of the sun was claimed to have occurred severral times.

For more information, visit:http://www.miraclehunter.com/

L'Ile-Bouchard, France (1947)

Title: Our Lady of Prayer

Investigated: 1947

Approved: for Faith Expression on Dec 8, 2001 by Andre Vingt–Trois, Archbishop of Tours. On May 21 and 22, 2004, Archbishop André Vingt–Trois approved the message of the Virgin, together with the bishop of Puy, Bishop and Henri Brincard and Mons. Louis Brigues, Bishop of Angers.

Visionaries: Jacqueline Aubry (12), Jeanette Aubry (7), Nicole Robin (10), Laura Croizon (8)

First Apparition: Dec 8,1947

Last Apparition: Dec 14 , 1947

Number of Apparitions: 9

Miracles & Signs: Miraculous ray of sunlight

Summary: In the parish church of St. Gilles, in L'Ile Bouchard south of Tours, from the 8th to the 14th of December 1947, four children witnessed the apparition of the Virgin Mary and an angel. She asked that they pray for France and construct a grotto at the location.

For more information, visit: http://www.miraclehunter.com/

Tre Fontane, Italy (1947)

Title: The Virgin of Revelation

Investigated: 1947

Approved: The Vicariate of Rome approves the cult of the Virgin of Revelation in 1947.

Visionaries: Bruno Cornacchiola

First Apparition: April 12, 1947

Last Apparition: April 12, 1947

Number of Apparitions: 1+

Miracles & Signs: Conversion of Bruno Cornacchiola

Notes: Not fully approved because of Bruno's character and subsequent 27 claims.

For more information, visit: http://www.miraclehunter.com

Balestrino, Italy (1949)

Investigated: 1947

Approved: The Vicar General stated that although the message did not contain theological errors, it did not meet a supernatural character (1969). Archbishop Mario Olivieri, opened a new investigation and crowned the statue venerated in the chapel. (1992)

Visionary: Caterina Richero

First Apparition: 1949

Last Apparition:

Number of Apparitions:

Miracles & Signs: spiritual fruits and conversions

For more information, visit: http://www.miraclehunter.com/

Ngome, South Africa (1955)

Title: Mary, Tabernacle of the Most High

Investigated:1976

Approved: in 1989 for Faith Expression Bishop Manuset Biyase

Visionaries: Sr. Reinolda May

First Apparition: Aug 22, 1955

Last Apparition: May 2, 1971

Number of Apparitions:10

For more information, visit: http://www.miraclehunter.com/

Fostoria, OH USA (1956)

Title: Our Lady of America

Investigated:

Approved: for Faith Expression by Monsignor Paul F. Leibold, Archbishop of the Cincinnati diocese

Visionaries: Sr. Mildred Mary Neuzil

First Apparition: Sept 25, 1956

Last Apparition: Dec 20, 1959

Number of Apparitions: Many

Miracles & Signs:

Summary: Sr. Mary Ephrem (Mildred Neuzil), of the Precious Blood Sisters and later a Contemplative of the Indwelling Trinity reportedly received apparitions of the Blessed Virgin Mary as well as of Our Lord, St. Joseph, St. Gabriel, and St. Michael. She said she was asked by the Blessed Virgin Mary to draw a picture according to the vision of Our Lady of America and have a statue constructed accordingly and placed after a solemn procession into the National Shrine of the Immaculate Conception, in Washington, D.C. as Our Lady of America.

For more information, visit: http://www.miraclehunter.com/

Natividade, Brazil (1967)

Investigated:

Approved: The diocesan bishop allowed the spreading of the messages and is building a sanctuary.

Visionaries: Dr. Sebastian Fausto de Faria

First Apparition: May 9, 1967

Last Apparition: 1968

Number of Apparitions:

Summary: The Virgin appeared as "the Immaculate Mother of Jesus" and stated that the divine motherhood was the origin and foundation of her own existence. In her messages, mainly directed to the Church, she claimed to be bringing faith and love to Christians traumatized by strife.

Cefala Diana, Italy (1967)

Investigated:

Approved: A church was built from 1967 and consecrated June 22, 1969 by Cardinal Francesco Carpino, Archbishop of Palermo.

Visionaries: Roberto Castelluci (11), Antonino Barberia (8), Francisco di Marto (12), Antonio Bellavia (10)

First Apparition: May 26, 1967

Last Apparition: May 26, 1967

Number of Apparitions: 2

Summary: 4 children claimed to see Our Lady of Sorrows in tears. The same appearance was repeated later in front of many people, when the children ran in town to announce the big event and then led everyone to the place of the apparition.

For more information, visit: http://www.miraclehunter.com/

Santa Domenica di Placanica, Italy (1968)

Title: Madonna Dello Scoglio

Investigated:

Approved: The local Bishop Mons. Morosini, approved the devotion for Faith Expression by declaring the "Scoglio" an official Catholic shrine on December 8, 2007.

Visionaries: Brother Cosimo Fragomeni

First Apparition: May 11, 1968

Last Apparition: May 14, 1968

Number of Apparitions: 4

For more information, visit: http://www.miraclehunter.com/

Belpasso, Italy (1986)

Investigated:

Approved: for Faith Expression – The Archbishop of Catania blessed the temple built to house the rock of appearances and has raised it to the status of Diocesan Shrine.

Visionaries: Rosario Toscano

First Apparition: May 11, 1986

Last Apparition: May 1, 1988

Number of Apparitions: 32

For more information, visit: http://www.miraclehunter.com/

Salta, Argentina (1990)

Title: Virgen del Cerro ("Virgin of the Hill")

Investigated: 2003–2006

Approved: for Faith Expression – Archbishop Mario Cargnello gave permission for the celebration of the mass at the closing ceremony of the pilgrim year 2011. In 2006, he released a *non constat* statement.

Visionaries: Maria Livia Galiano de Obeid

First Apparition: 1990

Last Apparition: Ongoing

Number of Apparitions: Many

Miracles & Signs: Miraculous cures, liberation from demons

For more information, visit: http://www.miraclehunter.com/

Aokpe, Nigeria (1992)

Title: Our Lady Mediatrix of All Graces

Investigated:

Approved: for Faith Expression – Bishop Orgah granted the Imprimatur to the publication of the account of the apparitions and gave his permission to pilgrimages. His predecessor Archbishop John Onaiyekan gave permission for the construction of the shrine.

Visionaries: Christiana Agbo (12)

First Apparition: Oct 1992

Last Apparition: 2004

Number of Apparitions: Many

Miracles & Signs: Eucharistic miracle, solar miracles

For more information, visit: http://www.miraclehunter.com

APPENDIX VII

Unapproved Marian Apparitions

The Catholic Church has been very cautious to approve purported miraculous events. In fact, in the twentieth century, of the hundreds of public claims of Marian apparitions, there have been only nine with episcopal approval (four of those with Vatican approval) and a handful of other Marian apparitions that have not received official approval but have been approved for faith expression at the site. A total of twenty-two apparitions throughout history have been investigated and have received episcopal approval. Additionally, there have been four Egyptian Marian apparitions approved by the Coptic Orthodox Church in the last fifty years.

Throughout history 308 Marian apparitions are attributed to Saints or Blesseds. They are generally unofficially recognized by Church authorities. Only seven Popes throughout history have witnessed Marian apparitions.

The list of "unapproved" Marian apparitions below includes three types of apparition claims:

- Uninvestigated Marian apparition claims (including several to saints);
- Investigated Marian apparition claims that have been determined to not have any supernatural character;
- Investigated Marian apparition claims that have not been determined to have any supernatural character.

YEAR	PLACE	# PEOPLE INVOLVED	APPROVAL OF SUPERNATURAL CHARACTER
1900	Lucca (Italy)	several people	N.A.
1900	Tanganika (Africa)	2 women	No decision
1900	Peking (China)	Crowd	No decision
1900	Loublande, Vendée (France)	Sr. Claire Ferchaud (1896–1972)	Negative decision
1902	Campitello, Corsica (France)	Maddalena Parsi	No decision
1904	Zdunska–Wola (Poland)	St. Maximilian Kolbe	No decision
1909	Grey (France)	Pere Jean Edouard Lamy	No decision
1909	Bordeaux (France)	Marie Mesmin	No decision
1910	Sandy, Utah (USA)	Cora Evans (nee Yorgason) (6)	No decision

YEAR	PLACE	# PEOPLE INVOLVED	APPROVAL OF SUPERNATURAL CHARACTER
1910	Alexandria (Egypt)	F. Bruno (future Cyril VI)	No decision
1911	Bruxelles (Belgium)	Berthe Petit	No decision
1913	Alzonne (France)	15 people	No decision
1914	Hrushiv (Ukraine)	22 people	No decision
Sept 8, 1914	Versailles (France)	Marcelle Planchon (23)	No decision
1917	Barral (Portugal)	Severino Alves (a young shepherd)	No decision
1917	Battle of la Marne (France)	soldiers	No decision
1918	Turin (Italy)	Flora Manfrinati	No decision
1918	San Giovanni (Italy)	St. Padre Pio	No decision
1918	Muzillac, Bretagna, Morbihan, Diocesi of Vannes (France)	3 children	No investigation
1920	Catania (Italy)	Ven. Lucia Mangano (religious)	No decision
1920	Verdun, Quebec (Canada)	Emma Blanche Curotte	No decision
1920	Vistula River, Warsaw (Poland)	Soldiers ("Miracle at the Vistula")	No decision
1923	Bayonne, NJ (USA)	Ven. Sister Miriam Teresa (Teresa Demjanovich) 23	No decision
1924	Cenusco sul Naviglio (Italy)	Title: Madonna of the Dv Elisabetta Reaelli	No decision
1926	Marlemont (France)	Maria P. (6)	No decision
1925	Tuy (Spain)	Sister Lucia dos Santos	No decision
May 31, 1927	Messina (Italy)	St. Annibale Maria di Francia	No decision
1928	Ferdrupt, Vosges (France)	Marcelle George (13) and Madeleine Hing-ray(6)	Negative decision
1929	Pontevedra (Spain)	Sister Lucia dos Santos	No decision
1930	Campinas (Brazil)	Sr. Amalia Aguirre	No decision
1931	Stenbergen (Holland)	1 woman	No decision

YEAR	PLACE	# PEOPLE INVOLVED	APPROVAL OF SUPERNATURAL CHARACTER
1931	Ezquioga – Ezkioga (Spain)	Andrés (7) and Antonia (11) Bereciartua and crowd	Negative decision
1931	Izurdiaga (Spain)	2 young women	Negative decision
1931	Zumarraga (Spain)	(see 1931 Ezquioga)	Negative decision
1931	Ormaiztegui (Spain)	(see 1931 Ezquioga)	Negative decision
June 15, 1931	Albiztur (Spain)	4 girl (age 8 – 15)	Negative decision
1931	Bacaicoa (Spain)	(see 1931 Ezquioga)	Negative decision
1931	Irañeta (Spain)	(see 1931 Ezquioga)	Negative decision
1931	La Pailly (France)	Pere Lamy	No decision
1932	Marmagen (Germany)	Odile Knoll (40)	No decision
1932	Metz (France)	nun	No decision
1933	Beauraing (Belgium)	Tilman Côme (58)	No decision
1933	Crollon, near Mont–St–Michel (France)	Adrien Angot (boy) and two friends	No decision – not investigated
1933	Onkerzele (Belgium)	Mrs. Nieke von den Dijk	Negative decision
1933	Harcy (France)	1 man (37) and many others	No decision
1933	Houlteau–Chaineux (Belgium)	Georges Duanime (37), Jeanne Edmonds (5), Charles Gillet (5)	No decision
1933	Lokeren–Naastveld (Belgium)	Bertonia Holtkamp and Joseph–Henri Kempenaers	Established as not supernatural (August 25, 1934 Archbishop of Malines and Bishop of Ghent)
1933	Etikhove (Belgium)	Maurice Van Rokegem and Omer Eneman (40)	Negative decision
1933	Herzele (Belgium)	Jules de Vuyst & Crowd	Negative decision
1933	Olsene (Belgium)	Maurice Vandembroeck	Negative decision
1933	Berchem–Anvers (Belgium)	Many people claimed apparitions following Beauraing	Negative decision
1933	Foy Notre–Dame (Belgium)	M. (19)	No decision – uninvestigated

YEAR	PLACE	# PEOPLE INVOLVED	APPROVAL OF SUPERNATURAL CHARACTER
1933	Melin–Micheroux (Belgium)	Mathieu Lovens	No decision
1933	Tubize (Belgium)	Many people claimed apparitions following Beauraing	Negative decision
1933	Verviers (Belgium)	Many people claimed apparitions following Beauraing	Negative decision
1933	Wilrijk (Belgium)	Many people claimed apparitions following Beauraing	Negative decision
1933	Wielsbeke (Belgium)	1 woman	No decision
March 23, 1934	Roggliswil (Switzerland)	Melchior Kleen–Hode	Negative decision – January 25, 1935
1934	Lucerne (Switzerland)	1 woman	No decision
1934	Marpingen (Germany)	E.B., an opponent of Nazism	No decision
1935	Rome (Italy)	1 woman	No decision
1935	Itri, Valmontana (Italy)	Luigina Sinapi (Teen-age girl)	No decision
1936	Milan (Italy)	Bl. Maria Pierina De Micheli (22)	No decision
1936	Bouxieres–aux–Dames (France)	Adeline Pietrquin (28) and Gabrielle Hanus (26)	Negative decision
1936	Ham–sur–Sambre (Belgium)	Emelda Scocky (11) and Adeline Pietrquin (28)	Negative decision
1937	Voltago–Belluno (Italy)	5 young shepherds and a boy	Negative decision
1937	Bettin (Italy)	Padre Gino	Negative decision
1937	Oberbruck (France)	Antoinette Lauber (15)	No decision
1937	Heede–im–Emsland (Germany)	Margaret Gansferth, Greta Gansferth, Anna Schulte, Susanna Bruns	No decision
1937	Saint–Bonnet de Mon-tauroux (France)	Henriette Dejean (15)	No decision – not investigated
1938	San Vincenzo Valle di Rovereto (Italy, Dio-cese of Sora–Aquino–Pontecorvo)	Filomena Carnevale (1926–1959)– stig-matic shepherdess	Positive investigation of Filomena; no formal approval of apparition

YEAR	PLACE	# PEOPLE INVOLVED	APPROVAL OF SUPERNATURAL CHARACTER
1938	Saint–Pierre–la–Cour (France)	children	No decision
1938	Madrid (Spain)	Maria Nieves Saiz (7)	No decision
1938	Kerizinen, Brittany (France)	Jeanne–Louise Ramonet (28)	Negative decision (1956, 1971, 1837, 1975)
1938	Bochum (Germany)	Ursula Hibbeln	No decision
May 31,1938	Milan (Italy)	Sr. Mary Pierina De Micheli	No decision
1938	Oberpleis (Germany)	1 woman	No decision
1938 and on	Paravati (Italy)	Natuzza Evolo	No decision
1939	Kerrytown (Ireland)	Crowd	No decision
1939	Dublin (Ireland)	N.A.	No decision
1939	Saint–Placide (Canada)	Thérèse Gay (12)	No decision
1939	Kallikulam, Tamilnad (India)	6 young people (Gnana Athikkam, S.P. John, M.G.Thomas, D.Thasan, R.Thasan, M.A.Thasani)	No decision
1939	Hungary	Sister Maria Natalia (38)	No decision
1939	Krakow (Poland)	Rev. Francis Marianus Nowakowski	No decision
1940	Holsterhausen, Dorsten (Germany)		No decision
1940	Ortoncourt (France)	Mme. Jeanette Tochet	No decision
1940	Bodonnou (France)	Theresa Coat	Negative decision
March 25, 1941	Alto de Umbe (Spain)	Felipa Sistiago de Arrieta (33)	No decision
1942	Cornamona (Irelande)	1 girl	No decision
1943	Girkalnis (Lithuania)	Crowd	Negative decision
1943	Athis–Mons (France)	Crowd	Negative decision
1943	Paris (France)	Mr. & Ms. Debord	No decision
1943	Warsaw (Poland)	Wadysawa Papis	No decision
1944	Ghiaie–di–Bonate (Italy)	Adelaide Roncalli (7)	Negative decision
1944	Balasar (Portugal)	Alexandrina Marta da Costa	No decision

YEAR	PLACE	# PEOPLE INVOLVED	APPROVAL OF SUPERNATURAL CHARACTER
1944	Mississippi (USA)	Claude Newman (prisoner)	No decision
1945	Georgia (USA)	James Wilburn Chauncey (Baptist)	No decision
1945	Italy	Marcelina Barossa (10)	No decision
1945	Bronx, NY (USA)	Joseph Vitolo (9)	No decision
1945	Fehrbach (Germany)		No decision
1945	Heroldsbach (Germany)		No decision
1945	Munich (Germany)		No decision
1945	Niderhbach (Germany)		No decision
1945	Pfaffenhofen (Germany)		No decision
1945	Remagen (Germany)		No decision
1945	Rodalben (Germany)		No decision
1945	Wurzburg (Germany)		No decision
1945	Ardhee, County Tyrone (Ireland)		No decision
1946	Suwon (Korea)	Theresa Hwang	Negative decision
1946	Espis (France)	Gilles Bouhours (5)	Negative decision
1946	Pasman, Dalmatia	Adults & children	No decision
Dec 10, 1946	Vilar–Chao (Portugal)	Amelia Nahiridade de la Navidad Rodriques	No decision
1947	Montichiari (Italy)	Pierina Guilli	Not established as supernatural
1947	Casanova Staffora (Italy)	Angela Volpini (7)	Negative decision
Aug 23, 1947	Forsweiler Tannhausen (Germany)	Mrs. T. Paula (40) & 4 children	Negative decision
1947	Urucaina (Brazil)	1 religious	Negative decision
1947	Tannhausen (Germany)	Mrs. T. Paula	No decision
1947	Pleskop near Vannes (France)	Therese Le Cam, Annik and Monique Goasguen	No decision
1947	Vorstenbosch (Holland)	Anton & Berta van der Velden	No decision

YEAR	PLACE	# PEOPLE INVOLVED	APPROVAL OF SUPERNATURAL CHARACTER
July 2, 1947	St. Emmerich–Berg (Hungary)	Klara Làszloné	No decision
1947	Grottamore (Italy)	1 child	No decision
1947	Ille Napoleon (France)	3 little boys	No decision
Nov 1, 1947	Kayl (Luxembourg)	Emily Wanding (10)	No decision
1948	MARTA DI BOL-SENA near Viterbo (Italy)	4 Children and Others	Established as not supernatural (1948 – bishop of Montefiascone; 1952 – Archbishop Adelchi Albanesi, Bishop of Viterbo
1948	Gimigliano (Italy)	Anita Feerici (Teenage girl) and others	Negative decision
1948	Montlucon (France)	1 religious	Negative decision
1948	Cluj (Romania)	Crowd	Negative decision
1948	Aspang (Austria)	Crowd of men	No decision
1948	Liart (France)	Louis Mercier and 11 Others	No decision
1948	St. Jeanaux Bois (France)	Mrs Lucie Manceauu (23)	No decision
1948	Lipa (Philippines)	Teresita Castillo	Negative decision
1948	Tor–Pignattiaira (Italy)	Bruno Bolotte (13)	No decision
1948	Marina de Pisa (Italy)	3 children and many adults	No decision
1948	Maria Bolsena (Italy)	4 little girls and some adults	No decision
1948	Zischowicz (Czechoslovakia)	2 girls	No decision
1948	Altenmarkt (Austria)	Katharina Kainhofer	No decision
1948	Caserta (Italy)	Teresa Musco(5)	No decision
1949	Lublin (Poland)	Crowd	Negative decision
1949	Zo–Se (China)	1 religious	Negative decision
1949	Fehrbach (Germany)	Senta Roos (Teenage girl)	Negative decision
1949	Hasznos (Hungary)	Crowd	Negative decision

YEAR	PLACE	# PEOPLE INVOLVED	APPROVAL OF SUPERNATURAL CHARACTER
1949	Balestrino (Italy)	Caterina Richero (9)	Non constat de supernaturalitate (1969) Approved for Faith Expression (1991)
1949	Gimigliano (Italy)	A young girl	Negative decision
1949	Heroldsbach (Germany)	Four children	Negative decision
1949	Necedah, WI (U.S.A.)	Mary Ann Van Hoof (neé Bieber) (1909–1984)	Negative decision
1949	Hersolsbach (Bavaria)	Crowd of 300	No decision
1949	Ceggia (Italy)	Mariolina Baldissin	No decision
1950	Girgenti (Malta)	Guza Mifsud	No decision
March 14, 1950	Acquaviva Platani (Italy)	Pia Mallia (12)	Negative decision
1950	Saint–Eugène de Gamby (Canada)	3 children	No decision
1950	Ribera (Italy)	2 children	No decision
1950	Denver, CO (USA)	Mary Ellen (15)	No decision
1950	Remagen (Germany)	20 children	No decision
1950	Perregaux (Algeria)	1 woman	No decision
1950	Guarciano (Italy)	A child	No decision
1950	Casalicchio (Italy)	Tina Mallia (12)	No decision
1950	Binghamton (U.S.A.)	1 woman	No decision
1950	Belmuttet (Ireland)	Teenage girl	No decision
1950	Bienvenuda–Usagre (Spain)	1 man	No decision
1950	Padoue (Italy)	1 woman	No decision
1951	Amarossi (Italy)	Teenage girl	No decision
1951	Arluno (Italy)	Luigia Nova (39)	No investigation
1951	Oriolo Calabro (Italy)	1 man	No decision
1951	Casalicontrada (Italy)	1 man	Negative decision
1951	Dugny (France)	3 people	No decision
1951	Tangua (Brazil)	Young girl	No decision
1951	Tinos (Greece)	N.A.	No decision
1951	Baggio (Italy)	Young girl	No decision
1951	Poland	Barbara Klossowna	No decision

YEAR	PLACE	# PEOPLE INVOLVED	APPROVAL OF SUPERNATURAL CHARACTER
1951	New York (USA)	Frank, Laity brotherhood of the passion of Christ	No decision
1952	Bergame (Italy)	1 woman	No decision
1952	Orria (Italy)	Crowd	No decision
1952	Rome (Italy)	1 woman	No decision
July 1952	Rodalben (Germany)	Annelise Walzig	Negative decision
1952	Niederbach (Germany)	1 man	No decision
1952	India	Fr. Louis M. Shourish, S.J.	No decision
1952	Gerpinnes (Belgium)	Rosette Colmet	No decision
1953	Caserta (Italy)	Maria Valtorta (1897–1961)	Negative decision
1953	Cossirano (Italy)	Young girl	Negative decision
1953	Bivigliano (Italy)	Galileo Sacrestani (49)	No decision
1953	Hubersent (France)	3 children/1 adult	Negative decision
1953	San Saba di Sparta (Italy)	Rosario Pino (8)	Negative decision
1953	Rome (Italy)	Teenage girl	No decision
1953	Philadelphia (U.S.A)	1 woman	No decision
1953	Frignano Maggiore (Italy)	Teenage girl	No decision
1953	Calabro di Mileto (Italy)	Bl. Mother Elena Aiello	No decision
April 23, 1953	Sabana Grande (Puerto Rico)	Juan Angel Pinto Collado (8), Bertita Pinto, and two girls Isidra and Ramonita	Negative decision
Dec 20, 1953	Dubovytsya (Ukraine)	Hanya	No decision
1953	Calais (France)	O. Lavoisier (10) and 50 others	No decision
1953	Cossirano (Italy)	several children	No decision
July 18, 1954	Jerusalem	several children	No decision
1954	Seredne (Ukraine)	Anna and Several people	No decision
1954	Montichiari (Italy)		No decision
1954	Astuna (Italy)		No decision
1954	Liceta (Italy)		No decision

YEAR	PLACE	# PEOPLE INVOLVED	APPROVAL OF SUPERNATURAL CHARACTER
1954	Ribera (Italy)	2 children	No decision
1954	Casa Cicchio (Italy)		No decision
1954	Rombia (Italy)		No decision
1954	Arluno (Italy)		No decision
1954	Marta (Italy)		No decision
1954	Cisterna (Italy)		No decision
1954	Balestrino (Italy)		No decision
1954	Lazise (Italy)	Bruno Buratto – a boy	Negative – Uniinvestigated
1954	Catane (Italy)	A boy	No decision
1954	Vittoria (Italy)	2 sisters	No decision
1954	Mezzolombardo (Italy)	1 man	No decision
1954	Palerme (Italy)	Several children	No decision
1954	Angri (Italy)	Sultana Ricci (31)	No decision
1954	Sasso Marconi (Italy)	1 woman	No decision
1954	Marche–en–Famenne (Belgium)	N.A.	No decision
1954	Eisenberg (Austria)	Aloisia Lex (6)	Negative decision
1954	Colombera di Avenza (Italy)	1 man	No decision
1954	Pingsdorf (Germany)	2 women	No decision
1954	Saint–Tropez (France)	N.A.	No decision
1954	Calabria (Italy)	Mother Elena Aiello	No decision
1954	Newcastle (Great Britain)	N.A.	No decision
1954	Bande (Luxembourg)	Several children	No decision
1954	Cosenza (Italy)	1 religious	No decision
1954	Ibdes (Spain)	Several children	No decision
1954	Pombia (Italy)	1 woman	No decision
1954	Windy Gap (N. Ireland)	Seamnus Quail	No decision
1955	Zululand (South Africa)	Reinolda May, Benedictine nun	No Investigation
February 1955	Reggio Emilia (Italy)	Rosa Soncini (50)	Negative decision
1955	Itauna (Brazil)	1 man	No decision
1955	San Vincenzo (Italy)	1 woman	No decision
1955	Rome (Italy)	1 woman	No decision

YEAR	PLACE	# PEOPLE INVOLVED	APPROVAL OF SUPERNATURAL CHARACTER
1955	Theriot, LA (USA)	Claire Rose Champagne	No decision
1955	Hungary	1 religious	No decision
May 31,1956	Urbania (Italy)	Augusta Tangini and 1 other person	No decision
1956	Assoro (Italy)	4 children	No decision
1956	Urbania (Italy)	Several children	Negative decision
Sept 15, 1957	Rocca Corneta (Italy)	Crying statue	Negative decision –1967
1957	Sausalito (U.S.A.)	1 man	No decision
1957	Cracovie (Poland)	1 woman	No decision
1957	Gasp, (Canada)	N.A.	No decision
1958	Saint Jovite (Canada)	Gaston Tremblay ("Apostles of the infinite")	Negative
1958	Quebec (Canada)	Marie–Paule Giguère (37) – "Army of Mary"	Negative
1958	Jorcas (Spain)	N.A.	No decision
1958	Villa Barone (Italy)	1 woman	No decision
June 1, 1958	Turczovka (Slovakia)	Matousch Laschut (42)	Declared site of pilgrimage and prayer – Msgr. Tomass Galis Oct 19, 2008
1958	Vallemaio (Italy)	1 family	No decision
1958	Mantoue (Italy)	A child	No decision
1958	Milan (Italy)	N.A.	No decision
1958	Terni (Italy)	2 children	No decision
1958	Turzovka (Czechoslovakia)	Matous Lasuta	No decision
1958	Abbeyleix (Ireland)	Josephine Dayton	No decision
1959	Scheggia (Italy)	4 children	No decision
May 9, 1959	MALÈ, Trent (ITALY)	Laura Bertini (d. 1994)	Negative decision (March 9, 2002 – Luigi Bressan Archbishop of Trento)
Oct 7, 1959	Warsaw (Poland)	Many people	No decision
Oct 7, 1959	Warsaw (Poland)	Many people	No decision
1959	Stornarella (Italy)	1 man	No decision

YEAR	PLACE	# PEOPLE INVOLVED	APPROVAL OF SUPERNATURAL CHARACTER
1959	Ascona (Switzerland)	N.A.	No decision
1960	Neuweier (Germany)	Erwin Wiehl	No decision
1960	Balestrino (France)	Caterina Richero	No decision
1960	Acqua Voltri (Italy)	A boy	No decision
1960	Paravati (Italy)	Natuzza Evolo	No decision
1960	Thierenbach (France)	1 man	No decision
1961	Garabandal (Spain)	Mari Loli Mazon (12), Jacinta Gonzalez (12), Mari Cruz Gonzalez (11), Conchita Gonzalez (12)	Not established as supernatural
1961	Craveggia (Italy)	1 woman	Negative decision
September 29, 1961	San Damiano (Italy)	Mama Rosa Quattrini	Negative decision – 1980, 2005
1961	Budapest (Hungary)	Mrs. Erzsebet Szanto Kindelmann (49)	No decision – Imprimatur for writings of seer
Feb 18, 1962	Ladeira do Pinheiro (Portugal)	Maria do Conciçao Mendes	Established as not supernatural (Feb 4, 1965; June 17, 1977)
1962	Chiari (Italy)	1 woman	No decision
1962	Skiemonys, Janonis, (Lithuania)	Ramute m–Mapiukaite	No decision
1962	MONTE FASCE (Italy)	Padre Bonaventura e Giliana Faglia	No decision
1963	Saigon (Vietnam)	several nuns in a convent	No investigation
1963	Verceil (Italy)	2 men	No decision
1963	Vietnam	Rosa Maria (novice)	No decision
1964	Turczovka (Slovakia)	1 man	No decision
1965	Fribourg (Switzerland)	A girl	No decision
May 1965	Aleppo (Syroa)	Mariette Korbage (19)	No decision
1965	Conchar (Spain)	1 woman	No decision
1965	Belgium	Marguerite	No decision
1966	Porto–San–Stefano (Italy)	Enzo Alocci	No decision
1966	Ain–el–Del (Lebanon)	Teenage boy	No decision
1966	Cabra (Philippines)	Teenage girl	No decision

YEAR	PLACE	# PEOPLE INVOLVED	APPROVAL OF SUPERNATURAL CHARACTER
1966	Liège (Belgium)	N.A.	No decision
1966	Rome (Italy)	Teenage girl	No decision
1966	Ventebbio (Italy)	1 priest	Negative decision
June 12, 1967	Raccuja, Messina (Italy)	Many people (animated statue)	No investigation
Sept 9, 1967	Ulzio (Italy)	1 woman	No investigation
1967	Nativitade (Brazil)	1 man	No decision
1967	Raccula (Italy)	N.A.	No decision
1967	Edenvale, Johannesburg (South Africa)	Domitilla Hyams	No decision
1967	Fribourg (Switzerland)	1 woman	No decision
Oct 1967	Bohan–Mortsel (Belgium)	Leon Theunis and D Wittenwrogel	Negative decision
1967	Mont–Laurier (Canada)	1 woman	No decision
1967	Quebec (Canada)	1 girl	No decision
1967	Oulx (Italy)	1 woman	No decision
1968	Florence (Italy)	Mama Carmela Carabelli (58)	No decision
1968	St–Bruno–de–Chambly (Canada)	Several children	No decision
1968	Anse–aux–Gascons (Canada)	Several children	No decision
1968	Fort Kent (U.S.A.)	Young boy	No decision
1968	Maille (France)	4 children	No decision
1968	Palmar de Troya (Spain)	Clemente and 4 young girls	Negative decision
May 11, 1968	SANTA DOMENICA DI PLACANICA (Italy)	Cosimo Fragomeni now Brother Cosimo	Approved for Faith Expression – 2008
1969	Naples (Italy)	Brother Elia (7)	No decision
1969	Florence (Italy)	1 person	No decision
1969	Barcelone (Spain)	N.A.	No decision
1969	Mexico (Mexico)	1 religious	No decision
1969	Suodziai (Lithuania)	Anele Matjosaitis	No decision
1969	Cairo (Egypt)	Mrs. Camille Basaly	No decision
1969	Mouseitbe (Lebanon)	72 boys, Bishop & Others	No decision

YEAR	PLACE	# PEOPLE INVOLVED	APPROVAL OF SUPERNATURAL CHARACTER
August 16, 1969	White Lake, New York (USA)	Mary MacKillop	
1970	Lecce (Italy)	Angelo Chiaratti (15)	Negative decision
June 18, 1970	Bayside (U.S.A.)	Veronica Leuken	Established as not supernatural (Archbishop Minerva of Salerno / Bishop Francis Mugavero of Brooklyn)
1970	Vladimir (Russia)	Josyp Terelya	No decision
1970	Tajique, NM (USA)	Fr. Molnar	No decision
Oct 1, 1971	Amman (Jordan)	cloistered monk	No decision
1971	Pendiamo (Columbia)	Young girl	No decision
1971	Crèteil (France)	N.A.	No decision
1971	Luke Saint John (Canada)	N.A.	No decision
1971	San Vicens del Horts (Spain)	1 man	No decision
1971	Kafr Atalla (Egypt)	Many	No decision
1971	Beirut (Lebanon)	Crowd of school children	No decision
1971	New York (USA)	A.W.	No decision
1972	El Mimbral (Spain)	Several people	No decision
1972	Porziano (Italy)	Several people	No decision
1972	Ravenna (Italy)	Several children	No decision
1972	Drummondville (Canada)	N.A.	No decision
1972	Milan (Italy)	Fr. Stefano Gobbi	No decision
1973	Nitape (Peru)	1 religious & several children	No decision
1973	Mortzel (Belgium)	N.A.	Negative decision
1973	Belgrade (Yugoslavia)	Julka	No decision
1973	Lincoln, NE (USA)	Dr. Mary Jane Even	Not established as supernatural – Warning against writings (1995 – Diocese of Lincoln)
1974	Atene (Greece)	1 woman	No decision
1974	Dozul (France)	M. Aumont	Negative decision

YEAR	PLACE	# PEOPLE INVOLVED	APPROVAL OF SUPERNATURAL CHARACTER
1974	Derval (France)	1 man	Negative decision
1974	Putot–en–Auge (France)	Madeleine	No decision
1974	Gallinaro (Italy)	1 person	No decision
1974	Cinquefrondi (Italy)	1 woman	No decision
1974	Canada	Brother Joseph Francis	No decision
1974	Rome (Italy)	Mother Elena Patriarca Leonardi	No decision
	Anversa (Belgium)	Eric Bonte "Frere Elie" (1930–1996)	No investigation
1975	New Orleans (USA)	Johnny Hernandez	No decision
1975	Altai (Siberia)	Agnes Ritter (49)	No decision
1975	Dugny (France)	Teenage girl	No decision
1975	Kenya	Muthoni	No decision
1975	Binh Loi / Trieu (Vietnam)	Stephen Ho Ngoc Anh (soldier)	No decision
1976	Bislig, Surigao del Sur (Phillipines)	Consuelo Nalagan ("Mother") Royo	No decision
July 16, 1976	Berlicum (Holland)	Elisabeth Sleutjes	Negative decision
1976	Cerdanyola (Spain)	N.A.	Negative decision
1976	Olmos (Peru)	Young girl	Negative decision
1976	Puylaurens (France)	1 man	Negative decision
1976	Deir–el–Ahmar (Lebanon)	Fr. Boutros Mounsef	No decision
1977	Rostov (U.S.S.R.)	N.A.	No decision
1977	Kharkov (U.S.S.R.)	N.A.	No decision
1977	Leningrad (U.S.S.R.)	N.A.	No decision
1977	Le Fréchou (France)	Fr. Jean Marie	Negative decision
1977	Lamezia Terne (Italy)	Young man	No decision
1978	Chiang Si (China)	various witnesses	No decision
1979	Palestine (Beirut)	Many People	No decision
1980	Agropoli, Salerno (Italy)	Armida	No decision
1980	Paulina, Louisiana (USA)	Fr. Albert Hebert	No decision
1980	El Escorial (Spain)	Luz Amparo Cuevas	Negative decision
1980	Ede Oballa (Nigeria)	1 man	Negative decision

YEAR	PLACE	# PEOPLE INVOLVED	APPROVAL OF SUPERNATURAL CHARACTER
Nov 6, 1980	Wu Fung Chi (Taiwan)	9 Buddhist men	Investigated – Approved for Faith Expression
1981	Medjugorje (Bosnia–Herzegovinia)	Ivanka Ivankovich, Mirjana Dragicevic, Vicka Ivankovic, Ivan Dragivecic, Marija Pavlovic , Jakov Colo	Not established as supernatural (1991) Currently under Vatican investigation (2010)
1981	Worcester, MA (USA)	Eileen George	No decision
1981	La Talaudière (France)	Blandine Piegay	Negative – Not established as supernatural / No devotion (April 16, 1982, Bishop Rousset of Saint–Etienne)
1981	Seoul (Korea)	Rev. McAlear & Liz Brennan	No decision
1981	Rome (Italy)	1 woman	No decision
1981	Thornton, California (USA)	Manuel Pitta	No decision
1982	Cankton, Louisiana (USA)	Genevieve Huckady	
1982	Blackwatertown (Ireland)	Eileen McPhillips, Patrinne McConville and Maria McClements (17)	No decision
1982	Izbicno (Bosnia–Herzegovinia)	2 children	No decision
1982	Arguello (Argentina)	1 man, then several others	No decision
1982	Damascus, Syria	Mary (Myrna) Kourbet Al–Akhras	Approval by Syrian Catholic Church
1982	Nowra (Australia)	William Kamm (The Little Pebble)	Established as not supernatural – Bishop of Wollongong
1982	Canton (U.S.A.)	1 woman	Negative decision
1983	Marpingen (Germany)	Margaretha Kunz	Negative decision
June 12, 1983	Penablanca (Chili)	Miguel Angel Poblete	Negative decision
1983	Olawa (Poland)	Casimierz Domanski	Negative decision
February 1983	Surbiton (Great Britain)	Patricia de Menezes	Negative decision

YEAR	PLACE	# PEOPLE INVOLVED	APPROVAL OF SUPERNATURAL CHARACTER
1983	Israel	Thousands of Arab Christians	No decision
1983	Tel Aviv	Hundreds of People	No decision
1983	Baguio City (Philippines)	Many People	No decision
July 21, 1984	BOITSFORT (BELGIUM)	André Pestiaux	Negative decision
1984	Availles–Limouzine (France)	Marie Madeleine Chêne	No investigation
1984	Kernéguez (France)	1 woman	No decision
Sept 14, 1984	Montpinchon (France)	Ivanof Gayet, his cousin, Josiane Halbourt and others	No decision
1984	Jall–el–Dib (Lebanon)	Young girl	No decision
1984	Gargallo di Carpi (Italy)	Gian Carlo Varini	Negative decision
1984	Crotone (Italy)	Several people	No decision
1984	Mushasha (Burundi)	1 man	No decision
1984	Kinshasa (Zaire)	1 man	No decision
1984	Bakersfield (U.S.A.)	Crowd	No decision
1984	Guatemala	Carmen	No decision
1984	Surrey (England)	Patricia de Menezes	No decision
April 28, 1985	Valencia (Spain)	Ángel Muñoz (24)	Negative decision
1985	Port–a–Prince (Haiti)	Sister Altagrace Doresca (nun – Order of the Consecrated Virgins)	No decision – approval of publication of messages
1985	Nowy Dwor (Poland)	Robert Rzepkowski (10)	Negative decision – Uninvestigated
1985	Vadiakkado (India)	Mary Anna	No decision
1985	Lvov (Ukraine)	N.A.	No decision
1985	Naju (South Korea)	Julia Kim	Negative decision
1985	Melleray (Ireland)	Ursula O'Rourke, Breda Coleman	No decision
1985	Carns (Ireland)	4 young shepherd girls	No decision
March 25, 1985	Schio (Italy)	Renato Baron	Negative decision
1985	Oliveta Citra (Italy)	Anita Rio (8 children total)	No decision

YEAR	PLACE	# PEOPLE INVOLVED	APPROVAL OF SUPERNATURAL CHARACTER
1985	Sofferetti (Italy)	Several people	No decision
1985	Bisceglie (Italy)	Young girl	No decision
1985	Belluno (Italy)	2 Teenagers	No decision
1985	Floridia (Italy)	8 children	No decision
1985	Casavatore (Italy)	Several children	No decision
1985	Casavatore (Italy)	Several children	No decision
1985	Salzburg (Austria)	Mrs Elfriede Hickl	No decision
Feb 2, 1986	Rouen (France)	Stephane Michel (30)	Not investigated
May 11, 1986	Belpasso (Italy)	Rosario Toscano	Approval of Faith Expression
1986	Wilmington, CA (USA)	Patricia Soto	No investigation
1986	Burkina Faso	Marie Rose Kaboré	No decision
1986	Mazzano (Italy)	1 woman	No decision
1986	MONTEFANERA (Italy)	Paola Albertini	Negative decision (March 6, 2006 – Vicar General Monsignor Corrado Pizziolo)
1986	Tierra Blanca (Mexico)	Elba (13) & Zenaia (11)	No decision
1986	Cardito (Italy)	Teenage girl	No decision
1986	Sezze (Italy)	Several people	No decision
1986	Campobasso (Italy)	N.A.	No decision
1986	Giubiasco (Italy)	Pino Casagrande (62)	No decision
1986	Verviers (Belgium)	N.A.	No decision
1986	Nsimalen (Cameroon)	Belinga Luc Marc and 6 other children	Negative decision
1986	Bilychi (Ukraine)	Josyp Terelya, Kizyn Navy	No decision
1986	Santa Fe, NM (U.S.A.)	Vange Gonzales	No decision
1986	Manila (Philippines)	soldiers	No decision
1986	Blue Mountains (Australia)	Paul	No decision
1986	Eastpointe, MI	Catherine Lanni	No decision
1986	Monzambano (Italy)	Salvatore Caputo	Established as not supernatural (March 9, 2002 – Archbishop Luigi Bressan of Trento)

YEAR	PLACE	# PEOPLE INVOLVED	APPROVAL OF SUPERNATURAL CHARACTER
April 3, 1987	Amsterdam (Paesi Bassi)	agnostics	No decision
May 13, 1987	AURACH–FISCHBA-CHA U (Germany)	Mrs. Monica Hofer	No decision
October 13, 1987	Matera (ITALY)	Nicolina Taddonio	Established as not supernatural (bishops of Andria)
1987	Borgosesia (Italy)	1 man	No decision
1987	Curitiba (Brazil)	3 or 4 persons	Negative decision
1987	Hrushiv (Ukraine)	Kizyn Maria	No decision
1987	Zarvanystya (Ukraine)	Chornij Zenovia	No decision
1987	Pochayiv (Ukraine)	Several people	No decision
1987	Crosia, Italy	Anna Biasa, Vincenzo Fullone	No decision
1987	Esmeraldas (Ecuador)	Teenage boy	No decision
1987	Inchigella (Ireland)	Rosemary O'Sullivan	No decision
May 30, 1987	Bessbrook (Ireland)	Beulah Lynch and Mark Trenor	No investigation
1987	Mayfield (Ireland)	Sally Ann Considine & Judy Considine	Not established as supernatural (Bishop of Cork, Bishop Michael Murphy)
1987	Granstown (Ireland)	N.A.	No decision
Dec 17 & 18, 1987	Mulevala (Mozambique)	Crowds of Catholics, Protestants, Muslims and others in five surrounding villages	No decision
1987	Belpasso (Italy)	Rosario Toscano (15)	Approved for faith expression (Bishop of Gurué authorized construction of sanctuary)
1987	Crosia (Italy)	Anna Biasa, Vincenzo Fullone	No decision
1987	Ft. Worth, Texas USA	Annie Kirkwood	No decision
1987	Rome (Italy)	Anna Wings / Sister Anna Ali	No decision
1987	Barton, Australia	Sr. Kate Douglas	No decision
1987	Michigan USA	Miriamante	No decision
1987	Anguera, Bahia Brazil	Pedro Regis Alves (18)	No decision

YEAR	PLACE	# PEOPLE INVOLVED	APPROVAL OF SUPERNATURAL CHARACTER
1987	El Ranchilo, TX USA	Friar David Lopez	No decision
1987	Mutwal (Sri Lanka)	"Privileged Soul"	No decision
December 1987	Kew (Australia)	Debra Geileskey	Negative – Uninvestigated
1988	Syria / Cleveland, OH (USA)	Dr. Issam Nemeh	No decision
1988	LINGUAGLOSSA (Italy)	Salvatore Marchesi	No decision
1988	Maracaibo (Venezuela)	José Luis Matheus Barboza and Juan–Antonio Gil	Negative – Uninvestigated
1988	Yardville/Marlboro, NJ (USA)	Joseph Januszkiewscz	No decision
1988	Hustusco (Mexico)	3 people	No decision
1988	Lubbock, TX (U.S.A.)	Mary Constancio, Theresa Verner and Mike Slate	Negative decision (Bishop Michael J. Sheehan, Bishop of Lubbock)
1988	Scottsdale (U.S.A.)	Father Jack Spaulding and nine young people (Gianna	
Talone–Sullivan, Mary Cook, Susan Evans, Steve and Wendy Nelson, James Pauley, Jim Kupanoff, Annie Ross Fitch, Stefanie Staab)	Negative decision (Established as not Supernatural)		
1988	Phoenix (U.S.A.)	Estella Ruiz	Negative decision
1988	Grosby (U.S.A.)	N.A.	No decision
1988	Tickfaw, LA (U.S.A.)	Alfredo Ramone	No decision
Aug 24, 1988	El Cajas / Cuenca (Ecuador)	Patricia Talbot	Not established as supernatural (1989)
1988	Burlington, Ontario (Canada)	Zdenko (Jim) Singer	No decision
1988	Cachiche (Perù)	Many people	No decision
1988	Waterloo, NY (USA)	Lena Shipley	No decision
1988	Scottsdale, AZ and Springs Colorado, CO, (USA)	Harriet Hammons	No decision

YEAR	PLACE	# PEOPLE INVOLVED	APPROVAL OF SUPERNATURAL CHARACTER
1988	Marches (Italy)	Filomena Agostini, Rosina Marinucci	No decision
1988	Paris (France)	Bassan Assaf	No decision
1988	Sydney (Australia)	Valentina Papagan	No decision
1988	Mbuye (Uganda)	Many People	No decision
1988	Masinde, Kayanza (Burundi)	Euzebie (4)	Under Investigation
1989	Cortnadreha (Ireland)	Christina Gallagher	Not established as supernatural – 1996 Michael Neary, Archbishop of Tuam
1989	Manila (Philippines)	Fr. Fernando Suarez	No decision
1989	Kurescek (Slovenia)	Franz Spelic "Smarevski"	No decision
1989	Chotyne (Poland)	Stanislaw Kochmar	No decision
1989	Zarvanystya (Ukraine)	Chornij Zenovia	No decision
1989	Austin, TX (USA)	Janie Gauze	No decision
March 31, 1989	Agoo (Philippines)	Judiel Nieval	Negative decision
1989	Zagabria (Croatia)	Marta Marija Serdar	No decision
1989	Zarvanystya (Ukraine)	Chornij Zenovia	No decision
1989	Porto S. Elpidio, Sicily	Giorgio Bongiovanni	No decision
1989	Guazapa (San Salvador)	Bessy Rodríguez	Negative decision
Jan 19, 1989	Ascoli Piceno (Italy)	1 woman (40)	No decision
May 24, 1990	MAMMALEDI, Syracuse (ITALY)	Giuseppe Auricchia (74)	Established as not supernatural
Sept 1990	TEGUCIGALPA (HONDURAS)	Girls from orphanage	Negative decision
Nov 10, 1990	Anosivolakely (Madagascar)	Patrice Raharimanana	No decision
1990	Atlanta, GA (USA)	Joan Holland	No decision
1990	Melbourne (Australia)	Josefina–Maria Zavadal	No decision
1990	Santa Maria, CA (USA)	Carol Nole	No decision
1990	Marmora, Ontario (Canada)	Many people	No decision
1990	Denver, CO (U.S.A.)	Theresa Lopez	Negative decision
1990	Conyers, GA (U.S.A.)	Nancy Fowler	No decision
1990	Hillside, IL (U.S.A.)	Joseph Reinholtz	No decision

YEAR	PLACE	# PEOPLE INVOLVED	APPROVAL OF SUPERNATURAL CHARACTER
1990	Litmanova (Slovakia)	Ivetka Korcakova (22) and Katka Ceselkova (23)	Apparition site declared place of prayer and pilgrimage (2004, 2008)
1990	Beaumont–du–Ventoux (France)	1 woman	No decision
1990	Winterset, IA (USA)	Marv Kucera	No decision
1990	Wisconsin, USA	Joanne Kriva	No decision
1990	L'Avenir, Quebec, (Canada)	Sr. Marie–Danielle	No decision
1990	Guatemala	Sr. Hermana Guadalupe	No decision
1990	Sydney (Australia)	Geraldine Doyle	No decision
1990	Salta, Argentina	Maria Livia Galiano de Obeid	Not established as supernatural (2006)
1991	mother of 4 children (27)	mother of 4 children (27)	Not established as supernatural
Feb 7th, 1991	Jacarei, São Paulo (Brazil)	Marcos Tadeu (13)	Not established as supernatural (Bishop Nelson Westrupp)
March 1991	Kettle River, Minnesota (USA)	Steve Marino	Not established as supernatural (1993 – Bishop Robert Banks of Green Bay)
1991	Quezon City (Phillipines)	Carmelo Cortez	No decision
1991	Honesdale, PA (USA)	Alix Fils–Aime'	No decision
1991	Ellsworth, Ohio (USA)	1 boy (17)	No decision
1991	Holving (France)	1 woman (66)	No decision
Aug 15, 1991	Mozul (Iraq)	Dina Basher (14)	No decision
1991	Arkansas/Texas (U.S.A.)	Cyndi Cain	No decision
1991	Bretagen, France	Mama Marie Claudine	No decision
1991	Quezon City (Phillipines)	Carmello, Puring, Rowel Darang, Lola Thelma	No decision
1991	San Bruno, CA (U.S.A.)	Carlos Lopez, Jorge Zavala	No decision
1991	Woombye, (Australia)	Susanna D'Amore	No decision

YEAR	PLACE	# PEOPLE INVOLVED	APPROVAL OF SUPERNATURAL CHARACTER
1991	Lake Ridge, VA (USA)	Fr. James Bruse	No decision
1991	San Juan (Puerto Rico)	Luz Diaz	No decision
1991	Pennsylvania (USA)	Jack Marie Smith	No decision
Dec 16, 1991	Dallas, TX (USA)	Maureen Cox	No decision
May 20,1992	Manduria (Italy)	Debora Marasco (19)	Established as not supernatural (2002, 2012 Vincenzo Pisanello, Bishop of Oria)
Aug 1992	JOINVILLE–LE–PONT (France)	Lydie	No decision
Sept 27, 1992	Settequerce – Bolzano, South Tyrol (Italy)	Nello "Toni" Rizzati	No decision
Oct 1992	Aokpe (Nigeria)	Christiana Inehu Agbo (12)	Approval of Faith Expression
1992	Washington, DC (USA)	John Downs	No decision
1992	MARINA Giampilieri (Italy)	Pina Scutellà	No decision
1992	Moscow (Russia)	N.A.	Negative decision
1992	Scottsdale, AZ (USA)	Carol Ameche (Peterson)	No decision
1992	Falmouth, KY (U.S.A.)	Sandy	No decision
1992	Enfield, CT (U.S.A.)	Neil Harrington, Jr.	Negative decision
1992	Belo Horizonte, Minas Gerais (Brazil)	Raymundo Lopes	No decision
1992	Steubenville, OH (USA)	Tony Fernwalt	No decision
1992	California, (USA)	Denise Estrada	No decision
1992	Santa Maria, CA (USA)	Sadie Jaramillo	No decision
1992	Toledo, OR (USA)	Sally Steadman	No decision
1992	Denver, CO (USA)	Veronica Garcia	No decision
March 1993	Auckland (New Zealand)	a few people	No decision
1993	Arc–Wattripont, Wallonia, (Belgium)	a boy	Not investigated
1993	Rome (Italy)	Marisa Rossi	No decision
1993	Ajmer (India)	NA	No decision

YEAR	PLACE	# PEOPLE INVOLVED	APPROVAL OF SUPERNATURAL CHARACTER
1993	Thu Duc (Vietnam)	1 girl	No decision
1993	Arc–Watripont (Belgium)	1 boy	No decision
1993	Manila (Philippines)	Allan Rudio (14)	Negative decision
1993	Belleville, IL (USA)	Ray Doiron	No decision
1993	Cincinnati (U.S.A.)	Rita Ring	No decision
1993	New S. Wales (Australia)	Mathew Kelly	No decision
1993	Bennington, VT (USA)	Laura Zink	No decision
1993	Toowoomba, (Australia)	Debra Geileskey	No decision
1993	Goulburn (Australia)	Pamela Dunn	No decision
1993	Balingasag, (Philippines)	Wengen Joson	No decision
1993	Derlan, NJ (USA)	Michael McColgan	No decision
1993	Ottowa (Canada)	Stephen Ley	No decision
1993	Surrey, BC (Canada)	Lorna Keras, Adriana Kerssens	No decision
1993	Scarborough, Ontario (Canada)	Eddie Virrey	No decision
1993	Kingston, Ontario, (Canada)	Emma de Guzman	No decision
1993	Rochester, NY (U.S.A.)	John Leary	Negative decision – July 7, 2000
1994	Arlington, VA (USA)	Joseph B. Reyes	No decision
1994	Hollywood, FL USA	Rosa Lopez	No decision
1994	Middleton, OH (USA)	Daniel Mohn	No decision
July 30, 1994	New York, NY (USA)	Franz Joseph Keiler	No investigation
1994	Conchabamba (Bolivia)	Catalina (Katya) Rivas	April 2, 1998 – Imprimatur to messages from the Archbishop Mons. Rene Fernandez of Cochabamba; recognition of supernaturality of bleeding statue
1994	Emmitsburg, MD (USA)	Gianna Talone Sullivan	Negative decision
1994	Sarasota, FL, USA	Peter C. Gruters	No decision

YEAR	PLACE	# PEOPLE INVOLVED	APPROVAL OF SUPERNATURAL CHARACTER
March 20, 1994	Niteroi (BRAZIL)	Marianna Luiza Gilio–Guzzo and sons Felipo and David	Uninvestigated
April 23, 1994	Baturite (BRAZIL)	José Ernane,	No decision
Sept 24, 1994	Batim, Goa (India)	Suor Mary Rodrigues, Martino Almedia, Iveta Fernandes Gomes (52)	No decision
1994	Dechtice (Slovakia)	Martin Gavenda, Mária Gavendova, Lucia Vadikova, Martina Kalasova, Adriana Kudelova, Simona Kumpanova, Jozef Danko	No decision
1994	Itapiranga, Amazonas (Brazil)	Edson Glauber and Maria do Carmo	No decision
June 3, 1995	Aleppo (Syria)	Josephine H. (46)	No decision
1995	Anna Rosa (Italy)	mother of two	No decision
1995	Manu Ariki Mara (New Zealand)	200 people	No decision
1995	Olo, Enugu State (Nigeria)	Barnabas Nwoye	No decision
1995	Maryland (USA)	Chris Courtis	No decision
1995	Santa Maria, CA (USA)	Sadie Jaramillo	No decision
1995	Cookstown (Ireland)	Patrick Rushe	No decision
1995	Sterling, Kansas (USA)	Patricia Mundorf	No decision
1995	Strabane (Ireland)	Margo Doherty	No decision
1995	Minnesota (USA)	Little Mary	No decision
June 8, 1996	Santa Fe, NM (USA)	Vangie Gonzales	Under investigation
June 21, 1996	San Francisco, CA (USA)	Herco Rose	Negative decision
1996	Clearwater, FL, (USA)	Many people	No decision
1996	Sisquoc, CA (USA)	Barbara Mattias	No decision
1996	Brooklyn, NY (USA)	Terrence Ross	Negative decision
1996	Dijon (France)	Eliane Deschamps	Negative decision
1996	Elyria, OH (U.S.A.)	Maureen Sweeney Kyle (48)	Negative decision
1996	Vitória da Conquista, Bahia (Brazil)	Fabiana Oliveira	No decision

YEAR	PLACE	# PEOPLE INVOLVED	APPROVAL OF SUPERNATURAL CHARACTER
1996	New Jersey (USA)	Michael Diamond	No decision
1996	Hazelton, PA (USA)	Mary Ellen Lukas	No decision
1996	Midwest (USA)	Barbara Rose Centelli	No decision
1996	Canberra (Australia)	Carmel Masters	No decision
1996	Olo (Nigeria)	Barnabas Nwoye	No decision – approval of publication of messages
1996	Sara Piqui (Costa Rica)	Many people	No decision
1996	MARTINCAMP (France)	Nicole	Established as not supernatural (Diocese of Rouen)
1997	Platina (Brazil)		No decision
1997	Perry, Michigan (USA)	Carolyn Kwiecinski	No decision
1997	Minnesota (USA)	Fr. Andrew Wingate	No decision
1997	Platina (Brazil)	Francisco Ovídio da Silva	No decision
1997	Zagreb (Croatia)	Mirna	No decision
1997	El Dorado, TX (U.S.A.)	Augustine Halvorsen	No decision
1997	Sataua (Samoa)	Suor Ruth Augustus	No decision
December 1997	Agen (France)	"Little Dominic"	No decision
1998	Montreal (Canada)		No decision
1998	Pocito (Argentina)	Gabriel Pizarro	No decision
1998	Greenfield, MA (USA)	John Snide	No decision
1998	Santa Fe, New Mexico (USA)	Michelle Rios Rice Hennelly	No decision
1998	St. John's (Antigua)	Don Gerard Critch	No decision
1998	Montreal, Quebec (Canada)	Delmis	No decision
1998	Saskatoon, Saskatche-wan (CAN)	Carmen Humphrey	No decision
July 21, 1999	Lanús, Buenos Aires (Argentina)	Marcia (b. 2/22/83)	No decision
1999	Houston, TX (USA)	Vincent Uher	No decision
1999	Algarve (Portugal)	Fernando Pires	No decision
1999	Quebec, Canda	Micheline Boisvert	No decision
1999	Marpingen (Germany)	Christine Ney, Marion Guttma, Judith Hiber	Not established as supernatural